ECONOMICS AND
THE GLOBAL ENVIRONMENT

CHARLES S. PEARSON
The Johns Hopkins University

CAMBRIDGE
UNIVERSITY PRESS

PUBLISHED BY THE PRESS SYNDICATE OF THE UNIVERSITY OF CAMBRIDGE
The Pitt Building, Trumpington Street, Cambridge, United Kingdom

CAMBRIDGE UNIVERSITY PRESS
The Edinburgh Building, Cambridge CB2 2RU, UK   http://www.cup.cam.ac.uk
40 West 20th Street, New York, NY 10011-4211, USA   http://www.cup.org
10 Stamford Road, Oakleigh, Melbourne 3166, Australia
Ruiz de Alarcón 13, 28014 Madrid, Spain

First published 2000

Printed in the United States of America

Typeface Times 11/14 pt.   *System* QuarkXPress™ [BTS]

A catalog record for this book is available from the British Library.

Library of Congress Cataloging in Publication data
Pearson, Charles S.
Economics and the global environment / Charles S. Pearson.
p. cm.
ISBN 0-521-77002-5 (hb) – ISBN 0-521-77988-X (pbk.)
1. Environmental economics. 2. Sustainable development. 3. Environmental
policy – International cooperation. I. Title.
HD75.6. P438 2000
333.7 – dc21   99-054674

ISBN   0 521 77002 5   hardback
ISBN   0 521 77988 x   paperback

ECONOMICS AND
THE GLOBAL ENVIRONMENT

Economics and the Global Environment is a pathbreaking, comprehensive analysis of how economic and environmental systems mesh in the international context. The book investigates how environmental resources, such as global climate, genetic diversity, and transboundary pollution, can be managed in an international system of sovereign states without a "Global Environment Protection Agency." It also considers how traditional international economics can be expanded to accommodate environmental values. Until recently, trade theory and trade policy neglected pollution and environmental degradation. This situation has changed dramatically, and the controversial and corrosive issues of trade and the environment, illustrated by the trade debacle at the WTO meeting in Seattle in 1999, are given careful analysis by the author. These topics are enriched by a concise presentation of the principles of environmental economics and by a thoughtful treatment of sustainable development. The book will appeal to students and practitioners of trade and development, as well as the environmental community. The economic analysis is rigorous yet accessible to this wide audience, and it is reinforced by skillful use of empirical material and case studies.

Charles S. Pearson is Professor and Director of the International Economics Program at the Paul H. Nitze School of Advanced International Studies, The Johns Hopkins University, Washington, D.C., and he has held senior adjunct positions at the East West Center and World Resources Institute. His international university teaching includes appointments at Thammasat University (Thailand), the International University of Japan, and at centers in Nanking, China (Nanjing), and Bologna, Italy. Professor Pearson has written extensively on international environmental issues, including the pioneering book, *Environment: North and South*, and *Multinational Corporations: Environment and the Third World*. He also teaches and publishes in the areas of trade policy and economic integration. Professor Pearson has been a consultant on international environmental economics with the OECD, UNCTAD, ESCAP, ASEAN, the World Bank, U.S. government agencies, and with the private sector.

To Sue
with love

Nature is indeed the eternal problem, and when it is solved, we know not only Nature but ourselves; the problem of Nature is the problem of human life.

—D. T. Suzuki, *Zen Buddism*

Contents

List of Tables   *page* xii
List of Figures   xiv
Preface   xix
Acknowledgments   xxiii

1   Introduction and Plan of the Book   1
    1   The Theme and Thesis   1
    2   Stepping Back   4
    3   Internationalizing Environmental Economics   7
    4   Plan of the Book   11
    5   A Cautionary Note   15

Part 1   The Basics

Note to Part 1   19

2   Interactions and Trade-Offs   21
    1   Introduction   21
    2   Linkages   22
    3   Trade-Offs and Complementarities   27
    4   Evolution Over Time   34
    Appendix 2.1 Derivation of Production Possibility
    Curves   38

3   The Roots of Environmental Degradation   42
    1   Introduction   42
    2   Consumer Surplus and Producer Surplus as
        Welfare Measures   43
    3   Efficiency and Equity   50

vii

4 Market and Government Failures and
   Environmental Degradation   53
5 The Coase Theorem   67
Appendix 3.1 Exact Welfare Measures: Compensating and
Equivalent Variation and Surplus   70

4 Issues of Time   77
1 Introduction   77
2 Discounting   78
3 An Environmental Discount Rate?   86
4 Examples of Discounting and Intertemporal Resource
   Allocation   95
5 Intergenerational Efficiency, Equity, and Sustainability   108

5 How Clean is Clean Enough?   114
1 Introduction   114
2 Optimal Environmental Protection   115
3 Concepts of Environmental Value   120
4 Techniques for Monetary Valuation   123
5 Alternatives to Monetary Valuation   136
6 Valuing Life and Health   138
7 Conclusions   140
Appendix 5.1 Resolving WTP and WTA Discrepancies   140

6 The Government's Tool Kit   144
1 Introduction   144
2 Promoting Coasian Markets   145
3 Command-and-Control versus Market-Based Instruments   148
4 Effluent and Emission Taxes versus Tradeable Permits   155
5 Subsidies   161
6 Double Dividends and the Choice of Tools in a
   Second-Best World   162
7 The Tools in Practice   163

Part 2   Trade and Environment

Note to Part 2   169

7 Trade and Environment: An Overview of Theory   172
1 Introduction   172
2 Environment and Comparative Advantage   172

3 Trade Theory and Environment: Early Contributions 176
4 The North-South Controversy 183
5 Theory of Policy and Policy Coordination 189
6 Terms of Trade and Factor Mobility 193
7 Strategic Behavior in Trade and Environmental Policy 197

8 Theory of Trade and Environment: A Diagrammatic
Exposition 200
1 Introduction 200
2 Summary of the Cases 200
3 The Six Cases in Detail 203

9 Theory of Policy: Partial Equilibrium, Terms of Trade,
and Distributional Issues 236
1 Introduction 236
2 Welfare Analytics – The Basics 237
3 The Murky World of the Second-Best 241
4 Who Gains and Who Loses? Distribution Questions 248

10 Trade-Environment Policy: Evolution of the Debate
and Taxonomy of the Issues 258
1 Introduction 258
2 Evolution of the Issue 259
3 Sorting Out Trade-Environment Policy: A Taxonomy 264

11 Institutional and Policy Responses: OECD,
WTO/GATT, EU, and NAFTA 283
1 Introduction 283
2 The OECD and the Polluter Pays Principle 283
3 The GATT, the WTO, and the Environment 288
4 Trade and Environment in the European Union
and NAFTA 299

12 Empirical Studies 307
1 Introduction 307
2 Competitiveness Questions 307
3 Trade Effects of Product and Packaging Standards,
Ecolabelling, and Multilateral Environmental Agreements 323
4 Impact of Trade and Trade Liberalization on the
Environment 333

Part 3   Transnational Pollution and Management of International Resources

Note to Part 3   341

13   International Environmental Externalities: Theory
     and Policy Responses   343
     1   Introduction and Classification   343
     2   Theoretical Illustrations   345
     3   Policy Responses   358
     4   A Potpourri of Evidence   361
     Appendix 13.1 Negotiating MEAs   378

14   Economics and Global Warming   385
     1   Introduction   385
     2   Analytical Complexities and Factual Background   386
     3   Global Warming in a Cost-Benefit Framework   399
     4   The International Context   403
     5   Approaches and Tools   412
     6   Taxes and Quotas   415
     7   International Response   425

15   Economics and Ocean Fisheries   430
     1   Introduction   430
     2   Theory   432
     3   Enclosure   443
     4   Examples from Fisheries Management   446

Part 4   Sustainable Development

Note to Part 4   461

16   Perspectives on Sustainable Development   463
     1   Introduction   463
     2   Changing Views on Resource Limits   464
     3   The Equity Roots   469
     4   What Is To Be Sustained?   472
     5   Policies for Sustainable Development   479
     6   The International Dimension   481

17   Measuring Sustainable Development   485
     1   Introduction   485
     2   Revising National Income Accounts: A Green NNP?   487

3   Some Examples of Green Accounting   501
4   An Environmental Kuznets Curve?   507
Appendix 17.1 User-Cost and Net-Price Methods to Value
Depletion of Natural Capital   510

18   Trade, Environment, and Sustainable Development:
     Thailand's Mixed Experience   514
     Sitanon Jesdapipat
     1   Introduction   514
     2   Thailand's Trade-Environment Profile   514
     3   Environmental Measures Affecting Thai Trade   520
     4   Impacts on Specific Sectors   528
     5   Challenges and Opportunities for Sustainable
          Development   537
     6   A Concluding Thought   541

19   Looking Back, Looking Forward   543

References   551
Index   573

Tables

3.1	Externality flows	*page* 57
3A.1	Comparing CV and EV	72
4.1	Profit streams	108
5.1	Valuation approaches	123
5.2	Consumer surplus – option one	130
5.3	Deriving data for demand curve	133
8.1	The six cases	202
8.2	Initial equilibrium point c_0	216
8.3	Initial equilibrium point c_1	216
9.1	Welfare and trade effects of policies	241
12.1	U.S. pollution-abatement and control expenditures, 1994	317
12.2	Composition of U.S. pollution-abatement and control spending, 1994	317
12.3	U.S. pollution-abatement and control expenditures 1972–1994	318
12.4	U.S. pollution-abatement cost as percent value of shipments and pollution-abatement capital expenditures as percent new capital expenditures, by industry, 1993	319
12.5	Food product detentions by FDA, by reason for detention	324
12.6	Product detained by type of product	325
12.7	Products detained by country or region of origin	325
12.8	Estimated exports from Asia of "sensitive" products subject to environmental product measures in selected OECD markets	328
12.9	Estimated exports from Asia of "sensitive" products subject to environmental product measures in selected OECD markets	329
13.1	GEF projects by priority area	368

13.2	Debt-for-nature swaps, 1987–1994	372
13A.1	Welfare under six negotiation scenarios	384
14.1	Changes in greenhouse gas concentrations	389
14.2	World CO_2 emissions by source, 1992	389
14.3	Sources of anthropogenic methane emission, 1991	390
14.4	Carbon content of fossil fuels	390
14.5	Cumulative CO_2 emission by country and region 1800–1988	391
14.6	CO_2 emissions from industrial sources, 1992	392
14.7	Methane emission by region and activity, 1991	393
14.8	Projections of energy consumption	397
14.9	Monetary damages estimates by region from doubling CO_2	404
17.1	Comparing traditional and green measures of national output: Papua New Guinea	506
18.1	Distribution of Thai exports by sector	517
18.2	Thailand's top ten exports, 1994	518
18.3	Estimates of hazardous waste generation in Thailand	527

Figures

2.1 Environment-economic flow model   *page* 22

2.2 Maximizing social welfare in a trade-off between conventional output (Q) and services derived from directly consumed environmental services (E_C)   29

2.3 Relationship between conventional output (Q) and environmental quality that affects production functions (E_Q): a positive range   32

2.4 Possible consumption path with increased production capacity and (ultimately) a strong demand for directly consumed environmental services   36

3.1 Consumer and producer surplus   43

3.2 Welfare effects of correcting production externality   46

3.3 A second-best problem: monopoly and production externality   50

3.4 Optimal supply of public good   55

3.5 Open-access common property resource under excess supply and scarcity   61

3.6 Inefficiencies in a simple oil reservoir example   62

3.7 Example of market failure in road congestion   64

3A.1 Deriving compensating variation measure of welfare change   73

3A.2 Deriving equivalent variation measure of welfare change   74

4.1 Maximizing utility: equilibrium between present and future consumption   80

4.2 Saving and investment schedules determine discount (interest) rate   82

4.3 Discount rates with taxes   82

4.4 Price of fixed asset subject to income elastic demand   89

4.5 Misallocation of man-made and environmental capital due to failure to include externality and user costs 92

4.6 Discount rates with various environmental "corrections" 93

4.7 Present value of $1,000 30 years hence at 1, 5, and 10 percent discount rates 95

4.8 Intertemporal efficiency: allocation of fixed resource over two time periods 96

4.9 Intertemporal efficiency at various discount rates 98

4.10 Optimal exploitation rate and time path of price of fixed resource 102

4.11 Two time period optimal extraction model with increasing marginal extraction costs 104

4.12 Optimal fallow period model with positive cropping costs 106

5.1 Determining monetary cost-benefit functions and optimal pollution abatement 116

5.2 Classification of environmental values 121

5.3 Identifying the costs of environmental degradation to consumers and producers 125

5.4 Allocation of cost of soil depletion between labor and landowners 126

5.5 Hedonic pricing model to monetize welfare effect of improving air quality 128

5.6 Travel cost approach: visit rates and travel costs 131

5.7 Inferred demand curve for recreation site from travel cost/visit rate data 134

5A.1 Explaining discrepancies between WTP and WTA 142

6.1 Efficiency in allocating abatement 150

6.2 The convexity complication: multiple equilibria of MC and MB 155

6.3 Supply and demand for tradeable pollution permits 157

6.4 Taxes and tradeable permits under uncertainty: shallow MC 159

6.5 Taxes and tradeable permits under uncertainty: steep MC 160

8.1 Case 1: Environment does not enter utility function 204

8.2 Case 1: Introducing environment to utility function 205

8.3 Case 1: Introducing trade 206

8.4 Case 2: Effect on environment of introducing trade and effects of introducing Pigovian externality tax 208

8.5	Case 2: Effects on trade and welfare of direct control of pollution	211
8.6	Case 3: Effects of introducing a separate pollution-abatement activity	212
8.7	Case 4: Heckscher-Ohlin model; effects of trade on environment	218
8.8	Case 4: Heckscher-Ohlin model; effects of environment on trade	221
8.9	Case 5: Heckscher-Ohlin model; production possibility surface	223
8.10	Case 5: Projection of production possibility surface on AE and AB planes	224
8.11	Case 5: Introducing trade to Figure 8.10	226
8.12	Case 5: Introducing environmental protection to an initial trade situation	227
8.13	Case 6: Negative effect of pollution in manufacturing sector on production function for agriculture	230
8.14	Case 6: Three production possibility curves: no pollution, pollution without pollution abatement, and optimal pollutional abatement	231
8.15	Case 6: Introducing trade	233
9.1	Externalities in import competing production	238
9.2	Externality – export industry	239
9.3	Inefficiency of using trade measures for production externality	242
9.4	A second-best illustration	244
9.5	Second-best Pigovian tax with terms of trade effect	247
9.6	Environmental subsidy to export	251
9.7	Distributional effects of import vs. export taxes for externalities	253
9.8	Distributional effects of externality tax and tradeable permit with changes in foreign demand	256
13.1	Pollution abatement in internationally shared resource: one polluter	346
13.2	Mutual reciprocal pollution of internationally shared resource	348
13.3	Allocating cost of public good	351
13.4	Reciprocal pollution, strategic behavior	352
13A.1	A noncooperative, suboptimal international pollution-abatement game with Nash equilibrium	381

13A.2 A noncooperative, suboptimal international pollution-
abatement game with Stackelberg-type strategy 382
14.1 Carbon emissions per capita 394
14.2 Carbon emissions per unit GNP 395
14.3 Possible paths to climate stabilization 398
14.4 The costs of a carbon tax by region: four models 408
15.1 Fish stock and fish stock growth rate 434
15.2 Relations between fishing effort, fish stock,
and harvest rate 436
15.3 Fishing effort, fish stock, and harvest rate:
Isoquant diagram 437
15.4 Fishing model with costs and revenues 438
15.5 Northeast U.S. commercial fish landings 1965–1996 454
18.1 Thai exports, imports, and GDP 516

Preface

This book has roots in a research seminar on international environmental issues that I have taught for several years at the Paul H. Nitze School of Advanced International Studies, The Johns Hopkins University. The seminar members have been graduate students of international relations with varied training in economics. My contribution has been to provide enough theory, drawn from international and environmental economics, to provide a coherent analytical framework for understanding environmental issues, especially in an international context. Their contributions have mainly been policy-oriented research, sometimes using economic concepts and tools and sometimes using legal, institutional, or political approaches. This combination of theory and policy has been successful in the classroom, and I hope it will carry over in the book. My experience is that although the merging of environmental and international economics is rather new, and at many points is breaking new ground, a clear exposition of basic principles and concepts helps bring some analytical rigor to what are frequently confused public policy debates.

Interest in international environmental issues among students and the general public has increased greatly in recent years for several reasons. Some global environmental threats such as climate change and the thinning of the atmospheric ozone shield, although not absent or unknown in the 1970s, have taken on greater urgency and have moved up the international policy agenda. The 1991 decision against the United States in a famous trade case with Mexico concerning tuna fishing and dolphin mortality was a watershed event in alerting the environmental community to links between international trade and environmental protection. International interest was also stimulated by the 1992 United Nations Conference on Environment and Development (Rio Conference) 20 years after the landmark 1972 UN Conference on the Human Environment (Stockholm Conference). More broadly, the concept of "sustainable development" with its emphasis on the need to conserve environmental and natural resources for future generations has gained a solid foothold in the United Nations system and the World Bank, and is gaining support in the developing world. Popular interest in international environmental questions has also been tweaked by a number of public debates, most prominently the creation of NAFTA, although the tone often has been shrill and the economics rather shallow.

A merging of international and environmental economics can also be detected in academic writings, although it is far from complete. There are many good textbooks on international economics but most have not systematically included environmental considerations. Environmental and natural resource economic texts are more likely to have sections that examine international concerns, but by and large the international dimensions, and especially trade, is not given a central place. There is, however, a growing body of analytical work that does investigate the nexus between international economics and the environment. That literature generally falls in one of two categories: the management of international environmental resources, for example, global climate change, and the interactions between international trade and environmental regulations. Even here, however, the analysis often takes an institutional or legal approach, or exists in scattered sources – technical journal articles, specialized reports, and working papers with a relatively narrow audience and focus. After protracted definitional debates, the economic literature on sustainable development now concentrates on intertemporal resource use with little attention to its international context. Thus there appears to be a need to consolidate and integrate three broad areas of research and policy discussion: the links between trade and environment; transnational pollution and management of international environmental resources; and the now fashionable notion of sustainable development.

Two features of the book deserve comment. First, the emphasis is on the contribution that the discipline of economics can make to the understanding of international environmental issues. Economics brings a sophisticated and powerful set of concepts and theories for explaining the roots of environmental degradation and devising efficient policies. But economics must be supplemented by legal and political analysis if the policies are to be implemented and effective. Also, a full understanding of international issues requires contributions from the environmental and ecological sciences. Communication between economists and ecologists remains difficult, in part because of basic differences in conceptual approaches. For example, economists tend to assume continuous functional relations, use marginal analysis, assume substitutability of inputs, and try whenever possible to measure in monetary units. Ecologists are more likely to use the concepts of threshold and irreversibility, stress the scale of an activity, and concentrate on physical measurement. Communication between the environmental community and international economists and trade officials was also quite limited until recently. By and large, economists and trade negotiators paid scant attention to the environmental consequences of international trade, and gave little attention to the environmental determinants of international production and consumption. Environmental analysts and activists were perhaps even less inclined to consider the environmental implications of the international economic system.

In the last few years, these perspectives have started to converge. International environmental economics is becoming a growth sector in the economics profession, international trade has become a central concern for many in the environmental community, and trade officials are starting to consider environmental viewpoints. But communication among the groups has been guarded, and this is especially noticeable at the intersection of economic and environmental policy making. One reason is the scarcity of analytical studies that present the basic principles of environmental and international economics in an integrated fashion and are easily accessible to those with modest training in economics. The intention of this book is to make these principles available to a larger audience, including students and policy makers in the environmental area. At the same time, I hope the book will broaden the understanding of those whose principal interest lies in international economics, but who wish to understand how the economic system interacts with environmental systems.

To accomplish this objective, the opening section of the book – The Basics – is a compact presentation of the main principles and theory of environmental economics. This section provides the concepts and tools needed to understand the international implications of economic-environmental interactions. Also, the book makes extensive use of diagrammatic presentation and minimal use of mathematics. This treatment is both a plus and a minus. The hope is that diagrammatic presentation of basic theory will broaden the potential audience while preserving sufficient rigor. At the same time, both environmental and international economic theory can be expressed in mathematical form, often with increased precision. Thus the approach has an opportunity cost. The goal is an acceptable compromise between accessibility and precision in presentational style, resulting in an integrated analysis that has something to offer readers from both the economic and the environmental communities.

A second feature of the book is that the subject is broadly construed to include not only the question of trade and environment, but also the theory and practice of managing international environmental externalities and resources and the related issues of sustainable development. One reason for linking trade-environment questions with the management of international environmental resources is that both have a common analytic base in environmental economics, and both involve deficiencies in markets. International trade becomes distorted if environmental costs are neglected in prices and hence in production and consumption decisions. On the other side, an economic distortion arises precisely because there are no functioning market prices and no trade in international environmental services such as biodiversity or wilderness preservation. In both cases, prices are distorted or absent, and international markets are not efficient. Another, practical, reason for linking the two sets of questions is that trade measures are increasingly used as carrots or sticks in agreements to manage international environmental resources, and that these agreements themselves have trade consequences. Finally, recent efforts at achieving sustainable development, which often involve increased government regulation to address market failures, are occurring at the same time as the worldwide trend toward deregulation, privatization, and a more outward view on economic policies, especially trade liberalization. The complementarity or conflict between the pursuit of sustainability and the liberalization of the internal and external economy are of interest in this book.

Integrating trade-environment issues, transnational externalities, and sustainable development, the book blends theoretical, empirical, and policy analysis. The reason is straightforward: The effects and efficiency of policy cannot be assessed without a theoretical framework. And a feeling for the quantitative importance of interactions between economic and environmental systems – for example, the competitive effect on international trade of strict environmental controls – is desirable to identify policy needs.

Acknowledgments

My debts for help in researching and writing this book are many and varied. I wish to thank my friends and colleagues who have read various versions and chapters, and whose comments have been of great help. They are Edward Barbier, W. Max Corden, Judith Dean, David Fernandez, Isaiah Frank, John Kellenberg, Steven Landefeld, Jaime Marquez, Irving Mintzer, Morris Morkre, James Riedel, Wendy Takacs, Robert Weiner, Frank Weiss, and I. William Zartman. I also thank the participants in seminars based on various chapters and held at SAIS, Johns Hopkins, the University of Bologna, and, at an early stage, UNCTAD, INSEAD, and Cornell University. My understanding of trade and environment issues has been greatly increased over the years through many discussions with Rene Vossenaar, Veena Jha and Roland Molarus at UNCTAD, Bill Long, Candice Stevens and Michael Potier at OECD, Tiziana Bonapace at ESCAP, Dhannan Sunoto and Filemon A. Uriarte, Jr., at ASEAN, Richard Eglin at WTO, and Dan Esty and Steve Charnovitz of the Global Environment and Trade Study.

A second round of thanks goes to my seminar students and research assistants at SAIS over many years. I especially would like to mention Ainoa Doughty, Christopher Dymond, Anna Hansson, and Esben Pederson, all of whom proved to be most able researchers; Bruce Schlein and Michele Quadt, who are master makers of complex diagrams; Flora Paoli for her editing skills; and Walter Weaver for his many contributions. Patricia Calvano, assisted by Lisa Blaydes, performed exemplary service in typing and retyping the many drafts, and without their help I would have been helpless. The entire staff of the SAIS library has been extremely accommodating and professional to a fault, and I am most grateful.

A third round of thanks goes to Dr. Sitanon Jesdapipat of the Thailand

Environment Institute and Chulalongkorn University, who is the principal author of Chapter 18, and whose knowledge of Thailand's environment is unparalleled.

Finally, my wife, Sue Pearson, gave me what I value most, the peace to work and the smile that encourages.

1

Introduction and Plan of the Book

1 The Theme and Thesis

The central theme of this book is the meshing of economic and environmental systems in an international context. Broadly speaking, the systems interact at two levels. The first is the interaction between international trade and investment and the environment, and the second is transnational pollution and the management of international environmental resources. The trade-environment nexus raises a number of interesting questions. How do trade and foreign investment affect environmental quality? What are "pollution havens"? Do the rules of a liberal trade system as exemplified by the General Agreement Tariffs Trade/World Trade Organization support or undermine environmental protection?[1] Are environmental regulations used as covert trade barriers? Is comparative advantage determined by environmental resource endowments? Should poor countries specialize in producing "dirty" products?

Transnational pollution and the protection of international environmental resources such as a biological diversity and global climate raise equally interesting questions. What is the economic explanation for transnational pollution, and how can international environmental resources be protected? Who should pay? How can international environmental agreements be reached when environmental values, attitudes toward risk, and abatement cost burdens differ greatly, and nations assert sovereign rights? Are trade sanctions useful tools to prevent "free riders" and to enforce management of international resources? What are the connections between trade liberalization, international environmental agreements, and the attractive but

---

1 The General Agreement on Tariffs and Trade (GATT) was incorporated into the newly created World Trade Organization (WTO) in 1995.

vague concept of sustainable development? Is liberal trade consistent with sustainable development?

The relations between the international economy and environmental objectives can be controversial. The conflicts generally fall in two groups, between the trade and the environmental communities, and between the industrial North and the developing South. For example, many environmental organizations in the United States were skeptical of the North American Free Trade Association (NAFTA), and virtually all were opposed to the implementing legislation for the Uruguay Round Agreements and the creation of the World Trade Organization (WTO). In the North–South context, the 1984 Bhopal disaster, which killed 2,500 people in India, illustrates how environmental protection can fall between the cracks in joint venture arrangements between multinational corporations, in this case Union Carbide, and local partners. Trade and trade liberalization in developing countries can intensify environmental stress in export sectors, and sometimes provoke consumer opposition and boycotts in importing countries in the North. The harvesting and export of tropical timber and the conversion of mangrove forests in Southeast Asia for shrimp and prawn export are examples. There is widespread concern in developing countries that the industrial North, after squandering much of its environmental patrimony and fouling parts of the global commons, will engage in some form of "eco-imperialism" in which trade measures will be used to deny market access. The use or abuse of international environmental resources such as ocean fisheries, biological diversity, and the atmosphere is also contentious. These latter controversies raise questions of intercountry efficiency and equity, but they also raise serious questions of intergenerational fairness.

Some of the conflicts between international economic activity and environmental protection are real and are not easily resolved. Some, however, reflect either poor trade policy or poor environmental policy. And some could be defused with better understanding and communication among different interest groups. A basic thesis of this book is that economic analysis provides an extremely useful tool kit for understanding the apparent conflicts and for devising policies that will remedy or moderate damages to trade and environmental systems. This point is worth emphasizing. A liberal trade system confers many benefits and should not be lightly compromised to secure international environmental objectives. At the same time, the putative benefits of trade are illusionary if the prices of traded products do not incorporate the environmental costs of production and consumption. Market prices matter.

The *absence* of markets also matters. Transnational pollution and mismanagement of international environmental resources occur precisely because no property rights and hence no markets exist. These can be thought of as international market failures. Examples are the absent or incomplete international markets for wilderness recreation, wildlife, genetic resources, open access ocean fisheries, and greenhouse gas emissions. As demonstrated throughout the book, the task of establishing property rights, creating markets, and correcting market price distortions is greatly complicated by the international character of these problems. The tools of economic analysis, however, can be productively deployed for a deeper understanding of the issues and for the creation of policies that advance international economic *and* environmental interests.

Although we conclude that there are few *fundamental* conflicts between a liberal trade system and strong environmental protection, points of friction exist and are corrosive, and their resolution will not come about automatically. One reason is that until very recently the trade policy system evolved and operated independently of environmental concerns. Trade ministries and environmental agencies did not communicate with one another. Theory and experience, however, suggest that the two sets of policies require coordination, as trade does affect the environment, and environmental protection has implications for trade and the rules governing international trade. Another reason for considering trade and environment together is that some environmental effects are by their nature transnational or international in character, and trade measures offer a superficially attractive method for controlling transnational pollution and achieving international environmental objectives.

At a more fundamental level than policy frictions, there can be conflicts between the values held by environmentalists and the values implicit in a liberal economic system, although the differences should not be pushed too far. Historically, liberal economics has emphasized efficiency and consumer sovereignty. Environmentalists are more likely to emphasize stewardship, intergenerational equity, and an intrinsic value for environmental resources. A divergence of value systems would occur in the absence of world trade and investment. But the ethical questions become more difficult and urgent in an international context. Economic decisions in one country impinge on environmental conditions in other countries. Markets for many environmental services are either rudimentary or nonexistent. Thus there is exceptional reliance on public policy to protect the public's environmental interest, but the willingness and ability of governments to reflect the environmental values of their citizens vary greatly among countries. One cannot glibly assert that the environmental consequences of trade are simply matters to be left to national authorities in other countries; environmentalists are not parochial in their concerns. At the same time care must be taken not to impose one country's environmental values on another, especially when the economic costs are borne by the second country. While eco-imperialism may be too strong a term, the coercive use of trade measures to achieve a wide range of noncommercial, international objectives, from human rights to arms control, is not uncommon.

Ethical questions also arise in allocating the cost of environmental protection internationally. Who is to bear the cost of environmental protection, the producing (exporting) country or the consuming (importing) country? Which regime is more efficient? Will market structures permit environmental protection costs to be passed forward to consumers? The conflating of efficiency and equity and the related issue of stewardship is, perhaps, most acute in the discussion of global warming, a problem in which the international and intergenerational incidence of costs and benefits is central.

Economics cannot answer purely ethical questions. But it can greatly help in sorting out the issues, identifying more and less efficient policy measures, and tracing through the equity implications of trade and environmental policies. In succeeding chapters we use basic economic tools to analyze three broad areas in which international economic and environmental systems intersect. These areas are the reciprocal relations between international trade (and investment) and environment; international environmental externalities, sometimes known as international spillovers, in which economic activities in one country have a direct effect on international environmental resources or the environment of other countries; and ongoing efforts to redirect economic development toward sustainability.

2 Stepping Back

Before exploring why international economic-environmental issues have become prominent, it is useful to step back and say a word about the treatment of the environment in economics. All economic activity is embedded directly or indirectly in an environment matrix, if the environment is understood to mean nature (or natural resources) whether commercialized or not. This implies a reciprocal relation between economic and environmental systems. Environmental and natural resources are inputs into economic production and provide directly consumed services of economic value. As a consequence, economic output and welfare are determined in part by the availability and quality of environmental inputs. The inputs may or may not pass through organized markets, and their value may or may not be recognized. At the same time all economic activity has environmental effects, from resource extraction, through processing and transport, to consumption (a misleading term as goods are not physically consumed but are ultimately disposed of in environmental media). Moreover, environmental protection itself is an economic activity requiring conventional economic inputs of labor, capital, and technology. Thus, environmental quality may suffer from the disposal of residuals resulting from economic activity, but that damage often can be moderated or reversed with economic inputs. The reciprocal relations between economic and environmental systems would exist in autarky. The internationalization of economic systems and the globalization of environmental threats simply underscore the intimate, mutual relation of economic activity and the environment, and the need to analyze the interactions from an international perspective. Understanding these interactions is a central purpose of this book.

The historical record of economics in focusing on the interactions between economic activity and the environmental matrix within which that activity takes place is checkered. The classical economists did give a central importance to land, a shorthand description for natural resources. Diminishing marginal returns in agriculture were important in the classical growth model and for the Malthusian pessimism concerning long-run wage stagnation. But modern growth theory, building on the Harrod Domar model of the 1940s and the Solow-Swan model of the 1950s, and the so-called "new growth theory" of the last two decades, which attempts to endogenize technological progress, almost totally ignores natural and environmental resource inputs and the waste flows and environmental stress created by economic activity. In similar fashion, none of the popular economic development theories of the early postwar era – the big push, unbalanced growth, foreign exchange constraint (two-gap), or dualistic labor surplus models – paid more than minimal attention to natural and environmental resources. The labor surplus model did stress the need to maintain agricultural productivity if the rural sector were to be a source of savings, labor, and agricultural surplus to fuel industrial development. But neither resource degradation nor pollution played a significant role. "Until very recently, environmental resources made but perfunctory appearances in government planning models, and were cheerfully ignored in most of what goes by the name of development economics" (Dasgupta, Mäler, and Vercelli 1997, p. v).

Recent thinking on economic development still displays some divisions. Most mainstream development economists are primarily concerned with restoring a proper balance for markets, the price system, and the private sector as the engines of economic growth and development, after the excesses and failures of government planning, state enterprises, and especially import substitution policy. But at the same time the connection between poverty and abuse of environmental resources and the need to conserve natural resources are receiving increased attention under the rubric of sustainable development.[2]

Although explicit consideration of the environment was absent from the growth and development literature during much of the 20th century, two early strands of modern environmental economics did emerge. The formalization of externality theory by Pigou in the 1920s has become a centerpiece of environmental economics, although it was viewed mainly as a bucolic footnote for decades. The Coase Theorem, dating to 1960, also deals with externality theory but leads to quite different policy conclusions. Whereas Pigou's analysis suggests a policy of government taxes to correct externalities, Coase emphasizes that if property rights are well defined, costless bargaining between polluters and victims can lead to efficient outcomes without direct government involvement.[3]

The second strand is anchored in natural resource theory. Hotelling (1931) pioneered research on the optimal rate of extraction of exhaustible resources. His conclusion, that under certain conditions the price of a resource would increase at the relevant discount rate, remains a centerpiece of exhaustible resource theory. The larger questions of whether the price/market system on its own leads to intertemporal efficiency, and whether intertemporal efficiency is consistent with intergenerational fairness, continue to be debated in discussions of sustainability. Gordon (1954) investigated the yield of a renewable resource in an open-access common property resource context, and subsequent models have built on this base. The critical insight that open-access resources invite excessive exploitation is behind current efforts to manage international environmental resources. This earlier work on externalities and optimal exploitation of natural resources laid the basis for modern environmental economics.

As a result of this theoretical foundation, when the environment became a high priority in the late 1960s and early 1970s, the discipline of economics

---

2 As illustration, the authoritative *Handbook of Development Economics*, edited by Hollis Chenery, Jere Behrman, and T. N. Srinivasan, included for the first time in 1995 a chapter on environment and development.

3 The term "polluters and victims" has a pejorative tone, but is widely used in the literature. David Pearce and R. Kerry Turner (1990) use the term "sufferer" instead of victim. More neutral phrases such as "externality generators and recipients" are awkward. Strictly speaking, there is no necessary reason why rights should always be awarded to victims over polluters on either equity or efficiency grounds. See Chapter 3.

was able to offer a "tight" theory explaining the roots of environmental degradation and providing insight into corrective policies. However, economics had not yet fully incorporated environment into economic-growth and development models, and the efficiency-equity issue remained unresolved.[4] Subsequent contributions to environmental economics over the past two decades have focused on methods for valuing environmental damages, refining notions of sustainability, and evaluating the instruments available to government for environmental protection, especially market-based measures such as pollution taxes and tradeable permits.[5] Placing these advances in an international context is the subject of this study.

3 Internationalizing Environmental Economics

Although fashionable and controversial, the international issues dealt with in subsequent chapters are not entirely new. The trade-environment nexus first received analytical and policy attention in the early 1970s partly as a consequence of the 1972 United Nations Conference on the Human Environment. Regional and global environmental disputes also have a long and rich history. The 1909 U.S.-Canadian Boundary Waters Treaty prohibited pollution by one nation that would injure the health or property of the other. A number of water treaties in Europe, including agreements between France and Switzerland (1904), Denmark and Germany (1922), and Belgium and Germany (1929), included clauses that limited or prohibited pollution (Lester 1963). Regional management of national waters and water quality also has a long history. Between 1904 and 1930, seven multipurpose water authorities were created in the Ruhr area of Germany (Kneese and Bower 1968). Transboundary air pollution led to the Trial Smelter dispute between the United States and Canada in the 1930s and its resolution is regarded as a major benchmark in the evolution of international environmental law. With respect to conserving international resources, the threat posed by long-distance trawler fleets led to the North Sea Fisheries Convention as early as 1882. Conservation motives also led to the Bering Sea Fur Seal Arbitration between the United States and Great Britain in 1893 and a multilateral con-

---

4 Major contributions in the 1970s include growth-theoretical work on resources by Solow (1974) and Dasgupta and Heal (1979), and intergenerational equity analysis by Page (1977). Allen Kneese and his colleagues at Resources for the Future were at the center of analytical and policy research at this time.

5 The contributions of Pigou, Hotelling, Gordon, and Coase are all within what might be called mainstream economics. A number of economists have worked further from this core, including Kenneth Boulding, Robert Costanza, Herman Daly, and Nicholas Georgescu-Roegen. Charles Perrings (1987) links materials flows (the materials balances model) with externality theory. Formal models of economic-environmental growth are developed by Andrea Beltratti (1996).

vention on sealing including Russia and Japan in 1911. The latter is interesting, as the United States and Russia operated as agents for the parties,
with proceeds from the seal harvest split among all parties – an early form
of least-cost management and international compensation (Christy and
Scott 1965; Johnston 1965). Global environmental threats such as atmospheric ozone depletion and greenhouse gas emissions were first recognized
in the 1960s and early 1970s, although they received little public attention
until the late 1980s. Concern for soil erosion, extinction of species, deforestation, and the depletion of exhaustible resources, the hallmarks of unsustainable natural resource development, also can be traced back decades and
sometimes centuries, although the focus was generally at the local or
national rather than the international or global level.

The current intensity of interest in economic-environmental interactions
at the international level is, however, unprecedented. There are several
reasons. First, the environmental problems identified decades ago appeared
mainly to involve local pollution or degradation. But these have been
superseded by the emergence of newly recognized, serious threats to the
global environment, including atmospheric and climate change, pervasive
destruction of coral reefs, and deforestation and loss of biological diversity
on a scale that creates international spillovers and requires international
response. Regional environmental problems have also captured headlines,
including the smokey haze from Indonesian forest fires that covered
much of Southeast Asia in 1997 and pollution from Mexican fires affecting
southern portions of the United States in 1998. The pollution and degradation of resource systems has coincided with renewed interest in
conservation of natural resources and a new appreciation of valuable
basic ecological functions, analyzed under the rubric of sustainable development. Population and economic growth, together with accelerating
technological change, are changing our view from a nearly empty to a nearly
full world.

A second reason for the intensity of interest is the astonishing advance in
internationalizing the global economy through trade, investment, and technology flows. Not only does the integration of the global economy make
ostensibly domestic environmental policies international in their effects, but
it deepens what some have described as the "global ecological shadow" cast
by the economic activity of the industrial countries (MacNeill, Winsemius,
and Yakushiji 1991). International trade separates in a spatial sense the
environmental effects of producing goods from the point of consumption. It
follows that consumption in one country can affect the environment in other
countries even when there are no direct pollution spillovers. In both per-

ception and fact, environmental policies affect international trade, and trade affects environmental conditions on an unprecedented scale.

Finally, the current interest in the environment reflects mounting evidence that poverty itself contributes to environmental degradation in poor countries, especially of the productive resource base, and that this degradation may have international consequences. This awareness underpins the evolving concept of sustainable development. Recasting development strategy in poor countries toward sustainability, however, has taken place in the difficult international economic context of an extended debt crisis and structural adjustment programs during the past decade. Internal and external market liberalization in the developing South can sharpen potential or perceived conflicts between economic activity and environmental protection. All three of these new, or newly recognized, international interactions between economic and environmental systems were at the center of the 1987 Brundtland Commission Report, *Our Common Future*; were very much evident at the 1992 United Nations Earth Summit in Rio; and are with us today.

Environmental economics has roots in domestic resource management but can contribute to analysis and policy response to international environmental issues. There are, however, special features at the international level that are muted or not present at the national level. Four of these features deserve mention. First, there is no supranational Environmental Protection Agency that can establish environmental standards internationally and compel compliance. Agreement on environmental objectives and implementation requires either voluntary negotiations and commitments among sovereign states, perhaps accompanied by compensatory payments, or by some form of coercion. This means that the institutional context within which international environmental policy is made is quite different and more complicated than at the national level. The absence of a supranational EPA also invites the use of trade measures for securing environmental objectives.

Second, environmentalists often have a global welfare perspective, but do not have well-developed markets or political institutions through which they can express their preferences. This creates a dysfunction between the geographic scope of their concern and their ability to exercise extraterritorial influence. This dysfunction has also encouraged the use of restrictive trade measures to secure international environmental objectives. In trade policy the unit of analysis for welfare calculation is often the national level. For example, much of the strategic trade policy literature identifies conditions under which government intervention, using protection or subsidies, can switch monopolistic profits to home country producers or capture industries with significant positive technological externalities. Even when economists take a more cosmopolitan view of trade, or, as in neoclassic trade theory, when they assert that liberal trade is a positive-sum game, the practitioners of trade policy often respond to domestic political pressures and defend their initiatives in terms of national advantage and national welfare. In contrast, the environmental community places less stress on national welfare and gives greater weight to protection of environmental resources regardless of their geographic location. Also, the environmental community in the United States is accustomed to achieving its objectives through legislation, not improvement in markets *per se*. Without an effective international legal regime and without a functioning international market for environmental services, the incongruity between environmentalists' international objectives and the means available to them to obtain these objectives again directs attention to the use of trade measures.

A third special feature at the international level is that the notion of open and closed systems is quite different for environmental and economic questions. True, both the global environment and the global economy are closed systems (except for solar flux). But each national economy interacts with other economies through trade and investment by choice and policy. Thus national economies are more or less "open" depending largely on national policies. In contrast, national environmental resources are in essence arbitrary divisions of a global biosphere. The degree of "openness" is more an ecological and environmental attribute or endowment, and less a matter of policy discretion. A country cannot control transnational pollution and the quality of its environment as easily as it controls trade at its border. Put somewhat differently, economic activity by one country can have an environmental impact on others either directly through transboundary pollution and use of international common property resources such as the oceans, or indirectly, through trade. Economic activity and the associated environmental effects are not congruent in a spatial sense. This, of course, is also true within countries. But within countries trade is generally unrestricted, citizens can freely move among regions, welfare is more apt to identify with the national level, and interregional welfare redistribution mechanisms are more likely to be in place. Most important, national political structures are more highly developed. For all these institutional reasons, the spatial incongruence between economic activity and its environmental consequences is different at the international than the national level.

Fourth, economic relations among countries are subject to a special web of rules and regulations, many of which are codified in the General Agreement on Tariffs and Trade (GATT) and now the broader World Trade Organization (WTO). The process of developing a comparable web of international environmental regulations is in its infancy. This raises the possibility of conflicts between the trade *policy* system and environmental objectives, conflicts that are generally absent or can be more easily mediated at the national level. It has also led some experts to support the creation of a "Global Environmental Organization" to bring various environmental initiatives such as the Global Environmental Facility and the United Nations Environmental Programme under one institutional roof and to work with WTO in sorting out trade-environment issues (Esty 1994; Runge 1994b).

Internationalizing environmental economics is only part of the story. There is also a need to add an environmental component to traditional trade theory. The main pillar of that theory remains the concept of comparative advantage, which explains the pattern of trade and the gains from trade. A primary task is to investigate whether environmental resources are a determinant of comparative advantage and, if so, how that affects trade patterns and the gains from trade. An impressive body of theory exists for the analysis of trade policy, but it will be productive to add an environmental component as well.

4 Plan of the Book

This book is organized in four major sections, the latter three corresponding to the main areas where economic and environmental systems intersect at the international level: the relations between trade and environment, international environmental spillovers and management of international resources, and sustainable development.

Part 1, The Basics, prepares the way. Its purpose is to provide a theoretical framework and analytical tools with which the three international topics can be examined. Chapter 2 starts by considering the reciprocal relationships between economic activity and the natural environment. It describes the threefold economic role of the environment, as a producer good entering production functions; as a consumer good, providing directly consumed services; and as a sink or repository for waste disposal. It then investigates alleged trade-offs between economic activity and environmental quality. Chapter 3 sets out a conventional economic interpretation of the roots of environmental deterioration. This interpretation involves the notion of market failure and the underlying concepts of externalities, public goods, and open-access common property resources. The underpinnings are from welfare economics. The main conclusion is that in many instances the price/market system, if left unregulated, fails to allocate resources efficiently, resulting in excessive use and abuse of the environment. Government policy failures that contribute to environmental degradation are also noted.

Time plays an important role in resource-allocation questions, and Chapter 4 explores intertemporal issues. These include the roles of discounting, intergenerational equity, and aspects of sustainability. The next two chapters address two central policy questions that follow from the implied invitation for government to correct market failures and improve social welfare. Chapter 5 asks the question, "How clean is clean enough?" As might be expected from a discipline characterized by incremental analysis and money as a measuring rod, the answer is where marginal costs of cleanup match the incremental benefits of environmental damages prevented. "Clean" becomes relative. This answer leads to a discussion of concepts of value, and of techniques for placing monetary values on environmental services. The second policy question, addressed in Chapter 6, is what instruments for environmental protection should governments employ? The range is from environmental zoning to so-called "command and control" measures (for example, physical-effluent and emission standards) to market-friendly measures such as taxes and tradeable permit systems. Taken together, Chapters 2 to 6 are a primer on environmental economics and policy and pave the way for international analysis.

Part 2 (Chapters 7 to 12) examines the relations between international trade, investment, and the environment. The overarching issues are the melding of trade theory and environmental economics, the extent of conflicts between liberal trade and environmental protection, and how those conflicts can be resolved. Chapters 7, 8, and 9 are primarily theoretical, including a review of trade and the environment as it is developed in the literature, and illustrations of how trade theory can be modified to account for the environment. These chapters present simple models showing how the environment can be fitted into traditional comparative advantage, and the conditions under which trade alters optional environmental policy.

Trade-environment policy issues are investigated in Chapters 10 and 11. Chapter 10 offers both a history and a taxonomy, or organizing framework, within which most issues can be discussed. It examines the competitive effects of differential environmental regulations, environmentally related product standards and ecolabelling, and other policy issues. Chapter 11 analyzes the roles of the international economic institutions that deal with trade-environment issues. GATT is the principal set of rules governing a liberal trade regime, but it has been under attack by many environmentalists as insensitive to environmental objectives. The Organization for Economic Cooperation and Development (OECD) has been an important forum for developing trade-environment policies and is perhaps best known for its Polluter Pays Principle (PPP). This chapter traces the evolution of OECD principles bridging trade-environment policies and examines the compatibility of GATT rules with environmental objectives. It also examines the trade-environment issue in two formal integration arrangements, the European Union (EU) and NAFTA. Finally, the effects of environmental regulations on trade, and the effects of trade on environmental resources, are very much empirical questions. Chapter 12 summarizes the major quantitative studies assessing these effects.

Whereas Part 2 examines indirect trade linkages between economic activity and the environment, Part 3 (Chapters 13 to 15) analyzes direct spillovers arising from transboundary pollution and exploitation of international common property resources. Unlike Part 2 issues, which presume markets for trade in goods and services, Part 3 issues arise in large measure because of the *absence* of international markets for environmental services. Chapter 13 presents the basic theory of international externalities involving pollution and internationally shared resources. The absence of a supranational environmental protection agency suggests the desirability of a Coase-like bargaining solution, but ambiguities in regard to property rights and underdeveloped mechanisms for making international payments (compensation or bribes) create special difficulties, as do strategic and free-riding behavior. Nevertheless, Chapter 13 presents a number of examples in managing international environmental externalities and also a potpourri of evidence drawn from diverse experiences. Chapters 14 and 15 examine these issues further using case studies. Chapter 14 addresses the international economic, political, and ethical aspects of what is perhaps the preeminent environmental challenge, global warming. While the tools of economic analysis are essential, broader questions of equity within and among generations play a critical role. Chapter 15 analyzes ocean fisheries by describing the basic economics of renewable resources such as fisheries and providing a number of examples illustrating how the inefficiencies of open-access fisheries resources have been dealt with.

Part 4 (Chapters 16 to 18) turns to the topic of sustainable development in a more concrete fashion. The inclusion of sustainable development in this book requires a word of explanation. In a strict sense, sustainable development could be analyzed at an abstract level without introducing the international dimensions, but some richness would be lost. Developing countries are engaged in two fundamental restructurings: liberalization of internal and external markets, which binds them even more closely to the international economic system, and recasting development strategies, which had paid too little attention to protecting their natural and environmental resource base, toward sustainability. These restructurings are mirrored in development-assistance agencies such as the World Bank, which now promotes trade liberalization and privatization, but which also declares support for sustainable development and makes environmental protection a criterion for funding.

The interface of these two restructurings holds our interest. Market liberalization gives freer reins to the price system in allocation of resources. Structural adjustment programs lead to greater openness to trade, investment, and technology. Both imply less government intervention. Restructuring for sustainable development, however, involves correcting private market failures and often can mean a stronger role for government intervention. How can governments devise a sophisticated program of deregulation where markets can be efficient and greater regulation where markets fail to protect the environment? More broadly, do environmental protection efforts among industrial countries, working through trade, investment, and technology flows, support or undermine sustainable development in poor countries? Do environmental and natural-resource protection policies in poor countries support or undermine their internal and external market liberalization and trade objectives? But sustainability is also a challenge for rich countries. A central economic and ethical question of sustainability is how we should value the future. Rich countries consume a disproportionate share of global environmental resources. What is an efficient and equitable allocation of environmental resources over intergenerational time?

Chapter 16 traces the roots of the sustainability concept and explores a variety of analytical approaches. While there remains ambiguity to the term, protection of environmental resources is recognized as a central element. Chapter 17 takes up measurement questions. Accounting systems are management tools. It is now recognized that traditional national income accounting, by failing to account properly for environmental and natural-resource effects, is misleading and can lead to policy errors. This chapter explains these failures and reviews attempts at "greening" national income accounts. It also examines the empirical evidence relating environmental variables and per capita income, the so-called "inverted U" hypothesis. Chapter 18 uses a case-study approach to analyze the interaction of trade and sustainable development in Thailand, a country characterized by great success over two decades in terms of conventional economic growth, but one in which the cost of environmental degradation was unnecessarily large. Chapter 19 pulls together various strands woven through the four sections of the book and presents a summary and conclusion.

5 A Cautionary Note

A basic premise of this book is that economics offers considerable insight into the management of trade-environment relations and international environmental resources. But it is worth emphasizing certain limits to economics. One has to do with imperfect knowledge. In many instances we do not know the outcome of critical economic-environment interactions. If the environmental effects of greenhouse gases are uncertain, economic valuations of the benefits of abatement are necessarily uncertain. A second limitation is the great difficulty in placing monetary values on environmental services. And yet a prominent feature of environmental services is that they often are not marketed and are unpriced by the market. Techniques for ascribing implicit, or shadow, prices remain imperfect. Third, as explained in Chapter 3, the Theory of the Second Best places severe limits on our ability to say that a particular policy unambiguously improves welfare without detailed analysis. The gist of that theory is that if multiple distortions exist and market prices do not reflect social costs and benefits (typical of environmental situations), the removal of *one* of these distortions may or may not improve welfare. While economics can be credited with this insight, the theory suggests great caution in proposing policy. A fourth limit is the inability of economics to make interpersonal and intergenerational welfare comparisons. The former is especially important in an international context that lacks political mechanisms for income redistribution or compensation. The latter is also critical, as environmental decisions made today can have long-term consequences, and yet future generations cannot participate in those decisions. Fifth, and even more fundamental, the principal *numeraire* for conventional welfare economics, on which environmental economics is grounded, is "willingness to pay." In this framework values are anthropocentric and no weight is given to intrinsic values of, say, wildlife or wilderness. The ethical justification for using individual human preferences for establishing all environmental values can be questioned. Moreover, willingness to pay means nothing without ability to pay. Hence environmental values are contingent on global and national distributions of income and wealth, another point at which economic analysis is open to ethical challenge. These are serious limits to economic analysis and policy. Nevertheless, all economic life will have environmental repercussions with or without economic analysis. Imperfect though it may be, careful use of economic tools and cautious interpretations are likely to improve efficiency in the use of environmental resources, and can clarify the equity consequences.

As a final note, some readers may be puzzled as to why population growth plays such a small role in this analysis. A popular view is that a population explosion is at the center of environmental stress. In rich countries, a greater number of people implies more production and consumption, and hence more pressure on resources and the environment. In poor countries, high population growth rates coupled with poverty are thought to encourage abusive natural resource practices, as the ratio of the population to the natural resource base breaches some critical limits. Both propositions have a kernel of truth, but I am reluctant to give them a central place in the subsequent analysis. One hesitation is that simple ratios of, say, population density or natural resources per capita are not accurate indicators of environmental quality. The Netherlands illustrates that high density is compatible with high income and what is generally considered a good environment. (High levels of consumption, however, *may* create stress in other countries through trade.)

A second hesitation is that population growth rates are slowing quite dramatically. Whereas world population increased 128 percent in the 45-year period 1950–1995, the UN estimate over the longer 55-year period 1995–2050 is for a 65 percent increase. Indeed, between 1992 and 1998, the UN revised downward its long-term stabilization estimate by about 6 percent due to larger declines in fertility rates than previously projected (United Nations 1998). The world average fertility rate dropped from 4.5 in the 1970–75 period to 3.1 in the 1990–95 period (World Resources Institute 1996, Table 8.2). While local instances of population exceeding environmental carrying capacity may occur, the role of population growth in long-term environmental degradation appears somewhat less urgent than it did three decades ago. In the end I have decided that a proper treatment of population would add to the length and complexity of the book but would yield diminishing returns.[6]

6 For the view that population growth creates external costs to society in poor *and* rich countries, see Kerstin Lindahl-Kiessling and Hans Landsberg (1994).

Part 1

The Basics

2

Interactions and Trade-Offs

A
be
1 Introduction

economic activity and environmental resources interact in a number of
ways. We need a framework or model to sort out the channels. The framework should capture the important relations, but not be so complex that the
details obscure the main connections. One purpose in this chapter is to reconcile two different views of the relationship between economic activity and
environmental quality. A popular view is that there is a trade-off between
the two – improvements in environmental quality can only be obtained by
sacrificing some output of conventional goods and services. A second view,
associated with the concept of sustainable development, is that environmental protection is necessary to support conventional economic output,
and failure to maintain environmental quality undermines income and
output, at least in the longer run. The second view suggests a positive relation between conventional economic output and environmental quality. We
show in this chapter that elements of both views are valid and can be reconciled if one recognizes a dual role for the environment: to provide valuable services that are directly consumed (environment as a consumption
good) and to provide inputs into the production of conventional goods
(environment as a producer good). A second purpose of this chapter is to
sketch out how economic-environmental connections might change as economic output and income grows. What factors are likely to determine the
longer run relations between gross domestic product (GDP) and environmental quality?

The chapter starts by presenting a simplified flow model linking economic
activity to natural and environmental resources. It continues with an inves-
tigation of the trade-off between economic activity and environmental
quality, and provides an initial, simple interpretation of sustainable/unsus-

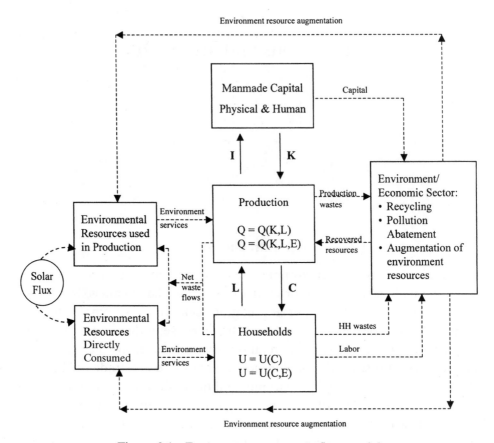

Figure 2.1. *Environment-economic flow model*

tainable development. This analysis is based on a static allocation model to help fix our understanding of economic-environmental interactions. The formal model and proofs are in Appendix 2.1. The chapter concludes by identifying possible longer run interactions between the economic and environment systems as growth proceeds. The role of time is considered further in subsequent chapters, especially Chapters 4 and 16.

2 Linkages

Figure 2.1 illustrates a simplified flow model linking economic activity with natural and environmental resources. The capital, production, and household boxes linked by solid-line flow arrows are the heart of a basic, conventional economic model. The services of labor, human capital, and physical capital are inputs to the production sector. Output, in the form of consumption and investment goods and services, flows to households or to augment the stock of man-made capital. A production function, $Q = Q(K, L)$, describes the technologies of production, and a utility function, $U = U(C)$, captures social welfare, where Q is output, K and L are capital and labor inputs, U is utility or social welfare, and C is the flow of consumption goods. This is essentially a static model, so we suppress investment and increases in the stock of capital, and output and consumption are identical.

The core economic model can be extended by adding natural and environmental resource boxes and specifying their links to the production and household sectors, and by incorporating recycling, resource recovery, pollution abatement, and environmental augmentation activities. In making these extensions certain changes are in order. First, the utility function must be expanded to include directly consumed environmental services. These may be life support or amenity services. By life support services we mean such *desiderata* as clean air and potable water. Amenity services include scenic and recreational areas, aesthetic enjoyment of wildlife, and the like. The absence of markets and market prices for these services in no way implies they are of little or no economic value.

Second, the production function for conventional goods is expanded to include a flow of environmental resource services that contribute positively to production. These might be broken down as renewable versus nonrenewable, energy versus nonenergy, commercialized versus noncommercialized, and so forth. Natural resources whose supply cannot be increased in human time scales (e.g., coal) are termed "nonrenewable," although the rate at which they can be discovered and exploited is not fixed. Natural and environmental resources capable of regeneration or replenishment to maintain a constant flow of services are termed "renewable" (e.g., fisheries). The distinction is not always sharp, however, as renewable resources such as soils and fisheries can be "mined" or depleted. Viewed as producer goods, environmental resources include such commercialized natural resources as fossil fuels and ores. But they also include surface water for agriculture, the natural fertility of soils, industrial process water, genetic resources useful for plant breeding or new pharmaceuticals, and many more. They also include environmental systems maintenance processes such as the recycling of nutrients, hydrology cycles, and filtering pollutants. This is natural capital performing ecological services. The substitutability of conventional production inputs (physical and human capital, labor) for environmental inputs to production is critical and much debated. Chapter 17 explores the issue in the context of sustainable development.

As inputs into production, environmental services may or may not be

owned or purchased in organized markets. As we will see, the absence of
property rights and well functioning markets for environmental resource
services is, perhaps, the central explanation for environmental degradation.
At this point, however, the key consideration is that environmental
resources make a positive contribution to production of conventional economic goods, and that this contribution is likely to be most visible in natural
resource-based sectors. It follows that a decline in environmental resources
or their quality will tend to reduce conventional economic output. Eroded
soils are one example.

It is useful at this point to elaborate on what is meant by "environment"
and "environmental services." The first is a stock concept and can be measured by indices of air and water quality, ore deposits, genetic diversity, and
so forth. Viewed as a stock, environment can be called natural capital. The
quantity and quality of natural capital provide a flow of services that enter
utility (welfare) functions and production functions. It is useful to think of
these services as "gifts of nature" even when their full utilization may require
some complementary inputs such as transportation to recreation sites, or
logging costs for harvesting timber. It follows that if the stocks are drawn
down through pollution, overfishing, salinization of soils or otherwise, the
flow of environmental services entering utility and production functions
diminishes. The total economic value of ecological systems and natural
capital stock is large, but difficult to measure.[1]

A third relation to consider is the effects of economic activity – production and consumption – on the quantity and quality of environmental
resources. At first glance we expect a negative relationship. Higher levels of
economic output (consumption) imply a higher level of materials throughput in the economic system. At higher levels of throughput there are greater
waste flows (residuals) in the form of materials and heat. These residuals
occur at all stages – extraction, initial processing, transport, manufacture, and
consumption (disposal). The materials balance-accounting approach, which
traces physical materials through the economic system, shows that in a
closed economy the gross mass of materials extracted from the natural environment, after adjusting for inventory changes, is equal to that mass of residuals discharged back to the natural environment.[2] This corresponds to the
first law of thermodynamics. Moreover, economic activity not only creates

1   Economics has difficulty in measuring nonmarginal changes in production inputs, in part because they
    create general equilibrium effects. The methods for monetizing (valuing) environmental services dis-
    cussed in Chapter 5 generally use a partial equilibrium framework.
2   The materials balances model developed by Alan Kneese, Robert Ayres, and Ralph d'Arge (1970)
    traces the mass of material extracted from the environment through the economic system to its ulti-
    mate disposal. See also Chapter 16.

residuals, but can lead directly to environmental degradation through loss of wilderness areas and species habitat. Some activities – for example, ill-conceived nature tourism – can directly degrade the environmental resource base on which the service is produced and consumed. These reasons suggest a negative relation between the level of economic output and environmental quality.

On reflection, however, the negative relation between economic output and environmental quality may be modified for one of several reasons. Environmental resources may possess some inherent *assimilative capacity* for absorbing wastes and rendering them harmless. Examples are the ability of water to absorb some waste heat without degradation, the decomposition of organic materials through natural processes, and the dispersal of atmospheric emissions through air currents and wind patterns to levels that are harmless (i.e., have no measurable effect on directly consumed environmental services or on production processes). If *unused* assimilative capacity is present, the negative relation between output and environmental quality is severed.

Also, output increase may be accompanied by a sustained increase in recycling and resource recovery. This would be more likely if there were an increase in the relative price of virgin raw materials, perhaps through a severance tax, or a policy of charging full social cost for waste disposal in environmental media. Also, if the virgin materials are commercialized, increasing scarcity may induce a price increase, encouraging recycling. An increase in recycling and resource recovery would decrease the throughput of virgin materials, reduce waste flows, and moderate stress on environmental resources in extraction.

Finally, at higher levels of income and output, there may be a sustained shift toward a less materials-intensive composition of output and consumption. In other words, the ratio of materials (in physical measures) to output (income) in monetary terms may decline. For example, the consumption of steel in tons per unit GDP in Japan declined by 17 percent in the decade 1985–1995. More broadly, OECD consumption of metals and minerals per unit GDP fell 42 percent over the three decades from 1960 to 1990 (World Bank 1995a, p. 40).[3] A reduction of materials use per dollar of GDP can be the result of technology change that is materials saving (e.g., miniaturization, improved auto mileage) or due to high income elasticity of demand for

---

3 However, merely substituting lighter materials for heavier materials (e.g., plastics for steel) may not decrease environmental stress. Worldwide, the consumption of energy per dollar of real output declined by about 1 percent annually from 1970 to 1995 (World Resources Institute, 1998, p. 13).

materials-sparing goods and services. A decrease in materials intensity, like an increase in recycling, may be the result of market forces or policy measures. In an open economy trade will create a wedge between the materials intensity of national production and national consumption. However, we expect that there are limits to unused assimilative capacity, opportunities for recycling and resource recovery, and shifts toward less materials-intensive production. At some point a negative relation between economic output and environmental quality is likely to reemerge unless additional deliberate action is taken to maintain environmental quality. This does not imply that environmental quality must ultimately fall as output increases, but rather that the environmental damage needs to be controlled through deliberate waste-management policies.

The fourth modification to the simple economic model recognizes that environmental degradation can be slowed or arrested (and indeed environmental quality can be restored or augmented) with the use of capital, labor, and technology. Thus we should incorporate the possibility that environmental resources or their quality often can be maintained (produced) with the application of conventional inputs. Soils or rangeland can be restored, wild trout streams can be rehabilitated, pollution can be abated or directed toward less damaging sites or media, and toxic waste dumps can be cleaned up.[4] But the cost of such protection or restoration is the diversion of capital and labor away from the production of conventional goods and services. To the extent that the degradation of environmental resources is prevented, or new environmental resources are created, a fully employed economy must shift resources away from conventional production. In this sense there is an opportunity cost to environmental protection.

To summarize, there are four major modifications to make to the basic economic model in Figure 2.1: (1) accounting for directly consumed environmental services in utility functions, (2) recognizing the positive contribution of environmental services in production functions, (3) incorporating the detrimental effects of economic activity and associated waste flows on quality or quantity of environmental resources, and (4) adding a new environmental-economic sector that "produces" pollution abatement, recycling, rehabilitation, and augmentation of environmental resources using conventional capital and labor inputs.

These four modifications are incorporated in Figure 2.1 by expanding the production and utility functions and by introducing the dashed directional arrows linking the old and new boxes. The environment-economic produc-

---

4 Some environmental effects cannot be reversed. Extinction of species is an example.

tion sector, like the original production sector, uses capital and labor to produce recycling, pollution abatement, and the augmentation of environmental resources. These economic activities reduce the net waste flow to the environmental resources boxes and reduce the environmental degradation associated with the initial extraction or exploitation of virgin resources. In this fashion the environmental-economic production sector helps maintain the flows of environmental services to the conventional production and household sectors. However, an opportunity cost arises from the diversion of capital and labor away from conventional production. One important feature the flow model does not capture is time. Specifically, pollutants may accumulate in the environment or their effects may be lagged. The introduction of time complicates the analysis, and a discussion of its implications is deferred until Chapter 4. Also, the activities identified in Figure 2.1 have a spatial dimension, and for environmental management purposes physical modeling of waste flows in airsheds and watersheds is needed.

3 Trade-Offs and Complementarities

3.1 An Allocation Model

This section presents an intuitive description of a static allocation model linking economic and environmental systems. The formal model is presented in the Appendix. Our main purpose is to reconcile two very different views of how economic activity and environmental quality interact. The first view concludes that there is a negative relation, or trade-off, between conventional economic output and environmental quality. The second view holds that over some range there is a positive relation between economic output and environmental quality. As it turns out, the two views can be reconciled by making a clear distinction between environmental services that are directly consumed (i.e., enter utility functions), and environmental services that make a positive contribution to the production of conventional economic output. Put somewhat differently, environmental services are both consumer and producer goods. This distinction is illustrated in Figure 2.1 by the two dashed arrows flowing to the production and household boxes. The distinction also becomes useful in analyzing trade-environment models (Chapters 7 and 8), and in Part 4 discussions of sustainable development.

We start by classifying *all* productive resources, called R, into three groups: the conventional production inputs of labor, physical capital such as machinery and transport infrastructure, and human capital, grouped into a single composite production input called K; environmental resources whose services enter production functions (e.g., fertile soils), denoted E_Q; and environmental resources whose services are directly consumed (e.g., outdoor recreation), denoted E_C. The production function for conventional economic output, denoted Q, requires K and E_Q as inputs. The substitutability of K and E_Q in production is much disputed and is at the heart of the debate on sustainability rules (Chapter 16). In our formal model we assume an elasticity of substitution of one in a simple Cobb-Douglas relation. Second, we recognize the negative relation between economic output Q and the environmental resource variables E_Q and E_C through environmental degradation parameters. Higher economic output tends to degrade the quantity or quality of E_Q and E_C. Third, we recognize that conventional production inputs denoted by K can also be used for pollution abatement and environmental protection, slowing or reversing any decline in E_Q and E_C. Examples of sustaining E_Q would be erosion control measures and restoration of soil fertility through organic mulching. Depleted renewable resources such as fisheries can also be stabilized and restored by curtailing fishing effort and restocking, and this would entail an opportunity cost in current yields forgone. This restraint would operate in much the same fashion as devoting some portion of K to the protection of E_Q. Examples of maintaining E_C would include expenditures on pollution abatement to stabilize or improve air quality in urban centers. For simplicity we assume that the negative effects of Q on E_Q and E_C, and the positive effects of devoting K to environmental protection, are immediate, not cumulative. In a more realistic, complex model time lags would need to be introduced. Finally, we acknowledge that utility, or social welfare, depends on the consumption of conventional economic goods, Q, and the services derived from one type of environmental resource, E_C. We assume a traditional welfare function with positive but diminishing marginal utilities for the consumption of both.

The basic problem is to allocate an endowment of resources, R, so as to maximize welfare or utility. This boils down to allocating the composite conventional input K among three activities – producing conventional output, protecting or augmenting E_C, and protecting or augmenting E_Q – to maximize social welfare. The solution is best illustrated using production possibility or transformation curves that specify combinations of conventional output and the environmental variables that can be achieved, given the total resource endowment and the environmental degradation and pollution abatement functions described in the previous paragraph. We do this in two versions.

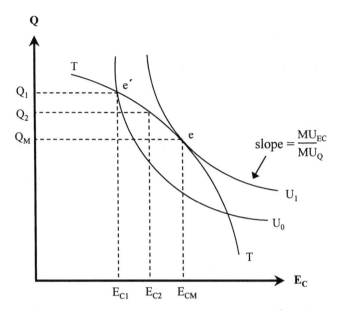

Figure 2.2. *Maximizing social welfare in a trade-off between conventional output (Q) and services derived from directly consumed environmental services (E_C)*

Version 1 The first version of the model concentrates on the relation between conventional output, Q, and the stock of environmental resources whose services are directly consumed, E_C. To separate this relation, assume that there is no pollution feedback from economic output to E_Q, which is fixed at some arbitrary initial value. Therefore, pollution from production and consumption has a negative effect on E_C alone, and this negative effect can be offset by devoting a portion of K to environmental protection. For any initial endowment of resources R, there are pairs of Q and E_C that are technically feasible, and these pairs form the transformation curve between Q and E_C.

Figure 2.2 illustrates the transformation curve, *TT*. Given resources and the functional relations, the combination Q_1, E_{C1} represents one feasible combination of conventional output and environmental quality. To obtain a higher level of environmental quality, say E_{C2}, it is necessary to sacrifice some conventional economic output by moving to Q_2. This shift is accomplished by reallocating some K away from conventional production toward environmental protection and augmentation. Thus conventional output has an opportunity cost measured by forgoing directly consumed environmental services; in similar fashion environmental quality improvement has an opportunity cost in terms of conventional output forgone. The math in

Appendix 2.1 demonstrates that the transformation curve has a negative slope, and is concave to the origin. This implies that there are *increasing* opportunity costs at higher levels of environmental quality. This feature is typical of most production possibility (transformation) curves.

The maximization problem is solved by superimposing on Figure 2.2 a set of social indifference curves, U_O, U_1, ... Social welfare is maximized at the point of tangency, e, (Q_M, E_{CM}). The slope of the indifference curves measures the ratio of the marginal utilities of E_C and Q. Thus we arrive at a standard result; welfare is maximized when the opportunity cost of environment in terms of conventional output forgone is just equal to the ratio of their marginal utilities. This ratio can also be interpreted as the relative price of environmental quality. With E_{CM} and Q_M determined, the allocation of K as between producing output and protecting the environment is also determined. This solution is sustainable in the sense that with unchanged total resources and technological relations, output levels and environmental quality can be maintained indefinitely.

A few additional comments are in order before analyzing the pollution that affects production functions. First, it is clear that countries will differ in their optimal solutions. Differences in incomes and environmental preferences will be reflected in different utility functions. *Ceteris paribus*, we would expect rich countries to choose a higher ratio of E_C to Q than poor countries, especially if the directly consumed environmental services are of the amenity type such as scenic attractions, recreation, and absence of nuisance odors and noise (environmental degradation of productive resources is another matter, and is considered next). Also, countries will differ in their production possibility curves, depending on individual environmental degradation coefficients, their ability to offset degradation through abatement and other efforts, and their initial endowment of environmental resources and conventional production inputs. These differences are explained in Chapters 8 and 9, which consider international trade based on differences in environmental supply and demand. Second, as analyzed in the next chapter, it is unlikely that the price-market system alone will achieve the optimal solution. The essential reason is that many directly consumed environmental services do not pass through markets, and there is no incentive to conserve or augment them. The pure market solution is likely to be suboptimal, say, at point e' in Figure 2.2. The task of environmental and economic policy is then to move from e' toward e to improve social welfare.

Version Two It is now time to consider the role of E_Q, environmental resources whose services enter conventional production, and the feedback from economic activity on the quantity and quality of these resources. To keep the analysis as simple as possible, assume that economic activity has no negative effect on environmental resources whose services are directly consumed, and hence there is no need to allocate the composite input K to its protection. E_C is fixed at some initial level. We follow the same general procedure of building a production possibility curve between Q and E_Q, but the result is quite different. Over some range, there is a positive relation between Q and E_Q.

Consider any initial level of E_Q. Assume a policy of maintaining this level with appropriate investments of labor, physical capital, and the like. Examples might include planting windbreaks and ground cover to stabilize soils, expenditures on exploration and development of nonrenewable energy sources to maintain energy supplies, or effluent filtration to maintain water quality in downstream fisheries. The amount of K used to maintain E_Q will depend on the extent to which E_Q is "exploited," which depends on the level of conventional output, Q. With fixed total resource inputs, R, and having committed to maintaining E_Q at its initial level, some of the composite input K must be devoted to environmental protection, though some will be available to work with E_Q to produce conventional output Q. We illustrate that as point e_o in Figure 2.3. Some of the input K is devoted to maintaining E_Q and some is contributing to conventional production, thus establishing one point, Q_O, E_{QO}, on the transformation curve *TT*.

Now assume a reallocation of K toward further protecting and augmenting the environmental resource, E_Q. While this will divert a larger fraction of K away from direct economic production, it will increase the availability of E_Q, itself an input into production of Q. So long as the marginal productivity of K *indirectly* supporting economic output by augmenting E_Q is greater than its direct marginal productivity in producing Q, there will be a positive range to the Q–E_Q production possibility curve as illustrated in Figure 2.3.

Thus, within a certain range, investments in maintaining or augmenting the stock of productive environmental resources are consistent with increases in conventional economic output. The negative trade-off between environmental protection and economic activity disappears, and a positive relation emerges. This might be termed a "sustainable" range, in which failure to protect productive environmental resources in a misguided effort to increase output of conventional economic goods undermines the productive base itself. (Chapter 17 introduces a broader concept of sustainability in which time plays a role. The allocation model in this chapter does not consider progressive resource degradation.) The existence of a positive rela-

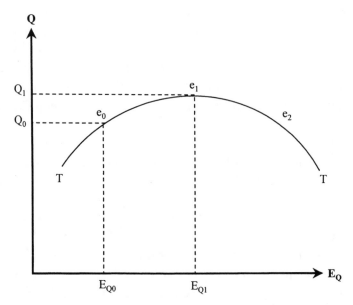

Figure 2.3. *Relationship between conventional output (Q) and environmental quality that affects production functions (E_Q): a positive range*

tion between environmental quality and economic output would surely argue for at least minimal environmental protection measures even in poor countries, where preference for environmental amenities incorporated in E_C may be limited, but where environmental resources used in production, E_Q, are crucial. By separating the two types of environmental resources, E_Q and E_C, something useful can be said concerning the appropriate environmental protection policies in both rich and poor countries. Also, the apparent conflict between those who hold the view that environmental protection is at the expense of economic output and those who argue that sustainable development permits increased economic production *and* improved environmental protection is bridged.

The positive region of Q and E_Q illustrated in Figure 2.3 will have an upper bound, however. The principal reason is that the marginal productivity of the environmental resource input E_Q will decline and the marginal productivity of conventional inputs K_Q will increase as K is converted to E_Q. Moreover, the larger Q is, the greater is the potential for environmental degradation, and hence the greater the need for environmental protection expenditures. An upper bound for output Q will be reached at point e_1 where the ratio of the marginal productivities of K_Q to E_Q is just equal to the rate at which K_Q can be converted to E_Q. As shown, further conversion of K_Q to

E_Q to obtain point e_2 would reduce economic output. Although not formally incorporated into the model, the environmental degradation relation is unlikely to be linear but rather exhibit increasing marginal degradation with increases in economic output. This would imply increasingly larger inputs of the composite resource for abatement, leaving progressively smaller amounts to produce economic output. Also, inputs to maintain environmental quality are likely to show diminishing marginal returns, further reducing the amount of the composite input available for economic output. Both of these modifications would also tend to put an upper bound on Q.

In the second version the objective of policy would be to maximize Q. The level of E_Q enters the social welfare function indirectly, only through its contribution to economic output. If the environment were at some level below E_{Q1}, it would be rational to build up E_Q. If it were above E_{Q1}, it would be rational to draw down E_Q. *A priori*, it is not clear where any specific economy is situated. As discussed in the next chapter, government and market failures often lead to inadequate protection of environmental resources, and this suggests some level below E_{Q1}. But a country richly endowed in natural and environmental resources and at a relatively low level of industrial development may find itself above the E_{Q1}, and thus find it rational to deplete some of its environmental stock without replacement.[5] The static allocation model presented in this chapter cannot provide a full answer, as much depends on how the converted natural capital is used, in particular whether it is used for current consumption or to build productive capacity, a question addressed in subsequent chapters. The renewable/nonrenewable character of the natural capital is also important, as are substitution opportunities among types of natural capital.

The preceding sketches out the bare outlines of a static system linking economic and environmental variables. One variation, not explored here, would be to incorporate the concept of assimilative capacity, in which the effect of economic output on environmental resources E_Q and E_C is zero, not negative, over some range. A second variation would be to assume that the negative pollution effects of economic output on E_Q and E_C are lagged, rather than immediate. In that event, *un*sustainable development would exhibit short-run economic growth and longer-run economic and welfare decline. Finally, for completeness, we should point out that if an economy is operating inefficiently, well below its production frontier because of distor-

---

5 The logic of this version of the model is similar to obtaining maximum sustainable yields for renewable resources. See Chapters 4 and 15.

tions and poor policy, it will also be possible to increase economic output *and* environmental quality. For example, the large energy subsidies that characterized the former Soviet Union, and which are still present in many countries, are inefficient in purely economic terms. Allowing market price to equal marginal social costs would improve resource allocation, increase conventional output, *and* reduce energy-related pollution. This notion underlies the so-called no regrets measures to control global warming (see Chapter 14).

4 Evolution over Time

The assumption thus far is that institutional arrangements are in place to provide for pollution abatement and the maintenance or augmentation of environmental capital. If property rights and markets for environmental services functioned well, there would be little need for government policy. But as explained in the following chapter, the main features of environmental resources are their common property nature and the failure of markets to allocate resources efficiently. In the absence of corrective policy, an economy that started with a particular endowment of environmental resources, E_Q and E_C, would tend to devote insufficient conventional inputs to their protection. Initially it may achieve a higher measured GDP but welfare derived from directly consumed environmental services would suffer. Also, over time, the depletion of environmental capital whose services are inputs to economic production would cause conventional economic output to decline or grow at a suboptimal rate. Both might be considered characteristics of unsustainable development.

Setting aside this institutional uncertainty, how might the environmental and economic variables of the model evolve over time? In particular, is the system consistent with the scattered evidence that measured pollution levels follow an "inverted U" path, increasing as per capita income grows, reaching a maximum, and then declining at yet higher income levels?[6] Four channels need consideration: a scale effect, a demand effect, a composition effect, and a productivity effect. The scale effect by itself should be positive. An increase in productive resources over time (physical and human capital, labor) shifts the production possibility curve between Q and E_C outward, allowing for higher consumption of both Q and E_C, provided that the increase in productive resources is not totally absorbed in incremental pollution abatement. It may be necessary to increase expenditure on main-

6 See also Chapter 17.

taining the stocks of environmental capital, but those expenditures can be accommodated out of increased productive capacity (Scott 1995). For example, an economy that initially devoted 5 percent of its productive inputs to the maintenance of E_C and 5 percent to the maintenance of E_O could maintain these levels while devoting 90 percent of incremental physical and human capital and labor force growth to the production of conventional economic output. The outward shift in the production possibility curve need not be uniform, however, and might be biased toward either conventional economic goods or directly consumed environmental services. This would depend on the relative marginal productivities of inputs in the production of Q and E_C and on the strength of the negative relation between economic output and the stock of environmental capital whose services support economic production. Thus, even with homothetic preferences,[7] while the absolute production of economic goods and directly consumed environmental services would increase, their shares in production and consumption could change. On balance it seems likely that the outward shift in the production possibility curve would be biased toward conventional goods, Q, as environmental amenities directly consumed could require natural assets in fixed supply such as wilderness recreation.[8]

Other changes may be the result of preferences and demand. Specifically, if the income elasticity of demand for directly consumed environmental services, E_C, is sufficiently high as compared to the income elasticity of demand for economic goods and services, the welfare share derived from E_C may increase. This seems especially likely if E_C consists in large part of amenity services, and per capita income passes some threshold level. Translating this preference set for environmental services into effective demand is not necessarily a mechanical market process. It may involve institutional and policy changes to create or simulate the market in a political process. Figure 2.4 illustrates a possible consumption path, with biased outward shifts in the production possibility curve, and social preferences drawn such that the share of E_C in total consumption first declines from e_1 to e_2 and subsequently increases from e_2 to e_3.

An output-composition effect is also likely as the economy grows, but its impact is ambiguous. Poor economies tend to be highly dependent on their

---

7 Homothetic preferences imply that the ratio of goods consumed depend on their relative prices but not on income levels. This is a convenient if arbitrary assumption to eliminate the effects of income change.

8 The economic reasoning behind this conclusion is simple. An increase in conventional production inputs (labor and physical and human capital) allows an increase in both Q and E_C. But a presumption that the supply of natural assets, such as wilderness areas and fresh water, is inelastic implies that the expansion of E_C is more severely limited by the law of diminishing marginal returns.

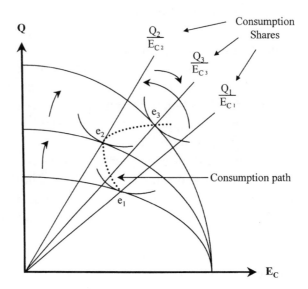

Figure 2.4. *Possible consumption path with increased production capacity and (ultimately) a strong demand for directly consumed environmental services*

natural resource base and hence the amount of resources needed to maintain or augment environmental capital, E_Q, may be relatively large. Rich countries with large tertiary sectors may be able to expand in sectors where adverse environmental effects are generally small. (We defer a discussion of the effect of trade on the composition of output until Part 2.) If so, the composition effect, separate for the scale effect, should be positive as countries enjoy economic growth and move away from natural-resource production. Environmental degradation per unit GDP would decline and a smaller fraction of incremental resources would be needed to maintain the environmental base. But before arriving at this happy state, the economy could go through an industrialization phase, in which environmental stress on natural resources were transformed into industrial pollution, and the productive resources necessary for pollution abatement would take an increasing fraction of incremental output.

Thinking through the composition effects is not easy. The composition of output and consumption depends on both supply and demand factors. Moreover, international trade drives a wedge between the bundle of goods produced and the bundle of goods consumed within an economy. Finally, pollution, or environmental degradation generally, arises from both production and consumption activities and can have its principal effect on directly consumed environmental services or on environmental services entering economic production processes. For all these reasons it is difficult to draw firm conclusions with regard to the environmental consequences of economic growth arising from changes in the composition of output and consumption.

The final channel for consideration is the marginal productivity of resources devoted to maintaining or augmenting the environmental resource base, E_Q and E_C. Their marginal productivity is likely to decline, implying larger increments of capital and labor to maintain the same level and quality of environmental resources. The empirical basis for this assertion rests on numerous firm and industry-specific studies that show increasing marginal abatement costs as pollution levels are reduced. There is a presumption that this relation also holds at the level of the aggregate economy, although the diversity of pollutants, their spatial dispersion, and the compositional shifts in output make empirical documentation difficult. If the marginal productivity effect is significant, it would work against the benign conclusion drawn from the scale effect. Progressively larger fractions of input growth would be needed simply to stabilize environmental quality.

To summarize the argument thus far, it is relatively easy to build a model that simultaneously exhibits a negative trade-off between output of conventional economic goods, Q, and directly consumed environmental services derived from E_C, but which also displays a range within which protection of environmental resources used in production, E_Q, and conventional output are positively related. This is called a sustainable region, although a full notion of sustainability requires a time dimension. Environmental protection measures are warranted in the first instance as environmental services contribute to utility or welfare, but such services bear an opportunity cost in conventional economic output foregone. Environmental protection measures are also warranted in the second instance, but only to the point where their contribution to conventional production is equal to their opportunity cost. How this economic-environmental system changes over time depends first on institutional behavior to compensate for market failures and second on the four supply and demand factors enumerated previously. Improving the quality and quantity of environmental services does appear compatible with economic growth, at least to the point where the bite taken by diminishing marginal productivity in environmental protection and increasing marginal damages begins to dominate. Technological improvements that are materials- and energy-saving and that reduce the cost of recycling and pollution abatement will also ease the economic environment trade-off.

Appendix 2.1

Derivation of Production Possibility Curves

This appendix sets out the formal model underlying section 3. Consider the following system. Specific forms of more general functional relations are used to assist the exposition.

$U=U(Q,E_c)$	utility (social welfare) function	(1)
$U'_Q, U'_{EC}>0$	(positive marginal utilities)	
$U''_Q, U''_{EC}<0$	(diminishing marginal utilities)	
$Q=A\,K_Q^\alpha\,E_Q^\beta$	production function for conventional economic goods	(2)
$\alpha+\beta=1$		
$\Delta E_C=-bQ+cK_{EC}$	environmental degradation and pollution abatement function for E_C	(3)
$\Delta E_Q=-gQ+hK_{EQ}$	environmental degradation and abatement function for E_Q	(4)
$K=K_Q+K_{EC}+K_{EQ}$	allocation of conventional production inputs	(5)
$E=E_Q+E_C$	allocation of environmental resources	(6)
$R=K+E$	allocation of conventional production inputs and environmental resources	(7)
$R=R^*$	endowment of total production inputs and environmental resources	(8)

Where:

U	is utility or social welfare
Q	is output of conventional economic goods and services
E_C	is the stock of environmental resources whose services are directly consumed
E_Q	is the stock of environmental resources whose services enter production functions
ΔE_C and ΔE_Q	are changes in the quantity (or quality) of E_C and E_Q
K	is the composite production input (labor, physical capital, human capital) allocated to producing economic output (K_Q), to maintaining or augmenting environmental resources whose services are directly consumed (K_{EC}) and to maintaining or augmenting environmental resources whose services enter production functions (K_{EQ})
R	is total resources, that is, the sum of environmental resources and the composite production input

The utility function (1) incorporates directly consumed environmental services in social welfare, and assumes a traditional form with positive but diminishing marginal utilities. Equation (2) is a Cobb-Douglas–type production function with K and E_Q as inputs. This implies positive but diminishing marginal products for K and E_Q, and constant returns to scale.[9] Equations (3) and (4) include the environmental degradation parameters b and g and the environmental protection-augmentation parameters c and h. The equations are linear for convenience; in the real world, marginal degradation is likely to exceed the average, and marginal productivity of protective measures is likely to be below average productivity. Equations (5), (6), and (7) are allocation identities and imply full employment. Equation (8) fixes the totality of resources at R*.

Version One of this model concentrates on Q and E_C, directly consumed environmental services, and assumes E_Q is fixed at E_Q^*. With no pollution feedback from output Q to E_Q, K_{EQ} is zero, and we use Equations (2), (3), (5), (6), (7), and (8) to derive a production possibility curve between E_C and Q. It is computationally convenient to assume coefficient values of A=1, and $\alpha=\beta=\frac{1}{2}$ in Equation (2). Then

From (6) $E_C = E - E_Q^*$

From (7) $E_C = R - K - E_Q^*$

From (8) $E_C = R^* - K - E_Q^*$

From (5) $E_C = R^* - K_Q - K_{EC} - E_Q^*$

From (3) $E_C = R^* - K_Q - (b/c)Q - E_Q^*$

for $\Delta E_C = 0$

From (2) $Q^2 = K_Q E_Q^*$ for $\alpha, \beta = \frac{1}{2}, A = 1$

or $K_Q = \dfrac{Q^2}{E_Q^*}$.

Substituting,

$$E_C = R^* - E_Q^* - \frac{Q^2}{E_Q^*} - \left(\frac{b}{c}\right)Q,$$

or E_C as a function of Q and the parameters. The negative slope and concave property of the production possibility curve can be derived with the first and second derivatives,

$$\frac{dE_C}{dQ} = -\frac{2Q}{E_Q^*} - \frac{b}{c} < 0$$

$$\frac{d^2 E_C}{dQ} = \frac{-2}{E_Q^*} < 0.$$

Version Two of this model concentrates on Q and E_Q, environmental resources whose services enter production functions, and assumes E_C is fixed at E_C^*. With no pollution feedback from Q to E_C, K_{EC} is zero, and we use Equations (2), (4), (5), (6),

---

9 An alternative modelling of environment and conventional economic output, popular in trade-environmental models, views environmental protection as a simple diversion of resources from economic output. While not wrong, this formulation leads to a negative trade-off between output and environment and fails to address the serious problems, especially in developing countries, in which environmental deterioration erodes the productive capacity of the economy itself.

(7), and (8). Again, it is computationally convenient to assume coefficient values of $A=1$, $\alpha=\frac{1}{2}$, $\beta=\frac{1}{2}$ in Equation (2), and $g=h$ in Equation (4).
Then we use:

$$\text{From (2) } Q=(K_Q)^{0.5} (E_Q)^{0.5}$$

$$\text{From (4) } \Delta E_Q=-Q+K_{EQ}$$

$$\text{From (5) } K=K_Q+K_{EQ}$$

$$\text{From (6) } E=E_Q+E_C^*$$

$$\text{From (7) } R=K+E$$

$$\text{From (8) } R=R^*$$

Note that R^* and E_C^* are fixed parameters.
Defining

$$n=R^*-E_C^*,$$

equations (5), (6), (7), and (8) can be used to write:

$$n=K_Q+K_{EQ}+E_Q.$$

In equilibrium, the degradation of environmental capital E_Q caused by production of Q must be offset by a sufficient allocation of capital for pollution abatement, so that from (4)

$$\Delta E_Q=-Q+K_{EQ}=0$$

Or substituting back

$$K_{EQ}=Q$$
$$n=K_Q+Q+E_Q$$

Or

$$K_Q=n-Q-E_Q.$$

Substituting back in the production function (2) we derive the relation between Q and E_Q

$$Q=(n-Q-E_Q)^{0.5} (E_Q)^{0.5}.$$

This produces the humped curve TT illustrated in Figure 2.3.[10]

To determine maximum output, Q_{MAX}, square both sides and use implicit differentiation,

$$Q^2=nE_Q-E_QQ-E_Q^2$$

10 A numerical example may help. Assume coefficient values of α, $\beta=\frac{1}{2}$ and h, g, $A=1$. Let the initial endowments be $K=130$, $E=9$, and $E_C=0$ so that their total $R^*=139$. The equation system can be solved so that $Q=30$, $K_Q=100$, and $K_{EQ}=30$. Note that the amount spent on abatement, K_{EQ}, is just sufficient to hold the environmental resource E_Q at an equilibrium level ($gQ=hK_{EQ}$). Now assume total R^* is reallocated so that $K=278/3$ and $E_Q=139/3$. Note that R^* remains 139. Solving the system, $Q-139/3=46.33$ and now $K_Q=139.3$, $K_{EG}=139/3$. Again the amount directed to abatement is just sufficient to stabilize the environmental resource at the new higher level of output. The reallocation of the fixed level of total resources, R^*, allows an output increase from 30 to 46.33, and an improvement in environmental quality from 9 to 46.33.

$$2Q\frac{dQ}{dE_Q}=n-E_Q\frac{dQ}{dE_Q}-Q-2E_Q$$

Or

$$\frac{dQ}{dE_Q}=\frac{n-Q-2E_Q}{2Q+E_Q}.$$

Set equal to zero,

$$n=Q+2E_Q$$

but also

$$n=K_Q+Q+E_Q$$

or

$$Q+2E_Q=K_Q+Q+E_Q$$

implies $\quad K_Q=E_Q.$

And, if $\quad Q^2=K_Q E_Q$

then $\quad Q=K_Q=E_Q \ (=K_{EQ})$

finally, with

$$n=K_Q+Q+E_Q=K_Q+K_{EQ}+E_Q$$

$$Q_{MAX}=\frac{n}{3}$$

and the available resources, n, are allocated

$$K_Q=K_{EQ}=E_Q=\frac{n}{3}.$$

Thus, if total manmade and environmental resources, R*, were 300, and if environmental resources whose services are directly consumed were 90, the value of n would be 210 and the maximum output of Q would be 210/3 or 70 units.

3

The Roots of Environmental Degradation

1 Introduction

This chapter explains the causes of environmental degradation, using the analytical tools of microeconomics, especially environmental economics. Before investigating the root causes, however, it is useful to develop a monetary measure of welfare using the concepts of consumer surplus and producer surplus and to relate welfare to the concepts of efficiency and equity. Section 2 introduces consumer and producer surplus. For marketed goods, consumer surplus and producer surplus are convenient to estimate but are not exact measures of welfare, and the appendix to this chapter explores more precise measures. Section 3 uses these concepts to illustrate efficient and inefficient allocations of resources and to relate efficiency to equity. Section 4 analyzes three interrelated sources of inefficiency in the allocation of environmental resources, collectively known as market failures. They are public goods, externalities, and open-access common property resources. The common thread to the three is defective or nonexistent property rights. Section 4 also examines so-called government failures, which also frequently contribute to environmental degradation. Finally, Section 5 presents the influential Coase Theorem, which concludes that in some situations a private "market" might be developed between those who generate environmental externalities (in short, polluters) and those who bear the cost of externalities (victims). Under certain conditions such a market can be shown to allocate resources efficiently *regardless of the initial system of property rights*, and this strategy has been proposed as an alternative to more direct government regulation of the environment. The insights of the Coase Theorem and its focus on negotiations between affected parties may be especially useful in an international context, in which there is no supranational environmental protection agency with

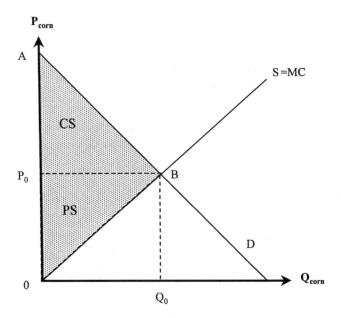

Figure 3.1. *Consumer and producer surplus*

the authority to regulate externalities and remedy international market failures.

2 Consumer Surplus and Producer Surplus as Welfare Measures

The first task is to find a monetary measure of welfare or utility. A logical starting point is to assume that consumption expenditures on final goods reveal underlying welfare or utility. *Consumer surplus* (CS) can be defined as the excess of utility that consumers receive over the amount they actually pay in the purchase of final goods and services. The notion is explained using Figure 3.1, which depicts the market for a final good, say, "corn." The market demand curve, D, shows the amounts consumers would be willing to buy at alternative prices (willingness to pay for alternative amounts of corn); the market supply curve, S, shows the amounts farmers would supply at these prices; P_0 and Q_0 are the market clearing equilibrium price and quantity.

The area under the demand curve up to level Q_0, area $OABQ_0$, can be interpreted as the utility or welfare consumers derive from consuming Q_0 units of the product. The amount they actually pay, however, is area OP_0BQ_0, and the difference, the triangle P_0AB, is CS. This is a monetary measure of their *net* welfare from purchasing Q_0 units of corn. A change in CS is a measure of welfare gain or loss.[1] If the product in question is an intermediate good, say, fertilizer purchased by farmers for the production of corn, the demand curve is *derived* from consumers' demand for corn, and the consumer surplus in the fertilizer market can ultimately be traced to consumers' willingness to pay for the final good, corn.

Turning to the supply curve, in competitive markets with no externalities S reflects the marginal private and social costs of producing corn. It follows that the area under the supply curve up to the level Q_0, area OBQ_0, represents total variable costs of producing corn. In the long run, when all of the inputs to production are variable (land, labor, capital, and intermediate inputs), this area measures the total economic cost of production. Total revenue to farmers in this market is the area OP_0BQ_0 and, with total production costs of OBQ_0, the difference, triangle OP_0B, is *producer surplus* (PS). In industries characterized by perfectly elastic input supplies, the long-run supply curve is horizontal (barring technological change) and PS disappears. In natural resource sectors, however, one expects increasing scarcity of inputs and hence a positive PS or scarcity rent even in a long-run competitive equilibrium.

Production cost (supply) schedules and their associated producer surplus can also be traced to consumers' willingness to pay for final goods. Specifically, the *opportunity cost* of the inputs to corn production, on which the supply curve is built, is the value of output forgone elsewhere in the economy by using the inputs in corn production. That value is of course ultimately determined by consumers' willingness to pay for these other goods and services. In this fashion both the benefits of producing corn and the costs of producing corn are directly or indirectly derived from consumers' willingness to pay, and that willingness to pay is assumed to reflect the utility or welfare derived from consumption.

Returning to Figure 3.1, if the welfare derived from consuming Q_0 units of the good is the area $OABQ_0$ and if the economic (opportunity) cost of producing Q_0 is OBQ_0, then the shaded area OAB is a monetary measure of net social welfare from producing the product, and is composed of consumer surplus and producer surplus. We can write welfare, W, as

$$W = CS + PS = P_0AB + OP_0B.$$

And we also have a measure of changes in welfare,

$$\Delta W = \Delta CS + \Delta PS.$$

---

1 The *market* CS is built up from individuals' consumer surplus. A change in market CS only measures *social* welfare change if all incomes are given equal weight, a serious limit explored in Section 3.

This formulation is especially useful as it allows decomposing welfare gains and losses as between consumers and producers, an important tool in understanding the political economy of environmental policy. Also, while the example is posed in terms of a conventional economic good, corn, the concepts of CS and PS also apply to environmental goods such as clean water, biodiversity, or scenic amenities. As explained in Chapter 5, one difficulty in estimating CS and PS for environmental goods is that market supply-and-demand information is often lacking.

The concepts of consumer and producer surplus can be used to analyze a variety of economic issues ranging from the welfare effects of monopoly to tariff policy. We use CS and PS to analyze a simple pollution externality problem in Figure 3.2 (externalities are described more fully in Section 4). In Figure 3.2a, S is private marginal supply costs, D is demand for some marketed product such as steel or paper. In the absence of regulation, the market equilibrium is at H with a price P_0 and quantity Q_0. Assume each unit of production causes (uncompensated) environmental damages to victims equal to a constant monetary amount, OE. In that event, the *social* costs of production (private costs plus cost to victims) are given by S', the social marginal cost. The victims can either be individuals whose utility is adversely affected or producers if the externality enters production functions with a negative sign. Figure 3.2b abstracts from the same information to create the net marginal welfare curve of consumers and producers taken together, MW_{c+P}, and is derived from the CS and PS in Figure 3.2a. Net marginal welfare to producers and consumers becomes negative at output levels above Q_0. The constant marginal cost to victims is represented by MC_v. Either part of Figure 3.2 can be used to analyze social welfare before regulation, or

$$W = CS + PS - VC$$

where VC is cost to victims.

In Figure 3.2a,

$$W = AHO - OECH = ABE - BCH$$

In Figure 3.2b we see that at the unregulated equilibrium Q_0, $MC_v > MW_{c+P}$, a signal that welfare is not maximized.

In this example, social welfare from the unregulated production of good X may be positive or negative, depending on the relative size of the triangles ABE and BCH in Figure 3.2a. If $ABE < BCH$, social welfare would improve by eliminating the production of the good. That extreme result, however, is unlikely to maximize social welfare. In general, the preferable

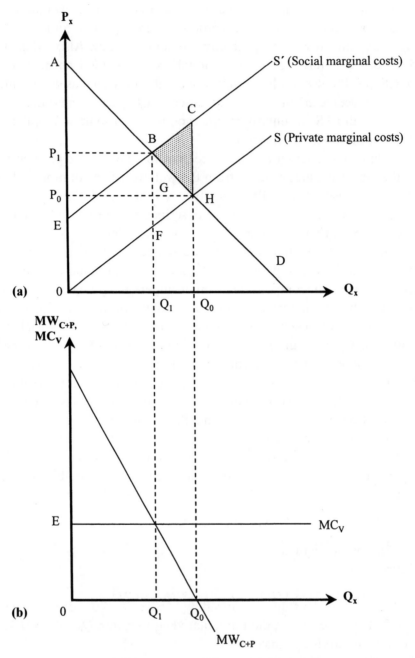

Figure 3.2. *Welfare effects of correcting production externality*

policy would be to reduce the externality to the point at which its remaining marginal cost or damages is just equal to the marginal benefit to producers and consumers of X production. Assume that no direct pollution abatement is available, so all pollution reduction must come from decreasing output. In that event, the costs of reducing pollution are the losses of consumer and producer surplus. Assume that in some fashion output is restricted to Q_1 with a market clearing price of P_1. This might be accomplished by a production tax equal to CH or by direct regulation. A tax equal to marginal damages at the optimal level is called a *Pigovian tax* and is examined in Chapter 6. To avoid involving taxpayers' welfare, assume direct regulation. Then

$$W' = CS' + PS' - VC'$$

where primes indicate the new levels, and in Figure 3.2a we see

$$W' = ABP_1 + P_1BFO - OEBF$$
$$= ABE$$

Comparing W and W', $\Delta W = BCH$, or the welfare increase measured by the shaded area BCH. Note that at the new equilibrium Q_1 price equals social marginal cost, and in Figure 3.2b

$$MC_v = MW_{c+P}.$$

The optimal level of production from the point of view of society is where the marginal costs to victims is just equal to the marginal welfare (benefit) to producers and consumers. Notice also that neither pollution nor victims' cost is completely eliminated at this optimal output level. The new lower level for victims' cost is $OEBF$, and victims' welfare is improved by $FBCH$ as compared to the unregulated situation (shown in Figure 3.2a).

Finally, note that an environmental policy to improve social welfare can have major distributional consequences. In this example, the net social welfare gain is the shaded triangle BCH. But the policy of restricting output to its socially optimal level Q_1 creates major *transfers* of welfare. As shown in Figure 3.2, consumer surplus is reduced by the area P_0P_1BH due to higher prices. Producers' welfare is increased by area P_0P_1BG due to higher prices for its remaining sales, but diminished by the area GHF, the surplus it had enjoyed on the production in the output range Q_1Q_0. A direct restriction on output may increase producers' welfare. Victims of pollution are unambiguously better off by area $FBCH$, an amount exceeding the social welfare gain of BCH. As explained in more detail in Chapter 6, the *distribution* of gains and losses depends very much on how the environmental policy is implemented. (A more realistic example would allow for a separate activity, pollution abatement, the costs of which would reduce producer surplus.)

To recapitulate, in an unregulated market too much X was being produced. Although the marginal utility was equal to the marginal private cost of production at Q_0, the marginal social costs exceeded marginal benefits as measured by producer and consumer surplus. Restricting output to Q_1 brings marginal social costs and marginal benefits into alignment and maximizes social welfare. But this was accompanied by major transfers of welfare between the three groups: consumers, producers, and pollution victims. Also, at the socially optimal level, pollution damages are not eliminated but just reduced. Finally, and to repeat, a statement that social welfare has unambiguously improved is only valid if all incomes are weighted equally.

The ideas embodied in Figure 3.2 are so central that some elaboration is justified. First, this example is cast in terms of the optimal level of output of the good (service). Because we have assumed pollution damages to be related to output, we have inferred the optimal level of pollution from the optimal level of output. Also, we have inferred the optimal level of pollution damages abated (area *FBCH*). Had we wished, we could have cast the problem as determining the optimal level of pollution or the optimal level of pollution abatement, and inferred the optimal level of output of good X, with the same results. Some analysts set up the problem as determining optimal output, some as optimal pollution, and some as optimal pollution abatement, but they all amount to the same thing. Second, although pollution itself has no true market and market price, we have inferred a hypothetical shadow price to a unit of pollution equal to the marginal damages of pollution at the optimal output level. This price is equal to the vertical distance between *S* and *S'* in Figure 3.2a and would be the basis for a Pigovian tax. Third, it is useful to remember the important assumptions in this simple model: pollution is treated as a flow, with immediate, not cumulative damages; these damages can be monetized; pollution is a consequence of production, not consumption; pollution can only be controlled by reducing output (although the same basic conclusions would hold if a separate activity of pollution abatement were available).[2]

---

2 In many cases pollution damages are related to both the current flow and accumulated stock of the pollutant in the ambient environment. For example, ozone depletion by chlorofluorocarbons (CFCs) and atmospheric carbon dioxide contributing to global warming are stock pollutants, where damage at a point in time is related to accumulated concentrations. Determining the efficient time path of the flow of such persistent pollutants is considerably more difficult, as the model needs to consider the

Two extensions need to be made to the foregoing discussion of consumer and producer surplus as welfare measures. First, exact measures of welfare cannot be based directly on market demand curves, and the theoretically superior measures involve the concepts of compensating variation and equivalent variation. These more sophisticated concepts are explained in the appendix to this chapter. Under certain conditions, however, CS and PS provide good approximations and are easier to calculate empirically. The second extension involves the Theory of the Second Best. Figure 3.2 is restricted to a single distortion due to the externality. In the real world multiple distortions may be present. The Theory of the Second Best reminds us that to remove one distortion in the economy (e.g., monopoly or a production externality) while leaving other distortions present *may or may not* improve welfare. The Theory of the Second Best is a general cautionary principle addressing partial policy measures. It has special relevance to environmental and resource management policies where distortions frequently remain widespread despite partial corrective policies. For example, a strict air pollution control regime may shunt wastes to more damaging and less regulated water and solid waste disposal methods, possibly creating more, not less, damage.

To illustrate the potentially ambiguous results of policy in a second-best world, consider a standard monopoly situation illustrated in Figure 3.3, perhaps a sole producer of steel whose production creates pollution. D represents the demand schedule and MC the monopolist's long-run private marginal costs. If this market were perfectly competitive and there were no pollution, Q_0 and P_0 would be the market equilibrium, and social welfare would be measured by the area ABO. If it were monopolized, however, the owner would maximize profits where marginal revenue (MR) equals marginal private costs (MC), and produce Q_m with a market clearing price P_m.[3] The social welfare loss from the monopoly is the shaded area CGB (the transfer from consumer surplus to producer surplus can also be seen).

Now assume pollution damages such that the marginal social costs of production are represented by the line OGF. Thus there are multiple distortions, with the monopoly suggesting too little output and the pollution

discounting of future utilities and the time rate of decay of the persistent pollutant (i.e., how rapidly atmospheric carbon dioxide is absorbed into the oceans where presumably it is harmless). In general, the efficient solution to the stock pollutant problem requires that the present value of future damages from a unit of pollution be equal to the cost of abating that unit of pollution. The solution also establishes a shadow price for pollution, but in this case the shadow price is not constant but rises over time. For a clear exposition see Perman, Ma, and McGilvray (1996, Chap. 8).

3 For a linear demand curve the marginal revenue curve is twice as steep as the demand curve.

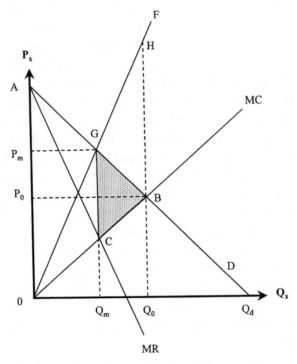

Figure 3.3. *A second-best problem: monopoly and production externality*

suggesting too much output. As constructed, any output change from Q_m would reduce social welfare. For example, an environmental policy to restrict output below Q_m would reduce pollution damages but the marginal loss to producers and consumers combined would outweigh the marginal gain to victims. A policy to move to competitive equilibrium Q_0 would also cause social losses. Pollution damages would increase by $CGHB$, but producer plus consumer surplus would only increase by CGB. In this example, no single environmental or antimonopoly policy is warranted. In general, to achieve a first best solution, two policy measures to deal with the monopoly and externality distortions are needed. As explored in Chapter 9, the existence of trade distortions complicates the analysis of optimal environmental policy in an open economy.

3 Efficiency and Equity

The basic notion of efficiency is implicit in the preceding discussion. Resources are allocated in an efficient manner if it is not possible to rearrange them in a fashion that can improve one person's welfare without reducing the welfare of another. This is known as the Pareto criterion or Pareto optimality. Microeconomic textbooks demonstrate that a perfectly competitive economy with no externalities will be efficient, with relative commodity and input prices providing the signaling and adjustment mechanism. Nevertheless, the criteria for efficiency remain incomplete *unless an optimal distribution of income can be specified.* Many resource allocations can satisfy the Pareto criterion, depending on income distribution patterns. The optimality of income distribution, however, cannot be established on a rigorous scientific basis, for it requires interpersonal comparisons of welfare (utility), for which there is no objective benchmark. To be specific, there is no reason to believe that a particular efficient economy is equitable or just. If ownership of productive assets is unequally distributed, income will be unequal. Whether or not any specific distribution of income, equal or unequal, is equitable is an ethical question, not an economic question.

The importance of this limitation is considerable in natural and environmental resource economics. Consider again the pollution example in Figure 3.2. To make the example concrete, suppose that the pollution damages productive resources owned by the victims (say, a commercial fishery), so that the monetary value of the damages can be relatively easily measured as the decrease in the net value of output of the fishery. The earlier discussion showed that a reduction in output of the polluting industry yields a net social welfare gain, with victims gaining, consumers losing, and producers either gaining or losing depending on market conditions. If consumers are compensated for their losses out of the victims' and producers' gain, then all parties are either no worse off or better off, and one can say that welfare has increased, a Pareto improvement. If compensation does not occur, the result is ambiguous. The uncompensated welfare loss to consumers *may* weigh more heavily in a social welfare function than the net gain to victims and producers. This would be more likely if consumers were poor and producers and victims were rich. The more general point is that virtually any environmental policy is likely to be associated with uncompensated welfare loss by at least one group in society, and flat statements about social welfare improvement become suspect. Economists often bypass this problem by asserting that the policy change increases the total availability of goods so that compensation *could* be paid with a net gain remaining,[4] and by noting that society has other mechanisms such as the tax system for achieving desir-

---

4 Sometimes known as the Hicks-Kaldor hypothetical compensation test. Compensation or transfers are apt to create additional costs if the money is generated through taxes.

able income distribution, if actual payment is desired. But strong statements about welfare improvement without compensation remain on conceptually weak ground.

Possible conflicts between economically based notions of efficiency and ethically based notions of equity or fairness are common in the management of the environment. At its most basic, all environmental policy involves a rearrangement of property rights. While the ostensible motivation may be efficiency, there are always equity consequences as some rights are withdrawn and others conferred. Conversely, some policies are motivated by equity concerns but they, too, will have efficiency consequences. As explained in Chapter 11, the Polluter Pays Principle (PPP) of financing environmental protection had its origins as an efficiency principle but is now widely interpreted and supported on "fairness" grounds. The simple example in Figure 3.2 is another illustration. An efficient solution leaves some pollution damages remaining, and one could make an ethically based argument that this is not acceptable. Also, ethically based social welfare functions become complicated in an international context. Should they be national or global in scope? What right or obligation does an environmentalist have to protect wildlife internationally, and how is that to be reconciled with efficiency in economic development? As examined in Parts 2 and 3, the connection between efficiency and equity becomes more complex in an international context where the vehicles for international compensation are primitive, and the geographic scope of social welfare functions uncertain.

The preceding discussion examines static efficiency in the distribution of goods and allocation of resources. Dynamic efficiency refers to the allocation of resources and goods over time. One appealing criterion for establishing dynamic efficiency is to allocate the resource over time so as to maximize the net present value of the use of the resource. To do this requires a discount rate and hence some notion of pure time preference, expected income growth, and the marginal utility of income. The first example given in the following chapter illustrates the simplest type of dynamic efficiency problems, and can be interpreted using the consumer and producer surplus concepts. The uneasy relation between efficiency and equity also arises in intertemporal decisions on resource use. Indeed, achieving a fair *and* efficient use of natural and environmental resources over generational time has emerged as a core issue in the sustainable development and the global-warming debates, and we return to it in subsequent chapters.

4 Market and Government Failures and Environmental Degradation

There are many explanations for environmental degradation and excessive exploitation of natural resources. Ignorance of long-term effects is surely one. Social and cultural value systems that place high priority on immediate material consumption have also been implicated. In this section we focus on circumstances in which the economic system fails to give proper value to the environment, and on failures of policy and political systems, the so-called government failures.

Economics recognizes four situations in which the price/market system fails to achieve efficiency. They are public goods, externalities, open-access common property resources, and market power.[5] Collectively, they are known as the sources of market failure. Three of the four – public goods, externalities, and common property resources – are central to the economic explanation of the roots of environmental degradation. The fourth, market power as exhibited in situations of monopoly, monopsony, oligopoly, etc., is not directly relevant. Although critical to understanding environmental and natural resource abuse, the first three are not limited in their explanatory power to environmental analysis. Other economic problems such as congestion can also be analyzed with these concepts. There is often some overlap and reinforcement among the three that needs to be sorted out, but as explained in the next section, the adequacy of property rights is at the core of all three.

4.1 Public Goods

A *pure public good* has two characteristics: nonrivalry in consumption and nonexcludability. *Nonrivalry* simply means that the consumption of a good or service by one party does not diminish the availability of the good or service for others. *Nonexcludability* means that for technical or cost reasons, it is not feasible to exclude consumers from using the good or service once it has been produced. *Nonrivalry* and nonexcludability both contribute to a failure of the price-market system. If a consumer cannot be excluded from using the good or service, he or she will have no incentive to purchase it.

---

5 Arguably, merit goods whose social value exceeds their private value are a fifth example. Imperfect or asymmetric information might also qualify. Randall (1983), with some reason, finds the overlap and definitional fuzziness of these four concepts too confusing, and would substitute a twofold classification of goods based on rivalry in consumption and excludability.

Hence the potential producer, with no prospects for sales or revenue, will have no incentive to bear the costs of production, and little or none of the good or service will be produced. Consumers would act as free riders. Moreover, if there is no incremental cost to supplying the good or service to an additional consumer (nonrivalry in consumption, implying no opportunity or user cost), the appropriate economic price for the good or service is zero. Once produced, it would be inefficient to exclude anyone from use. It follows that the private market system will fail to produce an appropriate supply of public goods.

Classic examples of pure public goods include national defense and the services of a lighthouse (although private lighthouses have existed). Knowledge itself, for example, the invention of the calculus, has the quality of a public good, although transmitting knowledge (education) does not. Also some forms of knowledge, especially intellectual property, can secure excludability through the legal devices of patents and copyright privileges. Environmental examples of public goods may include clear air for breathing, visual amenities, the ozone layer, and genetic resources, although the ability to exclude may exist for some of these, especially genetic resources. Notice that without the ability to exclude there is no ability to charge, and hence no incentive for ownership and traditional property rights. Notice also that public goods can be either produced or exist as gifts of nature.

The terminology of public goods can be confusing. Gifts of nature such as biodiversity and the global climate system are sometimes called privately produced public goods, as their level or quality is in large part a function of private activity. It is perhaps more helpful to turn the concept of public good around, and consider pollution or the degradation of these gifts of nature as a "public bad." An individual has little ability to easily exclude his or her consumption of dirty air, and consumption by one person does not diminish the amount of dirty air consumed by others; these are the same attributes that public goods exhibit. In this sense, air pollution may be termed a privately produced public bad, and just as the market fails to produce sufficient public goods, it produces excessive amounts of public bads.

The policy issue is how much of the public good or service to provide. In the case of produced public goods, for example, lighthouses, while the short-run marginal cost of providing for additional consumption is zero, the long-run cost of production (which includes the building and equipment) is positive. Hence, for efficiency the production costs should be set against the benefits. But in the absence of market prices, these benefits are difficult to estimate and monetize. For naturally occurring public goods such as the ozone layer (gifts of nature), the question is similar – how much of the good

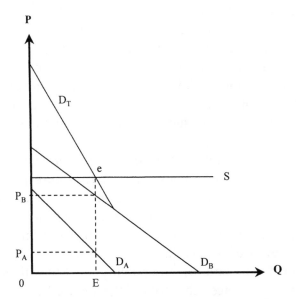

Figure 3.4. *Optimal supply of public good*

or service should be protected from encroachment by competing uses? Once again the cost of protection, which is now an opportunity cost, should be set against the benefits of protection. Unlike *rival goods*, such as airline tickets or hamburgers, where use by one excludes use by another, determining the optimal provision of public goods proceeds by vertically summing imputed demand curves to obtain a (social) willingness to pay, or demand curve. This is illustrated in Figure 3.4. Assuming they can be estimated, individual demand by consumers A and B (D_A, D_B) for a public good such as lighthouse services are summed to total demand D_T, and the area under D_T represents the consumer surplus derived by A and B.[6] The marginal costs of supply are described by S, and the intersection of D_T and S at e indicates optimal supply OE. The implicit prices P_B and P_A cannot be charged, however, as the consumers cannot be excluded from use. In fact, optimal provision of public goods is complicated for two reasons. First, individuals' demand for the public good or service cannot be observed from market behavior, and, if queried, they may behave strategically and provide inaccurate information. Second, unlike private goods where consumers adjust quantities purchased to market prices to maximize their welfare, public goods are provided in fixed quantities. Optimal provision of public goods must then involve variation in "pricing" among consumers rather than

---

6 Individual demand curves for rival goods are summed horizontally to obtain the market demand curve.

variation in quantity, so that each is satisfied with the quantity supplied. These problems are considered in the context of transnational pollution and the allocation of environmental protection costs in Chapters 13 and 14. The issue is critical in an international context because, unlike public goods provided by national governments, no international agency has the authority to tax countries. Efficiency and equity in the provision of international public goods are pursued through negotiations, and cannot be delinked.

Pure public goods are relatively rare and *congestible public goods* are an important variation, falling somewhere between pure public and private goods. They maintain the characteristic of nonexcludability, but at some level of capacity utilization the use by one consumer interferes with the use by another. Congestible public goods lose the attribute of nonrivalry. Historically, with low levels of demand a resource such as an ocean fishery might be best described as a (natural) pure public good. But with increased fishing activity and more advanced technology, the service becomes economically scarce and one fisherman's effort affects the catch of another. Congestible public goods are thought to be a frequent source of environmental problems – overfishing, congestion, and amenity losses from crowding in public parks, and so on. In fact, air and some water pollution might well be considered an example of congestible public goods. The use of environmental media by individuals or firms for waste disposal services interferes with the beneficial use of that media (e.g., drinking or breathing) by others and hence the medium is "congested." In this case the public policy problem is to allocate the now scarce resource in an efficient fashion between competing uses. However, prevalence of true congestible public goods is open to question. In many cases users *could* be excluded if property rights were rearranged. In practice, congestible public goods shade into the problem of open-access common property resources, considered in Section 4.3.

4.2 *Externalities*

The concept of public goods is closely related to another explanatory concept, externalities. An externality can be defined as the incidental but not necessarily unanticipated effect caused by the actions of one economic agent on the welfare of another economic agent, in which the effect does not pass through markets. Economic agents can be producers, consumers, or government. The effects can be positive (external economies) or negative (external diseconomies or external costs). The word "incidental" rules out such activities as mugging and charity, the purpose of which is to affect welfare.

Table 3.1. *Externality flows*

Sectors of origin	Sectors of impact	
	Producers	Consumers
Producers	a_{11}	a_{12}
Consumers	a_{21}	a_{22}

Also, although incidental, the effects can often be anticipated, as many routine pollution externalities demonstrate. Finally, the stipulation that the effect does not pass through markets rules out such activities as bidding between two agents in an auction leading to price change and welfare shifts. Environmentally related externalities are a subgroup of externalities and are generally thought to be negative. They need not be, however. A favorite bucolic example in old textbooks was the reciprocal externalities enjoyed by beekeepers and orchard owners in the pollination of fruit trees. Positive externalities between firms tend to be internalized through merger.

It is useful to classify externalities along a number of dimensions. One dimension, shown in Table 3.1, is by origin and impact.

Cell a_{11} would include the honeybee/orchard example but also a large number of negative externalities in which the activities of one industry directly affect the productivity of other industries. Cell a_{12} would include the old standby (now archaic) example of a factory emitting smoke and resulting in sooty laundry, as well as the negative welfare effects felt by wilderness enthusiasts of, say, commercial clear-cutting of forests, or damage to recreational fishermen from agricultural chemical runoff entering prime fishing streams. Externalities flowing from consumers to producers (a_{21}) are less common but might include road congestion from private auto use increasing commercial transport costs. Externalities among consumers (a_{22}) include urban air pollution from private auto use and other causes. The origin of the externality is important (i.e., producers versus consumers) in devising appropriate restrictions.

Other useful externality classifications include:

• Unidirectional versus reciprocal; for example, upstream deforestation contributing to downstream flooding versus joint pollution by littoral countries on the Baltic Sea
• Domestic versus international; for example, local noise pollution from airport traffic versus pollution of international rivers such as the Rhine

- Immediate versus delayed damages; as, for example, nuisance noise versus global warming
- Tangible versus intangible damages; for example, flood damages to structures and crops versus aesthetic loss as scenic areas are degraded

The last is mentioned to emphasize that many environmental services entering utility functions are intangible but of real value. An externality that damages a scenic vista is every bit as damaging as increases in urban ozone concentration, so long as people are willing to pay an equal amount for preservation or for cleanup. Notice also that in an unregulated situation, pollution externalities "trump" beneficial uses of the resource. Waste disposal reduces recreation value but recreation does not physically reduce the waste-disposal function of the environment. This is a fundamental point as it implies that even if recreation and waste disposal are equally valuable, an unregulated market always produces too much pollution, not too much recreation.

The inefficiency associated with unregulated environmental externalities was illustrated earlier in Figure 3.2. The problem arises because those responsible for the externality have no incentive to curb it, as the benefits of such an action (damages avoided) would accrue to others. Indeed, in competitive conditions an environmentally responsible firm that unilaterally incurred substantial pollution abatement costs might be driven out of business. In this sense, unregulated externalities illustrate a failure of the price-market system to allocate resources efficiently, and are an invitation to governments to intervene and improve the social welfare.

The connection between externalities and public goods becomes evident. With a public good, it is not possible to exclude users. With a positive externality, the agent producing the externality cannot appropriate and charge for his beneficial effect. With a negative externality, the victim is the unwilling recipient of the effect and cannot himself directly exclude the effect. The producer does not bear the cost but shifts it to the victim. The lack of excludability is central to both the public goods and externality problems. Moreover, for a *congestible* public good, the cost inflicted by one user on another can itself be considered an externality. For instance, with multiple use of a body of water for fishing, recreation, and waste disposal, the activity producing wastes creates an externality borne by the fishing and recreation interests. The solution rests in either clarifying property rights and negotiating between the polluters and victims for compensation or mitigation of the externality or, more likely, appealing to a collective unit such as the government to offset the market failure. Recall, however, that even with optimum pollution abatement, some pollution remains. An efficient solution can be achieved while some uncompensated costs continue to be borne by pollutees.

4.3 Common Property Resources

Whereas public goods are defined by their attributes (nonrivalry, nonexcludability), and the term *externality* refers to a cost or benefit transmitted from one agent to another, the term *common property resources* (CPR) refers to ownership or property rights, and offers a complementary insight into market failure.[7] The term itself is a bit vague. A useful distinction can be made between a resource that belongs to everyone, *res communis*, and a resource that belongs to no one, *res nullius*. *Res nullius* may be the appropriate (efficient) legal regime for resources that are not economically scarce. Writing in the 17th century before a modern fishing industry, Grotius, the father of the freedom-of-the-seas doctrine, recognized this and anticipated but dismissed the oceans as a congestible public good: "The vagrant waters of the sea are . . . necessarily free. The right of occupation rests upon the fact that most things become exhausted by promiscuous use and that appropriation consequently is the condition for their utility to human beings. But this is not the case with the sea; it can be exhausted neither by navigation nor by fishing, that is to say, neither of the two ways in which it can be used."[8]

Unlike pure public goods for which excludability is not possible, CPRs can exhibit free or restricted access. Examples of resources that at one time were free-access CPRs include ocean fisheries, the geostationary orbit (for communications satellites), most road systems in the United States, and much commonly held grazing land. The last was made famous by a biologist, Garrett Hardin, in his 1968 article "The Tragedy of the Commons." Overgrazing of communally held pasture was used as a metaphor for increased pollution of shared air, water, and land resources (less well known is that the article is mainly an indictment of leaving family size up to individuals – "freedom to breed will bring ruin to all" [Hardin 1968]). Unless restricted by regulation, air and water resources exhibit free access for waste disposal purposes. Not all CPR market failures are environmental. Congestion inefficiencies can arise in CPR situations, but with no direct environmental component.

---

7 For formal theory of CPRs, see Dasgupta and Heal (1979, Chap. 3).
8 Quoted by L. H. J. Legault (1971).

The economic inefficiency, or market failure, associated with open-access common property resources is that there is a strong tendency toward overuse or overexploitation. An individual finds it in her narrow self-interest to exploit the resources to the point where her private marginal costs equal her private marginal revenue. But in doing so, each individual generates an external cost borne by other users in the form of lower fish catch, reduced fodder, degraded soil, and so forth. The *social* cost of exploiting the resource exceeds the individual private cost, and the productivity of the resource is impaired. In this sense, open-access common property resources are closely linked to congestible public goods.

In an exceptionally interesting analysis, the economist Harold Demsetz (1967) has argued that "a primary function of property rights is guiding incentives to achieve a greater internalization of externalities" and that "property rights develop when gains from internalization become larger than the costs of internalization." The extension of national jurisdiction over a 200-mile fishing zone, starting with Peru in 1952 and completed by the United States in 1976, is a good illustration. Increasing demand and technological improvements have made ocean fisheries, once a resource in excess supply, economically scarce. The first step of establishing national property rights in 200-mile zones has been accomplished. The second step, developing fishing access restrictions appropriate for communal or national property, is analyzed in Chapter 15.

The two dominant responses to open-access common property resources are to privatize through private property rights or to have an external agency, most likely government, restrict access. As examined in Chapter 6, economists generally prefer tax or tradeable license systems if government restrictions are chosen. But privatization and government restrictions are not the only options. There are many instances in natural resource management in which stable institutions of self-governance by the participants themselves emerge, and control access without resort to external government involvement (Ostrom 1990). This third approach has been studied mainly in relatively small-scale, renewable resource situations, but the lessons may be important for international common property resources precisely because there is no effective international government to award property rights or to enforce restrictions on access.

4.4 Illustrations

A few simplified examples can illustrate these open-access CPR concepts. As previously noted, free access may be the appropriate regime for

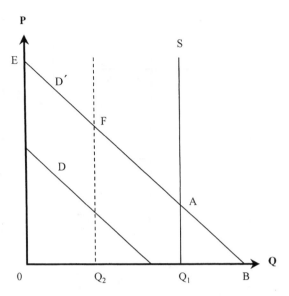

Figure 3.5. *Open-access common property resource under excess supply and scarcity*

resources in excess supply. Consider Figure 3.5. Given demand, D, and a fixed supply, S, the resource is in excess supply at a zero price. Under these circumstances welfare is maximized (consumer surplus is maximized) with a zero price. Because it is in excess supply, there is no point to limiting its use, and no incentive for private ownership. If, however, demand (or supply) shifts to make the resource economically scarce, say, to D', a common-property free-access regime is no longer appropriate. Free access on a first come, first served basis would not ensure that the resource would go to the highest valued uses. More specifically, if the users represented by the segment of the demand curve AB are first comers, and users EF are late comers who are denied access, the welfare gain to the former is measured by consumer surplus as ABQ_1, and is far less than the welfare loss to the latter, $OEFQ_2$. Efficiency requires allocation to highest valued uses. Observe, however, that if property rights could be established and the good in question is transferable, there is ample incentive for a market to develop between the two groups. The first comers would be sellers and the late comers would be buyers. The initial allocation is less important for efficiency than the marketability of the good.

The free-access common property resource concept is also useful in evaluating the efficient use of oil reservoirs. Assume an oil reservoir with surface ownership and mineral rights owned by several individuals. In such a situa-

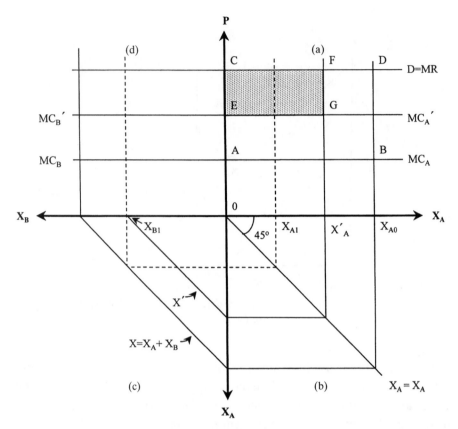

Figure 3.6. *Inefficiencies in a simple oil reservoir example*

tion there are two potential sources of inefficiency – each surface owner, in an effort to tap the most oil for himself, will drill a large number of wells, and total investment in well drilling will exceed the efficient level. Second, each surface owner will pump as rapidly as possible, exceeding the technologically efficient pumping rate, dissipating underground gas or water pressure, and reducing total recoverable oil. The essence of the inefficiency is again externalities. By pumping oil, each surface owner creates an external cost (reduced yield) for every other surface owner, yet has no incentive to take these external costs into account in his drilling and pumping plans. The response to this problem in the United States was output restrictions under the National Industrial Recovery Act and the 1935 Conolly "Hot Oil" Act, which followed decades of attempts to regulate the number, location, and extraction rates of oil wells (Yergin 1991).

Figure 3.6 is a highly simplified illustration of the oil reservoir problem. Assume oil underground in fixed supply, X. Assume the resource is common property and two firms, A and B, engage in extraction. Assume each faces the same, constant, marginal costs of extraction, $MC_A = MC_B$. Assume the oil pool is small relative to the total oil market so that the demand and marginal revenue can be represented by a horizontal demand curve, D. Finally, assume that price reflects social marginal utility. Figure 3.6a is the situation from the perspective of owner A. The X_A axis measures A's production of oil. Figure 3.6b, with the 45° line, simply transforms the horizontal X_A axis to a vertical X_A axis. Figure 3.6c shows total resource availability, $X = X_A + X_B$. Figure 3.6d is the situation from the point of view of B (measuring B's production of oil from right to left).

If there were no externalities in production, society would be indifferent on efficiency grounds as to whether A or B produced. If A gets the jump, it would produce at X_{A0} (all the oil) leaving no oil for B. Total cost of production is $OABX_{A0}$, total revenue and utility is $OCDX_{A0}$, and $ACDB$ is the rent from the resource accruing to A. Alternatively, the two firms may split output. A may produce at X_{A1}, leaving X_{B1} available for B's production. The total rent would be the same, although distribution would be different. In practice, however, in their eagerness to obtain the rent, A and B would have an incentive to drill too many wells and to pump beyond the technologically efficient rate, decreasing the oil field gas pressure and either decreasing total recoverable oil or increasing the marginal cost of recovery. This can be represented by shifting inward the total recovered resource from X to X' and increasing marginal cost to $MC_A' = MC_B'$. The result would be to reduce total rent. If, for example, A still had the jump on B, it would produce at X_A', leaving nothing for B. But total rent (and hence total net welfare) would be reduced from $ACDB$ to the shaded area $ECFG$, a loss due to reduced output and higher extraction cost. Again the distribution of this (smaller) rent is indeterminant, but the loss of welfare to society from the dissipation of rent is clear. Also, as explained in the following chapter, resources such as oil may have a user cost – the value lost to users in the future from current consumption. This feature may introduce a further inefficiency. Neither A nor B has any incentive to defer production, as that would benefit the other and not themselves. Therefore, the rush to exploit would provide no incentive for conservation, and the user cost would be neglected in the exploitation decision, an intertemporal inefficiency.

A simple example can also illustrate the inefficiency of congestion in a common property resource such as a road. Consider Figure 3.7. Figure 3.7a represents a typical current road user, A, where use is measured in vehicle miles per day. His demand for road use services is D, his marginal costs of road use (gas, oil, tires, time) is given by MC_A, his utility maximizing road

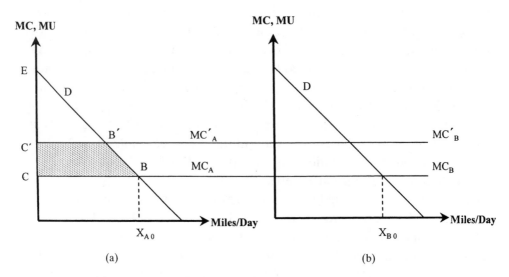

Figure 3.7. *Example of market failure in road congestion*

use is given by X_{A0}, and his consumer surplus is the triangle *CEB*. Assume there are many such users, and the road is fully utilized just to the point of congestion, where one additional vehicle would slow everyone's travel. Now consider the new road user B in Figure 3.7b. She too has a demand curve and the same basic marginal cost, MC_B. Based on her private calculus of benefits and costs, she chooses to drive X_{B0} vehicle miles and maximizes her private benefits.

But the introduction of B slows traffic for everyone, increasing marginal costs to MC'_A and MC'_B. This is shown for the typical established road user A, whose consumer surplus shrinks by the shaded area *CC'B'B*. The sum of the increased costs incurred by others as the result of B's action represents true social costs, but they are not borne home to B, except to the extent that she too has higher marginal costs due to slower traffic. B therefore has no incentive to modify her behavior. In the absence of private property rights to the road (private ownership), some restriction on access, or a mechanism through which existing users "bribe" B to take the bus, congestion and inefficiency result. Actually, this is a little unfair on B; there is no reason why she should be considered the marginal driver – removal of A from the road would have an equally beneficial result.

These examples of market failure are sufficient to demonstrate the central points. The combination of public goods, externalities, and inadequate user restrictions on common property resources amounts to a powerful explanation of environmental degradation and abusive use of natural resources. They also point toward solutions: collective action for the provision of public goods; internalization of externalities either through the extension of property rights, private negotiation of restrictions on externalities, or public restrictions; and limitations on excessive use of common property resources. It is worth reemphasizing that all three sources of market failure – public goods, externalities, and common property resources – are related to defective or nonexistent property rights (i.e., either exclusive ownership rights to benefits, the transferability or marketability of those rights, or enforcement, are defective). It does not follow, however, that privatization of environmental resources through the granting of property rights is either the most efficient or equitable response in every case. Finally, the central role of deficient property rights lies at the heart of the sustainability issue. Future generations have no effective "rights" to today's resources and no voice in their exploitation.

4.5 Government Failure

It would be inaccurate and misleading to attribute all environmental degradation to market failures. The dismal examples in Eastern Europe and the Soviet Union of the failure to protect environmental resources during the decades when markets were suppressed and central economic planning prevailed are ample evidence. Moreover, it would be naive to assume that wherever market failure exists, government corrective policy can necessarily obtain efficiency. It is now recognized that government policy itself is implicated in a good deal of environmental degradation. And when corrective policies addressing market failures are undertaken by government, the results often fall short of expectations or are unnecessarily costly. The public policy task is twofold – to review existing government policies and identify where these policies inadvertently contribute to abuse of environmental resources, and to design corrective policies for mitigating failures of the price-market system that are effective and efficient.

Securing these objectives is complicated by different opinions regarding the appropriate role of government. On one end of the spectrum are those who believe that if property rights were clarified and if private markets were allowed to develop under the protection of a secure legal regime, many environmental problems would either disappear or be satisfactorily managed. Proponents of this view also tend to believe that policy makers and bureaucratic regulators often serve special interests or promote their own parochial objectives over the public interest. At the other end of the spectrum are those who believe that effective private markets often cannot be created, or that their distributional consequences would be unacceptable. They also argue that existing problems with particular environmental policies, such as inefficiencies associated with the use of quantitative effluent and emission discharge limits, can be remedied. Increased attention to market-friendly government measures helps bridge these extremes, and are examined in Chapter 6. Indeed, casting the debate in the stark terms of market solutions versus government intervention is not always revealing. The creation of private markets requires clarifying property rights, and this necessarily involves government. This is true for a tradeable permit system for, say, lead or sulfur dioxide, or for establishing property rights to genetically engineered organisms, both of which are market-oriented interventions. The real struggle is to acquire or retain property rights, and the relevant economic question is the appropriate balance between direct regulation by government and indirect regulation through market-oriented instruments.

Government failure *per se* occurs when the incentives of politicians and bureaucrats do not coincide with the public interest. Economics provides some insight into the sources of government failure, especially in the analysis of lobbying and rent seeking, and in the public choice literature that identifies bureaucratic interests such as agency budget growth, and career-enhancement opportunities in a revolving door system. There is nothing unique in government failure in the environmental area except, perhaps, the scale of the rearrangement of property rights that has accompanied environmental policy in the past three decades and hence the scope of these failures. Setting aside these difficulties, two other problems with government policy should be mentioned. First, the mechanism for expressing individuals' environmental preferences through collective action is absent or muted in undemocratic systems. It is not surprising that unresponsive governments fail to seek, let alone obtain, maximum social welfare. Even in such situations, however, organized environmental pressure groups may exist and force undemocratic governments to pay some attention to the environment. At a more practical level, the information required of regulators to devise reasonably efficient environmental policies may not be available. Some types of policies, however, are less information-intensive than others or are more apt to generate useful information. The questions of uncertainty and information are explored more thoroughly in Chapters 5 and 6. The special problems of government failure in an international context are considered in Parts 2 and 3.

5 The Coase Theorem

It is useful to close this chapter on the market and government failures that are at the root of environmental degradation with a brief review of the Coase Theorem (Coase 1960). Assume two parties, a "polluter" and a "victim." If property rights are awarded to the polluter and allow waste disposal in environmental media, the victim may "bribe" or "buy" clean air or water from the polluter, creating a marketlike solution. Alternatively, if property rights are given to the victim, the polluter may "compensate" the victim or "buy" the right to pollute. If transactions costs are minimal, the Coase Theorem states that the resulting allocation of resources will be efficient – that is, the resource will be dedicated to its highest valued use – *regardless of the initial allocation of property rights*. This result holds whether the problem is framed as an either/or decision – to pollute or not to pollute – or whether it is framed as a marginal decision – that is, to determine the optimal level at which pollution should take place. Moreover, the theorem states that the resulting allocation of the resource will not only be efficient, but will be *the same*, regardless of initial allocation of property rights, provided that the income effect of owning the property right is negligible.[9] Creation of a "market" in the Coase solution internalizes the externality but does not necessarily bring pollution to a zero level.[10]

Figure 3.2 has already set the stage for the analysis. Recall that moving from Q_0 to Q_1 there is a welfare improvement for victims of *FBCH*, and producers and consumers show a combined net loss of *BHF*. Thus if polluters are awarded property rights – the right to pollute – a bargain seems feasible. Victims could offer a payment of up to a monetary value of *FBCH* to secure a reduction of output from Q_0 to Q_1 and still be no worse off, whereas producers and consumers would presumably be willing to accept any payment greater than *BHF* and be better off with restricted output. If instead of allocating rights to polluters, the right to be free of pollution were given to the potential victims, the efficient output level Q_1 might also result from a bargain (market). Producer and consumer interests combined could offer a compensation payment up to the amount *ABFO* to be allowed to produce at the level Q_1, whereas victims would presumably accept anything greater than *EBFO* and be better off than at zero output. Again a bargain seems feasible. Figure 3.2b makes clear that any reduction of output below

---

9 Or that preferences are quasilinear, meaning that a utility function is linear in at least one good. On an indifference map of quasilinear preferences, indifference curves are vertically shifted versions of one another.
10 More precisely, but in economic jargon, the Pareto-relevant externality is eliminated.

Q_1 would not maximize welfare as the marginal welfare loss to consumers plus producers would exceed the marginal welfare gain to victims. (In the notation of Figure 3.2, MW_{C+P} lost $> MC_v$ avoided.) Regardless of the initial allocation of property rights, the market would tend to settle at output level Q_1.

Figure 3.2a also illustrates an extremely important point – although the resource allocation and efficiency results of a Coasian market may be independent of initial allocation of rights, the resulting welfare distribution certainly is not. If producers and consumers are given the right, their welfare is at least the area $ABFO$ and possibly $ABFO$ plus $BCHF$ (the distribution of the social welfare gain BCH will be determined by relative bargaining skills). If victims are given rights, the maximum welfare producers and consumers can expect is only ABE, which, if not clever in the bargaining, might dwindle to zero. The welfare consequences for victims is equally strong. If they receive rights and accept compensation for output up to Q_1, their maximum welfare net of residual environmental damages is the area ABE. If they must buy pollution reduction, the best they can do is reduce their welfare losses from $ECHO$ to $EBHO$.

The Coase Theorem yields strong propositions and needs elaboration. In the first place, there have to be well-defined property rights for a market to work. One group or another has to have an unambiguous right to use the resource for a particular purpose, *and* be able to "sell" this right if they desire. For example, a no-smoking rule for domestic U.S. airline flights is a limited property right granted to nonsmoking air passengers, but a Coase-like solution is not possible because nonsmoking passengers are not allowed to sell their rights to smokers. An efficient outcome is no longer assured by market process because a market is not legal. It is conceivable, although not likely, that the collective utility gain for nonsmokers from the rule is less than the welfare loss of the addicted passengers. In that event, the resource, cabin air, is misallocated and all could be made better off through a bargain. Moreover, the flat ban on smoking precludes a marginal solution, where marginal costs and marginal benefits are equalized and limited smoking results. Environmental problems frequently involve marginal solutions, and unless justified by ethical considerations or by avoiding excessive enforcement costs, bans are likely to be inefficient.[11]

---

11 In this contrived example, it is likely that transactions costs would be prohibitive regardless of the allocation of rights. No market sprang up among passengers in the decades when smoking on airline flights was permitted. If transactions costs themselves are a function of the allocation of rights, this further qualifies the identical resource allocation conclusion of the Coase Theorem. See Bromley (1989).

Achieving an efficient result regardless of the allocation of property rights by creating a market also requires that transactions costs be minimal. By transactions costs, we mean the real economic costs of aggregating the collective interests of the two groups – the polluters and the victims – negotiating an agreement, and then enforcing the agreement. Frequently, polluters and victims are numerous and dispersed, and the transactions costs become prohibitive. Indeed, transactions costs escalate when there is some ambiguity about property rights and disputes are settled in the judicial system. Enforcement costs may also be prohibitive, but then again enforcement costs may also be high when more direct government intervention is used. In the Figure 3.2 example, producers would have to join with consumers to negotiate with the victim, an unlikely coalition.

Along these same lines, the market for the externality may perform poorly because of strategic behavior by either polluters or victims. If rights are given to polluters, individual victims may follow a "free-rider" strategy and fail to "pay" for their share of bribes in the expectation that other victims will pick up the tab. If all behave in this fashion, too little is bid for pollution abatement. At the same time, if polluters are awarded rights, they have an incentive to threaten pollutive activity when no such activity was actually contemplated, in order to extort payment from victims. This can be termed *environmental mugging*. Symmetrical strategic behavior may arise if rights are given to victims. The free-rider and the extortion behavior both raise questions about the practicality of a Coase-type solution.

We should also acknowledge that the information cost to individuals of learning what their true environmental preferences are, and how they would be affected by a particular economic activity, may be extraordinarily high. For example, it may be far more efficient for the government rather than private individuals to collect information on the health hazards of lead emissions (information is a public good). Having assembled the information, it may be an efficient next step for government to set some minimum lead pollution abatement levels, rather than relying on informed individuals to strike their own transactions with lead polluters.

Also, bear in mind that even when the results are equally efficient in the two property rights allocation schemes, the resulting allocation of the resource will not be identical unless income effects are negligible. If rights are given to polluters, their wealth is enhanced, and they will presumably demand a somewhat higher sum to curtail their pollution. Conversely, if victims are given rights, they have a higher real income base, and their demand for compensation will be correspondingly higher. In specific instances such as smoking on a single air flight, the income effect may be small, but in aggregate the nonmonetary income or utility derived from environmental services may be large. In that event, the initial allocation of rights to the resource may have a substantial effect on the resource use, even if the market is functioning well (Mishan 1988). Recall also that there can be many Pareto-efficient resource allocation patterns depending on income distribution patterns.

Finally we stress the very different welfare distributional consequences of a legal regime that awards rights to polluters versus rights to victims. These differences in distribution are exceptionally important in a political economy context. The most cost-effective strategy for either victims or polluters may be to lobby for a legal regime change rather than spend their resources on pollution abatement or on buying the desired level of pollution (abatement) in a Coasian market. Such expenditure comes close to rent seeking and the so-called directly unproductive behavior, which is well known in public-choice and trade literature. On a more subtle level, the Coase Theorem makes us look more closely at the ethical basis of the terms "polluter" and "victim." The heart of the problem is conflict in use of an environmental resource. *A priori*, it is not always clear that one use is more equitable or just than another, and the terms polluter and victim may prejudge the fair allocation of rights. It is not always clear who is the moral victim. As seen in later chapters, the simple polluter-victim terminology may not correspond to equitable environmental obligations of rich and poor countries. The distribution question raised by the Coase Theorem is also relevant for the Polluter Pays Principle, discussed in detail in Chapter 11.

All of these dimensions of the Coase Theorem – the preference for creating markets rather than direct intervention, the clarification of property rights, the question of transactions costs, enforcement and free riders, and the distributional questions – take on great importance in the context of international externalities. The reason is simple. In the absence of an international environmental protection agency, Coase-type negotiations among countries may provide a useful explanatory model for analyzing and resolving international externalities. This approach is explored in more depth in Parts 2 and 3.

Appendix 3.1

Exact Welfare Measures: Compensating and Equivalent Variation and Surplus

Consumer surplus as described in Chapter 3 is not an exact measure of welfare. The reason is that market, or Marshallian, demand curves incorporate the effects of both price change and the real income (utility) change arising from the price change itself.

For example, if a consumer faces 10 percent lower food prices and unchanged money income, the increase in quantity of food purchased reflects a substitution toward food due to relative price change, *and* his or her increase in real income. An exact measure of welfare change from the price change requires stripping the income effect from the price-substitution effect.

There is a second complication. Environmental goods and services are often *public goods* supplied in fixed amount or quality by government. Not only is there no direct market price data for estimating welfare, but individuals cannot directly adjust the quantity they consume, as they can with conventional market goods. For example, the quality of air in an urban environment is "supplied" by public authorities through regulation, and individuals are faced with a fixed air quality and cannot purchase better or worse air. This Appendix first explains how exact measures of welfare can be derived for marketed goods and services, where consumers adjust quantity demanded to market prices. It then considers welfare measures for public goods, which are supplied in fixed amounts.[12]

Welfare Measures of Price Changes

The welfare effects of a price change on an individual can take one of two reference points; the prechange welfare level or the postchange welfare level. The first is a measure of compensating variation (CV); the second is a measure of equivalent variation (EV). If a price decrease is contemplated, CV is interpreted as the maximum amount an individual would be willing to pay (WTP) to enjoy the price reduction. If a price increase is contemplated, CV is interpreted as the minimum amount an individual would be willing to accept (WTA) that would restore him to his initial welfare level. If CV payments are actually made following a price change, the individual is returned to his initial welfare level.

EV takes the postprice change welfare level as the reference point. For a price reduction, EV is the minimum amount an individual would be willing to accept (WTA) to forgo the price decline. For a price increase, EV measures the maximum amount an individual would be willing to pay (WTP) to avoid the price increase. If EV payments are actually made following a price change (*to* the individual for price increase, *by* the individual for a price reduction), his welfare is at the postprice change level.

Neither the CV nor the EV measure of welfare change from a price change is inherently superior. If one takes the view that consumers have an implicit right to their current welfare levels, CV is the appropriate measure. If consumers have an implicit right to the postprice change welfare level, EV measures the amount they would either pay or receive to maintain that welfare level.

---

12 In practice, consumers can sometimes adjust their consumption of a public good by moving to areas where it is supplied in greater or lesser amounts. An important example is the housing market where the consumption of clean air or dirty air is determined by where one buys a house. The variation in housing prices across air pollution zones is the empirical basis for many hedonic price models described in the Chapter 5.

Table 3A.1. *Comparing CV and EV*

	Welfare Reference Point		
	Initial preprice change welfare level (CV)		Subsequent postprice change welfare level (EV)
Price decrease	CV (WTP)	<	EV (WTA)
Price increase	CV (WTA)	>	EV (WTP)

Relative Size of CV and EV and Diagrammatic Illustrations

A price *decrease* increases real income and welfare. It follows that for normal goods the amount one would be willing to pay for a price reduction is less than the amount one would be willing to accept as compensation to forgo the same price decline, because the income base for WTP is less than the income base for WTA. The first, WTP, proceeds from the initial, low income reference point. The second, WTA, proceeds from the subsequent higher income reference point. This implies that for a price decrease WTP<WTA and therefore CV<EV. A price *increase* decreases real income and welfare. It follows that for normal goods, the amount one would be willing to pay to avoid the price increase is less than the amount one would be willing to accept in compensation for the price increase. In this instance willingness to pay proceeds from subsequent lower welfare level, and willingness to accept proceeds from the initial higher income level. This implies that for a price increase WTP<WTA and CV>EV. These results are summarized in Table 3A.1.

In short, there are theoretical reasons for believing that WTP<WTA. The empirical significance is explored in Appendix 5.1.

The derivation of CV and EV measures of welfare and their relation to Marshallian consumer surplus are illustrated in Figures 3A.1 and 3A.2. Part *a* in both figures contains representative indifference curves from the utility function, $U=f(X, C)$, where X is the good in question, C is a composite of all other goods, and $U_1>U_0$. The budget constraint is depicted by the line nn, whose slope is the initial price of X relative to the price of C, or P_{x0}/P_{c0}. Consumer utility is maximized at equilibrium point e, and X_0 of X is purchased. The point P_{x0}, X_0 is shown in part *b* as one point R on the demand curve.

Now consider a decrease in the price of X, shifting the slope of the budget line to nn' and equilibrium to point e'. The consumption of X rises to X_1 and a new point on the Marshallian demand curve, D_M, is established at S in the lower panel. Until now the analysis is identical in Figures 3A.1 and 3A.2. As is well known, the increase in consumption, $X_0 X_1$, can be decomposed into a pure price-substitution effect and

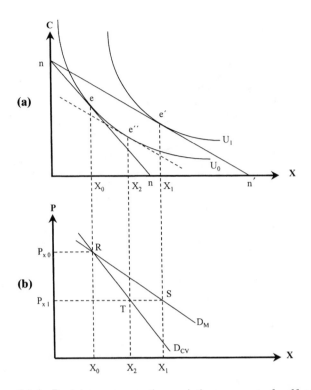

Figure 3A.1. *Deriving compensating variation measure of welfare change*

an income effect, the latter arising from the real income increase represented by U_1 $> U_0$. To decompose, in Figure 3A.1a, hold the consumer at her initial income level U_0, but apply the new relative prices, P_{x1}/P_{c0}. The equilibrium point is e'' and the amount demanded is X_2. The increase $X_0 X_2$ is solely due to the relative price change, as real income has been held at its initial level U_0. The quantity increase $X_2 X_1$ is due to the income change associated with the price decline. The resulting demand curve traced out in the lower quadrant, D_{cv}, provides the *compensating variation* measure of change in consumer surplus. For the price change from P_{x0} to P_{x1}, consumer surplus measured by the Marshallian demand curve is the area P_{x0} $RSTP_{x1}$, and, for the income-compensated demand curve, it is the smaller amount $P_{x0}RTP_{x1}$. The latter is the maximum amount of money the consumer would be willing to pay to secure the price P_{x1}. If she paid this amount, her welfare would be its initial level U_0.

Figure 3A.2 illustrates *equivalent variation*. Again, initial prices lead to equilibria of e and X_0 in part a, and P_{x0} and X_0 in part b. Again, a decrease in the price of X leads to e', X_1 in Figure 3A.2a and the Marshallian demand curve D_M in Figure 3A.2b. Now, however, take the postprice change perspective and ask what is the monetary payment that the consumer would be willing to accept if she is asked to forgo the price decrease. To answer this, hold the consumer at her postprice change utility level, U_I, and find the tangent of the original relative price line at point e''.

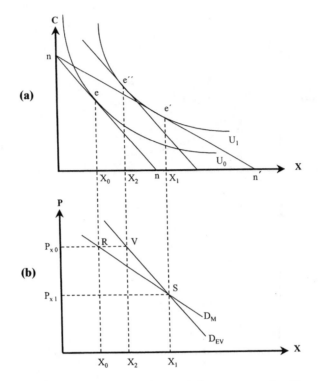

Figure 3A.2. *Deriving equivalent variation measure of welfare change*

The resulting quantity, X_2, represents the amount the consumer would buy if her real income were U_I and the prices were P_{X0}/P_{C0}. This establishes a point P_{X0}, X_2, labeled V in part b, and can be used to trace out the equivalent variation demand curve, D_{EV}. Now the consumer surplus change from reducing price from P_{X0} to P_{X1} is the area $P_{x0}RVSP_{x1}$, larger than the Marshallian consumer surplus $P_{x0}RSP_{x1}$. The preceding analyzes a price decrease; a price increase leads to symmetrical conclusions.

To summarize, CV and EV are exact measures of welfare change following a price change, although their reference points or benchmarks for measuring welfare change differ. Marshallian consumer surplus falls somewhere between CV and EV. Unfortunately, CV and EV are difficult to estimate empirically as compared to Marshallian consumer surplus, which is based on market data. Robert Willig has shown that the error in using Marshallian surplus (the concept of consumer surplus as developed in the text of this chapter) is small if the income elasticity of demand for the good is low (if zero, no error) and the ratio of consumer surplus from the good to total expenditures by the consumer is small (e.g., shoelaces). When these conditions do not hold he provides a method for adjusting Marshallian surplus to approximate CV or EV (Willig 1976). One conclusion from Willig's work is that theoretically CV and EV should be reasonably close in size, implying that consumers WTP and WTA should also be reasonably similar in size. The empirical evidence does not fully support this, and we return to the question in the appendix to Chapter 5.

Welfare Measures of Changes in Environmental Quality

When environmental services such as air or water quality are supplied as public goods, two analytical difficulties are encountered. First, as noted in the previous section, the quantity (quality) is supplied in fixed amounts, and individuals cannot adjust the quantity they consume. Second, there is no information from market prices to indicate utility or welfare. However, at a theoretical level it is possible to construct analogies to CV and EV that measure welfare changes from increases and decreases in environmental quality, and these are known as compensating surplus and equivalent surplus in the literature (Bishop and Woodward 1995). Compensating surplus is to be interpreted as the maximum amount of money an individual would be willing to pay to obtain an environmental quality increase or the minimum amount of money an individual would be willing to accept in compensation for an environmental quality decrease. Either the payment or receipt of compensation would restore him to his initial welfare level. Equivalent surplus takes the postenvironmental change welfare level as the reference point or benchmark. For a quality increase it is the minimum amount of money the individual would be willing to accept to forgo the quality increase, and for a quality decrease it is the maximum he would be willing to pay to avoid the quality decrease. For the same reasons that we expect WTP<WTA for a price change, we also expect WTP<WTA for an environmental quality change.

To derive compensating and equivalent surpluses, it is necessary to conceptualize "virtual" demand curves, the prices individuals would be willing to pay for various quantities (or qualities) of the environmental service if the service were marketed, and if the individuals could adjust the amount they purchase. The compensating surplus demand curve would then measure the amount that would be purchased at alternative prices holding the individual at his initial utility level, and the equivalent surplus demand curve would measure the amounts that would be purchased holding the individual at his postenvironmental change utility level. (Obviously utility functions would now include both marketed goods and the public good.) If these demand curves were specified, it would be possible to calculate welfare changes from increasing or decreasing the supply of the environmental public good.

The empirical problem of measuring compensating surplus and equivalent surplus can be addressed in one of two ways. First, individuals could be asked directly how much they value environmental change. This is the contingent valuation approach. Alternatively, the demand for the environmental good can be inferred from demand for marketed goods with environmental attributes (the hedonic price method) or from surrogate market behavior (for example, the travel cost method). These valuation techniques are explained in Chapter 5. More broadly, we should keep in mind that these exact measures of welfare change are a counsel of perfection. Even in the simplest cases where demand curves can be derived from market behavior, any theoretical error from using the Marshallian consumer surplus approximation of welfare changes is apt to be small relative to errors arising from uncertainties in the data.

The question of welfare gained or lost from environmental policy takes on special difficulties in an international context, in which national governments ostensibly act as agents for their citizens, and in which a supranational authority for managing environmental resources is absent. The latter raises the salience of welfare distributional issues among countries and hence the importance of welfare measurement. But because governments imperfectly reflect the welfare of their citizens, and because the mechanisms for international compensation are so crude, the insights of welfare theory and measurement may not be directly useful.

4

Issues of Time

1 Introduction

Chapter 2 presented a simplified explanation of principal linkages between economic activity and the natural environment. However, it skirted certain important intertemporal issues that need to be addressed. For example, waste flows today may accumulate and affect production and welfare in the future. Depletion of exhaustible resources today increases their future scarcity and price. Preferences for conventional economic goods and services versus environmental services may change as income grows. The introduction of time raises the question of dynamic efficiency, the optimal allocation of resources over time. But it also raises complex questions of equity, involving a fair or just allocation of these resources among different generations. Agreeing on a just distribution of income at a point in time is itself difficult. The inability of future generations to make their preferences known in current environmental and resource decisions that will affect them, the absence of secure methods for making intergenerational transfers, and the increasing uncertainty surrounding long-lived environmental effects all make intergenerational equity questions extraordinarily difficult. They cannot be avoided, however, as economic activity today casts a shadow in time on environmental conditions and welfare in the future. In thinking about time and the environment, it is useful to categorize natural and environmental resources into three types: (1) strictly renewable (sunlight, which cannot be borrowed by the present generation from the next), (2) exhaustible (resources such as forests or soils, which are capable of renewal or regeneration, but which may also be exhausted if the rate of exploitation exceeds the regeneration rate), and (3) strictly nonrenewable (fossil fuels, which cannot be regenerated in human time scale, but whose economic supply may be augmented by discovery and technological progress). Time plays a critical role in the latter two types.

Section 2 starts with a discussion of discounting, the procedure by which future benefits and costs are expressed in present value terms. The mechanics of discounting are simple, but choosing the "correct" discount rate is not. It involves economic theory, empirical observation, and ethical choices. This section explores the concept of a social rate of time preference. Section 3 examines the arguments for and against a special discount rate when environmental effects are significant. Section 4 illustrates the importance of the discount rate in a variety of intertemporal resource allocation choices. Starting with a very simple model illustrating a dynamically efficient allocation of a fixed resource, the section continues with analysis of the role of the discount rate in nonrenewable and exhaustible resource use situations. This involves a discussion of optimal exploitation and extraction rates. Section 5 returns to the question of intergenerational equity and the concept of sustainability. It also suggests how discount rate issues might be modified in an explicit *international* context.

2 Discounting

Because policies and projects create economic costs and benefits that occur through time, it is necessary to give weights to costs and benefits that occur at different points in time. This is true when one is considering a single project – do its benefits exceed its costs? – or when choosing among projects that have different time profiles of net benefits (benefits minus costs). One solution would be to choose unitary weights – the value of one dollar of benefits (costs) today and one dollar a year from now would be the same, at one dollar. Unitary weights are generally unsatisfactory. When applied to the benefit stream they imply that society is indifferent regarding present and future consumption if the future benefit of the project is a consumption good. If unitary weights are applied to the cost stream, they imply that the input in question cannot be used productively in the intervening period. If we assume a positive time preference for current over future consumption, and if we assume there are investment opportunities available such that a unit of resources when invested today will yield greater output in the future (positive marginal productivity of capital), we should weight benefits today as greater than the same benefit accruing in the future. Similarly, we should weight costs incurred in the future less than costs incurred today. Discounting is then the mechanism through which one finds the present value of future benefits and costs.

The notion of discounting is easy to understand in financial terms. A dollar of income today can be used for immediate consumption, generally preferred by individuals to future consumption, or invested to yield a higher income in the future. A dollar of expenditure today drawn from savings has an opportunity cost in interest earnings foregone, and a dollar of expenditure drawn from borrowed funds has an explicit interest cost. The argument has a parallel in terms of real resources. "Corn" made available today can be "invested" and yield a larger crop next year. At the same time, refraining from corn consumption today (saving) requires a positive payment for the disutility of deferred consumption.

The general formula for establishing net present value for a project of n years is

$$NPV = \sum_{t=1}^{t=n} \frac{B_t - C_t}{(1+r)^t}$$

where B_t, C_t, are benefits and costs at time t, and r is the discount rate.[1] This formula for discounting to establish NPV is the cornerstone of evaluating projects or policies with costs and benefits occurring through time. If NPV >0, the project should be undertaken.[2]

The preceding suggests two approaches to determining the discount rate. First, one wishes to take account of individuals' pure time preference for present over future consumption. The pure time preference may be modified if we expect income and consumption to be higher in the future, and if we assume diminishing marginal utility of consumption (i.e., the incremental utility of a unit of consumption, while positive, is less at higher income levels than at lower income levels). The implication of this modification is that if income (consumption) growth is expected, the appropriate discount rate is higher than the pure time preference.

The second approach is to estimate and use the marginal productivity of capital, the yield or return that can be expected from the marginal unit of consumption foregone today and used to invest and build the stock of pro-

---

1 Another useful formula is for the present value of an annuity of $1 for n years discounted at r,

$$a = \frac{1 - \dfrac{1}{(1+r)^n}}{r}$$

where a is an annuity factor. For an infinite annuity this reduces to

$$a = \frac{1}{r}$$

This gives the present or capitalized value of a permanent gain (or loss) of $1 annually, in perpetuity.

2 The internal rate of return (IRR) is an alternative decision criterion. The IRR is the rate at which cost and benefit streams must be discounted so that NPV is zero. If the IRR exceeds the social discount rate, the project should be undertaken.

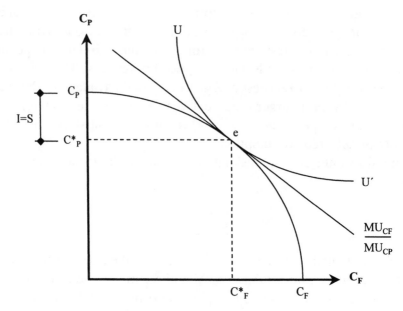

Figure 4.1. *Maximizing utility: equilibrium between present and future consumption*

ductive resources. It assumes that a set of investment opportunities exists at a point in time and that they can be ranked by their yield or return. In this approach, the discount rate measures the return on the marginal project. If the discount rate were incorrectly set higher than the return on the marginal project, some socially desirable projects would not be undertaken. If the discount rate were lower, qualifying projects would exceed available investment funds. Correctly set, the discount rate equals the return on the marginal project when the investment budget is just exhausted.

These two approaches are consistent in principle and are combined in Figure 4.1. The first step is to establish an intertemporal social utility function, $U = f(C_P, C_F)$, where C_P is present consumption and C_F is future consumption, say, one year later. The function assumes diminishing marginal utility to both C_P and C_F. The indifference curve *UU'* represents combinations of present and future consumption with constant utility. The second step is to determine the ability to transform present into future output (a production possibility curve over time), which is determined by the investment opportunities available. These opportunities are ranked and arrayed from highest to lowest rates of return. The resulting transformation function is illustrated in Figure 4.1 as $C_P C_F$. Note that the slope of the line tangent to both curves at *e* can be thought of as the "price" of future consumption over the "price" of present consumption. It reflects the relative marginal utility of future over present consumption – the amount by which people discount future consumption on the margin. The slope of the tangent also measures the marginal rate of transformation of present into future consumption, as determined by investment opportunities. It can be thought of as the opportunity cost of future consumption as measured by present consumption foregone.

In equilibrium with no distortions, the level of present consumption that maximizes utility is C_P^*, and the difference between C_P^* and C_P is the amount of present consumption foregone, or savings, S, that is available for investment, I. Thus preferences and the transformation curve, which may be thought of as demand and supply, both help determine the relative price of present and future consumption. If, for example, the slope of $C_p C_F$ is 0.8 at e, the implication is that 0.8 unit of present consumption yield the same utility as one unit of future consumption, and also that 0.8 unit of output not consumed today (i.e., saved) can be transformed, through investment, to yield 1 unit in the future. The discount rate that would make 1 unit in the future equivalent to 0.8 unit today is 0.25 or 25 percent (i.e., present value =future value/(1+r), or r=0.25). It should also be clear from Figure 4.1 that if the marginal utility of present versus future consumption were higher (due, perhaps, to poverty), the appropriate discount rate would be higher even if there were no change in investment opportunities.

In equilibrium with no distortions in the economy the discount (interest) rate is such that savings equals investment (See Figure 4.2). It is immaterial whether one considers r_e as individuals' rate of time preference for current over future consumption, that is, the amount they require in compensation for deferring consumption, or the rate of return on the marginal investment, that is, the opportunity cost of capital on the margin – they are both the same. In practice, however, because of capital market distortions, including taxes, the rate received by savers is not equal to the rate of return on the marginal investment. Also, the appropriate *social* rate of discount may not be the same as the rate determined in private markets. Specifically, private savings and investment may fall short of socially desirable levels. Another complicating factor is that if projects are supported with government funds, government investment will affect private savings, consumption, and investment behavior, and these effects should be incorporated. Finally, questions have been raised as to whether environmental effects and projects should have their own discount rate. We examine some of these complications.

Consider Figure 4.3, which includes a proportional tax on savings and a proportional tax on investment returns. S_n is savers' willingness to save

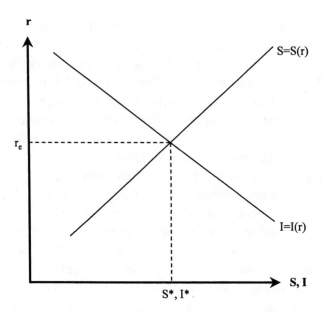

Figure 4.2. *Saving and investment schedules determine discount (interest) rate*

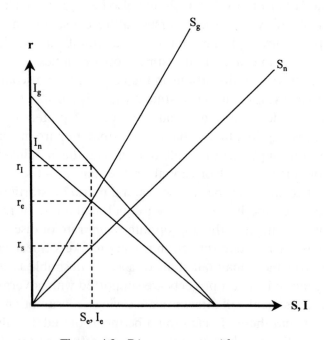

Figure 4.3. *Discount rates with taxes*

(forego consumption). If the earnings on savings are subject to a proportional tax of, say, 40 percent, S_g indicates the gross savings necessary to yield S_n, net savings. I_g is the schedule of gross rates of return on investment and declines as I increases due to progressively inferior investment opportunities. If investment returns are also taxed at a proportional rate, say, 25 percent, then I_n becomes the schedule of investment returns net of the 25 percent tax. S_e, I_e represent the equilibrium level of S and I in this (distorted) market. At S_e, I_e the marginal investment earns a gross return of r_I, which, after subtracting the 25 percent tax, leaves a net return of r_e. In turn, r_e is the gross rate of return to savers, who, after taxes, receive a net return of r_s, which encourages them to save just the amount S_e that is also justified for investment, I_e.

But the introduction of taxes poses a conceptual and empirical problem. Now r_s, which measures the time preference of individuals, is less than r_I, which measures the rate of return of the marginal investment. The problem is apparent. Should we value resources (funds) used in public projects at (1) the opportunity cost of capital (the marginal productivity of capital in the private sector, r_I), (2) the marginal time preference of savers, r_s, or (3) some weighted average of the two, or should we (4) ignore the evidence from the private sector and find some other device for evaluating public expenditures?

The first, second, and fourth alternatives are not attractive. The first alternative assumes that public investments simply displace the most efficient private investment. It does not account for consumers' time preferences, consider the effects of the government project on private savings and consumption, or consider subsequent savings or reinvestment effects in either the private or the public sector. If the second alternative is adopted, the implicit assumption is that government secures its funds (resources) by displacing only private consumption, and the displacement effects on efficient private investments earning r_1 are ignored. In fact, government projects earning the low rate of r_s may displace some private investments earning the higher r_I rate, and this would be a misallocation of capital. The fourth alternative would be to assume government resources are fixed and its expenditures do not affect private savings and investment behavior. In that event, a discount rate could be chosen such that acceptable government projects just exhaust government funds. The discount rate is then a mere rationing device for government investments, and has little relation to the time preference or investment opportunities in the private sector. In fact, government funds are not fixed and government investments overlap with private investments, so that treating the discount rate as a rationing device is not desirable.

We are left with the third alternative, which takes account of private time preferences, r_s, and private investment opportunities, r_I. At this point there are two approaches. The first approach uses units of consumption as the basic measuring rod or *numeraire*. This involves "shadow pricing" investment to determine its consumption equivalent value and discounting all of the project's costs and benefits at the *social* rate of time preference (SRTP). The second approach uses government income as the measuring rod, or *numeraire*. This involves "shadow pricing" consumption to determine its investment or government income value, and discounting all of the project costs and benefits at the accounting rate of interest (ARI). Both approaches have been used, and the choice is a matter of convenience and taste. Notice the implicit but questionable assumption that marginal government income will be used for investment, not current government consumption. The first approach is now explained in nontechnical fashion to illustrate the complexities. The exposition is a bit tedious. But discount rates play a crucial role in many environmental decisions, and understanding their strengths and weaknesses is important.

A first step in the first approach is to estimate the shadow price of investment. If the return in perpetuity of a unit of private investment is assumed to be r_I, and the time preference of savers is r_s, the shadow price of investment is simply r_I/r_s (resources invested have a higher value in consumption units than resources consumed).[3] Obviously if r_I equals r_s, which would be the case in a perfect undistorted market, there is no need for shadow pricing investment and the exercise is greatly simplified. On the other hand, both r_s and r_I may change over time, so that the shadow price of investment may rise or, more likely, fall over time. If so, the discount rate calculated on the basis of the shadow price of capital will change over time. This complication is frequently ignored, but is relevant for long-lived investment projects. There has been some theoretical discussion of hyperbolic discount rates that decline over time, but few practical applications. As noted below, an explicit consideration of environmental effects may also justify a declining discount rate over time.

Assuming $r_I > r_s$, the next step is to trace through the effects of the government expenditure on private consumption and savings (investment) to determine the magnitude of investment that needs to be shadow priced. In

---

3 Consider an infinite time horizon, where $r_I = 20\%$ and $r_s = 10\%$. Then \$1 devoted to investment would yield a stream of benefits of \$0.2 per year in perpetuity. If that stream is discounted at savers' rate of time preference (to measure it in consumption units) its net present value is \$2.

$$\left(NPV = \frac{a}{r_s} = \frac{0.2}{0.1} = \$2 \right)$$

This indicates a shadow price for investment of 2, or r_I/r_s.

principle, one should look at both the financing of the project (how much is financed out of reduced consumption and how much displaces private investment?) and the consequences of the project (whose income and hence savings and consumption behavior is altered by the project?). The latter is particularly difficult for several reasons. First, income effects should be traced through to different income classes in society if they have different marginal propensities to save and consume. Second, the data should include transfers, for example, losses to existing asset holders in one region and gains to asset holders in another region, if their savings/consumption behavior differ and if the consequences are to be accurately measured. Transfers can be large relative to the net welfare gains from a project, and the distributional and hence savings consequences of transfers may be important. Third, with long-lived projects one must be concerned with distributional and savings consequences in the medium and distant future, which are difficult to estimate.

Having established the shadow price, or premium on investment, by seeking r_s and r_1, and by considering the savings and investment versus consumption consequences of the project, the next step is to determine if the *social* rate of time preference differs from the time preference of individuals as reflected in r_s. As generally formulated, the time preference of savers is a function of three variables, a pure time preference arising from impatience, the expected future consumption level (income) of savers, and an assumption of diminishing marginal utility from incremental consumption. If we express the impatience parameter as p, we can write $r_s = p + (c)(n)$ where c is the expected consumption growth rate and n is elasticity of marginal utility with respect to consumption.[4] Thus if p=0.05, c=0.03,

---

4 The percentage change in marginal utility divided by the percentage change in consumption. Using the notation c for consumption, u for utility, and a parameter, n, which indicates the strength of diminishing marginal utility, and if we use a mathematically convenient utility function,

$$u = \frac{1}{1-n}c^{1-n}$$

and its marginal utility function,

$$mu = c^{-n}$$

then

$$\frac{d(mu)}{dc} = -nc^{-n-1}$$

and the elasticity

$$E_{mu,c} = \frac{d(mu)}{dc} \cdot \frac{c}{mu} = -n.$$

If we choose n=0 we are assuming constant marginal utility. If we choose n=1, and we assume that incomes in 10 years will be double their current value, then the present value of a marginal dollar 10 years hence is about 50 cents, disregarding any impatience for present over future consumption.

and n=1.5, this implies a time preference for savers, taking into account their expected income growth and an assumed diminishing marginal utility of consumption, of 0.095, or a 9.5 percent discount rate on future consumption.

All of these parameters may have to be adjusted to arrive at a social (not private savers') rate of time preference. Specifically, while individuals acting as individuals may exhibit "impatience," it is not clear that society should exhibit impatience to the same degree or indeed any at all. These adjustments are discussed next in the context of an environmental discount rate and are not pursued here. For the moment we simply note that in this first approach we would wish to convert the savers' rate of time preference into an SRTP before discounting the project's cost and benefits, which have now shadow-priced investment units into their consumption equivalents. In effect, the procedure, by shadow-pricing investment and giving it a premium, *devalues* consumption and in principle leads to higher investment and economic growth.

We must confess that much of this discussion has a rather stale flavor to it. The underlying premise of putting a premium on government income goes back decades when it was widely believed that private savings rates in developing countries were too low, capital was the principal scarce resource, and government had a major responsibility to accelerate development. In this view, government investment would occupy a large share of total investment, and diverting income to the public till would not be squandered but would be used productively. More recent evidence of high marginal private savings rates in many developing countries, privatization as a reaction against the dead hand (and financial drain) of investment in state enterprises, and contributions in the public choice literature cautioning against "government failure" in a misguided effort to correct market failures all weaken the case for deliberately selecting projects on the basis of their contributions to savings and government income. And indeed the World Bank appears to be in full retreat from using different private and public sector income weights, the method the Bank itself helped develop in the 1970s (Jenkins 1997).

3 An Environmental Discount Rate?

An important question is whether environmental projects require some adjustment of discount rates, or, to be more extreme, whether discounting itself is inappropriate for environmental effects. Before addressing this question, however, we need to dispose of three misconceptions. First, "high" discount rates do not necessarily work against environmental protection, and "low" discount rates are not necessarily conservation-friendly. True, high discount rates give little weight, in present value terms, to long-term environmental damages; the present value of environmental protection projects such as control of soil erosion are reduced; and in most economic models, high discount rates are associated with high depletion and harvest rates for natural resources. Nevertheless, high discount rates also bias selection against projects with long benefit streams, as are typically characteristic of natural resource development projects. Thus high discount rates in practice may discourage large-scale hydroelectric ventures, major mining projects, agricultural colonialization schemes, and similar projects that may have high environmental damage profiles. More broadly, high real interest rates are likely to slow overall investment and growth, indirectly slowing the rate of materials throughput in the economy. *Ceteris paribus*, natural resource extraction rates and pollution emission rates are slowed. In short, the conservationist faces a dilemma, desiring low discount rates for assessing long-term environmental costs (making current expenditures for protection more attractive) and high rates to discourage long-lived natural resource development projects with inevitable environmental quality losses (Norgaard and Howarth 1992).

Second, suggestions for adjusting discount rates to account for environmental uncertainty and risk are dubious. At first glance such adjustments look attractive. The environmental consequences of projects are uncertain, risks are asymmetrical (positive environmental surprises are rare), and the analyst might be tempted to add on a risk premium to the discount rate to account for possible negative environmental consequences. On reflection, this is not good practice. The premium is either entirely arbitrary, or based on an implicit probability distribution of a set of outcomes. If such an implicit distribution exists, it should be made explicit and applied directly to the calculation of the expected value of the relevant cost or benefit. The result will be as desired; projects with large, asymmetrically negative environmental risks will have lower and perhaps negative net present values, without any need to juggle the discount rate. The more difficult situations are those of very low probability of a very large or catastrophic loss in the future, or when uncertainty is so great that no probability distribution is available (e.g., serious nuclear accidents). These are not discount rate issues *per se*. Rather, this class of problems falls within the theory of decision making under uncertainty, and the precautionary principle is relevant. When the outcome involves generational time, ethical considerations are necessarily germane, and a strategy of minimizing maximum losses may be an appropriate adjunct to net present value analysis. Global warming, examined in Chapter 14, is a possible example (Perrings 1991).

Third, it has been suggested that a low discount rate is appropriate in situations involving irreplaceable environmental assets, the present values of which at conventional discount rates apparently do not justify protection. As a hypothetical example, consider a unique scenic attraction, the Grand Canyon, the current recreational and aesthetic value of which is assumed to be properly measured at $10 million annually. With a social rate of time discount of, say, 8 percent, the capitalized present value would appear to be $125 million.[5] Any development project that has a net present value of benefits minus costs in excess of $125 million would appear to dominate the opportunity cost (recreation foregone), and an irreplaceable environmental asset would be lost. Applying an "environmental" discount rate of, say, 2 percent to the stream of recreational benefits would immediately increase the opportunity cost from $125 million to $500 million and (perhaps) save the resource.

The problem, however, is misspecified. With a positive income elasticity of demand and increasing income, an irreplaceable environmental asset in fixed supply will have a benefit stream the (relative) value of which increases over time.[6] Assume real income growth of 3 percent, and an income elasticity of demand of 2 percent (a 1 percent growth in income, *ceteris paribus*, increases demand by 2 percent). In that event, the increasing demand, represented by $d_0, d_1, d_2 \ldots$, in Figure 4.4, increases the real price (value) of the asset by 6 percent per year ($P_t = P_0 e^{xt}$, where $x = (g)(n)$, or the income growth rate g multiplied by the income elasticity of demand n). Still assuming the initial year value is $10 million, discounting the (increasing) benefits stream at 8 percent gives a present value of $500 million, again, perhaps, sufficient to save the resource from development. If the price (value) of the resource grows at a *faster* rate than the discount rate, the present value of the resource is infinite. Moreover, the benefits from the development alternative, say, production of hydropower, may exhibit a declining price if technological improvements tend to lower real energy prices. This would further tilt the decision toward the conservation alternative. In short, preservation might be accomplished by manipulation of the discount rate, but the more direct and appropriate method is to adjust the benefit stream to reflect increasing rel-

5 Using the formula for the present value of an infinite annuity,

$$a = \frac{1}{r}.$$

6 For extensions and illustrations of this line of argument, see Krutilla and Fisher (1985).

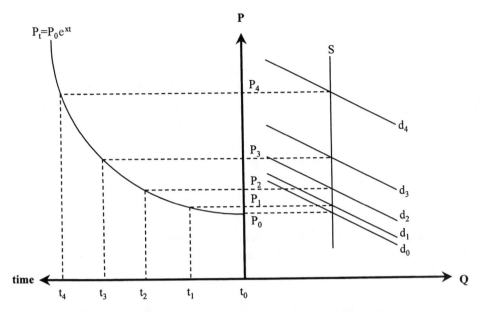

Figure 4.4. *Price of fixed asset subject to income elastic demand*

ative scarcity and hence demand and price. Choosing the "correct" environmental discount rate would in any event require the same information on future valuation. Moreover, manipulating the discount rate would mean alternative projects are evaluated at different discount rates – an invitation for arbitrary allocation of resources.

Setting aside these misconceptions, there are more compelling reasons why the discount rate might need adjustment when environmental considerations are taken into account. We start with the framework elaborated earlier, in which the discount rate emerges from the shadow pricing of investment, which earned a rate of return of r_I, into consumption terms; costs and benefits are then discounted at $r=p+(c)(n)$, where p is "impatience," c is expected growth in consumption, and n reflects diminishing marginal utility of consumption expressed in elasticity form.[7] First, estimates of r_I, the marginal productivity of capital from private investment, may be too high and hence the premium on investment too high. Historically, the productivity of commercial investments has not accounted for environmental exter-

---

7 The technical literature draws a distinction between discounting utility and discounting future consumption. The expression $r=p+(c\ n)$ is known as the consumption discount rate, or "how fast the value of a small increment in consumption changes if its date is delayed." Note that r can be negative if the rate of growth of consumption, c, is negative. In that event, the process of discounting would actually be awarding a premium to future consumption.

nalities. Nor have they fully accounted for depletion of natural capital. Studies indicate that national income growth can be overstated by failing to incorporate depletion of natural and environmental resources. They also show that measured rates of return to investment in extractive sectors overstate the real rate of return because they combine the return to physical capital invested in the sector with the royalty associated with the resource. (See Chapter 17.) Adjusting for these factors lowers the real productivity of capital, lowers the shadow price of capital, and, because the discount rate blends the opportunity cost of capital and savers' time preference, lowers the appropriate discount rate itself.

Second, c, the estimated growth of per capita consumption, may be too high. Per capita consumption data are inevitably drawn from marketed goods and services. Directly consumed environmental services are excluded. If such environmental goods and services (clean air and water, recreation and amenities) are becoming increasingly scarce, the growth of real per capita consumption, broadly defined to include directly consumed environmental services, is likely to be less than conventionally measured consumption growth. In that event, the SRTP (the discount rate) should be adjusted downward. It would be ironic if the failure to account for nonmarketed environmental consumption resulted in artificially high discount rates, which in turn discouraged the preservation of remaining environmental services. Both the adjustment of r_I and the adjustment of c are relevant for environmental damages with long time horizons. If global warming erodes the productivity of investment in, say, agriculture, and if it reduces the consumption of nonmarketed, directly consumed environmental services, the appropriate discount rate should be adjusted downward. This downward adjustment would justify a more aggressive greenhouse gas abatement program.

Third, estimates of n, the elasticity of marginal utility with respect to consumption, may be inappropriate. This parameter cannot be directly observed. The suggestions for determining a value for n include looking at government policy (including progressive tax systems) to judge social concern for income equality and to review past government decisions on investment projects, so as to infer from them government preferences for income equality (Squire and van der Tak 1975, pp. 103–104). This is almost circular; to determine an appropriate decision by government in one instance one looks to see how it acted on other decisions. This is a general criticism, unrelated to environment. The more specific point is that estimates of n, an interpersonal weighting parameter, are also used for intertemporal weighting or capturing intergenerational equity. It is a considerable leap to argue that the social values placed on consumption of groups at different income levels at a point in time are also the identical social values for consumption levels of future generations over long periods of time. Whether the appropriate n reflecting intergenerational consumption levels is higher or lower than the interpersonal n is not known; neither can be determined by objective analysis.

This leaves p, the impatience parameter. In fact, p, the pure time preference, is related to n. The welfare of future generations can be taken into account either by a lower p or by choosing a lower n for any positive c, implying that the rate at which marginal utility falls with increasing consumption is reduced. Both have the effect of reducing the SRTP and presumably increasing current savings and investment, assisting the growth of the capital stock and hence improving welfare in the future.

The use of a positive p in determining the *social* rate of time preference has been subject to a number of criticisms apart from the environmental implications. Some are intuitive but difficult to formalize. For example, individuals in their personal behavior may have a specific preference for distributing their consumption stream over time, but individuals acting in their social role might have a different intertemporal utility function, in which the social utility function gives greater weight to future welfare. In that event, there is justification for government acting in the social interest to override the expressed time preference of individual savers, acting in their individual capacities, as expressed in r_s.

Two other arguments supporting a social discount rate below the rate emerging from private savings decisions have been suggested (Lind 1982; Marglin 1963; Sen 1967). The first is known as the isolation paradox. It rests on the notion that individuals derive satisfaction not only from their own consumption but also from the consumption of other individuals, including future generations. A market failure arises because of the absence of collective action and enforcement, and because any individual's utility gain from providing for future generations is trivial compared to the gain he or she would receive from others' provisions for the future. Individuals, acting as individuals, therefore do not restrain their current consumption, even though if they did so collectively, all would gain. In this sense, the welfare of future generations has the quality of a public good. The "assurance problem" is related. The basic premise is that individuals would choose to make greater provision for future generations if they were assured that others were doing likewise. In the absence of this assurance, private decisions lead to suboptimal savings and the welfare of future generations is inadequately considered even in relation to the preferences of current generations. While

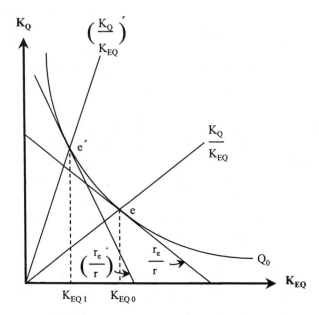

Figure 4.5. *Misallocation of man-made and environmental capital due to failure to include externality and user costs*

developed independent of environmental considerations, these arguments for a social discount rate at variance with market rates take on greater force when considering the conservation of natural and environmental resources. The literature on the social rate of time discount grew out of a desire to accelerate economic growth and was part and parcel of the mind-set that government had a large role to play in achieving development. The current concern is very different – assuring future generations of having adequate supplies of environmental capital. When actions today result in uncompensated environmental damage in the future, discounting reduces the value the present generation attaches to these damages. It is difficult to find justification for this practice in moral philosophy.

Consider Figure 4.5, which illustrates the point made earlier, that the marginal productivity of capital as conventionally measured may be too high. The representative isoquant Q_0 is derived from a neoclassical production function in which man-made capital and environmental capital (K_Q, K_{EQ}) produce conventional economic output. If environmental capital is underpriced because externality and user costs are not internalized, the initial (distorted) equilibrium point may be at e, with an implied input price ratio of r_e/r, where r is the price of man-made capital and r_e is the price of

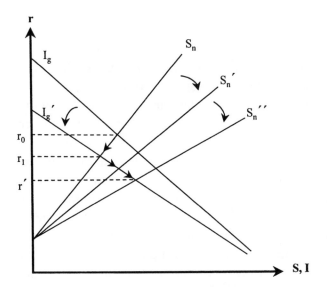

Figure 4.6. *Discount rates with various environmental "corrections"*

environmental capital. Full inclusion of externality and user costs would increase r_e relative to r, moving the input point to e'. This conserves K_{EQ}, but also reduces the rate of return to man-made capital, as shown by $(r_e/r)' > (r_e/r)$. In this fashion, the underpricing of environmental capital (r_e) overstates the return or price for man-made capital. An environmental policy that would correctly price environmental capital would not only conserve its use but would reduce the apparent return to man-made capital. This adjustment has been formalized by Weitzman (1994).[8]

Now carry these notions over to Figure 4.6, which reconstructs Figure 4.3 but without taxes.[9] S_n and I_g were the original supply-and-demand schedules for savings and investment. Correcting the social costs of investment for the true externality and user costs shifts the investment curve to I_g'. At the same time, if measured estimates of per capita consumption growth, c, are judged too "high" for the reasons given above, S_n is shifted down to S_n' (increased savings). And if the assurance and isolation paradox arguments are accepted, S_n' is still too high, and the social savings curve should be shifted down to S_n''. By itself, reducing the investment schedule

8 Weitzman shows that in a simple model in which environmental degradation is a positive function of economic activity but can be controlled by environmental spending, the social rate of discount is both lower than the private (market) rate in an otherwise undistorted economy, and the social rate of discount is likely to fall over time.
9 As suggested by Pezzey (1992, Figures 15 and 16).

from I_g to I'_g would reduce the market clearing interest rate (discount rate) from r_0 to r_1 and lead to lower savings and investment. The effect on welfare of future generations is uncertain. Lower investment would decrease future capital stock. But incorporating user and externality costs would tend to conserve natural capital available to future generations. As drawn, the double shift of the savings schedule from S_n to S''_n would further reduce the discount rate but would be consistent with higher savings and investments.

An additional line of argument suggests that by incorporating environmental considerations the appropriate discount rate itself might decline in the future. This is relevant to long-lived environmental effects such as global warming. Consider an initial situation in which environmental degradation is held in check by expending some fraction of national income on abatement. Now consider an incremental increase in investment which, if pollution were absent, would earn a return of i, the private marginal productivity of capital. But in fact some of the production and consumption made possible by the investment must be devoted to abating the increment in pollution if environmental disamenities are to be held constant, and therefore the social rate of return is something less than i. The larger the fraction of income needed to control pollution and the less efficient abatement spending is in controlling pollution, the greater the gap between the social and private rates of return. If the share of environmental spending increases and if it has declining marginal efficiency, one would expect the environmentally adjusted social rate of discount to decline over time (Weitzman 1994).

Most of the preceding paragraphs represent a tinkering with the discount rate. Except for the general point that high discount rates slow down overall investment and hence tend to slow the overall use of environmental resources, and except for situations characterized by great uncertainty and potentially catastrophic consequences, the introduction of environmental considerations suggests a lower but still positive discount rate, uniform across all policies and projects, not just environmental projects. In other words, a separate discount rate for environmental projects is not warranted. Environmental considerations do point toward a lower social rate of time discount than has traditionally been used. Still, a lower discount rate does not assure the interests of future generations and further arguments are explored in the final section of this Chapter.[10]

---

10 A lower discount rate also slides over the questions of how the interest rate in private sector investments is to be adjusted downward and how the government is to acquire the additional resources for public investments implied by the lower discount rate.

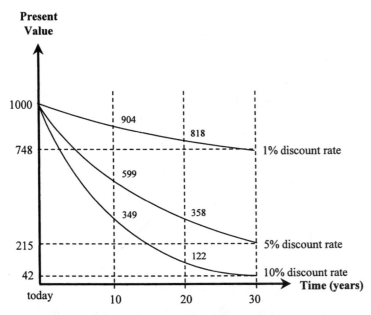

Figure 4.7. *Present value of $1,000 30 years hence at 1, 5, and 10 percent discount rates*

4 Examples of Discounting and Intertemporal Resource Allocation

It is hard to exaggerate the importance of the discount rate in allocating resources over time. The present values of $1,000 received 30 years from now discounted at 1 and 10 percent – two rates that have been suggested in the literature for U.S. government projects[11] – are $748 and $42, respectively. The disparity increases over time, making long-lived natural and environmental resource allocation decisions especially sensitive. Figure 4.7 illustrates the power of discounting. It shows the present value of $1,000 received today and 10, 20, and 30 years hence at 1, 5, and 10 percent discount rates.

This section presents some illustrations of efficiency in the allocation of resources over time and the effects of discounting. The principal purpose is to show the role of the discount rate in intertemporal allocation problems for both nonrenewable and renewable resources. The exposition starts with a simple case of allocating a fixed supply of a resource over two time periods. This is extended to a natural resource extraction model first without and

11 One percent is the average real return on 91-day Treasury notes over a 35-year period. Quirk and Terasawa (1991) argue for a rate in excess of 10 percent.

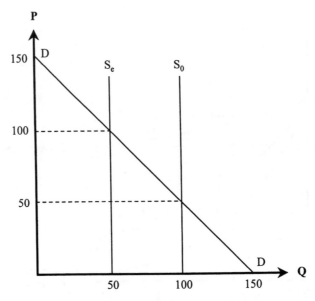

Figure 4.8. *Intertemporal efficiency: allocation of fixed resource over two time periods*

then with extraction costs. The section concludes with an example of a renewable but potentially depletable natural resource.

4.1 Resources in Fixed Supply

Consider first the problem of allocating a fixed supply of a resource effi-ciently over two time periods, t=0 and t=1. Efficiency is defined as maxi-mizing the net present value derived from the resources use.[12] For simplicity and to give numerical content to the example, assume 100 units of the resource are available, the same linear demand schedule for the resource exists in the two periods, Q=150−P, and there are no extraction or produc-tion costs. The situation is shown in Figure 4.8. *DD* is the representative demand curve. If the entire stock is used in the first period, S_0=100, and the value or consumer surplus is simply the area to the left of S_0 under the demand curve, or 10,000: (50)(100)+(100)(100)(0.5). This is clearly an inef-ficient allocation (and quite possibly inequitable). If one unit could be shifted from t_0 to t_1, current welfare would be reduced by approximately 50

---

12 This approach is known as discounted utilitarianism. See also Tietenberg (1996, Chap. 2).

(its marginal value in t_0), and that unit valued one year from now would be approximately 150. Consumption of the resource today creates a *user cost* in the next time period; the opportunity cost of using the last unit today is its value in consumption in the next time period. A moment's reflection will reveal that the present value of the marginal user cost in both (all) time periods must be equalized, otherwise total welfare (efficiency) can be increased by shifting units from periods of low to high marginal value.

If the value of future consumption is not discounted, the optimum (efficient) allocation of the fixed stock is at $S_e=50$ for each time period. The market clearing price is then 100, and the total value *in each time period* is the area to the left of S_e and below the demand curve, or 6,250: $(100 \times 50) + (50)(50)(0.5)$. For the two time periods together, the value is 12,500. The marginal user cost in both periods is \$100 and the resource is allocated efficiently over time. It also appears equitable, as each "generation" receives the same quantity, 50 units.

Now consider a positive discount rate, say 20 percent.[13] The demand curve in the first time period, $Q_0=150-P_0$, is unaffected. But the demand curve in t_1, expressed in present value terms, is now $Q_1=150-P_0 (1.2)$. Consider the top part of Figure 4.9, where D_0D represents demand in the original time period and D_1D is the present value of the demand curve for t_1. The problem is to allocate the fixed supply of 100 between the two time periods in order to maximize the present value of consumer surplus. The graphic solution is shown in the figure, where Q_0 is the amount used in t_0, Q_1 is the amount used in t_1. The trick is to find an allocation Q_0, Q_1 such that the marginal user cost in the first period is equal to the (discounted) marginal user cost in the second period, and the total consumption of the resource equals its supply (i.e., $Q_0+Q_1=S_0$). P_0 is such a marginal user cost. Given the price P_0 in t_0, Q_0 is consumed, leaving Q_1 for t_1. The price in t_1 is now P_1 and $P_1=P_0 (1.2)$.

The algebraic solution is to use the two demand equations and the total supply equation:

$$Q_0 = 150 - P_0$$
$$Q_1 = 150 - P_0(1+r)$$
$$Q_0 + Q_1 = Q$$

13 Large discount rates are easier to illustrate. They would also be appropriate if the consumption periods are separated by several years.

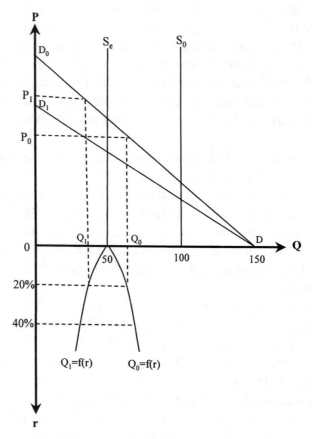

Figure 4.9. *Intertemporal efficiency at various discount rates*

solving for Q_0

$$Q_0 = \frac{Q - 150 + 150(1+r)}{1 + (1+r)}$$

for r=0.2, Q=100:

$$Q_0 = 59.09$$

and, by substitution,

$$Q_1 = 40.91$$
$$P_0 = 90.91$$
$$P_1 = 109.09$$

Note that the present value of the price in time t_1 ($P_1/1+r$) is equal to the price P_0. The present value of the marginal user cost is the same in both time periods. The total discounted value (revenue plus consumer surplus) over the two periods can be easily calculated and shown to be greater than either immediate consumption ($Q_0=100$, $Q_1=O$) or equal consumption in both periods ($Q_0=Q_1=50$).[14]

Although simplified, this two-period optimal allocation model illustrates a number of fundamental results. First, no other allocation will produce a higher present value than Q_0Q_1 as determined in the previous example. Second, the positive discount rate results in a disproportionate share consumed in the first period. What is efficient may not be perceived as "fair." Third, the price of the resource increases at the rate of the discount [$P_t=P_0(1+r)^t$]. Finally, the higher the discount rate, the more "inequitable" the intertemporal distribution appears to be. The demand curve expressed in present value terms at a 40 percent discount rate would fall below D_1D (not shown). The user cost of consuming the resource in the first period would fall further due to the higher discount on future consumption, and a greater share of the resource would be consumed in the initial time period. For convenience, the positive relation between Q_0 and the discount rate r and the negative relation between Q_1 and r are shown in the lower part of Figure 4.9, illustrating the increasing intertemporal "inequity" as the discount rate increases.

Nevertheless, an efficient allocation *need not* be inequitable as compared to an equal distribution of the resource between the two periods if investment opportunities earning a return equal to the discount rate are available. At a 20 percent discount rate the efficient allocation is $Q_0=59.09$, $Q_1=40.91$. Let 8.264 be set aside from consumption in t_0 and be invested at 20 percent. The resulting consumption in the two periods, $C_0=59.09-8.264=50.83$, and $C_1=40.91+(1.2)(8.264)=50.83$, is equal. Also, by efficient allocation it is possible to enjoy higher consumption in both periods. But as pointed out in the following section, one's confidence in achieving intertemporal equity requires that a sinking fund be set up, with continued reinvestment, sometimes for long periods of time.

This simple example also casts doubt on the contention that discounting always amounts to a bias against future generations. Two responses, the first rather weak and the second somewhat stronger, are possible. First, it is true that positive discount rates reduce the present value of future benefits. But projects whose stream of net benefits (gross benefits less costs) are constant over time are unaffected by discounting; the ratio of cumulative benefits to

---

14 An efficient distribution has a net present value of 11,534. Equal use in the two time periods has a net present value of 11,458.

cumulative costs is the same whether discounted at a 0 or 10 percent rate. However, such projects are rare. More frequent are projects whose benefits are near-term and whose environmental costs are long-term. For example, discounting increases the net present value of offshore tin dredging, where the near-term benefits are mining revenues and the long-term costs are loss of coral reefs and recreational potential. At the same time, discounting makes less attractive environmental protection projects, such as soil-erosion control, with near-term costs and long-term benefits. The environmentalist sees an apparent bias in discounting future environmental costs and discounting the benefits of environmental protection. But even so, discounting does not necessarily disadvantage future generations – avoiding current costs and securing near-term benefits frees up resources in the near term that can be reinvested at a positive rate, thus increasing the wealth and income of future generations. The key question is whether the net proceeds in the near term are consumed currently or invested to secure future benefits. The discount rate not only reflects impatience for current consumption but also opportunities for productive investment.

This two-period resource allocation model can be extended to approach a basic natural resource extraction model. Consider a natural resource in fixed supply (R_0 at time t_0) and a linear market demand curve assumed constant over time. For the moment, neglect any extraction costs or other complications such as new discoveries, imperfect markets, and the like. The task is to find the optimal rate of exploitation over time in order to maximize the net present value of the resource. In doing so, we wish to determine the initial price, P_0, and its time path, as well as the total length of time before the resource is exhausted. The solution makes use of Hotelling's rule, which says that the optimal extraction rate for a fixed resource with no extraction costs is such that the rate of increase in the price of the resource, η_p, should be just equal to the discount rate (Hotelling 1931). An alternative and equivalent formulation is given by the exponential growth equation

$$P_t = P_0 \, e^{rt},$$

where r is the discount rate and P is the price of the resource. The intuitive understanding of this rule is as follows. Resource owners will convert their natural resource capital into financial capital through extraction and earn a return, r, so long as r exceeds the return on the unexploited natural resource, which is nothing more than the rate at which its price increases. Thus, if $r > \eta_p$, the extraction rate will increase, and for $r < \eta_p$, resource owners will cut back on current extraction and conserve the resource in the expectation of higher future prices. At an extraction rate such that the rate of price increase just equals the discount rate, the net present value of the resource is maximized for the same reason as in the earlier two-period model – the marginal user cost as reflected in then current prices, when discounted, are equal for all time periods. It is not possible to shift use of the resource from one time period to another and increase the net present value derived from using the resource.

Stating the rate at which the resource price will increase over time, however, does not complete the problem. One must still find the number of years over which the resource is to be exploited and the initial price of the resource. These are not arbitrary choices. Only one combination of resource lifetime and initial price results for a given discount rate. The trick is to determine the resource lifetime, T, and the initial price, P_0, so that at time T the price has increased to a level such that demand for the resource dwindles to zero *and* the resource is fully exhausted.[15] This makes intuitive sense. It would be wasteful to have a solution in which a high price forced demand to zero when some of the resources had not been used. By the same token, it would be uneconomic to exhaust the resource too quickly at a price less than some future user would have been willing to pay.

These ideas are illustrated in Figure 4.10.[16] Quadrant 4 contains the (reversed) demand curve for the resource. Note the horizontal axis, Q, measures the amount of resource use per market period, a flow variable. When Q is traced over time, as in quadrant 3, the area under the curve will measure the cumulative amount of the resource extracted from t_0 to any subsequent time, t_n. Quadrant 1 indicates the time path of the resource price. The rate of growth of price will be determined by the discount rate, as in $P_t = P_0 e^{rt}$, but there is a separate time path for each initial P on the vertical axis. The choice of P_0 is critical. As seen in quadrant 1, it will determine the length of time it will take for prices to rise to the level at which demand falls to zero. Also, the choice of P_0 working through the demand curve in quadrant 4 will determine the initial rate of exploitation, Q_0. The resource extraction curve in quadrant 3 itself is set by the time path of prices that, working through the demand curve, determine the time path of resource exploitation. Thus for every initial Q, there is a separate time path for exploitation. Put somewhat differently, given the discount rate and the demand curve, a particular P_0 determines a particular time path for prices in quadrant 1 and a particu-

---

15 The problem is often framed with a so-called "backup technology" that puts an upper limit on the price increase for the resource in question. This adds a note of realism and also facilitates nonlinear demand curves.

16 This diagram is similar to David Pearce and R. Kerry Turner (1990), although the cumulative extraction curve is reversed and they include a backup technology.

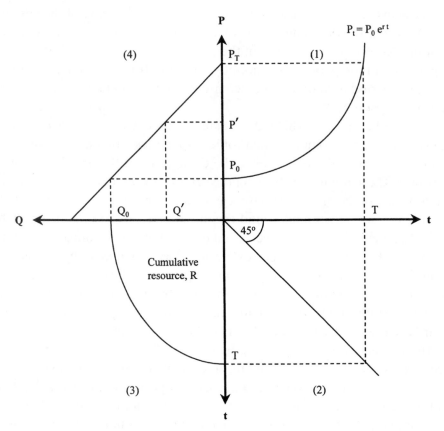

Figure 4.10. *Optimal exploitation rate and time path of price of fixed resource*

lar time path for resource extraction in quadrant 3. The system is solved by choosing Q_0, P_0 such that the cumulative area under the resource exploitation curve in quadrant 3 is just equal to the initial stock of the resource. Note that P_0, Q_0 in the diagram lead to exhaustion of the resource at time T, which is also the time at which the price has risen to P_T and demand has dwindled to zero. Given the initial resource stock, the demand curve, and the discount rate, a higher initial price and a lower initial quantity extracted, say P' and Q', would have prices reach P_T with some fraction of the resource remaining; choosing an initial price below P_0 and an initial quantity larger than Q_0 would exhaust the stock of resources before P had reached P_T, implying unsatisfied market demand and a misallocation of resources. Finally, it should be clear that, *ceteris paribus*, the higher the discount rate, the lower the initial price, the more rapid the price increase, and the *shorter the time period* within which the resource is used up. As expected, high discount rates favor current over future consumption of nonrenewable natural resources.[17]

Another step toward realism is to introduce extraction costs, and more specifically to make extraction costs a positive function of the amount of the resource that has been exploited (depleted). *Ceteris paribus*, we would expect that as mineral deposits and oil reservoirs are mined, the marginal cost of additional extraction will rise. Thus we have a second notion of user cost – in addition to the notion of user cost as the opportunity cost of fore-going consumption in the future, extraction today increases extraction costs in the future. Although this is essentially a problem of allocating the resource over several time periods, it is convenient to use a two-period time frame and to consider allocation from the perspective of a single resource owner.

Michael Toman has presented a neat diagrammatic exposition of the problem (Toman 1986).[18] Suppose a single owner of a stock of resources, R, wishes to determine extraction rates in periods t_0 and t_1, under certain knowledge of prices today (t_0) and in the future (t_1). Assume further that the marginal costs of extraction are positively related to the rate of extraction and to the amount of the resource that has been depleted. It follows that in determining the profit-maximizing level of output today, the resource owner must take account of the user costs he imposes on himself in the next time period due to higher extraction costs. Consider Figure 4.11. Part a represents the present time period; part b represents the future at t_1. If marginal costs in the two time periods were independent, the optimal outputs are Q_0 at t_0 and Q_1 at t_1.[19] Profits are the area under the price line and above the marginal cost curves, and the present value of future profits can easily be calculated with the appropriate discount rate. If, however, the depletion implied by Q_0 in the first period increased marginal costs in the second period, then the marginal cost curve in the lower panel shifts to MC_1', the optimal output decreases to Q_1', and second-period profits are reduced by the area *ABCD*. This represents the depletion-induced increase in costs and reduction in profits that, when discounted, is the "user cost" that should be added to the marginal cost curve in Figure 4.11a. In general, for every output level in the first period, a second-period user cost can be calculated. In the figure we have added the user cost to MC_0 to get the total marginal cost

17 It may be noted that in this illustration if the price elasticity of demand at P_0 is less than one, value of the resource used in each period grows initially and then declines.
18 Toman also considers expenditures for resource exploration and additions to supply.
19 That is, $MC_0 = P_0 =$ marginal revenue in the first time period, and $MC_1 = P_1 =$ marginal revenue in the subsequent time period.

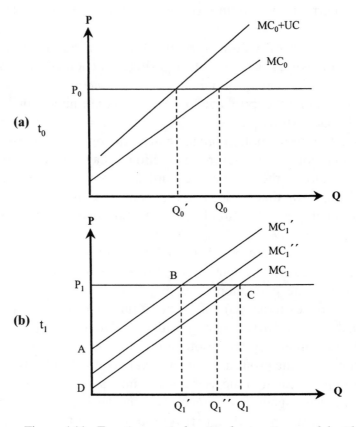

Figure 4.11. *Two time period optimal extraction model with increasing marginal extraction costs*

($MC_0 + UC$) in the initial period. Having done so, the optimal first period output drops to Q_0', the second-period marginal cost corresponding to Q_0' is MC_1'', and the optimal second-period output settles at Q_1''. The net result is to hold both initial and subsequent output below the levels that would have obtained had not the two marginal cost curves been linked through the depletion effect. To have ignored the user cost in the initial period would have led to larger immediate profits but higher costs and lower future profits. Although not featured in the model, the higher the discount rate, the smaller the present value of the user cost, and hence the higher the extraction rate in the initial time period.

More generally the introduction of extraction costs, discovery of new deposits, and technological progress may alter Hotelling's conclusion that the price, or scarcity rent, of nonrenewable resources rises monotonically (Krautkraemer 1998). Farzin (1992) has shown that the price path of the resource may be nonmonotonic and may indeed first decline and then increase. This helps reconcile empirical studies that fail to show steadily rising prices for exhaustible natural resources.

4.2 Time and Renewable Resources

Time and the discount rate enter renewable resource management decisions in two ways. First, unlike nonrenewable resources, renewable resources regenerate themselves over time, and this introduces a biological growth function with a time dimension to the calculations. Second, as with nonrenewable resources, the asset owner must decide the rate and timing of converting her natural resources to financial assets so as to maximize the present value of her income stream. The discount rate, as the rate of return on alternative investments, obviously enters this decision. Economic models of these decisions generally take one of two forms. The first is the optimal harvest rate model for resources such as fish stocks. Chapter 16 investigates this type of model in the context of ocean fisheries. The second type analyzes the optimal harvest cycle for long-lived biological resources such as forests. The general rule is to harvest when the rate of increase in the value of trees is equal to the opportunity cost of capital, which brings together the discount rate and the biological growth rate of the trees themselves.[20]

In this chapter we examine a variation of the latter analytical question – the optimal fallow period for soil resources, whose productivity can be depleted by cropping and restored by resting the soil for moisture and nutrient accumulation. A similar model might also be used for analyzing slash and burn (swidden) agriculture as practiced in the tropics. The model serves to illustrate three points: that optimal economic management may imply some reduction in average soil quality, that a positive discount rate will also tend to lower average soil quality, and that introducing positive harvesting costs will tend to increase average soil quality.[21] To keep the exposition simple and focused, we assume no open-access common property and externality problems, although harvest cycle and optimal extraction rate models frequently include these complexities.

Consider a farmer with full property rights who must decide how often to crop his land. Assume that soil quality, measured in yield per hectare (ha) per crop, increases with the length of fallow up to some maximum yield. Although it is natural to think of the fallow period in years, for expositional

---

20 For a basic forestry model see Lesser, Dodds, and Zerbe (1997, Chap. 16).
21 These results parallel the results of the fisheries model in Chapter 16. The economics of soil conservation has a long history. See Bunce (1942).

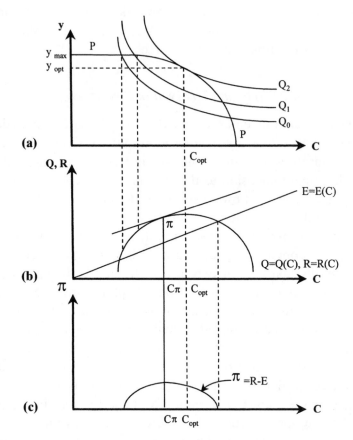

Figure 4.12. *Optimal fallow period model with positive cropping costs*

convenience assume the fallow period is infinitely divisible. Without going into detail, we can assume a crop yield function showing positive but diminishing returns with a longer fallow period up to some maximum biological yield. At the same time the number of crops planted and harvested over any arbitrarily long time period T is inversely related to the length of the fallow period. Thus there is a trade-off between yield per ha per crop and number of crops. It can be shown that total agricultural output over the long time horizon T is maximized when the yield is less than its biological maximum.[22] This implies shorter fallow and more crops than would obtain if the soil were managed to obtain its highest average quality.

Figure 4.12 illustrates the situation. In part a the vertical axis, y, measures yield per ha per crop. The horizontal axis, C, measures the number of crops

22 For the formal model, see Charles Pearson and Anthony Pryor (1978, Chap. 4 Appendix, p. 246).

in the arbitrarily long time horizon. The curve *PP* (a type of production possibility curve) represents the trade-off between yield per crop and number of crops. It is convex to the origin to reflect diminishing marginal returns to increased fallow period.[23] Q_0, Q_1, and Q_2 are measures of total output Q over the period T and are rectangular hyperbolas (i.e., Q=yC). Maximum total output is Q_2, and this determines the optimum yield (soil quality) y_{opt} and the optimum number of crops in the period C_{opt} (and hence the optimum fallow period). Note that the optimum yield y_{opt} is less than the biological maximum yield, implying a lower average soil quality than is possible to obtain. The environmental resource, soil, is maintained at its maximum economic yield, which is less than its maximum productivity. The economically optimal fallow period is less than the fallow period that yields the largest crop per ha. This occurs even if the discount rate is zero, a point worth stressing. The reason is that to increase fallow, soil quality, and yields, it would be necessary to reduce the total number of crops that could be harvested.

The analysis can be modified to take account of cropping costs, and a positive time preference and hence discounting. These work in opposite directions. Figure 4.12b illustrates $Q=Q(C)$, the relation between total output Q over the period T, and the number of crops harvested in T, with output maximized at C_{opt}. If the price of the crop is constant, this also serves as a total revenue function, R=R(C). Assume expenditures E for planting and harvesting are a linear function of the number of crops, $E=E\ (C)$. Profits, π, are then *R* minus *E*, measured by the vertical difference between the two curves, and the profit maximizing number of crops (where marginal revenue equals marginal costs) is shown as C_π in the middle panel. For clarity, profits are also shown in the bottom panel. The implication is that the introduction of positive cropping costs reduces the profit-maximizing number of crops over the period T from C_{opt} to C_π. The further implication is that the economically optimal rotation period, as measured by the fallow period, lengthens. In general, the higher the cropping costs, the longer the fallow period and the higher the average productivity of the soil.[24]

The final adjustment is to recognize that different cropping and fallow decisions generate different time streams of revenues and costs and hence different time streams of profits. Specifically, a cropping strategy of long

---

23 The horizontal segment reflects the assumption that yields reach some biological maximum.
24 A higher price for the output, if constant over the period T, would shift the revenue and profit curves upward but not disturb the profit-maximizing number of crops and length of fallow. This example assumes cropping costs are related to the number of crops harvested, not the quantity harvested per crop.

Table 4.1. *Profit streams*

Time (t)	Cropping strategy		
	1	2	3
1			
2	10		
3		15	
4	10		
5			
6	10	15	30
Total profit	30	30	30
NPV profit at 10%	20.7	19.7	16.9

fallow and high yields throws more of the output and profit toward the end of the time stream, where it is heavily discounted, whereas a short fallow, lower yield strategy that generates the same total output and profits brings output and profits closer in time. For example, consider three profit streams from three rotation strategies with the same total profits (Table 4.1). (For simplicity we now assume any difference in yield from the three strategies is offset by different harvest costs so that the total undiscounted profits are the same.)

The net present value of profits from the first short fallow strategy exceeds the net present value of the other two strategies, and its attractiveness increases as the discount rate increases. A positive discount rate will tend to lead to lower average soil fertility over the long term. Put somewhat differently, high discount rates increase the opportunity cost of waiting for higher yields and encourage more frequent cropping with lower yields, a result consistent with the optimal extraction models for renewal resources such as fisheries and optimal harvest cycle models for forests.

5 Intergenerational Efficiency, Equity, and Sustainability

As analyzed in the preceding section, dynamic efficiency implies maximizing the net present value of a resource using the appropriate social rate of time discount. What are the intergenerational equity implications? At one level it can be argued that efficiency is not necessarily inconsistent with an equitable distribution of resource use over time. The increased output from efficient allocation can be set aside, invested, and used to compensate future generations for any environmental resource loss they may suffer as the result of current usage. If the opportunity cost of capital is used for the discount rate, the use of the resource today earns a positive return, that if reinvested, may be able to fully compensate society in the future. For example, faced with a choice of using fossil fuel or more expensive solar energy today, the real resources freed up by using fossil fuel could be invested in other productive investments that would accumulate and may be sufficient to compensate for losses from global warming in the future. It is important to remember that this has to be done in real, not financial, terms. Although individuals can transfer financial resources to their heirs over time, the only way a society can increase its future welfare is by bequeathing a larger net stock of real productive resources – physical, human, intellectual, and environmental capital. Keep in mind also that the social rate of discount may well change over time. In particular, the marginal productivity of capital may fall (or rise) so that the reinvestment may not accumulate at the rate based on current estimates.

But this line of argument is grounded partly on faith. Recall that the traditional efficiency criterion, known as the Pareto criterion, requires that the beneficiaries of a policy or project *could* compensate the losers and still be better off. Thus the Pareto criterion only requires a potential Pareto improvement.[25] This criterion has been widely accepted in decisions that do not involve long periods of time or intergenerational transfers. For example, reducing a tariff will benefit consumers but harm asset owners in the import competing industry, and the welfare changes tend to be immediate or near term. The Pareto criterion is satisfied if consumers could compensate welfare loss in the import-competing industry and still be better off. The Pareto criterion commands widespread support in many economic policy decisions because political institutions and instruments exist, at least in democratic societies, for achieving a socially equitable distribution. These include progressive tax systems, welfare payments, direct provision of government services, and the like. Thus efficiency can be pursued in individual projects and policies with some confidence that distributional equity can be achieved through other channels.[26]

This confidence falters and must be replaced in part by faith in situations involving intergenerational welfare transfers. There is no political mechanism that connects and represents the interests of future generations to the present one. Their voices are not heard (and indeed their preferences are

---

25 In contrast, an actual Pareto improvement requires that no one be made worse off and at least one person be made better off. The Pareto criterion is also known as the Kaldor-Hicks hypothetical compensation test.
26 The efficiency aspects of the distributional policies raise separate questions.

not known). Nor are there secure mechanisms for transferring real wealth or capital over long periods of time. The absence of such mechanisms has led Mishan to label this situation a *potential* potential Pareto improvement, with the first potential the *possibility* but not the certainty of reinvestment through time, and the second potential being the conventional, hypothetical character of the compensation at some future date (Mishan 1988, p. 300).

The notion of *potential* potential intergenerational compensation makes environmentalists properly nervous. To achieve the potential compensation requires that a fraction of the current gain actually be invested and continue to be reinvested in some form of real sinking fund, so that the accumulated resources are indeed available in the future. This implies enormous confidence in a social agency that will, over long periods, scrupulously protect the sinking fund from raiding for interim consumption. If the resource itself and not the sinking fund were set aside today, it, too, would be vulnerable to raiding at some interim future point. But there may well be a practical difference between using the resource today (and hoping sufficient proceeds for future compensation are continually reinvested) and refraining from current use of the resources (and hoping that the current restraint is continued). Nevertheless, a conundrum persists. Abstaining from using resources today may reduce current income, savings, and investment and, by slowing the accumulation of assets, work to impoverish future generations.

All this has a very abstract flavor. But intergenerational equity considerations are highly relevant for current environmental problems. How much nuclear waste should be left to future generations, and how do we compensate them for storage costs and possible radiation disasters? What climate will prevail 50 or 100 years from now? What will be the soil quality, fish stocks, gene pools, and wilderness areas? As discussed, manipulating the discount rate *may* increase conservation, but it does not answer the ethical questions. Indeed, setting too low a discount rate or using a zero discount rate may be unethical, as it neglects the real productivity of resources and, by misallocation, can impoverish future generations. Moreover, accepting a low discount rate for long-lived environmental protection projects such as curtailment of global warming can divert development funds and welfare improvement among today's poor.

Does the newly popular concept of sustainable development, considered more fully in Chapter 16, help resolve the intergenerational efficiency-equity issue? One concept of sustainability requires that a nondeclining stock of total capital (physical, human, natural) be maintained through time, and a second more restrictive concept requires that the stock of natural capital be nondeclining through time. These sustainability concepts help by focusing attention on capital broadly defined as the source of welfare. If intergenerational equity is considered to be nondeclining utility or welfare, then a minimum condition appears to be the maintenance of the stock of total capital. Indeed, a requirement that either total capital or natural capital be maintained over time is a way of imposing an equity requirement *prior* to seeking an efficient solution. In essence, such a requirement represents implicit rights to resources for future generations.

Norgaard and Howarth (1992) argue strongly that the intergenerational distribution of rights to resources should first be established on some acceptable moral basis and then an efficient allocation of resources should be sought. The basis for their argument is that instead of viewing the discount rate purely as a tool for achieving efficiency – using it as a criterion for choosing among investment projects with the highest net present value – we should recognize that it is inseparable from equity considerations. It is well known from welfare economics that the set of Pareto-efficient prices depends on the initial distribution of wealth or assets. For each distribution, a unique set of efficient prices emerges. Norgaard and Howarth take this insight one step further. For each distribution of welfare across generations, a unique set of prices, including the discount rate, emerges. It follows that if there is a concern for sustainability, and that concern is based on some ethical principles underlying a *fair* distribution of welfare across generations, an appropriate starting point is to determine each generation's access or rights to resources and the intergenerational transfers of real resources (physical, human, and natural capital) this implies. Once this is done, a specific discount rate emerges and can be used to efficiently allocate resources available to the present generation. This line of thinking inverts the conventional process – instead of seeking a discount rate that ensures intergenerational equity, equity or rights to resources are first determined and the discount rate is a result.[27]

The problem of what resources should be transferred across generations remains. The first concept of sustainability, maintaining the total stock of capital but allowing for substitutions among broad categories (physical, human, and natural capital), is attractive and permissive. But this raises a serious question of the substitutability of natural and other types of capital. If they are not substitutable, the criterion of maintaining total capital is not

---

27 It also helps resolve the problem of an intertemporally efficient resource allocation that leaves future generations worse off than ourselves. See Chapter 16.

sufficient – one cannot simply cut a virgin forest and replace it with a factory or a collection of newly minted PhDs (whose human capital incidentally may depreciate rather more rapidly than commonly believed). Maintaining the total stock must be accompanied by nondeclining environmental capital. Substitutability itself has to be addressed from both a consumption and a production point of view – how readily can virtual reality entertainment devices substitute for wilderness recreation in utility functions, and how easily can man-made capital substitute for natural capital in the production of goods and services? Asking these questions reveals the essential role of some form of natural resources in all forms of "made" output. While the mix of natural-resource-based inputs in production may change from, say, soil-grown to hydroponically grown vegetables, all production can be traced back directly or indirectly to an environmental matrix.

If full substitution is not feasible, the more restrictive criterion is to maintain the stock of natural resources so that future generations have at least the same environmental options as ourselves. But even here the problems are numerous and perhaps insoluble. What is to be done about using exhaustible resources? What substitutions among categories of natural capital are permissible? Can one mile of rehabilitated trout stream substitute for one barrel of petroleum and still keep the stock of natural capital constant? Can a school of cod be substituted for a run of salmon? What is the geographic scope for maintaining the stock of natural assets – the provincial, national, or global level? More fundamentally, the second sustainability criterion may be a desirable guide if it could be made operational, but it does not assure intergenerational equity. The unknown character of future preferences, the uncertainty of technological change, and the absence of a secure mechanism for intergenerational transfers are again at work.

The discount rate and intergenerational equity literature is quite vague with respect to the appropriate geographic unit for analysis. It is, of course, commonplace to suggest that the social rate of time preference for poor countries is higher than for rich countries due to generally greater scarcity and higher returns to capital and the immediacy of current consumption needs in the former. This suggests that discount rates should be uniform within countries but may differ internationally. And indeed practitioners of benefit-cost analysis and project evaluation virtually always look for national-level parameters such as discount rates and shadow price for capital.[28] Differences among countries in their social rates of time discount

---

28 This practice can be challenged (Lind 1990). The internationalization of capital markets may affect the appropriate discount rate for government expenditures.

can create a number of problems in the management of environmental resources. We mention three briefly here, and return to them in subsequent chapters. First, the solution to global environmental threats such as global warming will require international action. Even if the incidence of net benefits from prevention measures were equal across countries, different countries using different discount rates would calculate the present value of those benefits quite differently. Countries would have different willingness to engage in costly, near-term preventative measures.

Second, if social rates of time preference are actually used by governments to manipulate the rate of extraction of nonrenewable resources, the pattern of production may be biased toward poor countries with high discount rates and immediate consumption needs. The more rapid the current depletion, the lower the current price. If the resources are traded internationally, the poor country by virtue of its high discount rate engages in rapid extraction with perhaps unfavorable terms of trade. When its reserves are near depletion, the balance of production may shift to the richer countries who then enjoy relatively large reserves that can be more slowly exploited and sold at higher prices. In theory, of course, the poor country could borrow against its assets, bolster current consumption, and wait for improved prices to help service its loans. But this assumes perfect international capital markets.

Third, economic models can be constructed showing that the higher the discount rate, the more likely will be the extinction of a species (Pearce and Turner 1990, Chap. 17). The essential reason is that if the species grows slowly and if the returns to other investments are high, hunting the species to extinction may be economic. This would be more likely in open-access regimes. The international problem arises when individuals or groups in one country, the "rich" low-discount country, have an interest in species preservation in a second, "poor" high-discount country. Without a market to express their preferences, and in the absence of any authority to regulate resource depletion in the second country, the differential in discount rates may lead to unwarranted species extinction. These three examples of new complexities when moving from national- to international-level analysis are in fact variations of a single problem. Differences among countries in time preferences as well as differences in relative current valuations create unique difficulties in international environmental management. These and other sustainability issues are considered in greater detail in Chapter 16.

5

How Clean Is Clean Enough?

1 Introduction

Chapter 3 explains the roots of environmental degradation in terms of private market and government policy failures. Private market failure invites government intervention to improve social welfare. Government policies that inadvertently damage environmental and natural resources need to be modified. Before action is taken, however, it is necessary to refine the objectives of policy. Measures to protect and conserve environmental resources involve substantial economic costs. The opportunity cost of pollution abatement, or the protection of wilderness areas and endangered species, is the output of conventional economic goods and services foregone, while the benefits are, of course, environmental damages avoided.[1] The shorthand question can be framed as "how clean is clean enough?"

Section 2 provides an analytical framework for answering this question. Not surprisingly, it concludes that at a high level of abstraction the optimal level of environmental protection is such that the marginal costs of protection equal the marginal benefits of damages avoided. This is equivalent to saying that *total* social costs (abatement costs thought of as opportunity costs plus residual environmental damage costs) are minimized. To operationalize this goal requires knowledge of pollution abatement (environmental protection) technologies and their costs. But it also requires linking pollution abatement to environmental quality; investigating the effects of environmental quality on human health, biological and ecological systems, and other resources; and establishing monetary values for environmental damages (or

---

1 It is customary to use the terms environmental damage and damage functions to describe environmental changes with negative effects on utility or production functions. This does not imply all environmental changes are detrimental. Converting scrub forest to productive cropland, for example, is an environmental change that involves net benefits, not damages.

damages avoided). Section 3 looks more closely at economic valuation and discusses concepts of environmental value as they have evolved in the literature. Section 4 explains some specific techniques for monetary valuation of environmental damages. Section 5 discusses alternative approaches to establishing environmental standards when defensible monetary valuation techniques are not available, and Section 6 considers the vexing problem of valuing human health and life. Appendix 5.1 examines the troubling discrepancy between willingness to pay and willingness to accept compensation estimates in contingent valuation studies.

2 Optimal Environmental Protection

Pollution is only one aspect of environmental degradation. Congestion, loss of habitat for wildlife, soil erosion, and increases in environmentally related disease vectors are other examples. Nevertheless, we can use pollution as a generic example of how optimal environmental protection levels are established. The relevant question may come in two parts: First, at what level or scale should pollution abatement be contemplated? Second, given the appropriate level, should the abatement activity be undertaken or not? The quick answer to the first question is the level of abatement such that marginal costs of abatement equal marginal benefits of damages avoided. The quick answer to the second question is whether, at the optimal level, total benefits from abatement exceed or fall short of total abatement costs.[2] In some situations there is no choice of scale, level, or intensity, and the only relevant question is whether benefits exceed costs, discounted where appropriate. But the latter possibility is relatively rare. For example, the decision whether or not to construct a waste-water treatment plant still confronts the questions of plant capacity and of appropriate water purity standards, which are scale questions. The creation of a national park confronts an optimal size question. Another, more frequent, variation occurs when a particular economic activity has unavoidable environmental consequences, the damages from which cannot be mitigated. For example, flooding a pristine river valley to construct an irrigation dam and hydroelectric facility might destroy a wilderness recreation area. In that event, the relevant question is whether the discounted net benefits of the development project exceed the discounted net benefits arising from its use as a recreation area. This question

2 If abatement costs and benefits (C and B) are functions of abatement (A), then determine if B > A where

$$\frac{dC}{dA} = \frac{dB}{dA}$$

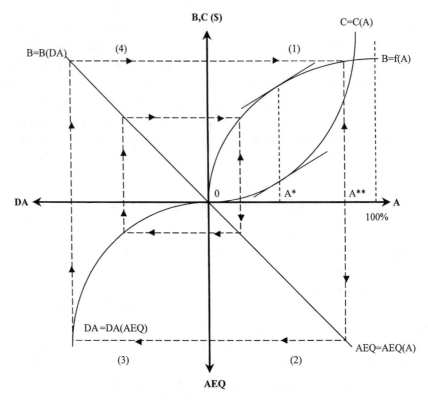

Figure 5.1. *Determining monetary cost-benefit functions and*
optimal pollution abatement

too can be framed as a benefit-cost question in which recreation values foregone are treated as an opportunity cost.

Figure 5.1 illustrates the steps that may be necessary in selecting an
optimal pollution abatement level (Pearson and Pryor 1978). It also illustrates some of the complexity of the task. Quadrant 1 measures pollution
abatement on the horizontal axis, ranging from 0 to 100 percent (no pollution discharge). The monetary value of total abatement costs and benefits is
measured on the vertical axis. An arbitrary cost function, $C=C(A)$, has been
drawn where C is abatement costs and A measures pollution abated. The
shape of the function conforms to theory and empirical evidence that marginal abatement costs rise, often quite steeply, as one approaches zero waste
discharge (100 percent abatement). In principle, data for the abatement costs
function should be available from engineering cost studies. The range of
abatement techniques and technologies is costed out to derive a least-cost
set of abatement activities at alternative abatement levels. For example,

water pollution abatement for a specific industrial plant may be accomplished by varying combinations of process change, in-plant recycling of wastes, on-site lagooning, and end-of-pipe treatment. $C=C\ (A)$ may be subject to kinks and discontinuities. Separating abatement costs from other production costs may also be difficult, especially for process change. Obviously, cost figures should be the net of the value of recovered resources, energy savings, and the like. If several pollution sources are present, $C=C$ (A) should be interpreted as a least-cost function, where the marginal cost of abatement is equalized among different sources.[3] Care must also be taken that a particular form of pollution abatement, say, restricting air pollution from waste incineration, does not merely shunt the pollutant to another medium, say, ocean disposal. The cost function in Figure 5.1 is most easily understood in the context of a single emission source. But the basic conclusion that marginal abatement costs rise is likely to be valid in more complex situations.

Constructing a pollution abatement benefit function, $B=f\ (A)$, is more difficult. As illustrated in the diagram, it may involve a three-step process, moving from abatement levels to ambient environmental quality to physical environmental damages to monetary valuation of physical damages. Quadrant 2 contains an arbitrary functional relation between abatement levels and ambient environmental quality levels, $AEQ=AEQ\ (A)$. To establish this, uncontrolled pollution, $A=0$, and no waste discharge, $A=100$ percent, are taken as benchmarks. The effects of various levels of emissions (effluents) expressed, say, as milligrams of pollutant per cubic meter of water discharge per day on an index of ambient air or water quality, is then estimated. This requires knowledge of the production process and may involve complicated pollution dispersion and concentration models, as well as models that capture the accumulation of pollutants over time. A variety of ambient environmental quality indices may be needed such as biological oxygen demand (BOD) for water quality and carbon monoxide in parts per million for air quality. Moreover, ambient environmental quality may need to be measured at many locations. The next step is to relate ambient environmental quality to biological, physical, health, and other environmental damages. As shown in quadrant 3, damages avoided *(DA)* are a positive function of ambient quality, or $DA=DA(AEQ)$. The curvature reflects a widely accepted assumption that marginal damages rise as ambient air and water quality deteriorate, or conversely, marginal damages avoided fall as ambient air and water quality improve. There may be threshold levels of

3 See Chapter 6. If the least-cost solution is not available, a second-best problem arises.

assimilative capacity below which further improvements in ambient quality involve no avoidance of environmental damages. There may also be a range in which the environment is so polluted that all damages have been wrought, and marginal damages dwindle to zero.[4] Finally, if the damage is to renewable resources, say, forests, there may be complicated lagged relations for dieback and regeneration of trees, and dynamic modelling may be appropriate.[5]

To this point, damages and damages avoided are in nonmonetary units – fish kills, worker absentee rates due to respiratory illness, corrosion rates to structures from atmospheric sulfur dioxide, decline in crop yields due to salinization of soils, and so forth. The construction of $DA = DA \ (AEQ)$ may be very difficult, involving complex ecological relations, discontinuities, irreversibilities, and perhaps time, and the exact relation is likely to be quite uncertain. In any event, quadrants 2 and 3 are primarily tasks for physical and ecological scientists and not economists, although economists may have something to say about averting behavior and adjustments in economic activity, for example, shifting cropping patterns if farmers are confronted by degraded soils.

Quadrant 4 attempts to place monetary values on the benefits of environmental damages avoided through the relation $B = B \ (DA)$, and returns the analysis to economics. If defensible monetary values can be found, it then is an easy task to transfer $B = B \ (DA)$ to quadrant 1, and a pollution abatement benefit function, $B = f \ (A)$, can be traced out. In this fashion, starting from the A axis in quadrant 1 and traveling clockwise along the dashed lines the monetary value of abatement efforts are established. Both the benefit and cost functions are discounted to calculate present value. The optimal pollution abatement level is then established in the diagram at A^*, where the vertical distance between B and C is greatest and where marginal costs and benefits are equal. To go beyond A^* to, say, A^{**}, would still result in positive net benefits, but the incremental costs would exceed the incremental benefits. If the cost function everywhere lies above the benefit function, no abatement is warranted.[6]

The analytical process underlying Figure 5.1 is useful for heuristic purposes but may not be fully operational. Even when good abatement cost data are available, the models and data underlying the ambient quality and environmental damages functions may be inadequate. We also emphasize that analysis of pollution abatement benefits should include indirect as well

---

4 This relates to the "nonconvexity" issue and is considered in Chapter 6. For a thorough discussion, see Paul Burrows (1995)
5 For an illustration, see Sohngen and Mendelsohn (1998).
6 This would imply that at all abatement levels, marginal costs exceed marginal benefits.

as direct effects. For significant pollution abatement measures, this implies that the "ripple" effects throughout the economy should, in principle, be captured. One technique is computable general equilibrium (CGE) modelling, now widely used to assess other policy measures such as trade liberalization. CGE models are also capable of estimating terms-of-trade changes. For small open economies the terms of trade change consequent to a pollution abatement policy may dominate the more direct measurement of domestic costs and benefits. In an interesting application of CGE, Lars Bergman has shown that while a sulfur emission reduction program might increase productivity in the Swedish forest sector, the additional costs are disproportionately borne by two export sectors that cannot pass along cost increases into international prices. The result is that output in these sectors decreases, and output in sectors that can affect terms of trade increases. Consequently, one of the important costs of reducing sulfur emissions is indirect terms of trade loss, a finding that would be overlooked in partial equilibrium analysis.[7]

In another example, Beausejour et al. (1995), using a CGE model of the U.S. and Canadian economies, have shown that the real income cost of controlling carbon emissions through a carbon tax rises more rapidly than the tax rate, implying increasing marginal abatement costs. This is consistent with tax theory, which concludes that the excess burden of a tax is an increasing function of its rate. In a general equilibrium approach, indirect effects of an abatement policy may be important and may affect the shape and position of the abatement cost function. For example, in the Beausejour model, the carbon tax produces significant reductions in other pollutants as well, namely, nitrogen oxide and volatile organic compounds. These incidental benefits might be included to derive a net carbon abatement cost function, or simply added to the abatement benefit function. Also, a carbon tax may substitute for other, more distortive taxes leading to additional incidental benefits. In principle, it is better to use a general equilibrium approach to estimating abatement cost functions, but this advantage must be traded off against the additional complexities of general equilibrium modelling.

The remainder of this chapter focuses on the problem of valuation illustrated in quadrant 4. It should be kept in mind that the results of the valuation can be no better than the information contained in the prior two functional relations.

---

7 See Bergman (1995, pp. 153–70). For more on environmental policy and terms of trade, see Chapter 9.

3 Concepts of Environmental Value

Chapter 3 explained how in competitive markets price reflects consumers' valuation of a good as revealed by their marginal willingness to pay and also the marginal costs of production. If the good in question is an intermediate good (i.e., an input in production), the willingness to pay reflects the value of its marginal product, which is ultimately derived from consumers' valuation of some other final product. Chapter 3 also argued that changes in consumer surplus – the area above the price line and below the demand curve – is a reasonable measure of changes in individuals' welfare, although consumer surplus may need modification to find compensating and equivalent variation and surplus as discussed in the appendix to that chapter. One must also be properly cautious in interpreting market prices to reflect economic values because of market power, government taxes and subsidies, and the recognition that prices need not reflect the optimal distribution of income. These complications are discussed in the literature on shadow pricing in cost-benefit analysis.

The valuation of environmental goods and services confronts additional difficulties. In many cases, these goods and services do not pass through organized markets and hence there are no prices to reflect values. Nevertheless, if a serious attempt is to be made to compare the monetary costs of environmental protection with the benefits, an effort must be made to compute implicit prices or values. Abstract discussion of environmental values makes heavy use of classification systems. Figure 5.2 illustrates one such system. It is conventional in the economics literature to begin discussion of valuation by distinguishing between *use value* and *intrinsic value*, the latter sometimes termed *existence* or *nonuse value*. (Use value is not the same as the user cost discussed in the previous chapter.) Use value can then be classified in one of at least three ways. The first is to distinguish among environmental services that are inputs into production functions (whether or not marketed), and environmental services that enter directly into individuals' utility functions. These are sometimes called producer goods and consumer goods. Chapter 2 employs this distinction. This approach leads more or less directly to various techniques for valuation discussed in Section 3. The second approach is to break out *direct use value* and *indirect use value*. Direct use value includes products made possible by the environmental (natural) resource, such as timber or fish. Indirect use value includes ecosystem support functions, such as climate regulation, nutrient cycling and soil formation, and maintaining hydrological systems and flood control, that indirectly support economic activity. Indirect use values are clearly economic

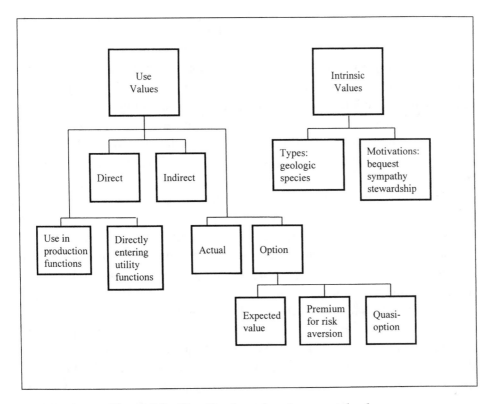

Figure 5.2. *Classification of environmental values*

values, but because they are not marketed and because they are indirect, their monetary value must be inferred. The third approach is to subclassify use value into *actual use value* and *option value*. Both actual use value and option value could, of course, be further broken out into services entering production and utility functions.

This last approach leads to classifying the value of an environmental resource as: Total Value = Actual Use Value + Option Value + Intrinsic (Existence) Value (Pearce and Turner 1990, Chap. 9). Actual use values are more or less self-evident – process water for industrial purposes, recreation services, potable water, and so forth. Option value is more problematic. Its narrowest interpretation is the expected value that would be obtained when the environmental service is actually consumed or used in the future. An aquifer that is expected to be tapped later for agricultural use is an example. A broader interpretation would include willingness to pay for maintaining an option to use the resource when future conditions are uncertain. The more adverse to risk individuals are, the larger this option value is. Because these uses are expected to materialize over time, option value may accrue to the individual at some point in the future, or to future generations. One difficulty is that the preferences of future generations, and hence the option value, cannot be known with certainty. There is a concern that traditional measures of consumer surplus or the more exact compensating surplus do not fully capture option values. Finally, quasioption value is the additional payment that individuals may be willing to pay to maintain an option to use the resource because the knowledge base is expected to improve. Certain genetic resources may have no known use today but through scientific progress may have positive use value in the future. They would possess quasioption value.[8]

Intrinsic (existence) values are more fuzzy and less susceptible to economic analysis than use values. While intrinsic values are often thought to derive from people's preferences, by definition they do not derive from use or option to use. Contingent valuation, described next, may be used for estimating monetary values. Resources possessing intrinsic value are thought to include unique geological formations (e.g., Iquasu Falls in Brazil), complex ecosystems such as tropical forests, and entire species (e.g., glamour species). As the examples indicate, the same resource may possess both use (actual and option) and intrinsic values. At this point, discussion often veers in the direction of identifying motives underlying the preferences for maintaining intrinsic values. These motives may include *bequest*, *sympathy*, *stewardship*, and a host of social, cultural, and religious values. Intrinsic values may or may not be in conflict with use values. Hunting whales for food may pit use value against intrinsic value; excursions to view whales do not. Consequently, one cannot always simply add together use and intrinsic values. At a yet deeper level, some assert that there are intrinsic values in nature, and that other species and their members have "moral standing" independent of humans and their preferences.

To summarize, there is no single accepted classification of values. Indeed, the availability of communications media to document or portray remote and unique environmental resources such as the ocean depths or polar bears blurs the distinction between use and intrinsic (existence) values. In itself this is no great problem, as valuation techniques are not congruent with taxonomies of value. In general, economists fall back on willingness to pay as evidence of preferences and hence values. But this is an anthropocentric

---

8 Note that the concept of option values does not always support immediate environmental protection. Using real resources for protection today creates sunk costs that cannot be recovered. If, on the basis of improved knowledge or better technology, lower expenditures become warranted, we have foreclosed these options by incurring sunk costs today. This is relevant in the global warming debate. See Chapter 14. Most of the analysis has focused on option values and quasioption values in estimating the benefits of environmental protection rather than their costs. For discussion, see Richard Ready (1995) and Theodore Graham-Tomasi (1995).

view. If one believes the earth and its species possess inherent rights and intrinsic value, these values cannot be derived from willingness to pay calculations, no matter how cleverly done.

This leads to a final comment on environmental values. Economists tend to accept the notion that the preferences of individuals are sovereign and the formation of these preferences is exogenous to the discipline of economics. It follows that values ascribed to environmental goods and services, once uncovered, are the proper units for decisions. But if one accepts that communal values have some legitimacy or that there is some moral obligation to shape social values, merely uncovering individual preferences and values is not sufficient, and a more pluralistic approach to environmental decision making is needed (Norton and Toman 1995).

4 Techniques for Monetary Valuation

Once again there is a choice in classification systems. One approach is to classify by types of environmental damages and then identify available techniques. For example, we might classify most environmental damages as falling into one of four categories:

Productive resources
Human health
Amenities
Environmental and ecological systems

and proceed to apply appropriate valuation techniques. At a more abstract level, some economists offer a twofold classification of valuation approaches, illustrated in Table 5.1 (Freeman 1993; Markandya 1992; Mitchell and Carson 1989). Generally speaking, directly observed behavior is preferred if data are available. The choice between hypothetical and observed depends on the specifics of the situation. In some cases one technique can be used to confirm the results from a second technique. For example, a hedonic pricing model to value damages from excessive noise, which is inferred from observed behavior, may be used to verify a contingent valuation study that is based on hypothetical questions.

A third closely related system is to rank techniques according to their direct reliance on market data (Hufschmidt, James, Meister, Bower, and Dixon 1983), shown in the following lists.

Market value/productivity approaches include:
- Opportunity cost
- Human capital

Table 5.1. *Valuation approaches*

	Observed behavior	Hypothetical
Direct	market price; simulated markets	willingness-to-pay questions
Inferred	travel cost; property value (hedonic pricing); defensive expenditure; wage models	contingent ranking

Surrogate market approaches include:
- Property value (hedonic price)
- Wage models
- Travel cost

Survey-based approaches include:
- Contingent valuation
- Contingent ranking

Rather than proposing an ideal classification system, it is perhaps more productive to give a brief description of some of these techniques. The objective is not to be exhaustive, but to give a flavor of each.

4.1 Damage to Productive Resources (Freeman 1993)

Damages that directly affect production functions are generally the easiest to monetize. Pollution damages to a commercial fishery can be measured by the value of reduced catch, adjusted for any change in the use of complementary resources such as labor and fishing gear. In similar fashion, soil degradation that forces a shift to lower-valued crops, for example, wheat to barley, might be measured by either the change in the market price of the land, its rental value, or the reduction in net revenues due to shifting from one crop to another, depending on which data are most easily available and reliable. Air pollution that increases corrosion and shortens the lifetime of bridges and roads can be measured as the net discounted cost of higher maintenance and accelerated replacement. Soil erosion that leads to downstream siltation and reduction in the lifetime of hydroelectric reservoirs can be reasonably readily costed. The mechanics for such valuation are widely known in cost-benefit literature. Care should be taken to strip market prices of transfers (e.g., taxes), and shadow prices may be necessary in the presence of foreign exchange distortions, monopoly pricing, and the like.

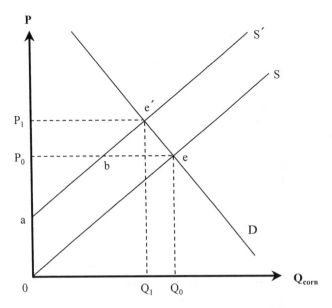

Figure 5.3. *Identifying the costs of environmental degradation to consumers and producers*

Care also should be taken in tracing through who actually bears the cost of the environmental damages. When the effects of environmental degradation work through production functions, the damage costs may be borne by consumers, producers, or the suppliers of factor inputs, depending on market structure. To illustrate, consider a simple example in which agricultural output, corn (C), is produced by a fixed amount of land (T) and a variable input labor (L), as illustrated in Figure 5.3. With a fixed quality of soil, the corn market is in equilibrium at e with price P_0 quantity Q_0. A deterioration in soil quality increases production costs, shifting supply from S to S'. Price moves to P_1, quantity to Q_1. The total social welfare loss is the loss of consumer surplus plus producer surplus, or the area $oae'e$. In this example, consumers are the big losers, with consumer surplus shrinking by $P_0P_1e'e$. The effect on producers is less clear; they sell less but at a higher price. Specifically, producer surplus, which originally was OP_0e, is now aP_1e'. To determine producers' net welfare change, one must compare their gain, $P_0P_1e'b$, with their loss, $oabe$.

The effects of environmental damages can also be traced back to input markets (Figure 5.4). Figure 5.4a displays the production of corn as a function of the variable input labor, $Q_c=f(L)$, with land fixed. Figure 5.4b displays the marginal physical product of labor MP_L, and Figure 5.4c shows the

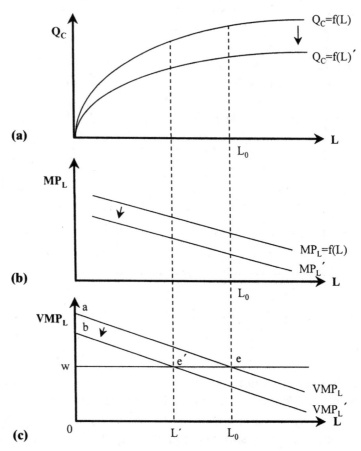

Figure 5.4. *Allocation of cost of soil depletion between labor and landowners*

value of the marginal product, $VMP_L = (P_0)(MP_L)$, where P_0 is the initial price of corn. Labor supply is assumed perfectly elastic at the wage rate w. Before the loss of soil quality, profit-maximizing employment of labor is at L_0, value of output of corn in the bottom panel is the area under the VMP_L curve, $OaeL_0$, which is distributed as wages (area $OweL_0$), and rent, or the return to land, as area wae. The soil deterioration shifts the production function (part a) to $Q = f(L)'$, shifting the MP_L and the VMP_L down. If there were no change in product price (i.e., infinitely elastic demand for corn), the wage bill shrinks to $Owe'L'$ and rent to wbe'. Assuming labor can be reemployed productively elsewhere, the entire cost is borne by the landowner in the form of reduced rent, which is likely to be capitalized into lower land price. More likely there is a transitional cost to labor before it is reemployed. If, as in Figure 5.3, corn demand is not perfectly elastic, the increased price shifts the VMP curve back upward (not shown) and the cost of environ-mental deterioration is shared by consumers, through higher price, and landowners, through lower rent and land price. The distribution of environ-mental damage costs as between input owners and consumers is extremely important when international trade is introduced.

The proceding analysis assumes the environmental damage is to pro-duction for the market economy. In developing countries some resources such as fuelwood are used directly by households, and the economic cost of a deterioration in their quality or availability must be estimated using a non-monetary household production function. For example, an increasing scarcity of firewood could be monetized by the earnings foregone due to additional time spent collecting wood or possibly by the incremental cost of substituting kerosene for wood. Similar techniques could be used to value changes in access to potable water. Productive resources should be broadly defined to include environmental resource services that indirectly support economic production (a major part of indirect use values). For example, tropical wetlands can help prevent storm and flood damage, act as nurseries for natural fisheries, and perform other regulatory functions. The opportunity cost of converting wetlands to alternative uses such as agricul-ture should be included in benefit-cost analysis, with the cost based on the value of flood damages (e.g., crop loss) and lost fish production (Barbier 1994).

4.2 Hedonic Pricing Techniques[9]

The hedonic pricing technique attempts to infer implicit prices and willing-ness to pay for environmental quality by examining a marketed good that possesses environmental attributes. This technique is an example of the sur-rogate market approach. Many environmentally related hedonic price studies examine the housing market, although the technique can be used for other market prices with environmental characteristics, for example, wage differentials to infer monetary valuation of different working conditions, including risk of injury or death.

The basic premise is that in a well-functioning housing market prices reflect the totality of characteristics providing utility. These characteristics include structure (house size, number of rooms), location and neighborhood (access to shopping, transportation), crime rates, taxes, and environmental characteristics (most often air quality but possibly noise, visual amenities,

---

9 Ian Bateman (1993) gives a clear exposition of this method.

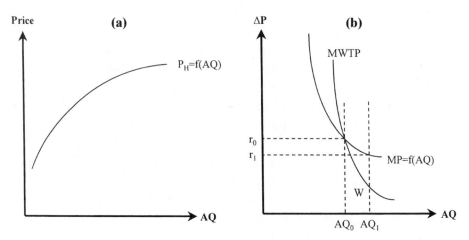

Figure 5.5. *Hedonic pricing model to monetize welfare effect of improving air quality*

etc.). If the relevant data are available, a regression equation can be estimated, with house prices the dependent variable and the structure, neighborhood, and environmental characteristics as explanatory variables. Holding other variables constant, the regression equation quantifies the relation of housing prices, P_H, and the environmental variable air quality. This is shown as the relation $P_H = f (AQ)$ in Figure 5.5a. Given the hedonic price function in part a, its *slope* can be measured and drawn in Figure 5.5b. It is identified as *MP* as it is a marginal (implicit) price schedule showing how much house prices increase as air quality increases. As drawn, the *increase* in house prices falls as air quality increases, although other shapes are possible. The schedule *MP* indicates the incremental price or cost for buying a house with better air quality that a house buyer faces. For example, a small increase in air quality above the level AQ_0 would cost the home buyer an additional amount r_0, and a small increase above the level AQ_1 would cost an additional amount r_1. If home buyers attempt to maximize their utility, they will choose a home with an environmental quality level such that the incremental cost they pay is just equal to their marginal willingness to pay. Figure 5.5b shows the marginal willingness to pay (*MWTP*) schedule for one such home buyer, who chooses a house with air quality AQ_0.

The next step is to ask how much welfare would increase if the authorities provided a nonmarginal change in air quality, say, from AQ_0 to AQ_1. For the existing homeowner who has already purchased her home, this welfare increase is measured by the area W, the area under her *MWTP* schedule between air quality levels AQ_0 and AQ_1. The difficulty is that individual *MWTP* schedules cannot be directly observed, although we know that points along the *MP* schedule represent points on individuals' *MWTP* schedules. One solution would be to make some arbitrary assumption about the shape of the individuals' *MWTP* schedule. A second technique used at this point is to attempt to estimate another regression in which the demand for environmental quality (MWTP) is estimated as a function of household characteristics (e.g., income, family size) as well as environmental quality. If successful, this will yield MWTP functions, and from these the welfare improvement from moving from AQ_0 to AQ_1 for the individual can be measured and then summed over all affected individuals to obtain the total welfare gain.[10]

The limitations to hedonic pricing techniques applied to housing are evident. At a very basic level it requires that individuals can perceive variations in environmental quality and have good price and environmental quality information, and that the relevant housing market is competitive, open, and in equilibrium. Beyond this, there are theoretical questions about specifying the hedonic price function and other theoretical difficulties in specifying the supply-demand interactions to estimate the marginal willingness to pay functions. The data requirements are high throughout. Nevertheless, there is general agreement that the hedonic pricing technique can develop useful information on the valuation of environmental damages and the benefits of environmental improvement. Many empirical studies have shown positive valuation attributable to environmental characteristics such as good air quality.

4.3 Travel Cost Techniques *(Bateman 1993)*

The travel cost approach is a surrogate market technique but also requires survey-based information. The method mainly has been used to value recreation experiences at outdoor sites where the entrance fee is either zero or set at some arbitrary level. Even when fees are charged, they tend to remain fixed, and direct estimation of demand schedules is not feasible. The objective of travel cost studies is to measure consumer surplus or welfare associated with visits to the site, or to estimate the increment in consumer surplus should the quality of the recreational service be improved. In more sophis-

---

10 If individuals were identical or if the change in AQ were very small, the MP schedule could be used directly without the second regression equation. Pearce and Turner state that most studies stop at the point of estimating the MP schedule. For further discussion of the theory and empirical difficulties, see A. Myrick Freeman III (1993).

Table 5.2. *Consumer surplus – option one*

Zone	Population	Visits per year	Visit rate (3)/(2)	Travel cost per visit	Total consumer surplus $
(1)	(2)	(3)	(4)	(5)	(6)
1	10,000	200	0.02	10	4,000
2	12,000	180	0.15	20	2,700
3	15,000	150	0.01	30	1,500
4	16,000	80	0.005	40	400
5	20,000	0	0	50	0
Totals:		610			8,600

ticated studies, particular attributes of a site such as quality of fishing can be measured.

The basic approach starts with the estimation of a regression equation explaining the number of visits to a recreation site on the basis of the travel cost to the site and socio-economic variables such as income levels, education, etc. The data are drawn from visitor surveys. The geographic origin of the visitor is identified, and visits are allocated into travel cost zones with each zone representing a different cost of travel to the site. The dependent variable in the regression equation is the visitor rate by zone (visits per zonal population from zones $1 \ldots n$), and the hypothesis that visit rates are inversely related to travel cost is tested. The influence of other variables that affect visit rates such as income and education is accounted for, so that a statistical relation between travel cost and visit rates is identified. As illustrated in the following numerical example, this allows the creation of a "whole experience" demand curve relating visit rates to visit cost (travel costs). At this point two options are available to the analyst. In the first, the area under the demand curve corresponding to each zone is calculated (graphically or mathematically, as the integral over the appropriate range). This yields average consumer surplus per person by zone, which can be scaled up to total consumer surplus by zone by multiplying by zonal population, and then summing for all visitors.

This procedure is illustrated in a hypothetical numerical example in Table 5.2 and Figure 5.6. Consider the table. Travel cost zones 1 through 5 are established and the respective travel costs are entered in column 5. The data on population by zone are entered in column 2 and the total visits and visitor rates are entered in columns 3 and 4. Visit rates and travel costs for the five

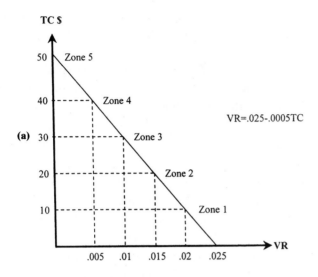

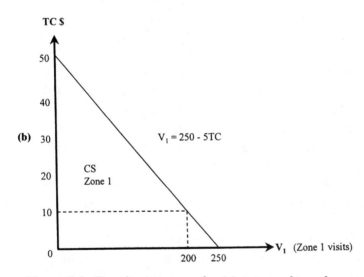

Figure 5.6. *Travel cost approach: visit rates and travel costs*

zones are plotted in Figure 5.6a. The numbers have been chosen to yield a simple linear curve, $VR = 0.025 - 0.0005TC$, where VR is visit rate and TC is travel cost. The next step is to calculate the consumer surplus for visitors from each zone, or the area above their zonal travel cost and below their demand curve.

The visit rates shown in Figure 5.6a can be scaled up to zone 1 population (10,000) to obtain a demand curve for visits by zone 1 residents, $V_1 =$

250–5TC. This demand curve is shown in Figure 5.6b, and the area above their travel cost ($10) and below their demand curve can be approximated as $4,000 (i.e., $(50-10)(200)(\frac{1}{2})$). Using the same visit rate function but with zone-specific population and travel cost data, consumer surplus for zones 2 through 5 can be calculated and are entered in Table 5.2, column 6. The sum of the surpluses for the 610 visitors is $8,600.

Following this option does not separate out demand for the recreation site itself from the total experience of travel plus recreation. In fact, the total visitors to the site of 610 is only one point on the demand schedule for the site itself, corresponding to a zero admission price. The second option attempts to measure the demand for the recreation site itself. The fundamental assumption is that visitors would respond to a fee or price for the recreation experience in the same fashion they respond to travel cost. This permits using their revealed behavior in responding to travel cost to estimate their behavior if fees were imposed. The numerical example found a total of 610 persons per year with a zero fee. Continuing this example, suppose a fee of $10 were imposed. Total cost (travel cost plus fee) for zone 1 residents would then be $20. The estimated visit rate function indicates a visit rate of 0.015 and with a zone 1 population of 10,000, this translates into 150 visits per year from zone 1 residents. Similar calculations show visits from zones 2, 3, 4, and 5 to be 120, 75, 0, and 0, respectively. This sums to 345 visits per year and establishes a second point in the demand curve corresponding to a $10 fee. Table 5.3 works out the numbers for fees ranging from 0 to $30, and Figure 5.7 displays the constructed demand curve. With a $40 fee, visits drop to zero. Note that the horizontal axis is now total visits per year from all zones, and the vertical axis measures hypothetical fees. Using linear segments the total area under the curve can be approximated as can consumer surplus at various entrance fees.

There are many theoretical and empirical difficulties with the travel cost method, some of which have been surmounted by more sophisticated studies than is illustrated in this example. One difficulty has already been mentioned – the assumption that users would respond to an admission charge in the same fashion they respond to travel costs. Also, if congestion is present or likely, individuals' utility functions are interdependent, and simple additive consumer surplus models are not satisfactory. Also, demand for any particular site is also a function of the availability and cost of other recreation sites, and data on the quality of the sites and elasticity of substitution among them may be required. On a more practical level, there are problems in calculating the appropriate cost of travel, including time cost, and in attributing cost and utility to the site being analyzed when recreation excursions

Table 5.3. *Deriving data for demand curve*

Zone	Population	Visit Rate	Total Visits
Fee = $0			
1	10,000	0.02	200
2	12,000	0.015	180
3	15,000	0.01	150
4	16,000	0.005	80
5	20,000	0	0
Total:			610
Fee = $10			
1	10,000	0.015	150
2	12,000	0.01	120
3	15,000	0.005	75
4	16,000	0	0
Total:			345
Fee = $20			
1	10,000	0.01	100
2	12,000	0.005	60
3	15,000	0	0
Total:			160
Fee = $30			
1	10,000	0.005	50
2	12,000	0	0
Total:			50

include visits to multiple sites. Also, the method is more appropriate for measuring the benefits of an existing site than a proposed site because of the hypothetical aspect, unless the proposed site has a good existing duplicate in terms of quality, location, etc. Finally, the travel cost method does not capture option and existence values discussed earlier. Nevertheless, a large number of studies have been conducted and, when done in conjunction with contingent valuation methods, the travel cost approach is being used with increasing confidence.

4.4 Contingent Valuation Techniques

The hedonic pricing and travel cost approaches infer utility (welfare) derived from environmental services from observed behavior. Adequate

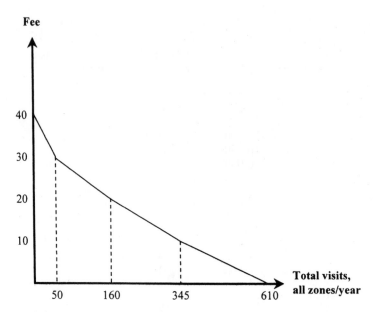

Figure 5.7. *Inferred demand curve for recreation site from travel cost/visit rate data*

surrogate market data may not be available, however. Equally important, these techniques do not measure intrinsic or nonuse value as described earlier in this chapter. An alternative is to question individuals directly. This has the great advantage of eliciting values where no market or market behavior exists. But the equally great disadvantage is the inevitable hypothetical nature of the exercise. Economists generally feel more comfortable working with preferences as revealed in the marketplace.

There are several variations of contingent valuation and the related contingent ranking technique (Freeman 1993; Markandya 1992; Mitchel and Carson 1989; Pearce and Markandya 1989; and Sinden and Worrell 1979).[11] In its simplest form, the respondent is asked how much he or she is willing to pay for an environmental service or his/her willingness to accept compensation for the loss of the service. It may be difficult for the respondent to answer, as the service has not been priced. As an alternative, an iterative bidding process may be used, in which, after careful description of the service in question, the interviewer offers a starting point bid in monetary terms, and if the response is positive, the "price" is increased incrementally until the respondent balks at paying a higher price. However, a bidding game

11 Ian Bateman and R. Kerry Turner (1993) give a particularly clear exposition of contingent valuation. For critique of contingent valuation, see Arild Vatn and Daniel Bromley (1995).

may introduce a starting point bias, described next. The bidding approach can be used to elicit both willingness to pay and willingness to accept compensation. Another variation is a simple trade-off game. The respondent is offered varying combinations of money and environmental services and asked to rank these combinations according to his/her preferences. This permits calculating a monetary valuation of a change in environmental quality without requiring the respondent to directly state a price. If the service is a pure public good, with zero marginal cost of supply to another user, the responses to the survey can be added to obtain a total willingness to pay. Trade-off games shade into contingent ranking methods. These techniques require the respondent to rank or order alternative bundles of goods (services). The bundles will have two or more attributes. The rankings can then be analyzed to estimate rates of substitution among attributes or characteristics, and if one of the goods has monetary value, the rankings can be used to infer a willingness to pay for the environmental attribute or service.

Because contingent valuation is hypothetical rather than behavior-based, considerable attention has been paid to the reliability of the results and the identification of biases. A *strategic bias* can arise if the respondent understates her preference in the hopes that the price she will pay is thereby reduced, a variation of the free rider problem. Alternatively, she may overstate her preference if she believes the service will be provided free, as a public good. *Design bias* can arise if either the starting bid by the interviewer in a bidding game influences the respondents, or the method of payment proposed has an effect on the respondent (i.e., entrance fee versus an additional local tax obligation). *Information bias* may arise if clear, accurate, and intelligible information is not made available to the respondent. All information on a proposed environmental change is by its nature deficient in describing the actual change, and reducing information bias is a matter of minimizing this deficiency. Finally, a *hypothetical bias* may exist in that the respondent is not capable of attaching accurate monetary values to changes in environmental quality. The respondent may not take the hypothetical question seriously. Or he may find it impossible to place a monetary value on a service for which he has never had to actually pay. Respondents may also lodge *protest bids* if they believe they have rights to certain environmental services without payment. Despite these limitations, contingent valuation has become an increasingly important technique for establishing monetary values for a large range of nonmarketed environmental services.

5 Alternatives to Monetary Valuation

In some instances it is not possible to estimate defensible monetary values for environmental damages or environmental improvements. This tends to occur in the areas of health and safety, for damages to basic ecological functions, and for intrinsic (existence) values. Rather than taint formal benefit-cost analysis with arbitrary and unconvincing values, it may be more appropriate to seek out alternative guides for decision makers. Economic analysis continues to play a role, but at a more modest level.

One alternative, appropriate for deciding between two mutually exclusive uses of an environmental site, is to calculate the opportunity cost of foregoing development to preserve unmarketed environmental services. An example might be development of a river system for hydropower versus its use as a wilderness recreation area. If the incremental economic cost of supplying electricity from an alternative source, say fossil fuels, can be calculated, that cost can be compared to the recreational services foregone. This avoids a direct monetary valuation of recreation. The question is framed: is the value of recreational services likely to be greater or less than the monetized difference between hydro and fossil fuel production of electricity? With data on expected recreation use, this could also be reduced to the monetized opportunity cost of one visit or day of recreation, a format that the decision maker may find easier to visualize. If, as would be likely in this example, the alternative source of electricity – fossil fuels – also generates environmental damages, the comparison would be between recreation foregone and the incremental monetary cost plus the unmonitized environmental damages incurred by using fossil fuels, a more complicated choice for the decision maker. Still, a serious effort to identify and quantify (not monetize) environmental effects should improve decision making.

A second alternative is to examine averting and defensive expenditures to provide a minimum estimate of damages. For example, if individuals incur the additional expenditures of double glazing and otherwise soundproofing their homes in the presence of serious noise pollution, these expenditures provide a minimum estimate of environmental damages. Expenditures for medical treatment of environment-related respiratory disease may also provide a minimum estimate of environmental damage costs, although the socialization of medical costs through insurance and government involvement makes data on individuals' expenditures suspect. Obviously, unless averting and defensive expenditures completely offset the environmental damages (disamenity from noise, adverse health effects), the full welfare loss is underestimated. Also, averting behavior and defensive expenditures are limited by individuals' incomes and there may be important distributional consequences that society will wish to consider.

A third alternative is the so-called replacement project approach. It may be possible in some instances to fully replace the environmental service suffering deterioration with the creation of a new project supplying services of equal or greater value. The cost of the replacement project is then treated as a cost to be attributed to the original project. For example, offshore tin dredging may spoil one recreation site, but the facility might be replicated elsewhere. Hufschmidt et al. (1983, p. 266) gives an illustrative example of offsetting upland soil erosion in Korea by nutrient replacement and the actual return of soils deposited downstream to their original sites. The weakness of the replacement cost approach, of course, is lack of evidence that the costs of replacement are justified. In essence, the replacement cost approach implicitly assumes the benefit-cost ratio for replacement is always one or greater. While perhaps technically feasible to replace the damaged asset, it may be more economic to forego replacement and simply accept the original environmental deterioration. Averting and defensive expenditure approaches tend to underestimate damage costs; uncritical use of the replacement project approach can overestimate damage costs. Moreover, in many environmental protection decisions, the group suffering losses may not coincide with the group gaining from the replacement project, and important distributional and equity issues would be involved. Still, this approach is in general conformity with one prominent view of sustainability, that the stock of natural capital be maintained while substitutions within the stock are possible. The U.S. policy of no net loss in wetlands is consistent with this approach.

Cost effectiveness, or least-cost analysis, is perhaps the most useful of the alternative approaches.[12] The idea is simple. An environmental standard or level of environmental quality is established without explicit regard to the monetary value of the standard's benefits. Examples might be a decision to reduce the incidence of schistosomiasis by 80 percent, or reduce marine pollution due to petroleum discharge by oil tankers 50 percent, or reduce a steel plant's SO_2 emissions from 30 tons per day to 15 tons per day. All that is required is that the objective have some physically measurable dimension. The analytical step is to achieve this objective at least cost by considering various abatement and protection technologies singly or in combination. For example, schistosomiasis, a water-borne disease spread by snails and aggravated by irrigation development projects in the tropics, can be controlled by

---

12 Least-cost analysis is always a part of full benefit-cost analysis.

a variety of techniques ranging from molluscides, to lining irrigation canals, to improved sanitation facilities. The task is to find the most cost-effective (least cost) combination of techniques to achieve the objective. As another example, erosion from logging steep slopes can be controlled by choosing among alternative logging methods (tractor skidding, high lead, helicopter removal), each with different cost structures, or by increasingly stringent technical requirements on logging road construction, or by establishing protective strips along water courses. Again the task is to find the least-cost combination of techniques that reaches the objective. Ideally, the analysis leads to a cost function as described in Figure 5.1, so that the marginal cost of moving from a lower to a higher level of protection can be calculated. This does not resolve the full benefit-cost question or indicate an optimum level of environmental protection, but the explicit consideration of alternative technologies, their costs, and their effectiveness is a useful first step in making rational choices with regard to environmental protection. Cost effectiveness analysis can also be used in conjunction with the establishment of safe minimum standards, which are widely used in the area of health and safety, and which have been proposed for conservation policy. As discussed in Chapter 14, much of the economic analysis of controlling global warming takes a least-cost (cost-effectiveness) approach.

6 Valuing Life and Health

There is no unique technique for placing monetary values on human mortality and morbidity arising from environmental quality changes. But the importance of health benefits in establishing environmental policy justifies at least a brief description of various approaches. The productivity approach measures damage to health by its effect on economic output. A second approach attempts to measure willingness to pay for good health, either from inferential evidence or from direct survey data (i.e., surrogate market and contingent valuation approaches).

The productivity approach views individuals as productive capital. If individuals suffer premature mortality due to environmental causes (e.g., air or water pollution), or if their productivity as measured by days lost from work is impaired due to morbidity, the value of the economic output foregone is the damage. If wages reflect marginal productivity, lost wages and earnings are the measurement tool. The attraction of the productivity approach is clear enough. If statistical links can be made between pollution abatement levels and environmental quality, and between environmental quality and mortality/morbidity (quadrants 2 and 3 of Figure 5.1), it is relatively easy to then monetize these losses (quadrant 4), and a monetary benefit function from environmental protection and pollution abatement can be calculated.[13]

It is easy to poke fun at the productivity approach. Should the future earnings of the prematurely dead be net or gross of their own projected consumption? Should one include the net present value of premature burial costs? It is also easy to find ethical objections. With positive discount rates and long years of schooling (negative earnings), the deaths of infants have little if any economic cost. Older individuals, past their productive years, have zero or negative economic value. The most devastating criticism, however, is that the productivity approach, by emphasizing the productive role of individuals, violates the basic premise of welfare economics that the value of a good or service is to be measured by willingness to pay. While the productivity approach may be an appropriate starting point for estimating compensation to survivors in legal actions following a wrongful death, as it often is, it is inadequate as a measure of welfare effects from environmental changes.

That leaves willingness-to-pay techniques. Two initial points need be made. First, it should be clear that any meaningful discussion must be restricted to a change in the *risk* of death. Faced with the certainty of death, virtually everyone would commit all of their resources and all borrowed funds to avoid that outcome. It follows that analysts try to estimate the value of a *statistical* life. Typically the question is what is the benefit of reducing the risk, in any one year, of dying from an environmentally related illness from, say, 3 in 10,000 to 2 in 10,000. Fortunately, the notion of a statistical life is harmonious with many environmental policies, which cannot identify specific individuals as beneficiaries. Second, it should be reiterated that the concept of "willingness to pay" is bounded by ability to pay. The existing distribution of income matters. Any measure of aggregate willingness to pay for environmental protection has an inescapable ethical component.

Willingness-to-pay (or willingness to accept compensation for increased risk) estimates involving health effects can involve a range of techniques. Hedonic wage models using relative wages and mortality/morbidity information on the risks of various occupations are one method. Inferences from consumption expenditures on safety devices – seat belts, airbags, antilock brakes, smoke detectors – are another. Survey responses are a third. All of

---

13 Landefeld and Seskin (1993) trace the origins of the productivity approach (i.e., human capital) to Sir William Petty, writing in 1699, "Political Arithmetick, or a Discourse Concerning the Extent and Value of Lands, People, Buildings, Etc., London."

these require reasonably accurate information on risks, and become inappropriate when the risks are unknown even to the expert.

7 Conclusions

This chapter starts with a clear and simple message – pollution abatement and environmental protection should be pursued to the point at which marginal benefits equal marginal costs. The prescription starts to run into trouble, however, in translating the message into operational terms. The data necessary to transform protection measures into ambient environmental quality, and environmental quality into physical environmental damages and damages avoided (quadrants 2 and 3 of Figure 5.1), may not be available. Setting these difficulties aside, the concept of environmental value becomes murky when intrinsic values are introduced. The valuation challenge arises from the lack of markets and prices for many environmental services. Economists have responded with considerable ingenuity, attempting to measure productivity effects, inferring values from surrogate market transactions, and by direct survey. Despite theoretical and empirical advances, some environmental effects resist monetization, and alternative methods, mainly least-cost analysis, seem most appropriate. In any event, the *process* of benefit-cost and least-cost analysis, which lays out assumptions and encourages consideration of alternatives, is likely to improve decision making. That process is quite general and equally applicable to rich and poor countries. One international complication, however, is when the costs (benefits) of environmental protection are not congruent with national boundaries. As shown in Part 3, the answer to the question how clean is clean enough will vary from country to country, and vary with the incidence of costs and benefits among countries.

Appendix 5.1

Resolving WTP and WTA Discrepancies

One unresolved feature of contingent valuation studies alluded to in Appendix 3.1 deserves greater attention. This centers on empirical evidence from contingent valuation studies that willingness to pay is often far less than willingness to accept compensation when changes in the supply of environmental services are contemplated. Contingent valuation does not rely on Marshallian demand curves, and therefore the validity of Marshallian consumer surplus versus compensating variation and equivalent variation as a measure of welfare change are not directly relevant. But the conclusion drawn from Willig's work, that the divergence between CV and EV should be "small," is relevant. An accumulation of contingent valuation studies showed that contrary to initial theoretical expectation, the ratio of WTA to WTP for environmental services can be large, ranging from 1.6 to 6.5. To illustrate, individuals might be willing to pay an average $100 to eliminate smoking on domestic air flights, but would require up to $650 to compensate them for accepting smoking if they were granted the right to smoke-free flights.[14] The impact of these findings casts some doubt on the validity of the contingent valuation method. The findings also underscore the importance of the property rights regime – whether individuals have a right to existing pollution levels but must pay for an improvement, or whether they have a right to a cleaner environment and should receive compensation if the improvement is not forthcoming.

There are three explanations for this apparent conflict between theory and empirical studies, and they are not mutually exclusive. The first explanation refines earlier theory and tends to rehabilitate contingent valuation. Specifically, for unpriced environmental goods, the divergence between WTA and WTP is shown to be a function of the income elasticity of demand for the environmental good, the elasticity of substitution of the environmental good for other goods, and the size of the Marshallian consumer surplus relative to total income. The larger the income elasticity of demand for the environmental good and the lower the elasticity of substitution between the environmental good and other marketed goods, the greater the expected discrepancy between WTP and WTA measures. In the view of Bateman and Turner (1993), WTA/WTP ratios of 4 and above are not inconsistent with theory. Surely some types of environmental services have high-income elasticity of demand (wilderness recreation) and low elasticities of substitution. Environmental services that are viewed as necessities – potable water – or that represent unique assets – the Grand Canyon – may have low substitution elasticities. Still, as Freeman (1993, p. 178) points out, large WTP–WTA divergences are also found in simulated markets involving commonplace goods, not exotic or life-supportive environmental services.

A second explanation does cast some doubt on WTA estimates. Individuals are accustomed to valuing conventional goods and services according to their willingness to pay. They make shopping decisions of this sort every day. Even when the good or service is nonmarketed, as is typical of environmental services, they may have little mental difficulty in envisioning a purchase. However, except for their sale of labor services and an occasional yard or garage sale, individuals have little opportunity to exercise a willingness to accept monetary compensation, and certainly little experience in receiving compensation to forego a price decline or to endure a deterioration in an unmarketed environmental service. Hence their responses to WTA-type questions may be unreliable due to the novelty of the question itself. While plausible, this line of argument has limits. In any market transaction, for example, potatoes at the grocery store, a WTP for potatoes with money is, by definition, a WTA compensation in the form of potatoes for money. But this view of exchange

---

14 Differences in WTA and WTP are summarized by Pearce and Markandya (1989).

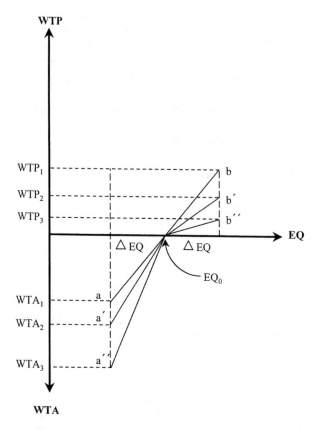

Figure 5A.1. *Explaining discrepancies between WTP and WTA*

is unconventional, and the novelty of trying to state a WTA payment may distort responses to a contingent valuation survey.

The third explanation also has a common sense plausibility although it tends to undercut traditional utility theory. Basically it argues that individuals react asymmetrically to an increase versus a decrease in the provision of environmental services, and perhaps other goods. The idea is illustrated in Figure 5A.1 (Bateman and Turner 1993; Brookshire, Randall, and Stoll 1980). The horizontal axis measures the provision of an environmental good or service indexed by EQ. The vertical axis measures WTP(+) and WTA(−). The initial point is EQ_0. The reference curve ab is drawn at 45°. If income elasticity of demand is close to zero, and if the degree of substitutability between the environmental good and other goods is very high, we expect a marginal increase or decrease in environmental services, ΔEQ plus or minus, to generate a WTP about equal to a WTA compensation. In the diagram, WTP_1 equals WTA_1. According to the first explanation, the appropriate curve may be $a'b'$, and $WTP_2 < WTA_2$. If, however, individuals feel a strong *right* to their existing consumption at EQ_0, the kinked curve $a''b''$ may best describe their welfare. Any decrement in environmental quality would require a large compensation payment (WTA_3), while their WTP for an improvement (WTP_3) is modest. This explanation for the divergence of WTP and WTA grows out of prospect theory. It has a strong intuitive appeal and is consistent with pervasive examples of individuals resisting loss more vigorously than pursuing gains. It also helps explain the frequency of "protest" answers in contingent valuation studies.

6

The Government's Tool Kit

1 Introduction

Chapter 3 provides the rationale for government response to market failure: externalities, public goods, and open-access resources. Chapter 5 demonstrates that the optimal level of pollution abatement or environmental protection in general is where the marginal cost of abatement equals the marginal benefit of environmental damages avoided. The marginal analysis provides an efficiency criterion for guiding government intervention and regulation. This chapter investigates the policy tools at the government's disposal.[1]

Selecting the appropriate policy tool is sometimes cast as a simple choice between directly setting effluent and emission standards for individual pollution sources and the use of effluent/emission charges or taxes. The first is known as the command-and-control approach and the second as the incentive or market-based approach. While this is an analytically useful distinction, it does not fully reveal the diversity of tools available nor the ambiguities in classifying various policy instruments. The full array of government tools includes, in addition to command-and-control and market-based instruments, the provision of information, for example, regarding "clean" technologies when private information markets are imperfect; the use of publicity and moral suasion; the clarification or limitation of private property rights through zoning and through the establishment and enforcement of liability rules; and regulating the use of state-owned property such as national forests and military installations.[2]

---

1 Many excellent texts and collections treat government environmental policy. See Baumol and Oates (1988), Bromley (1995), Dorfman and Dorfman (1993), Goodstein (1995a), Markandya and Richardson (1992), Pearce and Turner (1990), Perman et al. (1996), and Tietenberg (1996).
2 Goodstein challenges the conventional view that environmental degradation results from inadequate property rights regimes and can be remedied with clarification of property rights and improving markets through taxes or tradeable permits. He asserts that a particular technology, once chosen, generates reinforcement feedbacks that entrench it in the economy (path-dependent technology choice). The public policy challenge, then, is to encourage sustainable technologies (Goodstein 1995b).

Command-and-control measures themselves cover a wide spectrum, ranging from bans and prohibitions on products and production techniques, for example, banning the use of DDT or clear-cutting techniques in forestry, to more flexible measures such as product performance standards (product *design* standards tend to be inflexible), and "bubble" policies in which a firm must meet an overall cap on a plant's emissions, but can choose which of several pollution sources within the facility to abate. Incentive or market-based instruments also cover a variety of tools, often with quite different distributional and enforcement characteristics: taxes, tradeable permit schemes, subsidies for pollution abatement or soil conservation, deposit-refund schemes, and more. And the distinction between command-and-control measures and market-based instruments is not always sharp. An effluent standard enforced by fines has some of the attributes of an incentive tax system.

The economic literature on environmental regulations emphasizes efficiency as the principal criterion for policy analysis. But other criteria for selecting tools are also important. These include distributional effects, the ease and effectiveness of implementation and enforcement, political acceptability, information requirements, geographic flexibility, behavior under uncertainty, and encouragement or discouragement of rent-seeking activities. Of these, differences in distributional effects may be most important. Environmental policy involves a rearrangement of property rights, and the incidence of costs and benefits from such rearrangements raises equity or fairness questions and also lies at the heart of the political economy of environmental regulation.

This chapter first examines the scope for encouraging Coasian-type bargaining among the parties to an externality. It then presents the conventional economic efficiency arguments for incentive or market-based instruments over command-and-control measures. This is followed by a mainly theoretical analysis of the advantages and disadvantages of the principal economic instruments: taxes, tradeable permits, and subsidies. The possibility of a "double dividend" and the additional complexities of environmental taxes in a second-best world of continuing distortions are also considered. The final section looks briefly at actual experience. Although the discussion in this chapter is couched in terms of national level tools, it is useful to keep in mind how they might be deployed in an international context.

2 Promoting Coasian Markets

As explained earlier, the Coase Theorem has two elements. First, with clear property rights and minimal transaction costs, the parties to an externality can create a "market" in the externality leading to a Pareto-efficient solution. The market internalizes the Pareto-relevant externality but does not generally eliminate all pollution. Second, under certain conditions the resource allocation results of Coasian bargaining will be the same regardless of which party is awarded rights to the environmental resource in question. The relevant conditions are that there is perfect competition, that the income effects of the property rights allocation be negligible, and that the incidence of the transaction costs (borne by externality generator or recipient) be the same regardless of the initial allocation of property rights.[3] A solution closely related to a Coasian market is merger, in which two firms linked by a production externality merge and internalize the externality.

At first glance, the Coasian bargaining approach looks attractive. An economy may be able to move toward or achieve Pareto-efficient resource allocation without pervasive government regulation. And society's distributional or equity objectives can be separately attended to in the initial allocation of rights to the resource. If equity is thought to reside with the victims, they can be granted the rights and market them as they desire. Moreover, Coasian bargaining solutions may be especially attractive for international externalities, where there is no supranational environmental protection agency with the authority to issue abatement directives or impose pollution taxes.

On closer inspection, however, the number of situations for which Coasian bargaining is feasible and desirable is limited. First, Coase-like solutions do not fully eliminate the role of government, which must establish or clarify property rights and provide enforcement mechanisms. The assignment of initial property rights will be subject to special interest groups lobbying and rent seeking, not unlike the lobbying associated with direct use of command-and-control or economic instruments. Moreover, in establishing property rights, governments often neglect to make the rights marketable, thus precluding subsequent bargaining and Coase-like solutions. Rigid land use zoning or prohibitions on smoking in public areas may be efficient under certain circumstances, but they bar a market or bargaining solution. Also, because many environmental externalities are indirect, cumulative, and uncertain and because resort to the legal system has well-known inefficiencies, the enforcement costs of Coasian bargains may be large. Moreover, many externalities are intertemporal, and future generations are simply not

---

3 As Bromley (1989) shows, if the incidence of transactions costs depends on the initial allocation, the offer curves of polluters and victims will shift from one rights regime to another in addition to shifts arising from income effects.

present to make bargains. In that case, a pure Coasian solution between private parties to the externality cannot take place, and government becomes an (imperfect) advocate of the missing parties. Finally, the establishment of rights to international common property resources, a necessary condition for Coasian bargaining, is itself difficult in an international context without supranational authority.

A second limit on Coasian markets is that many environmental externalities involve substantial numbers of participants, either generating the externality or receiving it, or on both sides. Auto emissions, sulfur dioxide emissions, water eutrophication through the use of nitrogen fertilizers, and noise externalities in the vicinity of airports are all examples. Under these circumstances, the transactions costs of aggregating the interests of all affected parties, negotiating an optimal abatement level, and then enforcing the market agreement will preclude a purely private bargain, even if the allocation of rights is quite clear. Indeed, in some instances (as illustrated in Figure 3.2), the externality recipients (the victims) would be required to negotiate with two groups whose internal interests diverge, producers and consumers of the product generating the externality, a highly unlikely prospect. Moreover, as is well known in the large-number case, individuals will tend to act as free riders in the negotiations, undermining the negotiations themselves. In such cases, individuals would treat the outcome of negotiations as beyond their control and therefore would be unwilling to bear any transactions cost (Baumol and Oates 1988; Buchanan 1967). In short, when transactions costs are substantial and when the number of participants is large, Coasian solutions to environmental externalities are generally ruled out. It does not follow, however, that government intervention should necessarily follow. The essential case for government intervention requires that either it acts as agent for the "missing" parties, its own transactions costs are lower, it has superior information, or it should act paternalistically.

Two other considerations are worth noting. First, even when Coase-type bargains result in efficient resource allocation, the equity consequences depend on which party is given the initial rights. While it is theoretically possible to separate efficiency and equity, the laws of physics give the advantage to the polluters. When rights are unclear, the polluter uses air and water for waste disposal, interfering with and trumping beneficial uses for, say, breathing or recreation. Thus, common law practice may build in a bias for waste disposal over other resource uses. That bias may be reinforced if polluters are small in number relative to victims. As is well known from tariff theory, a small number of producers are often willing

to invest larger sums of money in lobbying for protection than are consumers, whose interests are diffused over a large population. By analogy,
awarding initial rights and hence the equity consequences of Coasian bargains, may have a built-in bias against pollution victims. A second consideration is that Coase-type bargains can be subject to threats and extortions. If
polluters must be bribed into reducing pollution, they can threaten pollution levels beyond what is in their own self-interest in order to "extort"
payment.[4]

Despite the limits to Coasian bargaining, some examples can be cited. An
active commercial market between orchard owners and bee keepers exists,
internalizing the pollenization externality of honey production. "Sunshine
rights" are said to be marketed in urban areas in Japan in which a property
owner can sell to developers his access to sunlight if the price is right. Resort
hotels sometimes buy adjacent land and keep it vacant to provide a scenic
buffer and preclude externalities of unsightly development. Conservation
organizations buy up development rights from farmers to maintain open
spaces. Perhaps most important, a central point in Coase, that markets can
be created and used to allocate environmental resources efficiently, has
helped establish the legitimacy of tradeable permit systems. Such schemes
generally do not entail bargaining between polluters and victims (although
this is not ruled out), but they do clarify property rights and let a market
sort out the actual use of the permits.

3 Command-and-Control versus Market-Based Instruments

Once the limited potential of a Coasian bargain is accepted, the principal
choice for government is between direct regulation, that is, setting standards
with which polluters must comply, and more indirect tools that use economic
incentives and disincentives to alter polluters' behavior. There is a consensus among economists that indirect economic measures are likely to be more
efficient than direct command-and-control measures. A basic premise for
this belief is that polluters have better knowledge of least-cost pollution
abatement methods than do government regulators, and economic measures
can utilize this knowledge. The superiority can be illustrated by comparing

4 The possibility for extortion is symmetrical. If initial rights to zero discharges are given to "victims,"
and if some waste discharges do no damage, victims could demand compensation for all discharges
whether or not they involve damages. There is also a hint of Panglossian optimism in excessive reliance
on Coase-type solutions. If markets can internalize Pareto-relevant externalities, then any remaining
pollution must be efficient, and no further abatement effort is needed or warranted.

a crude system of command-and-control standards and an effluent tax system. It is important to remember that the alleged efficiency advantage of the tax tool exists whether or not the pollution-abatement objective is designed to achieve Pareto optimality.

Consider a situation in which there are multiple pollution sources, each with a different marginal cost of abatement. Assume the objective of government is to reduce total pollution flows by a fixed amount, say, 50 percent of current levels. This objective may represent an attempt to achieve Pareto optimality or be chosen on more arbitrary grounds. A crude command-and-control directive might require all sources to curtail emissions by 50 percent. In contrast, a uniform tax on pollutants of X dollars per unit emitted might be employed. The command-and-control measure, by setting a fixed emission reduction for all polluters, would neglect differences among pollution sources as to marginal abatement costs, and the objective would not be obtained at least cost. High abatement cost sources would be required to undertake too much abatement, while low abatement costs sources would do too little. Economic efficiency requires that the marginal abatement costs of all sources be equal. This is exactly what a uniform emissions tax would accomplish.[5] Individual polluters confronting the tax would abate up to the point where their marginal abatement costs equaled the per unit emissions tax but not beyond. In this fashion, marginal abatement costs would be equalized among pollution sources, and the abatement objective would be obtained at least cost.

This fundamental point can be easily illustrated. Assume two polluters, A and B, contributing equal amounts of pollution, 50 tons each. With no regulation or taxes, total pollution equals 100 tons. Assume different marginal abatement cost functions, MCA_A and MCA_B.[6] Figure 6.1 displays the situation with pollution abatement (not pollution) measured on the horizontal axis. Assume the authorities wish to get pollution down to 50 tons total. If each source were ordered to reduce pollution by 50 percent to 25 tons, the objective would be achieved. This would be inefficient, however, as the $MCA_A > MCA_B$ at the 25-ton limit. The same pollution target could be achieved by shifting some of the abatement burden away from the high abatement-cost firm A, to the low abatement-cost firm B. The least-cost allocation of abatement burden is where $MCA_A = MCA_B$ *and* total pollution is limited to 50 tons. In the diagram, this is 15 tons abatement for Firm A, 35

---

5 This assumes one unit of pollution from source *i* carries the same damage as a unit from source *j*.
6 The diagram illustrates the specific marginal abatement cost functions: $MCA_A = 10/15 \ PA_A$; $MCA_B = 10/35 \ PA_B$, where PA_A and PA_B are pollution abated by A and B measured in tons.

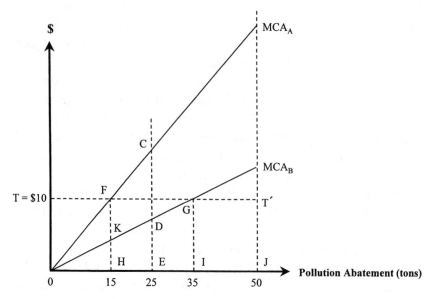

Figure 6.1. *Efficiency in allocating abatement*

tons abatement for firm B.[7] This efficient allocation of abatement would automatically be achieved with a tax, T, of $10 per ton, given the specific pollution abatement functions in this example.[8]

This is a highly contrived example. The question immediately arises as to why the regulators do not recognize the abatement cost differences and adopt standards accordingly – a 30 percent abatement for A and a 70 percent abatement for B. One answer is that it may be politically difficult to set different abatement requirements for different sources.[9] A more compelling answer is that in general regulators would not know the details of abatement cost functions for individual sources and could not specify least-cost standards for various firms. Moreover, polluters would have an incentive to supply erroneous cost data to regulators, overstating their costs. In contrast, a uniform pollution tax obliges individual polluters to investigate their own abatement cost situation to determine at what point marginal abatement costs start to exceed the tax.

7 The inefficiency of a flat 50 percent reduction directive can also be seen by comparing total abatement costs, the areas under the marginal abatement schedules, under the two solutions.
8 Total costs are minimized when $MCA_A = MCA_B = T$ and $PA_A + PA_B = 50$ tons. Solve and obtain T=$10, $PA_A = 15$ tons, and $PA_B = 35$ tons. Tax payments are $350 for A and $150 for B. Abatement costs are $75 for A and $175 for B. Thus total tax and abatement costs are $425 for A and $325 for B. Tax payments are of course transfers, not economic costs.
9 Polluter B may claim it unfair to face 70 percent abatement and greater total abatement costs.

But this answer points to a possible weakness of the tax approach (and distinguishes it from the tradeable permits approach considered next). If regulators do not know individual abatement cost functions, they will not know the tax rate that will secure the overall pollution abatement objective. If the tax is set too low, too much pollution results, and vice versa. While it is possible to set a tax, observe the response, and adjust the tax as appropriate (the iterative approach), frequent adjustments of tax rates are politically difficult and may lead to transitional inefficiencies as polluters commit resources to meet one tax and then must adjust to subsequent changes.

Figure 6.1 also illustrates another major difference between command-and-control and tax measures, and may explain why polluters often prefer command-and-control measures. Under the command-and-control approach, polluters A and B will only bear the cost of their pollution abatement (areas *OCE* and *ODE,* respectively). (They may attempt to pass on these costs to consumers, but that would be consistent with the Polluter Pays Principle discussed in Chapter 11.) Under the tax approach, however, they would pay the $10 for each ton of residual pollution, or the areas *HFT'J* for A and *IGT'J* for B plus their abatement costs *OFH* and *OGI*. In essence, they would pay for the socially desired level of abatement plus a "rent" for remaining waste disposal services. While in principle this rent could be rebated in lump sum payments, the amount of rebates could not be tied to the amount of abatement without undermining the incentives of the pollution tax. Using the numerical example, total costs for A and B would be $297 under the command-and-control measure and $750 under the tax system.

To summarize, the static efficiency advantage of the tax measure is that it can achieve a target level of pollution abatement at least cost by equalizing marginal abatement costs among polluters.[10] The tax tool can also have important dynamic efficiency advantages. Specifically, under the tax approach a firm has incentive to continually seek out new, lower cost-abatement techniques, thus lowering its abatement levels and its tax payment. In contrast, under the command-and-control approach, the firm may attempt to lower its abatement costs but would have no incentive to reduce pollution below the standard set by regulators. Indeed, development of new cost-saving technology might induce regulators to set tighter standards. Finally, as Goodstein points out, the command-and-control approach frequently sets tighter standards for new facilities than old, polluting ones.

---

10 For formal proof and qualifications, see Baumol and Oates (1988, Chap. 11).

Under these circumstances, firms may be reluctant to scrap and replace old facilities (Goodstein 1995a, Chap. 14). A uniform tax would remove this disincentive to employ new, cleaner technology.[11]

The static and dynamic efficiency benefits of the tax tool, and its parsimonious need for information, are major advantages. But before proceeding to a comparison of taxes with the other major incentive-based tool, tradeable permits, some complications that undermine the apparent simplicity of taxes should be mentioned. Some of the difficulties relate to environmental taxes generally, and some are specific to Pigovian taxes, which seek optimal solutions. First, if taxes on uniformly mixed pollutants are to be efficient, they must be set on the basis of effluent and emission flows, not on the process or product that generates them. For example, if the objective is to reduce carbon emissions, a uniform tax on fossil fuels would be inefficient as it would not distinguish among the carbon content of different fuels. A tax on electricity would be even more inefficient, as it would not accomplish the desired shift to renewable energy technologies. Indeed, either a fuel tax or an electricity tax *might* worsen welfare by creating costly by-product distortions.[12] It is the carbon in fuels that should be taxed.

Second, to be efficient the tax must be based on the *effects* of the emissions. Not all units of pollutant emissions are equally damaging. Much depends on the spatial pattern of their disposal in relation to the location and vulnerability of receptors. For example, carbon monoxide emissions are more damaging in urban than rural areas. Also, damages may depend on the extent to which pollutants are diluted when emitted and the manner in which the emissions are distributed over time. For example, the potential damages from discharging waste heat or organic matter into a water body depend on the location of the outfall and whether the discharge is uniform or occurs in surges. For pollutants that become uniformly mixed on a global scale, such as chlorofluorocarbons (ozone depletion) or CO_2 (global warming), the damage from one specific unit is the same as from any other unit of the same chemical. But in many other cases, efficient taxes would require different tax rates for different polluters and for different emission patterns, and the burden of acquiring information on individual damage

---

11 The incentive to innovate in pollution-abatement technology can also be seen in Figure 6.1. Consider firm A, which under the tax system emits 35 tons of pollutants. Assume this is also the limit set under a command-and-control approach. If A could innovate and achieve the marginal abatement cost schedule of B, it would reduce its total expenditure by *OFG* in the tax scheme. In contrast, if the 35-ton standard remains, its cost saving from innovation is only *OFK*, a weaker incentive.

12 This point parallels the theory of domestic distortions in the trade literature. Corrective policies should be applied as closely as possible to the source of the distortion to avoid byproduct distortions. See Chapter 9.

functions could not easily be shifted to polluters as is the case with abatement cost functions.[13] In short, for efficiency it would be necessary to develop a matrix of transfer coefficients relating the effects of unit emissions from various sources at different locations (and perhaps at different times and on multiple receptors) and adjust tax rates to these coefficients (Tietenberg 1996, p. 343). Incidentally, this same complication applies to tradeable permit schemes and command-and-control measures if they attempt efficient pollution control.

A third complication relevant to Pigovian taxes is that the rate should reflect marginal damages at the optimal, not current, level of pollution. Empirical evidence on current marginal damages will overstate the appropriate tax rate for optimal abatement if total damages increase at an increasing rate, which may often be the case (see Figure 5.1). The need to estimate marginal damages at optimum levels is a difficult requirement to meet, and suggests that efficient Pigovian taxes are more of an ideal than a reality. Also, in a second-best world, as explained in Chapter 3, the simple Pigovian tax prescription may not improve efficiency.

A final complication is the so-called nonconvexity issue. Figure 5.1 illustrates a typical benefit function for pollution abatement to be positive but have a decreasing rate. The assumption was that marginal damages from pollution increase, and marginal benefits from pollution abatement decrease. This led to the conclusion that the optimal level of pollution abatement was where marginal benefits of abatement were equal to the monotonically rising marginal cost curve. We have taken this conclusion as the basis for asserting that a Pigovian tax, set at this marginal damage rate at the optimum (if it could be calculated), would internalize the externality and yield a Pareto optimum outcome. Unfortunately, things are not so simple. Environmental damages may not rise at a constant or increasing rate, and hence the marginal analysis underlying the Pigovian tax prescription may be incorrect. One reason may be that beyond some pollution level, total damages cease to rise (a saturation point). Water too polluted for drinking, fishing, or swimming may be an example. An additional, marginal unit of pollution would create no marginal damages; by the same logic, a marginal unit of abatement would have no benefit. Reliance on marginal analysis would suggest a zero Pigovian tax and the regulators would conclude, perhaps incorrectly, that no cleanup is desirable. Another example would be a production externality between two firms (Starrett and Zeckhauser 1992).[14] If

---

13 The information needed, of course, differs. The transfer coefficients would depend on hydrological and meteorological variables, dilution factors, and the like.

14 Starrett and Zeckhauser (1992) also show that Coase-like bargains could fail in these circumstances.

sufficiently severe, one firm may be driven out of business, in which case additional pollution by the first firm would have zero marginal damages and there would be zero marginal benefits from abatement. Again, the margin-based Pigovian tax would be set at zero. In neither situation, however, can we be sure that social welfare is maximized. If these nonconvexities were rare, they would do little to undermine the Pigovian tax tool. Some theoretical literature concludes that if environmental externalities are sufficiently strong, the externalities themselves will produce nonconvexities. In that event, correcting prices through marginal-based Pigovian taxes may or may not improve social welfare (Baumol and Oates 1988, Chap. 8).

The nonconvexity complication is readily illustrated. Consider a simple example of an upstream chemical plant, the "polluter," and a downstream fishery. If the chemical plant is operated at zero output, the downstream fishery is unaffected and, if efficiently managed, yields economic rent. At a positive output of chemicals and pollution, the fishery suffers, and rent is reduced. At a sufficiently high level of chemical output and pollution, the fishery collapses and its rents disappear. Additional pollution beyond that level will have no marginal damages. This situation is illustrated in Figure 6.2.[15] In part a the total abatement cost function for the chemical plant rises at an increasing rate as 100 percent abatement is approached. In the range O-PA^* pollution remains sufficiently high that no fishing occurs and the benefits of modest abatement in this range are zero. At higher abatement levels the rent from the fishery becomes positive and increasing but at a diminishing rate as represented by B. The corresponding marginal curves are shown in Figure 6.2b. Marginal benefits are zero over the range O-PA^*, then jump and remain positive but declining. If marginal analysis is used, there are multiple equilibria. Marginal cost equals marginal benefits at three levels of abatement – zero, PA^* and PA^{**}.

It becomes clear that a Pigovian tax set at either zero, or at ot, where marginal costs equal marginal benefits, would be inefficient. As drawn, the social optimum occurs with abatement PA^{**} and a tax rate ot^*. Also note that if the cost function were everywhere above the benefit function in Figure 6.2a, the social optimum would be zero pollution abatement.[16] In short, with convexities we can no longer rely on marginal analysis to inform us as to the size or direction a tax should nudge resource allocation. It is necessary to undertake a more complex analysis involving the entire range of the cost

15 Goodstein (1995a, Chap. T1) presents a similar diagram.
16 PA^* represents an inefficient and unstable equilibrium. Any small departure, either more or less abatement, will improve social welfare and indicate even higher (or lower) levels of abatement are warranted.

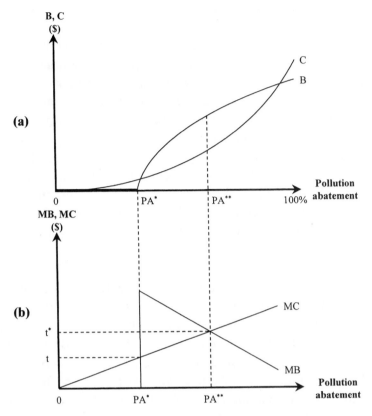

Figure 6.2. *The convexity complication: multiple equilibria of MC and MB*

and benefit functions to determine which of several equilibria maximize social welfare. This example of nonconvexities has a parallel in trade-environment theory, and is considered again in Chapter 8.

4 Effluent and Emission Taxes versus Tradeable Permits

In tradeable permit schemes the regulatory authorities set a maximum quantity of pollutants to be discharged over some fixed time period, divide that quantity into "rights" or permits, and auction or otherwise distribute the permits to polluters who are then free to buy additional permits or sell their excess. In essence, the government has created limited property rights, providing the foundation for a private market. By promoting a private market, this resembles a Coasian approach. But unlike Coasian markets, the transactions are generally among polluters themselves, and not between polluters and victims. (In principle, victims could buy pollution permits and refrain from using them, thus reducing pollution. But free-rider behavior makes this unlikely.)

Tradeable permit schemes share several advantages with effluent and emission taxes. Like a pollution tax, tradeable permits are able to achieve a desired level of abatement at least cost by equalizing marginal abatement costs among various pollution sources. Again, like taxes, the tradeable permit tool accomplishes efficient allocation of abatement effort without detailed knowledge by regulators of individual polluters' marginal abatement cost functions. And, similar to the Coase Theorem, the ultimate allocation of abatement effort among polluters under certain circumstances is independent of the initial allocation of the permits. Finally, if the permits' market is competitive, the market price for permits and the emissions tax will be the same if the tax and permit tools are used to achieve the same abatement objective.[17]

These features can be illustrated again using Figure 6.1. As noted earlier, if the objective is to limit total pollution to 50 tons, this can be accomplished by an emission tax of OT with residual emissions by A of 35 tons and residual emissions of B at 15 tons. Assume instead the authorities set an overall cap of 50 tons, divided that notationally into 1-ton units, and simply gave the permits to one or the other polluters in some arbitrary fashion. Assume B receives all the permits totaling 50 tons, and assume A and B ignore their duopoly status and act competitively. A's demand for permits is set by its marginal abatement cost curve relative to permit price; at a zero permit price, it demands permits for 50 tons, at permit price of OT (equals $10), it demands 35 tons, and so on. A's demand schedule is illustrated in Figure 6.3. B's supply of permits' schedules is determined by its abatement costs relative to the price of a permit. So long as the permit price exceeds its marginal abatement costs, it is willing to sell permits. The market clearing price for permits, where A's demand is equal to B's supply, is OT (equals $10), the same as the tax rate, and the quantity of permits changing hands is 35.[18]

It is obvious that the same permit price would result if A were given the entire set of permits, but the volume changing hands would shrink to 15. Also, the welfare distributional effects would also be very different. If B receives the entire batch of permits, its net welfare position is +$175 ($350

---

17 This parallels the trade literature on the equivalence of tariffs (a tax tool) and import quotas (a quantity tool).
18 If $MCA_A = 10/15\ PA_A$, then A's demand for permits is $Q_{DP,A} = 50 - 1.5\ P$, where P is the price of a 1-ton permit. If $MCA_B = 10/35\ PA_B$, then B's supply of permits for sale is $Q_{SP,B} = 35/10\ P$. Setting supply equal to demand and solving, $P = \$10$, $Q_{SP,B} = Q_{DP,A} = 35$.

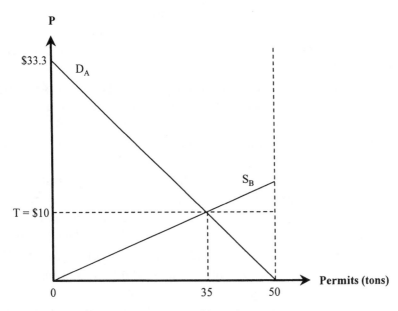

Figure 6.3. *Supply and demand for tradeable pollution permits*

in permit sales receipts less $175 in abatement costs) and A's net welfare position is −$425 ($350 in permit purchases plus $75 in abatement costs). If A receives the entire batch of permits, its net welfare position is +$75 and B's net welfare position is −$325. This example illustrates how a permit system allows the authorities to determine distributional objectives while achieving efficiency by choosing the initial distribution of permits. Tradeable permit schemes allow the separation of efficiency and equity goals more easily than uniform taxes, but create lobbying pressures in the allocation decision that taxes avoid.[19] Finally, note that if the initial distribution were 35 permits to A and 15 permits to B, there would be no transactions in the permit market.

Taxes and tradeable permits differ in several other important respects. First, with taxes, the government receives revenues and the financial burden of pollution abatement is carried by the polluters (who may pass on the additional costs to consumers, market conditions permitting). As explained earlier, the financial cost would include a payment for residual pollution. With tradeable permits, the financial burden on polluters would be less, unless the permits were auctioned. The polluters' net cost as a group would

19 Distributional objectives could be met in a tax system if taxes are rebated in lump-sum fashion. Some European water pollution abatement schemes attempt this.

be restricted to their actual pollution abatement expenditures without any rental payment for residual disposal. Moreover, the government could determine the transfers among the polluters by its initial allocation of permits.

Whether the lower financial burden on polluters (loss of tax revenue to government) and the increased flexibility given to regulators in distributing abatement costs among polluters are advantages of tradeable permits is debatable. As examined in the next section, an argument can be made that pollution tax revenue can replace other, more distorting taxes and thus bring double benefits, the so-called double dividend thesis. But it can also be argued that the greater cost burden from taxes would generate stronger opposition by business and would slow desirable environmental protection measures. The additional flexibility in allocating cost burdens by allocating initial permits may be an important advantage of a permit system. But at the same time the allocation of valuable quantitative rights to emit pollu-tants, like any government-sponsored quota scheme, invites lobbying and possible corruption. As Chapter 14 points out, a system of internationally tradeable carbon emission permits, and the disproportionate allocation of these permits to developing countries, could be an important inducement for them to participate in efforts to control global warming.

A second major difference arises from uncertainty (Baumol and Oates 1988, Chap. 5; Weitzman 1974).[20] A tax tool sets the marginal abatement cost with certainty, but unless individual abatement cost functions are known to the regulator, the resulting quantity of pollution is uncertain. A tradeable permit scheme sets the total quantity of pollutants, but unless the abatement cost functions are known, the cost of the policy is uncertain.[21] If society has a strong preference for knowing in advance the quantity of pollution, trade-able permits (or command-and-control standards) are superior. If the strong preference is for certainty in costs, taxes are superior.

There is an additional difference. If there is uncertainty with regard to marginal abatement costs, then the tax tool is superior to tradeable permits when the slope of the marginal cost curve is greater than the slope of the marginal benefit curve, and tradeable permits are superior when the mar-ginal benefit curve has the steeper slope. This is illustrated in Figures 6.4 and 6.5. In Figure 6.4 the marginal benefits of pollution abatement are indicated

---

20 The question of taxes versus permits under uncertainty has arisen in the context of global warming. See Chapter 14, Section 6.

21 In trade theory the price effect of a tariff by a small country is known, but the quantity effect on imports is not known with certainty. A quota on imports sets the quantity but the price impact is less certain.

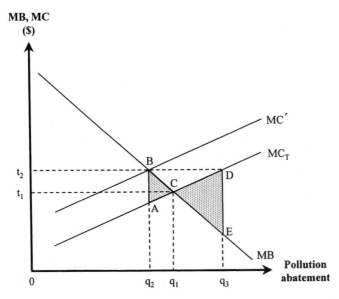

Figure 6.4. *Taxes and tradeable permits under uncertainty: shallow MC*

by *MB*. MC_T represents the true marginal abatement cost curve and is drawn with a shallower slope (in absolute value) than *MB*. The optimal level of abatement is q_1, which could be achieved by either a tax $0t_1$ or a permit system with total permits such that q_1 units of abatement was achieved. If the regulators erroneously estimate the marginal cost curve to be *MC'*, they would either set a tax of ot_2 or issue permits sufficient to achieve abatement level q_2. The permit tool would result in a suboptimal level of abatement, $q_2 > q_1$, or excessive pollution. A tax of t_2, however, would result in pollution abatement of q_3, or excessive pollution abatement and pollution brought below its social optimum. As can be seen in the diagram, the social welfare costs of the mistake are not equal. The social costs of the tradeable permit scheme is the shaded area *ABC* (suboptimal pollution abatement); the excess social welfare costs of the tax scheme is the larger shaded area *CDE* (excessive pollution abatement).

Figure 6.5 completes the argument. The marginal abatement cost curves are now drawn steeper than the marginal benefit curve, and again we assume an erroneous overestimation of abatement costs (i.e., *MC'* rather than MC_T). Again, the permit approach achieves the suboptimal abatement level q_2, and the tax approach yields the excessive abatement level q_3. But now, with the slope of the marginal cost curve exceeding the slope of the marginal benefit curve, the excess social welfare cost of the permit scheme is the large shaded

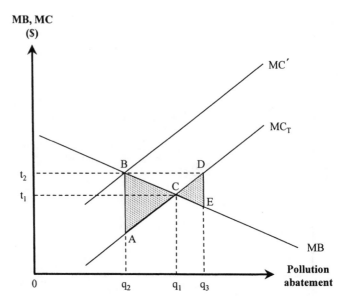

Figure 6.5. *Taxes and tradeable permits under uncertainty: steep MC*

area *ABC*, and the excess social welfare cost of excessive abatement with the tax tool is the smaller area *CDE*.

To summarize, if the marginal benefit curve is misestimated, either too much or too little abatement is achieved but welfare loss would be the same under a tax or a permit scheme. If the marginal cost curve is misestimated, too much or too little abatement is achieved but the size of the social welfare losses under tax and permit schemes will be unequal. Relatively steep benefit curves favor the permits scheme, and relatively steep cost curves favor the tax instrument. The practical significance of this difference is not clear, however, as empirical evidence of the relative steepness of MC and MB curves is often difficult to obtain.[22] Chapter 14 returns to the tax versus permit scheme under uncertainty issue in the context of global warming.

A final difference between the tax tool and the tradeable permit tool is their differential effects when inflation or economic growth is introduced. For example, a specific tax of X dollars per ton would have diminishing abatement effects if the general price level is rising, but a fixed cap on permits would keep the quantity of pollution and abatement constant (although the price of a permit would rise). Recall also that an efficient time

---

22 Roberts and Spence (1976) have developed a mixed regulatory scheme combining fees, subsidies, and permits that in theory can be used to minimize the social costs of misjudging abatement costs.

path for stock pollutants implies a rising shadow price for pollution over time. This suggests periodic upward adjustment in pollution taxes or, if tradeable permits are used, periodic reductions in permits outstanding.

5 Subsidies

The attractiveness of subsidies depends very much on their form and use. Obviously, subsidies for products whose production or consumption creates environmental externalities are undesirable, although they are pervasive in the natural resource sectors – energy, agriculture, forestry, fisheries, and minerals receive a disproportionate share of subsidies in most countries. The first and perhaps most important step governments might take toward environmental improvement is removal of such subsidies.

Subsidies to relieve industry of the financial burden of pollution abatement expenditures are also undesirable on economic efficiency grounds. Direct financial assistance, subsidized loans, and tax relief for pollution-abatement expenditures all have the effect of blocking the internalization of external costs in prices, thus continuing the divergence of market prices from social costs. Moreover, subsidizing pollution-abatement expenditures encourages inefficiencies in the choice of abatement techniques. Because they tend to be more easily documented and hence subsidized, firms are encouraged to use end-of-pipe treatment rather than change process techniques or input mix or take resource recovery measures. Nevertheless, some subsidy for pollution-abatement expenditures can be defended if it facilitates the introduction of new environmental protection laws or if it moderates transition costs such as plant closure and layoffs.

Two other types of subsidy appear to have more promise. The first is a subsidy linked to achieving a pollution-abatement objective. Such a subsidy might work as follows. The authorities establish a base level of pollution for a firm and then offer the firm a subsidy of a fixed amount per unit of abatement below that level. The subsidy is the carrot, whereas the tax was the stick in the earlier discussion. From the firm's perspective, continuing to pollute at its base level now carries an opportunity cost – the subsidy foregone. A profit-maximizing firm will then decide to undertake pollution abatement from its base level up to the point where its marginal abatement costs equal the subsidy rate, and the subsidy accomplishes the same abatement for the firm that an equivalent tax would have. Moreover, a uniform subsidy rate would equalize marginal abatement costs among polluters and apparently achieve least-cost (cost-effective) allocations of abatement among the several sources – the same desirable characteristic of the tax tool.

However, there are two critical differences between subsidies and taxes, both to the disadvantage of subsidies.[23] First, in the subsidy scheme the authorities must decide for each polluter a base level against which the abatement effort is measured and the subsidy paid. Not only is this unnecessary in the tax scheme, the need to establish an *a priori* base invites firms to increase their initial pollution levels to secure a larger subsidy payment. This amounts to extortion of the taxpayer. Perhaps more importantly, a subsidy scheme may be successful in inducing an individual *firm* to reduce pollution. But by maintaining profits and hence failing to drive out marginally profitable firms, and by offering an incentive for new firms to enter the industry, the *industry* output will be higher than under the tax scheme. With industry output higher, total pollution will increase rather than decrease. In short, there is little to recommend a subsidy tied to pollution abatement over a tax scheme, except the political economy argument that by maintaining industry profits, it may be easier to implement.

There is one final type of subsidy that has merit. Because of imperfect information, deficiencies in capital markets, or the public good character of technology, there may be insufficient investment in the production and dissemination of environmentally friendly technology, techniques, and products. The extent to which firms fail to adopt cost-effective, environmentally friendly production techniques is open to argument.[24] But if such market failures are pervasive, then an argument can be made for government subsidies for the development and use of such technologies and products.

6 Double Dividends and the Choice of Tools in a Second-Best World

Recent theoretical and empirical work suggests that the choices of appropriate policy instruments and the optimal level of pollution abatement depend upon the presence of nonenvironmental distortions (Parry 1995, 1999; Oates 1995; Goulder 1995; Repetto et al. 1992). The debate, which is not yet settled, starts with the double dividend hypothesis. This hypothesis asserts that environmental measures that raise government revenue, such as emission taxes or tradeable permits auctioned by governments, have *two* benefits. First, they reduce pollution and pollution damages, and second, the

---

23 From a political perspective, subsidies may be objectionable as they "reward" firms for behaving in the social interest but do not penalize them for residual pollution. In a general equilibrium framework, the possible inefficiency created by using tax money to pay the subsidies should also be considered.
24 For opposing views see Porter and van der Linde (1995) and Palmer, Oates, and Portney (1995).

revenues can be used to reduce existing distortive taxes on labor and capital, and hence improve overall efficiency.[25] In this view, the potential for efficiency gains from reforming the tax system reduce the economic cost of imposing the pollution taxes and, indeed, under certain circumstances may justify the measure even if the environmental benefits are minimal. In contrast, command-and-control measures such as technology requirements and emission caps, as well as freely distributed tradeable permits, do not raise government revenue, and subsidies require *additional* taxes if they are to be noninflationary. Therefore, command-and-control measures, free tradeable permits, and subsidies tied to pollution abatement are less attractive than tax and auctioned permit systems, as they do not carry the possibility of the double dividend.

The situation becomes more complicated, however, if distortions in the tax system are not fully eliminated – that is, the environmental taxes are imposed in a second-best world. In this case, it is necessary to investigate the "tax interaction" effect, in which an environmental tax magnifies preexisting tax distortions. The tax interaction effect may dominate the efficiency improvements from recycling environmental tax receipts. If there is a negative tax interaction effect, the magnitude of the double dividend is reduced or possibly becomes zero. Nevertheless, there remains a presumption that revenue-raising measures are less costly than nonrevenue-raising measures, especially when the level of abatement is "low."[26] Incorporating the tax-interaction effect also changes the optimal or Pigovian tax as described in Chapter 3. Because of the tax-interaction cost captured in a general equilibrium model with other tax distortions, the "second-best Pigovian tax" will be less than the optimal tax would have been in an undistorted economy. By implication, the level of abatement will be less, and the optimal level of pollution will be larger. These complexities are considered again in the chapter on global warming, a topic that has stimulated the current debate on the choice of instruments and the level of abatement.

7 The Tools in Practice

Despite their putative advantages, governments have been slow to adopt economic instruments for pollution control and environmental protection. In the United States the backbone of environmental regulation has relied

---

25 Taxes on labor reduce labor supply and distort labor versus leisure decisions; taxes on capital distort savings-investment decisions.

26 If the level of abatement is "high," the tax rate must be set high, the revenues collected will drop, and the benefits of revenue recycling will dwindle. If the tax on emissions is prohibitive, no revenue will be collected, and neither the tax nor the nonrevenue-raising instruments will generate a double dividend.

upon command-and-control type measures. More specifically, the original Clean Air Act (1969) identified so-called criteria air pollutants (e.g., particulates, SO_2, CO_2, nitrogen oxide) and directed the Environmental Protection Agency to establish national ambient air quality standards. The ambient standards were to be achieved by a combination of vehicle emission standards set by the EPA for mobile sources and, for stationary sources, technology-based regulations (i.e., new sources are required to meet new performance standards by installing the best technological system of pollution abatement commercially available). Water pollution also has to be controlled partly through technology-based controls (BPT, or best practical technology, and BAT, or best available technology), and partly by a nontradeable permit system that specifies legal pollution emission levels.

In Europe there has been greater reliance on effluent fees and charges, especially for water pollution. But an earlier survey conducted by the OECD reveals that only a small portion of the economic instruments actually employed by members are designed and operated to generate efficient, cost-minimizing behavior (OECD 1989). Many are designed for financial (revenues) purposes and are supplemental to direct controls. Revenues are used to finance government and private programs for water quality. Charges are frequently set below levels necessary to accomplish the pollution abatement objective. It is perhaps not surprising that the use of economic instruments has only made modest incursions. There is a deep-seated view that environmental resources are not mere commodities for which markets and prices can be established. Although command-and-control measures employing technology standards do not require zero emissions, their insistence on "best practical" or "best available" technology seems to many to be a reasonable compromise between concern for the environment and concern for the economy, especially when compared to a tax system in which corporations can continue to pollute, or a permit system that explicitly creates rights to pollute.

Moreover, the simple models already described, which demonstrate the least-cost character of tax and permit schemes, neglect important practical considerations. For example, for nonuniformly mixed pollutants, the emission tax rate has to reflect the transfer coefficients for individual sources (i.e., the amount by which concentration or damage of the pollutant will increase for each unit of pollution from that source). This means that different sources will face different tax rates, a result that may appear inequitable and invite endless squabbling. Even then, the tax rates would have to be adjusted in iterative fashion if ambient goals are not initially achieved, or to accommodate economic growth and inflation. Efficient tradeable permit schemes would also require the calculation of transfer coefficients by source. And in a situation in which there are several "receptors," a separate permit market would have to be established for each receptor, adding further complications to a new, artificial set of markets.

The redistributional and financial effects of economic instruments for pollution abatement have also slowed their introduction. While it is true that command-and-control-type measures including emission limits and technology standards impose compliance costs on firms, the financial impact has been moderated by (1) setting less stringent standards for old versus new plants, (2) government subsidies for the construction and operation of waste water treatment plants, (3) delay in implementing the standards, and (4) a variety of tax credits and low interest loans for pollution-abatement expenditures. While these measures may well have delayed desirable progress toward pollution control and undermined the efficiency rationale for the Polluter Pays Principle, they have also reduced private sector opposition to new, expensive pollution control legislation. In contrast, most tax schemes would oblige polluters to pay for both abatement and residual pollution. Tradeable permits, if auctioned, would impose a similar financial burden on industry. To illustrate the magnitudes, one study estimated that a taxlike control strategy for nitrogen, phosphorus compounds, and SO_2 for the EU might cost about \$18 billion per year after full implementation (Huppes et al. 1992).

Economic instruments need not impose such severe cost burdens, of course. Tax schemes combined with requirements that the funds be returned for environmental improvement in the sectors from which they originate, which is typical of French policy, moderate that burden. More generally, lump-sum distribution of effluent changes could moderate the overall financial burden on industry, although they should not compensate individual firms in the amount of their abatement expenditures if the efficiency of the tax is to be maintained. Nor is it necessary for permit schemes to impose the full burden of abatement costs plus permit purchase or firms. If the initial allocation of permits is based on historical pollution levels (grandfathering), and if the allocation is free, the financial burden is correspondingly reduced. And indeed the European introduction of emission taxes has been characterized by a recycling of receipts back to the sector of origin, and U.S. experiments with tradeable permits is characterized by grandfathering, to limit the financial burden on firms.

As economists have touted the advantage of economic instruments, policies have gradually shifted toward their use. In the United States the most important move away from command-and-control measures and toward economic instruments was the 1990 amendments to the Clean Air Act, which established a system for tradeable permits (allowances) for emission of sulfur dioxide by electric generating facilities. The heart of the regulation is to cut U.S. SO_2 emissions by 10 million tons from their 1990 level to about 9 million tons by 2000. This is to be accomplished by issuing marketable permits to U.S. utilities without charge, and equivalent to 30 to 50 percent of their 1985 emission levels. The permits are given, rather than auctioned (a small number of permits were withheld for auction by the EPA to jump-start a private market and ensure that new entrants were not frozen out). Enforcement is through in-plant monitoring systems certified by the EPA, and a fine of $2,000 per ton for excess emissions has been set.

The sulfur dioxide program is widely hailed as a success, so much so that an *international* permit trading system has become a centerpiece of U.S. proposals with respect to carbon emissions and global warming. The actual operation of the SO_2 scheme, however, has been somewhat surprising (Burtraw 1996; 1998). First, the cost of a permit established in the trading system is far less than originally anticipated. At the time of the amendments, some estimates placed the marginal cost of a permit at about $750/ton, but actual trades were $170/ton (1995) and the residual permits auctioned by the EPA were as low as $126/ton (Burtraw 1996). However, a direct comparison of *ex ante* marginal cost estimates with the current price of permit trades is misleading. Unrelated developments that reduced permit costs were trends in fuel markets that contributed to a decline in emission rates and increased competition in rail transport. Moreover, the current price of permit trades is not the same as long-run marginal costs. Second, the number and sizes of trades among utilities have been more modest than anticipated. Burtraw attributes the lower-cost/limited-trade results of the scheme to a second feature of the Clean Air Act – the setting of a performance standard for utilities *without* specifying how that standard is to be accomplished. Indeed, it is the emergence of low sulfur coal as a widely available low-cost compliance option that has driven down costs and reduced the need for emissions trading. Despite the lower-than-expected trading levels, the evidence suggests that the trading market since 1994 has been reasonably efficient (Joskow, Schmalensee, and Bailey 1998). In this instance, the role of the government has been to set the national emissions cap and to give full flexibility to the private sector and to the market system to seek out a least-cost compliance pattern, using permit trading in conjunction with other cost-reducing innovations.

Part 2

Trade and Environment

Note to Part 2

Trade-environment questions first arose in the early 1970s when all manner of environmental issues enjoyed great popularity. After the initial burst of theoretical, policy, and empirical research, interest waned, and it was not until the late 1980s that the topic reemerged in a rather controversial fashion. Even today most major textbooks on environmental economics and on international economics devote little attention to trade and environment. Outside of textbooks, however, there is a rapidly growing literature. And the interaction of trade and environment has become a high-priority policy issue at the national and international levels.

The over-arching theoretical and policy concerns are the effects of trade and trade policy on the environment and the effects that environmental conditions and environmental policies have on the level and pattern of international trade. One question that has received considerable attention is how traditional models explaining the level, composition, and gains from trade can be expanded to include environmental resources as determinants of comparative advantage. Another question is how international trade (and investment) affects the quality and availability of environmental resources. The answers depend very much on how the economic-environment interactions are modeled – for example, whether production or consumption pollution is assumed, and whether environmental degradation is modeled to affect production or utility functions. The theory of policy is also relevant. Different trade policies – tariffs, quotas, export restraints – may have different effects on the level and quality of environmental resources. At the same time, environmental policies, for example, strict pollution standards on domestic producers, may affect international competitive position and hence the level, pattern, and gains from trade.

The effects of international trade on the environment are not always obvious. Trade increases the relative price of the exportable product, and for natural-resource-based products, increases the rate of extraction. But trade may also contribute to conservation in the import-competing good. Reliance on imported oil allows the United States to conserve wildlife habitat in Alaska (but it may force environmental damage abroad). And, in any event, an increasing price for the exportable good does not necessarily cause greater damage. At world market prices, the natural resource producing the good has greater value, and stronger conservation efforts may be economically and financially justified. For example, international wildlife tourism, an exportable service, may strengthen the conservation of wildlife habitat. The ultimate results depend on how pervasive and persistent domestic market distortions are. As a general principle, however, the introduction of trade strengthens the need for domestic environmental protection policies.

Even in a very simple framework, in which a country has a comparative advantage in producing "polluting" goods, the effects of trade are not always obvious. As sketched out in Chapter 2, one of the determinants of environmental quality is the composition of output, which in the case of polluting exports would have a negative effect. But trade also tends to increase income growth. If, as is likely, the demand for environmental quality is income elastic, if the demand for relatively clean goods and services is also income elastic, and if trade facilitates the import of clean technology, the net result of introducing trade may be an improvement in the environment, even in countries that have an apparent comparative advantage in "dirty" products.

Nor are the effects of environmental regulations on the level and pattern of international trade always self-evident. For example, pollution standards on exports will tend to *increase* export earnings if foreign demand is sufficiently inelastic, and will also tend to shift the composition of output toward cleaner goods. And the trade effect of environmental regulations on import-competing products will depend in part on how environmental protection is financed.

Chapters 7, 8, and 9 consider trade and environment primarily on a theoretical level, including the theory of policy. Chapter 7 introduces the main issues and traces the evolution of the theoretical literature melding trade and environment. The early contributions concentrated on extending traditional, positive trade theory to incorporate environmental resources. More recently there has been greater attention given to policy instruments (both trade and environment), and to North-South trade-environment issues. Chapter 8 presents a series of general equilibrium "cases," or models exploring how the environment affects trade, and how the introduction of trade affects the environment and environmental policy. No single model captures all of the interactions, and it is instructive to compare results across different sets of trade-environment assumptions. The exposition is mainly diagrammatic. Chapter 9 uses the simpler tools of partial equilibrium analysis to investigate specific theoretical questions.

Trade-environment *policy* issues have spawned a large literature and are often controversial. It is useful to look at the roots of the conflict and to develop a framework for sorting out issues. In Chapter 10 a close examination suggests that some, though not all, conflict between liberal trade and environmental objectives could be resolved by better trade and/or environmental policies. Attempts to reconcile trade and environmental objectives have taken place in a number of fora, most importantly the OECD and in the GATT/WTO system, and in two major economic integration efforts, the EU and the NAFTA. These attempts can yield useful lessons and are examined in Chapter 11.

Finally, some feeling for the quantitative importance of trade-environment interactions is desirable. For example, do strict environmental regulations have a measurable effect on international competitive position? Is there evidence of a flight of "dirty" industry to developing countries? Do ecolabelling schemes create significant nontariff trade barriers? Will trade liberalization undermine environmental protection? The empirical evidence on trade-environmental interactions is presented in Chapter 12, which follows the taxonomy of policy issues introduced in Chapter 10. These six chapters investigate the theoretical, policy, and empirical questions. The trade-related aspects of transnational pollution and the management of international environmental resources are deferred to Part 3.

7

Trade and Environment: An Overview of Theory

1 Introduction

This chapter reviews trade models that include environmental resources and environmental policy. Our purpose is to explain how the environment has been fitted into trade theory and to describe some of the major conclusions. The presentation is more or less chronological but first makes some general observations about the environment and the theory of comparative advantage (Section 2). Early work through the mid-1980s was primarily concerned with modifying positive trade theory to incorporate environmental resources and drawing conclusions with respect to traditional trade theorems (Section 3). More recent work has a broader policy orientation: North-South trade-environment interactions and the effects of trade liberalization on the environment (Section 4) and trade-environment policy coordination (Section 5). The chapter continues with a discussion of the effects of lifting two restrictive conditions, the small-country, constant terms of trade assumption and the assumption of immobility of factors internationally (Section 6). Section 7 examines the integration of strategic trade theory and environmental policy.[1]

2 Environment and Comparative Advantage

The theory of comparative advantage asserts that countries will tend to specialize in the production and export of goods they produce relatively efficiently. Relative efficiency involves a double comparison, as among goods and as among countries. In the Ricardian one-factor input model, the source of relative efficiency is not explicit but resides implicitly in differences among countries in factor productivities. The Heckscher-Ohlin (H-O) two-

1 For a recent comprehensive but more technical treatment, see Michael Rauscher (1997).

factor model takes the analysis one step further, explaining relative cost differences in terms of differences among countries in factor endowments and differences among goods in factor intensities. A principal conclusion is that countries specialize in the production and export of goods that use intensively the factor of production with which they are relatively well endowed.

If one views the environment as providing services that directly and positively enter production functions, it is a fairly simple matter to accommodate environment in the Ricardian and the H-O models. In the Ricardian framework, environmental conditions conducive to the production of a good – for example, soil quality, availability of water, natural productive fisheries – help determine relative efficiency and hence the pattern of trade. Indeed this has long been obvious, and the contribution of Ricardo is not so much in explaining the pattern of trade but in demonstrating that relative, not absolute, costs are the basis for and gains from trade. The main challenges to update this theory are to incorporate the waste disposal function of the environment, to incorporate differences among countries in their demand for environmental quality, and to recognize that the productive services of the environment often are unpriced or involve externality and common property resource characteristics, in which case trade may magnify distortions and inefficiencies.

The H-O model can also be extended to include the productive services of the environment, and this too has been done in numerous three-factor models including labor, capital, and land – a proxy for natural resources, the latter itself a proxy for certain types of environmental services. The basic conclusion regarding trade patterns is unchanged. Countries relatively well endowed with environmental resources will tend to specialize in the production and export of goods that use these inputs intensively. To the extent that these inputs are commercialized – that is, pass through markets and are priced – the merging of trade theory and environmental economics has long been accomplished. Although perhaps fashionable, it is not novel to say that the natural environment, in this limited sense, is a determinant of comparative advantage. As in the Ricardian model, the interesting consequences of trade emerge when the waste disposal function of the environment is introduced and when the externality and common property resource characteristics of the environmental inputs are considered. Of these, the most serious policy question appears to be that natural-resource-based tradeable goods are priced below their social cost of production due to uncorrected environmental externalities.

Beyond this easy analysis, complications arise, and much depends on the purpose of the analysis and the specific assumptions. The models can be chosen to emphasize one of the three roles the environment plays – as a consumption good, directly entering utility functions; as a generally unpriced complementary input in conventional production functions; or providing assimilative capacity and waste disposal services for pollutants. Environmental damages can be viewed as arising from production or consumption. The damages can be local or transnational. A variety of production functions and utility functions can be chosen, for example, composite, single-factor inputs or multiple-factor production models, and fixed coefficient utility functions versus substitutability of environmental and conventional goods in consumption. Trade may be assumed free or subject to tariffs, subsidies, or quantitative restrictions. Environmental policy may be implemented through direct regulation, taxes, or tradeable permit schemes.

At a higher level of abstraction, the focus of the analysis can be on the effects of environmental policy on trade or the effects of trade and trade liberalization on the environment. In the former, the conventional questions of interest are the effects on the pattern of trade (comparative advantage), the volume of trade, the gains from trade and their international distribution, and factor earnings, an internal distribution question. The macroeconomic effects of environmental policy on the trade balance, unemployment, inflation, and the exchange rate are also of interest. If the focus of the analysis is on the effects of trade and trade liberalization on the environment, the interesting questions are the positive or negative effects of trade on the quality of environmental resources, the implications of trade and trade liberalization for optimal environmental policy, and the welfare consequences of trade after taking into account trade-environment interactions. There has also been considerable commercial interest in trade in environmentally "friendly" products and technology, but this poses few new theoretical questions.

Before presenting the important contributions to trade-environment theory, it is useful to distinguish two very different approaches to modelling environment and production. One approach, which is illustrated in the second version of the model presented in Chapter 2, in the Merrifield article discussed in Section 3, and again in one of the cases presented in Chapter 8, views the environment as making a direct, positive contribution to conventional output. Environmental *degradation* reduces the productivity of conventional inputs to production. A simple example is degraded soils reducing the productivity of capital and labor in agriculture. In this approach, pollution is a by-product of producing conventional economic goods. *Controlling* pollution or environmental degradation requires real resource inputs, capital and labor, and thus diverts them from conventional production. The analytical task is to choose the level of environmental protection or pollution abatement such that the marginal benefit of improved environmental protection and hence conventional output is equal to the marginal losses in conventional production from diverting resources to environmental protection. As shown in Chapter 2, this approach concludes that within certain limits there is a positive relation between environmental quality and conventional output, and that environmental protection may shift the production possibility curve for conventional goods outward.

A second approach, illustrated in the models discussed in Section 3 by Baumol and Oates (1988), Walter (1974; 1975), Grubel (1976), Siebert (1977; 1981), Pethig (1976), and McGuire (1982), emphasizes the waste disposal function or service of the environment. In this approach pollution is also viewed as an unwanted by-product of production, and the environment provides waste disposal services. In this sense, polluting production "uses up" environmental quality, and these authors treat this waste disposal service as a factor of production. In this fashion pollution is an output of production, but the use of the environment for waste disposal is viewed as an input to production. As in the first approach, *controlling* pollution requires real resources and diverts these resources from the production of conventional output. In the Walter, Grubel, Seibert, and McGuire models, there is an explicit activity of pollution abatement. In the Baumol and Oates and Pethig models, a cleaner environment is obtained by choosing a cleaner but less efficient technology for producing conventional goods. The results of explicit consideration of pollution-abatement activity or of shifting to a cleaner, less efficient technology are essentially the same – there is a negative relation between environmental quality and conventional output, and environmental protection shifts the production possibility curve for conventional goods inward. In these models the analytical task is to determine the optimal trade-off between environmental quality, which enters utility functions, and conventional economic output. This approach corresponds to the first version of the model presented in Chapter 2. Finally, in this second approach, goods can be ranked by their relative use of the environment for waste disposal. We can say that good A is "environment intensive" and good B is "labor intensive," if a unit of good A uses more waste disposal services relative to labor than does good B. Establishing the factor intensity of goods helps in extending traditional trade theory to include environmental services.

To summarize, in the first approach, environment is important as it enters into production functions, helps determine the output of conventional goods and services, and indirectly affects utility. In the second approach, environmental services are directly consumed and directly affect welfare, and the availability and quality of these services are determined by pollution incident to production and the amount of resources devoted to environmental protection. In both versions, however, pollution arises from production, not consumption, activities.

3 Trade Theory and Environment: Early Contributions

Baumol and Oates (1988, Chap. 16) present the simplest (although not the first) proposition linking the environment with trade and comparative advantage. Their discussion is a special case of the general proposition that comparative costs determine the international pattern of specialization and trade. Baumol and Oates consider two goods. The first is "clean," involving no production or consumption-related pollution externalities. The second good can be produced at a low cost by a polluting process or at a higher cost by a clean process. There is no explicit utility function nor are there any differences among countries in assimilative capacity. Pollution itself does not effect the production function of either good, although switching to the clean process (pollution abatement) does require real resources and hence increases costs. A country pursuing environmental protection by requiring the clean process will, in the absence of subsidies, decrease its comparative advantage (increase its comparative disadvantage) in the potentially polluting good and increase its comparative advantage in the clean good. Baumol and Oates point out that if developing countries choose uncontrolled pollution, while developed countries choose the clean process, developing countries will tend to specialize in the production and export of the world's dirty industries. They describe this as a peculiar form of export subsidy, implying but not stating that at least some minimal level of pollution abatement is warranted. This conclusion is at the heart of much of the theoretical and empirical work attempting to document and trace a migration of dirty industry from North to South.

   In an unrelated section and using partial equilibrium analysis, Baumol and Oates demonstrate that the balance-of-payments effect of undertaking pollution abatement can be positive or negative depending on the relative trade elasticities. If foreign demand for a country's export good is inelastic, choosing the expensive clean process over the dirty process will increase export earnings. The analysis concludes that a large country with market power can pass on some of its environmental protection costs to foreign consumers in the form of higher export prices (see Section 6). Also, the total employment effect may be positive if the clean process requires more labor per unit output than the dirty process, and if this outweighs the output decline. Both of these results would moderate concern in environmentally strict countries about industrial relocation to less strict countries.

The Baumol and Oates contribution is not based on a fully developed model. Ingo Walter (1974; 1975) made one of the earliest attempts at formally linking trade and environment. Unlike most other models, Walter stresses the role of environmental assimilative capacity in determining comparative advantage. Differences in assimilative capacity imply that equal pollution levels among countries will have different damages due to the presence or absence of physical characteristics – thermal inversions that trap air pollutants, the capacity of rivers to disperse and dilute pollutants, and so forth. The model also introduces the ideas that goods can be ranked by the pollution intensity of their production, and that the activity of pollution abatement itself has an inherent factor intensity that can be compared to factor intensities of other goods. Briefly, Walter's expositional model assumes (1) the social demand for environmental quality is positively related to income; (2) there is a positive linear relation between output and waste disposal and a nonlinear negative relation between waste disposal and environmental quality; (3) the shape of that negative relation is determined by a country's natural endowment of assimilative capacity; and (4) endowments of assimilative capacity differ among countries. Environmental protection policy can shift the output-environmental quality function through the diversion of resource inputs to pollution abatement, but only at the cost of reducing output of conventional goods. In this fashion, both the demand for environmental quality and the country's assimilative capacity determine the achievable level of conventional output and environmental quality.

It follows that under similar demand conditions, the "pricing" of hitherto free use of assimilative capacity will result in countries relatively well endowed with assimilative capacity to specialize in and export products whose production is pollution-intensive. On the demand side, countries at relatively low income levels and with weak demand for environmental quality will obtain a comparative advantage in the pollution-intensive goods. Elaborating on this basic structure, Walter builds a three-good model – importables, exportables, and the activity of environmental damage avoidance (pollution abatement). Using the basic H-O framework, Walter shows that if the pollution-abatement activity is intensive in the same factor as the exportable good, the introduction of an environmental protection program will reduce comparative advantage and specialization in that good and will also reduce trade. If pollution abatement is intensive in the same factor as the importable good, environmental protection will increase specialization (comparative advantage) and may expand trade. The Walter model, with its emphasis on assimilative capacity, resource diversion effects, and ranking of products by pollution intensity, laid the basis for much of the subsequent analysis. It did not, however, consider consumption pollution, the effects of pollution on the productivity of conventional resources, or the effects of trade changes on the environment and on optimal environmental policy.

Herbert Grubel (1976) using a similar H-O model, confirms that the introduction of environmental protection will tend to be antitrade biased if the activity of pollution abatement is intensive in the abundant factor (reducing exports), and protrade biased if pollution abatement is intensive in the scarce factor (reducing import-competing production and tending to expand imports). Additionally, Grubel makes the important contribution of demonstrating that the first-best method for dealing with an environmental externality associated with production is to eliminate it directly, rather than using a trade measure. For example, if the externality is in the production of an export good, say, a polluting industry such as pulp and paper, an export tax would shift production toward the cleaner import-competing product. But such a tax introduces by-product distortions and would be inferior to measures directly controlling the externality such as a pollution tax (see Chapters 6 and 9). A similar conclusion – that a consumption tax is superior to a tariff – is demonstrated when there is a consumption externality associated with the import-competing good. This important point is the basis for the widespread opposition of economists to using trade measures for environmental objectives.

An important element of conventional trade theory is the demonstration of welfare gains from trade. How does the introduction of the environment and environmental protection policies alter this conclusion? Horst Siebert (1977; 1987) addresses this question with a Ricardian-type model, using a single factor input that can be used to produce two tradeable commodities or can be used for pollution abatement. Pollution is modelled as a positive function of commodity output, with one commodity more pollution intensive than the other. Other assumptions are that (1) environment quality is negatively related to the flow of pollution (gross pollution net of pollution abated); (2) pollution abatement is accomplished through a pollution tax, which is transferred back to households; and (3) there is a social welfare function that includes consumption of the two commodities and the level of environmental quality. The important but not surprising conclusion from this model is that when a country specializes in and exports the pollution-intensive good and no pollution abatement is undertaken, environmental quality deteriorates and the gains from trade are eroded or possibly overwhelmed, so that trade can reduce welfare. A reduction in welfare is more likely if expansion of the export good has high marginal environmental damages. If the country imports the pollution-intensive good, an environmental improvement augments the conventional gains from trade. The conclusion that, with unregulated pollution, trade can decrease welfare is at the heart of the trade-environment policy debate, and underscores the need for coordinating trade and environment policy. For confirmation of this conclusion, see the models developed in the next chapter.

How does environmental policy affect trade and welfare? The introduction of a pollution tax on an export good will divert resources from its production, undermine apparent comparative advantage, and reduce trade and the gains from trade. In the limiting case, the environmental tax will return the country to autarky or even reverse the direction of trade. Nevertheless, welfare will be increased by the pollution tax so long as the social costs of production of the commodities (i.e., private marginal costs plus environmental damages) are greater than the value of the commodities foregone by imposing the tax. Alternatively, welfare will increase so long as an environmental tax, valued in commodities foregone, is less than the marginal environmental damage avoided. This, too, is an important conclusion. An appropriate environmental policy may diminish the gains from trade, but will improve total welfare. If the import-competing good is pollution-intensive, the pollution tax will increase specialization and comparative advantage, and the welfare gains from trade will be augmented by improved environmental quality. As in Walter's model, a central assumption is that pollution reduces utility directly, and not through adversely affecting production functions. The latter possibility is considered in Siebert's environment-production chapter (1987), in which he demonstrates that environmental protection may shift the production possibility curve outward rather than inward, but this approach is not carried through to his analysis of trade.

Another important trade-environment theory question is how environmental policies interact between countries, and whether trade shifts the burden of pollution from one country to another. Rüdiger Pethig (1976) addresses these questions with a Ricardian-type model, with one factor input (labor). Production creates a by-product, waste, the amount of which can be controlled by altering commodity output or by substituting (within limits) labor for waste emission in the production process. In that sense, the waste-absorptive role of the environment can be interpreted as a second factor of production, and the need for a separate activity, that is, pollution abatement, is finessed. Wastes are transformed into pollution (i.e., have negative welfare effects) above some minimum waste flow level. The welfare function includes consumption of both commodities (consumed in fixed proportions) and a normalized index of environmental quality, which is treated as pure public consumption good. The technology of production is such that one of the two commodities is unambiguously labor-intensive and the other environment-(waste)-intensive (i.e., no factor intensity reversal). Environmental policy is activated with either an emissions tax or a tradeable permits scheme, which are equally efficient.

In a two-country open economy (trade) situation, and in the absence of an environmental protection policy, the model leads to the conclusion that specialization and trade take place purely on the basis of comparative labor productivities (the traditional Ricardian result). However, trade will lead to a welfare loss in the country that specializes in the environment-intensive good (the good that uses more of the environment's waste disposal service) if the welfare loss from a deterioration in environmental quality exceeds the gains from trade as measured by the private consumption goods. This is essentially the same conclusion as in Siebert.

The introduction of environmental controls by one country will increase its comparative advantage if it exports the labor-intensive commodity, but if it initially exports the environment-intensive commodity, environmental controls will erode or potentially reverse its comparative advantage, switching it toward labor-intensive exports. If both countries institute environmental protection policies and have identical relative labor productivities, the country engaging in the least restrictive environmental protection policy will specialize in and export the environment-intensive good. Thus the two countries' welfare is interdependent, as strict pollution abatement in one country shifts production patterns and hence pollution even in the absence of transnational pollution. The more general point is that trade is the vehicle through which the burden of pollution can be shifted internationally, another critical issue in the trade-environment policy debate. Finally, Pethig demonstrates that even with different emission standards, the relative "price" of emissions in the two countries will tend to equalize, a result consistent with the traditional factor price equalization theorem.[2]

---

2 This conclusion must be interpreted carefully. This model is in the Ricardian tradition with only one explicit factor input. The traditional factor price equalization theorem is derived from the H-O two-factor input model.

Trade theory is also very much concerned with the effect of international trade on the prices of the factors of production. Two important theorems derived from the H-O trade model are that under certain conditions free trade leads to the equalization of factor prices internationally, and that an increase in the relative price of one commodity increases the relative and absolute (real) return to the factor of production that is used intensively in the production of that product (Stopler-Samuelson Theorem). Martin McGuire (1982) investigates the implication for these two theorems by first adding the environment as a factor of production (that is, as in the Pethig model, the environment provides a waste disposal service) and then by controlling pollution. His basic model consists of a polluting good (X) and a nonpolluting good (Y), both produced with capital and labor. Good X "uses" the waste disposal service of the environment in its production. As in the models discussed previously, pollution is a by-product of production. The environment is viewed as an input because it provides waste disposal services. As in the previous models (Walter, Grubel, Siebert, and Pethig), pollution does not directly impair the productivity of either labor or capital. In the absence of regulation, the environment is used for waste disposal to the point where the value of its marginal product in absorbing wastes is zero. If there is some direct regulation of pollution through emission limits, the relative cost of producing X rises as increasing amounts of capital and labor are used for abatement or a less efficient but cleaner production technology is used.

If the relative cost of producing X increases, and if the relative prices of X and Y are held constant as they would be for a small open economy facing fixed international terms of trade, the environmental regulation causes factor prices and capital and labor proportions to change. The return to the factor used intensively in the regulated product X must decrease. If the return to that factor decreases, and if the prices of X and Y are fixed, the income of that factor of production, as measured by its ability to buy X and Y, must decrease. (If the factor's income includes the quality of the environment, however, its *real income* need not decrease.) For example, if the polluting good X is labor-intensive, regulating pollution in X production would unambiguously lower labor's wage, measured by its command over goods X and Y.[3]

An intuitive explanation can be given. Regulation of X shifts the production possibility curve inward in a biased fashion, with a reduction of X production but no change in the Y anchor. With relative commodity prices fixed,

---

3 This result depends on production functions that are linear and homogenous and an assumption that the factor intensity of pollution abatement lies between the factor intensities of X and Y.

the composition of output must shift to a larger share of Y and a reduced share of X. The contraction of X and expansion of Y release more labor than can be absorbed at the prevailing wage, and wages must fall relative to the return to capital in order to increase the labor to capital ratio in both X and Y and absorb the excess labor. In a small open economy with no power to affect international prices, and neglecting the gain in welfare from better environmental quality, regulation of a product that pollutes will harm the factor that is used intensively in its production. Moreover, although commodity prices are equalized internationally through trade, factor prices are not. Unilateral imposition of pollution control on product X in this model changes the relative costs of producing X and Y. But trade demands that the relative prices and hence the relative costs of producing X and Y be equal internationally. This can only be accomplished by having the relative payment to capital and labor differ at home and abroad. In McGuire's words, "nonuniform regulation destroys factor price equalization."

These contributions are the main building blocks for extending traditional trade theory to incorporate the environment. The approach in both the Ricardian and H-O type models has been to treat pollution as a joint product of conventional production, and then to invert that insight by viewing the obverse of pollution, environmental quality, as an additional factor of production. None of the models reviewed here considers the possibility that pollution or environmental degradation reduces the productivity of conventional inputs to production. Because of this approach, all of analyses view pollution abatement (environmental protection) as shifting production possibility curves inward, and in that sense are at odds with the premise of sustainable development that environmental protection is consistent with increased conventional output (see Chapter 2).

This limited perspective is remedied in a comprehensive, comparative static, general equilibrium model constructed by John Merrifield (1988). Unlike the previous models, pollution impairs the productivity of conventional production inputs. The model includes two consumption goods and an intermediate good, pollution-abatement equipment, two primary factors, labor and capital, and two trading countries. Capital, goods, and pollution are all internationally mobile (i.e., transnational pollution is explicitly considered). Pollution arising from production damages the productivity of capital so that it becomes increasingly scarce relative to labor. Welfare in the two countries is indexed by consumption of the two goods (i.e., pollution does not directly enter utility functions). The returns to capital and labor and the terms of trade are endogenous and determined by pollution and pollution abatement, and both affect national welfare. Finally, two abatement strategies are investigated, a production tax and a regulatory measure establishing a minimum ratio between the use of pollution-abatement equipment and output of the final goods.

In applying the model to the particulars of the U.S.–Canadian acid rain dispute, Merrifield found that a production tax imposed by Canada would unambiguously raise Canadian welfare, as reduced output would improve its terms of trade and the decline in the return to capital would favor Canada as a net debtor *vis à vis* the United States (i.e., a lower return to capital reduces Canada's debt service payment to the United States). The return to capital declines because it becomes more "abundant" as pollution declines. By contrast, tightening the regulatory standard in Canada would have ambiguous effects. The initial effect diverts labor and capital from production of the tradeable goods to producing the intermediate good, that is, pollution-abatement equipment. This reduces emissions, tightens the capital market and pulls in capital from the United States. But the terms-of-trade effect is not certain. And in this model the second-round effects dominate. The reduced emissions *reduce* the scarcity of capital, decrease its price, and tend to increase production (and emissions) in both countries. In combining these effects, it is unclear if Canada's terms of trade improve and whether it benefits from a net reduction in the price of capital. One critical parameter is the damage coefficient, or the extent to which capital productivity changes when pollution changes. The larger this parameter, the more likely strict abatement will *increase* output. By treating pollution abatement as increasing the productivity of capital, Merrifield allows for the possibility that environmental protection is consistent with increased output of conventional goods. Total emissions do not increase, however, because of tighter regulatory standards.

4 The North-South Controversy

More recent theoretical work has tended to focus on North-South trade-environment issues and the assertion by some that trade harms the environment. The underlying issues are whether poor countries in the South have a comparative advantage in the products of "dirty" industries, whether there will be a shift of dirty industries toward "pollution havens" in the South, and whether trade contributes to a worldwide increase in pollution and environmental degradation. These are not merely abstract theoretical questions, but go to the heart of trade-environment disputes over the past decade.

Brian Copeland and M. Scott Taylor (1994) present an interesting model in which differences in assimilative capacity and other supply factors play no direct role, although the model can be extended to include them. Income differences between two sets of countries, North and South, lead to different demand for environmental quality (pollution abatement) and different levels of optimal pollution taxes and relative production costs, and hence determine the pattern of specialization and trade. Another feature of the model is that optimal environmental policy in the form of a pollution tax is endogenous, with government continuously setting the tax rate equal to marginal pollution damages. The modelling of pollution is similar to that presented by Pethig and others. Pollution is a by-product of production for a continuum of consumption goods. It can be regulated with an emissions tax through the substitution of a single resource input, labor, for pollution emissions. In essence, this describes two inputs to production functions – labor and pollution emissions. All pollution is local so that international externalities are absent. Again following Pethig and others, goods can be ranked by the pollution intensity of their production, with no factor intensity reversals. It is further assumed that labor in the North embodies greater human capital than labor in the South. This permits an arbitrarily large difference in labor wage, and hence income levels in North and South. Welfare functions in North and South include the vector of consumption goods and pollution, which enters with a negative sign. Environmental quality is assumed to be a normal good. Welfare functions are identical in the two countries, but of course income levels are not. As in most of the models reviewed earlier, the possibility that environmental deterioration has a negative effect on the productivity of conventional inputs to production is not considered. Environmental policy, conducted with pollution taxes, is adjusted to equate the marginal damage (welfare loss) caused by pollution with the tax. It follows that trade, even if pollution-increasing, is always welfare-improving.

With identical production technologies in North and South, trade takes place on the basis of relative costs. Given the higher pollution tax imposed in the North due to higher income and demand for environmental quality, the North will tend to specialize and export those commodities for which labor costs are high relative to pollution emission tax payments, that is, the relatively clean products.[4] The South specializes in the relatively dirty products. The relative cost differences between North and South provide the

---

4 Keep in mind that in this model pollution affects utility functions, not production functions. Because of the South's scarcity of environmental capital relative to labor, a model that focused on pollution affecting conventional production might conclude that the South should set *higher* pollution taxes than the North, which would alter the following conclusions.

basis for trade and the gains from trade without direct recourse to differences in assimilative capacity. This result, however, is partly an artifact of how pollution damages are introduced. Most of the paper assumes countries are identical in size and population density, implying similar physical damages per unit of pollution. In an interesting extension, Copeland and Taylor show that if the South were more densely populated, a unit of pollution might have greater utility loss. Its optimal pollution tax might then be higher than in the North, and hence the pattern of trade would reverse, with the poor South specializing in clean products and the North in dirty products. Systematic differences in assimilative capacity could also reverse the pattern of trade. Thus there is nothing inevitable about the South specializing in dirty products.

Returning to the standard assumption of the article (countries of similar size and population density), Copeland and Taylor analyze the effect of introducing trade on the global level of pollution and its incidence between North and South. To do so, they decompose pollution effects associated with moving from autarky to trade into scale, techniques, and composition effects (composition refers to the mix of dirty and clean industries). In the North, trade increases the scale of economic activity, thus increasing pollution, but this is partly offset as rising income pushes the optimal pollution tax higher, shifting the techniques of production toward less pollution. In this model, composition effects dominate the scale-and-techniques effect as the more pollution-intensive industries contract in the North. The reverse is true in the South; trade increases pollution even with optimal pollution abatement. The net *world* result of trade is an increase in pollution, as production of dirty industries is shifted to the South, with its lower income and lower pollution emissions tax, and production takes place with less stringent pollution-abatement techniques. The dominance of the composition over the scale-and-technique effects is, however, an artifact of the specific modelling of substitution possibilities in consumption and production.

Finally, the Copeland-Taylor model predicts that growth in the North arising from an increase in its human capital will have different consequences for pollution than growth in the South, even when North and South follow optimal pollution abatement. Specifically, if the North gets richer, world pollution increases, but if the South gets richer, world pollution falls. The intuitive explanation is that as the North grows, it attracts industries that on the margin are more polluting than its average, thus increasing the average pollution intensity of its production structure. In the South, the marginal industries that "migrate" to the North have lower than average pollution intensities, and hence the average pollution intensity of the remaining industries rises. Growth in the South, however, pulls in relatively clean industries, lowering average pollution intensity, while the release of relatively dirty industries on the margin in the North decreases the North's average pollution intensity. Also, economic growth in the South leads to an increase in its optimal pollution tax, thus reducing world pollution. Another interpretation of this surprising result is that as the South grows, the gap between North and South in their relative prices of labor and pollution (i.e., the pollution tax) shrinks, and the level of trade also falls. As trade falls, the world pollution attributable to trade must also fall. In the extreme, of course, equal incomes in North and South would eliminate trade in this model and thus render inoperative the increase in global pollution shown to be the result of trade.

Parenthetically, we note that the Copeland-Taylor model is a good illustration of why trade economists and environmentalists have difficulties communicating. The basic economic result is that trade increases welfare and trade is the vehicle through which environmental resources are efficiently used. The environmentalist, however, is apt to emphasize that trade increases world pollution and shifts the pollution burden from rich consuming countries to poor developing countries. Within the limits of the model, both sets of conclusions are valid. But with different value systems, the economist and the environmentalist are likely to judge the outcome differently.[5]

Moreover, the Copeland-Taylor model and its conclusion that trade increases world pollution depend critically on the assumption that pollution has local rather than global damages. In a companion paper, the same authors use a similar model but assume that pollution damages are international rather than local (Copeland and Taylor 1995b). In that event, and if countries are not too dissimilar with respect to income levels, the move from autarky to trade does *not* increase world pollution, although the source is shifted from North to South. The central reason is that trade will equalize factor prices, and as the environment is treated as a factor of production (that is, pollution is considered an "input" to production), the price of pollution as measured by the price of pollution permits equalizes internationally. If the relative price of the two inputs to production, labor, and "pollution" is equal across countries, they will choose the same combination

5 In another paper, Copeland and Taylor (1995a) extend their analysis by considering pollution generated by consumption, not production. Using much the same approach, they demonstrate that in autarky the relative producer price for the dirty good will be lower in the North than the South due to a higher pollution tax on the good, but the consumption price of the dirty good will be higher. This provides a basis for trade. After trade, the North is supplied with more of the clean good, and pollution levels fall. In the South trade leads to an increase in the consumption of dirty goods and an increase in pollution. It is worth pointing out that measuring and ranking goods according to a meaningful and comprehensive index of the pollution intensity of their consumption is fraught with difficulties.

of inputs in production. Hence, even though some pollution-intensive production is shifted from North to South, the relative use of labor and "pollution" in production will not change. To obtain this encouraging result, however, it is necessary to assume that the North responds to increasing transnational pollution originating in the South by tightening its own environmental standards. In fact, there is a hint of exploitation of the North by the South in this model. Copeland and Taylor assert that the South has a strategic advantage, in that their lower income levels allow them to commit to more pollution with the opening of trade. This transnational pollution adversely affects the North, which has a choice of accepting more global pollution, or cutting its own emissions and reducing or reversing its gains from trade. Although not modeled as explicitly strategic behavior (see Section 7), the analysis demonstrates one reason why the North may wish to link a free trade agreement with the South with an environmental agreement that limits the South's pollution emission levels, especially if pollution is transnational in character. NAFTA, with preexisting border pollution between the United States and Mexico (and the United States and Canada), may serve as an example. Chapter 14, which considers global warming, suggests a parallel argument – the North, in contemplating an agreement with the South to reduce carbon emissions, has some reason to be concerned with the trade effects arising from the agreement.

The conflicting conclusions between the first and second Copeland-Taylor models (trade does/does not increase global pollution) highlights the sensitivity of outcomes to model assumptions. This raises the question of whether these models, despite their technical sophistication, are sufficient to describe problems in the real world. For example, Copeland-Taylor, in their second (transnational pollution) model, list global warming and ozone depletion as the types of pollutants they have in mind. But it is easy to list features of global warming and ozone depletion that the model does not capture – CFCs and greenhouse gases are stock pollutants, and the time dimension is critical; physical (as well as monetary) damage functions differ among countries; abatement cost functions also differ; pollution has a negative effect on the productivity of conventional production inputs as well as its direct effect on utility. If the conclusions of these models are as sensitive to assumptions as they appear to be, it is difficult to be confident in the relevance of the models' conclusions for specific pollution problems.

More broadly, environmentalists and (sometimes) economists recognize that policy is seldom optimal. The Copeland-Taylor (1994) model described here assumes that governments would follow an optimal environmental policy. It concludes that specialization by the South in dirty industries is a natural working out of comparative advantage and is welfare-enhancing for both the North and South. In contrast, a model presented by Graciela Chichilnisky (1994) also addresses North–South environmental trade, but comes to very different conclusions because she does *not* assume optimal policy. According to her analysis, given current property rights regimes in the North and the South, the South overuses its environmental resources and sells its exports at less than social cost. Trade is distorted, and the North contributes to the problem by overconsuming the underpriced resource exports of the South. Thus the Chichilnisky model is very close to an exploitation model, although there is no suggestion that this occurs deliberately. The key to the Chichilnisky model is the assertion that environmental resources such as forests often exist as unregulated common property in developing countries, but similar resources tend to be subject to well-defined private property rights in the industrial countries.[6] Thus, unlike the Copeland-Taylor model, which assumed a powerful government agency capable of establishing and enforcing optimal environmental policy in both the North and the South, the Chichilnisky model starts from the inefficiency and overexploitation of unregulated common property. Because the external costs of resource use are not borne by those who harvest the resource (i.e., the externality costs imposed on other users of the fishery or forest), the quantity supplied at any given price in a common property regime exceeds the quantity that would be supplied if the resource were under private ownership. It follows that in a two-country (North–South) world in which both countries have the same technologies, the same homothetic preferences, and the same endowments of production inputs but different property rights regimes, the South would exhibit an *apparent* comparative advantage in environmental-intensive goods. With trade, the South would specialize in the production and export of environmentally intensive products, these goods would be sold at less than the social costs of production, and trade would exacerbate the inefficiencies associated with the common property regime. It is important to recognize that while trade may impoverish the environmental resource-exporting country, the source of the distortion is not trade, but defects in the market for environmental services. In this sense, the Chichilnisky model is simply an elaboration of the general proposition that if domestic distortions such as environmental externalities are left unattended, trade *can* worsen welfare.

Chichilnisky makes the further argument that a tax on natural resource

---

6 Brander and Taylor (1998) also consider the welfare effects of trade in open access natural resources. Not surprisingly, they conclude that "incomplete property rights in renewable resource sectors undermine the presumption that trade liberalization is necessarily welfare improving" (204).

extraction may increase rather than decrease the rate of exploitation of environmental resources. The gist of the argument is that the workers who harvest the resource tend to be immobile and have a low elasticity of substitution between work and leisure. As the price of the natural-resource-intensive good declines, the price of a second consumption good for these workers rises, and they devote greater effort to resource extraction.

One can quibble with the stylized facts underlying this model. Subsidies in rich countries also cause underpriced environmental resources. And the externalities associated with common property resources can also affect productivity in other sectors, a feature not considered. Over time the pattern of trade may reverse, as the South depletes its supply of environment-intensive goods, and a dynamic model might yield different and interesting conclusions. Nevertheless, the study does make useful contributions by extending the debate beyond pollution arising from industrial production to natural-resource-based trade, by drawing attention to the sale of exports at less than the full social costs of production, and by recognizing that actual and optimal policy may diverge widely in the real world. The conflicting conclusion among the various models of North-South trade underscores the need for critical scrutiny of assumptions.

5 Theory of Policy and Policy Coordination

Traditionally, trade policy and environmental policy have been formulated by separate government agencies with little or no coordination between them. This is undesirable, as trade policy affects the use of environmental resources, and environmental policy affects international trade. These interactions may be described as trade-environment *policy* spillovers, to distinguish them from physical pollution externalities. The policy coordination problem is relatively straightforward if there is only one trade distortion and one pollution externality distortion. Simultaneous trade policy reform and environmental policy reform using two instruments, say, tariff/subsidies and pollution taxes, can be used jointly to improve welfare, although the extent to which each instrument is used depends on the extent to which the other is used. If only one policy is used, a simple second-best type problem emerges, and welfare improvement is no longer assured. An example of a market power distortion and pollution distortion is given in Chapter 3. A partial equilibrium treatment of a terms-of-trade and a pollution externality situation is given in Chapter 9.

The policy coordination problem becomes more complex when multiple pollution externalities and multiple trade policy distortions exist and complete removal of all distortions is not feasible. For instance, restricting the disposal of a single pollutant at a single site and in a particular environmental medium may simply shunt the pollutant to another site or medium with higher damage costs, or substitute an even more damaging pollutant for the restricted one. The problem has long been recognized in the trade literature in the theory of the second best – reducing one tariff while leaving other tariffs in place may increase the distortive effect of other tariffs as trade is diverted from lower-cost to higher-cost sources, a central issue in customs union theory. Brian Copeland (1994) addresses policy reform with multiple distortions in both trade and environment, where the policy spillovers can flow between trade and the environment in both directions. This is an important practical question, as many developing countries are liberalizing trade and are concerned with the spillover to environmental resources, and many countries are reforming environmental policies and are concerned with trade effects. Interestingly, the two policy reforms are not symmetrical. Trade policy reform generally consists of *reducing* trade restrictions and trade subsidies. Environmental policy reform generally consists of *imposing* pollution taxes or otherwise restricting pollution emissions.

Copeland's basic model shares some characteristics with the Copeland-Taylor 1994 article. Pollution is a by-product of production. It adversely affects utility, but does not affect production functions. Also, this is not an optimizing model. Rather, it investigates whether small changes in trade or environmental policy will be welfare-improving, setting aside the issue of optimal policy. At first glance, it appears necessary to go to the specifics of each case and trace through all policy spillovers, sum their effects, and conclude whether a partial policy reform in either the trade or environment area improves welfare. Fortunately, a general rule has evolved in the second-best literature to the effect that *proportionate* reductions in all distortions will either not harm or will improve welfare. But with uncoordinated trade and environmental policy formation, such simultaneous proportionate policy reform in both areas is unlikely.

Copeland first shows that tariff reform without environmental reform will not harm and may improve welfare if tariffs are reduced equiproportionately and if the protected industries are pollution-damage-intensive.[7] Indeed, it may be desirable to go beyond trade neutrality and subsidize imports of the damage-intensive products (simultaneous environmental

---

7 The pollution damage intensity is defined over a number of pollutants and weighted by the difference between the pollution tax and the marginal damage of that pollutant. Thus if the pollutant tax is at its optimal level, that pollutant would have a zero weight in calculating damage intensity.

policy reform would of course be preferable). The idea behind this is straightforward. Tariff reduction reduces the trade distortion and, by shrinking domestic production of the good, also reduces environmental damages. Copeland further demonstrates that an equiproportional increase in pollution taxes toward their optimal level, with no change in tariffs or other trade reforms, will leave unchanged or increase welfare if the protected industries are pollution-damage-intensive. The tax increase works directly to correct the pollution distortion but also has a contractionary effect on the excessive output of the protected import-competing industries.

The Copeland model also investigates the use of quantitative restraints on trade and on pollution. In that event, the second-best policy spillover problem is very different. If all trade restraints are quotas, and *all* pollutants are subject to binding quantitative restrictions (i.e., absolute levels of effluents and emissions), then piecemeal policy reform, attacking any particular distortion, is welfare-improving. The explanation is simple – negative policy spillovers cannot occur because of binding quotas and quantitative restrictions.[8] For example, removing an import quota on an item that pollutes in consumption, say, an auto, will not increase pollution if auto pollution is strictly controlled by some quantitative limit. Recall, also, that quantitative limits on pollutants must have spatial, media, and dilution restrictions for this conclusion to hold. Partial restrictions on pollutants are not sufficient.

The use of trade measures to secure environmental objectives has been extensively analyzed. In contemplating their use, they should be compared to more direct measures such as pollution taxes, and if trade measures are to be used, price measures versus quantitative measures should be evaluated. A general conclusion from the theory of trade policy is that export and import bans and quantitative restraints are less efficient than tax/tariff measures. A general conclusion of environmental economics is similar: quantitative limits and bans on pollution are apt to be less efficient than tax or tradeable permit policies. These ideas are brought together in a pair of articles by Judith Dean (1995) and Dean and Gangopadhyay (1997) that investigate trade policy response to environmental externalities. The first study utilizes a two-good model in which the first good is an intermediate input to the second good and also produces "pollution" (environmental damages), which enters utility functions with a negative sign. The policy instrument examined is an export ban on the intermediate good, an extreme form of

---

8 By the same token, positive policy spillovers, in which removing one distortion tends to reduce a second distortion, cannot occur.

quantitative restraint. The real world context is the effects of an export ban on tropical logs, an input into wood-processing industries.

The first question Dean investigates is whether an export ban will achieve a socially optimal level of log harvest. The answer is that such a ban will leave harvest rates excessive *if* environmental damages grow rapidly as log harvesting rates increase, and leave harvest rates deficient *if* the harvest-damage rate increases slowly. The explanation is that if the elasticity of domestic demand for logs is sufficiently high, a ban on log exports diverts logs to the domestic processing industry, and if marginal damages from log harvesting rise rapidly, the harvest remains excessive. If the harvest-damage rate rises slowly, the export ban inflicts excessive trade and welfare losses. In other words, an export ban that resulted in an optimal log-harvest rate would be entirely coincidental. In contrast, an export tax could be found that brought the log-harvest rate to its optimal level, but the by-product distortion of subsidizing the log input into the domestic processing industry would make the export tax inferior to a production tax, a variation on the second-best optimal tariff concept. Dean also investigates the conditions under which a log export ban would improve social welfare as compared to a free trade policy. She finds that the more rapidly environmental damages rise with log harvesting, the more likely the ban will improve welfare. But this is also the condition under which the ban is less likely to reduce harvest rates to their optimal level.

In the second article the authors continue the examination of an export ban on logs, but change one feature and add two others. The change is that the externality in logging no longer affects utility directly, but damages the productivity of an input (land) in a third sector (agriculture). The two additions to the model are the introduction of a second distortion – unemployment in the urban, wood-processing sector – and presentation of separate short-run and long-run analyses. Rural-to-urban migration is assumed to result from a gap between the rural wage and the expected wage in the urban sector, which itself is the (fixed) urban wage adjusted for urban unemployment. The short-run–long-run distinction rests on whether rural land is mobile between logging and agriculture. A principal question of the analysis is whether the existence of unemployment strengthens the case for a trade restraint such as an export ban on logs. This is a relevant policy question, as many developing countries have restricted raw material exports to boost downstream processing industries.

Dean and Gangopadhyay show that in the short run the optimal export tax is lower when urban unemployment is introduced than without this second distortion, and that an export ban would aggravate urban unemployment. The intuitive explanation is that in both cases the trade restriction on logs depresses rural wages,[9] increases the wage gap, and increases migration and unemployment in the urban sector. In both the export tax and export ban cases, the depressed domestic price of logs does stimulate output and employment in the urban sector, but not enough to offset the influx of displaced rural labor. These conclusions are reversed in the long run. If agriculture is a labor-intensive sector, the export restriction on logs induces sufficient expansion of agriculture and the urban-processing sector to reduce total unemployment. In that event, an optimal export tax should be higher in an unemployment situation as compared to a full employment model. But as the authors point out, the more severe the environmental damages are, the smaller is the positive spillover effect from an log export tax on the unemployment distortion.

6 Terms of Trade and Factor Mobility

Several of the studies reviewed in this chapter drop the restrictive small-country assumption and allow for changes in the international terms of trade as measured by price of exports relative to imports. The question is potentially important because the terms of trade help determine the international distribution of the gains from trade. If there is a positive terms-of-trade effect, some of the cost of environmental protection can be shifted to consuming countries. In contrast, a small country has no international pricing power over either its imports or exports. In that event, the additional costs incurred for environmental protection cannot be shifted, but must be borne domestically in the form of reduced earnings for the factors of production. Therefore, the frequently heard assertion that a country that fails to undertake environmental protection is selling its products at below social cost, conferring an environmental subsidy, has a peculiar meaning. If the country were to impose costly environmental regulations on its export product, the international selling price would not change, but export volume would decline. As the quantity of exports declines, the marginal production cost falls to a level such that private costs plus marginal environmental protection cost just equal the fixed international price for its export. The country has incorporated environmental protection cost by reducing volume and moving down its marginal cost curve. On the import side, import-competing production must contract to

---

9 A necessary condition is that the result of declining marginal labor productivity in agriculture from shifting labor from logging to agriculture and the positive effect on the marginal productivity of labor in agriculture due to the reduced externality remains, on balance, negative.

accommodate new environmental protection costs in product price. A principal concern of small developing countries exporting price-sensitive commodities is not that they will suffer terms-of-trade deterioration, but that they will be unable to incorporate environmental protection costs in price without losing export earnings and increasing expenditures on imports. Trade equilibrium could be restored through a real exchange rate change, but to make that effective without a change in the price level, real domestic absorption and income must fall. It is this concern for a negative trade-balance effect that supports a coordinated environmental protection effort among exporters, so that in aggregate the exporters can overcome their small country status and shift environmental protection costs to consumers through higher export prices.

For a large country with market power over its exports and imports, some of the cost of environmental protection can be shifted abroad to consumers through higher export prices and lower world prices for its imports. In that event, the adverse trade-balance effect is moderated or eliminated. The extent of shifting depends on the elasticity of world demand for its exports and the world supply elasticity for its imports. One interesting situation, explored in Chapter 9, is a country that initially does not undertake environmental protection and is not exploiting its market power by taxing exports or imports. In that event it may secure welfare gains from improved terms of trade that are additional to the welfare gains from establishing environmental protection. Policy spillovers in a second-best world are not always negative.

The standard H-O model assumes factors are not mobile internationally. Several of the contributions reviewed here relax this assumption, at least with regard to capital. The results tend to reinforce the industrial relocation hypothesis that relatively dirty industry will tend to relocate in countries with relatively high assimilative capacity or whose income, preferences, and political structure lead to low environmental standards. This issue of capital flight to "pollution havens" was central to the NAFTA debate (see Chapter 11). The logic is straightforward. Pollution-intensive industries will be relatively severely impacted by the costs of stringent environmental regulation. If market conditions do not permit them to fully pass costs onto product price, profit rates fall, and *ceteris paribus*, they will tend to relocate in countries with lower standards, lower costs, and better returns to capital. If environmental standards respond to increasing pollution in the receiving country, there will be a limiting tendency to this industrial relocation, as standards among countries tend to converge over time.

As McGuire's model points out, however, in a simple two-country, two-product, two-factor model, the direction of factor movement depends on the factor intensity of the pollution-intensive product. For example, if a country is abundant in labor, and if it is the labor-intensive good that is subject to environmental regulations, the return to labor falls but the return to capital rises. If mobile, capital will flow *toward* the country undertaking environmental protection. Indeed, in his model capital will continue to flow into the country until the production of the pollution-intensive good is driven to zero and the country completely specializes in the "clean" product. Such a result is efficient if and only if one assumes that environmental standards in the form of taxes are set to equal marginal damage costs (and transnational pollution is absent). The model again illustrates the desirability of adjusting environmental policy to reflect trade and capital flows.

The Copeland model (1994) examining the conditions under which small changes in pollution policy will improve welfare also considers factor mobility. It demonstrates that in the absence of distortions in trade or in factors markets (i.e., only pollution distortions), the welfare gain from a small equiproportionate reform of pollution policy (i.e., an equiproportionate increase in all pollution taxes if they are initially too low) will be at least as large and possibly larger when factor mobility is allowed. This follows from the increased supply responsiveness to pollution taxes when factors are internationally mobile. But inwardly mobile factors may reduce welfare if they are directed toward a pollution-intensive sector with inadequate environmental protection. In this sense both trade and factor mobility tend to amplify environmental effects, strengthening the need for appropriate environmental policy.

Introducing international capital flows also directs attention to the relations between international debt and the environment. It has been argued that the massive external debts acquired by many developing countries in the 1970s and 1980s and the pressure to service those debts by increasing exports, especially exports of primary products, have contributed to unsustainable resource use in at least some developing countries (see Chapter 16). The Asian financial crisis of 1997 raises similar questions, although the origins of the Asian crisis are quite different. The argument has a certain plausibility. Regardless of how the debt was incurred, a heavily indebted country must generate a trade surplus if it is to meet its interest and principal repayment schedule. Even if natural-resource export prices are declining, which normally might reduce immediate pressure on resources, the price decline would be overridden by volume increases if a fixed target for foreign exchange is needed for debt service. Indeed, if several primary-product-exporting countries acted to increase export earnings, the combined effect would be to depress their export price and perhaps lead to higher exploitation rates.

Restrictive macroeconomic measures taken to deal with an external debt crisis can have mixed effects on the environment. The slowdown in domestic consumption may reduce or slow the growth of emissions from consumption, for example, slower growth of private auto use. Some environmentally harmful projects may be put on hold. And if imports of inputs used in the extractive industries were curtailed – for example, pesticides and fertilizer inputs to agriculture or machinery for clearing forests – there might be some short-term environmental relief. But on balance one would expect negative effects – curtailing domestic consumption merely frees up productive capacity for export with associated production pollution; imports of clean technology and pollution-abatement equipment may be cut back along with imports of environmentally damaging products and technology; governments with severe budget constraints are less likely to spend money on pollution abatement or impose strict pollution standards on industry.

The question of debt and environment has been investigated in a formal theoretical model by Michael Raucher (1997, Chap. 8). The problem is modeled as a dynamic optimization exercise in which one seeks the optimal time path of consumption and pollution emissions to maximize the present value of utility. Utility is determined by consumption and environmental quality; pollution arises from production but not consumption activities. A key to the model is that the interest rate paid on marginal debt is an increasing function of the level of external debt. This is certainly plausible as risk premiums would be expected to increase at higher debt levels. The solution to the basic model shows that, in the short and medium term, pollution emissions increase with higher initial levels of debt. In the long run, however, the optimal paths of consumption and emissions approach the same steady-state values regardless of initial debt levels. The intuitive understanding of these results is that because higher indebtedness increases the marginal cost of interest to the country, there is an incentive to reduce debt quickly. This is accomplished by exports, which require environmentally harmful production. The theoretical results tend to support assertions that the debt crises of the last two decades have had negative environmental effects. They also support some form of income transfers in the form of debt-for-nature swaps or other debt-relief assistance from rich creditor nations to poor debtor nations. Also, the stronger the transnational environmental effects of the debtor country's activity are (e.g., CO_2 released from deforestation), the stronger is the case for some form of international debt relief.

7 Strategic Behavior in Trade and Environmental Policy

Much of the analysis described in this chapter assumes competitive markets. In recent years, trade models based on oligopolistic market structures have proliferated, which has given rise to the analysis of strategic trade theory and strategic trade policy. The "strategic" term does not refer to either the centrality of certain industries in the economy or carry a military or defense connotation, but rather implies that the number of firms and governments is sufficiently small for the actions of one agent to affect the behavior of others. A popular approach has been to analyze "rent switching" trade policy, in which government policy is designed to encourage home output of goods whose marginal production costs are less than price, generating economic rent.[10] The strategic interaction is between and among firms and governments. Under quite specific conditions it can be shown that national welfare can be enhanced by activist government policy departing from free trade, including import restrictions and export subsidies. For the most part, however, such strategic trade measures are "beggar-thy-neighbor" and reduce world welfare.

A number of models have attempted to blend strategic trade policy and environmental policy. This is partly because the principal instruments of strategic trade policy, tariffs and export subsidies, are strictly controlled by GATT, and more indirect instruments such as environmental policy give governments a certain flexibility.[11] Also, as examined in Chapter 13, the management of international environmental resources frequently involves interactive behavior among governments, and trade policy becomes a tool of strategic environmental policy. At a more fundamental level, the determination of optimal environmental and trade policies becomes entangled, and what may appear optimal in a competitive context may be suboptimal when strategic interactions are considered. For example, if one assumes two monopolies in countries A and B that compete for sales in country C, and if the two firms "play Cournot" in the sense that each sets its output levels on the basis of the other's output level and each assumes that the other will not respond to its own output level, and if export subsidies are not available, then each government has an incentive to reduce its emission standards

---

10 This literature originates with James Brander and Barbara Spencer (1981).
11 For a sampling of these models, see Scott Barrett (1993), Klaus Conrad (1993), Michael Raucher (1994), and Alistair Ulph (1994).

to secure a greater share of the market for its own firms. Lax environmental regulations become the instrument through which the home industry receives an implicit subsidy. But this incentive is tempered by national welfare losses resulting from emission standards set below marginal social costs. Also, the conclusion that national welfare can be increased through rent switching can be easily reversed if the firms compete on the basis of price rather than quantity, or if the welfare of home country consumers is also considered. The analysis can also be extended to include foreign direct investments. Similar to the issue of tax competition, in which jurisdictions compete for foreign investment on the basis of low tax rates, environmental regulations set to attract foreign investment can be modeled in a strategic game framework. As in tax competition, the result is likely to be suboptimal environmental protection, even in the absence of transnational pollution.[12]

The results of these models, like the strategic trade literature on which they are built, depend very much on their specifics. At the broadest level one can conclude: (1) Trade and environmental policy should be jointly formulated. (2) From a narrow national welfare perspective, pollution taxes should be lowered, or subsidies to pollution abatement be increased, to the point where the marginal benefits from rent switching equal the marginal losses from excessive pollution. (3) The welfare for the home country engaged in strategic trade policy is likely to be enhanced if it has two policy instruments such as export subsidies *and* emission taxes to obtain its two objectives of rent switching and environmental protection. (4) The global result of mutual strategic behavior is likely to be suboptimal in these noncooperative games. (5) The presence of transnational pollution lowers the national cost of promoting pollution-intensive industries, but increases the prospects that foreign governments will retaliate.

In fact, there is a certain unreality about these models. In addition to the questionable Cournot assumption, many also assume that a credible subsidy by the home government will be meekly accepted by the foreign government. Some assume that all output is sold in third countries so that consumer welfare in the home country can be ignored. Some assume international market power, some do not; some assume transnational pollution, some do not; some assume pollution from production, a few assume consumption pollution; some model output competition, a few model price competition; some assume firms are internationally mobile, others do not; and virtually all finesse the time dimension of environmental protection and the longer-term

---

12 See, for example, Kanbur, Keen, van Wijnbergen (1995).

effects of environmental degradation on productive capacity. While it is undoubtedly true that governments consider the international competitive effects of their environmental regulations, and indeed are lobbied to do so by their industries, it seems unlikely that environmental standards can or should be set by some sophisticated policy model based on the often ambiguous results of strategic trade theory.

8

Theory of Trade and Environment: A Diagrammatic Exposition

1 Introduction

Chapter 7 described how trade-environment theory has evolved. This chapter takes the next step and uses diagrammatic analysis to clarify and illustrate the linkages. The six cases, or models, are in the general equilibrium tradition and for the most part are extensions of the basic Ricardian and Heckscher-Ohlin (H-O) trade models. The general equilibrium approach has advantages and disadvantages. Its strong point is the emphasis on the interconnections among the parts of a system – in this case an open economy operating in an environmental-resource matrix. But this advantage comes with a price. Even a simplified system will have a rather large number of variables, and diagrammatic analysis, which helps us "see" interconnections and feedbacks, tends to become complex.

We believe it is desirable for students and policy makers to understand connections within an integrated system, but we recognize that not everyone will have patience to work through the rather complicated analytical diagrams in this Chapter. Therefore we start with a verbal description of the six cases, and present the general conclusions. Those readers with sufficient stamina are invited to a more thorough presentation in subsequent sections.

2 Summary of the Cases

As initially analyzed in Chapter 2, we continue to view the environment in its dual role: providing valuable services that are directly consumed – environment as a consumption good – and providing services as inputs to the production of conventional goods – environment as a producer good. The overarching questions in all six cases are the effects of trade on the environment and on appropriate environmental policy, and the effects of introducing environmental protection policies on trade.

The first three cases are in the Ricardian tradition with a single factor input and constant opportunity costs of production. Case 1 treats the environment as a nontradeable consumption good, produced with the Ricardian input, whose quantity (quality) is unaffected by either production or consumption pollution. This simple model highlights the resource-diversion effect of environmental policy and allows a straightforward analysis of the effects of environmental policy measures on trade and the implications of trade for environmental policy. Case 2 adds the assumption that the production of one good generates pollution, and pollution has a negative effect on the environment and hence utility. The level of pollution can be altered by changing the composition of output. As in the other cases, we investigate the effects of trade on environment and welfare and the effects of environmental policy on trade. Case 3 continues the assumptions of case 2 but introduces pollution abatement as a separate activity requiring the Ricardian input. This reintroduces the resource-diversion effect of case 1.

Ricardian-type models, with their tendency toward complete specialization in production, can exaggerate positive and negative trade-environment linkages. In contrast, the more realistic increasing opportunity costs in the H-O model tend to produce incomplete specialization. Also, the use of two factors, capital and labor, allows for a meaningful analysis of income distribution. Case 4, paralleling case 1 but using a simple H-O approach, again considers the environment as a nontraded consumption good, whose level and quality is unaffected by either production or consumption pollution. Because we are using a two-factor model, the factor intensity of producing the environmental good becomes important. Case 4 draws conclusions not only regarding the effects of trade on the environment and the effects of environment on trade but also concerning the effects of both trade and environment on the internal distribution of income. Case 5, using the H-O framework, parallels Case 3 in that production of one good creates pollution, pollution has a negative effect on utility, and pollution abatement is modeled as a separate activity. Virtually all of the trade-theoretic literature treats environmental services as a consumption good, with little if any discussion of possible negative effects of pollution and environmental degradation on the productivity of conventional resources. This is unfortunate as it suggests that there is generally a negative trade-off between environmental quality and conventional production (see Chapter 2) and also, due to low incomes, developing countries should adopt low environmental standards. Neither proposition is flatly wrong, but both would be overturned

Table 8.1. *The six cases*

Case	Environmental services enter:	Model type	Negative feedback from production to environment via pollution	Pollution abatement (environmental enhancement), a separate activity
(1)	Utility functions	Ricardian (one input; constant opportunity cost)	No	Yes
(2)	Utility functions	Ricardian	Yes	No
(3)	Utility functions	Ricardian	Yes	Yes
(4)	Utility functions	H-O	No	Yes
(5)	Utility functions	H-O	Yes	Yes
(6)	Production functions	Mixed	Yes	Yes

if the majority of environmental externalities affected production rather than utility directly. Case 6 does precisely this by examining trade-environmental interactions when environmental deterioration affects the productivity of conventional inputs. The distinctions among the six cases are summarized in Table 8.1.

Although the six cases differ in their structure and assumptions, three general conclusions emerge. First, the introduction of trade in an autarkic economy will improve welfare if appropriate environmental protection policies are in place, but can contribute to environmental deterioration and welfare loss if such policies are not pursued. Second, the introduction of trade generally will require some *change* in environmental protection policy, suggesting that trade and environmental policies be jointly formulated. Third, the introduction of appropriate environmental protection measures in an open economy with uncorrected externalities will change the level, composition, and gains from trade, but will be welfare-improving. Notice the asymmetry in these conclusions. Introducing free trade will generally require a change in optimal environmental policy if welfare is to be maximized. But introducing an environmental policy will not generally require a change in optimal trade policy, which remains free trade. The reason is that in these models environmental policy counters an externality; anything other than free trade creates a distortion.

3 The Six Cases in Detail

3.1 Case 1: Ricardian, No Externalities

Consider first a simple economy consisting of three goods, A, B, and E. A and B are conventional tradeable goods. E is a nontradeable environmental good (service) with public good characteristics, implying that it will not be produced without government involvement. All three goods are produced under constant costs by a single, composite input "labor" (L), which is in fixed supply. Production and consumption of A and B involve no externalities. A and B are linked to E only through their competing use of the fixed resource L. It may be useful to think of E as *created* environmental services, for example, the services of new parks or the restoration of degraded environments, where the original cause of the degradation is no longer material in an economic sense. Toxic waste dump cleanup is an example.

Suppose there is a conventional social welfare function, $U = f(A, B)$, with positive but diminishing marginal utilities, to which E can be added in the course of the analysis. The analytical approach followed in this case and in the next four cases is to establish the initial pretrade, preenvironmental policy equilibrium and compare that solution first to trade, then to the introduction of environmental protection policy to correct the public good or externality distortions. With this approach we can draw conclusions regarding the effects of trade on environment and appropriate environmental policy and the effects of introducing environmental policy on trade.

Figure 8.1 illustrates the initial, pretrade situation. A three-dimensional goods space, ABE, is depicted. With a fixed supply of the labor input, the production surface is the lightly shaded surface *abe*. With utility restricted to goods A and B, consumption indifference curves u_0 and u_1 can be drawn in the AB plane. In autarky, equilibrium is at c_0 with production and consumption at a_0, b_0 and the environmental good E not produced. The slope of *ab* in the AB plane gives relative prices, P_B/P_A, and u_0 indicates social welfare. Now introduce the possibility of trade at fixed international prices $P_B^*/P_A^* < P_B/P_A$. The production surface remains *abe*, but with a higher relative price, production shifts to the product exhibiting comparative advantage, A, at point *a*. With trade, consumption *opportunities* are the points on the ab_2e surface, but because we are still excluding E from utility, only the ab_2 edge is relevant. Consumption at international prices moves to point c_1 (that is, consumption of a_1 b_1), utility increases to u_1, and we have the familiar trade triangle, with exports a_1a and imports a_1c_1 ($= Ob_1$).

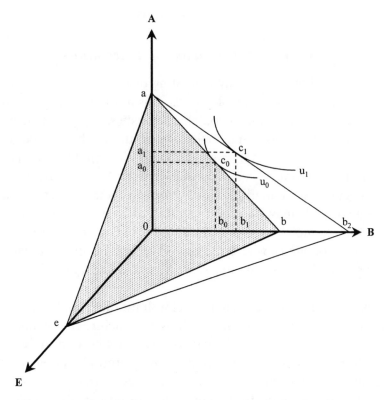

Figure 8.1. *Case 1: Environment does not enter utility function*

Now return to autarky, but allow the environmental good to enter the utility function, with A, B, and E all exhibiting positive marginal utilities. See Figure 8.2a. The production surface remains fixed at *abe*. A utility indifference surface in the three dimensions, ABE, for any given level of welfare may be visualized as a curved surface convex to the origin 0. Assume the production surface *abe* is tangent to the highest possible utility surface at some interior point, say, c_0, where welfare is maximized (for illustration, the tangency of the production surface and the highest positive utility surface are shown in Figure 8.2c). Production and consumption levels are a_0, b_0, and e_0. These output levels can be visualized by slicing through c_0 three times, parallel to the AB, AE, and BE planes. For ease of exposition, the transformation or production possibility curves between A and B are projected on the AB plane for two levels of environmental output, $E = 0$, and $E = e_0$. These transformation schedules are shown in Figure 8.2b, and are labelled *ab* (for $E = 0$) and $a'b'$ (for $E = e_0$). For higher levels of E, the transformation curve between A and B shrinks inward.

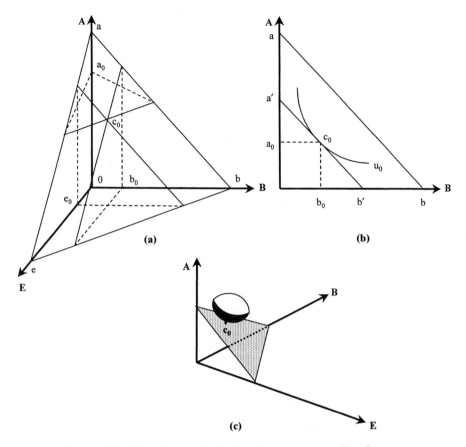

Figure 8.2. *Case 1: Introducing environment to utility function*

The results of shifting resources to produce a positive quantity of E are a decline in the production and consumption of goods A and B. This is the *resource-diversion* effect of reallocating labor input toward E production. The implicit price ratios are the slopes of the three lines cutting c_0 in Figure 8.2a, or P_B/P_A, P_A/P_E, and P_B/P_E. These price ratios reflect both the marginal rate of transformation of one good to another in production and the marginal rate of substitution (ratio of marginal utilities) in consumption. In Figure 8.2b, the transformation curve between the products A and B shifts inward from *ab* to *a'b'* and equilibrium is established at c_0. *However, the indifference curve u_0 no longer measures total welfare, as utility from the environment good, E, is not captured.* In this simple system there has to be a trade-off between E and conventional goods A and B, and the trade-off is fully determined by the production functions for A, B, and E and the social preferences among A, B, and E.

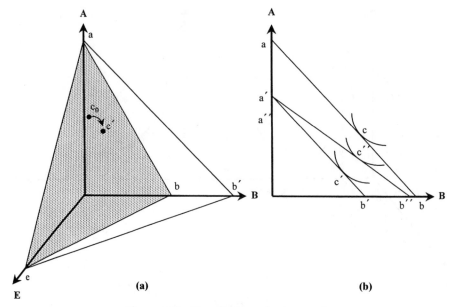

Figure 8.3. *Case 1: Introducing trade*

Now reintroduce trade, illustrated in Figure 8.3. The production surface
in Figure 8.3a remains unchanged at *abe*, as in previous diagrams. Assume
international prices $P_B^*/P_A^* < P_B/P_A$, which makes A the export good and B
the import good. Consumption opportunities now lie on the *ab'e* surface,
everywhere above the *abe* surface except along the edge *ae*. These changes
are also depicted in Figure 8.3b. The transformation function *ab* and the
equilibrium point *c* represent the pretrade position without the provision of
E. The optimal provision of E (pretrade) shrinks the AB transformation
curve to *a'b'* and equilibrium is at *c'*. Now introduce trade with the international price of A greater than the domestic price, so that A becomes the
export good and B the import good. At this point the key question is whether
the production of E is held at its initial pretrade level or whether the authorities recognize the change in relative prices and in income brought about by
the opportunity to trade, and respond by adjusting output of the public good
E. Suppose first that there is no response. With E held fixed, the AB transformation curve remains *a'b'* but the economy will specialize in A at point
a' and consume along the international price (trade) line *a'b''*, with consumption at *c''*.

We can draw the following conclusions. First, the opportunity to trade unambiguously improves welfare. Production and consumption of E remain fixed and consumption point c'' is superior to c'.[1] Second, the positive output of E reduces the output of the exportable good A ($a' < a$). This is simply the *resource-diversion* effect of allocating some labor input to the production of E. If A and B are consumed in fixed proportions, the volume and gains from trade will also fall but remain positive.[2]

However, it is unlikely that the level of E that was optimal in the pretrade situation will remain optimal in the posttrade situation. Trade has increased real income and has decreased the price of B relative to both A and E, and these will produce income and substitution effects (not shown). The optimal solution may involve more or less consumption of E and B depending on the specifics of the utility function. The important conclusions are that trade will improve welfare *and* alter optimal environmental policy. The implication is that trade and environmental policies should be coordinated.

To summarize this model, (1) welfare increases as a result of trade whether or not E adjusts from its initial to its subsequent optimal position, but the increase will be greater if E production responds to the income and price changes associated with trade, (2) the introduction of positive environmental output reduces the output of the exportable good, (3) trade is likely to be reduced, and (4) comparative advantage remains with the A good. We have drawn a possible new optimal consumption point at c' on the $ab'e$ surface (Figure 8.3a). We also conclude that trade will increase the production of the export good A, drive B production to zero, and increase or decrease the production and consumption of the environmental good E, depending on the relative strength of income and substitution effects. Consumption of B will rise due to income and substitution effects, and consumption of A may rise or fall.

3.2 Case 2: Ricardian, Externality in Production, No Separate Pollution-Abatement Activity

Case 1 makes the unrealistic assumption that the supply of the environmental good (service) is independent of production and consumption of conventional goods except through the resource-diversion channel. This case continues the Ricardian one-factor input assumption but assumes that production of one of the conventional goods has a negative effect on the quality

---

1 See part b. Having fixed E at its initial pretrade level, the consumption point c'' is better than the consumption point c' because more of both A and B can be consumed.

2 A positive output of E could conceivably increase the volume of trade if the income elasticity of demand for the exportable good A were sufficiently high.

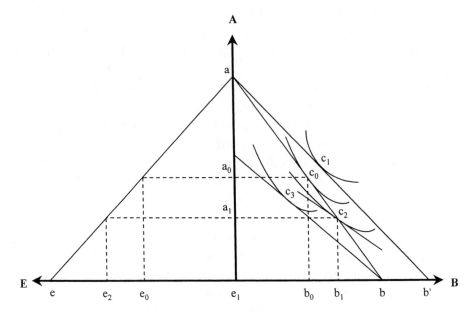

Figure 8.4. *Case 2: Effect on environment of introducing trade and effects of introducing Pigovian externality tax*

or quantity of the environmental good through "pollution."[3] We also assume that a separate activity of pollution abatement is not feasible, and pollution levels can only be controlled by altering the production of the polluting good. Specifically, assume that pollution is a joint product in the production of A, not B. For convenience, assume the relation between A production and pollution is linear and positive, and the relation between pollution and the environment, E, is linear and negative, so that:

$$E = e + \alpha A, \alpha < 0,$$

where e is environmental quality if there were no pollution. Notice that this model analyzes production, not consumption, pollution. To draw conclusions about the effect of trade on environment and the effect of environmental policy on trade, we need to investigate four situations: (1) autarky, no environmental policy; (2) trade, no environmental policy; (3) autarky, environmental policy; and (4) trade, environmental policy.

Figure 8.4 describes the initial autarkic situation and the effects of introducing trade. Given a fixed supply of labor input, *ab* is the conventional pro-

---

3 "Pollution" can be interpreted broadly to include environmental degradation associated with extraction, such as loss of wilderness areas and species habitats.

duction possibility (transformation) curve between A and B. The linear relations between production of A and pollution, and between pollution and the environmental good E, allow us to draw the relation ae in the AE space.[4] The level of the environmental good (service) increases to the left to a maximum of e when A production is zero and falls to e_1 when A production is at a.[5] If there is no trade and no explicit environmental policy, equilibrium is at point c_0, with output and consumption at a_0, b_0, and e_0. Still assuming no environmental policy, trade is introduced. If international prices, P_B^*/P_A^*, are less than the domestic autarky prices, trade leads to specialization in A at point a, and the country can trade at the international price line ab'. Welfare derived from the consumption of A and B at point c_1 increases, and the country enjoys the traditional gains from trade. But with production now specialized at a, the provision of the environmental good declines from e_0 to e_1, its minimum level. The economy has specialized in the production of the pollution-intensive good, and welfare derived from E must decline. Whether total welfare increases or decreases depends on netting the gains from trade against environmental losses, and ultimately on the explicit form of the utility function, the functions relating A output and pollution, and pollution and E, and on the divergence between autarky and international prices. This illustrates a typical second-best problem, where the removal of restrictions on trade in the presence of a second distortion, the environmental externality in the production of A, may or may not improve welfare. The net welfare gain or loss is analyzed further in Chapter 9. Note also that if international prices were such that B became the export good, specialization would be at b, and the country would enjoy both the gains from trade and an increase in the environmental good from e_0 to e. Trade would drive out the polluting industry. (In a closed global system pollution does not disappear, and trade is the vehicle for shunting pollution abroad where it may be more or less damaging.)

Now assume that in autarky pollution is controlled to its optimal level, a level allowing the environmental good to be e_2, somewhat higher than e_0. This might be accomplished by a Pigovian tax on the production of A, with revenues returned in costless fashion to consumers, or by more direct regulation of A. Either device increases the price of A relative to B. Let c_2 be the new, optimal equilibrium in Figure 8.4. Production and consumption of A

---

4 Case 1 assumed three production activities, A, B, E, and required a three-dimensional production surface. This case assumes only two production activities, A and B, and a two-dimensional production schedule is sufficient. However, the points in the AB space of Figure 8.4 no longer measure total utility as they do not capture the consumption of the environmental good E.

5 Thus E can be thought of as an arbitrary scale ranging from pristine at e to maximum polluted at e_1.

fall from a_0 to a_1, production and consumption of B rise to b_1, and supply of E increases to e_2. The relative price of A rises, as shown by the slope of the tangent line through c_2. (Recall that one cannot infer total utility from the points c_0, c_1, c_2 alone as they do not capture utility from E.) This is the optimal position in autarky.

Now introduce trade to the c_2 equilibrium. If a Pigovian tax on A is less than the divergence of prices set by the production possibility curve and the international terms of trade, production will specialize in A at point a despite the tax. Consumers, however, confront a set of relative prices that include the environmental tax on A production. Their consumption point lies some-where above c_0 and below c_1. It follows that the attempt to correct the externality through a Pigovian tax, which was successful in the autarkic situation, fails in the trade situation. Not only does the tax fail to discourage A production and thus fail to prevent the environmental good from declining to its lowest level e_1, but it distorts prices faced by consumers and does not permit attaining the c_1 consumption point. A sufficiently high pollution tax would reverse the pattern of trade; lead to specialization in the production and export of B; reduce net consumption and welfare from A and B to the interior of the AB transformation space, as shown by point c_3; but increase the supply of the environmental good to its maximum, e.[6]

The general conclusion is that a pollution tax is a very crude instrument in Ricardian-type models with their tendency toward complete specialization.[7] A direct limit on pollution or on the production of A would be more successful. Consider Figure 8.5. Instead of a pollution tax, let the authorities restrict A production to a_1 (or equivalently, restrict pollution to a level consistent with E at e_2). In autarky the relative prices of A and B adjust to clear the market at output level $a_1\, b_1$. These prices are shown as P_B'/P_A' in the diagram. Assume these market-clearing prices are greater than the international terms of trade, or $P_B^*/P_A^* < P_B'/P'_A$. There is still an opportunity for trade. Production will be at point c_2 (i.e., a_1, b_1), consumption will be at c_3, and A remains the export good. Comparing the autarky with environmen-

---

6 If the international terms of trade are such that B is the export good, no environmental policy is needed, as the polluting sector output is automatically driven to zero.

7 The underlying reason why a pollution tax is successful in autarky and not with trade needs some additional explanation. In the Ricardian model, in autarky relative costs and prices are determined by the technology of production, but the amounts of the A and B goods produced are determined by demand. Thus a tax on A alters consumer prices and the relative quantities of A and B produced and consumed. In contrast, with trade, international prices determine specialization in production. The introduction of a production tax on A has no effect on the composition of production until it is raised to a discontinuous point where A production is abandoned and replaced by B production for export. This discontinuity is inconsistent with the marginal cost-marginal benefit approach of Pigovian taxes. The practical implications do not appear important, however, if increasing opportunity costs are the norm. Allowing for pollution-abatement activity also eliminates the discontinuity.

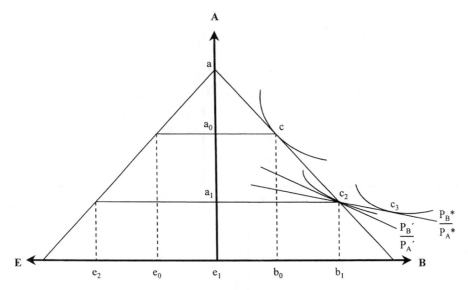

Figure 8.5. *Case 2: Effects on trade and welfare of direct control of pollution*

tal policy and the trade positions, E remains fixed at e_2, but the consumption point c_3 represents higher welfare then autarkic consumption of c_2. Unlike the pollution tax instrument, direct controls on pollution or A production allow for improvement in the environment while retaining (limited) gains from trade.[8]

3.3 Case 3: Ricardian, Externality in Production, Pollution-Abatement Activity

The assumptions of this case are similar to case 2 except that a third production activity, pollution abatement, is introduced. The level of the environmental good E then depends on two variables, the output of the polluting good A, and the amount of the primary resource, L, that is devoted to pollution abatement. Because L can now be allocated among three activities, the production of A and B and, through pollution abatement, to the production (maintenance) of the environmental good E, we return to a three-dimensional production surface, as shown in Figure 8.6a. The production surface is the shaded and tilted triangular plane *abe*. The extreme corners are at *a* (where B is zero and E is zero), at *b* (where A is zero and E is e_1), and at *e* (where A is a_1, B is zero, and E is e_1). The interpretation of E = 0 is

8 With trade it is unlikely that e_2 remains the optimal level of the environmental good.

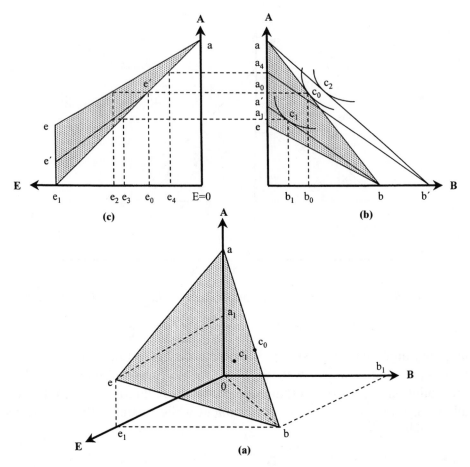

Figure 8.6. *Case 3: Effects of introducing a separate pollution-abatement activity*

that a low level of environmental services would prevail if all labor were devoted to A production and no effort at pollution abatement were undertaken.

Notice that the ABE production space is twice truncated, first along the ebe_1 face, and second along the $ab0$ face. The reason for cutting the ABE space at ebe_1 is that as one moves left along the edge ae, pollution is reduced as A production declines *and* labor is released from A production and allocated to pollution abatement. At the point e, A production has declined to the level a_1 and the combination of reduced pollution and labor released for pollution abatement means that pollution has been stopped. It follows that point e_1 represents a clean environment and maximum production of the environmental good E. Any further decline in A production releases labor for B production, and one moves along the *eb* edge, with declining A production, increasing B production and E fixed at its maximum e_1. The reason the ABE space is truncated, or cut, along the *ab0* face is that as A production declines and labor is released for B, there is an *automatic* increase in E. This is captured along the *ab* edge, with E increasing as A declines. It follows that efficient production must be a point on the production surface *abe*.

Before continuing, it is useful to project the production surface against the AB and AE planes, as is done in Figures 8.6b and c. This will facilitate the analysis of trade and environmental policy. In Figure 8.6b, line *ab* is the projection of the *ab* edge from part a. A movement from left to right along *ab* represents decreased A and increased B output. As A output falls, pollution falls, and the environmental good (service) E automatically increases. The line *eb* in part b is the projection of the *eb* edge from part a. Left to right along *eb*, A falls and B increases, but E is held at its maximum level e_1. Thus the lightly shaded triangle *abe* in Figure 8.6b is simply the two-dimensional projection on the AB plane of the production surface *abe* illustrated in Figure 8.6a.[9]

Figure 8.6c concentrates on the relation between A and E. The line *ae* is taken directly from part a and is the combination of A and E that can be produced with zero B output. The line ae_1 is the projection of edge *ab* from part a, and represents combinations of A and E that are possible if all the resources released from A are devoted to B production. Hence from right to left along ae_1, B output rises. Note that a line such as $e'e'$ describes A and E output for some constant positive level of B output. It follows that the only relevant surface in part c is the lightly shaded triangle aee_1. To summarize, in part c the point *e* represents maximum E, positive A output, and zero B output; the point *a* represents minimum E, maximum A, and zero B output; the point e_1 represents maximum E output, maximum B output, and zero A output.

Now consider E a good (service), which would be supplied free by nature at a level e_1 if there were no A production and its attendant pollution. Let E enter a conventional utility function, $U = f(A, B, E)$, exhibiting diminishing marginal utilities. Social welfare is maximized where the convex utility surface is tangent to the production surface, say, at point c_0 along the *ab* edge in Figure 8.6a. In that event and in autarky, output and consumption of A and B are determined at point c_0 (levels a_0 and b_0 in Figure 8.6b), and the environmental good is supplied at level e_0 as shown in Figure 8.6c. Even with

---

9 In part b, *eb* has a shallower slope than *ab* because left to right along *eb* labor is released from both A product *and* pollution abatement.

no explicit environmental policy, E exceeds its minimum, E = 0. Point c_0 is not a very interesting solution (except when trade is introduced). By assumption, the marginal utility gain from one more unit of E is less than the marginal utility loss from decreased production of the conventional goods A and B.[10]

Tangency of the convex utility surface to the production possibility surface *abe* at some interior point, say, c_1, is more interesting. In that event, a higher level of E can be achieved by sacrificing some conventional output and reallocating released labor to pollution abatement. Assume the production/consumption point c_1 in Figure 8.6a is realized by deliberate government policy. In Figure 8.6b this shifts the AB transformation curve inward to $a'b$, and sets a new equilibrium at c_1 indicating production and consumption levels $a_1 < a_0$ and $b_1 < b_0$. With A production now at a_1, the level of the environmental good increases to $e_2 > e_0$ (Figure 8.6c), and welfare is maximized. Incidentally, the shift from e_0 to e_2 in part c can be decomposed into that portion attributable to a decline in A production and its attendant pollution, $e_3 e_0$, and that portion attributable to deliberate pollution abatement, $e_2 e_3$.

Now consider trade. Our first autarky equilibrium is the point c_0 and our second will be the interior point c_1 shown in Figure 8.6a. Assume the international terms of trade are such that A is the export good, $P_B^*/P_A^* < P_B/P_A$. As shown earlier in Figure 8.3, the trade-consumption surface is anchored at points *a* and *e* but otherwise lies above the *abe* production surface (not drawn in Figure 8.6). Starting from autarky equilibrium c_0, and with the opportunity to trade, production specializes in A at point *a* in Figures 8.6a, b, and c. The effects are best seen in parts b and c. In part b production is at *a* and consumption at c_2 along the international terms-of-trade line ab'. Consumption of B increases (income plus substitution effect), consumption of A may increase or decrease (income *versus* substitution effect). Although the country enjoys the traditional gains from trade, the increase in A production causes pollution to increase and E to decline to its minimal level E = 0, shown in part c. The increase in pollution has eroded the gains from trade and may even reduce total welfare. While trade is the proximate cause of environmental degradation, the absence of explicit environmental policy is the underlying cause. Whereas a *laissez faire* environmental policy may have been optimal in autarky (i.e., if the initial equilibrium were at the edge solution c_0), trade makes an explicit policy desirable. Of course, if international prices were such that B becomes the export good, the country

---

10 c_0 is an "edge" solution.

specializes in B and enjoys both the conventional gains from trade and the elimination of the polluting industry.

Now consider the effects of trade if the autarky point were c_1 and an explicit optimal environmental protection policy were in place. Autarky output and consumption are a_1, b_1, and e_2. Again assume international prices such that A becomes the export good. There are three policy responses that the authorities could make. The first is to maintain at its initial level the allocation of the resource L to environmental protection. Specialization in A is then incomplete (some L allocated to pollution statement) at some level a_4, where $a' < a_4 < a$ (Figures 8.6b and c). Trade would take place somewhere along $a_4 b'$, but the volume of trade and gains from trade would be less than allowing for full specialization in A. Moreover, the environmental good E would decline from its autarky level e_2 toward e_4, and it is no longer certain that total welfare would increase. (The same level of L is devoted to abatement, but as A output increases pollution increases and E must decline.) A second policy choice would be to maintain output of the environmental good at its initial level e_2. This could be accomplished by further limiting specialization in A to a_0 (Figures 8.6b and c) and reallocating labor to increased pollution abatement. In essence, some of the labor released from B production goes to pollution abatement, holding E at e_2, and some goes to incomplete specialization in A at level a_0. But note that $a_0 < a_4$, further limiting the volume and gains from trade.

The first and second policy choices merely illustrate the trade-off between obtaining the environmental good and obtaining gains from specialization and trade. The third, optimal, policy would be to recognize that the opportunity to trade changes both income and relative prices of A, B, and E, and to seek a new optimum where the convex utility surface in Figure 8.6a is tangent to the trade/consumption surface. This would imply incomplete specialization in A and zero production of B. Production and consumption of E would most likely fall because their opportunity cost as measured by the gains from trade foregone would have increased. Nevertheless, with the new optimal environmental policy, trade must increase welfare as the trade/consumption surface lies above the production possibility surface.

Tables 8.2 and 8.3 may help keep these results straight.

General conclusions concerning trade-environment in the Ricardian models are as follows. First the introduction of environmental protection measures will tend to reduce the volume and gains from trade if the export good is pollution-intensive. If appropriate environmental policies are followed, however, the opportunity to trade increases welfare. Second,

Table 8.2. *Initial equilibrium point c_0*

	Production of A and B	Consumption of A and B	Environment
Autarky	a_0, b_0	a_0, b_0 (point c_0)	e_0
Trade	$a, B = 0$	point c_2	$E = 0$
Change	A↑, B↓	A↑↓, B↑	E↓

Table 8.3. *Initial equilibrium point c_1*

	Production of A and B	Consumption A and B	Environment
Autarky	a_1, b_1	a_1, b_1 (point c_1)	e_2
Trade (holding L devoted to E constant)	$a_4, B = 0$	along line $a_4 b'$	e_4
Trade (holding E constant)	$a_0, B = 0$	along a line $a_0 b'$ (not drawn)	e_2

trade will lead to environmental deterioration and may reduce welfare if production of the export good is pollution-intensive and no adjustment of environmental policy follows the introduction of trade. Third, and directly related, trade changes optimal environmental policy so that trade and environmental policy should be jointly considered. The new optimal policy may increase or decrease provision of the environmental good, depending on relative price and income effects. When designing the new optimal policy, a pollution tax may be less attractive than a more direct regulation of pollution, due to the tendency of Ricardian models toward complete specialization.

These conclusions are altered if the production of the export good is "clean," and the import-competing good is pollution-intensive. In that event, the opportunity to trade secures a double welfare increase, the traditional gains from trade, and the elimination of the polluting industry. What had been an optimal environmental policy in autarky may be relaxed or eliminated with trade. But joint consideration of trade and environmental policy remains desirable.

3.4 Case 4: H-O, No Externalities

Ricardian-type models have obvious limits because of the tendency toward complete specialization in production and reliance on a single-factor input. The standard H-O trade model, in which the pattern of comparative advantage and trade is the result of differences in relative factor endowments among countries and relative factor intensities in the production of goods, offers additional insights. Something meaningful can be said about the factor intensity of the environmental good. And something can be said about the effects of environmental policies on relative factor prices and the distribution of income.

This case, like the previous cases, assumes the environmental good, E, is not traded. It is produced through the application of conventional inputs, designated as capital (K) and labor (L), which can also be used to produce conventional tradeable goods A and B. As in case 1, there is no feedback from A and B production via pollution on E. The only connection between E and goods A and B is through the diversion of resource inputs, K and L. Also, similar to previous cases, the environmental good (service) directly enters utility functions with a positive sign and does not affect the production functions for A and B. Assume also that the endowments of K and L are fixed, and that the technology of production is such that A and E are equally capital-intensive relative to B, with no factor-intensity reversals.[11]

The production possibilities are depicted as the curved surface *abe* in Figure 8.7a. Note that the edges *ab* and *be* are curved, whereas the edge *ae* is linear. This follows from the assumption that A and E have the same factor intensity, and that intensity is different than B. Specifically, holding E production fixed, a reallocation of resources from A to B encounters increasing opportunity costs;[12] holding A production constant, a reallocation of resources from E to B encounters increasing opportunity costs; but a reallocation of resources from A to E, holding B production-constant, will have constant opportunity costs precisely because A and E are assumed to have identical factor intensities.

Figure 8.7a is an awkward representation of three dimensions (A, B, E) on a two-dimensional surface. It is useful to project the production possi-

---

11 That is, for any factor price ratio, w/r, $(K/L)_A = (K/L)_E > (K/L)_B$.

12 That is, the opportunity cost of increasing B production, measured by A production foregone, will increase. The reason is that resources released by A do not match resources absorbed by B (differing factor intensity). Because A is assumed capital-intensive and B labor-intensive, there is excess demand for labor and excess supply of capital. Factor prices change, with wages bid up and the return to capital bid down. Because B is labor-intensive, the cost of producing it goes up relative to the cost of producing A. Hence the opportunity cost of B rises.

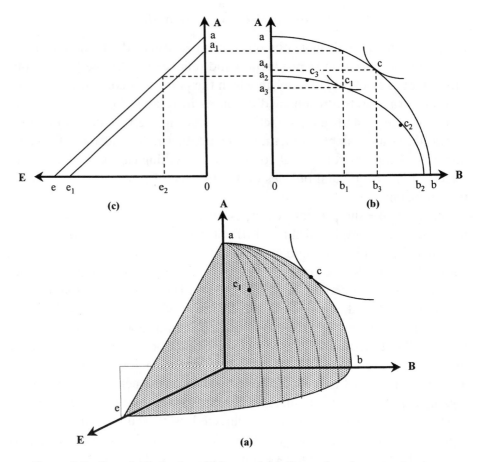

Figure 8.7. *Case 4: Heckscher-Ohlin model; effects of trade on environment*

bility surface on the AB and AE planes, as done in Figures 8.7b and c. The diagrammatic device is to trace out AB transformation curves holding E at various levels, and to trace out AE transformation functions holding B at various levels. In Figure 8.7c the linear relation *ae* is the production possibility curve holding B = 0. At some positive level of B output, say b_1, the AE production possibility curve shifts inward to $a_1 e_1$. In general, for every level of B output, a linear production possibility curve between A and E can be derived. At the same time, for every level of E output, a concave production possibility curve between A and B can be derived in Figure 8.7b. Consider, for example, output of E fixed at e_2. With zero production of B, A output is at a_2. With E still at e_2, it is possible to produce $a_3 b_1$, a second point in the AB production possibility curve. It is also possible to produce where A is zero, B is at b_2, and E is at e_2. The point A $= 0$, B $= b_2$, provides a third point and anchor for the production possibility curve between A and B, a_2b_2 corresponding to E $= e_2$.[13] In general, for successively higher levels of E output, the AB production possibility curve shrinks inward, as resources are reallocated toward E production. The shrinkage is not uniform, however, as expansion of E production, which is capital intensive, has a stronger effect on capital-intensive A production than labor-intensive B production.

With this foundation, we can follow either one of two analytical paths:

1 Establish equilibrium in the absence of trade or environmental preferences, then introduce environmental preferences, then introduce trade.

2 Establish initial equilibrium, then introduce trade, then introduce environmental preferences.

The first path addresses the effects of trade on environment; the second addresses the effects of environment on trade. Let us start with the first approach. In the absence of either trade or environmental preference, the utility function reduces to U $=$ f(A, B) and is tangent to the production possibility curve at some point along the *ab* edge, say, at point *c* in Figure 8.7a or at point *c* in Figure 8.7b. This equilibrium determines the entire system: production and consumption of A and B at levels a_4 and b_3 (Figure 8.7b); relative output prices P_B/P_A measured by the slope of *ab* at point *c*; the allocation of capital and labor between A and B; the relative prices of labor and capital, w/r; and the distribution of income between the owners of capital and labor.[14]

Now suppose a positive preference exists for the environmental good E, and the authorities respond by providing E as a public good. The utility function, U $=$f (A,B,E), now generates surfaces convex to the origin (Figure 8.7a), and the point of tangency of the production possibility surface *abe* with the highest possible utility surface maximizes social welfare. This tangency will be at some interior point on the *abe* surface, say, point c_1.[15] The effect of introducing production of the environmental good E on factor prices and the distribution of income depend critically on whether B output rises or falls. In the unlikely event that E and B are strongly complementary in

---

13 At e_2b_2, all resources are directed to either E or B; at e_2a_2, no B is produced.
14 With output of A and B fixed, there is only one efficient allocation of capital and labor between A and B production. With competitive input markets, the ratio of the marginal products of capital and labor equals the ratio of the prices of capital and labor. With fixed input supply of capital and labor, determining their relative prices also determines the distribution of income between capital and labor.
15 At c_1 the marginal rates of substitution in consumption between A and B, between A and E, and between B and E are equal to the slopes of the production-possibility surface in the AB, AE, and BE planes.

consumption, B output may increase. In that event there will be net excess demand for labor and net excess supply of capital at prevailing factor prices,[16] and factor prices and income distribution will shift in favor of labor. The more likely outcome is the substitution of E for both A and B consumption, net excess demand for capital and excess supply of labor, with factor prices and income distribution shifting toward capital.[17] These possibilities are depicted in Figures 8.7b and c. With strong complementarity between E and B, the production/consumption point could shift to point c_2 in part b; more likely it would shift to a position such as c_1. At c_1, output and consumption levels are a_3, b_1, e_2. The "cost" of the environmental good is A and B production foregone, that is $a_4 a_3$ and $b_3 b_1$.

The next step is to introduce trade. Assume international prices $P_B^*/P_A^* < P_B/P_A$ at the pretrade equilibrium point c_1. If output of the environmental good E is held constant at e_2, the country tends to specialize in A production and to export A in exchange for B. This means a leftward movement along $a_2 b_2$ toward a new production point, say, c_3. The commodity price, factor price, and income distribution effects are well known; the price of B declines relative to A, the labor wage falls relative to the return to capital, and the distribution of income shifts toward capital.

The more interesting question follows the second analytical path, that is, the comparison of trade with and without production of E, as shown in Figure 8.8, which reproduces Figure 8.7b. The parallel lines p^* and $p^{*\prime}$ represent international prices and determine two production points, c_4 (without E production) and c_3 (with E production at e_2). To concentrate on the supply side, assume A and B are consumed in fixed proportions along the ray oz_1. Without any E production, but with trade, output is at c_4, consumption is at g, and the trade triangle is composed of $c_4 f$ units of A exports and fg units of B imports. With positive production of E at some arbitrary level e_2, production is at c_3 and consumption is at j with $c_3 h$ units of A exports and hj units of B imports. Comparing the two trade triangles $c_4 fg$ and $c_3 hj$, it is clear that positive production of the nontradeable E reduces the volume of trade. However, it is also clear that trade improves welfare whether or not there is positive production of E. This can be seen by the consumption points j and g falling outside the respective transformation curves, $a_2 b_2$ and ab. The decline in trade is simply the resource-diversion effect from the tradeable to the nontradeable. But the *ratio* of A to B production also falls as positive production of E is introduced, indicated by the slopes of z_3 and z_2. Not only

16 By implication, the net change in A+E output must be negative.
17 Recall that A and E are assumed equally capital-intensive relative to B.

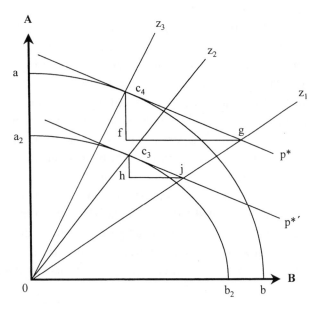

Figure 8.8. *Case 4: Heckscher-Ohlin model; effects of environment on trade*

has trade shrunk, but specialization in production has decreased. Diversion of the resource inputs, capital and labor, to capital-intensive E production has reduced comparative advantage in the export good A. This results from the similarity in capital intensity between E and the export good A. Had E been labor intensive, the volume of trade would also tend to shrink, but there would be greater specialization in A production.

The final step is to recognize that the opportunity to trade changes both real income and the implicit prices between A and E and between B and E. Thus the optimal provision of the environmental good E is likely to change. Little can be said *a priori* without further specification of the utility function. As compared to the autarkic equilibrium shown as point c_1 in Figures 8.7a and b, we expect a positive income effect on E if it is a normal good. However, the price of E rises relative to B. Thus the optimal consumption of E may rise or fall, but will likely fall relative to B. In general, the higher the income elasticity of demand for E and the stronger the complementarity of B and E in consumption, the more likely the optimal output of E will increase. Allocating increased resources to E would, of course, shift the AB transformation function and initiate second-round effects on production and trade, but these are not shown in the diagram.

Four conclusions can be drawn from case 4. First, quite apart from trade, the introduction of a capital-intensive environmental good tends to increase the price of the capital-intensive conventional good and shift factor prices and income distribution in favor of capital. Second, comparing the trade solution with and without provision of the environmental good, the provision of the environmental good reduces the volume of trade, the conventional gains from trade, and the extent of specialization. Third, while provision of the environmental good will reduce the gains from trade, trade is always welfare-increasing. The essential reason is that, like case 1 but unlike cases 2 and 3, there is no negative feedback from production to the environment via pollution. Fourth, as in the previous cases, trade changes the optimal provision of the environmental good, which may rise or fall depending on income and substitution effects. These results are consistent with the parallel case 1, but now take account of the factor intensity of producing the environmental good relative to the tradeable goods, and also allow conclusions concerning factor prices and income distribution.

3.5 Case 5: H-O, Externality in Production Affecting Utility Functions

This case continues with the H-O model. As in case 3, assume the production of one good, A, causes pollution, and that pollution diminishes the quantity of an environmental good, E, available for direct consumption. The two inputs to production, capital and labor, can be used for the production of goods A and B, or can be used for pollution abatement, thus indirectly supporting the availability of E. It follows that E output is negatively related to A output (via pollution) and positively related to inputs used for pollution abatement. For simplicity, assume that the relations (1) between A production and pollution and (2) between pollution and the availability of E are linear, the first positive and the second negative. Also, assume the activity of pollution abatement and the production of A are equally capital-intensive relative to B production.

Figure 8.9 depicts the production possibility surface for A, B, and E as *abe*. The edge *ae* holds B production at zero and traces out the (linear) production possibility curve between A and E. As A declines along *ae*, pollution declines *and* capital and labor are freed up for pollution abatement. At corner *e*, the combination of declining pollution from A and increasing pollution abatement brings pollution to zero and E to its maximum level.[18] Further declines in A production free up resources for B production along

---

18 We ignore the possibility that additional E can be "produced" beyond the level of zero pollution.

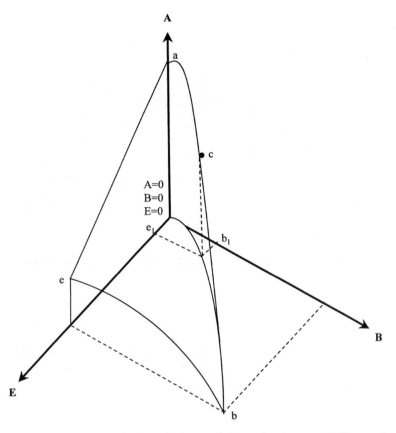

Figure 8.9. *Case 5: Heckscher-Ohlin model; production possibility surface*

the edge *eb* (concave due to different capital intensity between A and B). At corner *b*, B and E are at maximum levels; A output is zero. The edge *ab*, curved in both the AB and EB planes, traces out the loci of A, B, and E production if no deliberate pollution abatement is undertaken. For instance, moving from point *a* to point *c* reduces A production, allowing B to increase from b_0 to b_1. At the same time, reduced A output, working through reduced pollution, allows for an increase in availability of the environmental good from e_0 to e_1. While the edges *ae* and *eb* are production-possibility curves holding the third good constant, all goods, A, B, and E, change along the *ab* edge.

Figure 8.9 is again awkward, and it is useful to project the *abe* surface on the AE and AB planes, as is done in Figures 8.10a and b. The interpretation of this diagram is as follows. With fixed supply of capital and labor and with full employment, combinations of A, B, and E are restricted to the lightly

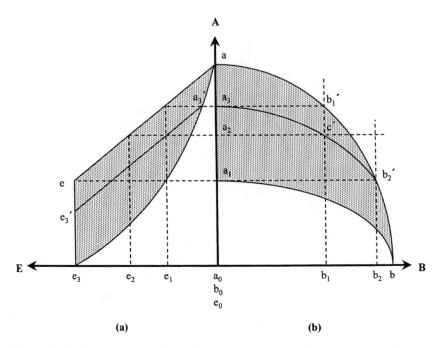

Figure 8.10. *Case 5: Projection of production possibility surface on AE and AB planes*

shaded area aee_3 in Figure 8.10a and the area aba_1 in Figure 8.10b. In general, fixing the output of one good identifies a production-possibility curve between the other two goods.[19] For example, in Figure 8.10a, if B is fixed at b_0, or zero B output, the production-possibility curve between A and E is the (linear) curve ae. If B is fixed at b_1, the AE trade-off is along $a_3'e_3'$. Alternatively, if we fix E at its maximum level e_3, the production possibility curve for A and B in Figure 8.10b is shown by a_1b. If we fix E at a lower level, say e_1, the AB production-possibility curve is a_3b_2'.[20] Note that the curves a_1b and a_3b_2' in Figure 8.10b are production-possibility curves for A-B, holding E at fixed levels. The outermost curve ab, however, is maximum AB combinations when E varies from e_0 to e_3. Finally, if we fix A at some intermediate

19 The exceptions are point a, where B and E are fixed at zero level, and point b, where A is fixed at zero and E is fixed at its maximum level, e_3. Fixing any two output variables, of course, determines the third.
20 Greater B output shrinks the AE production-possibility curves in part a; greater E output shrinks the AB production-possibility curve in part b.

level between a_1 and a, say, a_2, we can read off consistent pairs of B and E in parts b and a, respectively. For example, at the point a_2b_1 in Figure 8.10b, the corresponding E must be e_1. Alternatively, if we fix A at a_2 and subsequently fix B at b_0, this is consistent with an E output of e_2.

The preceding clarifies the supply capabilities of the economy. Now assume a social utility function, $U = f (A,B,E)$ with conventional properties (i.e., positive but diminishing marginal utilities). As in the previous cases, welfare will be maximized at the point of tangency of the production possibility surface *abe* (as depicted in Figure 8.9) and the highest possible utility surface. Again there are two possibilities. First, the tangency may be along the *ab* edge, say, at point *c*. In that event, environmental output at level e_1 (Figure 8.9) will be positive and exceed its minimum, $E=0$, but no specific allocation of capital and labor to pollution abatement is undertaken (or warranted). A second possibility, tangency at some interior point on the *abe* surface in Figure 8.9, would require diverting some capital and labor from A and B production to pollution abatement. Such a tangency can be represented by point *c'* in Figure 8.10. A, B, and E are determined at levels a_2, b_1, and e_1.

We now wish to analyze the introduction of trade. The effects will be determined by the initial situation and the policy response. Consider first an autarkic equilibrium in which there is no explicit environmental policy. (This would correspond to point *c* in Figure 8.9). The two-dimensional representation is given at point *c* in Figure 8.11b. Initial values of A, B, and E are a_1, b_1, and e_1. Assume that international prices for the two tradeable goods A and B are such that A becomes the export good. In the absence of any explicit environmental policy, production moves from *c* to *p'* with an expansion of A output and a contraction of B output. The availability of the environmental good, E, falls from e_1 to e_2 due to increased pollution. The consumption of A and B also responds to the relative price and real income change associated with trade. For expositional purposes we assume fixed AB consumption along the ray *occ'*, forming the familiar trade triangle *fp'c'* with *fp'* exports of A and *fc'* imports of B.[21] The welfare effect of trade can be positive or negative, depending on whether the welfare increase from A and B consumption exceeds or falls short of reduced availability of E. Note also that if international prices are such that B becomes the export good, welfare unambiguously improves through the traditional gains from trade and the increased availability of the environmental good.

21 More likely, consumption of B will increase relative to A as relative prices shift.

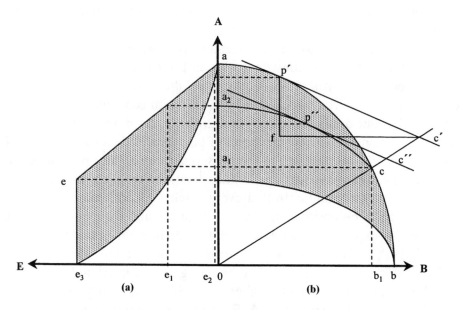

Figure 8.11. *Case 5: Introducing trade to Figure 8.10*

While trade *may* worsen welfare, if no explicit environmental policy is followed, a production point can be found that unambiguously increases welfare as the economy moves from autarky to trade. Suppose the authorities act to fix the environmental good at its initial pretrade level e_1 through appropriate pollution abatement. AB production possibilities are then along the curve a_2c. Production with trade is at p'' and the economy can trade along the international price line and consume at c'', superior to point c, while maintaining consumption of E at its initial level e_1. Welfare has clearly increased. But the volume of trade and gains from trade are less than they were at p'. As a more general point, the introduction of trade, by changing relative prices among A, B, and E, and by increasing real income, will determine a new optimal production and consumption set between A, B, and E, depending on the relevant elasticities. Optimal consumption of E may rise or fall. This again reinforces the desirability of joint consideration of trade and environment policy.

Much the same conclusions obtain if the initial autarky point is on the interior of the *abe* surface in Figure 8.9, indicating deliberate pollution abatement. The effects of trade are shown in the two-dimensional Figure 8.12. The initial equilibrium production and consumption is at point c, with A, B, and E at the levels a_1, b_1, and e_1. Note that the level e_1 is achieved

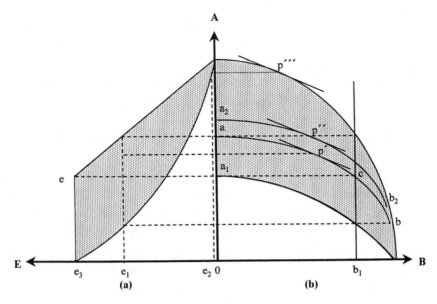

Figure 8.12. *Case 5: Introducing environmental protection to
an initial trade situation*

through the application of capital and labor to pollution abatement. If international prices are such that A is the potential export good, the market pressure is for an expansion of A output at the expense of B and possibly E. The
effects of trade depend on the environmental policy response. At one
extreme, the authorities could maintain a commitment to the initial level e_1,
production could move along the AB production-possibility curve to point
p', and trade could occur along the international price line. Note that because
A output increases, a commitment to e_1 requires a larger allocation of capital
and labor to pollution abatement; some of the resources released by B go
to A production and some to maintaining E at e_1. This response ensures an
increase in welfare, but may not be optimal.

A second response might be to hold the allocation of capital and labor
to pollution abatement constant. In that event, E would decline (higher A
output implying higher pollution) but the AB production possibility curve
would shift outward, illustrated by the curve a_2b_2. With production at p'', the
volume and gains from trade are larger than the first policy response, but
with some decline in E. The welfare effect is ambiguous. At the extreme,
the policy response to trade opportunities might be to abandon deliberate
efforts at pollution abatement and locate production at point p'''. While this
policy maximizes trade and the gains from trade, the environmental good

falls sharply to level e_2. Our reason for including this extreme is that it illustrates the effects of starting from a trade situation and introducing a deliberate environmental protection policy. Specifically, if the initial posttrade, preenvironmental policy situation is at p''', establishing an environmental goal equivalent to e_1 forces production to point p', and the effects of the environmental policy on reducing the volume and gains from trade become clear.

As a final point, the introduction of trade from an initial autarkic position has the effect of decreasing the production of B. The factor price and income distribution consequences are similar to earlier cases; with A and E assumed equally capital-intensive relative to B, the price of capital relative to labor increases and income distribution shifts away from labor. And if the initial situation is trade without deliberate environmental policy, as at point p''' in Figure 8.12, the introduction of positive environmental policy increases the absolute production of B, increasing the relative price of labor and shifting income distribution in its favor. At first glance this is a curious result, as pollution abatement (the production of E) was assumed to be capital intensive. But the positive environmental policy also involves declining production of A, and the net result will be excess supply of capital and excess demand for labor at initial prices.

3.6 Case 6: Externality in Production Affecting Production Functions

Cases 1 through 5 and most of the studies reviewed in Chapter 7 assume that the environmental good or service enters utility functions with a positive sign. This was not always obvious in the literature review, as the conventional treatment turned the problem around and considered the waste absorptive function of the environment as an "input" to production along with capital and labor. Nevertheless, in these models the diminished supply of environmental services resulting from pollution had a direct negative effect on utility, not a negative effect on conventional production functions. As shown in cases 1 through 5, this approach does permit the models to consider supply of environmental resources and demand for environmental services together with the pollution intensity of products in determining comparative advantage. It also permits analysis of the income-distributional effects of environmental policy in a trade context. Nevertheless, treating environmental externalities as direct negative effects on welfare diverts attention away from the frequent externalities that reside within and among production sectors. These seem especially important in developing countries that rely on natural-resource-based production, where evidence of environmental deterioration affecting production is widespread. The allocation model presented in Chapter 2 demonstrated that although there may be a negative trade-off between environmental quality and conventional output when environmental services are directly consumed (as confirmed in cases 1 through 5), there can be a *positive* relation between environment and conventional output when environment affects production functions.

Environmental externalities with an adverse effect on production can take a variety of forms. In some instances, the externality is contained within the sector itself – for example, the effects of soil erosion and salinization from inappropriate agricultural practices reducing agricultural yields. In other cases, the effects are between different production sectors: erosion from upland agriculture has been implicated in damages to coastal fisheries. In many instances, dynamic analysis is needed to capture the cumulative detrimental effect of environmental degradation on future production. In either event, and in contrast to the earlier cases, environmental protection then tends to expand rather than shrink the production-possibility curve.

This case analyzes a simple and rather artificial situation in which production in one sector, through "pollution," enters the production function for a second sector, with a negative sign. The example is static and does not accommodate cumulative environmental damages. As in the previous cases, the ultimate purpose is to analyze the effect of trade on the environment and the effect of the environment on trade, but first the autarkic situation must be examined. Assume two potentially tradeable products, manufactures (M) and agriculture (A). Manufacturing output is assumed to be a linear function of a composite input called labor (L), and it also produces pollution as a joint product. In turn, pollution has a negative linear relation with an index of environmental quality, E. Agriculture is produced with a neoclassical production function exhibiting constant returns to scale, with E and L as substitutable inputs in the relevant range. Labor can also be used in a third activity, pollution abatement. We assume a positive linear relation between the input of labor for pollution abatement and the environmental variable. Total labor supply is fixed at $\bar{L}$ and in the absence of pollution, E is fixed at $\bar{E}$. The utility function includes consumption of agriculture and manufactures, but, to keep the focus on production, does not include directly consumed environmental services. Thus the production functions for manufactures and agriculture are joined in an asymmetrical fashion. Increased production of agriculture merely diverts the composite input labor away from manufactures output, whereas increased production of manufacturers

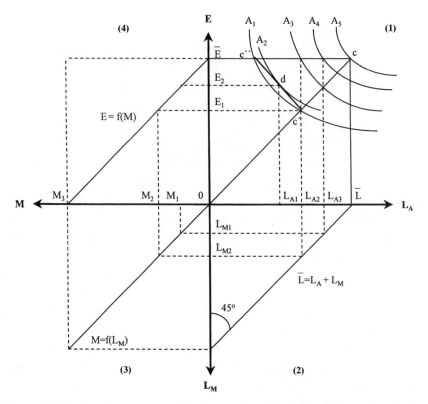

Figure 8.13. *Case 6: Negative effect of pollution in manufacturing sector on production function for agriculture*

involves both diversion of labor and, through pollution, reduces the availability of the environmental input for agricultural production.

We first wish to investigate the production-possibility curve between agriculture and manufactures. This is done with the aid of Figure 8.13. Quadrant 1 displays the total endowments of labor, $\bar{L}$, and the freely provided environmental input, $\bar{E}$. It also contains an isoquant map for agricultural production, $A_1 \ldots A_5$. Quadrant 2 allocates total labor supply, $\bar{L}$, as between agriculture (L_A) and manufactures (L_M). Quadrant 3 displays the linear production function for manufactures, and Quadrant 4 contains the negative linear relation between manufactures output, M, and the environmental variable when no pollution abatement is undertaken.

If there were no pollution associated with manufactures output, the production-possibility curve between A and M can be derived directly from Figure 8.13. For example, given an allocation of labor L_{A3} and L_{M1} and the endowment of the environmental input, $\bar{E}$, then A_4 and M_1 are produced.

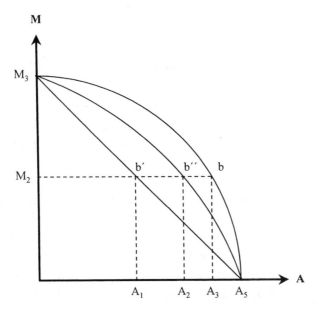

Figure 8.14. *Case 6: Three production possibility curves: no pollution, pollution without pollution abatement, and optimal pollutional abatement*

Given an allocation of L_{A2} and L_{M2}, A_3 and M_2 are produced. These trace out a concave production possibility curve M_3bA_5 in Figure 8.14. It is concave because with E fixed at $\bar{E}$, increasing labor devoted to agriculture encounters diminishing marginal returns (whereas labor devoted to manufacturing exhibits a constant marginal product).

If, instead, uncontrolled pollution from manufacturing is present, increasing the output of manufactures reduces the availability of E, and the resources available for agricultural output decline along the ray *oc* (Figure 8.13). For instance, starting from point *c*, a reallocation of L_{M2} labor away from agriculture to manufactures leaves L_{A2} in agriculture and decreases the environmental input from $\bar{E}$ to E_1. Agricultural output falls from A_5 to A_1. The implication is that for any agricultural labor allocation, $0 < L_A < \bar{L}$, the output of agriculture is *less* than it would have been without pollution. The *with*-pollution case traces out another production possibility curve, $M_3b'A_5$ in Figure 8.14. The constant returns-to-scale assumption in agriculture production now implies a linear production-possibility curve between A and M.[22] The two production-possibility curves M_3bA_5 and $M_3b'A_5$ in Figure 8.14

22 For presentational convenience, we assume the slopes of $M=f(L_M)$ and $E=f(M)$ are the same, thus establishing the locus of E and L along the ray *oc* in quadrant 1. With constant returns to scale in agriculture, this implies a linear relation between the output of manufactures and agriculture, that

have the same anchors because at M_3 no agriculture is produced and the pollution does no damage, and at A_5 there are no manufactures and hence no pollution.

However, the production-possibility curve $M_3b'A_5$ is unlikely to be an efficient allocation of resources. Consider, for example, point c' in Figure 8.13, representing a labor allocation of L_{A2}, L_{M2}, environmental input E_1, and output levels A_1 and M_2. If labor in manufacturing is held constant at L_{M2}, a portion of the remaining labor can be devoted to pollution abatement with an increase in E. The positive functional relation between labor allocated to pollution abatement and the environmental variable is shown by the linear segment $c'c''$ (quadrant 1). It follows that if the marginal product of L in environmental protection is greater than the slope of the A_1 isoquant at point c' (the ratio of the marginal products of labor and environment in the production of agriculture), it will be more efficient to devote some L to pollution abatement. Given manufactures output at M_2, agricultural output is maximized at level A_2, where the marginal product of labor in environmental protection is equal to the ratio of the marginal products of labor and environment in production of A (the slope of the A_2 isoquant). This is shown as point d in the figure, and the environment is partially restored to E_2. The optimum allocation of labor is thus $O\text{-}L_{A1}$ in agriculture, $L_{A1}\text{-}L_{A2}$ in pollution abatement, and $L_{A2}\text{-}\bar{L}$ $(=L_{M2})$ in manufactures. The output point in Figure 8.14 is labeled b'' and indicates output levels M_2 and A_2. The environmental variable is at level E_2.[23] A similar procedure at different levels of manufactures output generates the third production-possibility curve $M_3b''A_5$ in Figure 8.14. This lies everywhere above the linear schedule $M_3b'A_5$ except at the anchor points. At M_3, agricultural output is zero, so no damage is done to agriculture and no pollution abatement is warranted. At A_5, there is no manufactures output and hence no pollution. For intermediate points, however, efficient resource allocation requires some diversion of labor toward pollution abatement. The intuitive explanation is that so long as the marginal productivity of labor in protecting the environment and hence contributing indirectly to agricultural output is higher than its direct marginal productivity in agriculture, some labor should be allocated to environmental protection.

is, line $M_3b'A_5$ in Figure 8.14. If the slopes of the two functions differed, the locus of E and L in quadrant 1 would be linear and anchored at c but would not pass through the origin. In that event, the transformative curve between M_3 and A_5 in Figure 8.14 would still be anchored at M_3 and A_5 but would be somewhat concave. Within a certain range, the conclusions presented next would still hold.

23 If the slope of $c'c''$ exceeds the slope of the relevant A isoquant along the segment $\bar{E}c$, there is a corner solution, and the pollution abatement effort is sufficient to hold E at its maximum, $\bar{E}$.

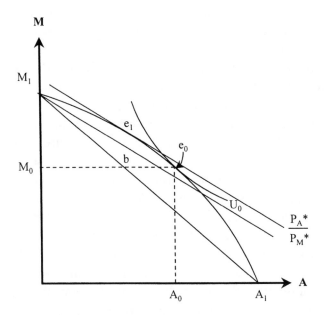

Figure 8.15. *Case 6: Introducing trade*

The preceding represents the supply side of the economy. Demand can be introduced using indifference curves between agriculture and manufactures, as shown in Figure 8.15 (recall that environment has no independent value except as an input to agriculture). In Figure 8.15 $M_1 b A_1$ is the inefficient linear transformation curve in which pollution abatement is neglected. The curve $M_1 e_0 A_1$ is efficient allocation. If optimal pollution policies are in place, general equilibrium is at e_0, with welfare reaching level U_0. This point determines A and M output at M_0 and A_0, the allocation of labor among agriculture, manufactures and pollution abatement, and the level of the environmental variable E. If pollution abatement is not in place, the economy is constrained to the linear curve $M_1 b A_1$ and a lower level of welfare (not shown).

The introduction of trade can have some unexpected results, in part due to a tendency toward complete specialization. Assume the initial autarky position is one of uncontrolled pollution, with production and consumption along the production-possibility curve $M_1 b A_1$ in Figure 8.15. If international prices are such that manufactures are the export good, production moves to point M_1. Pollution increases and the environment deteriorates, but trade *appears* to eliminate the need for pollution abatement, as the damaged sector, agriculture, is driven down to zero output. Welfare improves as compared to the initial autarky, no pollution-abatement situation, but may or may not reach the level U_0. Alternatively, if international prices are such that agriculture becomes the export good, production moves to point A_1. This also *appears* to eliminate the need for pollution abatement as the polluting sector, manufactures, is driven to zero output. Points M_1 and A_1 have very different environmental effects, but at both output points there is no *apparent* need for environmental protection.

Now assume that the autarkic situation included optimal environmental policy, and the economy was in equilibrium at e_0 (Figure 8.15). If the world-relative price of manufactures versus agriculture were sufficiently high or low, production would again be driven to either M_1 or A_1, and no pollution abatement would be needed or warranted.[24] If, however, international prices were closer to domestic autarky prices, for example, P_A^*/P_M^* as shown in the diagram, production would shift to point e_1, and some level of pollution abatement would be warranted. As can be seen in Figure 8.13, as the relative share of manufactures in total production increases, the level of E declines and ultimately the optimal amount of labor allocated to pollution abatement also declines. In this model, specialization in the "dirty" sector ultimately decreases the need for environmental protection. Of course, if trade expands the share of agriculture in total production, the level of E increases and the optimal amount of labor devoted to pollution abatement will also change.[25] Specializing in the "clean" industry may increase the need for environmental protection until specialization is complete.

The preceding examines the effect of trade on the environment and environmental policy. We can also note the effect of environmental policy on trade and welfare. As a starting point, consider in Figure 8.15 a posttrade, preenvironmental policy situation in which the country is producing at point M_1 and can trade along an international price line parallel to P_A^*/P_M^*. While it might appear that no environmental protection is warranted (as agricultural output is zero), in fact, pollution abatement would shift the entire production-possibility curve outward, except at the anchors; the new equilibrium would be at e_1, specialization would be incomplete, and welfare must improve as the country can now trade along P_A^*/P_M^*. The opportunity to trade *and* appropriate environmental policy both contribute to increasing welfare.[26] A failure to recognize the welfare-enhancing effects of pollution

---

24 This is, of course, a very static view. If pollution caused long-term damage to agricultural production, and relative prices changed over time, current pollution abatement could be warranted.

25 Up to this point where E reaches its maximum, $\bar{E}$, the corner solution.

26 Depending on demand, the introduction of environmental policy may reduce the volume of trade. Note also that similar results obtain if agriculture were the export good. While it might appear that no environmental policy was warranted because there was no pollution, welfare could be increased by incomplete specialization along the $e_0 A_1$ segment of the $M_1 e_0 A_1$ production-possibility curve provided international prices did not depart too radically from autarky prices.

abatement is similar to a policy failure due to nonconvexities discussed in Chapter 6.

To conclude, case 6 is generically different than cases 1 through 5 in that environmental degradation undermines productive capacity. The productive factor, labor, should be allocated so that its marginal productivity directly producing agriculture is equal to its indirect contribution, through pollution abatement, to maintaining the quality of the environmental variable that is also used in agricultural production. The introduction of trade changes the optimal production mix between agriculture and manufactures, and hence changes the optimal amount of pollution abatement. This underscores the desirability of joint consideration of trade and environmental policy. While it is possible that trade leads to complete specialization in either agriculture or manufactures, and no pollution abatement is warranted, specialization itself is not a sufficient condition for ignoring pollution. Some level of environmental protection could result in incomplete specialization and a higher level of welfare.

9

Theory of Policy: Partial Equilibrium, Terms of Trade, and Distributional Issues

1 Introduction

Partial equilibrium analysis has long been applied to trade policy and environmental policy. While the interconnections among markets and between aggregate production and consumption are suppressed, the greater simplicity of the partial equilibrium approach allows for a more detailed focus on particular market and policy features. This chapter extends and amplifies the general equilibrium analysis in Chapter 8 with partial equilibrium tools. The emphasis is again on the effects of trade and trade policy on the environment and the effects of environmental policy on trade.

Section 2 starts with a standard welfare economic analysis of externalities in production and consumption set in a trade context, and examines the effects of corrective environmental policies. It demonstrates how uncorrected production externalities constitute a subsidy and a distortion to international trade. As a general proposition, it is easy to show that the first-best policy response to externalities in production and consumption is to correct the distortion at its source, which means either controlling production if pollution abatement is not feasible or taking measures to control pollution, which will indirectly reduce output. Using trade policy in general will create by-product distortions and may worsen welfare. Nevertheless, first-best policies may be unavailable or ignored by governments. Section 3 delves into the murky world of the second-best. The analysis of trade policy with continuing domestic distortions has a long history (Johnson 1966) and its relevance to environmental externalities has been investigated by Anderson (1992b), Snape (1992), and Lloyd (1992), as well as by Copeland (1994) and Dean (1995), reviewed in the Chapter 7. Section 3 starts with the concept of an "optimal second-best" export or import tax. This is followed by a demonstration that ostensibly first-best policies such as Pigovian externality taxes may be counterproductive in a trade situation with imperfect competition domestically. The interaction of the so-called optimal tariff and environmental taxes is also considered.

Section 4 examines the effects of environmental policies on a country's international terms of trade and considers other distributional issues. One purpose is to clarify the widely used but ambiguous notion of internalizing environmental costs. Another distributional issue involves trade taxes imposed by the exporting versus the importing country. This section also compares trade and distributional effects of a variety of environmental policy instruments. These topics represent only a small fraction of the special cases that could be investigated, and we again defer analysis of trade policies for transnational pollution until later. As in Chapter 8, the approach is mainly diagrammatic to identify the range of outcomes rather than to present fully worked out mathematical models.

2 Welfare Analytics – The Basics

Consider first a small country producing a good the manufacture of which creates a negative externality such as pollution. It is immaterial whether the external cost directly reduces welfare or has a negative effect on other productive activity, as would be the case where upstream chemical pollution damages a downstream commercial fishery. Assume the externality is inherent in the production of the good rather than in the particular technique of production or combination of inputs employed. This allows us to focus on measures to restrict production, for example, a Pigovian tax on output, rather than measures to alter input combinations or production techniques such as an input tax.[1] The product under consideration can either compete against imports or be an exportable, depending on international price, which is held constant through the small-country assumption.

Figure 9.1 illustrates the import situation. S_p is the private marginal cost (supply) curve for good Q; S_s is marginal social costs including environmental damages; D_D is domestic demand; S_w represents world supply at world price P_1 (making Q an import-competing good). With no corrective environmental policies in place, Q_2 is produced domestically, Q_3 is consumed, and Q_2–Q_3 are imported. Using producer- and consumer-surplus concepts, we can identify welfare as consumer surplus plus producer surplus minus environmental costs. In Figure 9.1 notation we have

---

1 Thus in this simple example pollution is controlled by altering output of the traded good and not by a separate activity of pollution abatement. The latter could be accommodated with some additional complexity. See Chapters 3 and 8.

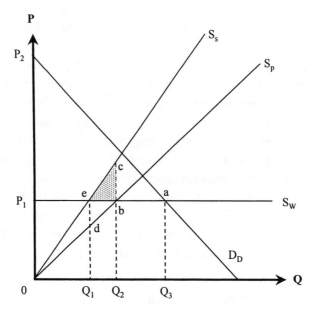

Figure 9.1. *Externalities in import competing production*

$$\text{welfare} = P_1 P_2 a + 0 P_1 b - 0cb$$

where $0cb$ is the monetary measure of environmental damages.

The welfare improvement from restricting production can be easily shown. Restricting production to the point where marginal social costs equal world price, output Q_1, would increase imports by $Q_1 Q_2$ and leave price and consumption unchanged at P_1 and Q_3, respectively.[2] Consumer surplus is unchanged but producer surplus is reduced by the area *deb*. Those who had borne the cost of the externality gain an amount equal to the area *decb*, for a net social welfare gain of the shaded area *ecb*. (A Pigovian tax set at the rate de/dQ_1 could have the same social welfare gain, but would transfer the tax revenue from producers to the government.)

Figure 9.2 illustrates the export situation. S_p and S_s are again private and social marginal costs, D_D is domestic demand, and D_w is world demand at price P_1. With no corrective environmental policies in place, Q_3 is produced, Q_1 is consumed domestically, and $Q_1 - Q_3$ are exported. Welfare is again consumer- and producer-surplus minus externality costs,

$$\text{welfare} = P_1 P_2 a + 0 P_1 b - 0cb$$

2 The policy of restricting output to control a production externality is analytically convenient but not fully realistic. More likely, government limits pollution and the producer responds by installing pollution-abatement equipment and, perhaps, restricting output.

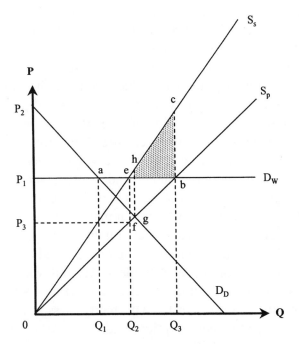

Figure 9.2. *Externality – export industry*

The welfare gain from restricting production to Q_2, where marginal social costs equal world price, can be shown. Price and consumer surplus are unchanged, exports decline to $Q_1 Q_2$, producer surplus declines by *ebf*, and the welfare of those who bear the externality damages improves by *ecbf*, for a net welfare gain of the shaded area *ecb*. (Notice that if the world price were only slightly higher than the autarky price, or if the environmental damage were sufficiently large, the optimal restriction in production could shift the product from an export to an import-competing good.)

The import-competing and export cases illustrated in Figures 9.1 and 9.2 lead to several conclusions. First, it is clear that if left uncorrected, the externality confers a "social subsidy" to the import-competing or export industry. In both cases, the marginal social cost of production exceeds the market price. Both lead to a trade distortion. In the one instance, there are deficient imports, and in the other instance, there are excessive exports. The welfare costs to the domestic economy of these distortions are the shaded areas *ecb*. The social subsidies are not financial (government grants or tax relief) and are borne directly by the victims of the pollution. The policy implications of social subsidies arising from inadequate environmental protection measures are considered in Chapters 10 and 11. Correcting the distortions will change domestic production and will appear to represent a loss of international competitiveness. This is the *competitive effect*, about which more will be said in Chapters 10 and 13. But in fact domestic welfare improves.

Second, Figure 9.2 also illustrates how in the absence of environmental policy the introduction of trade can reduce welfare. The autarkic equilibrium is at point g. The opportunity to trade at the world price P_1 creates a net producer-consumer welfare gain of abg. But the welfare loss from increased environmental costs is the area $ghcb$. If the area $ghcb$ exceeds the triangle abg, welfare falls. In general, the larger the divergence between social and private costs, the more likely trade will worsen welfare if externalities are not addressed. The situation is very different if one moves from autarky to imports of the polluting good. In that event, the traditional gains from trade are augmented by reduced externality damages. The basic point is that welfare may decline with trade if the uncorrected externality is associated with production of the exportable good, but will unambiguously increase if associated with production of the import-competing good.

The preceding analysis assumes the externality is associated with production. If instead, a negative consumption externality were present, the conclusions would be reversed. The social value of consumption is less than private value by the amount of the consumption externality. The introduction of trade at a world price below autarky price encourages domestic consumption, and the gains from trade are diminished by the associated increase in pollution damages. However, if the world trade price exceeds the autarky price, the domestic price rises to world price levels, domestic consumption falls, and the traditional gains from the export trade are augmented by a reduction in consumption-related externality costs. Also, in this situation the appropriate environmental policy – a Pigovian tax on consumption or some other more direct consumption restriction – has the effect of reducing imports in the import-competing situation and expanding exports in the exportables situation. Thus there may also be a positive "competitive effect" from introducing environmental protection policies. These conclusions are summarized in Table 9.1.

These conclusions rely on a number of restrictive assumptions: welfare is measured at the national level; the country is sufficiently small so its terms of trade are constant; pollution damages are local, not transnational; and general equilibrium effects are not important. The analysis does, however, underscore the importance of specific conditions: production versus consumption externalities; the location of the externality in the exportable or import-competing industry; and whether optimal environmental policies are or are not in place.

Table 9.1. *Welfare and trade effects of policies*

	Consumption externality	Production externality
Introduction of trade, no environmental policy		
import-competing good	W↑	W?
exportable good	W?	W↑
Introduction of environmental policy		
import-competing good	W↑ M↑	W↑ M↓
exportable good	W↑ X↓	W↑ X↑

Note: W is welfare; X is exports; M is imports.

3 The Murky World of the Second-Best

There is general agreement that the first-best method for dealing with a domestic distortion is with a domestic rather than a trade measure. The implication is that if an externality arises in, say, log harvesting, the market distortion is better approached through a production restriction on logging (tax) than an export restriction (tax). The straightforward reason is that an export tax creates a by-product distortion, to use Corden's term (Corden 1997). The by-product distortion involves an additional cost, not present with a simple output restriction. In some instances, however, the first-best policy measure may be unavailable or not feasible. This raises the question of whether a trade measure is a suitable second-best policy. This is a typical question in the general theory of the second-best, which postulates that the removal of one market distortion while leaving others in place may improve or harm welfare, depending on specific circumstances.[3]

The problem of using a trade measure for a domestic distortion is illustrated in Figure 9.3. Suppose a small country produces a natural resource product for domestic use and export, and suppose there is an environmental externality associated with its production such that social marginal production costs, S_s, exceed private marginal production costs, S_p. Similar to the analysis of Figure 9.2, the uncorrected production level is Q_4 in Figure 9.3. The optimal level, which would produce an environmental gain of *abdc* and social gain of *bdc*, could be achieved by a production tax of ab/aQ_3, reducing output to Q_3. If the production tax were unavailable, an export tax

---

3 Copeland (1994), Dean (1995), and Dean and Gangopadhyay (1997) are policy analyses of second-best situations.

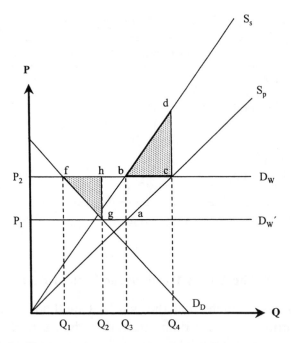

Figure 9.3. *Inefficiency of using trade measures for production externality*

at the same *ad valorem* level, ab/aQ_3, would also bring output to its target level Q_3. The export tax would shift the world demand curve as seen by domestic producers down from D_w to D'_w, reducing production from Q_4 to Q_3. But the export tax would also depress domestic price from P_2 to P_1 and divert $Q_1\,Q_2$ exports to additional domestic consumption. The incremental increase in domestic consumption of $Q_1\,Q_2$ has a value to consumers of $Q_1 fg Q_2$ (the area under the relevant portion of the demand curve) but is less than the export earnings foregone, $Q_1 fh Q_2$, by the amount of the shaded triangle *gfh*. This is the cost of the by-product distortion in consumption that was not present with the production tax or the direct restriction on output. If this cost exceeds the net environmental gain *bdc*, total social welfare will actually decline. In any event, it is clear that the welfare gain from the production tax, undiminished by any by-product distortion costs, must exceed the welfare change associated with the export tax. The general point is that the use of a trade measure to address a domestic distortion (production or consumption externality) is inferior to a policy that addresses the distortion directly (tax or direct control of the externality). All this assumes, of course, that the administrative costs of trade and domestic policies are *de minimis*.

The analysis can be taken one step further. Again, suppose the production restriction (direct or Pigovian tax) were for some reason unavailable, and the export tax were the only feasible policy. The question is then one of "optimal second-best" policy.[4] There is no longer any reason to believe that output level Q_3 in Figure 9.3 maximizes welfare – indeed, as just shown it may worsen welfare, while ostensibly protecting the environment. The optimal second-best export tax is such that on the margin the additional benefits from reducing the externality are just equal to the additional costs arising from the by-product distortion to prices. Although not drawn in Figure 9.3, this can be visualized by introducing small increases in the export tax, shifting D_w downward from its initial level. The benefit of a small increment in the tax is measured by the vertical distance between S_s and D_w, starting with the distance dc; the economic cost of the tax is the vertical distance between D_w and the domestic demand curve D_D, starting at point f. It is clear that the marginal benefits decline as the increasing tax moves production from Q_4 toward Q_3; the marginal costs rise as domestic consumption increases from Q_1 toward Q_2. The tax such that the two vertical distances are equal (marginal costs equals marginal benefit) is the optimal second-best export tax. This tax, although positive, leaves domestic production and pollution at a higher level than Q_3, the optimal level if a production tax were available. It also leaves welfare below the level that could be achieved if the appropriate production tax were available. Of course, in the event that there is no domestic consumption, an export tax is equivalent to a production tax, and the question of the optimal second-best tax does not arise.

The superiority of Pigovian taxes and similar measures over trade measures to correct production externalities quickly breaks down if other distortions persist, for example, trade restrictions and monopoly power. Indeed it is relatively easy to show that a Pigovian tax may harm welfare if a trade restraint remains in place, and that the removal of a trade restraint that protects a domestic monopolist may harm welfare if a domestic production externality remains in place. Consider a situation in which a domestic monopolist is protected from import competition through a quantitative restriction on imports (a quota) and in which domestic production creates a pollution externality.[5] A protected steel or chemical industry could serve as an example. Under these conditions, in which the monopolist has already restricted output below the socially optimal level, the *imposition of a*

---

4 This is not the same concept as the "optimal tariff," which is designed to alter terms of trade.
5 The appropriateness of Pigovian taxes in situations of imperfect competition has been investigated by Buchanan (1969) and Baumol and Oates (1988).

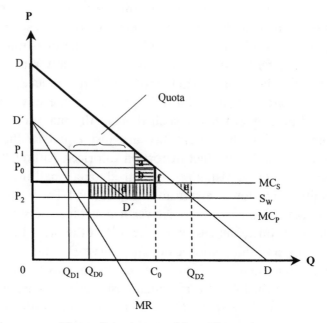

Figure 9.4. *A second-best illustration*

Pigovian tax would further restrict output and raise price. While the reduction in domestic production reduces externality damages, it also widens the distortive wedge between price and marginal social production cost. Conversely, the *removal of the trade restriction* without an appropriate externality tax could increase domestic output to the point where the marginal social costs of production exceed the social value of the product. Two policies are needed, one to correct the trade distortion and a second to address the environmental externality.

Figure 9.4 illustrates the problem. We assume an infinitely elastic foreign supply curve, S_W, (the small country assumption) to avoid terms of trade complications. We also assume that the quota rent is captured by domestic importers, and, for simplicity, that the marginal private and social costs of domestic production, MC_P and MC_S, are constant. The vertical distance between MC_P and MC_S represents the per unit cost, or damage, of the externality. Domestic demand is shown as DD. After subtracting the fixed import quota, the residual demand faced by the monopolist is $D'D'$. The monopolist's marginal revenue curve is then MR and with private marginal costs MC_P, the profit-maximizing domestic output is Q_{D0} permitting a market clearing price of P_0. Domestic production is Q_{D0} and imports, equal to the quota, are $Q_{D0}C_0$. Social welfare, consisting of consumer surplus, producer surplus, and the welfare of importers fortunate enough to obtain import licences minus the negative welfare effects endured by the victims of the externality, is the area outlined in bold. It is the area under the demand curve up to consumption level C_0 and above the kinked supply curve representing the social cost of domestic supply (MC_S) and imports (S_W).

A Pigovian tax set at the externality level would bring the monopolist's marginal cost curve up to MC_S, reduce domestic output to OQ_{D1} and increase price to P_1. The net social welfare loss due to the tax is indicated by the horizontally shaded areas $a+b$. The net loss occurs because the value consumers place on the lost consumption ($Q_{D1}Q_{D0}$) is greater than the social costs of its production.[6]

The removal of the import quota, eliminating the monopolist's market power, would also reduce welfare *if* the externality were left uncorrected. In that event, the domestic producer facing potential foreign competition would expand his output to Q_{D2}, just undercutting and eliminating imports. Price would fall to P_2. As drawn, net social welfare would decline following trade liberalization for two reasons. First, imports would be replaced by high social cost production, and second domestic production would expand to a level where social production costs (MC_S) exceed the price, P_2. These two losses are the vertically shaded areas d and e. Set against these losses as a gain is the smaller area, f. In summary, correction of either distortion, leaving the other in place, harms welfare. The optimal solution would be to eliminate the trade restraint *and* impose the Pigovian tax, in which case imports would supply the total market at a price P_2, and social welfare would be maximized. More generally, in the world of the second best where distortions persist, very little can be said about the welfare effects of partial removal of distortions without a close examination of the relevant facts.

We conclude that in a first-best world in which the only distortion is an environmental externality in production or consumption, the appropriate policy response should be directed at the source of distortion, and that a trade measure might worsen welfare. Furthermore, as a general proposition, if two domestic distortions are present, say, monopoly and an environmental externality, it would be desirable to have two separate policy instruments, and assign each to the relevant distortion. Lacking the two policy measures, it *might* still be desirable to use a trade measure even though both distor-

---

6 The distributional effects can also be tracked. Consumers and the domestic monopolist lose welfare; externality victims, government revenues, and the quota rent captured by importers with licences all increase.

tions are domestic in nature. But the trade measure may appear perverse – for example, restricting import despite a domestic monopoly. We now consider a slightly different situation in which there is a production externality and also a *trade* distortion in the form of international market power (Krutilla 1991).

The so-called optimal tariff is that restriction on imports or exports that equates the marginal benefit to a country from a terms-of-trade gain with the marginal cost of the trade distortion introduced by the tariff. The optimal tariff is only available to "large" countries that can affect the international price of their exports or imports. It is optimal only from the perspective of national welfare. From a cosmopolitan viewpoint, it is a "beggar thy neighbor" tariff and reduces global welfare. Conventional trade theory shows that the optimal export tariff is inversely related to the elasticity of world demand – the more elastic world demand, the lower the optimal tariff.[7] In the limit, a small country confronts an infinitely elastic demand and the optimal tariff is zero.

A general proposition in the theory of policy is that to achieve *n* policy objectives, *n* policy instruments are required. The implication is that for a large country with environmental externalities in production, it would be desirable to use a trade policy to secure terms-of-trade objectives (taking a parochial national view) and a Pigovian tax or other domestic measure to correct the environmental externality. This may not be possible, however, either because of international trade rules (most tariffs are "bound" in the GATT) or because of political or technical difficulties in imposing a corrective environmental tax. Two policy questions are then of interest: Is there a "second-best" Pigovian tax for the externality if trade measures are not available, and how does this differ from the traditional first-best Pigovian tax? Second, what is the optimal trade measure if policies to correct the externality are unavailable, and how does this differ from the conventional optimal tariff? A full analysis would consider both production and consumption pollution and would analyze import tariffs and export tariffs (the latter are generally not available to the United States). We restrict ourselves to a single situation, the use of a second-best Pigovian tax to obtain terms-of-trade welfare gains *and* address production pollution in an import-competing industry.[8]

Consider Figure 9.5. $S_{d,P}$ is domestic supply based on private costs. S_f is

---

7 One formulation of the optimal tariff rate, t, for a country is $t = 1/E - 1$, where E is the elasticity of import demand of the foreign offer curve.
8 For elaborations, see Krutilla (1991).

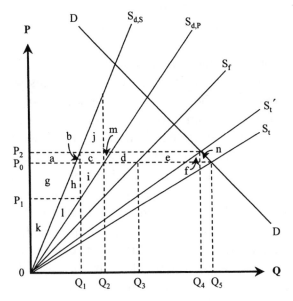

Figure 9.5. *Second-best Pigovian tax with terms of trade effect*

foreign supply, no longer perfectly elastic due to the large-country assumption. S_t is total supply, the horizontal addition of $S_{d,P}$ and S_f. DD is domestic demand. In the absence of either environmental or trade policy, equilibrium is at price P_0, with Q_2 produced domestically, Q_2 to Q_5 ($=0\,Q_3$) imported, and Q_5 consumed domestically. Now suppose that the social costs of production, including an environmental externality, can be represented by $S_{d,S}$. Assume the government responds by imposing a conventional Pigovian tax such that the tax equals marginal social damages, or a rate $P_1 P_2/OP_1$, and does so without regard to terms-of-trade consequences. The domestic supply curve inclusive of the tax shifts to $S_{d,S}$, and total supply shifts to S'_t. The results are that the world price for the good rises to P_2, the price net of the tax to producers falls to P_1, domestic production drops to Q_1, consumption falls to Q_4, and imports expand to $Q_1 Q_4 > Q_2 Q_5$.

The incidence of the tax is borne partly through higher consumer prices and partly through lower prices to domestic producers. But because of the increase in the quantity of imports, import prices also rise, an additional burden to domestic consumers. On the other hand, reduced domestic production has limited environmental damages. Unlike the standard Pigovian tax in a closed economy, the welfare effect is no longer necessarily positive. Netting out internal transfers, the welfare effect can be shown to be plus area j minus uncompensated domestic losses measured by areas $m+d+e+f+n$. The clear implication of Figure 9.5 is that net welfare loss is possible.[9]

A *second-best* optimal Pigovian tax would be lower than the standard tax and would trade off the marginal environmental gains with the marginal terms-of-trade losses. In other words, environmental policy would need to be adjusted toward lower standards (taxes) in light of terms-of-trade consideration.[10] Symmetrical results can be obtained if one works out the export example. In that case, the environmental tax has the effect of discouraging exports, increasing international price, and improving the terms of trade. The second-best optimal externalities tax would then be higher than the conventional tax. For completeness we should note that if the externality is in *consumption*, not production, the results are reversed. The second-best Pigovian tax is higher than the conventional tax in the case of an import good, and lower than the conventional tax in the case of an export good, because a consumption tax tends to decrease imports and improve the terms of trade, or increase exports, depressing the terms of trade. The general point is that optimal environmental policy will need adjustment when the terms of trade are variable. In similar fashion the optimal tariff will need adjustment when environmental externalities are present. Once again, the need to consider trade and environmental policies jointly is demonstrated.

4 Who Gains and Who Loses? Distribution Questions

Except for the discussion of the optimal tariff just described, we have assumed the country in question is "small" – that is, cannot influence international prices for its imports and exports. This section is concerned with distributional questions: who gains and who bears the cost of uncorrected

---

9 The net welfare change is the sum of changes in consumer surplus, plus producer surplus, plus government tax revenue, plus reduction in environmental damages,

$$\Delta W = \Delta CS + \Delta PS + \Delta T + \Delta ED$$

$$
\begin{aligned}
\Delta W &= (-)(a+b+c+m+d+e+f+n) && \Delta C \\
& (+)(-)(g+h+I) && \Delta PS \\
& (+)(a+b+g+h) && \Delta T \\
& (+)(i+c+j) && \Delta ED \\
&= j-(m+d+e+f+n)
\end{aligned}
$$

10 If tariffs are present, the externality tax expands imports and increases tariff revenue. This moderates the extent to which the second-best Pigovian tax is lower than the conventional first-best tax. If one started from a situation of excessive tariffs (i.e., tariffs above the optimal level set for terms-of-trade purposes), the optimal Pigovian tax would be higher than the conventional first-best tax.

externalities, and who gains and who loses from environmental protection policies? To address these questions will require relaxing the small-country assumption. In doing so, it is useful to sharpen the distinction between internalizing environmental costs and reflecting these internalized costs in product prices. Internalizing environmental costs is central to correct environmental policies. Without internalization, a wedge is driven between private and social costs distorting the decisions of producers and consumers, and incidentally creating trade distortions. This economic logic lies behind Principle 16 of the 1992 *Rio Declaration on Environment and Development*, which calls for national authorities to "endeavor to promote the internalization of environmental costs" and the related stricture that "the polluter should, in principle, bear the cost of pollution." The latter is known as the Polluter Pays Principle (PPP) and is examined in detail in Chapter 11. The ability to pass on internalized environmental costs into product prices is another matter, and of considerable concern, especially for developing countries exporting price-sensitive commodities.

We first consider the distributional consequences of uncorrected externalities, which brings us to the environmental subsidy issue. The first point to make is that in the absence of transnational pollution and in the absence of protective measures, an externality cost is borne in the country in which it occurs: The cost of a production externality is borne in the country of production and export; the cost of a consumption externality is borne by the country in which the product is consumed. This implies that the principal responsibility for corrective policies will differ between production and consumption externality situations. Furthermore, if an uncorrected production externality exists, production of that good receives an implicit subsidy. It does not follow, however, that the foreign consumer necessarily enjoys a subsidized, below-market price. If the exporting country is small, world market prices are unaffected. In this case, the implicit subsidy accrues to the producers of the pollution-intensive export and not the foreign consumer. By the same logic, import-competing firms in a small country receive an implicit subsidy if a production externality is left uncorrected. This results in excessive domestic production and a distortion in international trade.

The amount of the implicit subsidy is subject to different interpretations. Agreement on how the subsidy should be measured is important because there have been numerous proposals that importing countries should be allowed to apply countervailing duties on imports that receive implicit environmental subsidies. Consider the exportable case as illustrated in Figure 9.2. One definition of the implicit subsidy is the excess of social costs over private costs of production at the uncorrected output level Q_3. This is the area *0cb*. This view tends to exaggerate the subsidy as it implies that the optimal policy would be zero pollution and zero externality damages. It may be more reasonable to think of the subsidy as the difference between producer surplus in the uncorrected situation and producer surplus at the optimal level of production (Q_2 in Figure 9.2). But the subsidy calculation in this second approach depends very much on the manner in which the optimal level, Q_2, is to be reached. If it were done through direct restriction on production, the subsidy, defined as the difference in producer surplus with and without the correction would be the area *feb*. If it were done through a Pigovian tax and defined in similar fashion, the subsidy would then be the much larger area P_3P_1bf. The difference is that the tax forces the producer to pay marginal damage costs for the entire production. In contrast, the output restriction allows the producers to continue free use of the environment for waste disposal up to the optimum output level. While both are efficient, the former secures the rental value of the environment for the government, while the latter awards this value to producers. At this point refining the notion of the subsidy takes on an ethical coloration – who should get the rent?[11] In any event, determining the "correct" subsidy measure would bedevil any attempt to offset foreign environmental "subsidies" with border taxes – a proposal considered in more detail in Chapter 10.

Turning to international distribution, environmental protection measures internalize (some) environmental damage costs in the sense that these costs are no longer external to the producer. But in the small-country case with fixed international prices, this is accomplished by moving down the domestic supply curve rather than passing the costs on to consumers, foreign or domestic, in the form of higher prices. Thus, for a small country contemplating environmental protection measures, the principal trade concern is not an adverse movement in its terms of trade, but a loss of competitiveness in its export and import-competing industries. This *competitiveness effect* is examined in Chapters 10 and 12. Here we simply note that a small country can in principle restore a loss of competitiveness with a real depreciation of its currency, which would occur through market forces in a floating exchange rate regime. This exchange rate change has an added environmental benefit, as it will shift the composition of production toward relatively clean products, the production of which had been penalized in the initial, uncorrected externality situation.

11	In this particular example, the case for a countervailing duty on the part of the importing country is especially weak. By assumption, the exporting country is "small," and any incremental exports due to the environmental subsidy would simply displace imports from other sources by the importing country. Production, consumption, and price in the importing country is unaffected by the implicit subsidy.

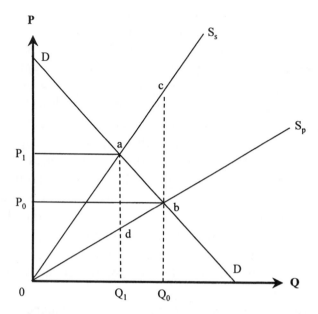

Figure 9.6. *Environmental subsidy to export*

The situation for a large country with some power over international prices is different. At least part of the cost of environmental protection measures can be shifted abroad. If, for example, the export sector is pollution-intensive, measures to internalize costs will remove a subsidy enjoyed by foreign and domestic consumers, and part of the cost is shifted abroad in the form of higher export prices. This is illustrated in Figure 9.6. S_p and S_s are private and social cost supply curves, D is export demand. An externality tax ad/dQ_1 reduces production and exports by Q_0Q_1 and prevents externality costs with a monetary value of $acbd$. It also pushes up export price from P_0 to P_1, eliminating the implicit export subsidy. While export earnings may rise or fall depending on elasticities, welfare must improve. On the other hand, if the import-competing sector is pollution-intensive and if the reference country has market power in this sector, environmental cost internalization measures will tend to increase imports, drive up world market prices and lead to an adverse terms-of-trade impact. Consumers in the importing country will pay higher prices due to their own environmental cost internalization measures and due to higher import prices even if their foreign suppliers undertake no environmental protection measures.[12]

12 It follows that the *trade partners* of countries engaged in serious environmental protection may enjoy higher prices for their exports but also pay more for their imports.

Some developing countries argue that individually they have little ability to pass on environmental protection costs in export prices because they tend to specialize in price-sensitive, homogeneous raw materials (elastic demand), whereas industrial countries that produce differentiated industrial products and confront a less price-elastic world demand can incorporate environmental protection costs in their export prices, tilting the international terms of trade against the developing countries. This argument is the basis for proposed collective action among developing country suppliers to simultaneously introduce environmental protection measures. If this can be accomplished, the exporters, acting together, may have sufficient market power to incorporate environmental protection costs in product price and improve their terms of trade. The logic of this argument only holds if pollution and environmental damages are predominantly in the exportables sector. It also requires that the demand for the export of an individual country be price-elastic and the demand for the collective supply of the product be less elastic.

Another distribution question concerns the equivalence or nonequivalence of taxes imposed by exporters *versus* taxes imposed by importers (Snape 1992). Assume a situation in which a product is produced in one country under constant private-cost conditions, but production involves an environmental externality. To keep it simple, assume that all of the output is exported to a second country. The model is depicted in Figure 9.7 with S_P, S_S, and DD the private supply, social supply, and foreign demand curves, respectively. P_0 and Q_0 are the initial price and quantity. In such a situation, the obvious policy would be an export (production) tax equal to the damages, so that the export price rises to P_1 and quantity falls to Q_1. The export tax removes the environmental subsidy to the foreign consumer, which initially was P_0P_1ab when measured by damages. Foreign welfare declines by P_0P_1cb, its consumer surplus; home country welfare increases by the export revenue collected as tax P_0P_1cd and by the reduction of environmental damages of $abcd$, for a net *world* welfare gain of abc. Notice that the redistribution from the trade partner to the home country P_0P_1cb can be large relative to the efficiency gain, similar to the large transfer versus efficiency effects found in many partial equilibrium trade models.[13]

Countries may be reluctant to tax production or exports to bring private and social costs into alignment because the volume of exports and possibly export revenues may shrink or because producers' interests may override

---

13 Snape points out that further export restriction, below Q_1, might secure monopoly profits but with a global welfare loss.

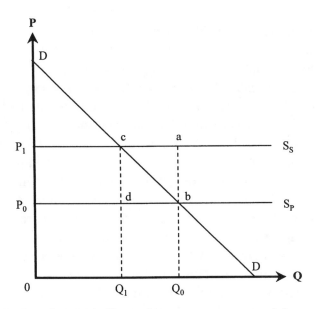

Figure 9.7. *Distributional effects of import vs. export taxes for externalities*

national interest. If the home country fails to act, the foreign (importing) country might consider an import tax set at cd/dQ_1 (again Figure 9.7). The motivation might be an altruistic concern for environmental deterioration in the polluting country, or it might be argued that the failure to act by the exporting country constitutes an environmental subsidy that should be countervailed.[14] If an import tax were imposed, the tax revenue P_0P_1cd now accrues to the importing country, and while the global benefits remain the same (area abc) the distribution of benefits shifts sharply away from the polluting country, where the welfare gain is reduced to the area abc.[15] The taxes imposed by importers and exporters are equivalent in terms of global efficiency, but have quite different distributional consequences. Indeed, confronted by a countervailing duty and reduced export volume, the polluting country might decide to scrap production entirely, removing from itself the burden of residual environmental damages, P_0P_1cd. While such a response would be inferior to a "strategic" export tax, and would reduce global

14 GATT/WTO rules regarding environmental subsidies and countervailing duties are considered in Chapter 11.
15 While it appears foolish to allow the tax revenue to accrue to the trade partner, such perversities are not unknown. In a famous case involving softwood lumber exports from Canada to the United States that were allegedly subsidized, the United States urged Canada to apply an export tax rather than apply its own countervailing duty, and Canada complied.

welfare, the exporting country would be better off with no production than continuing to export at level Q_1 and confronting the countervailing duty in its export market.

A third distributional issue concerns the instruments through which environmental protection is financed and mandated. For example, one extreme would be for the government to establish effluent and emission levels for firms (or plants) and provide direct financial subsidies to pay firms for pollution abatement costs. This approach would violate the Polluter Pays Principle (PPP) examined in Chapter 11. But it might be supported on the grounds of reducing transition costs, including unemployment, in highly polluting sectors. Also, such a policy helps maintain the international competitive position of these industries. A political economy rationale is that abatement-financing subsidies would reduce resistance in the business community to accelerated introduction of strict environmental controls. But subsidies for pollution abatement costs in the private sector would leave trade patterns distorted, with excessive domestic production of highly polluting export- and import-competing industries. For countries with some market power, tradeable goods prices would remain below social production costs, and the reference country would continue to subsidize the foreign consumption of its exports. At the macroeconomic level, the subsidies would tend to result in higher taxes on the "clean" sectors of the economy, putting them at an international competitive disadvantage.

Finally, different government policies for internalizing environmental externalities can have different international distributional consequences. Consider, for example, an externality tax versus a subsidy to industry for pollution abatement below some base level. An externality tax will increase average and marginal costs at the level of the firm. If an export industry is perfectly competitive, some firms will depart the industry, shifting long-run industry supply to the left, increasing price and reducing industry output, provided foreign demand is not perfectly inelastic. In this situation the foreign consumer bears some of the cost of the externality tax, and total pollution in the reference country is reduced. This was illustrated in Figure 9.6 for a pure export good.

In contrast, if the authorities attempt to control pollution by offering a subsidy per unit pollution *reduced* – also an incentive system – the result may be to reduce production and pollution at the level of an individual firm. But because such a subsidy reduces rather than increases long-run average costs, new firms will tend to enter the industry. The long-run result is a higher level of industry output, lower export price, and higher pollution levels – exactly opposite to the intention of the government policy.[16] In effect, the level of exports *increases* as a result of an attempt to control pollution, even though each firm sells where marginal cost equals price. Indeed, if the subsidized industry were initially in an import-competing sector, the environmental protection policy could conceivably turn it into an export good.

The international distributional effects of a Pareto tax versus a tradeable permit scheme can also be analyzed. In a simple system in which pollution from an export good is controlled through changing output levels, a tax and a permit system set to achieve the socially optimal pollution (output) level will have the same international distributional consequences when viewed in a static framework. Both will reduce industry output, raise export price, and reduce pollution. (If the permits are auctioned, the permit scheme will also tend to have the same internal distributional consequences as a pollution tax. But if permits are distributed without charge, the auction revenue foregone becomes a supplement to producer surplus under the permit scheme, and the internal distribution will differ; see Chapter 6.) However, the two systems will not necessarily have the same international effects when foreign demand changes. In a partial equilibrium context, an increase in export demand increases the Pareto optimal tax and also the optimal level of pollution permits. If the government does not adjust policy, however, the permit scheme has a greater effect on pushing up export prices than does the tax scheme. Thus the tax and the permit schemes would have different international distributional consequences. The essential reason is that the permit system acts as a quantitative restraint, whereas the environmental tax allows some quantity response to increased foreign demand.

The similarity of a Pareto tax and a tradeable permit scheme in pushing up export prices in a static context and their differences when foreign demand is changing are illustrated in Figure 9.8. The product is an export good. S_p is the private marginal cost supply curve, S_C is social marginal social cost supply curve inclusive of the environmental externality, and D_X is initial export demand. Assume the country does not attempt to exploit its market power but is concerned with correcting the environmental externality. The initial situation without environmental policy is output Q_0 and price P_0. Assume pollution can be controlled through output restriction, not pollution abatement. A Pareto-optimal tax of *ab* per unit output (a specific tax,

---

16 The same conclusion holds if the product is sold domestically, but results in an internal rather than external transfer. See Baumol and Oates (1988). Note that we are now considering a subsidy for reducing pollution below some base level and not simply subsidizing pollution-abatement expenditures by firms. See Chapter 6 for this distinction. The United States subsidizes farmers for taking environmentally sensitive farmland out of production.

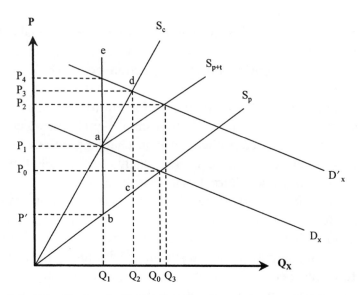

Figure 9.8. *Distributional effects of externality tax and tradeable permit with changes in foreign demand*

not an *ad valorem* tax) brings output down to its optimal level Q_1. Export price rises to P_1. The same result can be obtained with a permit scheme that sets total emissions equivalent to output Q_1. The effective supply curve becomes vertical along the segment *be*. Domestically the tax scheme distributes $P'P_1ab$ to the government; if permits are not auctioned but given free, their value to the producers is the same, $P'P_1ab$.

Now assume an increase in foreign demand to D'_X. An optimal environmental policy would require increasing the per unit tax to *cd* or expanding permits to allow production of Q_2. Suppose, however, that no policy adjustment takes place. With the tax per unit set at *ab*, the effective supply along the segment aS_{p+t} is at Q_3, and export price rises to P_2, less than social marginal cost. In the permit scheme, the supply of permits continues to be set equivalent to an output of Q_1. Export volume is constant and export price rises to P_4. In the first instance, under the tax, output is excessive and export price too low; in the second instance, under the permit scheme, output is deficient and price above marginal social production costs. The suboptimal permit system shifts more of the cost burden to the foreign consumer than does the suboptimal tax. The reason for the different outcome is that the permit system acts as a quantitative restraint severing domestic production from changes in foreign demand. The tax system, like a tariff, retains a link between foreign demand and domestic supply. (An *ad valorem* tax would automatically change as foreign demand changes.) This simply extends a standard result in trade policy theory – quantitative trade restraints such as export quotas become increasingly restrictive as compared to export taxes when foreign demand increases, and import quotas become increasingly restrictive as compared to import tariffs when domestic demand increases or foreign costs fall.

10

Trade-Environment Policy: Evolution of the Debate and Taxonomy of the Issues

1 Introduction

Trade-environment policy issues are complex and often controversial.[1] This chapter describes the evolution of the debate and presents an analytical framework for sorting out the relevant questions. Most trade-environment policy issues can be fitted into one of four categories: competitiveness questions and appropriate policy response; questions of market access and market opportunity, which include environmentally related product standards, ecolabelling, and "green" trade; the use of trade measures to secure international environmental objectives; and the effects of trade and trade liberalization on environmental and natural resources. The first three categories are concerned with the effects of environmental regulations on the international trade system. The fourth turns the question around and examines how trade and trade policy affect environmental objectives.

It is useful to start with three observations. First, although currently fashionable and much debated, trade-environment policy issues are not new, but were first addressed in the early 1970s. The interesting question is why discussions became increasingly strident in the early 1990s. Second, at a high level of generality there is no fundamental conflict between good trade policy and good environmental policy. Both require the internalization of the full social costs of production, including environmental protection costs, by either passing these costs forward to consumers in prices or backward to the factors of production. Often what appears to be a conflict between trade and environment is the result of either poor trade policy or inadequate environmental protection. There is an asymmetry, however. Good trade policy generally means removing government intervention in trade, whereas good environmental policy often involves increasing

1 For a balanced analysis see Daniel Esty (1994).

258

government intervention to correct market failures. The third point is that some of the conflicts between the trade community and the environmental community arises from rather different *modus operandi*. Konrad von Moltke (1994, p. 54) calls this a "veritable culture clash." Daniel Esty (1994) uses the terms "clash of cultures" and "cultural divide." Environmental organizations tend to be inclusionary and participatory, and they rely heavily on open discussion and active pressure from public opinion. The work of the World Commission on Environment and Development (Brundtland Commission) and the work of international scientific panels on ozone depletion and climate change are good examples of widespread, open, public participation. There are occasions when trade policy is openly and actively debated in public fora – NAFTA was an example. But for the most part, the specifics of trade policy are formulated and negotiated by specialized bureaucrats, with only modest and controlled input from the public. Negotiations are often secret. One example is the WTO trade dispute settlement process. The Uruguay Round Agreement creating the WTO has been criticized on the grounds that citizens and NGOs are prohibited from attending the hearings of dispute settlement panels and the standing appellate body, and that they have no right of access to the pleadings of the parties in disputes (Housman 1994).

2 Evolution of the Issue

Potential conflict between international trade and environment and efforts at reconciliation first surfaced in the early 1970s, about the time of the 1972 United Nations Conference on the Human Environment (Stockholm Conference). At that time the trade aspect was only a minor facet of a larger flowering of the environmental movement. That movement was greatly nourished by a series of influential and often pessimistic books and reports describing local and global environmental deterioration. Among these were Rachel Carson's *Silent Spring* (1962), tracing the effects of increasing use of pesticides; Barry Commoner's *Closing Circle* (1972), describing impending collapse from increasing toxic wastes; and Barbara Ward and Rene Dubos's *Only One Earth* (1972), a report to the Secretary General of the Stockholm Conference and a sober analysis stressing the planet's ecological unity and finite resources. Most influential was the report by Donella and Dennis Meadows and others, *The Limits to Growth* (1972), a report to the Club of Rome. Although much derided by economists, *The Limits*, published at the same time as the first oil crisis in 1972, provoked enormous public discussion and controversy. With a more restricted audience, *The Careless Tech-*

nology, edited by M. Taghi Farvar and John Milton, and published in 1972, detailed the pervasive failure of traditional development policies and projects in the Third World to anticipate and remedy adverse ecological consequences of economic development. The insights of that report led to reforms at the World Bank and other development assistance banks, and were ultimately picked up in the sustainable development movement. These studies and reports were reinforced by emerging scientific evidence that economic activity could produce global environmental threats. The possibility of global warming from CO_2 emissions, first speculated on in the 19th century, was rediscovered in the early 1970s, and the first scientific paper on chlorofluorocarbons and atmospheric ozone depletion was published about the same time.

Both domestic and international policy responded to rising environmental concerns. Within the United States, the 1969 National Environmental Policy Act created the Council on Environmental Quality, the administration and enforcement of environmental regulations were consolidated in the newly created Environmental Protection Agency in 1970, and the Clean Air Amendment Act became law in the same year. There was considerable international activity as well. The World Bank had created an environmental unit in 1970, although its staffing was scarcely adequate, considering the volume of its environmentally sensitive lending. The Founex (Switzerland) Symposium, in preparing for the Stockholm Conference, sought to bring developing countries into the environmental movement by redefining environmental degradation to include not only the "effluents of affluence" such as pollution and loss of wilderness and wildlife, but also the "pollution of poverty" – unsanitary water supplies, endemic disease, urban squalor. The desire to globalize the environment *problematique* also led to the decision to locate the newly created United Nations Environment Programme (UNEP) in Nairobi, the first UN specialized agency located in the Third World. The Stockholm Conference itself was followed by a series of issue-oriented global meetings sponsored by the United Nations, including water, desertification, habitat, and population.

In all this activity, trade-environment concerns played a relatively minor role and focused on a narrow set of issues. Moreover, the analysis and debate was carried on almost exclusively by economists and others in the trade community – environmentalists did not participate. The principal policy concerns were the international competitive impact of pollution-abatement costs, and the possibility that environmentally related product standards might be used as covert nontariff trade barriers. There was also some analysis of whether recycling and resource-recovery measures would affect the international markets for virgin materials. Although developing countries had an interest in these trade questions (and indeed the United Nations Conference on Trade and Development [UNCTAD] had a modest work program on trade and environment in the mid 1970s), the more publicized issue for developing countries was "additionality" – would donor countries provide *additional* resources to fund environmental protection in poor countries? The additionality question has echoes in current discussions of funding international environmental agreements such as the climate change convention.

In the United States, the major trade concern was possible loss of international competitiveness from strict pollution-abatement controls. For example, the 1972 Water Pollution Control legislation required the U.S. Commerce Department to conduct studies of the trade disadvantage that the United States might face as a result of abatement costs and the possibility of using border adjustments (import taxes and export rebates) to force a higher level of foreign environmental controls. The question of making pollution-abatement standards internationally uniform to avoid "pollution havens" was discussed in the 1972 report of the U.S. Council on Environmental Quality. Both issues still command attention in public debates today. Internationally, a GATT Working Group on Trade and Environment was established as early as 1971 but was not given an agenda and was not convened for 20 years.

It was left to the OECD to initiate serious policy work on trade and environment. In 1972, the OECD adopted "Recommendations of the Council on Guiding Principles Concerning International Economic Aspects of Environmental Policies." The best known recommendation is the Polluter Pays Principle, which is analyzed in Chapter 11. Here it is sufficient to note that the PPP originated as an efficiency, not equity, principle and can be correctly interpreted as a "no government subsidy" principle. The other two principles in the recommendations were that OECD governments were to renounce the use of border adjustments (export rebates and import surcharges) to offset international differences in environmental control costs and pledge that environmentally related product standards would not be used as covert trade barriers but that such standards be harmonized to the extent feasible. The recommendations also set up procedures for consultation should trade-environment disputes arise, but these procedures have not been used. At that time, the OECD's work was exclusively on how trade might be affected by environmental regulations. There was no policy concern for how trade might affect the environment.

By the late 1970s, the trade-environment issue was virtually comatose. Basic theoretical work expanding trade theory to include environment had been accomplished, the OECD had a policy framework in place, and a modest number of empirical studies were showing little significant trade effect. All this changed, however, by the beginning of the 1990s, when the trade-environment debate took on new life and a new level of contentiousness. How is this resurgence of policy interest to be explained? What is new since 1972?

Four factors have been at work. The first is increased global economic integration through trade and investment. This has been both market-driven and the result of more formal schemes such as the EC-92 initiative (a European attempt at creating a unified market), NAFTA, the Association of South East Asian Nations (ASEAN) Free Trade Area established in 1992, and most recently, the Asia Pacific Economic Cooperation (APEC) forum. Economic integration increases the importance of ostensibly domestic measures – for example, environmental, labor, and competition policies – in determining the location of production and the pattern of international trade. Thus economic integration underscores the putative importance of the competitiveness issue. Moreover, with open international borders and a desire to secure the benefits of a unified single market in formal integration schemes, the need to harmonize all forms of product standards, including environmentally related standards, takes on greater urgency.

The second factor has been a broadening of the earlier narrow concern for industrial pollution, to the protection of environmental and natural resources under the umbrella concept of sustainable development. Once natural resources are brought into the debate, the relevance of trade and trade policy to environment becomes far more evident. One might argue that industrial pollution control costs have been too small to have measurable trade effects, but one cannot argue that natural resource exploitation is unrelated to trade.

The third factor responsible for the resurgence of interest in trade and environment is that global environmental threats have moved from an earlier, limited, scientific debate to the center of international public policy discussions. As a consequence, the focus is now on multinational environmental protection agreements (MEAs) and other measures to change international environmental behavior. Trade measures offer a tempting method to secure and enforce MEAs or affect foreign environmental performance on a unilateral basis.

Finally, and perhaps most importantly, the environmental community has awakened to the possibility that international trade has environmental consequences and that trade policy can be a tool for securing environmental objectives. Two events triggered this awakening. One was the 1991 decision by the GATT dispute resolution panel, that found that a U.S. ban on imported tuna caught in a manner that unnecessarily killed dolphins was a violation of GATT rules. Many members of the environmental community viewed the decision as undermining domestic environmental legislation, in this particular case, the 1972 U.S. Marine Mammal Protection Act. The decision also sharpened the view of some that there has been a progressively narrower and more distorted interpretation of environmental disputes in GATT, especially Article XX, the general exceptions clause. The tuna-dolphin decision and the interpretation of Article XX are considered in more detail in Chapter 11.

The other event triggering the interest of the environmental community in trade was negotiations leading to the creation of NAFTA in 1993. The sudden interest by environmentalists in trade agreements is curious but ultimately understandable. Despite a long history of environmental disputes between the United States and Canada, including the 1935 Trail Smelter case involving transboundary air pollution, joint pollution of the Great Lakes, acid rain, and controversies over fisheries, and despite the fact that the 1987 U.S.-Canadian Free Trade Agreement was designed to deal with two contentious natural-resource issues – energy trade and subsidies to natural resources such as softwood lumber – environmentalists in the United States played a negligible role in negotiations leading to that agreement.[2] Five years later, environmental concerns were dominant in the NAFTA process. This reversal is also examined in Chapter 11.

By the mid-1990s, the public disagreement between the environmental and trade community had lost some of its earlier intensity. Trade-environment issues that were unresolved or unaddressed in the Uruguay Round were put on the agenda of the newly created Trade and Environment Committee of the WTO. But underlying issues and tensions have not been fully resolved. As described in Chapter 11, the WTO has yet to settle a number of trade-environment questions, including adjustments at the border for environmental taxes, the relation of trade rules to packaging and ecolabelling schemes, and ambiguities between trade measures in MEAs and WTO obligations. In the United States, in a replay of the earlier NAFTA debate, failure of Congress to grant fast-track trade negotiating authority to the President in 1997 was linked to international environmental standards. The trade-environment issue exploded in 1999 at the WTO ministerial meeting in Seattle. More broadly, some advocates of the so-called new protectionism argue that liberal trade causes worldwide

---

2 Some environmental groups in Canada did actively oppose the agreement. See Steven Shrybman (1991, 1991–92).

environmental damage.[3] It remains possible that protectionist interests will use the trade-environment concern to advance their own agenda (Van Grasstek 1992). And finally the uneasy truce with regard to environmental matters between North and South that was first struck in the Founex compromise over 25 years ago is in danger of breakdown. While developing-country governments have become aware of trade-environment linkages in their own countries, some also choose to see creeping eco-imperialism, as rich importing countries apply environmental conditionality to trade. There was a strong consensus among developing countries at the 1992 United Nations Conference on Environmernt and Development (UNCED) in Rio that trade measures *not* be used in pursuit of environmental objectives, but this has yet to be tested and may yet become a key issue in controlling global warming.

3 Sorting Out Trade-Environment Policy: A Taxonomy

The introduction of this chapter sketched out a fourfold classification of trade-environment policy issues. This framework corresponds to the analytical approach used by the OECD that separates the effects of environmental regulations on trade from the effects of trade on environmental and natural resources. It also conforms to the useful distinction between environmental effects occurring in production (extraction, processing, manufacture, transport) from environmental effects of consumption and disposal. The latter distinction is especially important in international trade, where the country of production and export bears the burden of production pollution, and the country of importation and consumption bears the burden of consumption pollution. Also, the distinction between production and consumption pollution conforms to GATT trade rules, which allow (within limits) trade restrictions on imports based on the characteristics of products themselves, but in general disallow trade restrictions based on the manner in which the products are produced.

3.1 Competitiveness Questions

Environmental regulation of production tends to raise costs and reduce an industry's international competitive position. The amount of the cost increase depends in part on the control measures chosen (i.e., zoning, emission and effluent discharge limits, taxes, technology or input requirements,

3 See, for example, Batra (1993).

etc.) and in part on who picks up the cost. In some instances, the regulations may *lower* industry's long-term costs through energy savings, in-plant resource recovery, accelerated investment in more productive equipment, and so forth. Nevertheless, in most cases environmental protection has both real and financial costs.

The international competitive effects of these cost increases may be modest to the point of no policy concern. This is more likely when: (1) foreign competitors are also undertaking pollution-abatement expenditures, (2) the financing of abatement expenditures is internationally harmonized under the Polluter Pays Principle, (3) environmental costs are passed backward to factor returns rather than forward in prices, and (4) the environmental protection costs are small relative to other production costs such as wages, raw materials, transport, and the like.[4] This last factor is of special importance, and the empirical evidence is examined in some detail in Chapter 12.

Even if environmental protection costs have a measurable effect on international competitive position, it does not follow that any policy response is necessarily warranted. First, in a floating exchange rate system a loss of competitiveness in a sector with high pollution-abatement costs starts an exchange rate adjustment that tends to improve the competitive position of clean industries. In that sense, the trade and exchange rate effects reinforce the pollution-abatement objective by shifting the structure of production toward clean industries. Second, and more fundamental, most countries have started from a situation of trade distortion, and, as they progressively tighten environmental regulations, some alteration in the level and pattern of trade is desirable on efficiency and environmental grounds.

The possibility of competitive loss has generated a number of policy proposals. The most controversial are for a system of import surcharges and export rebates to equalize environmental control costs internationally. These are sometimes known as *ecoduties*. Examples of such policy proposals include Section 6 of the 1972 U.S. Federal Water Pollution Control Act; the Copper Environmental Equalization Act, proposed in 1977 (not enacted); a proposal in 1993 by then U.S. House of Representatives majority leader Richard Gephardt for a "Green Section 301," which would allow ecoduties on imports produced in countries that did not meet U.S. environmental standards; and similar proposals by Senator Baucus in 1991 and Senator Boren in 1992.[5]

The purpose of these proposals may be to neutralize competitive loss or alter foreign environmental performance or both. Border adjustment

---

4 The environmental costs of purchased inputs can be cumulated through input-output analysis.
5 See Esty (1994). See also David Vogel (1995, pp. 208–210).

schemes have little support among economists and trade officials. The main objections are theoretical (some differences in costs reflect legitimate differences in comparative advantage when comparative advantage is extended to environmental resources – see Chapters 8 and 9), empirical (as reviewed in Chapter 12, differences in environmental protection costs may be too modest to affect trade), legal (border adjustments would violate current GATT rules), and practical (unilateral determination of differential cost margins would be an open invitation for protectionism). Despite these formidable objections, border adjustment schemes still garner some support from those who are committed to "fair" trade and those who see the schemes as a defense against egregious examples of pollution havens. Border adjustment measures also provide a potential confluence of interests between protectionists and environmentalists. Current discussions of "social dumping" also lends a patina of respectability to ecodumping duty schemes.

In analyzing such proposals, it is important to be clear as to what is being equalized or harmonized and what the economic effects will be. The following analysis refers to environmental regulations directed at production, and not at products. Clearly, a requirement that *ambient* environmental standards be equalized internationally is neither meaningful nor operational. Ambient environmental standards, for example, ground-level ozone concentrations in urban areas, are targets and not regulations. They can only be achieved by regulation (or taxing) of specific sources of pollution. Moreover, ambient air and water quality standards differ for different regions within the United States, and thus there is no single benchmark against which foreign ambient standards can be compared. Finally, there is little or no direct connection between ambient conditions and particular traded products, and thus no way of assigning any border adjustment to particular products.

Ambient standards are achieved through effluent and emission standards applied to particular production processes or, less commonly, through pollution taxes. A requirement that foreign manufacturing facilities, for example, cement production or nonferrous metal refining, meet the same air- and water-discharge (emission and effluent) standards as do U.S. firms or face adjustment charges at the border would be technically feasible (although it would lead to endless challenges). But such a scheme would not equalize environmental costs, as different facilities could have widely different pollution-abatement options and costs. Moreover, if countries do differ in their supply and demand for environmental quality, universal identical emission and effluent standards would undermine comparative advantage and erode the gains from trade.

Finally, a system of export rebates and input surcharges to offset international pollution-abatement *cost* differences would undermine the effectiveness of domestic environmental policy. It would tend to perpetuate excessive home production of pollution-intensive products. Import-competing firms would be given protection and exporters would have their pollution-abatement costs rebated at the border. The results would be that export price would be less the full social cost of production and import-competing firms would find their pollution-abatement costs to be "subsidized" by the protective effect of the import surcharge.

Less extreme proposals to mitigate the competitive effect of differential environmental controls have been suggested and may have merit. Harmonizing the *financing* of pollution-abatement costs under the Polluter Pays Principle is efficient, moderates trade effects, and has been official OECD and EU policy for many years. An agreement among principal suppliers of primary commodities to simultaneously internalize environmental protection costs will also moderate the adverse trade effects on a single country. A voluntary agreement among a number of countries to set common minimum standards for basic, pollution-intensive sectors such as cement and pulp and paper might avoid pernicious competition for foreign investment. The negotiation of economic integration arrangements such as Asean Free Trade Agreement (AFTA), APEC, or a Western Hemisphere Free Trade Agreement might provide an opportunity to align regional environmental standards as they apply to production. In a perfect world, the government of every country would set environmental standards and hence costs on the basis of a local calculus of costs and benefits and might not need these supplemental arrangements. But to rely exclusively on governments acting in the social interest may be a counsel of perfection. Finally, if there are compelling political, social, or short-run economic adjustment costs for industries losing competitive position due to stringent environmental regulations, temporary trade measures might be considered, but direct subsidies or wage subsidies to labor in these industries are apt to be more efficient.

3.2 Environmentally Related Product Standards and Market Access[6]

Many environmentally motivated regulations and standards are directed toward products rather than production processes. The distinction is important for trade, as product standards protect the health, safety, and

---

6 For broader analysis of product standards, see A. O. Sykes (1995).

environment of the importing and consuming country, whereas production standards protect the country of production and export. As explained in Chapter 11, GATT rules track the distinction between product and production standards, and subject to certain disciplines, allow importing countries to restrict imports based on product characteristics, but not production processes. However, it is not always possible to draw a bright line between product and production-related standards. For example, the most effective method for assuring the safety of meat for consumption may be the inspection of hygienic conditions in slaughterhouses (the process), rather than inspection of the meat product itself. The safety of imported fruits and vegetables or pharmaceuticals might best be assured by standards and inspection related to the production process. This issue of "product-related production and process methods" is explored further in Chapter 11 in the context of GATT rules.

Product standards is a generic term that loosely describes standards and regulations concerning the design, composition, and performance of products. The more precise terms are technical *standards*, which are established by various private and quasiprivate entities such as the International Organization for Standardization (ISO) and are voluntary, and technical *regulations*, which are established by governments and are mandatory. (Governments may choose to adopt and make mandatory standards developed by private entities.) Examples of environmentally related technical regulations are pesticide and heavy metal residue levels in food products, auto emission standards, and requirements for disposable packaging.

Other distinctions are analytically useful. "Compatibility standards and regulations" are established to achieve compatibility among products in use. Voltage standards for electrical appliances are an example. "Quality standards and regulations" deal with other product characteristics – materials, labelling, performance – and the main objectives are health, safety, and moderating environmental damages. By and large, compatibility is established through voluntary standards and market forces, and quality standards are a mix of technical standards and technical regulations. Another useful distinction is between design and performance standards (regulations). For example, if the objective is safety in low-speed auto crashes, a regulation may be written in terms of the design and materials for auto bumpers, or may be written to specify how bumpers perform when subject to test crashes. The economic case for design regulations is lower cost for regulators to determine compliance and monitor enforcement. For example, if the objective is to reduce pollution from oil-contaminated ballast water in oil tankers, a design regulation such as segregated ballast tanks may be easier to enforce then setting an oil-discharge performance standard. The case for performance regulations is that they encourage producers to seek low-cost methods for meeting the regulations, and they provide incentives for technical improvements.

A final distinction with an even fainter line is between environmentally related product measures and other types of product regulations. This is particularly true in the health and safety area, where it is often unproductive to attempt to categorize regulations as environmentally motivated or not. It is also true with many energy regulations such as the U.S. Corporate Average Fuel Economy (CAFE) regulations setting auto fleet mileage standards, the motivation for which includes energy security as well as pollution abatement. As a practical matter, the fuzzy area between environmental and nonenvironmental product regulations is not especially troubling, as environmental regulations raise no new conceptual issues going beyond long-standing product standard issues (except for the potentially important question of managing transboundary pollution).

Compatibility standards are of less interest to us than quality standards. Most environmentally related product standards address quality, not compatibility. Moreover, the market generally sorts out the proper balance between compatibility and incompatibility of products, with little direct government involvement.[7] Quality standards may also be sorted out by the market, but government involvement is more common. The two market failures that support such involvement are imperfect information and externalities in consumption. Information on the safety of a product is costly to acquire and has something of the character of a public good. It would be unreasonable to expect consumers acting individually to determine the health risk of pesticides in food products and, when at the grocery store, test food for pesticide residue levels. But such information is economically valuable and necessary if social welfare is the underlying objective. The market system provides some level of information and assurance through brand names, warranties, product liability laws, advertising, private certification schemes, and so forth. But it is more efficient in many instances for the government, acting in the collective interest, to establish health and safety standards and monitor products for compliance. At this point, however, the nature and extent of government action becomes murky. In which instances are mandatory *labelling* requirements sufficient, and in which instances are product-specific quality requirements necessary? Differing views on paternalism versus consumer sovereignty arise.

---

7 Firms with market power may attempt to establish industrywide product compatibility standards, decreasing effective competition, and inviting government intervention.

The second justification for environmentally related product standards are externalities in consumption and disposal. Examples include noise limits on consumer goods such as lawn mowers, bans on lead content of gasoline, biodegradability of detergents, auto emissions standards, recycled material content of paper and many more. When externalities in consumption and disposal are prominent, mere labelling requirements may be inadequate due to free riders and other market failure problems.

Trade Concerns Technical standards and regulation-related issues arise in a closed economy. But international trade introduces some complicating factors. One complication is that technical regulations and conformity procedures provide an attractive opportunity for governments to manipulate regulations and procedures in a fashion that protects domestic producers and discriminates against imports – in other words, the creation of covert, protectionist trade barriers. The Japanese ski standard is a well-known example. Arguing that snow in Japan is "different," the Japanese established a standard for the thickness of skis that differed from ISO standards, and that discouraged the sale of foreign skis in the Japanese market. The United States at one time required production safety testing of compressed gas cylinders to take place in the United States, precluding imports.[8]

Even when there is no protectionist intent, the proliferation of national product standards can create significant barriers to international trade.[9] The incremental costs of acquiring information on standards, modifying products, shortening production runs, and holding larger inventories can be considerable. The burden falls disproportionately on small suppliers to the market, which *de facto* tends to favor domestic producers over foreign exporters to the market. Both the possibility of covert protectionism and the additional costs of meeting a multitude of different standards in different markets supports the establishment of internationally harmonized standards.

The chief objection to internationally harmonized or uniform standards is that economic, social, and environmental conditions differ from one country to another, and what is appropriate in one set of circumstances may

8 At one time, United States exports of meat to Canada were temporarily embargoed in a dispute over inspection and certification for the hormone DES. When the inspection dispute was resolved, Canada imposed an import quota, leading to speculation that the DES issue was a protectionist pretext (Matthew Marks and Harold Malmgren 1975).
9 Just as a dominant firm may gain profit if its rivals confront cost increases from regulations, so countries may increase market share with well-crafted regulations. Regulations do not always favor domestic producers, however. There is some evidence that Japanese auto producers found it easier to comply with U.S. auto emission standards than did U.S. producers.

be inappropriate in another. Product health and safety standards for poor and rich countries may well differ if there are significant cost differences between low and high standards. Moreover, as evident in the hormone-fed beef dispute between the United States and the EU, countries may differ in their aversion to risk. Perhaps equally important, public support for a liberal trade system may be eroded if citizens feel their right to establish their own health, safety, and environmental standards at the national level is compromised. And there is a concern that international standards may be bid down to a least common denominator level – a variation of the "race to the bottom" argument. These concerns argue for a trade system that allows flexibility in setting product standards at the national level.

The environmental community has mixed views on international harmonization of product standards. On the one hand, harmonization *upward* to a high level may be effective in improving foreign environmental performance. On the other hand, harmonizing toward an average or to the lowest common denominator is objectionable, especially if it involves yielding standard-setting authority to others. From an economic perspective, the task is to balance the efficiency of differential product standards to reflect legitimate differences among countries in the supply and demand for environmental services, with the production and trade efficiencies associated with a single, uniform standard.

These are rather abstract considerations. Specific issues have emerged and are considered in more detail in Chapter 11: Should national-level product standards be based on scientific evidence, and how is that evidence to be evaluated? Should imports be restricted solely on the basis of their intrinsic characteristics, or should restrictions also be based on the environmental manner in which the products are produced (the process and production methods (PPM) issue)? How can environmentally motivated packaging requirements such as the Danish bottle bill and the German Packaging Ordinance be implemented with least disruption to trade? Are the GATT panel decisions regarding environmentally related product standards working against environmental objectives?

Ecolabelling, Environmental Product Certification, and Product Life-Cycle Management[10] These schemes fall somewhere between the technical regulation of products, which is mandatory and established by governments, and "green consumerism," which in its pure form is simply the expression by consumers in the marketplace of their preference for the purchase of products

---

10 See Organization for Economic Cooperation and Development (OECD), *Life-Cycle Management and Trade* (1994b).

that minimize or avoid environmental damage. An ecolabelling scheme informs consumers that a labeled product is environmentally superior (less damaging) than other products in the same category. It is a form of third-party product certification, with the certification done by a purely private organization, such as Green Seal in the United States, or by a mixed private-public entity, as in the Canadian system. In general, the intent of ecolabelling schemes is to *identify* such superior products to the consumer and allow the consumer to make an informed choice. The producer is presumably rewarded for an environmentally superior item by increased market share and perhaps a price premium. Thus, by improving information, ecolabels can improve the operation of the market system and in some cases may substitute for government-mandated product standards.

Ecolabelling can be distinguished from "single issue" labels, which address only one environmental aspect of a product, for example, its energy use. Ecolabels can also be distinguished from the more common warning labels, many mandatory, for dangerous or toxic substances. In principle, ecolabels are awarded after consideration of the full chain of economic activity – extraction, processing, production, transport, sale, use, and disposal – and for a variety of environmental criteria such as energy use, pollution, ecological disruption, recyclability, and degradability. In practice, the analysis requires a large amount of data and research. Because the importance of different environmental effects must be weighted, for example, energy use versus extent of recycling for glass versus plastics, the certification cannot escape arbitrary judgments.

Ecolabelling schemes fall within the broader, emerging activity of product life-cycle (PLC) management. PLC management involves three steps: an *inventory* stage, which quantifies physical effects; an *impact analysis* stage, which translates these physical effects into ambient environmental, biological, and ecological effects; and an *improvement analysis* stage, in which less environmentally damaging production techniques and product characteristics are sought. PLC management is not limited to ecolabel-granting organizations. It is also a tool for governments and corporations, although its development by all three groups is still in its infancy.

The trade policy questions surrounding ecolabelling are similar in some respects to product regulations. At a high level of abstraction, ecolabels improve consumer information and assist in the efficient functioning of international markets. While ecolabels will not replace technical regulations when the purpose of such regulations is consumer health and safety, and while ecolabels are inadequate in addressing consumption externalities and related free-rider problems, they do assist consumers in expressing their environmental preferences in the marketplace. To the extent that consumers are willing to pay incremental costs of environmentally "superior" products, ecolabels provide a public good – information – and market transactions reflect preferences more accurately.

But just as technical standards and regulations schemes may create non-tariff trade barriers, ecolabelling schemes may inadvertently or deliberately create impediments to trade. The specific problems include:

1 Product categories eligible for labels may be selected to favor domestic over foreign producers' interests.
2 The criteria for granting labels may favor domestic over foreign producers. (A German textile labelling scheme virtually required artificial dyes produced in Germany over natural dyes; Chile and Brazil have argued that ecolabel criteria for paper products that favors recycled paper over virgin pulp from sustainable plantation forestry are discriminatory.)
3 Discrimination may exist in the product classification system. Austria imposed a mandatory labelling requirement for tropical timber and products but did not impose similar requirements for temperate forest products. This was later withdrawn after ASEAN objections in GATT.
4 As with technical regulations, the cost of compliance may be much higher for small export suppliers (information costs, plant inspection and certification costs, and acquisition of approved inputs such as pesticide-free cotton, etc.) resulting in *de facto* protection of domestic producers.

In general, the criteria for granting ecolabels under life-cyle assessment (LCA) may be based on environmental conditions in the importing and consuming country and may be inappropriate in the country of production and export. Harmonized systems of ecolabels with some flexibility in criteria, depending on local conditions, and a form of mutual recognition for ecolabels would moderate some of the difficulties. But the inherent difficulties of life-cycle analysis, including tracking and weighing environmental effects at all product stages, may make such harmonized schemes unrealistic. It seems clear, however, that trade tensions created by ecolabelling have a North-South flavor to them and, correctly or not, many in the South believe ecolabelling schemes have an eco-imperialist and protectionist character. But criticism of ecolabels is not entirely limited to developing countries. Industry opposition has been reported in Europe and the United States (Salzman 1997, p. 11).

Procurement and ISO 14000 The ecolabelling issue blends into two other market-access obstacles, environmentally motivated government procurement and the ISO 14000 series. Discriminatory government procurement is a long-standing nontariff trade barrier (NTB) regulated to some extent by the WTO's Government Procurement Code. In recent years, some governments have added environmental criteria to their procurement policies, and the trade question is whether such criteria constitute a new NTB. In the United States, executive orders have been issued directing government agencies to buy products that use fewer ozone-depleting chemicals. The Clinton administration also sought a requirement that federal agencies purchase paper with at least 15 percent post-consumer waste content. State and local governments have also restricted their purchases of tropical timber and products, ostensibly on environmental grounds. While green consumerism in public procurement is not inherently against the interests of exporting countries, the potential for covert trade discrimination and the likelihood of increased costs for exporters are real, especially for smaller suppliers in developing countries.

The International Organization for Standardization (ISO) was founded in 1946 to promote international standards and facilitate domestic and international trade (incidentally, ISO is not an acronym but refers to the Greek word ISOS, meaning equal). Both public and private entities are represented in the form of national organizations with standardization interests. ISO standards are voluntary but are often made mandatory by member governments or become *de facto* standards for commerce. Until the 1980s, the ISO restricted its work to technical and manufacturing standards and was mainly interested in making product standards conformable. Typical examples include uniform size for freight containers and the thickness of credit cards. Subsequently, the ISO extended its activities to management and manufacturing systems with the ISO 9000 Standard Series on Quality Management and Assurance. Conforming to ISO 9000 standards has become an important condition for commercial activities. In some cases, suppliers must have third-party approval or registration of conformity to ISO 9000 quality management as a precondition for sales.

Starting in 1993, the ISO has further extended its work to environmental management systems (EMS) in its 14000 Series.[11] Standards are being developed in five areas: management systems, environmental audits, environ-

---

11 The ISO 14000 series includes 14001, which is the specific standard for environmental management; 14010–12, for environmental auditing; 14020–25, for environmental labelling; 14031, for environmental performance evaluations; and 14040–43, for life-cycle assessment guidelines. ISO 14001 is the most important and the only standard subject to certification.

mental labelling, environmental performance evaluation, and life-cycle assessment (Salzman 1997, p. 17). It is important to remember that the ISO 14000 Series sets *management* standards – it neither sets specific design and performance standards for products nor effluent and emission limits. One impetus for the ISO initiative was to preempt conflicting or inconsistent systems of environmental standards. These include the environmental management standards issued by the British Standards Institute (BS 7750) and the EU's Environmental Management Auditing Scheme (EMAS) standard.

The ISO 14000 initiative mirrors the broader trade issues of technical regulations, technical standards, and ecolabelling schemes. The ostensible purposes may be improvement in environmental performance and the facilitation of international trade. But unless carefully crafted, the 14000 Series can act as a trade barrier, as the use of the ISO 9000 Series in Europe has already been perceived. Specifically, if the environmental management standard is prescriptive, detailed, and costly to comply with, and if compliance requires strict criteria for subcontractor and suppliers' performance, it will be difficult for firms in developing countries to qualify. If, as expected, ISO registration becomes a condition for at least some types of international business, the trade barrier potential may be realized.[12] Once again there is a tension between the general desire for environmental improvement and the need to preserve flexibility in the face of internationally diverse economic and environmental conditions.

3.3 Trade Measures to Secure International Environmental Objectives

At the risk of some overlap, one can carve out a third category of trade-environment policy issues, the appropriate use of trade measures to secure international environmental objectives. This category merges on the margin of the competitiveness category. Ecodumping duties might be intended to maintain domestic competitiveness or to change foreign environmental practices. It also overlaps on the margin of the second category – extending product standards to include production and process methods – as the intent of PPM type restrictions also might be to change foreign practices. Nevertheless the increasing use of trade measures in international environmental agreements (MEAs) and on a more unilateral basis makes this a sufficiently distinct issue to warrant a separate category.

---

12 For example, Austrian policy requires a certified EMS for its government procurement (Cutter Information Corporation 1997).

MEAs with Trade Provisions There are about 900 legal instruments addressing international environmental resources (Esty 1994, p. 78). Of these, some 18 MEAs contain trade measures. There is no need to review them all, as three stand out in importance. The 1987 *Montreal Protocol on Substances that Deplete the Ozone Layer* is designed to limit emissions of CFCs and other chemicals that deplete atmospheric ozone. Among its trade measures are a ban on imports by parties from nonparties of CFCs and certain products that contain CFCs. Exports to nonparties are also restricted. The Protocol also restricts but does not eliminate trade in the controlled substances among parties and discourages the export of technologies for the production of the chemicals. As might be expected, production and trade restrictions have increased the price of CFCs, and considerable illegal trade in CFCs has been reported (Brack 1996). The Protocol has not been formally tested for consistency with the GATT. As analyzed in Chapter 13, it is generally believed that the trade sanctions were essential in dealing with the free-rider problem and making membership in the Protocol virtually universal.

The *Convention on International Trade in Endangered Species* (CITES) was signed in 1973 and came into force in 1975. As its name implies, CITES is designed to promote the conservation of endangered and threatened species by using various trade restrictions and bans. Three classes are identified: Appendix One species, where commercial trade is prohibited; Appendix Two species, which are in danger of becoming threatened with extinction, and where trade may be prohibited by the authorities of the exporting country; and Appendix Three species, in which flora and fauna are not at risk as species but are under protective measures in the country of origin. CITES is implemented through export and import permit schemes, which vary according to the species' status. Administration of the Convention is under the supervision of the Conference of the Parties and a standing committee, which can move species back and forth among categories, depending on the status of threats to their extinction.

The effectiveness of CITES, and more generally the effectiveness of using trade controls for species conservation, has been widely discussed (Barbier et al. 1990; Burgess 1994). One limitation is that international trade is less important than domestic trade for most wildlife, and international trade restrictions do not address the latter. A second problem is that habitat loss is more damaging than harvesting for many species. Thus harvesting and trade restrictions do not always get to the heart of the problem. Third, it is not clear that banning trade creates the best incentives for sustainable management of the species or that smuggling can be effectively controlled. Controlled harvest and trade of wildlife may generate revenue for conservation. A ban on marketing wildlife tends to reduce its asset value and incentive for conservation, at least to legal owners. The movement of the African elephants from Appendix Two to Appendix One status in 1989 and CITES's parallel restriction on elephant ivory trade have been particularly contentious. Zimbabwe recently obtained a partial exemption from the ban on ivory trade, but this may make detection and prohibition of trade in illegal ivory more difficult. CITES has not yet been directly challenged in the GATT.

The *Basel Convention on the Control of Transboundary Movement of Hazardous Wastes and their Disposal* was negotiated in 1989 and came into force in 1992.[13] While the vast majority of waste is recycled or disposed of in the country of origin, an estimated 10 percent of OECD wastes enter international trade. The Basel Convention is designed to bring transparency and "informed consent" to this trade. A basic premise is that, if unregulated, importing countries and especially developing countries may not have adequate waste-disposal facilities. The trade measures in the Basel Convention provide that countries have a right to ban waste imports. The Convention also prohibits the export of wastes to nonparties except under certain conditions and requires that waste exporters assure themselves that the receiving country will dispose of the wastes in an environmentally sound manner. A decision was adopted in March 1994 that requires all hazardous waste shipments for disposal from OECD to non-OECD countries be prohibited immediately, and that waste exports for recycling or resource recovery from OECD to non-OECD countries be prohibited by year end 1997. This decision may have been in response to the export to developing countries of excess wastes beyond the recycling capacity of European countries. While the goals of the Basel Convention are laudable, there are serious problems with regard to the definition of hazardous wastes, the maintenance of economically desirable trade in waste products to take advantage of scale economies in waste-disposal facilities, and the viability of trade for recycling and resource recovery. Also, some countries may have comparative advantage in waste-disposal activities. (Waste flows among states is a hot issue within the United States.)

In addition to these three MEAs, the Convention on Biodiversity and the Framework Convention on Climate Change (FCCC), negotiated within the UNCED process, will have trade consequences even though they do not contain explicit trade measures as an implementation or enforcement

---

13 For analysis, see Kalharina Kummer (1994) and Julie Bunn and David Blaney (1997).

mechanism. As examined in Chapter 15, obligations under the FCCC to reduce carbon emissions may have substantial effects on international competitive position, and carbon emission permits themselves might become internationally tradeable. Also, a serious dispute has arisen between major agricultural exporters (United States, Canada, Australia, Chile, Argentina, and Uruguay) and virtually all other countries concerning the regulation of trade in genetically altered products.[14] To summarize, major international environmental agreements have explicit or implicit trade restrictions. The purposes include an inducement to join the agreement and to improve the effectiveness of the controls. The consistency of these restrictions with GATT has not been fully worked out. And, as in the case of CITES, it is not always clear that trade restraints improve environmental conditions.

National Use At the national level, a number of environmental laws incorporate or contemplate trade restrictions. Some of these laws implement or enforce MEAs, while others are more unilateral in nature. The United States appears to be in the forefront and provides a useful illustration (Pearson 1994b). U.S. laws include the Marine Mammal Protection Act, which was the basis of the U.S. restriction on imports of tuna from Mexico; the Pelly Amendment to the Fisherman's Protective Act of 1967, which allows the president to ban imports of products from countries that diminish the effectiveness of international fisheries' conservation programs (see also Chapter 13); and the Lacey Act Amendments of 1981, which ban the importation of wild plants and animals taken in violation of United States and foreign law.

The trend appears toward greater use (or proposed use) of trade measures in environmental legislation. A U.S. International Trade Commission report found that 33 environmental bills introduced in the 101st Congress would have restricted trade or affected international trade policy (United States International Trade Commission 1991). A sampling includes one that would have authorized the president to take unilateral action under Section 301 of the Trade Act against countries that fail to protect endangered species; another that would have modified the U.S. Generalized System of Preferences (GSP) program and the Caribbean Basin Economic Recovery Act to require foreign countries to maintain certain environmental protection standards; a third that would have required the president to revoke most

---

14 The dispute has been played out in negotiations for a Biosafety Protocol to the Convention on Biological Diversity. One sticking point is whether or not WTO trade rules will take precedence over the protocol's trade provisions.

favored nation (MFN) status from countries that do not prohibit trade in ivory; and a fourth that bans imports of fish and marine animals from Japan, Korea, and Taiwan unless they prohibit driftnet fishing. Steve Charnovitz (1993a) has analyzed three U.S. environmental laws enacted in 1992, and their compatibility with GATT. The International Dolphin Conservation Act of 1992 authorizes the secretary of state to enter into an international agreement for a global moratorium on harvesting tuna through purse seine nets, and directs the U.S. Customs Service not to enforce the Marine Mammal Protection Act against countries that, *inter alia*, implement the moratorium by March 1994. Enforcement provisions include (1) a ban on imports of yellow tuna from countries not honoring their commitments, (2) restrictive quotas on fish and fish products in countries that do not take timely remedial actions, and (3) prohibition in the United States after May 1994 of the sale or transport of tuna that is not "dolphin safe." The High Seas Driftnet Fisheries Enforcement Act imposes mandatory sanctions on countries whose nations violate recent UN resolutions calling for a moratorium on driftnet fishing. If consultations with the offending country persistently fail, imports of fish, fish products, and sport fishing equipment from that country will be prohibited. The act expands potential Pelly Amendment sanctions to all imported products. Finally, the Wild Bird Conservation Act bans the importation of certain species of exotic birds and embargoes certain other species unless the exporting country effectively implements CITES, develops a management plan that ensures biological sustainability for the species, and minimizes the risk of inhumane treatment to birds during capture and transport. Charnovitz points out the significance of the last law is that it is designed to promote sustainable use by recognizing economic value and harnessing market forces to this end. While the United States has been most active, other examples can be found. The Netherlands unilaterally prohibited import trade in the Scottish red grouse, found only in Scotland. The European Court of Justice rejected this measure as it involved extrajurisdictional intent (Esty 1994, p. 265). The EU has a ban on imports of fur caught in countries that allow leghold traps although this has been challenged by Canada. It seems probable that such measures will be used more frequently in the future.

The temptation to employ trade measures to secure international environmental objectives is easy to understand. The fundamental dilemma of managing transnational externalities arises because the costs and benefits of environmental protection are not congruent with national borders. The dilemma is compounded when the valuation placed on environmental services differs substantially from country to country, for example, the value placed on glamour species by environmentalists in wealthy countries. With no supranational Environmental Protection Agency to directly compel compliance, and with greatly deficient international market mechanisms to arrive at a Coase-like bargaining solution, there is a strong temptation to use trade measures to induce or coerce other countries into taking environmental protection measures or to enforce MEAs.

In thinking about this problem, it is also useful to view trade measures as a device for dealing with the classic free-rider problem – countries that may benefit from an MEA *may* act strategically and withhold their support in the expectation that others will bear a disproportionate burden. But the use of coercive trade measures may create a symmetrical *forced-rider* problem. Countries with market power in the international trade system such as the United States may use that power to effectively compel others to engage in expensive environmental protection measures that go beyond their self-interest. In this light, trade "carrots" and trade "sticks" are not necessarily equally efficient. Quite apart from the resentment associated with the use of trade sticks, sometimes dubbed "eco-imperialism," the use of trade sanctions relieves the sanctioning country from the discipline of bearing the direct costs of the measures it seeks to impose.[15] Thus costs are shifted abroad, and the environmental objectives are not measured against a full consideration of the costs. In contrast, a system of carrots, in the form of side payments or trade concessions to induce compliance, keeps both costs and benefits within the calculus of the country desiring a change in foreign environmental performance. This is especially relevant when the protective measures arise from social value judgements, which may differ sharply from one country to another. For this reason, there is a presumption in favor of using trade incentives rather than sanctions to manage transnational externalities or affect foreign environmental performance.

3.4 Environmental Consequences of Trade

The fourth and final category of trade-environment policy issues turns the initial question around and focuses on the environmental impact of trade and trade policy on the environment. The basic theoretical points were examined in Chapters 8 and 9, which concluded: (1) that the effects of trade liberalization could be positive or negative depending in large part in whether the export or import sector was most environmentally sensitive, (2) that trade increases the need for appropriate domestic environmental

---

15 Rightly or wrongly, denying market access is perceived to harm the exporting country, although consumers in the importing country also suffer.

policies and, (3) that ideally trade and environmental policy should be jointly formulated. Empirical studies of the environmental impact of trade on the environment are reviewed in Chapter 12.

Much of the discussion remains speculative. A good example is the issue of the environmental effects of the existing level and structure of trade protection. Agricultural protectionism in OECD countries is often cited (Repetto 1993; Runge 1994a; Ward 1993). For example, intensive agriculture in the EU, protected from international competition through the Common Agricultural Policy, is said to result in increased pollution of air, soil, and water resources due to agricultural chemical use and livestock wastes, disturbance of wildlife habitat, and the loss of biological and genetic diversity. In the United States, restrictions on sugar imports, originally for revenue purposes dating in one form or another back to 1789, have more recently supported sugarcane production in Florida with allegedly devastating effects on the Everglades ecosystem (Repetto 1993). Also, by denying market access, agricultural trade protection is said to perpetuate poverty and associated abusive environmental practices in developing countries, including excessive and unsustainable exploitation of natural resources. Even more broadly, arguments have been made that high levels of OECD protection in textiles and garments, products in which developing countries have a demonstrated comparative advantage, frustrate the movement of poor people from rural areas where natural resources are overexploited, to employment in internationally competitive light manufacturing. A similar argument is made against the *structure* of protection in OECD countries, which tends toward higher rates of effective protection for intermediate and final products than for raw materials. The environmental connection is that developing countries are less able to shift production from natural resource exploitation to industrial output. This line of argument suggests that as trade liberalization under the Uruguay Round is implemented there will be a positive environmental effect.

But a change in the structure of production from raw materials to manufacturing may merely replace one set of environmental problems with another. In fact, tracing the environmental consequences of trade and trade liberalization is exceedingly difficult. As explained elsewhere, conventional analysis now distinguishes between scale, composition, and technique effects. In this framework, trade expands the scale of economic activity and, *ceteris paribus*, may create increased environmental stress as extraction, processing, consumption, and disposal all rise. Trade also changes the composition of output, and hence the vectors of pollution and natural-resource input demands. Trade can also change the techniques of production, perhaps toward less environmentally disruptive practices if relative prices or environmental regulations guide techniques in this direction. One can also argue that the increase in income resulting from an open trade regime can increase effective demand for pollution abatement through the political system, and that access to the international market for pollution-abatement equipment and environmental consulting services will also have positive environmental consequences.

These positive effects will not arise automatically, however. It is still unclear if, on balance, an increase in export price arising from trade liberalization increases unsustainable exploitation of renewable resources or, because of increased value, leads to additional conservation measures. The general point is that trade and trade liberalization underscore the need for environmental protection measures. This suggests that anticipatory policy based on trade-environment modelling is desirable. Thus far, attempts to anticipate the environmental effects of trade and trade liberalization have been spotty. The European Community, in planning for EC-92, did attempt to anticipate environmental effects in its Task Force Report on Environment and the Internal Market, and identified increased transport as potentially damaging to the environment. In the United States, under pressure from the environmental community, the U.S. Trade Representative (USTR) coordinated an interagency "review" of the environmental implications of NAFTA in 1992. The report asserted that NAFTA would enhance environmental protection by providing Mexico with additional resources, ease environmental problems at the border as economic activity in Mexico shifted southward, and would not lead to an environmentally motivated shift of U.S. manufacturing to Mexico. The review fell far short of a full environmental impact analysis (which was resisted by the Bush Administration) and was criticized by U.S. environmental groups as inadequate. Some have argued that the recent economic integration attempt in the Asia-Pacific region, APEC, should put environment in a central place on its agenda, but to date little has been done (Dua and Esty 1997).

11

Institutional and Policy Responses: OECD, WTO/GATT, EU, and NAFTA

1 Introduction

The trade-environment policy debate has taken place in a number of settings. This chapter analyzes the institutional responses to the four categories of policy issues set out in the previous chapter. The starting point is the earliest participant in the debate, the OECD, and in particular its Polluter Pays Principle. The PPP dates back to 1972 and is the most durable and arguably the most important bridge between trade and environment policy. This is followed by an examination of trade-environment within the GATT/WTO system. The chapter concludes with a discussion of trade-environment policy within two formal regional economic integration institutions, the European Union and the North American Free Trade Agreement.

2 The OECD and the Polluter Pays Principle

For over 25 years the OECD's "Guiding Principles" were the only explicit, internationally agreed-upon rules spanning trade and environmental policies.[1] Of these, the PPP has been the centerpiece. One might think that durability and prominence would have led to clarity. It has not. Interpretations of the PPP are more varied today than in the 1970s, and ambiguities remain.

The PPP as originally adopted by the OECD was a simple cost-allocation

---

[1] The PPP was adopted by the OECD in 1972 in "Recommendations of the Council on Guiding Principles Concerning International Economic Aspects of Environmental Policy" (Organization for Economic Cooperation and Development 1972) and further clarified in "Recommendation of the Council on the Implementation of the Polluter Pays Principle" (Organization for Economic Cooperation and Development 1974). It was first proposed, although not by name, by the U.S. Commission on International Trade and Investment Policy (1971). The original paper on this subject was Charles Pearson and Wendy Takacs (1971). For more recent analyses of the PPP, see Charles Pearson (1994a) and Candice Stevens (1994).

principle, designed to improve efficiency. In its original formulation, the PPP can be interpreted as a "no subsidization" principle. Environmental protection costs incurred in the private sector should not be offset by government subsidies. This formulation serves two efficiency objectives. First, it nudges market prices closer to the full social costs of production, a necessary condition for efficient resource allocation. Second, it helps prevent trade distortions arising from differences among countries in the financing of environmental protection. But the term itself is confusing. It is not pollution that the polluter is asked to pay for in the PPP, but pollution-abatement costs. Thus the PPP, which deals with pollution-abatement costs, is not identical to Principle 16 of the Rio Declaration on Environment and Development, which advocates "the internalization of environmental costs . . . taking into account the approach that the polluter should, in principle bear the cost of pollution. . . ." It is one thing to internalize environmental protection costs; it is another to internalize environmental damage costs. The two are only the same if the polluter is required to pay for residual environmental damages after he or she meets abatement objectives, a relatively rare situation.

A second source of semantic confusion is that although the polluting firm pays for abatement in the first instance, it is free to pass on cost increases in price to consumers, market conditions permitting. Thus the PPP is consistent with a "consumer pays principle." Third, although initially an efficiency principle, the PPP has come to convey a distinct equity or fairness quality. The implication of the term appears to be that it is fair or just for the polluter to pay, with the further implication that the payment be made to the victim of the pollution. Neither the moral inference nor restitution to victims, however, adds to the efficiency rationale for the PPP. Indeed, some analysts use the PPP to support the proposition that *countries* damaging international environmental resources should pay (compensate) countries burdened by damages, a normative proposition quite removed from the "no government subsidy" origin of the PPP.

Another source of confusion is how much the polluter should pay. In the original OECD formulation, the polluter was only obligated to pay for the pollution-prevention and control measures "decided by the public authorities to ensure that the environment is an acceptable state." Thus there is nothing in the original PPP that would effectively deal with a government that chose minimal environmental protection, so long as that government declared its standard to result in an acceptable state. The PPP does not call for optimal environmental policies. It cannot be used to support sanctions against a country choosing low standards and conferring on its firms an implicit environmental subsidy. Indeed, a separate OECD principle is an injunction against using border adjustment to equalize environmental costs. According to the OECD, such adjustments would be unnecessary and undesirable:

In accordance with the provisions of the GATT, differences in environmental policies should not lead to the introduction of compensating import levies or export rebates, or measures having an equivalent effect, designed to offset the consequences of these differences on prices. Effective implementation of the guiding principles set forth herewith will make it unnecessary and undesirable to resort to such measures (Organization for Economic Cooperation and Development 1972).

Even setting aside the contentious issue of implicit environmental subsidies, the amount the polluter should pay is not clear. As shown in Chapter 5, optimal environmental protection is obtained when marginal benefits equal marginal costs. In most instances, some residual level of pollution (environmental damage) remains. Thus the original PPP is consistent with the victim of pollution absorbing residual environmental damage costs, a variation of a Victim Pays Principle. In a 1975 elaboration, the OECD states that the PPP is *not* a principle of compensation for damages caused by pollution and the PPP is *not* intended to fully internalize the costs of pollution (Organization for Economic Cooperation and Development 1975, Forward, p. 6). That narrow view is under challenge. In a more recent (1991) document, an OECD recommendation calls for the "internalization of pollution prevention, control *and damage costs*" (Organization for Economic Cooperation and Development 1991; emphasis added). And, in a separate document, a draft report of the OECD Secretariat endorsed assigning the "cost of excessive pollution damage to the polluter" in the event of accidental pollution.

Finally, the PPP as originally envisioned by the OECD was narrowly intended to deal with pollution-abatement costs in the industrial sector. There was no vision of having the PPP apply to a wide range of environmental damage costs or protection measures in the natural resource and agriculture sectors, although the same efficiency objective would be served. Instead, the OECD has endorsed a separate User Pays Principle (UPP) as the natural resource analogue of the PPP. Under the UPP governments are supposed to find social prices and charge natural resource users accordingly. These charges would presumably include the financial costs of extraction and delivery of natural resources, but also any environmental costs, including user costs, and possibly option values and existence values as described in Chapter 5. But there has been no serious effort at operationalizing the

UPP or implementing it at the OECD level. This is a telling omission, as many studies have demonstrated the widespread environmental degradation associated with government subsidies for water, forest, and land uses.

To summarize, the PPP has evolved from a relatively straightforward, if narrow, no-subsidy cost-allocation principle to a rather messy concept in which equity and compensation to victims plays a role, and where it has been conflated with calls for the internalization of environmental damage costs. While not designed to deal with transnational pollution, some argue that the PPP is also the appropriate approach to assigning responsibility for international environmental damages.

Despite its ambiguities and muddied interpretation, the PPP has worked rather well within its limited scope. Four surveys carried out under a notification and consultation system established in the mid-1970s have concluded, on the basis of admittedly imperfect data, that OECD governments have not provided significant subsidies for industrial pollution abatement, and the impact on trade of such subsidies that do exist has been negligible (Stevens 1994). More recent data, however, indicate substantial subsidies ($1.5–2 billion annually) for development of clean technology, and these are likely to increase in global-warming programs (Stevens 1994, p. 584).[2] To our knowledge, only one significant trade dispute has involved an alleged violation of the PPP, the U.S.-EC Superfund case. As it happens, the Superfund dispute was handled under GATT, not OECD, dispute resolution procedures. The evidence suggests that the early and public commitment to the PPP has dissuaded OECD governments from extensive environmental subsidies, although this is difficult to prove.

There are several reasons for the apparent success of the PPP. First, as discussed in Chapter 12, industrial pollution-abatement costs have been less than initially anticipated, and most OECD countries moved at roughly the same pace in establishing more stringent environmental regulations. Both factors tend to reduce trade-competitiveness effects and hence some of the pressures for abatement subsidies. Also, the PPP has been implemented in a pragmatic fashion and explicitly allows for exceptions and derogations. These exceptions include the need for transitional assistance by governments to accelerate the introduction of new environmental measures, avoid exacerbating regional imbalances, and reduce labor adjustment costs. A recognition that the public goods character of research and development expenditures on pollution-abatement technology also may justify government assistance. To prevent the exceptions from becoming loopholes, the

2 Because technology has public goods characteristics, clean technology subsidies are not necessarily inefficient in the same sense that government subsidies for pollution abatement are.

OECD limits assistance to industries, areas, and plants where severe difficulty would otherwise result and requires that transitional time periods be set out in advance. Also, the PPP is consistent with a range of government measures, including effluent- and emission-discharge limits, pollution taxes, and tradeable permit schemes. This permits a flexible approach to pollution-abatement policy. Finally, as described next, the PPP is backed up by the relevant provisions of the GATT, which give some protection against egregious cases of government subsidy.

Together with the Guiding Principles' injunction against border adjustments to equalize environmental protection costs, the PPP represents the OECD's effort to deal with the competitiveness question. The OECD guidelines also tackled the issue of environmentally related product standards as potential trade barriers, or covert NTBs. The relevant principle straddles the question of harmonization versus independent national standards. Under the heading, Environmental Standards, the Guiding Principles first note that different national pollution standards may be justified due to differences in assimilative capacity and different levels of industrialization, but then states "where products are traded internationally and where there could be significant obstacles to trade, governments should seek common standards for polluting products" (OECD 1972, p. 15).[3] The principle has had little practical effect because, as described next, the question of product standards has been contested in the framework of the GATT and not the OECD. In its early work, the OECD did not address the last two categories of issues described in Chapter 10, (1) the use of trade measures in MEAs and in national legislation and (2) the impact of trade and trade liberalization on the environment.

In the early 1990s, the OECD undertook a substantial program to update its earlier work on trade and environment. This resulted in a number of useful studies and new empirical material in such areas as ecolabelling, product life-cycle analysis, and the impact of trade in the environment. But the effort fell short of its promise. Although the OECD reached agreement in 1993 on new *procedural* guidelines with respect to trade and environment (OECD 1993), it was unable to reach agreement on new substantive guidelines or principles.[4] With the formal establishment of the WTO's Commit-

---

3 Note also that the Stockholm Declaration from the 1972 UN Conference on the Human Environment acknowledged that internationally uniform environmental standards were not appropriate, but that to avoid impairing developing country market access, some effort at harmonizing standards should be made.

4 Procedural guidelines, analyzed by Raed Safadi, endorse transparency in policy development, government reviews of trade and environment policies, and cooperation among governments in addressing transboundary pollution (Safadi 1994). These are hardly in the same class as the 1972 Guidelines.

tee on Trade and Environment in 1995, the OECD sharply cut back on its analytical and policy work on trade and environment.

3 The GATT, the WTO, and the Environment

The GATT and the WTO are the institutional embodiment of a liberal trade system. Major GATT principles are nondiscrimination in trade with regard to tariffs and other regulations (the unconditional MFN principle); national treatment accorded to imports (imports once entered into the customs territory cannot be treated less favorably than domestic products with respect to internal taxes and regulations concerning distribution and conditions of sale); and a preference for tariffs over quotas when protection is warranted, together with a general prohibition against quantitative restrictions on trade except under specified situations. GATT does not regulate trade *per se*. It regulates national trade *regulations* that countries use to promote or restrict trade. By restricting trade *regulations* it presumably promotes trade liberalization, discourages domestic protectionist pressures, and limits the arbitrary use of market power in the international trade system. At the same time, GATT is not designed to eliminate all efforts at trade regulation. It permits tariffs (subject to binding), countervailing and antidumping duties in response to "unfair" trade practices, export taxes, exemptions from MFN for national security purposes, and other types of national regulations of trade, all subject to certain disciplines.

The overarching trade-environment issues are whether or not GATT inhibits or works against environmental protection measures undertaken by national governments, and whether GATT and the WTO should be reformed to become more positive agents for environmental protection. On the face of it, there does not appear to be any inherent reason why GATT principles are in serious conflict with environmental objectives. And until recently, the number of environmental disputes and their trade significance was modest, as described next. Indeed, between its establishment in 1979 and 1990 the Agreement on Technical Barriers to Trade (the Standards Code), which could be expected to have been a focal point for complaints, received some 378 environmentally related notifications of national regulations, but no cases were brought into or resolved under the Code's dispute settlement procedures.[5] Indeed, as late as 1986, environmentally related issues in GATT were so muted that they were not specifically included in the initial agenda for the Uruguay Round.

---

5 The United States did attempt to bring its hormone-fed beef dispute to the GATT but was blocked by the EC.

All this has changed. Many in the environmental community believe the GATT is insensitive to environmental concerns at best and needs considerable reform. Others in the trade policy community and also those in developing countries resist major environmental reform. The Uruguay Round Agreements, concluded in 1993, contain a number of provisions relevant to the trade-environment debate. But because environmental concerns were introduced late in the negotiating process, and because of a strong desire to bring to conclusion what was already a complicated and contentious exercise, the resolution of certain fundamental issues was laid over to post–Uruguay Round negotiations within the framework of the WTO's new Committee on Trade and Environment. That Committee issued its first comprehensive report in November 1996, but it is fair to say that major trade-environment policy issues are yet to be resolved.[6] This section on GATT/WTO proceeds by first looking at subsidies, border taxes, and border adjustments, which broadly relate to the competitiveness and pollution haven issues. It then analyzes the product standards, ecolabelling, and PPM issues, as well as the use of trade measures in MEAs.

3.1 Subsidies, Border Adjustments, and Taxes

GATT subsidy and border adjustment rules are complex and were significantly revised in the Uruguay Round. They have considerable relevance for the environment. In general, subsidies contingent on export performance are prohibited, except for primary products. For primary products, the subsidy should not allow the exporting country to capture more than an "equitable" share of world exports. Other subsidies are either "actionable" or "nonactionable," meaning they may or may not be subject to countervailing duties by importing countries. The 1979 GATT Subsidies Code made nonactionable subsidies for industrial redeployment to avoid congestion and environmental problems. The Uruguay Round went further, and because it extends the Subsidies Code obligations to all WTO members, expands the number of countries involved.[7] Specifically, Article 8 establishes as nonactionable (not subject to countervailing duties):

c) assistance to promote adaptation of existing facilities to new environmental requirements imposed by law and/or regulations which result in greater constraints and financial burden on firms, provided that the assistance:
   i) is a one-time nonrecurring measure; and
   ii) is limited to 20 percent of the cost of adaptation; and

---

6 For analysis of the CTE report, see Steve Charnovitz (1997).
7 Not all GATT members were parties to the 1979 Subsidies Code and bound by its terms.

iii) does not cover the cost of replacing and operating the assisted investment, which must be fully borne by firms; and

iv) is directly linked to and proportionate to a firm's planned reduction of nuisances and pollution, and does not cover any manufacturing cost savings which may be achieved; and

v) is available to all firms which can adopt the new equipment and/or production processes.

Moreover, the agreement also establishes as nonactionable certain subsidies for industrial research and precompetitive development activities, which would include *inter alia* research on pollution-prevention and environmental protection technologies. The rationales for exempting these forms of assistance from potential countervailing duty actions are to reduce short-term adjustment costs to firms (similar to the derogations permitted in the PPP) and the public good characteristic of research and development activities.

The agreement also clarified the concept of a subsidy by limiting GATT rules to *financial* contributions by governments. This makes it even less likely that implicit environmental subsidies arising from artificially low environmental standards could be justification for countervailing duties. Thus, although border adjustments to offset differential environmental control costs continue to exert some attraction, they would most probably be found inconsistent with present GATT/WTO rules.

The Agreement on Agriculture deals specifically with agricultural subsidies. In general, countries undertake a commitment to phased reduction of domestic support measures as indexed by an Aggregate Measurement of Support (AMS) calculation. But certain types of environmental subsidies are exempt from the support reduction commitment. They include payments by government as part of environmental or conservation programs and payments made to retire land and other agricultural resources from production. These provisions have the effect of easing restrictions on the use of environmental subsidies. Indirectly they respond to one criticism of the GATT by environmentalists: that it discourages the use of environmental subsidies to accelerate the introduction of stronger environmental rules.

The new GATT provisions do not resolve all issues, however. There is concern in the business community that subsidies for process change as well as end-of-pipe treatment open up a major loophole that may give an advantage to foreign competitors. Moreover, the new rules do not deal explicitly with certain special case subsidies: government assistance for remedial pollution cleanup, especially important in transition economies (there is no economic efficiency reason to burden current producers for earlier pollution for which they were not responsible); international subsidies in which country A "bribes" country B firms to undertake pollution abatement, a situation consistent with economically efficient management of transboundary pollution that is increasingly frequent; general distortion-correcting subsidies, for example, a subsidy to encourage the use of new clean technology; and the possibility that a tradeable permits scheme for SO_2 or carbon emissions, in which the government grants, not sells, permits, is construed to be an actionable subsidy.

Most important from the environmentalists' perspective, the new subsidy/countervailing rules do not permit the introduction of ecoduties to offset lower foreign environmental standards and costs. Indeed, as noted previously, the new GATT rules make countervailing against such implicit subsidies more unlikely, as the concept of subsidy was formally limited to financial contributions by governments in the form of direct transfer of funds, tax relief, or direct provision of goods and services. However, natural resource subsidies in the form of underpriced water, stumpage fees, or grazing rights on government land might still be actionable.

Rules concerning border adjustments for internal taxes can also have implications for environmental policy. GATT permits adjustment at the border for indirect taxes on "like" products, such as sales and value-added taxes. (i.e., rebated on exports and applied to imports). Thus the treatment of indirect taxes follows the *destination principle*, in which goods are taxed in the country of consumption. GATT does not permit adjustment at the border for direct taxes, for example, corporate income tax or taxes on wages. GATT rules with respect to direct taxes follow the *origin principle*. The theoretical justification for this distinction between direct and indirect taxes was the earlier view that indirect taxes are shifted forward to consumers, and direct taxes are borne by the factors of production. This is no longer believed to hold in all cases, but for practical reasons it has been retained in GATT rules. This treatment of direct and indirect taxes may encourage inefficient environmental policies. If pollution arises from a production process, it is inefficient to tax the product. But a product tax can be adjusted at the border and is more attractive to business interests.

GATT treatment of indirect taxes on *inputs* to production is murky. This is the old *taxes occultes* issue. The 1979 Subsidies Code permitted the remission of taxes on inputs that are *physically incorporated* into the product. The Uruguay Round goes further. The revised Subsidies Code permits a country to rebate indirect taxes on goods and services inputs if they are consumed in the production of the exported product, and the term *consumed* is clarified to include physically incorporated inputs, and "energy, fuels, and oil used in the production process." On the face of it, this would permit border adjustments for, say, fossil fuel taxes and possibly taxes pegged to the carbon content of fuels. This would be antithetical to environmental objectives; environmental externalities would not be internalized in the cost structure of traded goods. Indeed, one could argue that a carbon tax or effluent tax in general is simply a payment for the hitherto underpriced input to production called environmental services. From that perspective, no border adjustment is warranted. Not only does the GATT language work against the internalization of environmental taxes in production costs, but it is asymmetrical. The rebate at the border applies to exports. No explicit similar provision is made with respect to imports.[8]

The border tax adjustment–environment nexus has already produced a well-known dispute in GATT. In the 1988 U.S.-EC Superfund Case, the EC challenged a 1986 U.S. law that taxed certain U.S. feedstock chemicals and also taxed imported chemicals products to the extent these imported products used, as inputs, the same feedstock chemicals. The purpose of the tax was to finance pollution cleanup. The GATT panel found in favor of the United States, rejecting as irrelevant the EC's contention that the tax violated the PPP (an OECD stricture) and confirming the U.S. position that the tax on the imported chemicals was equal to the tax burden on like domestic production as a result of domestic producers bearing the tax on their inputs. The GATT panel also determined that the purpose of the tax (i.e., cleanup) was not relevant.

3.2 *Product Standards and the Exceptions Clause*

Environmentally related product measures have become a fertile ground for clashes between environmental and trade objectives, although the total number of GATT cases is not large. Two of GATT's major principles are involved – nondiscrimination and national treatment. Also, the interpretation of Article XX, the general exceptions provisions, is implicated. A brief review of GATT cases illustrates the difficulty of balancing liberal trade with environmental protection in the product standards area. Although GATT provisions with respect to nondiscrimination, national treatment, and a presumption against quantitative restraints are relevant, the key provisions in Article XX allow members to override other GATT obligations under the following circumstances:

---

8 One reason for this convoluted state is that GATT border tax adjustment mechanisms were designed to maintain the competitiveness of domestic producers. But environmental taxes are designed for a different purpose, to correct externalities.

Subject to the requirement that such measures are not applied in a manner which could constitute a means of arbitrary or unjustifiable discrimination between countries where the same conditions prevail, or a disguised restriction on international trade, nothing in this agreement shall be construed to prevent the adoption or enforcement by any contracting party of measures:

... (b) necessary to protect human, animal, or plant life or health

... (g) relating to the conservation of exhaustible natural resources if such measures are made effective in conjunction with restrictions on domestic production or consumption

The ambiguous and troubling terms are "arbitrary or unjustifiable discrimination," "disguised restriction on international trade," "necessary," and "related to."

In 1982, in retaliation for seizure of American fishing boats within Canada's 200-mile fishing zone, the United States barred the import of tuna and tuna products from Canada. Canada took the dispute to GATT and the United States justified its action partly as a conservative measure as allowed under Article XX (g). A GATT panel found, however, that the ban went beyond U.S. catch restrictions and was not accompanied by consumption limits. Hence it was not a legitimate conservation measure as contemplated by Article XX (g) and the U.S. position was rejected. A second fisheries dispute in 1988 between the United States and Canada involved a Canadian prohibition on the export of certain unprocessed herring and salmon caught in its waters. Canada defended the export restriction partly on the basis of Article XX (g), relating to the conservation of natural resources. The GATT panel interpreted the terms *relating to* and *in conjunction with* to mean *primarily aimed at*. Under this interpretation, it found that the Canadian measures were not primarily aimed at conservation of the herring and salmon stocks. In a follow-up case involving reworded Canadian regulations and resolved under the U.S.-Canadian Free Trade Agreement, the dispute settlement panel found that the Canadian landing requirement was not primarily aimed at conservation and rejected the Canadian defense.

A 1990 dispute between the United States and Thailand concerned Thai restrictions on imported cigarettes. Thailand defended its restrictions in part on Article XX (b), claiming the restrictions were necessary to protect human health. The GATT panel sided with the United States, asserting that the restrictions were not necessary as other means such as advertising limits and excise taxes could have been used to accomplish the objective. This decision contributed to evolution of a "least trade-restrictive" test – that is, the importing country is obliged to use the least trade-restrictive measure in accomplishing its environmental objective. The strict interpretation of "necessary" was also supported in a 1989 dispute concerning Section 337 of the U.S. Tariff Act, dealing with imports of products that violate U.S. patents. Although unrelated to the environment, that decision interpreted Article XX (b) to mean a measure is not "necessary" if an alternative measure, not inconsistent with GATT, is reasonably available.

The famous tuna-dolphin case between the United States and Mexico has been extensively analyzed and need not be recounted in detail.[9] Briefly, after a U.S. nongovernmental environmental organization (NGO) sued the Department of Commerce to enforce the Marine Mammal Protection Act (MMPA), the United States banned the import of tuna from Mexico, Venezuela, and Vanuata, and in a secondary embargo banned tuna imports from a number of other countries known to buy tuna from the three primary countries. The reason was that foreign fishing methods led to "excessive" incidental dolphin kills as defined in the MMPA. Mexico took the case to the GATT, where a dispute resolution panel rejected the U.S. defense based on Article XX (b) and (g). The panel stated that XX (b) applies only to activities within the jurisdiction of the importing country, the U.S. measure was not "necessary" in that other measures such as negotiating an international agreement to limit dolphin kills may have been available, and the particular scheme for calculating permissible dolphin kills put a special burden on trade and was not necessary. The most important features of the panel decision were the strong statements that the *process* through which a product is produced could not justify an import restriction, and that Article XX exceptions only applied to resources within the jurisdiction of the importing country (for a variety of reasons, the panel report was never officially sent to the GATT Council and adopted).[10]

In the Uruguay Round, the objective was to strike a balance between preserving national authority to set whatever standards a government deems appropriate for the protection of health, safety, and the environment and ensuring that such standards did not conflict with liberal trade. Two agreements were reached, one dealing with government regulations of products (Agreement on Technical Barriers to Trade, or TBT), and the second dealing

---

9 See, for example, Vogel (1995).

10 The EU challenged the secondary embargo, and a second GATT panel again found against the United States. The second panel did acknowledge, however, that a country might use an import restriction to protect resources outside its jurisdiction if the action were pursuant to an MEA. Three other highly publicized disputes, not reviewed here, are an EU ban on imports of hormone-fed beef affecting U.S. exports; the first case under WTO dispute settlement rules involving the import of reformulated ("cleaner") gasoline from Venezuela to the United States; and a U.S. restriction on imported shrimp that were caught by boats that do not use turtle-exclusion devices.

specifically with food, animal, and plant health and safety (Agreement on Sanitary and Phytosanitary Measures, or SPS) (Charnovitz 1994).

The TBT applies a so-called least trade-restrictive test to national regulations. More specifically, regulations "shall not be more trade-restrictive than necessary to fulfill a legitimate objective." It also requires that national regulations be based on relevant international standards where they exist, except when international standards would be ineffective or inappropriate for the fulfillment of legitimate objectives. If international standards are used, the burden of proof in showing they are inconsistent with the WTO rests with the exporting country raising the challenge. The TBT does state that developing countries are not expected to use international standards as a basis for their own technical regulations if such standards are not appropriate to their needs. But of course they would have to meet standards established in their export markets. The agreement also requires that conformity assessments, wherein imported products are judged to be in conformity with national regulations, "be not more strict or applied more strictly than necessary to give the importing member adequate confidence that products conform with the applicable technical regulations or standards." Finally, the TBT agreement, like the SPS agreement, requires national governments to take reasonable measures to ensure compliance by subnational governmental bodies.

The SPS Agreement also contains a modified least trade-restrictive test, by barring a particular measure if there is another measure "reasonably available, taking into account technical and economic feasibility, that achieves the appropriate level of protection and is significantly less restrictive to trade." The SPS also requires members to base their regulations on international standards where they exist (for example, as established by the Codex Alimentarius Commission). Notwithstanding this obligation, national standards that are higher than international standards can be established. But in doing so, members "shall avoid arbitrary or unjustifiable distinctions . . . if such distinctions result in discrimination or a disguised restriction on international trade." More generally, measures falling within SPS must be necessary and based on scientific principles. Taken together, these rules place considerable limits on the ability of governments to establish environmentally related technical regulations on products. They help explain why environmental groups in the United States almost uniformly opposed the Uruguay Round Agreements.

Ecolabelling and GATT The status of ecolabels in GATT is ambiguous and has yet to be sorted out. In general, mandatory labelling requirements are governed by the TBT agreement. Ecolabelling schemes, which may be purely private but which often involve governments and generally are voluntary, are somewhat different. The TBT does require that governments take reasonable steps to have nongovernmental bodies adopt a "Code of Good Practice for the Preparation, Adoption, and Application of Standards" but this code does not carry the same force as other TBT provisions. All of this is an untested area involving real conflicts of principle. In general, GATT shuns discrimination, but ecolabels are deliberately discriminatory, albeit on ostensibly environmental rather than protectionist basis. Nevertheless, they can *implicitly* discriminate, not only on the basis of the characteristics of products (which is not necessarily inconsistent with GATT), but on the basis of production process, which does not fit well with GATT principles. GATT itself is weak with regard to controlling private sector activity and the actions of subnational governments. But some ecolabelling initiatives have strong central government involvement and indeed involvement at the EU level, and it may be possible for a member to use its GATT rights against implicit discrimination.

The meshing of the ISO 14,000 Series and GATT also remains a gray area. The GATT's new TBT provisions do give a preference for international over national standards, but the TBT does not extend to management standards. For example, the ISO standards for environmental auditing or performance evaluation do not refer specifically to a product, for example, radiation emission standards for microwave ovens, and it is unclear how the TBT would become involved. Also, as noted earlier, the TBT applies to mandatory government standards and, in the first instance, ISO standards are voluntary.

The product standards issue merges into the PPM issue. At one extreme are product standards based on the physical characteristics of the product. There is no question that subject to certain GATT disciplines set out in the TBT and the SPS agreements, countries have a right to restrict imports if they fail to meet these product standards. At the other extreme are standards pertaining to methods by which a product is produced or harvested, but which do not show up in the physical characteristics of the product. Examples include the tuna-dolphin case, where the method by which the tuna are caught is unrelated to the characteristics of the product, tuna. By and large, GATT rules do not permit import restrictions based on the manner in which a product is produced (although goods produced by prison labor are an explicit exception). This treatment creates serious tension between environmentalists, who point out that often it is the production or harvest process that causes environmental degradation, and who would like to give governments authority to restrict imports of such products, and trade officials who generally oppose such restrictions on the grounds that they would invite arbitrary restrictions, encourage covert protection, and undermine liberal trade. An intermediate position would allow PPM-type restrictions *if* the environmental damage is transnational or harms a shared environmental resource such as a migratory species. The case for PPM restrictions would also be strengthened if the shared resources were protected through a MEA.

In between these two extremes GATT has carved out a third category, product-related PPMs. This category covers situations in which the consumption of the product may be harmful or environmentally damaging, but the most effective way of controlling the harm is through a process standard. An example is hygienic standards for slaughterhouses (a process standard) to ensure meat safety. Another example is regulation of pesticide applications in the cultivation of fruits and vegetables to minimize residues in the product. The SPS and TBT allow import restrictions for product-related PPMs, again subject to certain disciplines.

3.3 *The WTO and MEAs*

The relationship between MEAs with trade provisions and WTO rules remains unsettled. The trade provisions of MEAs are generally import or export bans, which are not allowed in GATT except when overridden by Article XX, the general exceptions clause. Article XX makes no explicit distinction between trade bans to implement an MEA and those that do not. Nor does it address trade restrictions that treat MEA members and non-members differently, as is the case for the Montreal Protocol. The (untested) legal question is whether and under what circumstances trade measures in MEAs are consistent with WTO rules. If they are not, the policy question is whether to amend WTO rules, grant waivers, or simply forgo the use of such measures.

The WTO's Committee on Trade and Environment took up the MEA issue and included it in its 1996 Report, but the results were inconclusive (World Trade Organization 1996). The report does acknowledge that "Trade measures based on specifically agreed-upon provisions can also be needed in certain cases to achieve the environmental objectives of an MEA, particularly where trade is directly related to the source of an environmental problem" but continued by stating "views differed as whether any modifications to the provisions of the multilateral trading system are required."

3.4 Unresolved Issues

On the surface, the principles of liberal trade embodied in the GATT/WTO system appear consistent with strong environmental protection. Below the surface, however, are a number of unresolved points of conflict that continue to trouble the environmental community and, if left unaddressed, can erode support for both liberal trade and environmental protection and provoke serious disputes. Many of the conflicts have a North-South confrontational quality. Some of the more important points of friction are:

1 Should countries have the right to adjust at the border their trade with countries following a "pollution haven" strategy that gains an "unfair" competitive advantage (the ecoduty issue)?
2 Are current subsidy rules adequate to deal with subsidies for remedial pollution cleanup, international subsidies for pollution abatement and environmental protection, and implicit subsidies when governments grant (not auction) tradeable pollution permits?
3 As energy, carbon, and environmental taxes become more common, are the trade rules with respect to taxes on inputs sufficiently clear? Does current GATT treatment encourage inefficient product taxes over more efficient pollution or input taxes?
4 Should Article XX permit trade restrictions to protect resources outside the jurisdiction of the importing country?
5 Should current GATT treatment of PPMs be liberalized so that trade measures can be used when environmental damage occurs in foreign production or harvest?
6 Is the ambiguous language of Article XX – "arbitrary or unjustifiable discrimination," "disguised restriction on international trade," "necessary," and "related to" – being interpreted too narrowly? Is the TBT's least trade-restrictive test a workable rule?
7 Is the SPS requirement that measures be based on scientific principles workable? Too narrow? Who is to evaluate these scientific principles?
8 How can ecolabelling schemes be made consistent with GATT principles, especially when they use PPMs as criteria? Will they harm developing country export prospects?
9 How are the trade provisions of MEAs (and implementing national legislation) to be reconciled with the WTO system?

4 Trade and Environment in the European Union and NAFTA

Formal economic integration increases the saliency of two trade-environment issues, the competitiveness question and the desirability of harmonizing environmentally related product standards. The disappearance of internal trade barriers within a free trade area and the greater mobility of capital within the region increase the importance of the members' national policies affecting production costs. For this reason, regionwide harmonization of environmental standards that affect *production costs* may appear more attractive. Harmonization of *product standards* is desirable to take full advantage of a single unified market and was one of the two main objectives of the EC-92 initiative. The negotiation of an economic integration arrangement also offers an opportunity for joint discussion of the environmental policies of the prospective members, as was the case in NAFTA and is again the case in the EU as it contemplates eastward expansion. Full harmonization, however, may prove difficult if members differ sharply in their environmental and economic circumstances and objectives, as was the case in NAFTA and is now evident in the expansion of the EU.

4.1 The EU

In considering the experience of the European Community (now the European Union), keep in mind its special features. The EU has supranational institutions, including the European Court of Justice, with authority to regulate environmental policies at the member state level. (It does not, however, have a large centralized fund for environmental protection to be allocated among member states.) The physical proximity of its members and the very high level of intraunion trade also strengthen the case for Unionwide efforts to deal with transnational pollution and harmonization of product regulation. Thus the trade-environment policy experience of the EU may not serve as a good model for less ambitious economic integration schemes. The Single European Act (1987) provided explicit legal authority for EC environmental actions.[11] The underlying principles are preventative action, rectification of environmental damage at its source, the PPP, the subsidiarity principle, and the doctrine of mutual recognition. Mutual recognition is explained later in this section. The subsidiarity

---

11 Prior to the Single European Act, the EC had adopted the PPP in 1975, and certain environmental measures were taken under the initial Treaty of Rome, including Article 100, which provided for harmonizing laws affecting the functioning of the common market.

principle means that the responsibility for environmental management should be at the lowest level of political or regulatory authority that has the competence to resolve the problem. Thus a specific land use issue such as rezoning for commercial purposes would be dealt with at the local level, while intra-EU transboundary pollution would require supranational decision making and control. In negotiating the Kyoto Protocol, for example, the EU had a common position on global warming, but the member states had different targets.

Thus far the potential competitive advantage accruing to EU members with "low" environmental standards for *production* pollution has not been a divisive issue. At a theoretical level, it has been argued that regulatory structures need not be harmonized *ex ante* within an integration area, but will emerge *ex post* through institutional competition as countries vie with one another through policy instruments (Siebert 1990). According to this theory, as dirty industry shifts to low-standard countries, the public's demand for tighter standards leads to convergence. This argument requires considerable faith in governments' responding fully and quickly to social preferences and also tends to minimize the importance of intraregional transboundary pollution. Probably more important explanations for the absence of an overt environment-competitive problem are the early adoption of the PPP by the EC, which prevents trade distortions based on different finance schemes for abatement costs, and the generally low costs of abatement in most industries. An additional explanation may be that the EU has the authority to issue directives covering all EU industrial activity. These directives differ greatly in their specificity. Some are very general, setting broad goals and encouraging cooperation; some set environmental quality standards, but leave members latitude in choosing methods of control and in setting emission limits for individual polluters. Some, however, are quite detailed, for example, a directive requiring environmental impact assessment (EIA) for large-scale, environmentally sensitive projects such as refineries, thermal power stations, and integrated chemical installations, as well as the EU-wide effluent and emission standards for asbestos. Merely requiring an EIA, however, is not the same as equalizing emission standards.

The prospects for competitive distortions arising from differential environmental costs of production has become somewhat more urgent with the prospective expansion of the EU eastward.[12] Similar to the U.S.–Mexico context described in Section 4.2, there is a real prospect that some pollution havens might emerge in Eastern Europe unless preventative steps are taken.

---

12 Ten countries are seeking membership. Of these ten, five are in a fast-track negotiating schedule, Poland, Hungary, the Czech Republic, Slovenia, and Estonia.

The resolution has been that perspective new members must align their national laws, rules, and procedures with the entire body of EU law contained in the *aquis communitare*, including its environmental directives, regulations, and decisions. A principal concern is the competitive effect: "The persistence of a gap between levels of environmental protection in present and new members would distort the functioning of the single market and could lead to a protectionist reaction" (European Commission 1995). The cost to prospective members of environmental alignment is estimated at $140 billion (3–5 percent of GDP over several decades), with the great bulk paid for by the applicants, not the EU (International Environmental Reporter 1997, European Report). To the extent that the costs are for remedial cleanup from the communist period and are paid for by current enterprises, there is a reverse distortion, with Eastern European firms penalized in EU trade.

In contrast to the earlier muted attention to competitiveness issues, harmonizing product standards has been difficult and controversial (Vogel 1995). Early efforts at product harmonization were ambitious, but the results were unimpressive. In the 1987 Single European Act, the Council was given authority to issue directives – the main regulatory device – by qualified majority rather than the prior unanimity requirement. Also, in two related decisions, the European Court rulings favored free internal trade over national product regulations. In *Cassis de Dijon*, the Court found a German law requiring minimum alcohol content of 25 percent in liqueurs to have no public health justification, and consequently, the lower-alcohol French liqueur, *Cassis de Dijon* could be legally sold throughout the EC. This was consistent with the then-emerging *doctrine of mutual recognition*, which holds that a member country could maintain its own standards on a product produced and sold within its territory, but could not prevent the sale in its territory of a product that met the standards of another member country. An exception would be made, however, if it could be shown that the restriction on the sale of the imported product was necessary to protect public health or defend the consumer. The great advantage of mutual recognition is that the need for harmonized product standards was restricted to standards affecting health and safety. The second European Court decision involved the German beer purity standard, Reinheitsgebot, and ruled that one member could not stop the importation and sale of a product containing additives that were legal in the exporting country and illegal in the importing country, except if it could be shown that the additive was harmful.

In some cases, however, trade has yielded to national environmental law.

The Danish bottle bill is a case in point. A Danish law requiring reusable containers for beer and soft drinks was supported by the Court over the objections of the European Commission and foreign producers within the EC, who argued that the measure was disproportionate to the environmental objective. This was a significant ruling as it favored an environmental regulation despite the fact that the regulation, while not overtly discriminatory, did have the effect of restricting trade.

The preceding simply touches the surface of product-harmonizing disputes in the EU. Other significant controversies have arisen with respect to EU-wide auto emission standards and the use of leaded gasoline, as well as recycling of packaging materials. The last originated in 1991 with a very ambitious German law requiring firms to take back and recycle packaging materials or establish a secondary system for waste-material collection and recycling. The ostensible purpose was to deal with a mounting solid-waste disposal problem, but one effect was to impede exports to the German market by other EU members and other exporters (Vogel 1995). A second effect was to overload the German waste-recycling facilities, leading to greatly increased waste exports from Germany to other EU members and the Third World. The increased waste supply also depressed waste prices and undercut recycling activities in other member countries, causing them to complain. The problem was partly resolved in 1994 with an EU-level packaging directive that went partway toward a harmonized system of disposal for waste packaging. In addition to attempts at product harmonization, the EU has also attempted a harmonized EU-wide ecolabelling scheme. As with product standards, one motive was to reduce potential trade barriers associated with six or eight different national schemes. The EU-level effort has sputtered, however, in part due to European industry opposition, and in part due to criticism from U.S. industry groups (Salzman 1997). Finally, to be complete, the EU has at least acknowledged the fourth category of trade-environment policy issues, the effects of trade on environment, when it commissioned a study of the environmental implications of the EC-92 single market initiative.

4.2 NAFTA

Unlike its predecessor, the U.S.-Canadian Free Trade Agreement, environmental questions were central and highly controversial in the NAFTA negotiations.[13] This is due in part to the well-documented and well-publicized

---

13 Concerns were raised by Canadian environmentalists (Shrybman 1991–92).

instances of pollution along the U.S.-Mexican border, and, in part to the large wage disparities between the United States and Mexico, which made the competitiveness and pollution haven issues more credible. It also is due in part to the 1992 GATT panel decision in the tuna-dolphin case between the United States and Mexico. That decision awakened the U.S. environmental community to the importance of trade for the environment, but also alerted environmentalists to the possibility of using trade measures for international environmental purposes. Also at that time, domestic politics within the United States were such that, however reluctantly, the Bush and later the Clinton administration needed to respond to environmentalists' concerns. Specifically, in the spring of 1991, the Bush administration needed fast track reauthorization to move NAFTA ahead, and in the summer and fall of 1993 the Clinton administration, to demonstrate its environmental credentials and win support for the agreement, also needed to respond to the environmental community's concerns.[14]

Broadly speaking, U.S. environmental groups had four objectives with regard to NAFTA. One was to move ahead on border cleanup including obtaining funding.[15] The second was to use NAFTA negotiations as a vehicle for better environmental policies and enforcement within Mexico (environmental laws in Mexico were much stronger than their enforcement). The third and critical objective was to maintain the independence and integrity of U.S. environmental standards and policy making – if there were to be harmonization it would be *up* to U.S. standards. Fourth, and equally important, environmentalists with an eye on the ongoing Uruguay Round wished to demonstrate that trade agreements could be "greened" without undue sacrifice of trade objectives. Whether NAFTA and its environmental side agreement are sufficiently green is disputed. While six major U.S. environmental groups ultimately supported NAFTA, some mainstream organizations such as the Sierra Club and Friends of the Earth did not (Esty 1994, p. 28).[16]

In what sense is NAFTA a green trade agreement? The hortatory language of the preamble sets as a primary objective the promotion of sustainable development and the expansion of trade in a manner consistent with environmental protection and conservation. While neither the term

---

14 Both the Bush and Clinton administrations preferred to keep environmental and trade negotiations separate, on "parallel tracks." The Clinton administration in an effort to demonstrate improvements in the Republican-sponsored NAFTA initiative, hived off separate labor and environmental side agreements to NAFTA.

15 U.S.–Mexican border environmental agreements date to the 1944 Water Treaty, which established the International Boundary and Water Commission.

16 *All* major groups opposed Uruguay Round Agreements.

sustainable development nor *environment* is found in GATT, there are ample precedents for including environmental objectives in international economic agreements. The 1983 International Tropical Timber Agreement has both trade and environmental objectives, the 1975 Convention Establishing the Latin American Economic System (SELA) has as an objective the protection and conservation of the environment, and the EC had made environment an explicit objective in its 1987 Single European Act.

The specific provisions, analyzed according to the fourfold classification introduced in Chapter 10, are as follows. With respect to competitiveness and the related pollution haven question there is no effort in NAFTA to equalize environmental control costs or environmental protection standards. There is, however, a statement that member countries *should not* (emphasis added) "waive or otherwise derogate from, or offer to waive or derogate from, such measures [health, safety, and environment] as an encouragement for the establishment, acquisition, expansion or retention in its territory of an investment of such investor." *Should not*, of course, does not carry the force of *shall not*. It is also interesting that this statement of intent is tied to attracting investment, not to gaining a trade advantage. As described next, trade sanctions may be used as a last resort against two of the three parties should they fail to enforce their domestic environmental regulations. Finally, NAFTA does permit environmental screening of new investment by host countries, which means that a member can protect against becoming a pollution haven if it so chooses.

With regard to product standards, NAFTA, like the Uruguay Round Agreement that followed, hived off sanitary and phytosanitary measures from other product standards. With regard to sanitary and phytosanitary protection levels, NAFTA reserves for each member the right to set what it believes are appropriate levels of protection for human, plant, and animal life, although in doing so members shall avoid arbitrary or unjustifiable distinctions in such levels, if such distinctions would constitute a disguised restriction on trade. (The agreement does endorse harmonization of standards as an objective.) But the trade measures that a member country can use to achieve this level of protection are circumscribed. The measures must be "necessary" to protect human, plant, or animal life (the interpretation of "necessary" in GATT has been disputed – see Section 3). And the measures must be based on "scientific principles" and not be maintained if there is no longer a scientific basis. The general standards chapter also reserves for each member the right to establish protection levels deemed appropriate, provided this is done in support of a "legitimate" objective. But in NAFTA, as in GATT, trade regulations cannot be based on the manner in which the product is produced (harvested, grown, or made) unless the production method is related to the characteristics of the product – the old PPM issue. If disputes arise with regard to product standards, NAFTA places the burden of proof on the complaining party to show that the product standard is inconsistent with NAFTA obligations. It also permits the country whose environmental law is challenged to have some choice in resolving the dispute within NAFTA or the GATT.

NAFTA also bears on the issue of the appropriate use of trade measures for international environmental objectives. It explicitly states that the trade obligations of certain specific MEAs (endangered species, ozone depletion, and hazardous wastes) take precedence over NAFTA's obligations, although this is subject to some qualifying language. Also, in the final compromise on the highly contested issue of NAFTA members using trade sanctions to enforce environmental regulations in other member countries, a side agreement dealing with the environment does allow such measures against the United States and Mexico but not against Canada. The sanctions provisions merit attention as they go to the heart of U.S. environmental concerns about NAFTA. At the time it was widely acknowledged that Mexican environmental laws were roughly equivalent in severity to those of the United States. But the general view was that the laws were not effectively enforced. From the environmentalists' perspective, nonenforcement would result in intensified border pollution, would encourage U.S. firms to relocate to Mexico, and might weaken environmental regulations at the state level in the United States as the states sought to retain production within their borders. At the same time there was resistance within the U.S., Mexican, and Canadian governments to the establishment of a supranational body with strong enforcement powers (Raustiala 1995, p. 31). The final compromise written into the environmental side agreement to NAFTA does permit trade sanctions to be employed in cases of a persistent pattern of failure to enforce environmental laws, but the route to these sanctions is so torturous as to make their imposition unlikely.[17] At the broadest level, the NAFTA process can be seen partly as an exercise in inducing Mexico to strengthen its envi-

---

17 The Secretariat of the Commission may accept a submission from any *private* group or person alleging that a party has failed to effectively enforce its environmental law. Moreover, any party may request consultations with another party concerning similar allegations. The parties are given 60 days to resolve the question informally. If unresolved, the commission's council may by two-thirds vote convene an arbitration panel. The panel initially reports within 180 days on factual findings and remedial recommendations, and the report is subject to commentary and rebuttal before a final report is issued. At that point, the disputing parties may agree on a satisfactory action plan. If this is not implemented, or if there is no agreement, the panel may then impose a "monetary enforcement assessment" (a fine), limited to 0.7 percent of trade between the two. Finally, if the fine is not paid within 180 days, the complainant may withdraw NAFTA benefits (i.e., tariff concessions) in an amount limited to that sufficient to collect the fine. For Canada, a panel fine will be filed in a domestic Canadian court and treated as a court order, thus exempting Canada from the possibility of trade sanctions.

ronmental laws and enforcement in return for the commercial gains from preferential access to the U.S. and Canadian markets.

Finally, with respect to anticipating the effects of trade on the environment, the NAFTA negotiation process contributed little. As noted previously, the U.S. government did conduct a perfunctory interagency review, but it was a minor effort and not even as thorough as the modest effort made by the EC in anticipating the environmental effects of EC-92. However, the side agreement did create the Commission on Environmental Cooperation, which has the authority to investigate the environmental effects of regional trade and investment liberalization. This effort is still at the stage of developing analytical methods.

12

Empirical Studies

1 Introduction

Chapter 10 suggested that most trade-environment policy issues can be placed into one of four categories. This classification also serves to group empirical studies, although the number of studies in each category and their quality is rather uneven. In Section 2 we start with those studies that primarily focus on competitiveness – the effects of environmental regulation of production on the level and pattern of international trade and investment. Section 3 considers empirical analyses of environmentally related product standards and ecolabelling, as well as the few studies analyzing the use of trade measures to achieve international environmental objectives. Section 4 reviews studies that measure the effects of trade and trade liberalization on environmental resources.

On the whole, the empirical or measurement work is not especially satisfying. One reason is that much of the analytical and public policy interest in trade-environment issues is of recent origin and the collection of relevant data is just starting. But even when the debate stretches back over two decades, as in the case of competitiveness, problems of definition, methodology, and data have made empirical work difficult. Nevertheless, it is important to get a sense of the quantitative importance of trade-environment questions, to inform current policy-making, and to guide future research.

2 Competitiveness Questions

A central hypothesis is that countries, or sectors within countries, confronting strict environmental regulations and high pollution-abatement costs may be placed at an international competitive disadvantage. Have differential environmental regulations among countries had a measurable impact on the level and pattern of international trade? Has there been relocation of dirty industries from North to South? Have differential environmental regulations affected the level and pattern of foreign direct investment? Approaches to answering these questions differ widely. Some studies are *ex post* analyses that look back and attempt to discern whether existing environmental regulations have had effects on trade. Some are *ex ante* and attempt to estimate the trade effects if prospective environmental regulations are put in place. Some studies use partial equilibrium analysis, some use computable general equilibrium (CGE) models. It is desirable to build the analysis on an input-output table, as environmental control costs can then be cumulated through an input-output matrix to obtain both direct pollution-abatement costs at the sector level and indirect costs that are passed forward in the price of intermediate inputs to production.

There is less variation in the scope of the analysis. Most studies have concentrated on industrial pollution and industrial pollution-control costs. Very few have systematically looked at the costs of environmental protection in agriculture and other natural resource-intensive sectors. This is unfortunate, as there appears to be significant distortions and relatively high environmental damage costs in agriculture and other natural resource sectors. Studies concentrating on industrial pollution-abatement costs neglect the trade consequences of protecting against broader environmental effects such as depletion of soils, overfishing, and disruption of ecosystems. Ideally one would wish to know the international trade consequences of a comprehensive environmental protection program that deals not only with industrial pollution, but also with these broader environmental effects.

Environmental protection cost data are central to empirical estimates of the trade-competitiveness question. Unfortunately, these data are not especially good. Many studies "follow the data" and use estimates of expenditures for end-of-pipe treatment and possibly process change. This approach risks neglecting the real costs (difficult to measure) of environmental zoning, delays and uncertainties in the permitting process, and the administrative costs of identifying and complying with environmental regulations. These more subtle costs can also affect competitive performance. On the international level, the OECD has published pollution-abatement cost data for member countries, but the country coverage is not complete, and annualized costs of capital expenditure as well as operation and maintenance costs are not always provided (annualized costs are preferable for trade analysis). Also, the sector disaggregation is not always consistent among countries. Finally, the extent of government subsidies for pollution-abatement costs requires better data if the trade effects are to be accurately measured.

There is little systematic knowledge of environmental protection costs in developing and transitional economies, although this is beginning to change. Even for the United States, where cost data are better than for most other countries, problems exist. For example, firms responding to the relevant Commerce Department survey were requested to estimate incremental capital expenditures as a result of environmental regulations. This would be quite clear in the case of end-of-pipe treatment facilities, but difficult and subjective when the regulations induce changes in production processes themselves. Also, the Commerce Department survey requested *net* expenditures, after deducting for cost savings from resource recovery and materials conservation, introducing another subjective estimate. Finally, expenditures for worker health and safety were not included in the estimates, although the distinction between measures protecting workers' health and measures reducing pollution can be arbitrary. Unfortunately, the collection and publication of U.S. pollution-abatement expenditure data, which had been a consistent, well-defined series for over two decades, was canceled for budget reasons as of September 1996.

Because U.S. pollution-abatement cost data have generally been better, they often are used as a proxy for pollution-abatement costs internationally. This is especially frequent in the various studies analyzing changes in the pattern of worldwide dirty industry trade.[1] The use of U.S. data to infer costs in other countries can introduce an additional bias. Pollution-abatement costs may vary depending on the location of the pollution firm, the age structure of the capital stock, access to technology, and relative factor input prices. If these variables differ systematically among countries, as they are likely to do, the reliability of studies based on U.S. cost data is reduced. To be specific, the ranking of industries with high pollution-abatement costs to identify dirty industries *might* be quite different in different countries. Finally, some studies use emissions measured in physical terms rather than abatement costs in examining trade-environment effects. Once again, the best data on emissions at the sector and plant level are in the industrial countries, especially the United States, and it is common to use U.S. data as a proxy for emission intensities by industry in developing countries (Eskeland and Harrison 1997). This may be satisfactory for ranking industries by their pollution intensity, but the absolute levels of pollution per unit product are likely to be very different in industrial and developing countries.

---

1 See, for example, Patrick Low and Alexander Yeats (1992).

2.1 A Sampling of Studies

Judith Dean (1992) has provided a comprehensive survey of empirical studies of competitive impact published through 1990. Although difficult to summarize due to differences in assumptions, data, and analytical methods, the general conclusion of the studies is that there has been no significant overall impact on trade competitiveness, nor is there evidence of significant industrial relocation as a result of differential environmental regulations. This does not rule out modest trade effects, some industrial relocation, and some foreign investment seeking low pollution-standard production locations by firms with high environmental control costs or facing onerous environmental regulations.

A study by J. D. Richardson and J. Mutti (1976) illustrates one of the earlier careful *ex ante* attempts to estimate the competitive effects of environmental controls. These researchers used a general equilibrium model with domestic and import demand and domestic supply equations for 81 industries linked together with an input-output model to calculate direct and indirect environmental control costs at the individual industry level. The approach was to estimate price effects from direct and indirect costs and use the price effects to estimate output impact through a weighted average of domestic and foreign demand elasticities. Thus the results describe the sensitivity of an industry to international competition as measured by its output, not the trade effect *per se*. The data were for the United States. Richardson and Mutti also analyzed three financing schemes: fully implementating of the Polluter Pays Principle, subsidizing private abatement costs through a value-added tax, and subsidizing costs through a general production tax. The price and output effects of environmental regulations were modest, generally falling below 2 percent, but with a few industries approaching 5 percent under the Polluter Pays Principle. With subsidization, the range of effects on price and output by industry was more muted, from −1.5 percent to +1.0 percent. This is to be expected because with subsidization the costs are dispersed more evenly across industries. To capture the full trade effects, of course, requires data on environmental control costs abroad and assumptions concerning compensatory exchange rate and macroeconomic policy, which were not included in the analysis.

Using a different methodology, James Tobey identifies five pollution-intensive industries – mining, paper, chemicals, steel, metals – and uses an augmented factor endowment model (Hecksher-Ohlin-Vanek) to test econometrically whether the stringency of environmental regulations was a statistically significant determinant of net exports (Tobey 1990). He could not demonstrate such a relationship, suggesting that environmental protection costs have no measurable effect on trade. The conclusion must be treated cautiously, however, as the variable measuring environmental stringency has certain weaknesses. Also, some other researchers suggest that environmental control costs have been systematically underestimated, leading to a downward bias in trade estimates.[2]

A number of studies have appeared since the review by Dean. The full array of research, both early and more recent, has been summarized by Adam Jaffee and his colleagues. That survey tends to confirm the earlier conclusion by Dean. Specifically, they state, "Overall, there is relatively little evidence to support the hypothesis that environmental regulations have had a large adverse effect on competitiveness, however that elusive term is defined" (Jaffee et al. 1995, p. 157).

Gene Grossman and Alan Krueger analyzed the composition of *maquiladora* production in Mexico, U.S. imports from Mexico under offshore assembly provisions of U.S. tariff law, and overall U.S. imports from Mexico (Grossman and Kruger 1993).[3] They found that, as expected, factor intensities and U.S. tariff rates were significant determinants of trade composition, but pollution-abatement costs (as measured in the United States) were not. This finding tends to undercut the pollution haven–industrial relocation hypothesis.

Robert Lucas and his colleagues examined the environment-trade-industrial relocation issue using the U.S. Environmental Protection Agency's Toxic Release Inventory Data, rather than the customary sector data on pollution-abatement costs (Lucas, Wheeler, and Hettige 1992). This method has the potential for better measurement of actual pollution levels (since actual releases of toxic materials are measured at the firm level), and the sector ranking of pollution intensity was found to be correlated with U.S. pollution-abatement expenditures by sector. Their findings from pooled cross-section regression analysis are consistent with the hypothesis that strict regulation of pollution-intensive industries in the OECD countries has led to some industrial relocation to developing countries. Nevertheless, their further finding, that countries relatively closed to international trade have experienced much greater increases in pollution-intensive output than open economies, modifies this conclusion. Specifically, the latter finding suggests

---

2 Gray and Shadbegian, cited by Jaffee et al. (1995, p. 152) initially estimated overall cost is three to four dollars for each dollar of reported compliance costs, but subsequent results cast some doubt on this.
3 These summaries are taken from Charles Pearson (1994b).

that the trade policy regime (closed versus open) may be more important than regulatory cost differences in explaining industrial relocation of dirty industries.

Patrick Low and Alexander Yeats (1992) identify dirty industries on the basis of U.S. pollution abatement cost data, and ask the question whether trade data indicate a migration of dirty industry production to developing countries. They find that (1) the share of dirty products in world trade declined from 19 to 16 percent from 1965 to 1988, (2) the share of world-wide dirty product trade exported from industrial countries declined from 78 percent in 1965 to 74 percent in 1988, with the share of developing and Eastern European countries rising from 22 to 26 percent, and the share of dirty products in the exports of Eastern Europe rising from 22 to 27 percent over the same period. These results are consistent with the industrial relocation hypothesis, but, on the other hand, may simply reflect a normal pattern in which developing countries move through a phase of heavy industry industrialization. The relatively rapid growth of dirty industry exports from Eastern Europe is consistent with the Lucas et al. conclusion regarding open and closed economies.

Piritta Sorsa, following the Low-Yeats approach and adopting their definition of dirty industry products (which she calls environmentally sensitive goods), finds somewhat different results (Sorsa 1993). Her data show that between 1970 and 1990 the share of dirty industry goods in world trade fell from 22 to 18 percent (consistent with Low-Yeats), but that the share of total dirty industry exports accounted for by industrial countries did not decline from 1970 to 1990.[4] She does find that imports of dirty industry products make up a larger share of U.S. and Japanese total imports in 1990 than in 1970.

Roland Mollerus (1995) has also analyzed dirty industry trade with special attention to the members of SELA. His data also confirm the declining importance of dirty industry exports as a fraction of world exports. From 1975 to 1990 the share of these exports in total manufactured exports of developed market economies fell from 26 to 20 percent, and the share of dirty industry exports in total manufactured exports of all developing countries fell by a similar amount, from 26 to 19 percent. This suggests little overall industrial reallocation, although because of rapid growth of all manufactured exports in developing countries, there was absolute growth in their dirty industry exports. When SELA exports are separated out from other developing countries the picture is somewhat different. The share of dirty

---

4 The rate was 81.3 percent in 1970, falling to 76.5 percent in 1980, but returning to 81.1 percent in 1990.

industry exports in SELA's manufactured exports from 1975 to 1990 only fell from 48 to 47 percent. This suggests that different country groups within the developing world have had somewhat different experiences. One limitation of the studies by Low and Yeats, Sorsa, and Mollerus is their use of value data. Changes in relative prices of dirty versus nondirty industry products may be responsible for any share changes, without any real relocation of industrial activity. Also, trade data do not reveal trends in dirty industry output for domestic consumption.

A study by Stephen Meyer (1992) examines interstate economic and environmental performance within the United States and casts light on the competitiveness and industrial relocation questions. Meyer uses an ordinal scale to rank states within the United States as to their environmental protection effort. He then tests whether economic performance (e.g., state-level gross product growth, employment growth, and manufacturing labor productivity) is negatively correlated with environmental protection effort. The analysis rejects the hypothesis that strong environmental regulation reduces economic performance; indeed, there was a generally positive relation between economic performance and environmental protection effort. While this study did not use trade data, it tends to strengthen the findings from international studies that differences among countries in environmental controls have had a minimal impact on competitiveness.

Another study by Patrick Low also bears on the competitiveness issue (Low 1992). His approach is to simulate the impact on Mexican exports, by Standard Industrial Classification (SIC) sector, if the United States were to remove its tariffs on Mexican imports and place a new tax on those imports equal to the pollution-abatement and control expenditures incurred by the industries in the United States. In effect, his approach implicitly assumes no pollution-abatement expenditures in Mexico. The simulation results show that such a tax would have a very modest adverse effect on Mexican exports to the United States, in the order of a 2 percent loss of export earnings. Turning this conclusion around, one can interpret the simulation to suggest that in a free trade agreement such as NAFTA, the export advantage that Mexico might realize from no pollution abatement would be at most a 2 percent export increase.

Changes in the composition of trade can be caused by many factors. Mani and Wheeler use the conventional approach of examining the relative shares of clean and dirty industries in trade, production, and consumption (Mani and Wheeler 1997). One innovation in their detailed examination of Japan is an attempt to separate out the effects of changes in energy, land, and capital prices from environmental regulations. Unfortunately, they have no direct measure of regulatory strictness and are forced to use per capita income as a proxy for both environmental strictness *and* the effects of low income elasticity of demand for pollution-intensive goods. In regression analysis, they find a strong, significant relation between per capita income in Japan and a decline in the ratio of its dirty-to-clean industry output. But this conflates the environmental regulation effect and the income elasticity effect, and separating the two is speculative. Overall they find evidence consistent with temporary pollution havens, but argue the pollution haven effects are not of major significance. They base this conclusion on the finding that most of the dirty industry output increase in developing countries is for domestic consumption at intermediate income levels where income elasticity of demand for these products is high, and evidence that environmental regulation increases with income. Both factors suggest that countries will outgrow any pollution-haven phase.

One other empirical study is relevant. Robert Repetto argues that profitability rather than the elusive concept of competitiveness is a better measure when investigating the economic effects of environmental regulation. He proceeds to test two competing hypotheses – first that better environmental performance at the level of the firm involves some sacrifice of profits, and a second and opposite hypothesis that firms pressured by strict environmental regulations may actually improve their productivity and profitability through resource savings and in-plant materials recovery, improved processes, and the like (Repetto 1995). The latter is known as the Porter hypothesis.[5] Using large data bases drawn from the U.S. Census of Manufacturers, the EPA's Toxic Release Inventory, the National Emissions Data Systems, the Aerometric Information Retrieval System, and the Commerce Department's Pollution Abatement and Control Expenditure surveys, Repetto calculates three physical emissions-to-shipment ratios: for toxic emissions, water-borne emissions (BOD plus suspended solids), and air particulate emissions, all at the establishment level for U.S. manufacturing. Two measures of profitability are used, gross operating margin and net return as percent of year-end book value of capital. Then, at the five-digit SIC code level, the analysis proceeds by calculating simple and partial correlation coefficients between the three measures of emissions-to-value of shipments and the two measures of profitability. A strong positive correlation between high level of emissions per unit shipment and profitability would support the first hypothesis; a strong negative correlation would support the competing Porter hypothesis. The overall conclusion using both

---

5 The Porter hypothesis is set forth and challenged in two articles, Michael Porter and Claas van der Linde (1995) and Karen Palmer, Wallace Oates, and Paul Portney (1995).

simple correlation and partial correlation, controlled for plant scale, age, and recent investment, is that the correlations between environmental performance and profitability are weak – there is no overall tendency for plants with superior environmental performance to be more or less profitable. Repetto draws the trade policy conclusion that there is no need for countervailing duties or other trade penalties directed at imports from countries with weaker standards, as there is no evidence that the competitiveness of U.S. firms has been impaired.

The apparently modest effects of environmental costs on international competitiveness should not be interpreted as meaning little or no impact of environmental regulations on productivity and welfare. One general equilibrium study of the United States, using a 35-sector disaggregation, concluded that environmental regulations have lowered measured annual GNP growth by 0.2 percent over the period 1973–1985. By cumulating this result, it suggests that current GNP is 2 to 3 percent below the level that would otherwise have been achieved (Jorgenson and Wilcoxen 1993b). The model did not, however, account for feedback of environmental protection to the productivity of the resource base, a channel that may be positive and large for developing countries. Nor did it include the benefits associated with a cleaner environment.

To summarize, the studies through 1990 suggest that there had been no significant overall loss of U.S. competitiveness (industrial relocation) due to strong environmental regulations. Some, not all, of the more recent studies are consistent with the competitive loss/industrial relocation hypothesis, but the effects appear small and may be the result of normal industrialization in developing countries, or the result of relatively closed trade regimes and not the result of differential environmental regulations. It should be remembered that these conclusions are limited to industrial pollution abatement efforts. Also, relatively new environmental regulations, such as the phase-in of U.S. Clean Air Act Amendments during the 1990s and prospective regulations of greenhouse gas emissions, may involve large costs and alter the conclusions. For example, a study by John Piggott, John Whalley, and Randall Wigle (1992), based on a six-region numerical general equilibrium model, shows world trade volume might fall by 50 percent from baseline projections by 2030 if global carbon emissions were cut by 50 percent using consumption-based measures. While that result is sensitive to the specifications of the model, and a 50 percent cut is unrealistic, it does suggest that empirical studies of pollution-abatement measures over the past 25 years may not be a good guide to the trade effects of controlling global warming (see also Chapter 14).

2.2 Explanations

There are a number of reasons why significant trade and investment effects
have not materialized. First, industrial countries have moved at roughly the
same speed to introduce environmental protection measures, and this has
tended to minimize cost differences among them. Cost differences have also
been moderated through the adoption of a common financing regime, the
Polluter Pays Principle, by OECD countries. While good, current, and comprehensive data on the extent to which governments derogate from the PPP
with implicit or explicit subsidies are not available, surveys conducted by the
OECD suggest that differences in financing regimes in the industrial sector
probably have a minimal effect on relative costs, and hence trade (OECD
1992). Most importantly, the costs of pollution abatement, while substantial,
have proved to be lower than anticipated.

Tables 12.1 to 12.4 provide information on U.S. pollution-abatement and
control expenditures and bear on the competitiveness question. Table 12.1
indicates that of total 1994 abatement expenditures of $121.8 billion, $76.6
billion, or 63 percent, was incurred by the business sector. This was about
1.1 percent of GDP. Of this, $49 billion (64 percent) was current expendi-
ture and $28 billion (36 percent) was capital expenditures. To put this in per-
spective, $28 billion represents 2.9 percent of gross fixed private investment
and about 10 percent of net fixed investment. Table 12.2 gives 1994 total and
business expenditures broken out by environmental media, air, water, and
solid wastes. The proportions are roughly equal although in recent years
solid waste disposal costs have been an increasing fraction of total business
pollution-abatement costs. Table 12.3 presents annual total and business
expenditures in current dollars and as percentage of GDP for 1972–1994.
Although total expenditures grew from $16.6 billion to $122 billion, they
were a remarkably stable percentage of GDP – 1.7 to 1.8 percent – over
most of the 20 years. Business expenditures were very stable at 1.0 to 1.1
percent GDP.

Averages for the business sector can conceal major differences among
industries. Table 12.4 presents U.S. pollution-abatement costs (capital expenditures plus operating costs) as a percentage of value of shipments and
abatement capital expenditures as the percentage of total capital expenditures at the two-digit SIC level. The highest costs are found in the expected
sectors – pulp and paper, chemicals, petroleum, coal, and primary metals.
Even in these industries, costs as a fraction of value of shipments are modest.
However, when abatement capital expenditures are expressed as a fraction
of total capital expenditures in that industry, the amounts appear much more

Table 12.1. *U.S. pollution-abatement and control expenditures, 1994*

Pollution Abatement	Billions $
Personal Consumption	
Motor Vehicle Devices	9.8
Business	
Capital Expenditure	27.7
Current Expenditure	48.9
Plant & Equipment	31.3
Public Sewer Systems[a]	12.4
Cost Recovered	(1.7)
Other	6.9
Subtotal	76.6
Government	
Public Sewer, fixed capital	12.8
Other	18.4
Subtotal	31.2
Regulation and Monitoring	2.2
Research and Development	2.0
Total	121.8

[a] Spending to operate public sewer systems is classified in the national income and product accounts as business spending.
Source: U.S. Department of Commerce, *Survey of Current Business*, Vol. 76, No. 9, Sept. 1996, Table 2, p. 50.

Table 12.2. *Composition of U.S. pollution-abatement and control spending, 1994*

Media	Total spending (in percentages)	Business spending (in percentages)
Air	30.9	32.6
Water	34.8	35.5
Solid Waste	34.3	34.0
Total	100.0	100.0

Source: Adapted from U.S. Department of Commerce, *Survey of Current Business*, Vol. 76, No. 9, Sept. 1996, Table 11, p. 63.

Table 12.3. *U.S. pollution-abatement and control expenditures 1972–1994*

Year	Total (billions 1987 dollars)	Percent GDP	By Business (billions 1987 dollars)	Percent GDP
1972	16.6	1.3	10.7	0.8
1973	19.3	1.4	12.2	0.9
1974	23.4	1.6	14.6	1.0
1975	28.3	1.7	16.4	1.0
1976	31.8	1.7	18.4	1.0
1977	35.1	1.7	21.0	1.0
1978	39.5	1.7	23.4	1.0
1979	45.3	1.8	27.0	1.1
1980	50.8	1.8	30.0	1.0
1981	54.4	1.7	32.5	1.0
1982	55.9	1.7	33.5	1.0
1983	59.1	1.7	35.0	1.0
1984	66.1	1.7	39.4	1.0
1985	71.4	1.7	42.0	1.0
1986	76.0	1.7	44.1	1.0
1987	78.9	1.7	45.7	1.0
1988	83.8	1.7	48.4	1.0
1989	88.5	1.6	52.2	0.9
1990	94.8	1.7	58.3	1.0
1991	97.9	1.7	61.1	1.1
1992	104.8	1.7	65.9	1.1
1993	110.1	1.7	69.0	1.1
1994	121.8	1.8	76.6	1.1

Source: Calculated from U.S. Department of Commerce, *Survey of Current Business*, No. 9, Sept, 1996, and Council of Economic Advisors, *Economic Report to the President*, 1996.

significant: 42 percent for petroleum and coal, 14 percent for primary metals, and 13 percent for chemicals.

Two additional reasons why thus far the aggregate trade-investment impact of differential environmental controls appears modest can be identified. First it is possible that governments have found ways to compensate business for pollution-abatement expenditures, and hence sector-specific effects on polluting industries have been avoided, although such compensation undermines the Polluter Pays Principle and leaves trade patterns distorted. As noted elsewhere, there is little evidence of derogations from the PPP among OECD countries, but the data are spotty and restricted to industrial pollution control. It may be easier for governments to offset environmentally related cost increases in agriculture, where the PPP is not

Table 12.4. *U.S. pollution-abatement costs as percent value of shipments and pollution-abatement capital expenditures as percent new capital expenditures, by industry, 1993*

SIC code industry	Pollution-abatement capital expenditures and operating costs as percent value of shipments	Pollution-abatement capital expenditures as percent new capital expenditures
All Industry	0.8	7.4
20 Food and Kindred Products	0.4	2.6
21 Tobacco Products	0.2	4.6
22 Textile Mill Products	0.4	1.8
24 Lumber and Wood Products	0.4	4.7
25 Furniture and Fixtures	0.4	4.6
26 Paper and Allied Products	2.0	10.2
27 Printing and Publishing	0.2	0.9
28 Chemicals	2.2	13.3
29 Petroleum & Coal Products	3.8	42.4
30 Rubber and Misc. Plastics	0.4	1.5
31 Leather & Leather Products	0.5	14.0
32 Stone, Clay & Glass Products	1.0	5.4
33 Primary Metals	1.8	10.2
34 Fabricated Metals Products	0.5	2.4
35 Machinery, except Electrical	0.2	1.5
36 Electrical & Electronic Products	0.4	2.0
37 Transportation Equipment	0.4	2.6
38 Instruments	0.4	2.9
39 Misc. Manufacturing	0.2	2.0

Source: Calculated from U.S. Department of Commerce, Bureau of the Census, *Pollution Abatement Cost and Expenditures: 1994*, report MA 200(94)-1 (Washington, D.C., GPO, 1996).

taken seriously and where multiple government subsidy programs already exist. Preliminary empirical findings by Eliste and Fredriksson show that in fact more stringent environmental regulations do cause greater government assistance to agricultural producers (Eliste and Fredriksson 1999).

Second, with regard to foreign direct investment, there is some evidence that for many industries clean technology is also efficient technology. It follows that the incentive to relocate abroad would be driven less by differential environmental standards and more by other determinants such as access to raw materials, labor costs, and so forth (Eskeland and Harrison

1997). Perhaps equally important, large multinational corporations face significant reputational risk if their environmental performance in developing countries is poor and widely publicized. This is the Union Carbide/Bhopal concern. There is now some empirical work showing that firm-specific, adverse environmental news does depress stock market values, not only for firms in the United States but also in a sample of developing countries (Dasgupta, Laplante, and Mamingi 1999). This market value effect may have also inhibited firms from exploiting differential environmental regulations or their enforcement, especially for larger firms with name identification. Small firms with little reputation at risk would be less affected. Finally, there is anecdotal evidence and some preliminary econometric work that suggests that foreign-owned facilities in developing countries are less polluting than their nationally owned counterparts (Eskeland and Harrison 1997; Pearson 1987).

2.3 The Competitiveness Question: Developing Countries

All of the studies reviewed in Section 2.1 approach the competitiveness question from the perspective of advanced industrial countries, and most use U.S. pollution or pollution-abatement cost data. The principal conclusion is that there is little or no evidence that strict environmental controls result in any significant loss of international competitiveness. It is tempting to infer from this conclusion that developing and transitional countries with weak standards (or weak enforcement) have not gained competitive advantage, and that they could proceed to internalize appropriate environmental protection costs without undue loss of export earnings or international market share. This in fact *may* be the case, but conclusions drawn from industrial country studies do not necessarily carry over to developing and transitional economies.

One reason is that developing countries rely more heavily on export of natural resources and natural-resource-based products than do industrial countries. Virtually all of the studies reviewed here focus on the relatively narrow issue of pollution abatement in the industrial (manufacturing) sector. The costs of appropriate environmental protection in the natural resource sector have not been well documented. Expressed as a fraction of value of shipments or value added they *may* be much higher than industrial pollution-abatement costs. Moreover, natural resource extraction and production often receive large implicit or explicit subsidies – water, energy, negligible rent and royalty payments. The first and most important step in fully internalizing social costs would be a removal of these subsidies. Unlike industrial production, where the measured costs concentrate on pollution abatement, full social costing of natural resources and natural-resource-based products would involve both the removal of existing subsidies *and* pollution-abatement and natural-resource-protection expenditures. While this is true for natural resource sectors of industrial countries as well, the greater reliance on these sectors in developing countries may produce a different and more substantial competitive result. Closely related, international markets for most natural resources are price-sensitive. This suggests that individual developing country exporters may find it more difficult to pass along environmental protection costs in price unless they are willing to accept loss of market share. Indeed, in some instances such as natural fisheries the appropriate environmental protection policy may be a limit on catch and therefore a cap on export revenues. While this may conserve the long-term yield of the fishery (or forest), the near-term effects on export earning may be negative and significant, especially if the policy is pursued unilaterally.

There are other reasons why increasing environmental protection in developing countries may have a different effect on competitiveness than in developed economies. First, access to pollution-abatement technology, for example, disposal of toxic wastes, may be more difficult or expensive. Second, the greater proportion of small- and medium-sized enterprises in the export sectors of developing countries suggests higher abatement costs per unit output. As noted later, the costs of complying with environmentally related product standards set in importing countries may be additional to domestic pollution-abatement costs.[6] Third, in highly polluted developing and transition economies, remedial pollution cleanup costs are large and additional to abatement in current production. The OECD countries have gradually tightened standards over almost three decades; developing and transitional countries confront accumulated pollution as well as a lag in standards.

For all these reasons, one cannot assert with confidence that the trade-competitive effect of substantial improvement in environmental protection in transition and developing countries will be negligible. Ultimately, it is an empirical question, and evidence is scattered and incomplete. There is some anecdotal evidence, but even that is contradictory. For example, a study of trade-environment linkages in Poland estimated that as a result of environ-

---

6 The leather and leather goods industry in India is a good example. Although a major exporter (7 percent of Indian exports in 1993–94) and employer (1.4 million workers), it is largely small scale, with over 2,000 tanneries alone. In 1990, only 22 percent of 436 small and medium tanneries surveyed treated effluents. See Jyoti Parikh (1994).

mental regulations, production costs in thermal power plants might increase by 30 to 40 percent, which would lead to a decline in export of fertilizers, plastics, cement, and other products, and would lead to the collapse of electricity exports by the largest power-exporting firm in Poland (Fiedor 1994). But another study of foreign trade and environment in China cites several cases in which environmental investments *improved* product quality and resulted in net savings to the enterprise, an example that supports the Porter hypothesis (Ruishu 1993).

The first systematic modelling study of environmental protection in production and trade competitiveness in a developing country that we are aware of was done by the Philippine Institute for Development Studies (Intal et al. 1994). Their work shows that the cost of preventing environmental damage from soil erosion plus the costs of a 90 percent reduction of air and water pollution would range from 0 to 6.1 percent of the value of output for the 60 economic sectors they examined. Only four sectors, however, had environmental damage and pollution-abatement costs that exceeded 2 percent of sector output (poultry, forestry, agricrop production, and livestock).[7] All of the industrial sectors fell below 2 percent and most were less than 0.5 percent. These results suggest that substantially stronger environmental protection measures could be implemented without any serious competitive effects. In further analysis, the authors calculated ratios of domestic resource cost to shadow exchange rates and official exchange rates, to calculate the social and private profitability of export sectors if environmental protection costs were increased and incorporated in total production costs. The results show that for the export sectors examined and in which the Philippines has a comparative advantage, the internalization of social costs would *not* reverse the social probability and comparative advantage, unless the social costs reached extremely high levels (e.g., 20 to 30 percent of production costs for aquaculture). But the analysis also shows that incorporating environmental protection costs, while maintaining existing distortions due to disequilibrium exchange rates and illiberal trade policy, could increase negative effective protection rates in some industries. This reinforces the desirability of coupling trade policy and environmental policy reform, a theoretical point made in Chapter 8.

A study by Beghin et al. combines the interaction of trade liberalization and increased environmental protection using a general equilibrium framework applied to Mexico. The abatement of a variety of pollutants through effluent and emission taxes, by itself, does indeed lead to a deterioration

---

7 This excluded public administration, which is apparently high due to the inclusion of urban water runoff damages and soil erosion from public lands.

in the Mexican trade balance and real GDP below baseline trends. And trade liberalization, by itself, increases GDP above baseline but also increases all pollutants (the scale effect dominates). When implemented jointly, however, the authors conclude that the two reforms are complementary – trade reform mitigates the contractionary effects of stronger environmental policy, and the abatement measures themselves dampen incremental pollution due to expanded trade (Beghin, Roland-Holst, and van der Mensbrugghe 1995).

Even if environmental protection measures have minimal effect on exports, the internal distribution of their costs may be significant and of concern. For example, Abdul Rahmin Khalid and J. D. Braden (1993) examined the stringent pollution control measures introduced in the Malaysian palm oil industry between 1978 and 1986. The industry was separated into three segments: production of fresh fruit bunches, initial processing to crude palm oil, and subsequent processing to refined palm oil for export. With fixed international prices for refined oil, typical of a small country, and inelastic supply of the fresh fruit, the pollution-abatement costs were pushed back through the processing chain to the fresh fruit producers. Export volume and value changed minimally, but the fresh fruit producers bore an estimated 84 percent of abatement costs by the processors, and the welfare loss to these farmers represented about 44 percent of the total value of the fresh fruit they produced. With small holders accounting for about half of fresh fruit production, the internal distribution effects appear to have been severe and negative, although the trade-competitive effect was minimal.

3 Trade Effects of Product and Packaging Standards, Ecolabelling, and Multilateral Environmental Agreements

The principal empirical question is whether environmentally related product standards, labelling, and related measures have had significant effects on international trade. The issue is of particular concern to developing country exporters. Evidence from both importing and exporting countries is relevant. Some empirical material is available from import detention records in the United States and from databases and case studies supported by UNCTAD, but the picture is far from complete.

The first source of information is the United States. In an earlier study, Pearson analyzed U.S. Food and Drug Administration (FDA) import detentions of food products for a single month in 1981 (Pearson 1982). The results showed a large number of shipment detentions (6,816 annualized) but with a small average value ($22,000). Most detentions were not for strictly envi-

Table 12.5. *Food product detentions by FDA, by reason for detention*

Reason for detention	Number of shipments detained	Percent of total shipments detained
A. Filth	89	11.9
B. Product decomposed	42	5.6
C. Salmonella	5	0.7
D. Other defects affecting health	43	5.7
E. Unsafe additives	79	10.6
F. Pesticide residues	24	3.2
G. Heavy metals	1	0.1
H. Substandard quality and short weight	6	0.8
I. LACF (Low acid canned food)	210	28.0
J. Improper labeling	250	33.4
Total	749	100.0

Note: Reasons for detention:
A: Filth includes insect, rodent, bird filth/damage, animal excreta; D: Other product defects affecting health include mold, poisonous/deleterious substances, *E. coli*/coliforms, alfa-toxin/mycotoxin, histamines, unfit for human consumption, damaged containers, water contaminated contents; H: Substandard quality includes substance omitted; I: LACF – manufacturer fails to register and/or file process for low acid canned foods; J: Improper labeling includes not labeled in English, ingredients not listed, failure to meet requirements of Fair Packaging Labeling Act (FPLA).
Source: FDA: Monthly Import Detention List: Report #93-01, January, 1993. As compiled in Pearson, 1994b.

ronmental reasons – about 4 percent of U.S. imports of fruits, vegetables, fish, and shellfish from developing countries were detained, but only 10 percent of the detained shipments were for pesticide residue and heavy metal contamination. The study was partially updated for January 1993 (Pearson 1994b). The results are reproduced as Tables 12.5 to 12.7.

Unfortunately, the FDA reports no longer include value data, and therefore the value of shipments detained is not known. The tables suggest that the two detention reasons most clearly environmental in nature, pesticide residues and heavy metal contamination, account for only 3.3 percent of detained shipments. The tables also show fish and shellfish, fruits and vegetables, and, surprisingly, spices are the products most frequently detained. Developing countries account for 60 percent of U.S. food imports and 76 percent of detained shipments. This may not be a meaningful comparison,

Table 12.6. *Product detained by type of product*

	Number of shipments detained	Percent of total shipments detained
Grain and grain products	38	5.1
Dairy products	18	2.4
Fish and shellfish	182	24.3
(shrimp)	(17)	(2.3)
Fruit and vegetables	210	28.0
(fruit)	(75)	(10.0)
(vegetables)	(125)	(16.7)
(nuts)	(10)	(1.3)
Spices	162	21.7
Coffee and cocoa	25	3.3
Other food products	114	15.2
Total	749	100.0

Source: FDA: Monthly Import Detention List: Report #93-01, January, 1993. As compiled in Pearson, 1994b.

Table 12.7. *Products detained by country or region of origin*

	Number of shipments	Percent of total detained shipments
India	23	3.1
Thailand	62	8.3
Hong Kong	60	8.0
People's Republic of China	42	5.6
Mexico	53	7.1
Philippines	71	9.5
Other developing countries	257	34.3
Total developing countries	568	75.8
Total developed countries	181	24.2
Total	749	100.0

Source: FDA: Monthly Import Detention List: Report #93-01, January, 1993. As compiled in Pearson, 1994b.

however, because of the composition of developing-country food exports to the United States and because the data are by number of shipments detained rather than by value of shipments detained.

Both NAFTA and the SPS and TBT agreements emerging from the Uruguay Round promote the use of international standards in national legislation. Differing national standards create costs and difficulties for exporters. The U.S. General Accounting Office (GAO) produced an interesting comparison of pesticide standards set by the United States and international standards set by the Codex Alimentarius (U.S. General Accounting Office 1991). A full one-to-one comparison by product and pesticide was not possible because of differences in definition and because EPA's set of pesticide-by-product standards is not totally congruent to the Codex set. For the 1,267 cases that could be compared, the United States had lower maximum residual levels (i.e., tighter standards) in 19 percent of the cases, Codex had lower maximum residual levels in 34 percent of cases, and the standards were about the same in 47 percent of cases. In other studies conducted by the GAO, the results showed that U.S. pesticide registration status coincided with registration status in five Latin American countries, indicating that as a dominant market the United States *de facto* exports its standards (U.S. General Accounting Office 1990). The GAO study also found that most FDA pesticide residue violations on imports were because the EPA had not established a specific pesticide tolerance for the product in question, and not because of excessive residue levels (for example, the EPA had tolerance level for bell peppers but not Mexican serrano peppers). This scattered evidence suggests that it is a bit artificial to separate environmental from other types of product standards, and that harmonizing standards at the international level will be slow and difficult. While the studies produced no evidence that the standards were being used as covert protectionist measures, they do not demonstrate that product standards are unimportant in trade.

A second source of empirical information is a database created at UNCTAD (Mollerus 1995). UNCTAD has identified a large number of environmentally related product measures by type, product, and importing country and has combined this with world trade data reported in the harmonized system (HS) for classification of goods. The measures are classified as prohibitions, standards and regulations, recycling requirements, ecolabelling, products controlled by the Montreal Protocol, and so on. The approach of linking environmental measures to trade data to measure the trade impact of environmental regulations is subject to a number of limitations. Product regulations may not conform to the HS system (e.g., packaging requirements). Not all products within the HS code may be regulated. Most important, the approach may identify the value of trade that is subject to a product-specific environmental measure, but does not indicate the severity of the trade impact, if any. Nevertheless, this work does provide additional information on the value, composition, and destination of trade subject to environmental measures. Also, measuring the extent of nontariff trade barriers by calculating the value of trade affected by them is an established procedure in the literature.

Roland Mollerus and Rafael Sanchez have used this database to identify exports from 14 Asian countries that are "sensitive" to environmental product measures.[8] Tables 12.8 and 12.9 summarize the main results. Table 12.8 shows that for the 14 Asian countries taken together, exports subject to some form of environmentally related product measure amounted to $47 billion, or about 15 percent of total exports from these countries to the selected OECD markets. Almost 30 percent of South Asia's exports to these markets fall in the sensitive category. This may be significant as the South Asian countries have more limited experience in exporting and thus may have greater difficulty in complying with environmental product standards applied in their export markets.[9] China stands out as having the lowest share of its sensitive exports destined for OECD markets and thus appears least vulnerable to environmentally related product standards in its export markets.

Table 12.9 shows the particular types of environmental measures that are important to the exporting regions. Because one export product can be subject to multiple measures in the same export market, the dollar value of exports subject to an environmental measure can be counted twice. With this caveat in mind, Table 12.9 reveals that for ASEAN exports the most important measures are standards and regulations ($5.3 billion), environmental labelling ($4.6 billion), and products controlled by the Montreal Protocol ($1.2 billion). For South Asia, the most important measures are ecolabelling ($1.7 billion) followed by standards and regulations ($0.9 billion). For East Asia the most important are also standards and regulations ($5.6 billion) followed by ecolabelling ($3.3 billion). Finally, for China, the most important are ecolabelling ($2.3 billion) and standards and regulations ($2.1 billion). The immediate conclusions are that two types of environmental measures dominate in quantitative (trade) terms, environmentally related standards and regulations and ecolabelling schemes, and that this pattern holds in the

8 Their summary tables are presented and discussed in Pearson (1996).
9 The country-level details show the percentages to be Bangladesh (48 percent), Pakistan (38 percent), Vietnam (34 percent), and India (25 percent).

Table 12.8. *Estimated exports from Asia of "sensitive" products subject to environmental product measures in selected OECD markets, 1993 value in U.S.$ million – export shares (in percentages)*

Market:		Sensitive exports to selected markets 1993 million U.S.$	Share of "sensitive" exports to selected OECD markets over total "sensitive" exports to all markets (in %)	Share of "sensitive" exports to total exports to selected markets (in %)
U.S.	ASEAN	2,453	18.5	5.6
	South Asia	479	25.5	7.0
	East Asia	3,557	22.5	6.6
	China	1,476	19.2	4.4
Japan	ASEAN	5,721	27.2	16.3
	South Asia	421	20.7	14.8
	East Asia	2,962	23.3	12.7
	China	1,718	25.4	8.4
European Union	ASEAN	6,597	29.7	20.3
	South Asia	4,992	53.2	48.2
	East Asia	9,509	22.1	28.1
	China	7,171	13.7	33.4
Total (U.S. + Japan + E.U.)	ASEAN	14,772	66.5	13.2
	South Asia	5,937	62.8	29.5
	East Asia	16,029	37.2	14.4
	China	10,365	19.9	13.7
Germany	ASEAN	2,382	5.0	26.2
	South Asia	2,053	12.5	73.3
	East Asia	983	2.7	32.4
	China	3,699	5.0	44.3
The Netherlands	ASEAN	3,485	3.1	1.9
	South Asia	320	4.3	45.0
	East Asia	983	2.7	27.5
	China	409	0.9	28.3

Note: ASEAN includes Brunei, Indonesia, Malaysia, Philippines, Singapore, Thailand, and Vietnam. South Asia includes Bangladesh, India, and Pakistan. East Asia includes Hong Kong, Republic of Korea, and Taiwan Province of China.
Source: Reported in Pearson (1996) and based on study by Roland Mollerus and Rafael Sanchez for ESCAP.

Table 12.9. *Estimated exports from Asia of "sensitive" products subject to environmental product measures in selected OECD markets (1993 value in U.S.$ million)*

Measure:		Total[a]	of which: U.S.	Japan	E.U.	Germany	The Netherlands
PR	ASEAN	1,991	1,776	62	153	84	2
	South Asia	306	208	8	90	25	9
	East Asia	614	213	50	321	42	5
	China	502	300	50	152	41	4
ST	ASEAN	5,300	1,705	2,934	670	2,170	70
	South Asia	839	371	405	164	1,058	17
	East Asia	5,586	7,636	1,737	1,808	2,260	203
	China	2,114	542	1,178	594	3,381	64
RR	ASEAN	468	75	393		15	28
	South Asia	31	30	1		6	1
	East Asia	1,435	1,245	189		338	36
	China	89	74	16		15	40
TC	ASEAN	192	124	68		7	24
	South Asia	94	93	1		6	7
	East Asia	1,743	1,598	145		338	36
	China	115	102	14		2	1
DR	ASEAN	110	54		56		
	South Asia	0	0		0		
	East Asia	280	147		132		
	China	63	21		41		
EL	ASEAN	4,604	436	2,472	1,695	56	428
	South Asia	1,653	1	8	1,645	7	298
	East Asia	3,303	325	866	2,112	467	694
	China	2,311	80	449	1,782	40	331
ML	ASEAN	700	253	130	277	1,426	5
	South Asia	88	0	0	88	1,566	9
	East Asia	1,019	367	29	603	2,199	17
	China	455	69	2	383	2,266	5
VA	ASEAN	0				51	371
	South Asia	0				10	17
	East Asia	0				61	127
	China	0				65	45
GP	ASEAN	0				293	26
	South Asia	0				13	16
	East Asia	0				201	44
	China	0				169	5

Table 12.9. *(cont.)*

Measure:		Total[a]	of which: U.S.	Japan	E.U.	Germany	The Netherlands
CS	ASEAN	1,219	277	538	403	5	28
	South Asia	54	21	3	31	1	2
	East Asia	2,899	1,115	735	1,049	12	88
	China	1,577	852	177	548	15	41

[a] Total = Sum of U.S., Japan and E.U. For country groupings, see Table 12.8.
Key: PR: prohibitions; ST: standards and regulations; RR: recycling and reuse measures; TC: taxes and charges; DR: deposit/refund schemes; EL: ecolabelling; ML: mandatory labeling; VA: voluntary agreements; GP: government procurement; CS: products controlled by the Montreal Protocol.
Source: Reported in Pearson (1996) and based on study by Roland Mollerus and Rafael Sanchez for ESCAP.

four subregions of interest, ASEAN, South Asia, East Asia, and China. At a more fundamental level, however, these results remain inconclusive. Without knowing the relative restrictiveness of the various measures, or their trade-distortive effect, if any, no firm conclusion can be drawn from these results. Nevertheless, the consistent ranking of standards and regulations and eco-labelling at the top suggests that these two types of measures are *potentially* the most significant for Asian exporters.

A third source of empirical information on product standards is various country and case studies that have been sponsored by UNCTAD. The questions these studies addressed include exporting countries' experience with the trade provisions of MEAs, ecolabelling, green trade, and so forth. The results are difficult to summarize in part because the various studies used different methodologies or address somewhat different questions. At some points the results are inconclusive or inconsistent. We summarize the results of the Colombia study as it is one of the more detailed and systematic (Gaviria et al. 1994).

The methodology of the Colombia study was a written survey of firms engaged in exporting, complemented by over 100 personal interviews at firms and interviews with representatives of all major business organizations. Sixty-seven percent of survey respondents reported they had not experienced any *international* (as opposed to national) environmental regulatory pressures, as compared to 16 percent that had. However, awareness of environmental regulations in foreign markets was weak. The majority of respondents stated they either lacked information on international environmental requirements and consumer preferences or felt the information they had was inadequate or unclear. The German Packaging Law was the most frequently cited external measure (16 percent of respondents) when an external measure was identified. The EU was the most frequently named source of external measures despite its low share in Colombian exports. Of 28 firms responding to a question on the competitive impact, 13 said that adapting to international environmental standards had a *positive* effect on their competitiveness, one felt it was negative, and 14 firms did not know. Of four fruit companies included in the survey, one reported that mandated input requirements raised cost by 6 percent, another reported packaging requirements raised costs by 2 percent.

With regard to ecolabels, 6 of 60 respondents possessed or had applied for labels, and 52 firms reported that they did not compete with foreign firms that had obtained ecolabels in overseas markets but 20 felt that if ecolabels became common it would affect their competitiveness. Ecolabels are or may become more important in cut flowers, clothing, leather products, and bananas, all significant export items. Colombian textile firms suspect the ecolabel is used as a protectionist device against non-European imports, especially private labelling schemes developed by producer interests in Germany. Ecolabelling of bananas under the Rainforest Alliance Smart Banana program is of some concern in Colombia if it expands in Costa Rica. Also, the EU's new strict quotas for Latin America's bananas may give preference to "environmentally certified" bananas and present difficulties for Colombia.

Of 60 firms responding, 10 reported being affected by the German Packaging Ordinance and only 9 of 26 responding felt the technical procedures in the law were clear. Of six fruit-exporting firms, four reported increased costs, but the costs were modest relative to total costs in two cases (1, 1, 4, and less than 5 percent). Again with regard to the German law, there was an earlier dispute over jute packaging of coffee but that had been resolved. Other difficulties centered on obtaining accurate, timely information and differences among European countries in national-level packaging requirements. The cut flower industry exporting to Europe reported that total packaging accounted for about 7.5 percent of total costs and incremental compliance costs were modest.

The Colombia study also examined the effects of the U.S. secondary embargo of tuna following its tuna-dolphin dispute with Mexico. It estimates that the incremental cost of modifying fishing technology to meet U.S. requirements was a modest 2.5 percent of operation costs for large purse seiners. Smaller fishing vessels may encounter higher costs. Moreover, the study estimates that up to $32 million in export revenues was lost during the embargo period. Further objections to the unilateral character of the U.S. embargo and the possibility that approved tuna fishing methods will result in greater catches of immature tuna and hence lower sustainable yield were also noted.

The government of Colombia analyzed the costs of the Montreal Protocol. It found that incremental and other costs for large Colombian industries would total up to about $80 million. A grant proposal to the Multilateral Fund of the Protocol had been submitted but the proportion of the costs, if any, that would be subsidized was not known. Moreover, certain export-oriented industries (flowers, bananas, meat) rely on refrigeration and will be affected by higher CFC and, ultimately, conversion costs. These costs and their export effects were not quantified.

With regard to phytosanitary regulations, pesticide residue tests in the U.S. market are said to be expensive ($200–$500 for each sample for strawberries), and Colombia firms allege the strict standards are to protect U.S. berry producers. Phytosanitary regulations are also important in the shrimp trade. Colombian processing firms, however, are export-oriented and report no difficulties in meeting foreign standards. Shrimp fishing vessels, however, must comply with a U.S. law mandating turtle exclusion devices (TEDs) if they are to export to the United States. The cost per vessel of TEDs is estimated at $400–$800 per vessel, a modest figure. Nevertheless, the measure is considered an unwarranted unilateral action and a study by the national fishing agency concluded that in 1992, prior to the installation of TEDs, only two turtles had been caught by Colombian fishing vessels. Finally, the study documents that the main environmental challenges facing the Colombian shrimp industry are not from external measures, but from serious overharvesting and conversion of mangrove forests.

Various other country studies sponsored by UNCTAD have tried to assess the trade effect on Asian countries of the phaseout of ozone-depleting substances under the Montreal Protocol. The results are both speculative and inconclusive. For example, the adjustment cost estimates for India range from $320 million to $2450 million, but except for some cost increase in refrigerated seafood and horticultural exports, most of the adjustment cost is borne domestically, not in the export sector. China reported a 63 percent drop in exports of refrigerators as a result of CFC restrictions in the Montreal Protocol, but that figure was not well documented. In Malaysia, CFCs were used in two important export sectors, electronics (as solvents) and refrigerators and air conditioners. While CFC prices have risen substantially, there is no evidence that this slowed export performance, which was robust in the first half of the 1990s. The explanations given in interviews are that some cost has been passed on in export prices and the introduction of CFC substitutes was accompanied by productivity-enhancing technological change. These sectors are made up of a few large, technologically sophisticated multinational firms, which makes adjustment easier. Singapore has used the price-market system to implement CFC controls, with an import quota for CFCs subsequently auctioned to domestic users. The report gave no overall estimate of export losses due to restricted use of CFCs, but states there was a perception that Singapore lost competitive advantage to electronics and refrigeration–air-conditioning competitor countries in the region, who received a 10-year grace period under the Montreal Protocol. Thailand's experience with product standards and MEAs is summarized in Chapter 18.

4 Impact of Trade and Trade Liberalization on the Environment

Empirical work on estimating the effects of trade and trade liberalization on environmental resources is just now emerging.[10] Before reviewing studies, it is important to reiterate three caveats. First, for environmental planning purposes, it is immaterial whether environmental stress associated with economic activity arises from production for domestic consumption or for export. Logging, overfishing, and toxic emissions are no more and no less damaging whether the product is exported than consumed domestically. The only legitimate reason to consider trade is its use as a tool for predicting the level and composition of production, so that natural resource inputs and pollution outputs can be anticipated. Second, if the analysis does attempt to identify environmental impacts of trade, the effects are only meaningful when measured against some counterfactual scenario. For example, a serious analysis of the environmental effects of NAFTA on Mexico should consider the economic and environmental profile of Mexico had NAFTA not been agreed to. Third, while it is easy to identify export demand as the proximate cause of environmental degradation in a particular sector, it does not follow that trade is "responsible" for the degradation

---

10 Empirical testing of Ricardian and H-O trade models do extend to commercialized natural resources, but their main focus is natural resources as a determinant of trade. The *recent* concern is with externalities in natural resource production, especially agriculture and mining. The 1970s boom and 1980s slump in U.S. agriculture and its growing dependence on international trade did stimulate studies of the effects of trade on land prices, agricultural inputs, and soil erosion associated with cultivation of marginal lands. See John Sutton (1988).

or that exports should be limited. In virtually all cases, the appropriate remedy lies in correcting government or private market failures, and this seldom involves a trade restriction.[11]

Attempts to measure the effects of trade and trade policy on the environment fall into three groups. The first group attempts to determine the impact of existing trade policies, the second group looks at broad trade liberalization agreements, and the third focuses on specific sectors. The methodologies range from presentation of descriptive statistics to regression analysis to CGE modelling.

Robert Lucas and his colleagues use regression analysis to test whether a trade-openness variable affects countries' rate of growth of toxic intensity. Toxic intensity is measured by toxic releases per unit value of manufacturing output (Lucas et al. 1992). The results suggest that rapidly growing, low- and middle-income *closed* economies exhibited rapid shifts toward toxic-intensive structures, especially in the 1980s. In contrast, open economics showed declines in the toxic intensity of their manufacturing during the 1970s and 1980s. This is consistent with the observation that low-income countries open to trade have exploited comparative advantage in labor-intensive manufactures that are generally characterized as low pollution intensity. These conclusions are also supported by pooled regression work on 25 Latin American countries over the same period done by Nancy Birdsall and David Wheeler (1993). Again, using an index of trade openness, they find that in the 1980s the toxic intensity growth rate for the decade was 35 percent annually for fast-growing, low-income, *closed* economies and 5 percent for *open* economies. For middle-income countries the results are 29 percent and –1.5 percent, respectively.

Liberal trade facilitates the import of clean technology and is generally accompanied by liberal policies *vis à vis* foreign direct investment. David Wheeler and Paul Martin (1992) tested the hypothesis that the rate of diffusion of clean technology in the world pulp industry was positively related to an index of domestic price distortions in different countries, a measure of the open or closed character of an economy. Thermomechanical pulping is a clean technology (in contrast to chemical-based pulp technologies). They found that the openness variable was significant in accelerating the timing of the adoption of the clean technology. A simulation showed that an open regime, by accelerating new, clean technology, would reduce pollution from 10 to 20 percent over a period of a decade.

These three studies suggest that open economies may have better envi-

---

11 Trade measures for transnational externalities are considered in Chapters 13 and 14.

ronmental performance if their comparative advantage is in relatively clean industries (e.g., labor-intensive manufacturing for low-income countries) or because of better access to clean technology. This is not always the case. The U.S. grains sector played the role of residual supplier to world trade in the 1970s and 1980s. During the years of booming world demand in the 1970s, U.S. cropping was extended to soils more prone to erosion, was accompanied by increased use of potentially damaging chemical inputs (pesticides, fertilizer), and used greater quantities of water (Runge, Houck, and Halbach 1988; Ogg and Sutton 1988; Runge 1994a). With the slump in the 1980s, Runge has suggested that in the interaction between U.S. environmental conservation policies and acreage controls to firm up prices, too little environmentally sensitive land was withdrawn from production.

Trade liberalization changes the level and composition of production and hence the stress on environmental resources. Grossman and Krueger produced an *ex ante* estimate of the effects of NAFTA on toxic emissions from manufacturing in Mexico, the United States, and Canada (Grossman and Krueger 1993). The method was to use the results of a CGE model to predict production changes by manufacturing sector, and to use toxic emission–output coefficients by sector from U.S. firm-level data (the Toxic Release Inventory). In this fashion, estimates of change in emissions by sector could be calculated. The result of trade liberalization without any induced capital flow shows a slight decline in aggregate toxic releases in Mexico, as it shifts out of chemicals and rubber and plastic products toward labor-intensive products. However, with positive capital flow to Mexico, all manufacturing sectors expand, as do toxic emissions. The model also predicted an increase in toxic releases in the United States, due mainly to expansion of chemicals production and also an expansion of toxic emissions in Canada, due namely to an expansion of primary metals production. The results should be treated with some caution as actual toxic emission coefficients in Mexico may be very different from the borrowed U.S. coefficients, and many aspects of environmental quality, for example, in agriculture, are not considered.

The same basic approach has been used by Michael Ferrantino and Linda Linkins to estimate the possible effects of the Uruguay Round and of full multilateral elimination of tariffs on manufactures on toxic emissions (Ferrantino and Linkins, forthcoming). As in the Grossman and Krueger study, a CGE model is used to estimate manufacturing output changes by sector and by region of the world, and then toxic emission–output coefficients from U.S. data are used to estimate changes in emissions by sector and region. The results show that full reduction of tariffs would decrease toxic emissions in China and Hong Kong (–7.7 percent); in a grouping composed of Africa, the Middle East, and South Asia (–2.9 percent); and in South East Asia (–2.5 percent). The effects in North America, Japan, and Europe would be modest (–0.1, +0.5, and +0.2 percent, respectively). The apparent reason for beneficial environmental effects in developing countries is their rather high levels of trade protection in pollution, capital, and energy-intensive industries, despite reductions agreed to in the Uruguay Round. Trade liberalization would shift some of this production back to developed countries.

In an effort to refine pollution emission coefficients, the study also estimates the implicit income elasticity of emissions per unit output for eight pollutants (e.g., SO_2, heavy metals, and BOD) over the per capita income range of \$2,000–\$12,000. These elasticities range from –0.15 for arsenic to –0.72 for smoke. The implication is that a 10 percent increase in per capita income leads to a 1.5 percent reduction in the arsenic emission coefficient and a 7.2 percent reduction in the smoke emission coefficient. In conducting the simulations, however, the elasticity is allowed to vary from 0 (assuming wideworld use of U.S. abatement regulations and technology) to –2. The results show that for midrange elasticities (e.g., –0.25 to –0.5), a full removal of all manufacturing tariffs would decrease global emissions by 0.55 to 0.66 percent, a modest global improvement. The reason is a relocation of heavy, dirty industry presently receiving protection in the South to the North, where environmental standards are higher and toxic emission coefficients are lower. At the extreme, if the coefficient elasticity were –2.0, global emissions would fall by 4.3 percent. Notice that this empirical simulation result is the opposite of the theoretical conclusion derived by Copeland and Taylor (1994), described in Chapter 7, that trade will increase world pollution. The different conclusion arises because the Copeland and Taylor model predicts that trade will cause production of dirty products to shift from North to South where they are subject to less stringent resolution, whereas this empirical exercise shows current dirty industry shifting from its protected status in the South to North as trade protection is dismantled.

Most empirical work examining the effects of trade on the environment has concentrated on how trade affects the *composition* of output and hence pollution levels. But trade also increases income growth and, through income, the demand for environmental quality. Using a data set on Chinese industrial water pollution by province for the period 1987–1995, Judith Dean separates a direct composition effect on pollution emissions from an indirect effect on emissions working through higher income. Her findings indicate a positive relation between China's terms of trade and its growth of emissions, indicating that China may have a static comparative advantage in pollution-intensive goods. But the study also finds that trade liberalization, working through the growth of income, tends to *reduce* pollution emissions (Dean 1999). This suggests that if the inverted U hypothesis, explored in Chapter 17, is correct, an open trade regime speeds a country's progress toward the environmental improvement range of the curve.

To conclude, we note that some sector-specific research on the link from trade to environmental quality has been published. The sectors include energy, transport, forestry, and agriculture (Markandya, Emerton, and Mwale 1998; OECD 1994a). The analytical challenge in the forestry sector is to disentangle the various factors contributing to deforestation – commercial logging for domestic consumption and export; extension of subsistence agriculture; commercialized agriculture including plantation crops, fuelwood, and so forth. The links between trade and deforestation can be quite indirect. For example, the direct effect of commercial logging for export may be small, but extension of logging roads to remote areas has been implicated in internal migration and the introduction of unsustainable farming practices.[12]

The empirical studies of the impact of agricultural trade liberalization on environmental resources has come to conflicting conclusions with regard to developing countries. Some studies conclude that trade liberalization will increase agricultural prices in developing countries and, with expanded production, would use more fragile lands, increase pressure in scarce water resources, and increase the use of chemical inputs. Kym Anderson (1992a) comes to a somewhat more optimistic conclusion.[13] He uses the results of a multicountry, multicommodity simulation model to determine price and production effects in the agriculture of trade liberalization. He then speculates on environmental impacts using estimates drawn from other studies of the responsiveness of inputs (land, chemicals) to price changes. The general conclusion is that some agricultural production would shift from chemical-intensive production in developed countries to more labor-intensive production in developing countries. Adverse environmental consequences in developing countries could be moderated by better enforcement of forest property rights, elimination of input subsidies, and the restraining effect of strict food safety standards in export markets. Moreover, Anderson argues that increased incomes and employment associated with trade liberalization would reduce natural resource stress arising from rural poverty.

---

12 For a detailed country-level analysis of the interaction between trade policy and deforestation in Indonesia, see Barbier, Bockstael, Burgess, and Strand (1995).
13 See also Anna Strutt and Kym Anderson (1998).

Part 3

Transnational Pollution and Management of
International Resources

Note to Part 3

No country can pursue environmental autarky. All share the global atmosphere and are connected by common watersheds, river systems, seas, and oceans. Valuable resources such as biodiversity and unique scenic attractions may exist within the territory of one country, but the condition of these resources is of widespread interest. Transfrontier pollution is the physical movement of pollutants outside the territory of the source country. A broader concept, international environmental spillovers (externalities), includes all instances in which the welfare of one country is affected by environmental performance of another country. The protection of regional and global environmental resources is the challenge of providing international public goods in a political system composed of sovereign national units.

The central problem of managing environmental spillovers can be simply stated. Countries pursuing their parochial self-interest are unlikely to fully account for the international environmental externalities they create. To do so would require them to bear pollution-abatement and environmental protection costs, the benefits of which would occur not to themselves, but to the international community. Neither the costs of environmental degradation nor the benefits of environmental protection are congruent with national borders. In a real sense, it is the absence of property rights and hence international markets for international environmental services that is the crux of the problem. At the same time, unlike domestic externalities, there is no supranational environmental protection agency that can compel protection measures or force the internalization of the externalities. For example, there is no supranational government that can levy an appropriate pollution tax on national governments or economic agents within countries. It follows that effective management of international environmental externalities must involve negotiations and bargaining among national governments. A reasonable minimum necessary condition for reaching a noncoercive agreement is that all participating countries must believe they are made better off (or at least no worse off) because of the agreement.

This condition has two major implications that distinguish international from domestic management of externalities. First, the distributional or equity aspects of a management scheme cannot be separated from efficiency considerations in negotiating the agreement. The expected net benefit (cost) to each negotiating party drives the negotiations. Second, in many circumstances an efficient allocation of environmental protection costs among parties to an agreement will imply net gains for some countries and net costs for other countries. To secure the participation of countries confronting net costs, an agreement will require some system of side payments to compensate for losses, or some system of sanctions or penalties to compel participation.

This is merely the bare bones of the problem. Many additional complications may be present, some of which are also present in managing purely domestic externalities. These complications include scientific and economic uncertainty surrounding the benefits and costs of environmental protection, strategic behavior in the negotiations, uncertainty with respect to legal regimes, government behavior that does not reflect the interests of its citizens, differences among countries with respect to environmental preferences and with respect to social discount rates, the equity implications of prior use and abuse of international commons for waste disposal, and many more.

The following three chapters explore the management of international environmental externalities (provision of international public goods). Chapter 13 presents a theoretical framework, discusses various approaches to management, and reviews evidence from selected international environmental arrangements. Chapters 14 and 15 illustrate the issues in two case studies: the international economics of global warming and the management of international fisheries. The emphasis on actual practice is deliberate. The formal theory of managing international externalities is highly abstract, involving strategic behavior and game theory, and tends toward pessimistic conclusions. It is useful to check theory against practice.

13

International Environmental Externalities: Theory and Policy Responses

1 Introduction and Classification

Controlling transnational pollution and managing international environmental resources requires negotiating agreements among two or more countries. The obstacles are formidable. There is no supranational authority to compel participation. International law and international property rights are weak, unsettled, or absent. An equitable distribution of the costs and benefits appears necessary, so that equity and efficiency must be simultaneously considered. At the same time, the instruments for international compensation are rudimentary, and the conditions for developing Coase-like markets are limited. Free-riding behavior is likely. Many of the more pressing issues involve scientific uncertainty and time lags, and many resist monetary valuation.

Section 2 starts with three simplified theoretical examples of reaching agreement on transnational externalities. The analytical foundations include the provision of public goods and, because of strategic interactions, game theory. Although the theoretical conclusions from simple models appear discouraging, some policy responses are feasible and welfare-improving, and these are discussed in Section 3. Section 4 tempers the abstract and theoretical discussion by examining eight specific cases or approaches to managing international externalities. The appendix to the chapter presents stylized examples of negotiations to underscore the sensitivity of the outcomes to the context and behavioral assumptions. Before getting started, however, it is useful to introduce a classification system.

International environmental externalities may be classified along three dimensions to aid analytical work. The first is to distinguish between unidirectional and reciprocal externalities. The former would describe international river pollution problems, for example, the salinity of the Colorado

River as it crosses into Mexico. The latter describes a situation in which two or more countries pollute each other's environment or a common property resource such as regional seas. Acid rain in Europe and in North America are examples. Global threats such as ozone depletion are a special case of reciprocal externalities. (Congestion of a common property resource such as a park or highway can be analyzed as a reciprocal externality problem, although generally not international in scope.) The distinction between unidirectional and reciprocal externalities is analytically useful because the response by polluters is likely to differ. Without strong international law, compensation, or coercion, there will be little effort by the source country to abate unidirectional pollution unless a large share of the damages accrue to itself.[1] As shown in this chapter, with reciprocal externalities affecting a shared resource, each country may find it in its self-interest to moderate pollution.

A second dimension is the number of countries involved – for example, the bilateral acid rain issue between the United States and Canada or the multiple country cases of ozone depletion and global warming. There may be one source and many victims, multiple sources and a single victim, or multiple sources and multiple victims. The theoretical literature on negotiations and on provision of collective goods suggests that small- and large-number cases are analytically distinct (Olson and Zeckhauser 1966). Specifically, small-number cases may encourage strategic behavior. This does not preclude agreements but does influence the use of analytical tools, especially game theory. Large-number cases are more prone to free-rider behavior. As a variation, there may be situations where the number of countries is large, but the interests of each country are very unequal. In that event, the number of countries may be less important than the behavior of the few for whom outcomes are important.

A third dimension that is analytically useful is whether the damages can be objectively measured. *Ceteris paribus*, it should be easier to negotiate international agreements when the externality, say, pollution, is measurable and the damage can be readily quantified. In that event, it is easier to reach agreement on the extent of the problem, the degree of restraint, and methods for monitoring. For example, the negotiation of target reductions for acid rain in Europe was greatly aided by models that could estimate source emissions and deposit rates by country. In contrast, where the alleged welfare loss is psychological or relates to option and existence values, as

---

1 Indeed, the incentive is to locate polluting industries downstream and downwind, close to an international border.

might be the case for protection of "glamour" species, disputes in identifying and quantifying loss and compensation may be frequent. The cultural value of whale hunting versus whale conservation is an example. Other characteristics of international spillovers are undoubtedly important in specific circumstances. These include the economic importance of the externality (large or trivial), the degree of scientific uncertainty surrounding the externality, and whether the environmental damages are immediate or cumulative and long lived.

2 Theoretical Illustrations

2.1 Three Models

The difficulties of managing international environmental externalities can be illustrated with some simplified examples. Consider first a situation in which two countries, A and B, share a resource such as a river system, airshed, or regional sea. Both make beneficial use of the resource (e.g., fishing, irrigation water, recreation) but only A pollutes. The international externality is unidirectional, as B does not create external costs for A. Some of the pollution damages are borne by A and some are borne by B, and hence the benefits of pollution abatement will be shared. The situation is illustrated in Figure 13.1 (Pearson 1976). The horizontal axis measures pollution-abatement effort by A up to the point of 100 percent abatement. The marginal cost of abatement to A (MC_A) has a positive slope, conforming to typical empirical evidence. Marginal benefits to A and to B (MB_A, MB_B) decline. The vertical addition of those two marginal benefits curves, MB_{A+B}, is the global marginal benefit function.

The optimal level of abatement from a global perspective is at Q_0. At that level, the incremental global benefits are equal to incremental abatement costs, and global welfare is maximized. Country A, however, acting in its parochial self-interest and not considering benefits conferred on B, will choose to abate at level Q_E, less than the global optimal. The extent by which unilateral action by A falls short of the global optimum abatement depends in part on the position of the two marginal benefit curves. If MB_A falls well above MB_B the divergence between the parochial equilibrium Q_E and the optimal level Q_0 will be small. In that event, most of the damage created by A will be borne by A, and we would expect that it would undertake a vigorous abatement effort in its own self-interest. At the opposite extreme, if the pollution damages to A were negligible, the MB_A curve would collapse toward the horizontal axis, and little or no abatement would be undertaken.

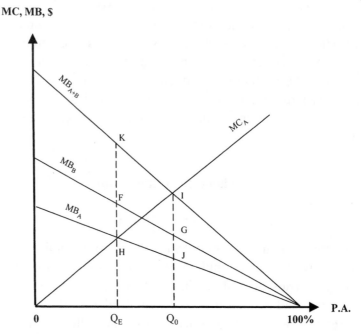

Figure 13.1. *Pollution abatement in internationally shared resource: one polluter*

The first conclusion, then, is that if the damages are primarily local (i.e., borne by the polluting state) unilateral actions may approximate the global optimum.

Figure 13.1 also illustrates the useful role that side payments might play in negotiating an international agreement. Starting from the equilibrium at Q_E, country B could pay an amount up to $Q_E\,FGQ_0$ to obtain the increment in abatement $Q_E\,Q_0$ and be no worse off, whereas the net cost to A of the additional abatement, after accounting for its own additional benefits of $Q_E\,HJQ_0$, would only be the area *HIJ*. The net global gain would be equal to the area *HKI*. Thus a Coase-like bargain is in principle possible. It would follow the Victim Pays Principle. There are a number of reasons why the agreement may not materialize, however. If the legal regime (property right) is unclear, country B may take the position that the polluter, A, should pay for the right to pollute. The dispute over property rights might forestall agreement. Indeed, A and B might dissipate the potential welfare gain by spending real resources on lobbying for favorable clarification of the law. Even if the law were clearly in favor of the polluter, bargaining difficulties would be present. For example, country A might act strategically, asserting that it would undertake *no* abatement unless compensated for the full amount of the benefits accruing to B, including the area under MB_B in the range OQ_E. This could be considered an example of environmental extortion, but the law of gravity and prevailing wind currents may put country A in a strong negotiating position.

Suppose B had clear property rights. In that event, A could afford to "buy" the right to pollute from B and the globally efficient outcome of Q_0 would remain feasible. But the payment would then flow from A to B with very different welfare distribution consequences. Also, as analysts of the Coase Theorem have shown, the allocation of property rights itself may affect the optimal level of abatement, as the wealth base from which the benefit functions are derived depends on the allocation of rights. Finally, if side payments are made the countries must agree on some "currency" for payment. Money payments would be the obvious choice, but may not be feasible because of negative public reaction and political realities. Other forms of currency are possible such as trade concessions, technological assistance, and so forth. In complex negotiations covering many issues, as was the case in the Law of the Sea negotiations, "payment" could be through concessions in quite unrelated areas. The danger from the environmentalists' point of view, however, is that undesirable environmental concessions become the payment vehicle for agreements on unrelated issues.

It is also worth pointing out that instead of payments, sanctions might be used. If, for example, country B had considerable market power in international trade, it might use that power to coerce country A to move from abatement level Q_E to the optimal level Q_0. As noted in previous chapters, the United States has used trade sanctions to achieve changes in foreign environmental practices. But the diagram reveals the asymmetric features of side payments versus sanctions. With side payments, country B is limited in its requests on A. Using coercive market power, however, it could demand 100 percent pollution abatement, clearly an uneconomic outcome.[2] Just as free-rider behavior may be globally inefficient, the threat of sanctions may lead to inefficient *forced-rider* behavior.

When two or more countries jointly pollute a shared resource and contemplate pollution abatement, the sharing of the cost burden becomes a central part of the negotiations. The efficiency criteria require that marginal abatement costs be equalized among all polluting countries, as well as equalizing global marginal costs and benefits. This introduces two difficulties in the negotiations. First, an efficient solution may not be perceived as equitable. Indeed, an efficient agreement might leave one or more countries

---

2 Sanctions themselves have efficiency costs. GATT rules place some limits on the coercive use of trade measures, but the limits are not absolute.

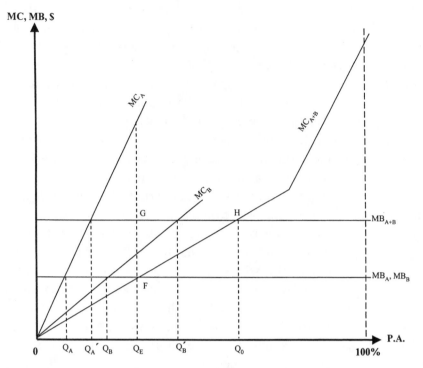

Figure 13.2. *Mutual reciprocal pollution of internationally shared resource*

worse off. This reinforces the desirability of a side payment mechanism. Second, the presence of several polluters can encourage strategic behavior and free-rider problems.

Consider a second situation, depicted in Figure 13.2, in which countries A and B are both polluting a shared resource that both use for beneficial purposes (i.e., reciprocal externalities). For simplicity, assume that both contribute equal amounts of pollution, but their marginal abatement costs, MC_A and MC_B, differ due to different alternatives for waste disposal. Also, for simplicity, assume the marginal benefits from abatement enjoyed by each country are equal and constant, MB_A, MB_B.[3] The global marginal benefit curve, MB_{A+B}, is the vertical sum of MB_A and MB_B. The global marginal abatement cost curve, MC_{A+B}, has been constructed so that at all levels of abatement the division of effort between A and B is efficient ($MC_A = MC_B$), so that MC_{A+B} is a least-cost abatement schedule. The global optimum is at Q_0 where $MC_{A+B} = MB_{A+B}$.

3 This example is constructed so that a unit of pollution creates identical damages for A and B, regardless of source.

The first point to note is that in the absence of any agreement, or indeed any consideration of each others behavior, some pollution abatement would be undertaken. But the total effort would be less than the optimum. Specifically, the two levels of parochial abatement would be Q_A and Q_B, and their sum, Q_E, is less than the global optimum, Q_0. What are the chances of improving on this situation with formal or informal cooperation? Clearly, a net welfare gain from moving from Q_E to Q_0 is possible (and would amount to area *FGH*). But efficient allocation of the abatement cost burden would require abatement of Q'_A by country A and Q'_B by country B. This requires a greater percentage and absolute effort by B than A and might be perceived as inequitable and therefore resisted. In contrast, an agreement calling for equal absolute and relative effort to achieve abatement level Q_0 would require each country to abate to Q_E. This would be inefficient, as at Q_E, $MC_A > MC_B$. (Global benefits would still exceed global costs but their difference would not be maximized.) But agreements requiring equal effort may have strong political appeal. In short, equity and efficiency goals may conflict.[4]

It would be a mistake to exaggerate the equity-efficiency conflict in this example. The empirical basis for establishing cost and benefit functions is likely to be shaky, and "efficiency" in allocating abatement effort chimerical. Moreover, in this example the knowledge that other countries will undertake to reduce pollution may encourage each country to balance larger prospective benefits against their own abatement costs and lead to greater abatement effort even with no formal agreement. Finally, unlike the following example, our assumption that the marginal abatement benefit schedules are constant implies that there is no advantage to following a strict free-rider strategy. For example, if country A observed that country B abated to the level Q_B, country A would still find it in its own interest to abate to level Q_A (A's marginal benefits exceeding its marginal costs up to abatement level Q_A).

The pollution-abatement model depicted in Figure 13.2 can be interpreted as an international public good, as one country's enjoyment of a cleaner environment does not reduce enjoyment by the second country. A vexing problem in the provision of public goods is that individual consumers of the good, in this case, countries A and B, cannot fully control the amount of the public good they consume. Unlike normal markets, where consumers maximize welfare by adjusting the quantity they purchase to the market price, the consumption of a public good by a consumer (or country) has to be equal

---

4 If equal effort is imposed as an additional constraint, the second-best global optimum is less than Q_0.

to the quantity supplied. Under these circumstances, the task is to choose the supply of the public good such that all consumers (countries) are satisfied. This can be accomplished by allocating the *cost* of supplying the public good in a fashion such that, given the cost allocation, each consumer (country) would choose the same quantity of public good. In essence, rather than adjusting quantity purchased to a common price, this method adjusts the "price" paid by individual consumers (countries) to a common quantity. These are called Lindahl Prices.[5] The calculation of Lindahl Prices is potentially useful in an international context, as they link the issue of the optimum provision of an international public good such as cleaning up regional seas or abating transborder SO_2 emissions with the issue of allocating the costs of cleanup.[6] Consider Figure 13.2 again. Assume that abatement is undertaken efficiently, along MC_{A+B}, but that allocating the cost of the abatement has not yet been decided. The amount of abatement A wishes to see depends on what fraction of the cost it must bear. From the figure, if it were obliged to bear all of the costs, its marginal costs and benefits would be equal at point F, or the pollution-abatement level Q_E. If it were allocated 50 percent of the costs, it would desire Q_0 of pollution abatement. A's "demand" for abatement is a function of the "price" it pays in terms of fraction of total abatement costs. At the same time, B's demand for abatement is a function of its share of total cost. What we seek is a level of pollution-abatement effort and a cost allocation such that both countries wish the same level of the public good and that level is globally efficient, and in aggregate their payments for pollution-abatement cover the cost of the pollution abatement.

The solution is illustrated in Figure 13.3. The left vertical axis measures the percentage of total abatement cost allocated to A. The right vertical scale measures (from top to bottom) the percentage of total abatement cost allocated to B. From left to right, the horizontal axis measures the amount of the public good supplied, in this case, pollution abatement. The curve D_A represents the amounts of pollution abatement country A desires at different percentage allocations. For instance, if it pays 100 percent of the cost, it selects Q_E units of abatement, and if it pays 50 percent, it chooses a higher level, Q_0 (recall that the actual abatement activities are divided among the countries in a least-cost fashion). At the same time, B's demand for abatement is measured against the inverted percent allocation scale on the right

5 For exposition in a domestic context, see Richard Musgrave (1959, Chap. 4). For possible use in an international context, see Robert Dorfman (1997).

6 In public finance terminology, the cost allocation follows the benefit principle – recipients of a public good are charged according to the benefit they receive – as opposed to allocation according to ability to pay.

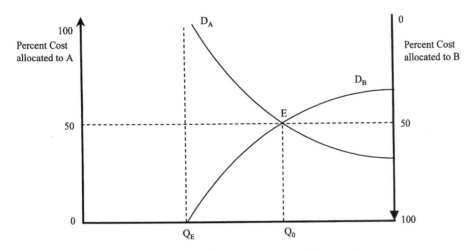

Figure 13.3. *Allocating cost of public good*

hand. The equilibrium at E simultaneously determines the appropriate supply of the public good, Q_0, and the allocation of costs between A and B. The allocation establishes the Lindahl Prices. In this example, because the benefit curves to A and B are assumed identical, the costs of the (efficient) abatement are shared equally at 50 percent. Note also that the equilibrium abatement Q_0 can be shown to be Pareto-efficient.

Casting the international public goods problem in terms of Lindahl Prices may be useful for analysis but does not resolve critical issues. First, this analysis follows the benefits principle of cost allocation rather than an ability-to-pay principle and may not be accepted by all countries. Second, note that in this example, even though the "solution" led to perfect cost sharing (i.e., both pay 50 percent of the total abatement cost), in fact money would have to change hands from A to B. The reason is that with efficient abatement, the cost of the abatement effort undertaken in B would exceed the abatement cost in A, and to equalize cost burden, A must pay B. Third, this analysis neglects strategic behavior by A or B or both. Finally, with many countries involved, the free-rider problem multiplies. These issues emerge in Chapter 14, in an examination of global warming.

Now consider another situation, our third model, in which the polluters have some incentive to act strategically (Figure 13.4). For simplicity and to highlight this behavior, assume the two polluting countries each contribute identical quantities of pollution to a shared resource, each has the same marginal abatement schedules (MC_A, MC_B), and each has the same

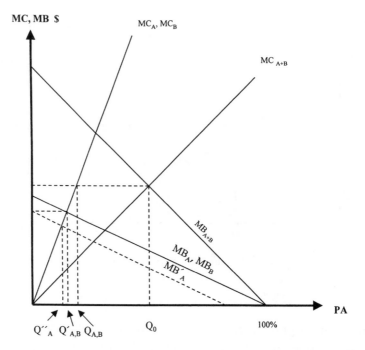

Figure 13.4. *Reciprocal pollution, strategic behavior*

declining marginal benefit function from pollution abatement, MB_A, MB_B.
The global marginal schedules assuming efficient allocation of abatement
costs are the curves MB_{A+B} and MC_{A+B}, indicating a global optimum abatement level Q_0 with individual country effort at $Q_{A,B}$. Acting in its parochial
interest, each country would abate to $Q'_{A,B}$, and total abatement would be
suboptimal.

   However, if either country anticipates the behavior of the other it would
have even less incentive to abate. For example, if A believes B will follow
its optimal strategy and abate to level $Q'_{A,B}$, the marginal benefit function for
A shifts to the dashed curve MB'_A. It follows that A's incentive to abate is
weakened, and it undertakes the lower level Q''_A. In essence, country A has
become a (partial) free rider on the other country's abatement effort. If free-
rider behavior is sufficiently widespread and severe, total abatement will fall
short of what purely unilateral action would accomplish. This example is
elaborated in the Appendix under a variety of negotiating formulas including coercion and using reaction functions and a Nash equilibrium.[7] A general

---

7 In game theory analysis, a Nash equilibrium is a set of strategies for the players in a game such that
   no player, acting unilaterally, could find another strategy that would improve his welfare. For an accessible and insightful treatment of international externalities using game theory, see Todd Sandler (1997).

conclusion is that outcomes are sensitive to the negotiation context and players' behavior – cooperative versus noncooperative, benevolent dictator, coercion, and so forth.

2.2 Further Theoretical Issues

Strategic behavior is not restricted to a situation of reciprocal externalities as in the previous example. A unidirectional externality with several downstream "victim" countries will face the same problem if they must collectively bribe the upstream country. Free-rider behavior also arises in negotiating restrictions on access to common property natural resources such as fisheries (Swanson 1991). If some fishing nations agree to restrict their fishing effort to a "sustainable" level, the rent that can be extracted by nonrestrained users is increased, and indeed their incentive for greater fishing effort is increased. The penalty for responsible behavior appears to be encouragement of irresponsible behavior.[8] This illustration, if taken seriously, also undermines the case for unilateral action to set an example for the international community. If one country undertook aggressive environmental protection in an effort to lead the international community by example, it might inadvertently allow other countries to delay or scale back their protection efforts.[9] For example, in the previous case if country B undertook its "fair" share of globally optimal abatement level $Q_{A,B}$, A would have an incentive to reduce its abatement effort even more, below Q_A''.

A further complication is that free-rider behavior may emerge *after* an international environmental agreement is signed unless it contains binding commitments. That is, the incentive to free ride affects not only the formation of the agreement, but the possibility of defections. The analytical question is under what circumstances agreements are *self-enforcing* – do all members find it in their interest to abide by the agreement? In a strategic context, one country may find it in its interests to join a MEA, anticipating benefits as others join, but subsequently decide to defect and free ride on others' abatement.

Scott Barrett investigates a formal model of international environmental

---

For a broader analysis see Partha Dasgupta, Karl-Göran Mäler, and Allessandro Vorcelli (1997). For formalization of a game theoretic analysis of negotiating pollution-abatement commitments in an incremental fashion, see Parkash Chander and Henry Tulkens (1992).

8 This has a parallel in cartel theory. The more restrictive is the cartel, the greater is the incentive for a single member to cheat and overship its quota. The main difference, of course, is that free riding in a cartel should *improve* social welfare by moderating the market power distortion.

9 A point also made by Barrett (1991).

agreements in which the number of signatories and the abatement levels of signatories and nonparticipants are determined endogenously. The model assumes that reciprocal externalities exist, all countries are identical, and all cost and benefit functions are known to all countries (Barrett 1994). The MEA is self-enforcing in the sense that every country is free to join or defect from the agreement depending on its net benefits or costs. This rules out the use of exogenous coercive measures. The central feature is that once a core set of countries agree on abatement they "reward" new participants by increasing their abatement effort and "punish" defectors by decreasing abatement. Thus each country continuously reviews its options – join or continue in the agreement if its benefits exceed its costs, defect or decline to join if the benefits of free riding exceed the costs.

The formal results are not encouraging. Barrett shows that (1) the number of signatories will be large if the ratio of national marginal abatement costs to global marginal benefits is small, but in that event the gains from cooperation versus noncooperation are small, and (2) that when this ratio is large and the potential gains from cooperation are large, the number of signatories will be small. This pessimistic conclusion tends to be confirmed in a second model that assumes repeat games. Repeat game models generally tend to favor cooperative behavior, as current noncooperative behavior can be sanctioned in subsequent rounds. However, Barrett shows in this particular model that if an MEA is to be resistant to renegotiation, it can only attract a large number of signatories when the gains from cooperation versus noncooperation are small, a result similar to his first model.[10]

Pessimistic conclusion about the scope and stability of international environmental agreements suggests that other elements might be usefully introduced in the negotiations. Consider, for example, a small group of countries that form an environmental coalition to reduce transnational pollution or protect an international environmental resource. To increase membership and approach optimal abatement, they could offer payments to new members financed out of gains from enlargement. This may encourage defection and create instability in the original coalition, however, unless they are formally bound or committed to the agreement. As an alternative to financial transfers to new members, Carraro and Siniscalco (1995) have suggested linking the environmental negotiation to a second agreement such as cooperative research and development, which produces a positive externality that is excludable. The intuition behind this is that by adding a

---

10 In speculating about the success of the Montreal Protocol, Barrett argues that the results of cooperation may not be significantly greater than they would have been under a noncooperative, unilateral regime.

potentially excludable benefit to the environmental agreement, the incentive to join (not free ride) and stay in the coalition (not defect) is strengthened. Whether there exist important opportunities to create positive excludable externalities in international negotiations is an open question. Other suggestions include linking trade and environment negotiations such that the "South" agrees to undertake some costly environmental protection measure with a positive international externality, say, conservation of tropical forests, and the "North" commits to lower trade barriers (Abrego et al. 1997). One game theory model shows that linked negotiations could improve the bargaining position of the South compared to stand-alone trade negotiations, but negotiations with cash side payments would be even more efficient and of greater benefit to the South. The authors also recognize that as a practical matter in a linkage negotiation the traditional and desirable trade disciplines such as most favored nation might be scrapped, with loss to all.

How the negotiation "game" plays out depends on the specifics of the externalities and how behavior is modelled. In general, the larger the number of players and the more uniform their interests, the more likely would be free-rider behavior.[11] A "small" number of free riders would not necessarily undermine the agreement and partial cooperation is likely to be better than no cooperative behavior. In a small-number situation, each player is likely to realize that noncooperative strategic behavior would doom any international effort at managing the externalities, and this puts a constraint on each player's behavior. But small-number games may be more likely to involve bluffing and misinformation. Giulio Ecchia and Marco Mariotti investigate a three-player game with two variations, the prisoner's dilemma case in which the immediate or myopic incentive for each country is to pollute, and a "chicken" case in which no cooperation among the three leads to an environmental "disaster" (Ecchia and Mariotti 1997). The innovative feature of the latter is that the players are not in fact myopic, but look down the road and anticipate a sequence of moves until an equilibrium is reached. Ecchia and Mariotti's conclusions are more encouraging than the Barrett analysis. In all of the cases they analyze either two of the three countries, or all three countries, will choose to cooperate.

Time also may play a critical role in assessing the prospects for cooperation. For example, Mäler (1991) presents a short-run illustrative model of acid rain in Europe and shows that with reasonable assumptions each country has an incentive to act as a free rider, provided the other European

---

11 The involvement of many countries would normally increase transactions and enforcement costs as well.

countries proceed to limit sulfur emissions. The model is then transformed into a long-run model by introducing a stock-flow relation for sulfur accumulation. In that context, and provided side payments are possible, Mäler concludes that once a cooperative strategy is agreed to, the incentives to free ride (defect) diminish. The reason appears to be that if one country found evidence of "cheating" it would itself break the agreement with losses to all. If this threat were recognized by each country, it would deter defections.

Three additional theoretical complications should be mentioned. First, multilateral treaty making generally proceeds in a sequential fashion (Swanson 1991). Typically, there is an agreement on text followed by a period in which the agreement is opened for signing and ratification. Only when a sufficient number of states ratify does it come into effect, after which the convention is open for subsequent accession.[12] This sequential process of acceptance and implementation may encourage free riding. If a subset of states agree to restrain their use of an international resource such as a fishery, or limit their waste disposal, the "holdout" states are rewarded by the behavior of the restraining states.[13] The incentive to abstain increases, the more states join the agreement. This holdout behavior arises from the free-rider incentive, although it might be justified by the recalcitrant state claiming that the net benefit was not satisfactory. In contrast, a negotiation procedure that requires all states either to move simultaneously toward restraint or not at all might reduce the free-rider incentive. This would be more likely if collapse of negotiations was seen as a realistic possibility. This alternative negotiation method is difficult, however, with international environmental agreements characterized by novelty, scientific uncertainty, and the need to build public support. These circumstances suggest that a step-by-step process – data collection, framework convention, and protocols with progressively more stringent (costly) obligations – may be more productive as it builds on better information and increasing trust.[14]

A second and related complication is that negotiations on side payments may be conflated with free-rider or strategic behavior. As illustrated in Figure 13.1, country A requires compensation to go beyond abatement effort Q_E. But it may also hold out for a payment from B for its efforts to move from zero abatement to level Q_E. The conflation of strategic behavior and the need for side payments seems more likely when the envi-

---

12 For example, the Convention on the Law of the Sea was opened for signature in 1982, but did not come into force until 1994.
13 Not unlike cartel behavior or Orderly Marketing Agreements in international trade.
14 For case studies of environmental negotiations, see Sjöstedt (1993).

ronmental damages in question are intangible, agreement on measurement is problematic, and the countries involved have very different preference functions. For example, rich and poor countries are likely to have quite different preferences with regard to species and habitat protection, and agreement on compensation for protection costs may be especially difficult to reach.

A third complication in reaching an efficient and equitable environmental protection agreement involves shunting the economic activity that generates the externality (i.e., pollution) from one country to another. More specifically, if a subset of countries agrees to limit pollution, trade and investment may be the vehicles through which the polluting activity is shifted to unrestrained countries. For example, there were initially serious concerns that if the use of ozone-depleting substances (ODS) was curtailed among some countries, its use might increase elsewhere as ODS-using industries sought new locations. There is inconclusive evidence of this happening (see Chapters 12 and 18). If the advanced industrial countries curtail fossil fuel use to moderate carbon emissions, international production cost patterns change, and fossil fuel intensive production may surge in unrestrained countries. One implication is the desirability of including the largest number of countries as possible at the outset, even if some of them currently make only a small contribution to the pollution externality.

The shunting problem just described connects international environmental agreements to trade policy. At first glance, it would appear that trade sanctions on nonmembers might serve two related purposes – encouraging participation (discouraging free riding) and reducing leakage. There are, however, problems. On a theoretical level, if nonmembers to an international environmental agreement are penalized by trade restriction, the members themselves bear a cost by foregoing the gains from trade. In that event, the threat of trade sanctions in an MEA may not be credible. It is true, of course, that many countries restrict imports and forgo trade gains – pursue protectionist policies – and in that sense do not act "rationally." But to model an MEA negotiation assuming rational behavior in promoting national environmental interest and irrational behavior with respect to trade seems suspect. If full rationality is assumed in both spheres, the prospects for substantial leakage might be sufficient to cause members to credibly use trade sanctions despite their trade costs, but the result remains uncertain (Barrett 1999). At a practical level, there are a host of problems. As outlined in Chapters 10 and 11, such trade measures would not be legal under WTO rules. If import restrictions were used, there is little reason to believe that the set of tariffs most effective at inducing membership would also be the most effective at stemming leakage. And, if trade sanctions were permitted, there would be a temptation to impose the environmental values of the MEA members on nonmembers, problematic if countries valued the public good provided by the MEA differently. This is the forced-rider problem in another guise.

3 Policy Responses

At first glance, these theoretical considerations suggest very formidable barriers to effective management of international externalities. And indeed the absence of a supranational EPA with authority to correct spillovers is a serious limitation. But the situation is not entirely bleak and the difficulties should not be exaggerated. At an abstract level, we can identify four grounds for a more optimistic view. First, as shown previously, in some circumstances it is in the narrow self-interest of states to curtail polluting activity and protect environmental resources, at least to the point where marginal abatement costs equal marginal damages to themselves. Such self-interest will also moderate, if not eliminate, the international externality. For example, one study estimates that the annual public health benefits of reducing atmospheric sulfate concentrations due to the 1990 U.S. Clean Air Act are $10.6 billion in the Eastern United States for 1997. But the incidental health benefits to Canada are estimated to be an additional $0.9 billion in the same year (U.S. EPA 1995, Tables S-2, S-3). Unilateral action has a positive spillover.

Second, there may be situations in which property rights can be clarified and at least a rudimentary commercial market developed. This would follow the Coasian tradition of creating "markets" for environmental services. For example, property rights to genetic resources for the development of pharmaceuticals and for plant breeding are being asserted by some developing countries. This allows for the negotiation of commercial agreements in which the resource owners are compensated for habitat and species protection costs, perhaps in the form of royalty payments linked to subsequent downstream profits. Broader schemes have been proposed for protecting habitat and biodiversity in developing countries by creating an international market for "transferable development rights" (Panayotou 1995). One idea is to separate development rights from land ownership and to market the rights to local and international organizations and others with an interest in conservation. Separating development rights from land ownership has been a conservation tool in the United States for many years. One might also argue that the protracted Law of the Sea negotiations, which formalized and legitimized national jurisdiction over fisheries resources within a 200-mile exclusive economic zone, were also a first step in rationalizing use of previously open-access fisheries resources. The 200-mile Exclusive Economic Zone has brought 90 percent of the world's commercial ocean fisheries within at least nominal national authority, although, as examined in Chapter 15, this does not guarantee efficient management. The development and commercialization of ecotourism is also a step in the direction of bringing some discipline to international externalities. By commercializing the environmental services implicit in ecotourism, there is, in principle, a vehicle through which environmental preferences of consumers can be translated into monetary payment to service providers. Purely private property rights, however, are unlikely to foster desirable promotion of ecotourism, and local government involvement is likely.

Third, although rudimentary, a system of side payments to entice the cooperation of countries facing net protection costs is not entirely absent. The Global Environmental Facility is one such vehicle. Other arrangements include debt-for-nature swaps and joint implementation arrangements. These are described later in this chapter. Another example is the 1995 pledge by the G-7 nations of $2.3 billion in loans and aid to help the Ukraine close Chernobyl and build new power plants. This can be interpreted as "buying" protection from nuclear accidents. One might also argue that the trade preferences contained in NAFTA are a *de facto* payment vehicle for improving Mexican environmental performance, with benefits to concerned environmentalists and border residents in the United States.

Fourth, although generally not first-best policy, trade and other economic sanctions may be used to discipline free-rider behavior. As explained below, the Montreal Protocol addressing ozone depletion uses both financial inducements and trade sanctions as carrots and sticks. Also, as described in Chapter 10, the United States has been in the forefront of using trade measures to enforce international environmental agreements and to accomplish more unilateral environmental objectives. The simple proposition that countries will not enter into an international environmental agreement unless they see net benefits may need to be modified in light of coercive international market power. There are, however, significant limits to using coercive trade measures to accomplish international environmental objectives. Subject to a few well-known exceptions, import quotas or tariffs create by-product distortions and inefficiencies, and these costs must be set against the presumed benefit of coercing other countries to limit international externalities.[15] As a legal matter, most tariffs are bound in GATT and cannot be increased unilaterally without offering compensation. As pointed out in Chapter 11, trade measures in MEAs are of uncertain legality. Trade liberalization inducements, as used in NAFTA, seem preferable.

These four avenues of policy response tend to moderate the apparently pessimistic implications of abstract theory. But it is also useful to question the underlying premises of that theory – that states know the interests of their citizens, can aggregate them in a meaningful fashion, and enter negotiations with the intent of maximizing narrow national welfare. A moment's reflection reveals these are tenuous assumptions at best. Even in the far more transparent arena of trade negotiations, the notion that governments objectively calculate and seek to maximize national welfare is not very persuasive. At a minimum one should acknowledge that governments respond to domestic constituencies and interest groups in formulating their negotiating positions. One implication is that if environmental groups have a cosmopolitan perspective and if they vigorously promote their interests, a country may willingly agree to international environmental protection measures from a cosmopolitan rather than a parochial perspective.

Moreover, the self-interest behavioral model just described gives little play for agreements based at least in part on national altruism, morality, guilt, and shame. We do not wish to push this too far, but examples of public-spirited and selfless behavior by individuals are not unknown, nor should the power of guilt and shame in molding social behavior be dismissed. Economics has a considerable literature attempting to explain why individuals voluntarily contribute to activities that they could enjoy even if they did not contribute. These activities range from office parties to environmental organizations that protect wildlife. Such behavior conflicts with assumptions of free-rider behavior in the supply of public goods. Theories explaining why voluntary contributions take place include altruistic preferences (people derive utility from improving others' welfare); assertions that individuals possess separate utility functions, one for self-interest, a second for group interest; and models of reciprocity based on moral considerations ("if others contribute, I have a moral obligation to do at least as much").[16] If it is plausible to elevate models of strategic interaction among individuals based on rationale self-interest to analyze behavior among countries as is implicit in the earlier theoretical models, it is equally plausi-

---

15 The exceptions include the optimal tariff, which exploits market power, and the strategic trade models involving rent switching in oligopolistic market structures. Both, however, are beggar-thy-neighbor policies and reduce world welfare.
16 See Howard Margolis (1991) and Robert Sugden (1984).

ble that some of the determinants of individuals' social behavior – guilt, shame and morality – may guide international environmental agreements. If so, prospects for effective management of international externalities are improved.

At an even more general level, the simple theory of international environmental externalities highlights the arbitrary nature of the international political system, in which the primary actors are nation states. There is no environmental basis for this division. Environmental resources and environmental degradation do not respect political borders. Nor do the preferences and concerns of environmentalists stop at the border. A general principle of public policy is that decisions should be made at the lowest political level that can effectively internalize their consequences. This means that a local environmental nuisance, for example, noise, might best be handled at the community level, whereas the decision to site an airport or oil refinery would require a regional authority. This is known as the subsidiarity principle, and is found in the EU's Single European Act. The logic of the subsidiarity principle suggests that as environmental problems shift from primarily local in nature toward regional and global scope, authority for managing externalities should be vested in broader political structures. To a limited degree, this is occurring. The clearest example is the environmental authority of the EU. At a much weaker level, some authority is granted to the trilateral North American Commission on Environmental Cooperation. But these are very modest steps. Some observers have suggested that other regional economic organizations such as APEC take on substantial environmental management functions including collective international action for environmental and natural resource protection (Dua and Esty 1997). Others, noting that the trade community has well-developed regulations and institutions (i.e., the GATT/WTO system), have suggested that international environmental interests need a parallel institutional structure, a World Environmental Organization (WEO) to work alongside the trade organization (Runge 1996b). Neither suggestion has met with overwhelming enthusiasm, but the linkage between international economic activity and the environment, and the proliferation of more or less freestanding MEAs with trade and investment implications, does suggest that new approaches to international environmental governance need consideration.

4 A Potpourri of Evidence

The preceding discussion is rather abstract. It is useful to take a quick look at various efforts at managing international environmental externalities to see if theory conforms with reality. The remainder of this chapter presents examples of managing international externalities.

4.1 International Conventions:
Ozone-Depleting Substances (ODS)
(Benedick 1991; Brack 1996; Szell 1993)

Chlorofluorocarbons were developed in the 1930s. In the three decades after War II, they were widely used in the industrial countries as refrigerants, propellants for spray cans, blowing and foaming agents, and industrial solvents. The first hint of environmental damage from CFCs came in 1974 in a paper by Molina and Roland (1974). New scientific research suggested that because of their stable structure, CFCs migrate slowly to the stratosphere where they can be broken down by solar radiation and release large quantities of chlorine, and that chlorine in the stratosphere could act as a catalyst and destroy ozone molecules. Ozone in the upper atmosphere serves as a shield against harmful ultraviolet (UV-B) radiation. Increased UV-B radiation is associated with increased skin cancers and eye cataracts. It is also implicated in suppression of the immune system, possible damage to phytoplankton and disruption to the aquatic food chain, yield reductions in agriculture, and global warming, although all of these are subject to scientific uncertainty.

Initial unilateral response in the United States was a 1978 prohibition on the use of CFCs as aerosol propellants in nonessential uses. The response in the EC was weaker – a 30 percent cutback in aerosol use from 1976 levels to take effect at the end of 1981. Internationally, the United Nations Environment Programme initiated technical work through the World Meteorological Organization in 1975, and in 1981 UNEP was authorized to work toward an international agreement designed to protect the ozone layer. This resulted in 1985 in a framework agreement, the Vienna Convention. This Convention created a general obligation for parties to take appropriate measures to protect the ozone layer but stopped short of identifying specific chemicals as ozone-depleting substances and did not specify particular control measures or target levels of reduction. A much stronger agreement, the Montreal Protocol, was signed in 1987. The Montreal Protocol specified controlled substances, and set increasingly stringent production and consumption limits, with 50 percent reductions from 1986 levels to be achieved by 1998. It also contained trade restrictions, which will be considered in this chapter. Partly in response to new scientific evidence, the Montreal Protocol was further strengthened by the 1990 London Revisions. These revisions include a scheduled total phaseout of CFCs, certain halons, and carbon tetrachloride by 2000; phaseout of methyl chloroform by 2005; and a nonbinding resolution calling for the phaseout of the CFC substitute, hydrochlorofluorocarbons (HCFCs), by 2040 and if possible by 2020.

By 1996, 140 countries had signed the Montreal Protocol including all major producers and consumers. How did this come about? Specifically, how was the deal structured to be attractive to virtually all countries, regardless of their contribution to the problem or their costs of compliance? The initial fault line in negotiations before the signing of the Montreal Protocol in September 1987 was between countries favoring strong controls (e.g., United States, Canada, New Zealand, and the Nordic countries) and certain members of the EC, notably France, Italy, and the United Kingdom. The latter group, according to Benedick, reflected the views of their chemical industries, which tended to minimize the threat of ozone depletion. Ultimately, the EC opponents, weakened by internal division, compromised with the strong-control advocates, although they were able to delay action on halons and were able to craft a production-plus-consumption cap more to their liking.[17]

The second major task was to make the agreement attractive to developing countries and obtain the largest possible number of signatures. The source of the ozone depletion problem was certainly not developing countries. A 1974 estimate of CFC 11 and 12 emissions put the industrial country share at 86 percent, centrally planned economies at 12 percent, and developing countries, including China, at less than 2 percent (Pearson and Pryor 1978, p. 275). A 1988 estimate placed the industrial country share of CFCs at 88 percent of global emissions (Benedick 1991, p. 149). But there was general agreement during the Montreal negotiations that limiting rapid growth in the use of ODS in developing countries, especially in the larger countries such as China, India, Brazil, and Mexico, was necessary if abatement in the North was not to be offset by increased emissions in the South. Moreover, there was a concern that without broad coverage, CFC "pollution havens" would spring up, and CFC-using industries such as electronics manufacturing might migrate to nonsignatories. This was the potential

17 European firms were substantial exporters of CFCs. Importing countries were fearful of a production cap, which would tend to give producers a monopoly position, and favored consumption caps. The compromise was to simultaneously cap "adjusted" production (production minus exports plus imports, which is apparent consumption) and production. The excess of domestic production over domestic consumption could supply net importing countries.

leakage problem and was ultimately resolved by virtual universal membership. The developing country perspective quite naturally emphasized that they were not the cause of the problem, and they should be compensated for incremental costs of foregoing ODS substances in their future development. Moreover, the most solidly documented benefit of ozone protection – reduction in the incidence of skin cancer – is of greater importance to countries with lightly pigmented populations, that is, the temperate zone industrial countries. In view of the opportunity cost of foregoing future use of CFCs and traditional free-rider behavior, the nonparticipation of developing countries was a real possibility.

In the end, both carrots and sticks were used. The Montreal Protocol allows developing countries with low initial consumption a grace period of 10 years within which consumption can increase to a per capita limit of 0.3 kilogram, well above then current levels. The protocol also contained a general and vague commitment to facilitate developing countries' access to environmentally safe alternatives and technology and to facilitate the provision of subsidies and other assistance for the use of alternative technology and substitute products. Nevertheless, China and India had not signed the Montreal protocol at the time of the London Revisions (June 1990). As further inducements, the London Revisions established a multilateral fund in the amount of $240 million over the first three years (if China and India were to become parties). The money was to be used by developing countries to cover incremental costs of complying with the control measures of the protocol. Finally, the London Revisions commit the parties to take every practical step to transfer the best available environmentally safe substitutes and technology to developing countries and to do so under fair and favorable conditions.

These inducements were backed up by trade restrictions. The Montreal Protocol prohibited exports and imports in bulk of controlled substances with nonparties; prohibited, starting in 1993, imports from nonparties of products containing controlled substances (e.g., air-conditioning units); and *contemplated* a restriction by 1994 of imports from nonparties of products *made* with controlled substances. This last would have been particularly onerous for exporters of consumer electronics, where CFCs were widely used as solvents. It became unnecessary, however, with the widespread accession to the protocol. These trade provisions provided substantial disincentives to free riding, and the relocation of industrial production using CFCs to nonparties. As a footnote, a number of country studies recently commissioned by UNCTAD suggest that compliance with the Montreal Protocol has not been especially disruptive in developing countries, in part because of assistance through the fund, and in part due to technology supplied through multinational firms in the air-conditioning, refrigeration, and electronics industries.[18]

4.2 Controlling Ocean Pollution by International Conventions – Early Examples

International pollution control and resource protection agreements vary greatly in the costs they impose on states. One would expect that agreements with minimal compliance costs would be relatively easy to achieve. Many of the agreements made through the Intergovernmental Maritime Consultative Organization (IMCO, now IMO) regarding maritime safety – shipboard navigational equipment, regulation of shipping lanes, and the like – are of this character and were easily reached. When potential compliance costs are larger, agreement may be more difficult. In that event, the choice may have to be between reaching a broad agreement with considerable discretion left to national government in implementation and negotiating an agreement with tougher and more costly obligations, but encountering long delays before entering into force. Two early ocean pollution conventions tend to bear this out.

The 1972 Ocean Dumping Convention[19] sets as a general obligation that parties *pledge* themselves to take all *practical* steps to prevent ocean pollution by dumping of wastes (emphasis added) and that parties take effective measures "according to their scientific, technical and economic capabilities" to prevent marine pollution caused by dumping. The convention prohibits dumping of products on a "black" list (e.g., mercury and cadmium, crude oil taken aboard for the purpose of dumping, and high-level radioactive waste). For products on a gray list, prior permits are needed (e.g., arsenic, lead, copper, zinc, cyanide, fluorides, and large quantities of acids and alkalis containing chromium). For all other wastes, a prior general permit is required. Permits are to be granted by national authorities after consideration of certain criteria relating to the dump site and dumped material, but also "the practical availability of alternative land based methods of treatment, disposal or elimination." The convention does not contain any enforcement mechanism and deferred considering procedures for dispute settlement. In summary, except for the short list of prohibited materials, the convention

---

18 See also Chapters 12 and 18. Recall also Barrett's conclusion that unilateral self-interest might have achieved much the same results as the Protocol. (Barrett 1994).
19 Technically, the Prevention of Marine Pollution by Dumping of Wastes and Other Matter. See Pearson (1975).

leaves maximum latitude to the parties themselves to determine how strictly ocean dumping is to be controlled.

The 1973 Prevention of Pollution from Ships Convention, which addressed oil and other pollution from normal tanker operations and accidental discharge, is another matter. The convention and the 1978 protocol to that convention, which together are known as MARPOL 73/78, contain expensive, mandatory design and equipment requirements. The most expensive of these is the requirement for new crude tankers over 20,000 tons to install segregated ballast tanks (SBTs) and crude oil washing (COW) equipment, and for existing tankers to be retrofitted with either SBTs or the less expensive COW equipment.[20] Various estimates placed the cost of SBTs for new ships at 2 to 9 percent of total construction costs, or an estimated $2 billion in new ship building costs over the period 1975 to 1990 (Mitchell 1993; 1994, p. 261). Thus, in contrast to the Ocean Dumping Convention, MARPOL 1973/78 contains specific, costly, mandatory design and operating standards, and is backed up by compulsory arbitration should a dispute arise.

In these circumstances, one would expect easy and rapid ratification of the Ocean Dumping Convention and difficulties with MARPOL 73/78. At first glance, this appears to have been the case. The Ocean Dumping Convention concluded in December 1972 and quickly came into force in August 1975. Although the original MARPOL was negotiated in 1973, it was not ratified by a sufficient number of countries and was folded into its own protocol in 1978, which itself came into force only in 1983.

Part of the explanation for the delay was resistance by oil and shipping interests and some maritime governments to costly equipment requirements for both oil- and chemical-pollution abatement. But in fact, the 1978 revisions included tighter and more expensive equipment requirements than were contained in the original 1973 version. The earlier version required SBTs on new tankers over 70,000 tons; the 1978 version required new tankers over 20,000 tons to install SBTs and COW equipment, and existing tankers over 40,000 to install either SBTs or the less expensive COW equipment. One reason why countries agreed to tighter standards was the U.S. threat to unilaterally require even more expensive measures, including a requirement for tankers to be constructed with double bottoms to reduce spillage in accidental groundings. More broadly, increased pressure from

---

20 Tankers take on seawater as ballast for return voyages to loading ports. When ballast water is pumped directly into cargo tanks, it mixes with oil residues and, when subsequently discharged, is a major source of marine oil pollution. Tanks also require washing before taking on a new load. COW is a technique that uses crude oil itself, not seawater, to wash tanks, thus reducing oily residue discharge from tank washing.

environmental groups and widely publicized oil spills created public pressure for more effective controls.

MARPOL 73/78 is interesting for another reason. Until the 1973 draft convention, the method of control relied on performance and discharge standards; no discharge within certain areas, and oil discharge limits expressed in parts per million in oily water discharge, or as a fraction of total cargo capacity. Moreover, the principal technological alternative to SBT was the load on top (LOT) system.[21] There is good evidence that SBT is the most expensive method for reducing international oil discharge, certainly more expensive than simple LOT. Its great advantage, however, is that as a design-equipment standard rather than performance standard, monitoring and compliance problems are minimal. In this case, there was a trade-off between cost and compliance, and the costlier but more certain design standard was chosen. It appears to have been effective, as discharges from tanker operations fell from 1.08 million tons in 1971 to 0.16 million tons in 1989 (Mitchell 1994, Table 3.1, p. 170).

4.3 Compensation Systems – The Global Environment Facility

The theory of international externalities suggests establishing a system in which countries benefiting from environmental protection can compensate countries that face net costs from reducing international externalities. Such a system can be defended on equity grounds – those who benefit should share in the costs. It also may be necessary on efficiency grounds – to ensure widespread participation in arrangements to protect international environmental resources. As a practical matter, the compensation generally will flow from North to South for three reasons: First, there is evidence that the South has greater opportunity for cost-effective protection measures, especially in greenhouse gas abatement and conservation of biological diversity. Second, the income disparities between North and South, which affect their priorities and preferences, point toward a North-South payment flow. Third, the historical record, in which the North has made disproportionate use of the global commons for waste disposal, creates an ethical presumption for North-to-South payments.

The Global Environment Facility (GEF) is the institutional response to this need. The GEF is a financial mechanism that provides grants and concessional financing for projects and programs to moderate global environ-

---

21 LOT consolidates ballast and tank-cleaning slops in a single tank. On return voyages, over time, the seawater settles and can be decanted, allowing the new cargo to be loaded on top.

Table 13.1. *GEF projects by priority area*
(cumulative through September 1998)

Area	Number of projects[a]	Allocation amount (millions $)	Percent total allocations
Biodiversity	117	773	39
Climate Change	85	775	39
Marine Environment	31	269	14
Ozone Depletion	14	113	6
Multiple Focal Areas[b]	8	64	3
Total		1,994	100

[a] Excludes enabling activity.
[b] Includes small grants program.
Source: Operational Report on GEF Programs 9/98, http://www.gefweb.com/OPERPORT/opers.hlm.

mental externalities. The three implementing organizations are the United Nations Development Programme (UNDP), the United Nations Environment Programme (UNEP), and the World Bank. The initial pilot program for the GEF ran from 1991 to 1994, at which time it was restructured and put on a permanent footing. The GEF also has been designated as the interim funding mechanism for the two agreements reached at the 1992 Rio Conference, the UN Convention on Climate Change and the Convention on Biological Diversity. The GEF Trust Fund was financed by $2 billion (over three years) in pledges, with contributions from industrial countries shared according to a formula originally used to fund the International Development Association (IDA), the soft loan window of the World Bank. Countries eligible to borrow from the World Bank are eligible to receive funds for the GEF. GEF funds are ostensibly additional to traditional development assistance, although this is difficult to document. "Additionality" in environmental aid funds has been a contentious issue since the 1972 Stockholm Conference.

Four priority areas for funding have been established: biodiversity, climate change, marine environment, and ozone depletion. (The GEF complements the activities of the Multilateral Fund set up by the London Amendments to the Montreal Protocol in financing ozone protection projects. The World Bank is an implementing agency for the Multilateral Fund.) Table 13.1 provides data on GEF projects by priority area. At first glance, the GEF fits very neatly into the theoretical framework for managing international externalities, although the level of funding is small relative to the need. As initially envisioned, it appeared that GEF funding would be limited to financing the *incremental* costs required to achieve global benefits (that is, in terms of Figure 13.1, GEF would pay for the incremental costs of moving from Q_E to Q_0). Moreover, the GEF was to select projects partly on the basis of cost effectiveness – i.e., maximizing global benefits per unit GEF subsidy. If carried through, this would aid in securing least-cost abatement, as illustrated in Figure 13.2. Finally, in its 1994 restructuring, the GEF adopted a formula for contributions by industrial countries based on IDA replenishment. Such a predetermined cost-sharing formula makes it unnecessary to trace through the benefits of abatement from individual projects to individual countries and assess them accordingly. Such a process would have been unworkable. In the current scheme, there is an implicit assumption that the totality of projects funded by the GEF produces global environmental benefits shared in reasonable proportion by the donor countries. Benefits are bought wholesale, not retail, saving transaction costs.

The GEF has found it difficult to implement these as operating principles (UNDP, UNEP, and World Bank 1994). The original idea appeared to be that the GEF would fund only the *net* incremental cost of a project – the gross incremental costs for securing global environmental benefits minus the national benefits that the country expected to obtain for itself (this would be the area HIJ in Figure 13.1). Distinguishing between domestic and international benefits proved very difficult in biodiversity and marine pollution-abatement projects, as well as the institution-building and capacity-development projects. As a result, there was pressure to treat all costs as incremental costs on the grounds that without GEF funding the project would not have been undertaken. Indeed, the recipient country has every incentive to claim that its domestic benefits are minimal (that is, GEF should fund the *entire* area $0IQ_0$ in Figure 13.1). Analysts, desiring to approve projects, tended to cooperate. Moreover, strict application of the incremental cost principle would rule out funding many demand side–management projects in the energy area, where the incremental costs were likely to be negative (i.e., economic benefits exceeding costs).[22] Finally, the criterion that projects be "cost effective" implies a common yardstick to compare projects – species saved per dollar spent, CO_2 abatement per dollar spent. In fact, the injunction that projects be cost effective is only operational if one can compare the benefits across projects in monetary units, which is not yet

---

22 Demand side management refers to reducing the consumption of energy/environment using activities. Examples include energy-efficient lighting and higher thermal insulation in building construction.

possible. The problem of defining and measuring incremental costs is also present in the UN Framework Convention on Climate Change, which requires developed countries to fund "agreed [upon] full incremental costs of implementing measures taken by developing countries."

The current GEF guidelines appear somewhat inconsistent (Global Environmental Facility 1996). First, complying with the climate and biodiversity conventions, the GEF funds *full* incremental costs. This could be interpreted to mean that if a country itself receives incremental benefits from its GEF project, those benefits would not be subtracted from GEF funding. In Figure 13.1 terms, this means that the GEF would fund the amount represented by $Q_E HIQ_0$, whereas the minimum necessary in theory to reach global optimum would be HIJ. Second, the guidelines state that if the GEF activity creates domestic benefits, they should not be counted in the incremental cost calculation, but if the GEF activity results in avoided (domestic) costs, these avoided domestic costs should be included in the incremental cost calculation. There is no economic rationale for treating benefits and avoided costs differently. Third, the guidelines state that no GEF project can have a negative domestic environmental impact (any potential negative impact must be fully mitigated). This is not an efficient restriction, as some environmental effects cannot be fully mitigated, and in some cases the cost of full mitigation greatly exceeds the damages prevented. Despite these questionable practices, the GEF remains a very positive innovation in managing international environmental resources.

4.4 Compensation Systems – Debt-for-Nature Swaps, a Quasiprivate Channel *(Crawford 1995)*

Debt-for-nature swaps, which were pioneered in the late 1980s, are an innovative channel for "buying" increased environmental protection. They are most frequently initiated by private sector NGOs in the North, but government agencies including U.S. Agency for International Development (USAID) and commercial banks have also been involved. Also the U.S. government's Enterprise for the Americas Initiative has conducted a similar operation, not for commercial bank debt, but for debt owed to the U.S. government. This includes debt owed to the Ex-Im Bank and the U.S. Commodity Credit Corporation.

The mechanics are as follows. Generally, after agreement with a debtor government, an NGO buys the country's debt on the secondary market for dollars at a substantial discount. The developing country central bank then converts the dollar debt into local currency or local currency bonds, which are then used by a designated local NGO for agreed-upon conservation measures. The deeper the discount is on the debt in the secondary market, the greater the face value of debt that can be purchased for dollars and, if agreeable to the debtor country, the greater the amount of local currency funds for conservation. See Table 13.2 for data on swaps, amounts, and conversion factors. The proceeds from swaps have been used for a variety of resource-conservation purposes, including establishment and operation of parks and nature reserves and reforestation in Costa Rica and inventory of endangered plants and animals and training of park wardens in Madagascar.

While generally at a modest scale and subject to various limitations, debt-for-nature swaps (and the related practice of converting debt owed to industrial country governments into environmental trust funds) offers an attractive vehicle through which developing countries receive some compensation from the international community for providing international public goods – preservation of tropical forests and species habitat. Moreover, in some instances the funds themselves lay the groundwork for commercialization of the services. Costa Rica, which participated in six debt-for-nature swaps, has established an extensive national park and reserve system (some 27 percent of national territory). As a result, nature tourism has become a major source of foreign exchange earnings. At a more speculative level, debt-for-nature swaps moderate external debt payment burdens. (It is possible that the purchase of the debt increases its price on the secondary market and does *not* reduce the effective debt, although it reduces the face value of the debt outstanding.) If debt payments had been implicated in unsustainable resource practices, including deforestation, the debt relief would have an indirect environmental benefit to the country additional to the provision of international public goods.[23] Debt-for-nature swaps were a feature of the debt crisis in Latin America in the 1980s, but have not been present in the Asian financial crisis starting in 1997.

4.5 Making a Market – Biodiversity

Developing countries and their tropical forests are a treasure-house of genetic and biochemical resources. Over one-half of total plant and animal species live in tropical forests. These genetic and biochemical resources are valuable in agriculture for plant breeding and in medicine for the development of pharmaceuticals. An estimated 25 percent of all prescriptions filled

---

23 The evidence that high external debt levels contribute to deforestation is not strong. See Raymond Gullison and Elizabeth Losos (1993) and also Todd Sandler (1993).

Table 13.2. *Debt-for-nature swaps, 1987–1994*

Date	Country	Purchaser	Cost to purchaser $	Face value of debt $	Conservation funds generated $[a]
1987	Bolivia	CI	100,000	650,000	250,000
1987	Ecuador	WWF	354,000	1,000,000	1,000,000
1988	Costa Rica	Netherlands	5,000,000	33,000,000	9,900,000
1988	Costa Rica	FPN/WWF	918,000	5,400,000	4,050,000
1989	Costa Rica	Sweden	3,500,000	24,500,000	17,100,000
1989	Costa Rica	TNC	784,000	5,600,000	1,680,000
1989	Ecuador	WWF/TNC/MBG	1,069,000	9,000,000	9,000,000
1989	Madagascar	WWF/USAID	950,000	2,111,000	2,111,000
1989	Philippines	WWF	200,000	390,000	390,000
1989	Zambia	WWF	454,000	2,270,000	2,270,000
1990	Costa Rica	Sweden/WWF/TNC	1,953,000	10,754,000	9,602,900
1990	Madagascar	WWF	446,000	919,000	919,000
1990	Poland	WWF	12,000	50,000	50,000
1990	Dom. Rep.	CTPR/TNC	116,000	582,000	582,000
1990	Philippines	WWF	439,000	900,000	900,000
1991	Costa Rica	RA/MCL/TNC	360,000	600,000	540,000
1991	Madagascar	CI	59,000	119,000	119,000
1991	Mexico	CI	180,000	250,000	250,000
1991	Ghana	DDC/CI/SI	250,000	1,000,000	1,000,000
1991	Nigeria	NCF	65,000	150,000	93,000
1991	Jamaica	TNC/USAID/CTPR	300,000	437,000	437,000
1991	Guatemala	TNC	75,000	100,000	90,000
1992	Philippines	WWF	5,000,000	9,847,000	8,816,000
1992	Guatemala	CI	1,200,000	1,334,000	1,334,000
1992	Brazil	TNC	748,000	2,200,000	2,200,000
1992	Panama	CI	30,000,000	30,000,000	30,000,000
1992	Mexico	CI	355,000	441,000	441,000
1992	Bolivia	TNC/WWF/JP Morgan	0	11,500,000	2,760,000
1993	Philippines	WWF	12,970,000	19,000,000	17,100,000
1993	Madagascar	WWF	909,000	1,868,000	1,868,000
1994	Madagascar	Deutsche Bank/WWF	0	1,340,000	1,072,000
1994	Jamaica	TNC/JCDT/SI	110,000	150,000	150,000

[a] U.S.$ equivalent in local currency. Conservation funds generated do not include interest on bonds when the government pays in bonds rather than cash.

Abbreviations: CI: Conservation International; CTPR: Conservation Trust of Puerto Rico; DDC: Debt for Development Coalition; FPN: National Parks Foundation of Costa Rica; MBG: Missouri Botanical Gardens; MCL: Monteverde Conservation League; NCF: Nigerian Conservation Foundation; TNC: The Nature Conservancy; RA: Rainforest Alliance; SI: Smithsonian Institute; USAID: United States Agency for International Development; WWF: World Wildlife Fund.

Source: Compiled by Jo-Ann Crawford, "Debt-for-Nature Swaps" (SAIS, mimeo, 1995), based on World Wildlife Fund Distribution Package dated June 1994; The Nature Conservancy, Officially Sanctioned and Funded Debt-for-Nature Swaps to date with Commercial Bank Debt (as of December 1992); and World Bank, World Debt Tables 1993–1994.

in the United States are based on ingredients extracted or derived from plants. Genetic diversity has contributed to improved plant strains and accounted for about one-half the gains in U.S. agriculture yield between 1930 and 1980 (Riedel et al. 1993; Sedjo 1992). At the same time, this richness has scarcely been tapped. Of an estimated 10 to 100 million living species, only 1.4 million have been described, and far fewer subject to chemical and genetic analysis (Simpson, Sedjo, and Reid 1996). This unexploited potential has led to the term "biodiversity prospecting" to describe the activity of seeking and screening genetic and biochemical resources from developing countries.

Biological resources have been described as nonrival, or public goods. It might be more accurate to say nonrival gifts of nature. *Nonrivalry* implies that the genetic and chemical information inherent in these goods is not exhausted by one user. While the potentially valuable information they contain is a gift of nature, the activity of protecting and conserving them can be considered a public good (service). The international management challenge is to devise methods by which developing countries, which typically bear the costs of conservation, are compensated by those who ultimately benefit from the downstream pharmaceutical and agricultural products. The current direction is to establish property rights and develop a commercial market. This is consistent with Demsetz's thesis (1967) that property rights to natural resources emerge when resources become commercially valuable and earlier open-access regimes become inefficient.

Intellectual property rights to new varieties of plants and animals developed by plant breeders and pharmaceutical firms are protected by patents in the United States and some other countries. These include novel DNA sequences, genes, plant varieties, and biotechnical processes. Such patent systems are a social compromise – granting monopoly rights to private firms in exchange for the investments made by the firms in the cost of developing products for the marketplace. Without intellectual property rights to downstream products, the effective demand for the genetic and chemical raw material located in developing countries would be greatly reduced. The raw material itself, however, has traditionally been of an open-access character, and little or no payment has been made. Hence the social value of conservation has exceeded its market value, and too little has been invested in conserving biodiversity.

This is changing. The Convention on Biological Diversity, signed at the Rio Conference on Environment and Development in 1992, rejects the notion that unimproved genetic and biochemical resources are the common heritage of mankind with free access, but instead asserts that biodiversity is a sovereign national resource, suitable for exploitation. A number of countries are proceeding to commercialize this resource through arrangements with pharmaceutical firms, research organizations, and firms specializing in the collection and screening of samples. The most widely cited agreement is between the Instituto Nacional de Biodiversidad (INBio) in Costa Rica and the drug firm, Merck and Co. (INBio itself was initially funded in part with debt-for-nature funds). That 1991 arrangement provides that INBio will provide Merck with chemical extracts from plants, insects, and microorganisms for subsequent drug screening in exchange for a $1.1 million payment, royalties on commercialized products, and technical assistance (Riedel et al. 1992, p. 1). In turn, INBio will contribute a portion of its budget and royalties to conservation activities in Costa Rica.

While the movement toward a commercial market in biodiversity is clear, the potential revenues for conservation appear modest and actual bioprospecting activity is limited (MacIllwain 1998). Simpson, Sedjo, and Ried have estimated that the maximum amount pharmaceutical firms might be willing to pay for preservation of a hectare of prime biological diversity (Western Ecuador) is $20.63, with values for other locations with fewer endemic plant species declining to $0.20 per hectare. These are estimates of the private returns. Social returns from option values and consumer surplus would be higher, but the authors still doubt that the value of conserving biodiverse raw material for pharmaceutical research would be substantial. This finding relates to habitat valued for pharmaceuticals – the authors do not attempt to measure other conservation values ranging from watershed protection to ecotourism.

4.6 Extending International Law – The Trail Smelter Precedent

The development of international environmental law is another avenue for managing externalities. The Trail Smelter Case between the United States and Canada is widely cited as an early and influential landmark in its development. A dispute arose over air pollution from a Canadian smelter in the 1920s and 1930s, with damages in Washington State. The United States and Canada agreed to send the dispute to binding arbitration by the U.S.-Canada International Joint Commission. In 1944, the Arbitration Tribunal found that damages had occurred and set an indemnity to be paid by Canada at $350,000 (USITC 1991). The decision stated that "no state has the right to use or permit the use of its territory in such a manner as to cause injury by fumes in or to the territory of another, or the property or persons therein, when the case is of serious consequence and the injury is established by clear and convincing evidence" (Dixon and McCorquodale 1991, p. 453). This principle was picked up and expanded in Principle 21 of the 1972 Stockholm Declaration on the Human Environment, which declares that in accordance with international law, states have "the responsibility to ensure that activities within their jurisdiction or control do not cause damage to the environment of other states or areas beyond the limits of national jurisdiction." The underlying principle has also been incorporated in a number of subsequent resolutions and declarations, including the 1974 UN Resolution on the Charter of Economic Rights and Duties of States and the Rio Declaration in 1992.

The extent to which resolutions and declarations actually affect behavior and reduce international environmental externalities is open to question. These declarations are known as "soft law" and although they establish norms for behavior, and may be useful in negotiating agreements on specific disputes, they lack traditional enforcement mechanisms. We also note that while the extension of international law helps clarify property rights to international resources and is a precondition for markets, the rights must be marketable if Coase-like solutions are sought.

4.7 Using Trade Measures – The Pelly Amendment and Elephant Ivory

In 1971, the United States passed the Pelly Amendment to the 1967 Fisherman's Protective Act. Under that legislation, the president has discretionary power to ban imports of fish products if the U.S. government unilaterally determines that the foreign fishing activity of a country diminishes the effectiveness of an international fisheries conservation program. This was extended in 1978 to include countries engaging in taking or trade that diminished the effectiveness of any international program for endangered or threatened species. In 1992, Pelly was further broadened, giving the president authority to ban imports of any product from the offending country. It should be noted that the Pelly Amendment was triggered by foreign persons and not foreign governments and is not limited to enforcing a treaty, but can be invoked in defense of international conservation programs.

Steve Charnovitz has analyzed the success of Pelly episodes over the period 1974–1993. He defines success as "a significant concurrent change in the policy of target government in the direction sought by the U.S. government (Charnovitz 1993a, p. 1). By this definition, he finds 50 percent of the Pelly episodes successful, 11 percent partially successful, and 39 percent unsuccessful. In no case were sanctions actually employed. Subsequently, however, the United States imposed trade sanctions against Taiwan for trade in rhino horns. Imports of wildlife products from Taiwan (e.g., coral jewelry, tropical fish) valued at $25 million per year were banned. Taiwan responded with an aggressive crackdown on illegal trade in tiger bone and rhino horn, and in just over a year the sanctions were suspended.

In contrast to the Pelly Amendment, which is essentially a unilateral sanctioning measure to increase the effectiveness (compliance) with international conservation programs, the 1973 Convention on International Trade in Endangered Species (CITES) is an international agreement whose centerpiece is trade restrictions. In 1989, the parties to the convention transferred the African elephant from an Appendix II listing to Appendix 1.[24] Under Appendix II, some international trade in elephant ivory and skin is allowed with appropriate permits; an Appendix I listing, reserved for currently endangered species, prohibits all trade in elephant products.

At first glance, a ban on international trade appears desirable. In the 1980s, the African elephant herd had declined from 1.2 million to about 600,000. The principal cause was illegal poaching for the international ivory trade. If trade restrictions cut off trade, demand would fall and, with lower poaching pressure, herd size could stabilize. However, the trade ban may have had unanticipated adverse consequences. One reason is that not all herds were equally threatened; certain countries such as Zimbabwe and Botswana claimed healthy populations and resisted transferring the elephant to Appendix I status. This is not necessarily free-rider behavior. If indeed their herds were sustainably managed, a trade ban would cut off the revenue flow and reduce the commercial value of the herd. As the "asset" value is reduced, there will be less incentive to invest in habitat preservation and herd management. The more general point is that if countries are asked to undertake expensive conservation measures, either they must be able to earn a return through sustainably managed yields, or they will require more direct compensation. Also, China and Hong Kong, major purchasers of ivory, declared reservations against the ban.

Two other points are relevant. First, the primary problem was illegal domestic harvesting and/or poaching. This (illegal) free-access regime meant, and means, that governments in African countries did not receive full returns for sustainable management of herds, and individual poachers have every incentive to deplete the resource. Trade restrictions do not directly deal with inadequate property rights or protection of state property and may

---

24 See Barbier et al. (1990), Barbier (1995a), and Joanne Burgess (1994).

weaken ability to control poaching. Second, as with many partial environmental measures, the restrictions on trade in African elephant ivory has shunted pressure and increased poaching of wild elephant herds in Asia, especially Laos.

4.8 Overarching Political Interests

From time to time, domestic or international political interests may ultimately dictate resolution of bilateral environmental disputes even when a narrowly defined economic advantage is questionable. Two examples are the salinity of the Colorado River as it crosses the U.S.-Mexican border and the acid rain controversy between the United States and Canada.

A 1944 treaty between the United States and Mexico guaranteed that a certain quantity of Colorado River water would be delivered to Mexico, but did not specify its quality. In the 1960s, there was a dramatic increase in the salinity of water delivered to Mexico in part due to new irrigation projects in the United States.[25] At the same time Mexican agriculture based on irrigation had boomed. Mexico protested, but the United States procrastinated in offering a solution. However, in 1972 President Nixon met with Mexican President Echeverria and agreed to find a definitive solution to the salinity issue. This was followed up in 1973 with a formal agreement between the two countries and in 1974 by the U.S. Salinity Control Act, which authorized certain actions including the construction of a $300 million desalinization facility at Yuma, Arizona. At about this time, there were important new discoveries of oil in Mexico, and additionally Mexico was pursuing an increasingly independent foreign policy *vis à vis* Central America and Cuba. It is reasonable to suppose that larger international political interests and a desire to cultivate good relations with Mexico played a role in resolving the festering environmental controversy over Colorado River water quality.

Larger foreign policy interests were also in play during the long drawn-out dispute between the United States and Canada concerning transboundary SO_2 and acid rain, but were not sufficient to bring the issue to a rapid conclusion. The dispute first arose from Canadian complaints during the Carter Administration, which promised to work for an early resolution. In 1981, President Reagan addressed the Canadian Parliament but made no significant concession on acid rain, and Prime Minister Trudeau again raised the issue later that year during the annual Summit meeting, but without

25 Lesser, Dodds, and Zerbe (1997) give a good account.

success.[26] Two meetings between President Reagan and Prime Minister Mulroney in 1984 and 1985 also failed to solve the issue. The elements of a resolution were finally worked out between Prime Minister Mulroney and President Bush in 1990 and formalized in a 1991 agreement concerning air quality. The United States agreed to reduce SO_2 by 10 million tons from 1980 levels by 2000 (consistent with Title IV of the U.S. Clean Air Act of 1990), and Canada committed to a reduction of emissions from seven eastern provinces of 2.3 million tons and a permanent national emissions cap of 3.2 million tons by 2000.[27] The lesson appears to be that even when international environmental issues reach the highest political level and are a major source of friction, they are not necessarily attended to immediately. Bui (1998) provides an interesting theoretical and empirical analysis of U.S.-Canadian acid-rain abatement. She finds that although joint abatement tactics by both countries would offer significant savings, the actual course of negotiations is consistent with a noncooperative Nash equilibrium, in which Canada attempts to free ride off U.S. abatement, and the United States has been reluctant to engage in joint action because it would bear *relatively* large abatement costs.

Appendix 13.1
Negotiating MEAs

The outcome of MEA negotiations are sensitive to context and behavioral assumptions. We illustrate this in a simple stylized example involving two countries and well-defined pollution-abatement cost and benefit functions, a variation of Figures 13.2 and 13.3 and related discussion in the chapter. Six situations are investigated: (1) each country pursuing its parochial interest oblivious to the actions of others (blind self-interest), (2) a benevolent dictator seeking global optimum, (3) full cooperation without a dictator, (4) a noncooperative Nash equilibrium, (5) a Stackelberg-type solution, and (6) coercive behavior. Cases 3 through 6 involve strategic behavior.

Assume two countries A and B emit equal amounts (20 units) of a uniformly mixed flow pollutant that damages the beneficial use of a shared environmental resource. Assume further that both countries experience the same damage functions and confront the same abatement cost functions. For concreteness, assume specific forms of the abatement benefit and cost functions:

$$B_A = 20E - 0.25(E)^2 \text{ in the range } 0 < E < 40 \tag{1}$$

$$B_B = 20E - 0.25(E)^2 \text{ in the range } 0 < E < 40 \tag{2}$$

---

26 For history of early dispute, see Chris Park (1987) and Anthony Scott (1986). See also Viki Golich and Terry Forrest-Young (1993).
27 See Carter and Trimble (1995).

$$C_A = (E_A)^2 \tag{3}$$

$$C_B = (E_B)^2 \tag{4}$$

$$E = E_A + E_B \tag{5}$$

where:

B_A and B_B are abatement benefits to A and B.
C_A and C_B are abatement cost functions for A and B.
E_A and E_B are physical units of pollution abated by A and B.
E is total abatement.

The corresponding marginal benefit (MB) and marginal cost (MC) functions are:

$$MB_A = 20 - 0.5E \tag{6}$$

$$MB_B = 20 - 0.5E \tag{7}$$

$$MC_A = 2E_A \tag{8}$$

$$MC_B = 2E_B \tag{9}$$

Define welfare as the gain from abatement as compared to no abatement:

$$W_A = B_A - C_A \tag{10}$$

$$W_B = B_B - C_B \tag{11}$$

$$W_G = W_A + W_B \text{ (global welfare)} \tag{12}$$

Case 1: Blind Self-Interest

If each country pursues its narrow self-interest without regard for the other, it will abate to the level where its marginal costs equal marginal benefits to itself:

for A

$$2E_A = 20 - 0.5 \ E_A$$

$$E_A = 8$$

for B

$$2E_B = 20 - 0.5E_B$$

$$E_B = 8$$

and

$$E = 16.$$

The welfare gains to A and B can be calculated:

$$W_A = 20E - 0.25 \ (E)^2 - (E_A)^2 = 192$$

$$W_B = 192$$

$$W_G = 384.$$

Case 2: Benevolent Dictator Seeking Global Optimum

Under the assumptions of this model (equal pollution levels, identical benefit and cost functions), a supranational authority pursuing an efficient global optimum would result in higher abatement efforts and higher national and global welfare levels than in case 1. To see this, derive the global marginal benefit and marginal cost functions (adding the national benefit functions vertically, as abatement is a public good) and set equal

$$MB_G = 40 - E$$

$$MC_G = E.$$

Solving,

$$E = 20,$$

and, because marginal abatement cost functions are identical,

$$E_A = E_B = 10,$$

welfare levels are

$$W_A = W_B = 200$$

$$W_G = 400.$$

We conclude from this example that a supranational authority can reach a global optimum so long as neither country is allowed to behave strategically.

Case 3: Cooperation with Positive Conjectures

Assume each country is aware of the benefits it confers on the other and is sufficiently trusting of the other that it anticipates that the other will respond positively if it initiates abatement. Then the marginal benefit function for A will include the effects of its abatement on itself and the anticipated effects of B's response. More specifically, the two countries would recognize the global optimal abatement of 20 units and, because in this example the costs and benefits are similar, share the abatement effort equally. The results of $E_A = E_B = 10$ and $W_A = W_B = 200$ are the same as for the benevolent dictator case.

Case 4: Noncooperative Suboptimal Nash Equilibrium

Assume instead that each country plays "Cournot," meaning that it sets its abatement according to the abatement chosen by the other and assumes the other will *not* respond. This case is best explained with a pair of reaction functions expressing A's abatement effort on the basis of B's effort, and B's effort on the basis of A's effort (Figure 13A.1). The reaction function for A can be derived from $MC_A = MB_A$,

$$2E_A = 20 - 0.5 (E_A + E_B)$$

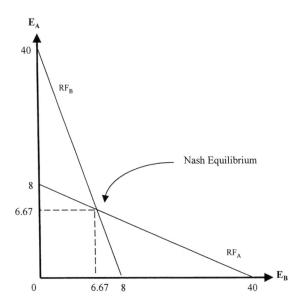

Figure 13A.1. *A noncooperative, suboptimal international pollution-abatement game with Nash equilibrium*

or

$$E_A = 8 - 0.2E_B \text{ (reaction function for A)}$$

and, in similar fashion, the reaction function for B

$$E_B = 8 - 0.2 E_A$$

or rearranging,

$$E_A = 40 - 5E_B. \text{ (reaction function for B)}$$

The two reaction functions can be solved for a Nash equilibrium at

$$E_A = 6.6667$$

$$E_B = 6.6667$$

$$E = 13.3333$$

and the welfare levels can be derived

$$W_A = 177.78$$

$$W_B = 177.78$$

$$W_G = 355.56.$$

Given the Cournot assumption that each tries to maximize its welfare subject to the abatement level chosen by the other, this is an equilibrium in the sense that neither has any incentive to alter their abatement level. The welfare levels are inferior to the previous three cases.

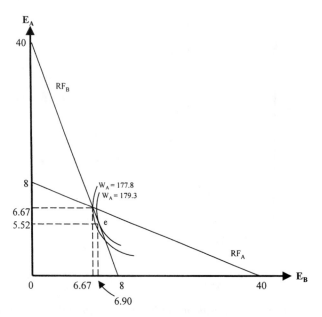

Figure 13A.2. *A noncooperative, suboptimal international pollution-abatement game with Stackelberg-Type strategy*

Case 5: Stackleberg-Type Negotiations

The Cournot assumption in case 4 is limiting as it assumes each country ascribes behavior to the other that it does not follow itself (i.e., A responds to B's abatement level but assumes B will not respond to A's level). The question arises as to why one country, say, A, does not establish a lower abatement level than the Nash equilibrium and "force" B into a higher abatement level, shifting welfare to A. Indeed, this may be the strategy.[28]

Consider Figure 13A.2, which repeats 13A.1 with the addition of two isowelfare curves for country A. The first curve, at welfare level 177.78, goes through the Nash equilibrium (E_A, $E_B = 6.667$). But if A chose a somewhat lower abatement level and B responded by maximizing its welfare along its reaction function, A could improve its welfare as compared to the Nash equilibrium. The maximum welfare A could achieve is the tangency of B's reaction function to the highest possible A isowelfare curve at point *e*.

This can be calculated:

$$\max W_A = B_A - C_A = 20\,(E_A + E_B) - 0.25\,(E_A + E_B)^2 - (E_A)^2,$$

---

28 In the classic Cournot market sharing duopoly model, A is constrained from doing so, as such a move would reduce its profits and hence lack credibility unless B responded by reducing output. The essence of the popular Brander-Spencer strategic trade model is that a government subsidy to the A firm would establish the credibility of expanded A output, and the B firm would reduce its output accordingly. There is no parallel profit constraint when government sets environmental policy.

subject to the constraint that $E_A = 40 - 5E_B$ (B's reaction function). After substitution and manipulation:

$$W_A = -29 (E_B)^2 + 400 E_B - 1200$$

for max:

$$\frac{dW_A}{dE_B} = -29 E_B + 400 = 0$$

and

$$E_B = 6.897$$
$$E_A = 5.517$$
$$E = 12.414.$$

Substituting into the welfare equations:

$$W_A = 179.31$$
$$W_B = 162.18$$
$$W_G = 341.49.$$

Thus a Stackelberg-type negotiation strategy could shift welfare from B to A but at an even lower global welfare level than the suboptimal Nash solution. The essential reason is that marginal abatement costs in A and B are no longer equalized. The realism of this case also can be questioned; if A attempts to gain advantage by reducing effort, so might B, and welfare would degenerate further. The possibility of retaliation by B may make A's aggressive strategy noncredible.

Case 6: A Coercive Solution

Assume A has coercive power over B through some exogenous measure, perhaps trade sanctions. A full use of that power would force B into complete abatement ($E_B = 20$). We can calculate the optimal amount of A's abatement:

$$MC_A = MB_A$$
$$2E_A = 20 - 0.5 (20 + E_A)$$
$$E_A = 4, E_B = 20, E = 24$$

and

$$W_A = 20 (24) - 0.25 (24)^2 - (4)^2$$
$$W_A = 320$$
$$W_B = -64$$
$$W_G = 256.$$

The coercive situation leads to excessive abatement and the lowest level of global welfare. The distribution of welfare has sharply shifted toward the coercing country.

Table 13A.1. *Welfare under six negotiation scenarios*

Case	Abatement effort			Welfare		
	E_A	E_B	E_G	W_A	W_B	W_G
1. Blind Self-Interest	8	8	16	192	192	384
2. Benevolent Dictator	10	10	20	200	200	400
3. Cooperation	10	10	20	200	200	400
4. Nash Equilibrium (Cournot Assumption)	6.67	6.67	13.33	177.78	177.78	355.56
5. Stackelberg Solution	5.52	6.90	12.41	179.31	162.18	341.44
6. Coercive Behavior	4	20	24	320	−64	256

Note: See text for symbols.

Country B is forced to abate well beyond the point where its marginal benefits equal its marginal costs and it has an absolute welfare loss. The attractiveness of this behavior to A is obvious: it obtains welfare of 320, well above its welfare in all of the other five negotiation situations. The results of the six cases are summarized in Table 13.A1.

Bluffs and Misinformation

A wide variety of outcomes is possible if bluffs and misinformation are allowed. Assume, for example, that A and B agree on a formula to share costs equally. This is reasonable as both enjoy the same benefits. However, both have an incentive to inflate their abatement costs, and, if accepted by the other, costs are exaggerated and abatement falls short of its optimum level. Also, when negotiations cover anticipated emissions, one country or the other, or both, may threaten to increase emissions beyond current levels in an effort to secure a better bargaining position. While this comes close to extortion, such behavior is not unknown in trade. For example, in the 19th century the United States imposed new so-called negotiating tariffs as a tool to beat down foreign tariff barriers. Bluffs and misinformation may play a role in allocating the costs of controlling greenhouse gas emissions among countries.

Summary and Relevance to MEAs

Within the limits of the model's assumptions, the conclusions from this exercise are quite encouraging. Case 3, full cooperation, leads to globally optimal abatement and the highest payoff for both A and B if coercive behavior is disallowed. But this is partly an artifact of the assumptions, especially identical cost and benefit functions that are known to both parties. Also, many international environmental externalities involve more than two countries, which increases the prospects for free riding and complicates the analysis by introducing coalition formation.

14

Economics and Global Warming

1 Introduction

In 1896, a Swedish scientist, Svante Arrhenius, calculated that as a result of emissions from fossil fuel consumption, a doubling of atmospheric carbon dioxide might raise global mean temperatures by 4°C to 6°C.[1] One hundred years after the initial calculations by Arrhenius, global warming has become the most important and controversial issue in international environmental relations. The theoretical prediction of increasing atmospheric concentrations of CO_2 was first confirmed in the 1970s by measurements at Mauna Loa (Hawaii), which showed an increase from 315 ppm (parts per million) in 1958 to 331 ppm in 1975 (Pearson and Pryor 1978, p. 267). Concentrations in the preindustrial era were about 280 ppm and reached 358 ppm by 1994. Global average temperature has increased between 0.3°C and 0.6°C (0.5 to 1.1°F) over the past century. How much of this is due to natural variability and how much to human activity is not known with certainty, but the 1996 report of the Intergovernmental Panel on Climate Change (IPCC) concludes that "the balance of evidence suggests that there is a discernable human influence on global climate" (J. T. Houghton et al. 1996, p. 5), and estimates temperature increases of 2°F to 6°F over the next 100 years.

This chapter emphasizes the international aspects of curtailing global warming.[2] Section 2 identifies some of the analytical complexities and provides factual background material. Section 3 casts global warming as a complex problem in cost-benefit analysis. Section 4 explicitly looks at the

---

1 Cited by William Cline (1992, p. 13).
2 The economic literature on global warming is vast and growing. The Bruce et al. IPCC volume dealing with economic and social impacts (1996) contains some 45 pages of references.

complications arising from the international character of global warming, and Section 5 continues this perspective in examining various measures to control emissions. Finally, Section 6 considers international actions taken to date, including the 1992 Framework Convention on Climate Change, the 1995 Berlin Climate Change Summit, and the Protocol to the FCCC signed in December 1997 in Kyoto. Before starting, it is worth noting that the science and economics of global warming are far from settled. For example, Mendelsohn (1999) argues that very recent research indicates global warming is much less serious and much less urgent than was believed in the early 1990s.

2 Analytical Complexities and Factual Background

Economic analysis of global warming poses formidable challenges. Much of the science on which the analysis rests remains uncertain. The uncertainties include emission rates for the various gases and their atmospheric lifetimes and concentrations; the effects of such concentrations on temperature, precipitation, and climate, especially at the regional, national, and local levels; and the effects of climate change on a wide range of variables of economic significance including agriculture, sea-level change, human health, biodiversity, and basic ecological and environmental systems. Uncertainties in the underlying science compound uncertainties in subsequent economic analysis. Nevertheless, economics can contribute to devising efficient and effective responses to global warming. In particular, skills in modelling and projecting economic-energy interactions, the principles of cost-benefit analysis, the ranking of policy instruments, and the theories of managing international resources can be productively employed.

Some of the more vexing problems in economic analysis of climate change arise from the very long time periods involved. Even with declining rates of emissions, which are not yet in sight, the time scale to stabilize atmospheric concentrations of long-lived greenhouse gases is decades to millennia, and the time scale to bring equilibrium to the climate system with stable concentrations is decades to centuries.[3] The long time scale highlights the critical and controversial role of discounting. It also requires projecting activity, technology, and other structural changes over much longer periods than economics is comfortable with. The time scale is not the only difficult feature. The size of potential damage and abatement costs dwarf all other environ-

---

3 Greenhouse gases are stock pollutants. Emissions are a flow. Changes in concentration are gross emission flows minus removals from the atmosphere through a variety of processes that operate on different time scales.

mental problems, and this means that policy mistakes – too much or too little expenditure on abatement, too early or too late – can have serious welfare consequences. For example, one model shows that an economically optimum abatement policy might yield net global benefits of $270 billion when discounted, but an attempt to stabilize emissions at 1990 levels, the first-stage target endorsed at the Rio Earth Summit, would lead to a net present value *loss* of $7 trillion relative to the optimum policy (Nordhaus 1993). In addition to these unique features, analysis of climate change confronts the conventional problems of environmental economics, that is, valuing the nonmarketed services of the climate system and the damages arising from climate change and finding policy measures that are effective and efficient.

These difficulties and challenges would arise even if the sources of and damages from climate change were restricted to a single country. But global warming is a transboundary environmental issue *par excellence*. All countries contribute in some degree and all countries would be affected should climate change (most harmed, although some could benefit). The multiplicity of sources and the pervasive effects of climate change mean that international management or at least coordinated national management will be necessary. In economic terms, a stable global climate is an international public good, and greenhouse gas emissions leading to global warming are privately produced international public "bads." As with other public goods, collective action is needed. Unilateral action by one country would not be sufficient to prevent global warming, which is best addressed by international action.

The international character of the problem has far-reaching implications, ranging from the need to negotiate, not impose, control regimes, to the selection of efficient regulatory instruments. Reaching an international agreement on objectives and implementing a global warming policy would be considerably easier if all countries were similar. They are not. As shown in this chapter, there are major relevant differences among countries with respect to (1) past, present, and prospective emissions; (2) vulnerability to global warming; (3) the costs of emissions control; (4) income levels and hence discount rates, valuation of damages, and willingness and ability to pay for controls; and (5) institutional capacity to formulate, implement, and enforce controls.

Countries are also linked together through international trade and capital flows. Serious efforts to control global warming will have significant effects on the international economic system, exchange rates, and the competitive position of individual industries and countries. Moreover, trade and investment can be the vehicles through which emissions controlled by one set of countries are shunted or leaked to uncontrolled countries, reducing the effectiveness of the control regime.

Finally, countries differ in their ethical, philosophical, and religious systems and beliefs. These differences manifest themselves with respect to values placed on environmental resources. They also shape countries' attitudes toward risk and toward interpersonal and intergenerational equity. These differences in deeply rooted value systems further complicate reaching an international agreement.

We now provide some background material. The main greenhouse gases are carbon dioxide, methane, nitrous oxide, and chlorofluorocarbons (also responsible for ozone depletion). Of these, carbon dioxide and methane are the most important contributors to human amplification of the natural background greenhouse effect, with CO_2 contributing an estimated 60 percent to global warming.[4] By 2100, the contribution of CO_2 is expected to rise to 75 percent.[5] The concentration of these gases in the atmosphere has increased since the preindustrial era and the increase is due to human economic activities. Table 14.1 shows preindustrial and current concentrations, and atmospheric lifetimes. Note that CFC-11, an ozone-depleting gas, is being controlled by the Montreal Protocol, but HCFC-22, a substitute for CFC-11, and CF_4 are not so controlled (Houghton et al. 1996, pp. 15, 19). Note also that currently measured (1994) levels of CO_2 are about 28 percent above preindustrial levels. Most of this increase is the result of fossil fuel use.

Table 14.2 presents world emissions of carbon dioxide from consumption of various fossil fuels, cement manufacture, and land use changes (deforestation). Fossil fuels account for about 82 percent and deforestation, about 15 percent. Table 14.3 shows the sources of global methane emissions. Agriculture and livestock together account for a little over 55 percent.

Reducing carbon emissions from fossil fuel consumption must be at the

---

4 Increases in the atmospheric concentration of greenhouse gases reduce the efficiency with which the Earth cools in space. Incoming radiation is "trapped," and tends to warm the lower atmosphere and surface. The scientific term for a change in energy in the Earth's atmosphere system is "radiative forcing."

5 One cannot directly compare emission rates of various gases to climate change for two reasons. First, the atmospheric lifetime of gases varies from about 12 years for methane to 50–200 years for CO_2 (the large range for CO_2 results from different sinks, for example, vegetation, soils, and the deep ocean). Second, greenhouse gases do not have the same radiative effects per unit mass emitted. The Global Warming Potential is an effort to put various gases on a comparable metric. With this measure, and using a 100-year time perspective, if a unit mass emission of carbon has an index of 1, the index for methane is 21, for nitrous oxide is 310, and for various hydrofluorocarbons, the range is 150 to 11,700 (Houghton et al. 1996, p. 22). The low index value of carbon is offset by the very large volume of emissions.

Table 14.1. *Changes in greenhouse gas concentrations*

	CO_2	CH_4	N_2	CFC-11	HCFC-22[a]	CF_4[b]
Pre-industrial concentration	⁓280 ppmv	⁓700 ppbv	⁓275 ppbv	zero	zero	zero
Concentration in 1994	358 ppmv	1,720 ppbv	312[e] ppbv	268[e] ppbv	110 pptv	72[e] pptv
Atmospheric lifetime (years)	50–200[c]	12[d]	120	50	12	50,000

Note: 1 ppbv = 1 part per billion by volume; 1 pptv = 1 part per trillion by volume, etc.
[a] A CFC substitute.
[b] A perfluorocarbon.
[c] No single lifetime for CO_2 can be defined because of the different rates of uptake by different sink processes.
[d] This has been defined as an adjustment time which takes into account the indirect effect of methane on its own lifetime.
[e] Estimated from 1992–93 data.
Source: Houghton et al., 1996, Table 1, p 15.

Table 14.2. *World CO_2 emissions by source, 1992*

	World carbon dioxide emissions	
	(Millions metric tons)	(in percentages)
Land Use Changes	4,000[a]	15.5
Gas Fuels	3,829	14.5
Liquid Fuels	9,050	34.2
Solid Fuels	8,588	32.5
Cement Manufacture	627	2.4
Gas Flaring	249	0.9
Total	26,443	100

[a] 1991 data.
Source: Based on World Resources Institute (1996), Tables 14.2 and 14.4.

center of any serious policy to mitigate greenhouse warming. Not all fossil fuels release the same quantity of carbon per unit of energy produced. Changing the fuel mix will be a central part of abatement policies. Table 14.4 shows the carbon emissions of various fuels per unit of energy produced. Coal is about 67 percent more carbon-intensive per unit of energy than

Table 14.3. *Sources of anthropogenic methane emission, 1991*

Sources	World emissions (millions metric tons)	(In percentages)
Solid Waste	43	16
Coal Mining	36	13
Oil and Gas Production	44	16
Wet Rice Agriculture	69	26
Livestock	81	30
Total	270	100

Source: Based on World Resources Institute (1996), Table 14.2.

Table 14.4. *Carbon content of fossil fuels*

Fuel	Tons carbon emitted per million BTU[a]
Coal	25
Oil	20
Natural Gas	15

[a] BTU: British thermal unit.
Source: Based on Watson et al. (1996), Box B-2, p. 80.

natural gas. Three important implications of these differences must be taken into account for a program to abate carbon emissions. First, if a fuel tax is used, it should be differentiated by fuel type, with the higher rates applied to the more carbon-intensive fuels. A uniform energy tax such as a BTU tax would bias the fuel mix away from low-carbon natural gas toward coal. Second, the economic costs of controlling carbon, country by country, will depend in part on their current and prospective fossil fuel trade and consumption mix. For example, a carbon tax would disproportionately affect coal-abundant countries such as China. Third, a tax policy to accelerate the near-term use of low-carbon fuels will alter the time pattern of emissions; but with gas and oil in relatively fixed supply, the ultimate cumulative level of carbon emissions might not be significantly reduced.[6]

6 The IPCC estimates *identified* global fossil fuel reserves at 50,000 EJ (exajoules), which would last 130 years at the 1990 global consumption rate of 385 EJ. Coal accounts for more than half. Estimates of resources remaining to be discovered are much larger. The *identified* fossil fuel reserves contain more carbon than is currently in the atmosphere.

Table 14.5. *Cumulative CO$_2$ emissions by country and region 1800–1988*

Region	Total CO$_2$ (in percentages)
1. OECD North America	27.7
2. OECD Europe	16.6
3. Eastern Europe	4.8
4. Former USSR	12.5
5. Japan	2.3
6. Oceania	1.9
7. China	6.0
8. India	4.5
9. Other Asia	5.0
10. North Africa & Mid East	1.7
11. Other Africa	5.2
12. Brazil	3.3
13. Other Latin America	6.5
Developed Countries (1–6)	67.8
Developing Countries (7–13)	32.2
World	100.0

Source: Bruce, et al. (1996), Table 3.1.

In contemplating international controls, it is useful to know greenhouse gas emissions, past, present, and future, by region or country. Table 14.5 presents estimates of cumulative emissions of CO$_2$ by country groups for the period 1800–1988. The OECD countries are responsible for about 50 percent; Eastern Europe and the former USSR, about 17 percent, and developing countries, including China, 33 percent. Historic shares have no effect on the efficiency of prospective emissions controls, but they have equity or fairness implications for the allocation of new controls. Table 14.6 displays by country and economic grouping CO$_2$ emissions from industrial sources for 1992. The United States accounts for about 22 percent of the total. Table 14.7 provides estimates for methane emissions from anthropogenic sources by activity and region. Tables 14.6 and 14.7 demonstrate quite clearly that different regions contribute different amounts of different greenhouse gases. Europe and North and Central America account for 58 percent of CO$_2$ from industrial sources, but only 32 percent of methane. Asia contributes 32 percent of industrial CO$_2$ and 50 percent of methane. Other data show Europe plus North and Central America account for 5 percent of CO$_2$ from

Table 14.6. *CO_2 emission from industrial sources, 1992*

Region or country	Total CO_2 emission from industrial sources (millions metric tons)	Percentage of total volume
Africa	715	3.2
Europe	6,866	30.7
France	362	1.6
Germany	878	3.9
Italy	407	1.8
Poland, Rep.	341	1.5
Russian Federation	2,103	9.4
Ukraine	611	2.7
United Kingdom	566	2.5
North and Central America	5,715	25.6
Canada	409	1.8
Mexico	332	1.5
United States	4,881	21.9
South America	605	2.7
Brazil	217	1
Asia	7,118	31.9
China	2,667	11.9
India	769	3.4
Japan	1,093	4.9
Korea, Rep.	290	1.3
Saudi Arabia	221	1
Oceania	297	1.3
Australia	268	1.2
World	22,339	100

Source: Based on World Resources Institute (1996), Table 14.1.

deforestation; Asia, 32 percent, and South America 44, percent. The disparities are of course related to income levels and industrial/agricultural structures.

Emissions of CO_2 per capita and per unit of economic activity vary greatly, and these differences will be important in devising an efficient and equitable control regime. Figure 14.1 displays the dramatic differences in per capita emissions between developed and developing countries, and substantial differences among countries at roughly equal income levels (eg., EU, Japan, and the United States). Figure 14.2 shows carbon emissions per unit GNP for selected countries and regions. National currency GNPs are compared

Table 14.7. *Methane emission by region and activity, 1991*
(1,000 metric tons)

	Percent world total	Solid waste	Coal mining	Oil and gas production	Wet rice agriculture	Livestock
Africa	7.6	1,700	1,700	6,000	2,400	9,000
Europe	19.5	17,000	6,600	15,000	420	14,000
North and Central America	12.9	11,000	6,100	8,200	590	9,200
South America	7.6	2,200	280	2,200	870	15,000
Asia	50.3	9,900	20,000	12,000	65,000	30,000
Oceania	2.1	690	1,400	310	75	3,300

Source: Based on World Resources Institute (1996), Table 14.2.

at purchasing power parity rather than market rates. Figure 14.2 hints at major differences in energy efficiency but should be interpreted cautiously. Differences in industrial/agricultural structures, available fuel mix including biomass, and errors associated with currency conversion are all potential explanations.

Future contributions to greenhouse gas emissions by country or region are speculative. The important variables in estimating emission levels and rates of growth for CO_2 are given in the Kaya identity:

$$CO_2 = \left(\frac{E}{Q}\right)\left(\frac{CO_2}{E}\right)\left(\frac{Q}{L}\right)(L)$$

or, in rates of growth,

$$\eta_{co2} = \eta_{\frac{E}{Q}} + \eta_{\frac{CO2}{E}} + \eta_{\frac{Q}{L}} + \eta_L$$

where:

E is units of energy.
Q is output of goods and services.
L is population.
η is rate of growth.

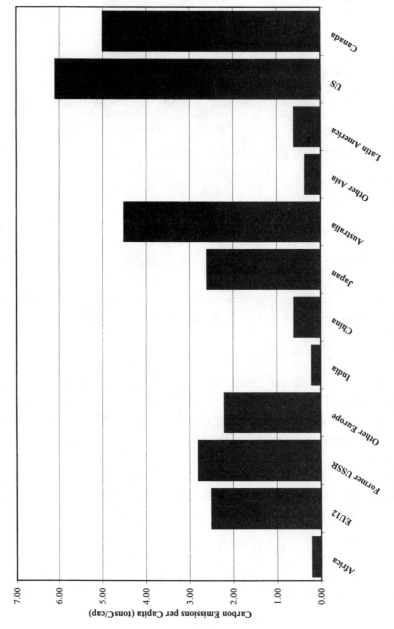

Figure 14.1. *Carbon emissions per capita. Source: Derived from Bruce (1996), Figure 3.1*

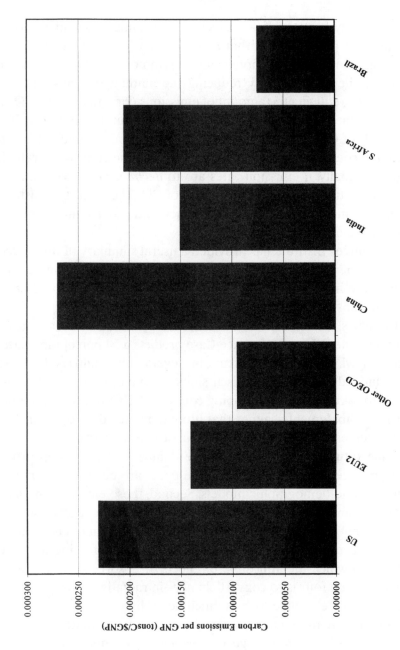

Figure 14.2. *Carbon emissions per unit GDP. Source: Derived from Bruce (1996), Figure 3.3*

The Kaya identity is useful for projecting CO_2 emissions and narrowing policy options. It basically says that if population is exogenous and if the feedback from emissions to economic output is minor, then the level of emissions can only be controlled by reducing the amount of energy per unit output (E/Q), by reducing the amount of emissions per unit energy (CO_2/E), or by reducing the rate of growth of per capita output. Furthermore, if the rate of growth of CO_2 is to stabilize, the energy-output coefficient and the carbon-energy coefficient must, in combination, decline at the same rate that output grows. Finally, if emission rates are to *decline*, which will be necessary to stabilize atmospheric concentrations of CO_2, there must be sustained and substantial increases in energy efficiency and movement toward less carbon-intensive energy sources.

World Resources Institute has provided a useful summary of three recent projections of energy consumption over the next 20 to 30 years and the percentage increase in 1990 CO_2 emission levels. As adapted in Table 14.8, the studies show substantial growth in energy use, and except for the World Energy Council's Ecologically Driven Case, substantial increases in CO_2 emission rates. The WEC's Reference Case predicts a 54 percent increase in energy use, of which four-fifths occurs in developing countries. In all scenarios, and indeed in virtually all discussions, the major growth in emissions is expected to take place in developing countries.[7] This reinforces the need to craft carbon-abatement regimes that ultimately include the major developing countries, especially China and India, due to their size.

Translating future emissions into future damages is a five-step process. First, plausible scenarios of emissions time paths are developed using economic, energy, and demographic models. Second, these emissions paths are converted to time-dated atmospheric concentration levels, taking into account atmospheric residence lifetimes and absorption models. Third, the time-dated concentrations are used to estimate radiative forcing, a measure of the extent to which the atmosphere reflects or absorbs solar and terrestrial radiation. Step four is to convert changes in radiative forcing into temperature and climate change with as much detail by region as possible. The final step before attempting to monetize damages is to estimate physical and biological effects of climate change, i.e., sea level rise, impacts on crops and health, and so forth.

The Intergovernmental Panel on Climate Change in 1992 presented six

---

7 A standard feature of most models is a rapid increase in the share of emissions accounted for by developing countries. For example, Nordhaus and Yang (1996) project that developing countries (including China), which accounted for one-third of 1990 emissions, will account for three-fourths of emissions in 2100.

Table 14.8. *Projections of energy consumption*

	World Energy Council scenarios				International Energy Agency scenarios		US Dept. of Energy reference scenario
	High growth	Modified growth	Reference	Ecologically driven	Capacity constraint	Energy savings	
Projection period	1990–2020	1990–2020	1990–2020	1990–2020	1992–2010	1992–2010	1990–2010
Economic growth, percent per year	High	Moderate	Moderate	Moderate	Moderate	Moderate	Moderate
OECD countries	2.4	2.4	2.4	2.4	2.5	2.5	2.3
Former Soviet Union and Central Europe	2.4	2.4	2.4	2.4	2.1	2.1	0.6
Developing countries	5.6	4.6	4.6	4.6	5.3	5.3	2.8–6.1[a]
World	3.8	3.3	3.3	3.3	3.1	3.1	2.7
Percent increase in world energy demand over projection period	98	84	54	30	44	34	36[b]
Percent increase in annual carbon dioxide emissions over 1990 levels	93	73	42	5	42	30	35[c]

[a] Varies by region: Africa 2.7%; Latin America, 3.7%; Middle East, 3.9%; Asia, 6.1%.
[b] Range=22% to 52%.
[c] Range=26% to 47%.
Source: World Resources Institute (1996), Box 12.2, Table 1.

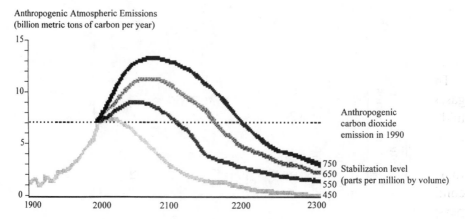

Figure 14.3. *Possible paths to climate stabilization. Source: Derived from
World Resources Institute (1996), Figure 14.4*

emissions scenarios (population in 2100 ranging from 6.4 billion to 17.6
billion; world GDP growth in 1990–2100 ranging from 1 to 2 percent; a
variety of energy-supply and price assumptions) (Watson et al. 1996, p. 3).
These were used in a 1994 IPCC report to calculate CO_2 emissions time
paths that would lead to eventual stabilization of atmospheric carbon at
various levels, ranging from 350 ppm to 750 ppm. As noted previously, the
current level is estimated to be 358 ppm (1994), compared to a preindustrial
level of 280 ppm. Figure 14.3, adapted from that report by the World
Resources Institute, illustrates four potential carbon emission time paths
leading to stabilization at four different concentrations, 450, 550, 650, and
750 ppm. Stabilization of concentrations does not occur until 2350. Recall
that even when concentrations stabilize, further global warming is expected
to continue for many years due in part to thermal inertia of the oceans. In
interpreting this chart, it is important to remember that for each stabilized
concentration target, there are numerous emissions time paths. At one
extreme, early efforts at control can obviate the need for severe controls
decades later, while modest early efforts may postpone serious reductions
to later decades. The economic efficiency of alternative time paths depends
in part on the social rate of time discount (willingness to accept abatement
costs early or late) and in part on incremental costs (or cost reductions)
expected with delayed emission reductions. The latter depends on expectations concerning the timing of new cost-saving and energy-efficient technologies, including the replacement of fossil fuels by renewable energy
sources. The chart leads to two conclusions. First, if concentrations are to be

stabilized at 750 ppm or less, at some point emissions will have to be brought well *below* current levels. Second, and quite obvious, the higher the ultimate concentration target is, the higher and longer emission flows can exceed current levels.

The current scientific consensus on the effects of prospective greenhouse gases on temperature and sea level is summarized by the IPCC: "for the midrange IPCC emission scenario . . . models project an increase in global mean surface air temperature relative to 1990 of about 2°C (3.6°F) by 2100." The range of temperature change in various scenarios is 1°C to 3.5°C (1.8°F to 6.3°F). Because of the thermal inertia of the oceans, temperatures would continue to increase beyond 2100 (Houghton et al. 1996, p. 6). To put this in perspective, the global mean temperature in the absence of human-induced emissions is estimated to be about 15°C.[8] The IPCC also estimates an increase in sea level of about 50 cm by 2100 (Houghton et al. 1996, p. 6). The range for sea-level rise is 15 cm to 95 cm. It is these projections together with estimates of regional climate change that are the raw material for estimating physical and biological effects, which in turn are inputs to environmental damage estimates. It should also be noted that temperature increase will not be uniform. The effects are estimated to be several times larger in the higher northern latitudes. In addition to sea-level changes, global warming is expected to influence ocean currents, precipitation, storm frequency, and other elements of weather, although regional predictions remain quite speculative.

3 Global Warming in a Cost-Benefit Framework

Setting aside for the moment the issues of equity and the international character of global warming, and deferring detailed consideration of abatement measures, the problem of global warming can be cast in a cost-benefit framework in which the time dimension and scientific and economic uncertainties play an unusually large role. One simplified formulation is that at any time, t, the optimal level of greenhouse gas emission reduction is such that the marginal cost of abatement of one unit of emissions is equal to the net present value of all future damages that would have resulted had that unit been released. Alternatively, for efficiency, one attempts to minimize the present value of abatement costs plus the future damages associated with residual greenhouse gas emissions.

It is immediately apparent that such a calculation would have to consider

8 Irving Mintzer, personal communication.

the costs and benefits of future defensive expenditures (e.g., building sea walls to protect against sea-level rise), adaptation expenditures (increased air conditioning), and residual damages for which adaptation is not feasible or cost effective.[9] The last would include irreversible changes and hence the estimation of lost option values and intrinsic values as discussed in Chapter 5. Furthermore, an efficient set of policies would have to solve for the optimum amount of abatement among various greenhouse gases (i.e., carbon, methane, etc.), which would involve separate estimates of their abatement costs and benefits. Such a calculation would also have to consider different techniques for abatement, or in the case of carbon, sequestration through reforestation, or deep ocean disposal, to establish a least-cost abatement function. These techniques range from switching to lower carbon fuels to accelerated research on renewable energy sources. The efficient time profile of abatement efforts would also have to be determined. Finally, the efficiency of various policy tools would be considered. In short, within an overarching cost-benefit calculus are nested a large number of subsidiary cost-effectiveness calculations. But benefit-cost analysis often confronts these complications, as well as optimal timing decisions.

One complex modelling exercise uses optimal control theory. Falk and Mendelson (1993), for example, present a model that specifies the optimal abatement path as reflected in the time path of the "price" of carbon. The price of carbon is the control variable and an abatement program could be implemented with a carbon tax equal to its price. The construction of the model allows for time variant damage functions, emissions rates, and abatement costs to take into account population, technical change, and economic growth. In one simulation, assuming a discount rate of 4 percent, and also assuming that the damages associated with a particular level of concentration grow at 2 percent per year, the price of carbon remains below $4 per ton for the first 50 years, but climbs to $27 in the 100th year (low-damage scenario), and reaches $168 in the high-damage scenario.

While a cost-benefit perspective can sharpen analysis and cast additional light on the global-warming problem, its usefulness for policy remains open to question. The very long time scales and associated uncertainties, combined with potentially irreversible effects, provide grounds for challenge. To be more specific, cost-benefit analysis requires the analyst to monetize damages to future generations and then to discount these damages to estimate their present value. But we do not know today what the structure of the economy will be like in four to six generations – the share of agricul-

---

9 On the complexities of "nonconvexity and self-defense" by victims, see Paul Burrows (1995).

ture, the spatial location of production, the technology employed – and hence we do not know the full nature of future damages. At best, we can ask what the effects of warming might be on today's economy, or what we think the future might look like. But this would only approximate the future. Even more fundamentally, we do not know the tastes and preferences of future generations and hence the value they would place on the whole array of marketed and nonmarketed goods and services that will be impacted by global warming. While we may infer the willingness to pay (and income distribution) of future generations from historical data on relative prices, income elasticities of demand, and so forth, the valuations remain *our* inferences of *their* valuations, a situation that makes economists uncomfortable.

The long time scales also invite a reconsideration of discounting. This is simultaneously an ethical, efficiency, and practical problem. There are two quite different perspectives leading to two different discount rates, and hence different views on the urgency of abating greenhouse gas emissions. Neither approach is totally satisfactory. Recall the formulation of the social rate of time preference presented in Chapter 4:

$$\text{SRTP} = r = p + cn$$

where p is "impatience," c is expected growth in consumption and n reflects diminishing marginal utility of income. Even if analysts could agree that the "impatience" parameter, p, is only appropriate for private, intragenerational decisions, and should be set at zero for social, intergenerational decisions, we must still determine c and n. The future growth rate of per capita consumption, c, can be projected from historical data, but it remains an estimate. For reasons given in Chapter 4, historical measured rates of c may overstate actual rates of consumption increase and thus bias the discount rate upward, leading to inadequate abatement efforts. Furthermore, c is not independent of r in the sense that per capita consumption is determined in part by expenditures on abatement, the amount of which we are using r to determine. In short, there is a circularity between c and r. The value of n, the elasticity of marginal utility with respect to consumption, is essentially unknowable in a scientific sense. Whatever evidence we have on n is likely to come from behavior toward risk in private decisions or from the revealed behavior of governments in their redistribution and tax policies.[10] Neither source provides a very firm base for social decisions. And even if the appro-

---

10 From time to time, the World Bank has attempted to use distributional weights by income groups in project evaluation, but the weights chosen (that is, the value of n) remain either arbitrary or simply reflect planners' preferences (Squire and van der Tak 1975).

priate *n* could be chosen for redistributive purposes within a country and, at a point in time, that *n* need not be "correct" for intergenerational comparisons of utility among countries at very different income levels.[11]

Given these difficulties, an alternative approach to the appropriate discount rate is to use the risk-adjusted opportunity cost of capital (thought to be considerably higher than SRTP). This has the apparent advantage of being grounded in empirical, market evidence. It can also be argued that because abatement expenditures will displace other productive investments with "high" rates of return, the well-being of future generations can best be secured by allocating investments to their most productive use, these increasing the total wealth of future generations. In this view, if a "high" discount rate based on the opportunity cost of capital diminishes the amount spent on abatement, the additional wealth generated by alternative investments can compensate future generations for higher damages from global warming. But this view also has problems. First, it is not clear how easily other wealth in the form of physical and human capital can substitute for environmental resources, including climate. Second, there is no secure mechanism through which the additional wealth can be transferred to future generations. It might be plundered by intervening generations. Third, even if transferred to generations damaged by global warming, there is no assurance that particular individuals (and countries) that bear the cost of warming will receive compensation. Without that assurance, it is difficult to assert that one discount rate is more efficient (in a dynamic sense) than another.

As might be expected when costs are near term and benefits very long term, the results of benefit-cost and optimal control models are highly sensitive to discount rates. To give only two examples, William Cline in an early study reports that the benefit-cost ratio of taking certain carbon-abatement measures increases from 0.86 to 1.52 when the SRTP is changed from 3 to 1.5 percent. Measures that failed a benefit-cost test at 3 percent easily pass the test at 1.5 percent. William Nordhaus and Zili Yang, in their recent model, find that by switching from a 3 percent SRTP to a 1 percent rate, the optimal carbon tax – which measures the stringency of abatement efforts – increases by a factor of 4 (Cline 1992; Nordhaus and Yang 1996).

The long time horizon also raises the issues of uncertainty and irre-

---

11 A value of *n* between 1 and 2 is often chosen. Using a convenient marginal utility function, $U(C) = C^{-n}$, a value of *n* set at 1.5 implies that an additional dollar of income to someone earning 25 percent of average income should be valued at about $8. In an international context, this implies we could vastly increase world welfare by transferring income from rich countries to poor ones within the present generation, but foreign aid budgets remain stuck at low levels, and there is no evidence that societies are willing to increase them.

versibilities. If the probabilities of different outcomes were known, an equivalent value could be calculated to include the expected outcome plus a risk-aversion premium.[12] But many of the probabilities in a cost-benefit calculus of global warming are unknown. Uncertainty and risk aversion support a precautionary policy stance, which may override the results of cost-benefit analysis. They also support investments in research and other activities that reduce uncertainty, including both scientific and economic research. The concept of option values, discussed in Chapter 5, is also relevant especially in relation to irreversibilities. Some positive price for maintaining an option to prevent an irreversible effect can be entered in as cost-benefit calculation, but the amount is unclear. At first glance, it would appear that option values would support a precautionary policy of early and aggressive abatement. But just as there are irreversibilities on the damage side, for instance, coastal flooding or species loss, there are irreversibilities on the abatement expenditure side. Real resources committed today for abatement cannot be recovered. If, over time, improved knowledge diminishes the threat of global warming, society has lost the option of using these resources for other productive purposes. In short, paying a premium for maintaining options in the face of uncertainty works on both abatement costs and abatement benefits.

4 The International Context

Studies estimating the damages from greenhouse warming and the costs of mitigation policies have been recently reviewed and reported by the IPCC. Here, we are concerned with the international aspects of these estimates and more particularly the linked questions of equity and efficiency in control regimes. In considering these questions, it is important to keep in mind the differences among countries in terms of their past, present, and prospective contributions to global warming (described in Section 2); their vulnerability to climate change and ability to adapt; and differences among countries in the costs of abating emissions. These features are important in devising an equitable and reasonably efficient regime for controlling emissions. If an international control regime is to have broad coverage and avoid the threat of carbon leakage to noncontrolled sources, it must be perceived as fair, and must be structured so that countries have an incentive to join based on their own national calculus of costs and benefits.

Before proceeding, it is necessary to raise two equity questions that have

---

12 Expected outcome is the weighted average outcome, where probabilities are the weights.

Table 14.9. *Monetary damages estimates by region from doubling CO_2*

Region	Billions $ (Fankhauser)	%GDP[a] (Fankhauser)	Billions $ (Tol)	%GDP[a] (Tol)
World[b]	269.6	1.4	315.7	1.9
European Union	63.6	1.4		
United States	61.0	1.3		
Other OECD	55.9	1.4		
OECD America			74.2	1.5
OEDC Europe			56.5	1.3
OECD Pacific			59.0	2.8
Total OECD	180.5	1.3	189.5	1.6
E. Europe/former USSR	18.2[c]	0.7[c]	−7.9	−0.3
Centrally Planned Asia	16.7[d]	4.7[d]	18.0	5.2
South and Southeast Asia			53.5	8.6
Africa			30.3	8.7
Latin America			31.0	4.3
Middle East			1.3	4.1
Total non-OECD	89.1	1.6	126.2	2.7

[a] Percentage of GDP figures are based on market exchange rate GDP. The order of magnitude of estimates does not change if uncorrected damage categories are purchasing-power-parity adjusted and expressed as a fraction of PPP-corrected GDP.
[b] Note that the GDP base may differ between the studies.
[c] Former Soviet Union only.
[d] China only.
Source: Based on Fankhauser 1995; Tol 1995; Cited in Bruce et al. (1996), Table 6.6.

direct efficiency implications. Both questions are rooted in the per capita income differences between rich and poor countries. The first question is how one should value identical physical damages, especially to human health, when income levels are very different. To be specific, some studies using either contingent valuation or hedonic wage models estimate that the value of a statistical life falls somewhere between $2 million and $9 million for developed countries. One preliminary study for India places it at $120,000 (Bruce et al. 1996, p. 197). Another study estimates additional annual deaths in non-OECD countries due to global 2.5°C warming to be 115,000. Evaluated at $0.2 million per life, this is $23 billion. Evaluated at $2 million, it is $230 billion, or nearly equal to the total world damages as estimated by Samuel Frankhauser (see Table 14.9). Clearly the value placed on human life can significantly effect estimates of optimal abatement efforts. Nor will discounting necessarily reduce the size of these estimates. It is reasonable to suppose that willingness to pay for preventing death will increase by at least the rate of increased real consumption, so that discounting a stream of rising benefits is largely a wash.

One suggestion is to scale the value of statistical life in different countries to average per capita incomes in these countries.[13] If deaths prevented were to be scaled to country level per capita income, the cost estimates would support more modest abatement efforts. With a disproportionate number of deaths expected in poor countries, their burden in the form of higher deaths from global warming would be correspondingly higher. But this conflicts with ethical principles that social policy should protect the least fortunate. It is not uncommon for governments to pursue policies and projects where income distribution weights favor the poor. It would be a strange ethical system that justified a premium on income to the poor and a discount on the cost of their death. Thus, at the international level the efficient level of abatement cannot be fully separated from the equity issue of valuing health damages in different countries.

The second point at which equity and efficiency become intermingled is with respect to choosing the appropriate discount rate in an international context (Schelling 1995). The case for a single discount rate at the national level is well established. Individuals can express their time preferences by adjusting their savings and consumption patterns to maximize their intertemporal utility. But due to substantial differences in time preferences between rich and poor countries and the incomplete mobility of capital (savings) among countries, the social rate of time discount is thought to be substantially higher in poor than rich countries. How is a globally efficient discount rate to be chosen? If global warming were analyzed from the perspective of India and its social rate of time preference, the resulting efficient level of emission abatement would likely be very much less than the level chosen if OECD time preferences were used. This problem arises whether one considers the discount rate as reflecting the time preference of consumers (savers) in the social rate of time preference or the opportunity cost of capital. The SRTP affects intergenerational equity or distribution. The opportunity cost of capital reflects investment opportunities. Both tend to be country specific. Using a "low" OECD rate to calculate the efficiency level of abatement effort (or its timing) would violate India's time preferences and neglect its current investment opportunities. Using a "high" Indian rate would have comparable results for the OECD. While it might be possible to

---

13 $VOSL_{LDC} = (VOSL_{DC})(Y^*_{LDC} / Y^*_{DC})$ where VOSL is value of statistical life, DC and LCD refer to developed and developing countries, and Y^* is average per capita income using purchasing-power parity exchange rates. It is possible, of course, that this issue is resolved by a worldwide convergence of income levels.

use a weighted average, that average would only be efficient if the weights corresponded to the allocation of the net costs of global warming (i.e., abatement costs, adaptation costs, and residual damage costs) as among countries and regions. But the allocation of these costs is essentially a distributional (equity) issue, and in this sense, also, the efficiency aspects of an international cost-benefit analysis of global warming cannot be separated from equity questions. The choice of a discount rate is the international analogue of the public-good–cost-allocation analysis using Lindahl Prices, which was discussed in Chapter 13.

There is a more practical reason for keeping distributional effects in mind. As argued in the previous chapter, a minimum necessary condition for securing participation in a broad-based control regime is that countries believe they are better off by joining, because their benefits would exceed their costs. If the regime fails to include the major prospective sources of greenhouse gas emissions, it will be ineffective. And the leakage problem through trade and investment channels will be exacerbated. Therefore, before turning to analysis of various control instruments, it is useful to summarize differences among countries in the likely damages from greenhouse warming and differences in marginal abatement costs.

Damages from global warming, measured in either physical or monetary units, will vary from country to country and region to region. Developing countries are thought to be more vulnerable than OECD countries because of their higher share of agriculture, forestry, and fisheries in GDP, which will be directly affected; the more immediate danger of sea-level change and tropical storms (e.g., in Bangladesh, Egypt, and China); and their more limited institutional capacity to adapt to climate change. The impact on agriculture is a good illustration. Temperature increases are expected to be greater at higher latitudes than in the tropics and subtropics where most developing countries are located. Agriculture in northern developed countries may benefit from warmer temperatures and longer growing seasons, but even modestly higher temperatures will have a negative effect on agricultural production in the tropics. The IPCC cites estimates of grain production *gains* of 4 to 14 percent in developed countries and *losses* of 9 to 12 percent in developing countries.[14]

Table 14.9 reports two studies that have attempted to estimate the cost of a doubling of atmospheric carbon dioxide (thought to increase average global temperature 2.5°C) on different regions. The costs are expressed as

---

14 This assumes positive benefits of CO_2 fertilization and "moderate" farmer adaptation (Bruce et al. 1996, p. 190).

percent regional GDP to make them comparable. The differences among regions are quite marked. In the Frankhauser (1995) study, the cost is 1.3 percent GDP for the OECD, 0.7 percent for the former Soviet Union (reflecting improved agriculture), and 4.7 percent for China. The Tol (1995) study is generally consistent, with the highest cost in developing countries, especially Asia, lower costs in industrial countries, and negative costs (i.e., benefits) in Eastern Europe and the former USSR.[15]

The costs of greenhouse gas control will also vary among regions and countries. The principal determinants will be opportunities for low-cost emissions reduction and the allocation of emissions-abatement obligations among countries. The latter is, in essence, the difference between baseline projections and controlled emissions plus or minus any international transfers to assist with emission reductions.[16] The available evidence suggests that marginal costs of carbon emissions reduction is lower in developing countries and transitional economies than in the industrial countries. The reason appears to be the existence of large inefficiencies in fossil fuel energy use. To take but one example, Grübler et al. estimate that of a world total reduction of industrial carbon emissions of 372 million tons that could be accomplished at either zero or at moderate costs, 257 million tons (69%), could be obtained in transition and developing countries (Grübler et al. 1993, cited in Bruce et al. 1996, Table 7.2). For carbon reductions in the next range (i.e., at costs less than $100 per ton) 80 percent could be obtained in transitional and developing countries.

If correct, the implication is that a least-cost global strategy of abating carbon emissions should concentrate on reducing emissions from transitional and developing countries. It does not follow, however, that transitional and developing countries will bear lower total costs than OECD countries. The reason is that developing countries are projected to increase energy consumption and hence CO_2 emissions more rapidly than industrial countries. More specifically, equal percentage reductions in emission growth will place a larger (relative) cost burden on developing countries. This is illustrated in Figure 14.4. Four models are used to estimate the costs, measured in percentage of GDP of carbon taxes imposed in each region sufficient to achieve a 2-percentage point reduction in the rate of growth of carbon emissions

---

15 The benchmark doubling of CO_2 used in these two studies could be reached by the middle of this century. Cline (1992) estimates a possible eightfold increase from preindustrial levels by 2275. This would imply a possible mean warming of 12°C. With these very large temperature changes, the economic damages are likely to increase disproportionately (Bruce et al. 1996, p. 205; Cline 1992).

16 The cost of abatement should be the measured net of any secondary benefits from reducing associated pollutants. These secondary benefits may be large, from 30 to 100 percent of abatement costs by some estimates (Bruce et al. 1996, p. 218).

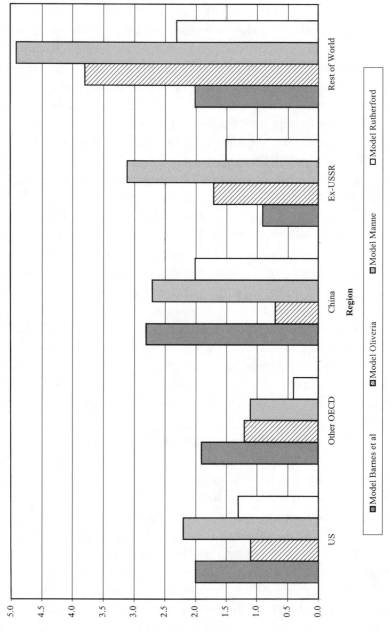

Figure 14.4. *The costs of a carbon tax by region: four models. Source: Derived from Dean (1995), Figure 1*

when measured from a "business as usual" baseline. The models generally agree that the costs for China and for "rest of world," a proxy for developing countries, will be considerably higher than for OECD countries. Moreover, simulations for costs in the years 2050 and 2100 show higher costs for all regions, but the highest costs still tend to be borne by developing countries.

To summarize the evidence thus far, developing countries appear to confront larger costs from global warming than do the OECD countries, at least when costs are measured as a fraction of GDP. At the same time, opportunities for low-cost emission reductions appear most prevalent in developing and transitional economies. This suggests that a globally efficient abatement program would concentrate efforts in developing countries and perhaps the former Soviet Union. Also, because of higher projected emission rates, an efficient abatement program would call for greater percentage reductions from baseline growth rates in developing countries. While the benefits of controlling greenhouse gas emissions appears weighted toward developing countries, they are unlikely to take on a disproportionate abatement cost burden due to their low incomes and urgent development needs and their equity-based argument that the industrial countries have been and are currently the major contributors to global warming. This all suggests that side payments from North to South through joint implementation, direct payments, or an inclusive emissions trading program as discussed later in the chapter would be a precondition for an efficient strategy.

The OECD countries face different prospects. They may expect relatively light damages from warming and face relatively high marginal costs if their abatement efforts were restricted to their own emissions.[17] If, however, they find a mechanism for financing abatement in developing and transitional economies, global costs of abatement could be significantly reduced. But with major financial transfers from North to South, the net benefits to the North would be reduced or perhaps eliminated.[18] Thus the preconditions for a cooperative solution are mixed.

These questions have been investigated in an innovative and sophisticated way by William Nordhaus and Zili Yang (1996). They construct a model in which the world is divided into 10 regions and investigate three policy sce-

---

17 The "relatively light damage costs" is very speculative.
18 If an efficient solution requires abatement, there must be some surplus of total benefits over costs, and the distribution of this surplus will be a central negotiating issue. The problem is further complicated as the surplus will not materialize for 50 to 100 years and in the interim all participants in an abatement regime would bear costs.

narios: (1) a "do-nothing" scenario in which no abatement policies are followed; (2) a cooperative scenario, in which abatement is optimal from a global perspective (i.e., present value of net abatement benefits is maximized) and abatement effort is efficiently allocated among regions to equate marginal abatement costs; (3) and a noncooperative scenario, in which each country acts in its narrow self-interest without regard for spillovers in other countries. The results are reassuring or disturbing, depending on one's perspective. One finding is that there is rather little difference in terms of carbon emissions, concentrations, or temperature change over the period 1990–2100 under the three separate scenarios. For example, in the do-nothing scenario, carbon emissions climb to about 38 billion tons (from the 1990 base of 8 billion tons) in 2100 but they also exceed 32 billion in the optimal cooperative scenario. Temperature increase under do-nothing reaches 3.1°C in 2100 as compared to 2.8°C in the optimal, cooperative scenario.[19] This suggests two conclusions. First, if the model is correct, even an optimal abatement policy would only work on the margin of climate change. The cost of severely limiting temperature increase is too high relative to the benefits. By implication, the Rio objective of rolling emissions back to 1990 levels is grossly uneconomic. Second, because the emissions, concentration, and temperature estimates are rather tightly clustered regardless of policy scenario, one can argue that failure to secure international cooperation, while costly, is not of overwhelming importance. This can be seen in a second finding. The authors' calculate that the cumulative world benefits over the next 100 years of the optimal, cooperative strategy would be $340 billion when discounted to the present, whereas they would be about $42 billion in the noncooperative, self-interest scenario. The inference is that cooperation versus noncooperation would produce a present value surplus of $300 billion. While this is not a trivial sum, it is small compared to the hundreds of trillions of dollars of world income and output over this time period.[20]

A third result of the model is that abatement effort will be truly minimal in the noncooperative scenario. The efficient carbon tax, a measure of abatement effort in the noncooperative scenario, is only 24¢/versus $6.19/ton in the cooperative scenario. This is not surprising, as only a few large emitters such as the United States and the European Union would find it in their

19 It should be kept in mind that the results are highly sensitive to the discount rate used (3 percent). If a 1 percent discount rate were used, the price of carbon would increase by a factor of 4, and presumably much stronger controls would be warranted.
20 To put this in perspective, an annuity with a present value of $300 billion is equivalent to a perpetual annual payment of $9 billion when discounted at 3 percent. Nine billion is approximately four-hundredths of one percent of 1990 world GDP of $21 trillion.

narrow self-interest to undertake any abatement. Smaller emitters would be full free riders. This result is consistent with the conclusions in Chapter 13 (Figure 13.2), which concluded that the larger the international spillovers are from abatement, the larger will be the gap between the equilibrium level of abatement and the global optimum. The final and perhaps most disturbing result of the model is that in the cooperative scenario, in which all countries undertake an efficient level of abatement, and marginal abatement costs among countries are equalized, the United States gains only $0.8 billion in present value terms as compared to the do-nothing strategy. Indeed, as compared to the noncooperative scenario, the United States is worse off by $2.1 billion in present value terms. The implication is that it would not be possible for the United States to finance major carbon abatement in developing countries and still receive net benefits under a cooperative scenario. According to the model and its underlying assumptions, if side payments or compensation from North to South is a precondition for an agreement, and if the United States requires positive net benefits, any limited side payments would have to come from Japan or the EU.

Let us try to summarize these considerations. The evidence suggests that it will be future generations in developing countries who would bear a disproportionate burden from global warming and who would be the major beneficiaries of an aggressive abatement policy. The evidence also suggests that a least-cost global abatement program would emphasize efforts in developing countries. For a variety of reasons including present poverty, high opportunity cost for capital, and their modest historical contribution to the problem, it is unlikely that developing countries would be willing to fund major, costly abatement in the near term, and thus they would look to the industrial countries for financing. It is not clear, however, that the United States and other industrial countries would reap major net benefits from an aggressive effort. Assuming the United States and other OECD countries did provide the bulk of the abatement effort, the intergenerational transfer would be from the currently wealthy to future generations in the South who, though probably better off than the poor today, would still be less wealthy than the rich North is today. This implies an international, intergenerational transfer from those with low marginal utility to those with higher marginal utility. By conventional analysis, this implies a low or even negative social rate of time discount for abatement activities and therefore supports an aggressive program (Schelling 1995). But this conclusion is an artifact of the redistributional character of abatement. If the international community is willing to engage in redistribution to improve global welfare, the more pressing need is probably to fund development projects that benefit today's poor.

From this perspective, the opportunity cost of capital for abatement should compete with the (relatively) high rates earned on current development projects.

5 Approaches and Tools

As stated before, a serious effort to moderate global warming must put control of carbon emissions as its centerpiece. However, before undertaking expensive restrictions on carbon, it would be desirable to know that such restrictions would be less costly than adaptation costs in the future, and that the benefits of early, aggressive action would outweigh the benefits of waiting. Furthermore, it would be desirable to first pursue all feasible low cost options for reducing carbon before turning to more expensive measures.

There is no consensus on the first two points. Our ability to estimate the present value of future defensive expenditures and adaptation costs (e.g., building seawalls, changing crop patterns) and compare these discounted costs with current emission control costs is greatly complicated by the discount rate and valuation uncertainties described previously, as well as the uncertainties surrounding the profile of physical and biological effects of warming and their implications for economic activity. In fact, there is no comprehensive survey of future adaptation options and their costs.[21] Nor is there a consensus that early action is more cost-efficient than waiting until our knowledge improves and uncertainties are reduced. In light of irreversibilities, discontinuities, and general uncertainty, the so-called precautionary principle would appear to apply, but it cuts both ways. Early, aggressive action might avoid potential catastrophic damages and reduce overall medium-term abatement costs by nudging new, long-lived, physical capital investments (transport, port facilities, power plants) toward less carbon-intensive development patterns. But there is also a positive value in waiting. Resources committed to abatement today cannot be recaptured if, with improved information, greenhouse warming turns out to be less serious than anticipated. There is, however, general agreement that investment in scientific and economic research to reduce uncertainties would be cost-effective and should play a prominent role in any approach to the problem.

The extent to which there are feasible, low-cost options for reducing emissions and enhancing sinks – the so-called no-regrets measures – is also dis-

---

21 The IPCC has surveyed the physical and biological impacts of climate change in some detail and identified certain adaptation options but stopped short of costing these actions.

puted (Bruce et al. 1996, Chaps. 8–9). This debate is often couched in terms of "top-down" and "bottom-up" modelling approaches, although more recent models are a partial blend of both. In general, top-down models tend to be more pessimistic than bottom-up models regarding low or negative abatement cost measures. Bottom-up models tend to work from cost-engineering studies of specific processes that reveal an efficiency gap between best available technologies and actual energy use. Hence they conclude that energy use can be cut at little or no economic cost. Top-down models are more aggregated and tend to assume that economies and economic agents are closer to their efficiency frontiers. The differences from bottom-up and top-down modelling are important for the types of policy as well as the aggressiveness of policies, goals, and timing. If a large efficiency gap in energy use exists, the appropriate policy measures are likely to be more diverse than the standard prescription of carbon taxes or tradeable permits and would include a provision for consumer information on energy efficiency, energy-efficient technical standards for products and processes, selective subsidies to overcome institutional barriers, and so forth. Both approaches, however, acknowledge that widespread energy and transportation subsidies work against carbon-emission reductions, and their removal should have a high priority. One study has estimated that removal of energy subsidies would reduce global carbon emissions by 18 percent below baseline in 2050 and increase global real income by 0.7 percent.[22] The IPCC concludes that improvements in energy efficiency of perhaps 10 to 30 percent could be achieved at negative to slightly positive costs (Bruce et al. 1996, p. 301). A U.S. study by five national laboratories for the Department of Energy estimates that an aggressive technology program together with a \$50/ton carbon tax would bring U.S. carbon emissions down to 1990 levels by 2010 (Interlaboratory Working Group on Energy Efficient and Low Carbon Technologies 1997). To put that in perspective, a \$50/ton carbon tax is equivalent to \$6.50/barrel or 15.4¢/gallon of gasoline. There is also some evidence that carbon sequestration through afforestation programs may be a significant part of a least-cost (net) emissions-reduction program. Some studies suggest that the physical potential for carbon sequestration is greatest in the tropics, but there is no clear conclusion whether sequestration costs will be higher or lower in developing countries (Bruce et al. 1996, pp. 345–356).

The advocates of no-regrets policies also call on the double dividend thesis discussed in Chapter 6. If carbon emissions are curtailed by a tax or by auc-

---

22 Bruce (1996, p. 73), citing J. M. Burniaux et al. (1992).

tioning tradeable permits, the revenues can be recycled and used to reduce other distortive taxes on labor and capital. If the efficiency gains are significant, the double dividend, by reducing the economic costs of the policy, support earlier and more serious abatement efforts. In one study, Jorgensen and Wilcoxen (1993a) found that a carbon tax yielding about $80 billion in 2020 would depress U.S. gross national product (GNP) by 1.7 percent below baseline if the revenues were returned to consumers as lump-sum payments, but would depress (GNP) by only 0.7 percent if the revenues were used to lower distortive labor taxes, and would *increase* GDP by 1.1 percent above baseline if used to lower distortionary taxes on capital (the lower tax on capital would increase after-tax returns and accelerate capital formation).

However, environmental taxes may interact with other taxes in a general equilibrium setting, and the size of the double dividend arising from a carbon tax in a second-best world is still unsettled. Goulder, for example, finds that recycling revenue from a carbon tax can lower the net cost of the tax, but states that it is unlikely that the net cost of the carbon tax would be brought to zero (Goulder 1995).[23] In a more recent study, Goulder, Parry, and Burtraw (1997) employ general equilibrium models of the United States to compare the cost-effectiveness of carbon taxes, quotas, fuel taxes, and command-and-control policies (performance standards and mandated technologies), all within a second-best world with preexisting distortive taxes on factor inputs. The analytical model assumes emissions are generated in production, and their effect is to decrease consumer utility, where utility is positive in consumption of economic goods and leisure and negative in the level of emissions (demand for economic goods and leisure are not dependent on the level of environmental quality indexed by emissions). Their conclusions have considerable policy significance. As they tend to equalize the marginal abatement costs among emission sources, emissions taxes and *tradeable* permits tend to be more efficient than nontradeable quotas and command-and-control measures. This study also emphasizes that if preexisting distortive taxes were present, all instruments would be more costly than they would be in a first-best tax-free world. This is because of the negative tax interaction effect. But nonauctioned quotas are *less* efficient (cost-effective) than emissions taxes and auctioned quotas, as they lack the positive revenue

23 A. Lans Bovenborg and Ruud A. deMooij's analysis (1994) concludes that recycling pollution taxes by cutting preexisting distortionary taxes on labor does produce a limited double dividend, but they also conclude that in a second-best, tax-distorted world the optimal environmental tax lies below the first-best Pigovian tax. For a current analysis see Parry (1999).

recycling effect.[24] The study also emphasizes that tax revenues should be recycled by cutting marginal tax rates rather than giving lump-sum distributions if the recycling effect is to be positive.

Finally, some analysts have identified a *triple* dividend. Reducing fossil fuel (carbon) emissions also reduces the emissions of and damages from other ground-level pollutants such as carbon monoxide and sulfur, and nitrogen oxides. The IPCC has summarized several studies quantifying the size of the triple dividend, and reports that it might offset 30 to 100 percent of carbon-abatement costs (Bruce et al. 1996, pp. 215–219). Roy Boyd, Kerry Krutilla, and W. Kip Viscusi's model suggests that taking into account the numerous pollutants associated with fossil fuel use, U.S. energy prices are lower than optimal, and with conservative assumptions, coal, oil, and natural gas prices should be 20, 10, or 5 percent higher, respectively (Boyd et al. 1995). The price increases are justified independent of their carbon-abatement benefits and thus reflect a variation of the no-regrets argument. According to their analysis, carbon reductions of 20 to 50 percent of baseline emissions could be attained without incurring a net loss in national welfare.[25]

The situation in transitional and developing countries is not well documented. There is of course considerable evidence that energy subsidies are extensive and presumably the removal of these subsidies would improve efficiency and contribute to carbon abatement at zero cost or possibly increased income. There is also evidence that, apart from subsidies, there are important technical efficiencies that could be achieved in energy use if informational, institutional, and market failure barriers could be overcome. There is very little evidence, however, as to whether the double dividend and tax-interaction effects would be substantial, or whether the incidental benefits of reducing collateral pollution would be important.

6 Taxes and Quotas

The two most frequently analyzed tools for reducing carbon emissions are carbon taxes and some form of tradeable quotas or permits (tradeable

---

24 The difference in cost effectiveness is most pronounced at modest abatement levels, and tends to converge at very high levels of abatement.

25 Robert Repetto and Duncan Austin (1997) provide a useful econometric analysis of the assumptions underlying 16 models that have been used to estimate the economic impact of carbon taxes. They find that differences in eight assumptions account for about 80 percent of the variation in predicted economic impacts among the 16 models. The critical assumptions include the scope for interfuel substitution, the availability and cost of nonfossil-fuel energy sources (i.e., backstop technology), the availability of a joint implementation option, the possible reduction in noncarbon pollution damages, and the recycling of carbon tax revenues to reduce other distortionary taxes.

permits generally refer to domestic schemes). With the signing of the Kyoto Protocol in 1997, interest increased in joint implementation projects, in which a firm or government of a developed country finances a specific emissions-reduction or sink-enhancement project in a developing country.[26] A carbon tax could be levied by an international agency or by national governments acting together or unilaterally. It is highly unlikely that governments will agree to surrender the revenues from any substantial tax to an international agency for redistribution, so the more relevant proposal would be for national-level taxes. This immediately raises three issues. Should the tax be equalized across fuels according to their carbon content? Should the tax be harmonized across countries and, if so, at what rate? What if any arrangement should be made to redistribute a portion of the tax revenues internationally? The first is essentially an efficiency question. The generally accepted answer is to equalize the tax by carbon content of fuels (e.g., a higher tax for coal than natural gas) to provide the correct incentives for fuel switching. This might be adjusted up or down for other externality costs specific to particular fuels. However, if the agreement to tax carbon is not universal, it can be shown that the taxes imposed by the participating countries may need to be differentiated by fuel type, depending on market conditions (Golombeck, Hagman, and Hoel 1994). The essential reason is to minimize carbon leakage, described later.

The second question is more complex. In general, a uniform tax across countries would provide the appropriate incentives so that the marginal costs of abatement would be equalized among sources, a necessary condition for least-cost emissions control (Chapter 6). But this principle has been challenged in an international context. Uzawa, for example, constructs a dynamic optimization model in which the optimal tax rate is an inverse function of per capita income levels in various countries (Uzawa 1991). In his numerical calculations, he puts the imputed price per ton of carbon at $150 in the United States and $4 in Indonesia. This radical difference appears to be the result of his assumptions that income cannot be freely transferred among countries, and the marginal utility of an extra unit of consumption in poor countries exceeds the marginal utility in rich countries. It follows that the burden of reducing emissions should be borne primarily by rich countries. In essence, differentiated taxes on carbon became an indirect vehicle for redressing intercountry income inequalities. While many analysts would agree that allocating the cost burden of carbon abatement should take into

---

26 Strictly speaking, the Kyoto agreement reserves the term *joint implementation* for arrangements among industrial countries, and calls similar arrangements between industrial and developing countries the "clean development mechanism."

account the ability to pay, most would stop short of attempting to redress existing income inequalities. (Also, nonuniform carbon taxes may be more efficient if preexisting distortive taxes differ among countries.)

The efficiency of an internationally uniform carbon tax or a tradeable permit system where permits are distributed in some arbitrary fashion has also been challenged on the grounds that climate is an international public good, supplied in fixed amounts to all. (Obviously, countries have different climates, but the public good is the control of global warming. The United States cannot choose a 2°C warming and India 6°C – one size will have to fit all.)[27] Because individuals (or countries) cannot adjust the quantity of the public good they consume, as they can with private goods, it is more difficult to fulfill one of the conditions for Pareto optimality, that the ratio of marginal utilities, or the marginal rate of substitution, between any two goods be equal for every participant in the market. In the case of carbon, one would expect that India, because of its poverty, would have a different rate of substitution between conventional goods and services and the public good, global warming, than would the United States. This suggests that the efficient carbon tax would be lower in India than in the United States. But differential taxes interfere with the efficiency objective of seeking least-cost abatement actions, which requires that marginal abatement costs be equalized among countries. In short, the inflexibility in the quantity consumed that characterizes public goods, removes one tool for achieving efficiency. One suggestion is to substitute a second tool, income redistribution, to salvage the efficiency implicit in equalizing marginal abatement costs. The redistribution could be made through the carbon tax revenues or, in the case of a permit system, by a disproportionate distribution of permits to low-income countries. In this fashion, the question of the globally efficient level of abatement is intimately tied to the distributional features of an abatement regime. Thus, in addition to offering net benefits to prospective members to induce them to join, the scheme should also have specific redistributional features if it is to be efficient. All of this becomes increasingly difficult because of serious uncertainties in national-level cost-benefit functions, because costs and benefits accrue to different generations, and because of strategic and free-rider behavior.[28]

---

27 Conversely, global warming can be considered an international public "bad" with the typical characteristics of nonexcludability and nonrivalry.

28 For elaboration, see Graciela Chichilinsky and Geoffrey Heal (1994; 1995). Their conclusion, that for Pareto efficiency the income allocated to abatement by each country be proportional to its income level, is consistent with Uzawa's conclusion that the imputed price per ton of carbon is proportional to a country's per capita income. This commingling of efficiency and distribution is closely related to the Lindahl Prices discussion in Chapter 13.

These objections to uniform taxes create disturbing issues at the interface of efficiency and equity and reinforce the need to consider them jointly. An efficient regime will also require the participation of all countries with significant emissions of carbon. This includes the major developing countries – India, China, Brazil, and the like. Without widespread participation, low-cost abatement opportunities will be lost and there will be an incentive to shift carbon-intensive economic activity to nonparticipating countries. But if countries are sovereign, not subject to coercion, and act in their narrow self-interest, the minimum necessary condition for participation is that each member considers itself no worse off by participating. This suggests a system of side payments, or compensation, from those with large net benefits (national damages avoided minus national abatement costs) to countries with unfavorable benefit-cost ratios. Presumably there will have to be substantial transfers of carbon tax revenues (or in some other payment vehicle) from OECD countries to developing countries. Transfers to the transitional economies of Eastern Europe and the former Soviet Union are more problematic. On the one hand, low-cost or no-regrets options may be so extensive that little or no compensation need be paid – self-interest will improve energy efficiency and reduce carbon emissions. But some studies show that Russia might enjoy a net gain from global warming, especially in agriculture. If so, it might need compensation to forgo the perceived benefits of global warming even if its marginal abatement costs were zero. Finally, at an abstract level, an optimal abatement program should yield a social surplus, and the distribution of this surplus is likely to be contentious.

The amounts of money needed to induce compliance cannot be estimated with any degree of precision and will in any event be determined by perceptions of benefits and costs and negotiating skills. An early study by Whalley and Wigle, however, provides a glimpse of the magnitudes. Their model suggests that revenues from a uniform global tax on carbon sufficient to reduce emissions by 50 percent below baseline over the period of 1990–2030 would generate some $46 trillion or about 10 percent of global GDP. If redistributed on the basis of population (not on the basis of national benefit-cost calculus), developing countries would receive $12 trillion net (international transfer minus taxes paid) or about 5 percent of their income over this period. The largest payer would be North America at $9 trillion (Whalley and Wigle 1991). However, their model results in an implausibly high carbon tax rate of $450/ton – well beyond what is currently discussed. Shah and Larsen have calculated that net payments and receipts from a global tax of $10 per ton, if distributed on the basis of population, would cost the United States 0.22 percent of its GDP and would benefit a sample of developing countries with large populations by about 2.5 percent of their GDP (Shah and Larsen 1992). If distributed by countries' shares in world GDP, the United States would gain by 0.03 percent of GDP and large developing countries in Asia would pay 0.7 percent of their GDP.

Before leaving the tax tool, it is useful to list specific issues that would have to be resolved: how to account for existing differences among countries in energy taxes; how to treat trade in fuels and energy-intensive products (important if taxes are not universal in coverage); where the appropriate point is in the extraction-processing-consumption chain to apply the tax; whether credit is given in the redistributive scheme to deforestation or reforestation activities; how to prevent erosion of the tax through government subsidies to energy-intensive industries; how to establish a tax that is sufficiently permanent to affect major investment decisions yet flexible enough to be adjusted for new information; how to monitor the use of energy and the collection of tax. The question of whether the carbon tax is production- or consumption-based is especially important in determining the international incidence of the tax. If it is production-based, net fossil fuel exporters (including the Organization of Petroleum Exporting Countries, or OPEC) tend to keep the tax; if it is consumption-based net fuel importers (of which the EU is the largest) keep the revenue. The welfare (and political) implications are large.

Internationally tradeable carbon-emission quotas are an alternative to harmonized national carbon taxes. (The Kyoto Protocol discussed later in this chapter is only a first step in this direction.) The concept has attractive qualities. Atmospheric carbon is uniformly mixed so that a unit emitted from any source creates the same damages. This avoids the need to calculate transfer coefficients as discussed in Chapter 6. Similar to a uniform carbon tax, the tradeable feature of such quotas will tend to equalize marginal abatement costs among countries, the criterion for least-cost abatement discussed earlier. In principle, these efficiency characteristics exist regardless of the initial allocation of quotas. A country with high abatement costs will buy quotas, and a country with low abatement costs will sell quotas when the quota price exceeds its marginal abatement cost. Subject to the caveats discussed later, international distributional objectives and incentives for participation can be separated from the efficient allocation of the abatement effort and addressed through the allocation of the quotas themselves. The international allocation of permits determines rights to emit carbon, but the tradeable feature allows these rights to be rented or sold, and not necessarily exercised by the country owning the right. Moreover, carbon-emission quotas by country are consistent with a variety of national control measures.

While one country may chose to implement its quota with a domestic permit scheme, a second may choose a national carbon tax set at a rate to achieve its quota target, and a third might choose more direct regulatory measures if that suited its domestic political and economic structure. If the efficiency gains from reducing other distortionary taxes were considered substantial, domestic permits could be auctioned or a carbon tax could be implemented. As compared to a tax, a system of national-level carbon emissions quotas would have a more certain effect on global emissions, although the cost would be less certain. Both systems would of course face monitoring and enforcement costs. Finally, in contrast to uniform national taxes with an international redistribution mechanism, national carbon quotas could finesse the need for large, *direct* financial transfers among countries. The distribution of wealth would be embedded in the quota-allocation process. While less than perfectly transparent, this feature might be politically useful, especially if tax revenues were to go to politically unpopular states. However, the exact income distributional consequences of a particular quota allocation would not be known ahead of time, as the market price of a permit would not yet be determined. Also, financial transfers would become more visible as the international marketing of permits proceeded.

A quota system may or may not be superior to a tax system in the presence of uncertainty. As explained in Chapter 6, if abatement costs are uncertain (as they are in the case of carbon), a tax instrument is superior if the marginal cost of abatement schedule is steeper than the marginal benefit curve, but the quantitative instrument (quotas) is superior if the benefit curve is steeper than the cost curve. Various estimates show steep abatement-cost curves after no-regrets options are exhausted. But if thresholds exist for higher levels of carbon concentration, damages and hence abatement-benefit curves could also be steep.[29] Although the issue is undecided, there is reason to believe that marginal benefits would be flatter than marginal costs, and hence the tax instrument would be superior to the permit system. One reason is that there are multiple types of damages from global warming, so that even if there were thresholds and discontinuities in one dimension, say, disruption of local agriculture, the summing of many damages would tend to smooth a gradually rising damage function, implying reasonably constant marginal damages. A second reason is that damages are associated with the *stock* of greenhouse gases and abatement policy reduces the *flow* of emissions. If the ratio of flow to stock is low, as would

---

29 A mixed system of taxes and quotas can limit the "cost" of error in checking abatement levels. See Marc Roberts and Michael Spence (1976).

be the case for CO_2, the marginal benefit of reducing the flow will have a minimal effect on the stock, and hence the *marginal* benefit should remain rather constant. William Pizer (1997) has provided some supporting evidence, estimating that the social gains from an optimal tax may be up to five times larger than the optimal gains from a permit policy.

Despite these attractive qualities, the difficulties in establishing a carbon quota regime are numerous. The first is to set the global "cap," the total world emissions over a year or several years. The second is to allocate that global cap in national quotas. This second task shares many similarities to the redistribution issue in a harmonized carbon tax scheme. The allocation has to be sufficiently attractive to secure widespread participation and to be perceived as fair. Without delving too deeply, a variety of allocation criteria have been proposed: historic responsibility for past emissions, which tilt allocations sharply away from OECD to developing countries; population, under the argument that everyone has an equal "right" to unused assimilative capacity (this would of course greatly favor large developing countries); current emission levels, which would strongly favor the United States and would fail to attract developing country participation; and formulas that would evenly divide the social surplus that should materialize if the global warming policy is efficient. This last criterion, which would have to incorporate estimates of differential damages, willingness to pay, and differences in abatement costs, is so fraught with uncertainties and so open to misrepresentation that it would be useless as a formula for negotiation. And it has the ethically unattractive feature of favoring countries that harm others.

One study estimates that allocation based on current emissions of CO_2 would give the North 72 percent of the global quotas and the South 28 percent, whereas if based on population, the North would receive 14 percent and the South, 86 percent.[30] A second study shows that if quotas were distributed on the basis of population and if permit price were $20/ton of carbon, the transfer from North America would be $22 billion annually (0.42 percent GNP) for permits. Receipts from permit sales would be $14 billion for China (4.3 percent GNP) and $40 billion for other developing countries (1.2 percent GNP). While these amounts might be sufficient to induce compliance by developing countries, it may be unrealistic to expect that the North would find them acceptable (Grubb and Sebenius 1992). It seems likely that if ultimately a global cap on carbon emissions is set, the allocation of national quotas will be determined by negotiations that meld a

---

30 North, including Eastern Europe and the former USSR. For calculations for 1988 emissions, see Arnulf Grübler and Nebojsa Nakićenović (1992).

variety of criteria, and the financial burden will be considerably heavier on the OECD countries.

A number of other difficult issues would have to be addressed, many of which would also arise with harmonized carbon taxes. They include the optimal duration for a permit (e.g., 2, 5, or 10 years); renegotiation of the global cap and its reallocation in the light of new information; the inclusion or exclusion of carbon sinks; whether the quota trading system should be extended to all greenhouse gases; whether time-dated permits could be "banked"; and monitoring and enforcement provisions. While these are formidable tasks, it should be kept in mind that many are common to any regulatory structure. Also, most analysts conclude that the cost savings from international emissions trading can be substantial. An OECD model estimates emissions trading would lower costs from 1.9 percent of world GDP in 2020 to 1.0 percent (Bruce et al. 1996, p. 339, Table 9.25).

A final issue common to both tax and quota schemes is incomplete coverage and carbon leakage. Carbon leakage will arise if the country coverage of an abatement scheme is incomplete, or if countries face nonuniform restrictions. There are two reinforcing channels for leakage, through production and trade and through energy prices. If some but not all countries restrict emissions, carbon-intensive production will tend to migrate to the unconstrained countries, partly through foreign investment. Even if foreign direct investment is negligible, differential rates of return on capital will reconfigure the pattern of world portfolio capital flows. Second, partial coverage will tend to reduce fossil fuel prices in unrestrained countries and lead to more carbon-intensive production methods. Both channels lead to increased carbon emissions in unrestrained countries, hence the carbon leakage problem. This creates two problems. First, the effectiveness of the abatement program is compromised or can only be attained at higher cost. Second, carbon leakage causes changes in comparative advantage, and may create trade balance and exchange rate difficulties.

Universal coverage with binding emissions-reduction targets is not now in the cards. As described in Section 7.3 the Kyoto Protocol only establishes binding targets for developed and (some) transitional economies. When the Protocol is submitted for ratification, or when there are subsequent efforts to enlarge the core group, some countries will decide that the side payments offered through trading or joint implementation are insufficient. Other countries may find the side payments they are requested to make too high. Smaller countries may decide on a free-rider strategy either overtly or with the pretext that the compensation structure is inadequate. The larger the group of unrestrained countries and the greater the carbon leakage, the higher the cost of meeting any given global emission target for participating countries. Also, one can anticipate that energy-intensive industries in participating countries will press for weaker controls as their competitive position declines. Incomplete initial coverage also raises the problem of defections from a carbon-abatement regime. Defection by one key member could trigger the unraveling of commitments.

Trade measures have been proposed to deal with the incomplete coverage and carbon-leakage issues. In principle, trade liberalization could be used as a carrot to induce participation, but whether that would be sufficient is not known.[31] Trade restrictions on countries failing to join an agreement or commit to reduction could serve two purposes. First, they would raise the cost of not joining, which might increase membership. There is no economic reason to limit the discriminatory trade restraints to energy or energy-intensive goods – any strong, blunt new tariff might serve this purpose. Second, the trade restrictions on imports from nonmembers could attempt to discriminate according to the carbon content of various products. This might help reduce carbon leakage, as the importation and consumption of carbon-intensive products by member countries would be reduced. However, the task of determining the differential tariff rates would be arduous and contentious, requiring detailed input/output analysis and documentation of the source of production inputs. There would be other disadvantages. Trade restrictions create their own distortions and entail welfare costs. Moreover, if members were to impose border adjustments on the carbon content of their imports from nonmembers, there would also be political pressure for them to rebate internal carbon taxes on their exports, and this would tend to increase the member countries' total carbon emissions. Trade restrictions on the carbon content of imports would also erode the liberal trade principle of nondiscrimination, be an administrative nightmare, and run afoul of current GATT/WTO rules. One model in which carbon abatement is limited to OECD countries suggests that serious reductions in emissions, in the neighborhood of 3 to 4 percent annually below baseline, would produce marginal leakage rates to non-OECD countries in the range of 40 percent, and would have high welfare costs as compared to universal agreement. Leakage could be controlled to some extent by OECD export subsidies for carbon-intensive goods, but only at high cost (Felder and Rutherford 1993).

The questions of free riders and the scope for trade sanctions has been studied in a game-theoretic context by a number of analysts. Simple game

---

31 A condition for Korean membership in the OECD was to become an Annex I country in the FCCC.

models tend to conclude that the problem of free riders is potentially severe. As explained in Chapter 13, unilateral action or action by a coalition of countries may actually reduce the incentive to abate in other countries below the level they otherwise would have attempted even without the carbon leakage set of issues. However, the analytic framework of simple game theory may not be appropriate. More sophisticated repeat game models tend to be more optimistic. Moreover, it is difficult for game theory models to capture the role of peer pressure, that is, the reputational aspirations to appear a good citizen in the world community and the pressures exerted by domestic and international interest groups for "enlightened" national policy.

The trade consequences of limiting global warming are more complicated than simply using trade measures to induce or coerce participation. If a global tradeable permit system were created and capped at 1990 global CO_2 emission levels, and if the permits were distributed in some politically acceptable pattern, there would most likely be substantial trade in the permits themselves. If, for example, developing countries received permits based in part on their share of world population, they would be suppliers to the world permit market. While permit sales would be welcomed for their foreign exchange, the effect would be to appreciate their currencies and put additional competitive pressure on their export- and import-competing industries. Rather than selling permits and perhaps losing competitiveness in their traditional exports, some countries might choose to use their "excess" permits to bid for foreign direct investment. In this fashion and through balancing current account changes, the level and pattern of world capital flows would be affected. There has been little study of the international trade and capital flow consequences of measures to control global warming.[32]

A final point relates to the trade-competitiveness effects of unilateral measures to abate carbon. Such measures will have a disproportionately contractionary effect on energy-intensive industries such as steel, nonferrous metals, paper products, and of course fossil fuels themselves. One can expect resistance from these sectors and requests for exemptions in order to preserve employment and export competitiveness. For example, Sweden, which has already imposed a CO_2 tax, has limited the tax liability of energy-intensive industries to help maintain exports of these products. But a nonuniform domestic carbon tax will either subvert the objective of reducing emissions or be inefficient, failing to equate marginal abatement costs

---

32 For initial work see McKibben, Shackleton, and Wilcoxen (1998).

among industries. The inefficiency is compounded because exemptions narrow the carbon tax base, and with higher marginal rates on remaining sectors, the tax distortion costs increase. One study of the German economy found that for a unilateral abatement policy, the welfare cost of exempting energy-intensive industries was roughly 20 percent higher than a uniform carbon tax for a target 30 percent reduction in emissions. While the tax exemption could save jobs in these industries, the cost per job saved would be high and could have been achieved more efficiently with a direct wage subsidy if preserving employment were a real constraint (Böhringer and Rutherford 1997).

7 International Response

7.1 The Convention

The Framework Convention on Climate Change, signed by 152 nations at the 1992 UN Conference on Environment and Development, was the initial international response to global warming. The objective of the convention is to achieve "stabilization of greenhouse gas concentrations in the atmosphere at a level that would prevent dangerous anthropogenic interference with the climate system," and this is to be achieved within a time frame that allows ecosystems to adapt naturally to climate change. The objective is noteworthy as it does not specify a particular numerical target for either concentrations or temperature change, implicitly acknowledges that some climate change will take place, and includes all greenhouse gases, not just carbon dioxide (Grubb et al. 1993).[33] The convention states that protection of the climate system should be on "the basis of equity and in accordance with [parties'] common but differentiated responsibilities and respective capabilities"; that "the developed country Parties should take the lead in combating climate change and the adverse effects thereof"; and that the "specific needs and special circumstances of developing country Parties . . . should be given full consideration." These provisions put the burden on the developed countries for reasons of equity and ability to pay, but stop short of tying that responsibility to past or current greenhouse gas emissions. The special conditions of low-lying island and coastal states and, indirectly, the unfavorable effects on the exporters of fossil fuels are recognized elsewhere. The convention also acknowledges the precautionary principle and warns that policies should be "cost-effective" and may be "carried out coopera-

---

33 See also *International Legal Affairs* (1992) for text; Mintzer and Leonard (1994).

tively by interested parties." This last provision opens the door for emissions trading and joint implementation. Furthermore, in an effort to prevent restrictive trade sanctions, the convention states that abatement measures "should not constitute a means of arbitrary or unjustifiable discrimination or a disguised restriction of international trade," language taken directly from GATT.

With regard to commitments, all parties are obligated to develop, publish, and distribute inventories of greenhouse gas emissions by source and removals by sinks and also to develop programs to mitigate climate change. The parties to Annex I (developed and certain transition countries) undertook an additional, qualified, and nonbinding obligation to abate emissions and enhance sinks with the aim of returning by 2000 to their 1990 emission levels. In a convoluted and ambiguous provision, developed countries are obligated to "provide such financial resources, including the transfer of technology, needed by the developing country Parties to meet the agreed full incremental cost of implementing measures that are covered in paragraph 1 of this Article, and that are agreed on between a developing country Party and the international entity . . . referred to in Article II." Paragraph 1 (which applies to all parties), in addition to its reporting requirements, calls for *inter alia* the development, application, and diffusion of technologies, practices, and policies that control or reduce greenhouse gas emissions. For example, it would appear that a developing country switching from a less expensive fossil fuel to a more expensive renewable energy source could request full funding of the incremental costs from the Global Environment Facility, the designated interim financial mechanism. The convention does not, however, provide the funding. More broadly, the convention's strategy followed the ozone-depletion model, to establish an international framework and leave critical details such as targets and timetables, instruments, funding, and enforcement to subsequent negotiations. Both equity and efficiency find a place in the convention, although the balance is weighted heavily on the equity aspect. Nothing in the convention would block a fully elaborated regime involving tradeable permits or harmonized carbon taxes, but the agreement is not a definitive step in that direction.

7.2 The 1995 Berlin Climate Summit

Although it was apparent by 1995 that the 1990 emissions-level targets were inadequate to meet the convention's goal of stabilizing concentrations below dangerous levels, and indeed that few Annex 1 countries would even meet the 1990 target, the Berlin Summit failed to set any new or binding targets. Instead, the parties agreed to negotiate binding quantitative emissions limits by 1997, which would become effective by 2005–2010. The Berlin agreement made clear that only developed countries would be required to establish abatement targets, but in a positive step it did clarify somewhat the possibility of joint implementation projects.

7.3 Kyoto

The agreement reached in 1997 at Kyoto sets specific emissions-reduction targets for developed (Annex 1) countries. Even if the Kyoto targets are met, however, atmospheric concentrations of most greenhouse gases will still be on an upward trend. (Many Kyoto supporters view the targets as a down payment on more aggressive abatement later.) The United States is to reduce net greenhouse gas emissions by 7 percent from 1990 levels by the period 2008–2012, with slightly larger reductions for the EU and slightly less from Japan.[34] This implies a reduction for the United States of about 30 percent below projected baseline emissions by 2010. Russia and other former communist countries, which have already dramatically reduced emissions through recession and restructuring, have 1990 levels as targets. Achieving targets in Europe will be assisted by the carbon-emissions reductions already accomplished through conversion of coal and natural gas in the UK utility sector and the closing of energy-inefficient industry in the former East Germany. The EU is to be treated as a "bubble," with an overall reduction of 8 percent from 1990 levels. There are no obligations for developing countries to limit emissions, making ratification by the U.S. Congress problematic.[35] Six greenhouse gases are covered, and allowance is made for carbon sinks (i.e., credits or debits for afforestation and deforestation since 1990). Ratification requires at least 55 parties, including Annex 1 countries that contributed 55 percent or more of Annex 1 countries' emissions in 1990.

Three "flexibility mechanisms" are authorized, but with no specifics: (1) emissions trading among Annex 1 countries; (2) joint implementation projects among Annex 1 countries, in which carbon abatement projects in one country receive funding and/or technology from a second country, which

---

34 Not all developed countries are obliged to cut. Australia, for example, is allowed an 8 percent increase over 1990 levels.

35 In July 1997 the U.S. Congress unanimously passed a resolution to the effect that it would not ratify any agreement unless developing countries also took on commitments to limit or reduce greenhouse gas emissions.

"earns" credits for some fraction of reduced emissions; and (3) the Clean Development Mechanism (CDM), which contemplates arrangements similar to joint implementation, but between Annex 1 and developing countries. The objective of these mechanisms clearly is to seek lower cost-abatement opportunities.

7.4 Post-Kyoto

The Kyoto Protocol left open many controversial and critical issues. Important features of emissions trading, such as whether trading will be among private agents or restricted to governments and how much of a country's obligation can be satisfied by international trades, are undecided. The rules for establishing baselines against which reductions can be measured in joint implementation and in CDM projects are left open. The protocol does not elaborate verification procedures, or spell out enforcement and sanctions for countries that fail to meet required targets. A subsequent meeting in Buenos Aires (1998) simply set a two-year deadline to negotiate these and other issues.

The cost of Kyoto to the United States is currently being analyzed and debated. The chair of the Council of Economic Advisors, Janet Yellen, has estimated the marginal cost of a ton of carbon abated would be $14 to $23, and the direct annual cost to the U.S. economy at $7 billion to $12 billion (0.1 percent GDP) in 2010, but this appears to be based on a series of optimistic assumptions, including unrestricted worldwide emissions trading (Yellen 1998). Charles Rivers Associates, a consulting firm under contract to the American Petroleum Institute, estimates that the price of carbon would rise from $14–$23 per ton to $193 per ton if there were no international trading, and total cost to the United States would be 1.1 percent of GDP (Bernstein and Montgomery, n.d.). The Energy Information Administration of the U.S. Department of Energy (1998), in an extreme scenario assuming that the U.S. Kyoto target was achieved entirely by domestic energy-related reductions (i.e., no sinks, no trading), estimated the cost to the United States in 2010 to be almost $400 billion (1992 dollars) or over 4 percent of GDP. These differences underscore the potential cost savings from some form of international emissions trading.

In a broader perspective, the Kyoto targets do not reflect a careful economic cost-benefit analysis of either the extent of emission reductions or their timing. Indeed, monetization of the benefits – the present value of future damages avoided – hardly enters the debates. Given the economic and scientific uncertainties described above, this may be inevitable. The arguments for proceeding are partly precautionary and partly political. Some level of abatement *may* avoid very large future costs. And without some early demonstration of commitment by the industrial countries, and especially the United States, the chance of action by developing countries is virtually nil.

15

Economics and Ocean Fisheries

1 Introduction

Ocean fisheries are a resource of great value but their efficient management leaves much to be desired. Total marine catch increased from about 60 million tons in the early 1970s to almost 91 million tons in 1995 (Food and Agriculture Organization [FAO] 1997). But increasing aggregate catch may simply imply unsustainable exploitation levels. The FAO estimates that for 1994, 35 percent of major fisheries were showing declining yields, 25 percent were at high exploitation levels, and 40 percent were capable of higher yields (and thus implying a need to reduced fishing pressure for restocking); no underdeveloped fisheries remain. It concludes that "given that few countries have established effective control of fishing capacity, these resources are in urgent need of management action to halt the increase in fishing capacity or to rehabilitate damaged resources" (FAO 1997, p. 43). The composition of the fish harvest is also shifting toward lower-valued species. The proportion of catch by weight of pelagic (that is, open ocean) fish, which except for tuna tend to be low-valued fish, has increased from 50 percent in 1950 to over 60 percent in 1994 (FAO 1997, p. 33). This is consistent with data showing that the proportion of the total catch used for fishmeal and fish oil has increased from about 16 percent in 1953 to about 28 percent in 1994. From an economic perspective, fishing effort is highly inefficient. The FAO reported in 1992 that annual gross revenues for the global fishing fleet were about $70 billion and annual operating costs, excluding debt servicing, were $92 billion. This implies not only a complete dissipation of fisheries' rents, but also industry losses and government subsidies of about $22 billion. The estimate was subsequently revised upward to $54 billion when capital costs were included (WRI 1994, p. 184). The industry is overcapitalized, which wastes real resources while increasing fishing pressure. Francis Christy, a fisheries economist, estimates the global fishing fleet is at least 30 percent and perhaps 100 percent larger than would be needed for efficient harvesting (*Resources for the Future* 1996, p. 17). While much of the fisheries problem can be traced to overfishing and inefficient management, pollution and destruction of coastal and coral habitat are also implicated.

The economics of ocean fisheries share many characteristics with international pollution. There is considerable scientific uncertainty concerning sustainable yields, natural fluctuations in stocks, recovery rates, and so forth, which complicate management. Free-access ocean fisheries are subject to overfishing and, like pollution, efficient management implies curtailing access or use. Until quite recently, most ocean fisheries were not under national jurisdiction, and supranational authority to restrict access was absent. This meant that, like international pollution control, agreements among fishing nations had to be structured with both efficiency and equity (distribution) objectives in mind. Even today, with the remarkable extension of national jurisdiction through exclusive economic zones (EEZs), which have brought over 90 percent of ocean fisheries under national control, some fish stocks straddle two or more national EEZs, some stocks straddle an EEZ and the adjacent high seas, and highly migratory species such as salmon pass through various jurisdictional areas, including internal waters. For this reason, and because not all coastal states fully utilize stocks within their EEZ, but license other states fishing rights, the management of ocean fisheries remains very much an international issue.

There are other similarities between international management of fisheries and pollution. Both can be approached through the concepts of common property resources and externalities. Restrictions on use can involve free-rider problems and strategic behavior. Restricting access to one species or area can shunt fishing pressure to other areas and species. As with pollution, fisheries management needs to determine efficient use levels *and* effective least-cost instruments for limiting access. Domestic interest groups are often active and influential in negotiating agreements and formulating policy.

There are, however, some important differences between international pollution and fisheries management. By and large, market values exist for fish and are frequently absent for pollution damages. The time scale for fisheries management and for global warming and ozone depletion are very different. The establishment of national property rights has gone much further for fisheries. And except for a few sea mammals (such as whales and dolphins) and turtles, conservation has a more straightforward commercial motivation.

This chapter starts with the simple theory of open access to biological resources such as fisheries, described in Section 2. The clear conclusion of this theory is that some restriction on access is necessary for efficient management. Section 3 traces the enclosure movement. International agreements on fisheries management have a long history, dating at least to the 1882 North Sea Overfishing Convention, but have a very spotty conservation record (Birnie and Boyle 1992, Chap. 13). Since 1952, when Chile, Ecuador, and Peru declared 200-mile maritime zones (patrimonial seas), the trend has been toward enclosure of ocean fisheries, bringing the biological resources within national jurisdiction. Like the partial commercialization of biodiversity briefly described in Chapter 13, the enclosure movement is consistent with Demsetz's thesis that property rights emerge when resources become commercially valuable and open-access regimes become increasingly inefficient. Once again, to check theory against practice, Section 4 examines four specific fisheries management examples: allocating access quotas within the EC, the turbot "war" between Spain and Canada, U.S. performance in its Northeast fishery since enclosure, and the tradeable permit system pioneered by New Zealand.

2 Theory

The economics of fisheries is complicated for several reasons. First, fish are a biological resource that over time both grow and produce more fish. This implies combining economic and biological modelling and also implies that dynamic analysis, with attention to the time paths of relevant variables, is desirable. Second, fisheries fall between strictly renewable resources such as sunlight, which cannot be borrowed from the future, and nonrenewable resources such as petroleum and coal, which cannot be renewed in human time scales. Fisheries can be harvested on a renewable basis, but they can also be "mined" and indeed brought to extinction. This introduces ambiguities in the concept of optimal exploitation. Third, harvesting fish is often "stock dependent." The more depleted the stock, the more difficult and expensive it is to harvest remaining stocks. While this offers some protection against extinction, it introduces a more complicated relation in the fisheries production and cost functions. Fourth, fisheries have historically been characterized by open access and the right of capture. Without well-defined property rights, they are subject to overfishing and dissipation of resource rents. This is especially relevant for fish resources outside national jurisdiction, including straddling stocks and migratory species (e.g., salmon), which present special international economic management problems.

This section presents the bare bones of simplified fisheries modelling. Even simple models illustrate important propositions, but for a fuller understanding, the reader should consult a good natural resource economics text.[1] Our purpose in the following discussion is to demonstrate three main propositions: first, the harvest rate and stock of fish that maximizes economic profits will not be identical to the maximum sustainable biological yield due to harvest costs; second, if a fishery exists as an open-access common property resource, fishing effort will be excessive and the rent from the fishery will be dissipated; third, the higher the discount rate is, the lower the optimal stock of fish and the greater the possibility that extinction is economically rational. All three propositions are relevant to domestic and international fisheries, but management, and especially restriction on access, are more problematic in the international context. We first investigate and compare optimal and open-access harvesting assuming a zero discount rate. We then investigate fisheries as an asset (capital) management problem with a positive discount rate.

2.1 A Simple Model

Consider first a biological relation between the stock of fish, S, measured in physical (biomass) terms and its growth per unit time, G(S), also in physical terms.[2] Growth is low if stocks are small and increases with S; past some level of the stock, however, food and other inputs become scarce and growth slows. To be concrete, assume the growth function, $G(S) = K_1 S(\bar{S} - S)$ where K_1 is a constant and $\bar{S}$ is the maximum stock that the fishery can sustain. This produces the humped growth curve G(S) illustrated in Figure 15.1. Undisturbed stocks below $\bar{S}$ will continue to grow until the capacity of the fishery is reached at $\bar{S}$, but the growth per unit time will slow past S_{MSY}.[3] If stocks exceed $\bar{S}$, they will decline over time and stabilize at $\bar{S}$. More realistic and more complicated models would shift the biological function to the right, establishing a minimum stock below which growth is negative, leading to extinction. The biological function used here is also a great simplification as it does not reflect natural fluctuations in stocks and does not consider interdependencies among species.

We are interested in comparing steady-state solutions, in which the rate of harvest per unit time, H, just offsets natural growth, G(S). The figure illus-

---

1 Classic works on fisheries include Clark (1976) and Gorden (1954).
2 Demographic details of the stock are suppressed. This exposition follows Neher (1990).
3 S_{MSY} is the fish stock associated with the maximum sustainable yield, or harvest rate. The term *sustainable yield* should be interpreted cautiously. It implies a single number but in reality the sustainable yield will vary according to climate, region, age structure, water quality, and other factors.

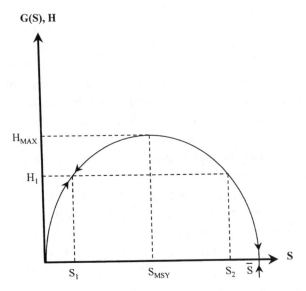

Figure 15.1. *Fish stock and fish stock growth rate*

trates two of many such harvest rates, H_1 and H_{MAX}. H_1 is consistent with two steady-state stocks, S_1 and S_2. That is, if the harvest rate is set at H_1, and the initial stock is at S_2, then harvest just offsets natural growth and the stock in the next time period remains S_2. The same is true for S_1.

At stock level S_{MSY} the fishery displays its highest natural rate of growth. If the initial stock is at S_{MSY}, a harvest rate H_{MAX} yields the largest sustainable physical yield, termed the maximum sustainable yield (MSY) by biologists. This stock level permits the highest sustained harvest over time. At first glance, S_{MSY} and H_{MAX} make appealing management targets as they maximize harvest and are sustainable. Indeed, they often were the targets in early fisheries management programs. From an economic/environmental perspective, however, there are three potential shortcomings. First, S_{MSY} does not reflect the costs of fishing. With the reasonable assumption that the lower the stock, the more difficult fish are to catch and hence the higher the costs per unit catch, it will be economically attractive to "thicken" the stock and establish a target stock somewhat *above* S_{MSY}. Although some harvest and revenue would be sacrificed, it would be justified if marginal fishing costs declined more than marginal revenue. Second, as explained later, in open-access fisheries it is highly likely that S_{MSY} is not a stable equilibrium as it will tend to invite additional fishing effort. Third, if there is a positive social discount rate, the opportunity cost of maintaining the stock at S_{MSY} is the real return forgone by not harvesting and converting some of this stock to alternative productive assets. The economic principle of adjusting asset holdings to equalize their rates of return suggest some drawdown of stock *below* S_{MSY}. In addition to these three considerations, there are other reasons for questioning S_{MSY} as the appropriate policy objective. The target species in the fishery may be significant in the food chain and its stock may help determine harvest levels of other valuable species. Or, as in the case of whales and certain other species, stocks may have direct value in utility functions. In that event, the socially desirable stock may exceed S_{MSY}.[4]

Consider the cost of fishing and its effect on the optimal stock of fish. The physical relations are established first and then the costs and revenues are introduced. Assume a simple production function, $H=K_2 LS$, where H is the harvest rate, K_2 is a constant representing the current technology of fishing, L is an index of commercial inputs to fishery (labor, nets, fuel, boats, etc.) that we combine and call labor, and S is again the stock. This production function states that if the stock is held constant, the greater the level of inputs (L) is, the greater the harvest will be; and if the level of L is held constant, the greater the stock is, the greater the harvest will be. To compare steady-state solutions, it is necessary to set the harvest rate equal to the growth rate, or $K_2 LS = K_1 S(\bar{S}-S)$

or

$$ L = \frac{K_1}{K_2}(\bar{S} - S). $$

Thus labor input is a linear inverse function of the stock, S.

The connection among these variables is shown in Figure 15.2. The upper part shows the biological growth function from Figure 15.1,

$$ G(S) = K_1 S(\bar{S} - S). $$

It also shows three production functions corresponding to fishing effort input levels L_1, L_2, L_3. The lower part shows the inverse linear relation between labor input and stock levels,

$$ L = \frac{K_1}{K_2}(\bar{S} - S), $$

which must be respected if we are restricted to steady-state fishing. Management objectives can be set in terms of harvest rate, fish stock, or

---

4 While environmentalists clearly have preferences for maintaining species, it is not so clear that they desire specific populations for commercialized fish species.

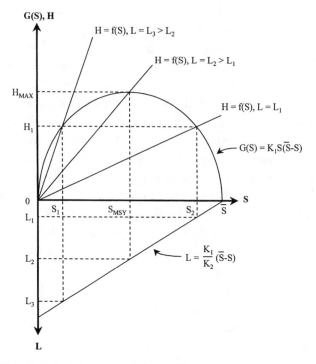

Figure 15.2. *Relations between fishing effort, fish stock, and harvest rate*

labor input levels, but the targets must be consistent. To illustrate, assume the initial and target stock is S_2. This implies a harvest rate of H_1 in the upper part and a labor input level of L_1 in the lower part. Alternatively, assume a management target harvest of H_{MAX}. This is consistent with a stock of S_{MSY} and an labor input level of L_2. Finally, if management dictates a labor input of L_3, this is consistent with a stock of S_1 and a sustainable harvest of H_1. But clearly H_1 could be achieved at the higher stock levels S_2 and a lower labor input L_1. Thus, setting aside the asset management issue considered later, the relevant ranges of target stocks and labor inputs are S_{MAX} to $\bar{S}$ and 0 to L_2. Finally, note that moving in the range $\bar{S}$ to S_{MSY}, fishing effort increases in a linear fashion, but the harvest, H, increases at a decreasing rate. This implies declining average and marginal product of labor (and cooperating resources) in fishing as stocks decline.[5]

It may be helpful to portray these production relations in the familiar

---

5 Moving left from $\bar{S}$ (i.e., increasing L), the average product of labor APL=H/L=K_2S. As S declines, the average product of labor declines.

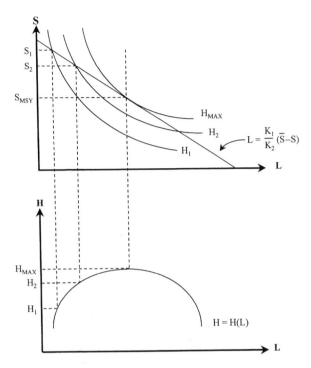

Figure 15.3. *Fishing effort, fish stock, and harvest rate: Isoquant diagram*

isoquant format (Figure 15.3). In the upper part the two inputs to the production function, S and L, are shown on the vertical and the horizontal axes. The multiplicative production function, $H=K_2LS$, allows substitution of inputs along each harvest level, $H_1<H_2<H_{MAX}$. However, because we are only concerned with steady-state harvesting, we are restricted to points along the line

$$L = \frac{K_1}{K_2}(\bar{S} - S).$$

Moving from zero to positive labor input, we can read off the corresponding increasing harvest levels H_1, H_2, H_{MAX} and the associated declining stock levels S_1, S_2, S_{MSY}. This traces out a labor-input, harvest-output production function in the lower part, $H=H(L)$, with maximum output at H_{MAX} (corresponding to MSY).

The remaining step is to convert these physical quantities into monetary units of costs (C) and revenue (R) and choose the stock, harvest rate, or labor input level that maximizes profits, defined as $\pi=R-C$. (Profits should

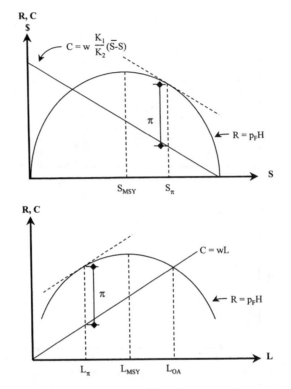

Figure 15.4. *Fishing model with costs and revenues*

now be considered to include the rent from the fishery.) This can be done using either the upper part of Figure 15.2 or the lower part of Figure 15.3, depending on whether we wish to work explicitly with the stock variable or L, the fisheries' input variable. For simplicity, assume the fishery to be "small" so that the price of fish, $\bar{p}_F$ is constant and the cost of labor input, w, is also constant. The problem is then to choose S (or H) that maximizes profits, $\pi = \bar{p}_F H - wL$, or, alternatively, to choose a level of labor input, L, that maximizes the same profit function.

The upper part of Figure 15.4 converts the growth (harvest) curve to a total revenue curve R by multiplying by the price of fish. The total cost curve C is simply the inverse linear relation between L and S,

$$L = \frac{K_1}{K_2}(\bar{S} - S)$$

multiplied by the price of labor, w. By visual inspection profits, the vertical difference between R and C, are greatest at stock level S_π, which falls to the right of S_{MSY}.[6] A similar result can be seen using labor input as the control variable. In the lower part of Figure 15.4, the total revenue curve R is the labor input: harvest output production function multiplied by the price of fish, and the total cost curve, C, is the linear function, $C=wL$. Again, profits are maximized at the labor input level L_π where the slopes of the curves are equal. This occurs at a lower level than L_{MSY}, implying that the harvest is below MSY and the stock higher than S_{MAX}. The two approaches, one focusing on S (and H) and the second focusing on L, are consistent.

We can now draw conclusions. First, the profit-maximizing stock, S_π, is greater than the maximum sustainable yield stock, S_{MSY}, so long as harvesting costs are positive. The reason was given earlier: "thicker" stocks reduce harvest effort and costs, and some sacrifice of harvest levels and revenues is justified by lower costs. Second, if fishing costs are sufficiently high, they will exceed revenues at all stock levels and no fishing will be economic. The stock will remain at its biological maximum, $\bar{S}$. Third, improved fishing technology (increasing the constant K_2 in the production function) will lower costs, increase fishing effort, increase harvest, and lower the sustainable stock. The same results hold for a decrease in the input costs, L. However, even if costs fell to zero, the profit-maximizing stock would not fall below the maximum sustainable yield level, S_{MSY}. This is *not* an extinction model if managed to maximize profits. Fourth, an increase in the price of fish would alter optimal S, H, and L in the same fashion as a decrease in costs, as described earlier. But in this simplified model (which excludes time) very high fish prices would simply push S_π closer to but not below S_{MSY}.

2.2 Open Access

The model previously described is a rationally managed idealized fishery. The growth function is stable and known to the managers; there is no threshold level below which stock cannot reproduce themselves and decline toward extinction; the age distribution of the catch is immaterial; and there are no significant interdependencies among species. The managers are indifferent between a dollar earned today and a dollar next year (zero discount rate), and, most importantly, the managers exercise prudent, effective, and

---

6 More formally, profits are maximized, when:

$$\frac{dC}{dS} = \frac{dR}{dS}$$

where R is revenue, C is cost, and S is stock.

efficient control on either the harvest level or fishing resource inputs. If any of these conditions do not obtain, the encouraging result of positive profits and stable stocks above S_{MSY} may not materialize.

We now compare these results to an open-access regime, a frequent condition in fisheries history and not unknown today. If profits defined as total revenue minus total costs (fixed plus variable) are positive, there is an incentive for existing fishing operations to expand and intensify operations and for new boats and crews to enter (perhaps displaced from other exhausted fisheries). If there is no limit on access, fishing effort will tend to expand to the point where total costs equal total revenue (level L_{OA} in Figure 15.4), and profits are squeezed to zero. Recall that profits include the rent from the fishery. Indeed effort will expand beyond that level if fixed costs are significant and exit from the fishery is slow. The operating rule for the individual boat with no alternative fishery is to fish so long as marginal revenue exceeds average variable costs (i.e., fuel, hired labor, etc.) This dissipation of profits (rent) occurs not because the new entrants are technologically less efficient, but because stocks are thinning and the average productivity of the resource inputs is declining. Also, if increased fishing pushes stock below S_{MSY}, the total revenue will shrink at fixed price for fish. Thus profits in open access can by squeezed by increasing cost and declining revenue. The profits are, of course, a measure of the social value of the fishery. If stock decline below S_{MSY}, the sustainable harvest declines, and fish prices may rise (a shift upward of the R curve in Figure 15.4). While this temporarily restores profits, it leads to increased fishing effort or delays exit from the industry and further depletes stocks. All this can be interpreted in terms of externality theory. Each participant in the fishery chooses a fishing level to maximize his/her individual profits, without regard for the costs imposed on others through lower catch – in economists' jargon, the fishery is characterized by reciprocal external diseconomies. Open-access fisheries also exemplify the so-called tragedy of the commons and illustrate the logic behind the enclosure of the seas, described in Section 3 following.

The clear conclusion is that some restriction on access that limits fishing effort or catch is needed. Not all tools are efficient, however. If fishing effort is limited by the number of boats, fishing days tend to expand; if limited by the number of boats and closed seasons, the size of boats and the sophistication of gear will be stepped up. If a patchwork of restrictions is built up, it is reasonably sure that fishing effort is inefficient and some or all of the profit from the fishery is dissipated through higher costs.[7] It would appear

---

7 For example, closed seasons for one species will increase downstream costs for processing plants left idle, and may simply shunt fishing pressure to other species.

that effectively administered catch limits, implemented through catch taxes or tradeable fishing quotas as described in Section 4, together with minimum net size to protect juveniles and closed spawning seasons, would be the most efficient package.

2.3 Time and the Discount Rate

In introducing the time value of money (and fish) it is useful to return to an efficiently managed fishery (i.e., limited access and profit maximization). To highlight the role of the discount rate, we make the unrealistic assumption that harvest costs are zero. The problem the managers confront is to adjust the portfolio of assets – fish in the sea, money in the bank – to maximize the flow of profits (or maximize the net present value of assets). The opportunity cost of holding fish as assets in the sea is the interest, r, forgone on financial investments. The opportunity cost of converting fish in the sea to financial assets is the natural growth of the fish stock lost by harvest plus any anticipated increase in the price of fish. We do not present a formal model incorporating the discount rate, but rather make some logical observations.[8] If we start with a virgin fishery at $\bar{S}$, and no fishing is done, there is no profit from conversion of fish to financial assets, there is no profit from growth of the stock, and the only possible profit is increased fish prices. But even these would not be realized until some positive harvesting took place. There is, however, an opportunity cost to zero harvest – the financial return from converting fish to money is sacrificed. If, in contrast, we start with a virgin fishery and immediately catch and convert all of the stock to financial assets, the profit or return is the discount (interest) rate times the value of the catch. The opportunity cost of immediate conversion to financial assets, however, is the loss of potential growth of the stock and its possible price appreciation.

It can be shown that in this *zero harvest cost, positive discount* model, the optimal steady-state fish stock and harvest rate is such that the rate of growth of the stock of fish, plus the expected rate of growth of fish prices (if any), are just equal to the discount rate. This appeals to common sense. On the margin, one would like to increase fishing effort up to the point where the incremental benefit of fishing (fish revenue invested at the discount rate r) is just equal to the incremental cost (reduced growth of fish stock and forgoing future price increases). This result leads to several conclusions.

First, the optimal steady-state stock will be below maximum sustainable

---

8 For simple formal models, see Neher (1990) and Pearce and Turner (1990). For a dynamic model using optimal control theory, see Gordon Munro and Anthony Scott (1985, Chap. 14, Vol. II).

yield if there is no expected price appreciation. The reason is that we have introduced a cost to holding assets in the form of fish – financial earnings forgone. Second, *ceteris paribus* the higher the discount rate is, the lower will be the optimal stock. A sufficiently high discount rate could lead to extinction of the stock (complete harvest) and be economically rational, and this would be more likely if the biological growth were slow.[9] Commercial whaling might be an example, but it is complicated by open-access characteristics. More generally, while including harvest costs tends to increase the optimal stock, including a positive discount rate tends to reduce the optimal stock, perhaps but not necessarily bringing it below threshold reproduction levels. Third, the expectation of increasing prices over time encourages conservation of the stock.

These conclusions pertain to a well-managed fishery with restricted access. The implication of open access is negative. The individual fisherperson has no incentive to conserve the stock; if not captured today, it may well be lost to other fisherpersons under the rule of capture. This is equivalent to an infinite discount rate and pushes fishing effort and hence total stocks below their optimal level. Indeed, if harvest costs are zero, the resource will be fully fished out. Positive harvest costs will offer some protection to the fishery, but again the net social value of the fishery (its rents) will be pushed to zero. As in the previous model, the dissipation of rents is the social cost of open-access fisheries. In a broad sense, the economic waste from open-access fisheries and the desire to appropriate rents to one's own country have been the driving force for enclosure of ocean fisheries.

The formal modelling should not obscure the fundamental intuitive conclusions from these simple cases. First, setting aside discount rates, the optimal fish stock in a rationally managed fishery will be above the stock that produces the maximum sustainable yield, (S_{MAX}) but below stock that the fishery is capable of supporting ($\bar{S}$). To maintain stocks at S_{MAX} would ignore the cost savings in fishing effort from more abundant stocks. To maintain stocks at $\bar{S}$ would mean that nothing could be harvested. Second, in this situation where discount rates are set aside, an *open-access* regime would increase fishing effort, increase harvest beyond its economic optimum, deplete stocks, and dissipate the rent from the fishing. Third, in an efficiently managed fishery the introduction of positive discount rates reduces the economically optimal stock of fish and, if the biological growth and harvest costs are low, can lead to extinction. If harvest costs are stock-dependent this is less likely. Fourth, an open-access regime acts as an infinite discount rate; no single fisherperson has incentive to conserve the stock. We note in

9 The initial stock size is also important but this requires dynamic analysis.

passing that the economics of fisheries casts light on the broader issues of extinction of species and sustainability. In poor countries with high discount rates for personal survival, and where at least some renewable resources remain open access, an economic explanation for abusive resource practices is apparent.

3 Enclosure

There are two broad approaches to resolving the problem of open-access ocean fisheries. The first is by international agreements, and the second is by extending national jurisdiction and putting into place national management schemes. Both have been difficult to pursue, in part because of the centuries-old doctrine of freedom of the seas and historic rights to capture on the high seas. As long as fishing technology remained primitive and supply was large relative to effective demand, open access was an efficient regime. But new fishing technology, including so-called industrial fishing, and increased demand have changed this.[10] Starting with the North Sea Overfishing Convention in 1882 and continuing until after World War II, the dominant approach was the negotiation of international fisheries agreements rather than extension of national jurisdiction. These early agreements and treaties were mainly concerned with establishing national limits and allocating access rather than conservation per se (Birnie and Boyle 1992). The commissions established by these agreements had certain regulatory authority in controlling fishing gear and open seasons, but none limited fishing entry or effort, and no convention provided for effective international enforcement. By and large these management agreements were not successful and many traditional fisheries in the early postwar period were in decline.

The first serious attempt at a more global framework for fisheries management was the 1958 Convention on Fishing and Conservation of the Living Resources of the High Seas, agreed to during the first United Nations Law of the Sea Conference (UNCLOS I). This convention, together with the Convention on the High Seas, reaffirmed the doctrine of the freedom of the high seas and open-access fishing rights, but did require cooperation among states in drawing up conservation measures. Moreover, it recognized the special interest of coastal states in fish stock in adjacent high seas, but gave them no effective exclusion or enforcement power. In short, the Conservation Convention contained broad principles, but would require detailed agreements by species and area if it were to be effective.

---

10 The product of industrial fishing is fish meal used as animal feed and fertilizers.

The North-East Atlantic Fisheries Convention of January 1959 is an example of the agreements concluded after the Geneva Convention. It established the North-East Atlantic Fisheries Commission, and divided the area covered by the agreement into regions, each dealt with by a regional committee made up of representatives from the coastal states for that region and from some of the states fishing for the same stocks in other waters. The commission was responsible for monitoring the state of fisheries and making recommendations based on the advice of the regional committees for conservation measures. Among the types of measures that the commission could recommend were the specification of minimum mesh sizes and fish sizes, restrictions concerning gear, and closed seasons and areas. On a two-thirds majority, the commission could also recommend total allowable catches (TACs). For the North-East Atlantic Fisheries Commission, as for other agreements concluded under the aegis of UNCLOS I, enforcement and the lack of an effective supranational authority were major weaknesses: contracting parties could opt out of recommendations they objected to and each contracting state was responsible for enforcement in its territories and in regard to its own nationals and its own vessels. Even then, such enforcement measures might be rejected by a two-thirds majority in the commission. Where each nation enforced the rules for its own nationals, it was difficult in practice for the measures envisaged in UNCLOS I to be imposed, and thus the weak preferential rights for coastal states established by the convention became meaningless. Similarly, the need to achieve consensus in the conservation measures adopted jointly meant that the protection afforded to stocks under such agreements was low.

While the international agreements route was foundering, the extension of national jurisdiction was gaining strength. Although authority for taking conservation measures was one motive, the more important was the desire on the part of coastal states to appropriate to themselves the economic benefits of their coastal fisheries. The process started in Latin America. In 1952, Chile, Ecuador, and Peru issued the Santiago Declaration in which they asserted sovereignty and jurisdiction up to 200 miles from their coasts, although they acknowledged navigational rights of innocent passage. By 1970, nine nations had unilaterally extended fisheries jurisdiction to 200 miles. The extension of fishing zones was accompanied by other encroachments. The 1958 UNCLOS I Convention on the Continental Shelf gave to coastal states sovereign rights over their continental shelf for exploiting the natural resources of the shelf – mainly offshore oil deposits. The Continental Shelf Convention itself followed a unilateral declaration by President Truman in 1948, in which he asserted U.S. rights over natural resources on its continental shelf, in particular petroleum reserves. In this same period, Canada had unilaterally asserted environmental protection rights of up to 100 miles in anticipation of possible oil shipments through Arctic waters. This process of extending jurisdiction can be described as the unbundling of rights to ocean resources, on the functional breakup of ocean space. The great prize was offshore oil, and assertion of coastal states' rights to oil reserves on the continental shelf. At the same time, the unbundling allowed, in principle, the maintenance of international rights of transit and navigation.

The end result of this process for fisheries was the 200-mile Exclusive Economic Zone (EEZ) agreed to in 1982 as part of UNCLOS III. Although the relevant convention did not enter into force until 1994, the EEZ gained wide acceptance in international customary law and has become the basis for management of ocean fisheries. Article 56 of the convention is the backbone of the EEZ regime and grants coastal states "sovereign rights for the purpose of exploring and exploiting, conserving and managing the natural resources, whether living or nonliving" to be found within the waters of the EEZ; furthermore, it grants coastal states jurisdiction with regard to "the protection and preservation of the marine environment." These sovereign rights are not to interfere with traditional freedoms of the sea, such as that of innocent passage. In this sense, the EEZ is importantly different from the territorial sea. Article 61, which applies Article 56 to the conservation of living resources, places an obligation on coastal states to manage the resources so as to maintain them at levels "which can produce the maximum sustainable yield, as qualified by relevant environmental and economic factors." In effect, this rather vague provision leaves coastal states with a great deal of latitude in setting management objectives for fisheries.

Article 61 is tempered by Article 62, dealing with the utilization of resources, and requires coastal states to grant other nations access to any surplus stocks not capable of being caught by the fishing fleet of the coastal state. However, since it is the coastal state that determines the maximum permissible catch, and thus how much of the stock can be considered "surplus," there is little guarantee that other nations will in fact be granted access. Furthermore, coastal states are permitted to impose conditions for granting access, such as the obligation to respect management rules, pay licensing fees, respect quotas, and contribute to scientific research. In a very real sense, then, coastal states under the EEZ regime are granted property rights over fish stocks within 200 miles of the baseline of their territorial seas; they are able to decide management targets, choose specific management tools, and sell or refuse to grant user rights to nationals of other states.

The EEZ, at least in principle, encloses the vast majority of the world's fish resources, and thus eliminates much of the open-access common resource nature of fisheries at the international level.

Acceptance of the EEZ concept does not fully assign property rights and remove all ocean fisheries questions from international relations, however. Four issues remain. First, there have been a massive number of boundary disputes related to the declaration of EEZs, estimated at 400 by Churchill (1993). Second, highly migratory species such as tuna move through various EEZs as well as the remaining high seas, and UNCLOS III simply requires cooperation in the management of such species. Property rights to these stocks remains ambiguous. Third, some stocks straddle an EEZ and the high seas, and rights to manage these stocks remain unclear. Closely related, some stocks overlap two or more EEZs, and the question of right of access remains. Fourth, in these instances in which a coastal state does not fully utilize stocks within its EEZ, disputes over rights to surplus stocks can arise. Most importantly, the device of the EEZ may moderate the international free-access problem, but it does not establish the effective *national* level policies to limit overfishing.

To summarize, after a long and often unsatisfactory experience with international agreements on fisheries management, the new approach has been to extend national jurisdiction. This has been motivated in part by conservation objectives, but more strongly by desires to appropriate to coastal states the wealth of the oceans. The new approach, however, does not settle all international property rights issues, nor does it guarantee efficient management at the national level. And indeed, the era of "creeping jurisdiction" may not be over. Chile has made proposals for a "mar presencial," an undefined area beyond and adjacent to the EEZ within which the coastal state would enjoy a role in the management and use of marine resources (Orrego Vicuna 1993).

4 Examples from Fisheries Management

The following examples illustrate different features of fisheries management, but, in one fashion or another, access restrictions are central to each. The first case examines how the EC allocated fishing rights within its congested waters and its attempts to improve fishing efficiency. The second case analyzes a serious dispute between Spain (and its backer, the EU) and Canada concerning straddling stocks. The third explores U.S. experience in managing its Northeast fisheries, and the final example illustrates the potential for individual tradeable fishing permits as a management tool.

4.1 The EC's Common Fisheries Policy *(Churchill 1992;*
Song 1995; Holden 1994)

The evolution of fisheries policy within the European Community, now the European Union, casts light on the three central questions in international resource management: (1) How is the resource to be protected against over-exploitation? (2) How are the resource rents to be distributed among participating countries? (3) Are the tools that are employed efficient? The first two questions are about limiting and allocating access and involve the clarification or rearrangement of property rights. Not surprisingly, historical legacies and domestic and international realities played a central role. With respect to the specific management tools, there is no evidence that at the community level efficient, market-oriented measures were sought to manage EC fisheries; internal and external politics were dominant.

Before starting, we note that because of its unique features, it is unclear whether fisheries management in the EC holds broader lessons for the management of international resources. First, as a supranational institution, the EC had the authority to establish and enforce a common fisheries policy. As set out in the Treaty of Rome, which established the European Economic Community, "the activities of this Community shall include . . . (d) the adoption of a common policy in the sphere of agriculture [Article 3] . . . 'Agricultural products' means the products of the soil, of stockfarming and of fisheries (Article 38)." In principle, this supranational authority sets the EC fisheries case apart from the great majority of international resource management questions, which are negotiated between sovereign states. In practice, however (and because of the structure of EC decision making), lobbying, negotiations, and compromise among member states was extensive and not unlike many international environmental negotiations.

Second, conservation and efficient management of its fisheries was only part of the EC's mandate. Up until 1977, when fishing zones were extended to 200 miles, the main component of the EC fisheries policy was not conservation (which would have been ineffective with its very limited territorial seas), but regulating the marketing of fish and providing structural assistance to the national fishing industries. Both of these functions worked at cross-purposes with conservation. The markets policy included price supports and price guides to help bolster producers' income, and reference prices below which duties on imports were imposed to protect the EC market. In this respect, like the Common Agricultural Policy, the purpose was not efficient trade but securing reasonable self-sufficiency and protecting producers' income. Elementary theory suggests that trade protection of an open-access common property resource invites abusive exploitation. The structural policy, first adopted in 1970, gave financial support for the modernization and expansion of the EC's fishing fleet. Engine power, a measure of fishing fleet capacity, increased from 2.0 million kilowatts in 1970 to 6.5 million kilowatts in 1987 (Holden 1994, p. 22). This expansion of fishing capacity increased fishing pressures and undermined conservation efforts.

A third feature that may make the EC fisheries story unique was that it took place under rapidly changing conditions. Externally, the major change was the move by most countries to 200-mile fishing zones. While this greatly expanded EC fishing waters and made EC-level conservation feasible, it also froze the EC fleet out of traditional distant water fishing grounds, shifted fishing effort to EC waters and, as described next, affected the allocation of catch quotas among EC members. The internal change was the absorption of new members into the EC, first the accession of Denmark, Norway, Ireland, and the UK in 1972 and then Spain and Portugal in 1986, all countries with major fishing interests. This meant a rearrangement of resource access rights among a larger set of claimants. In short, the Common Fisheries Policy (CFP) evolved simultaneously with broader membership and broader geographic scope, which complicated the formation of policy and may limit the generality of lessons to be learned.

Historical experiences may also make the EC case unique. These experiences include the boom and collapse of the North Sea herring catch, which rose from 500,000 tons in 1950 to 1.2 million tons in 1965 and crashed to less than 100,000 tons in the late 1970s, an early signal of overfishing and the need to control access. Another example, which prefigured the EC policy of special consideration for the social and economic interests of coastal communities, was the so-called first cod war between the United Kingdom and Iceland in 1958–1961. In resolving that conflict, the United Kingdom agreed to accept Iceland's 12-mile territorial sea in view of Iceland's reliance on coastal fisheries for its livelihood. The issue of special access for coastal states reemerged following the U.K. accession and its initial demands for an exclusive fishery zone of 50 miles.

Since 1983, the CFP's main device for preventing overfishing has been the establishment of annual total allowable catches (TACs) by species and location, and allocating the TACs in national quotas. *Access* to fisheries is governed by open-access principles dating to 1970. With some exceptions, any EC fishing vessel can fish in any area of community waters. The main exceptions are: a 12-mile coastal zone is reserved for local vessels (although some states maintain historic rights to fish in the outer 6 of the 12 miles of other member states); the right of Spanish and Portuguese ships to fish in the waters of other members is strictly limited until 2002; and a section of water north of Scotland (the Shetland Box) is restricted to small fishing vessels. Thus the distribution of fishing rents among members is governed by quotas on catch rather than carving up the fisheries into exclusive zones. The TACs are set by the Council of Ministers based on proposals by the EC Commission. In turn, the Commission receives advice from an advisory committee on fisheries management (ACFM). The advisory committee has been more concerned with maximum sustainable yield than maximum economic yield as described earlier. Indeed, the ACFM has stated its role as restricted to evaluating the biological consequences and biological constraints of management practices as set by the commission and the council. In numerous cases, especially before 1989, the TACs set by the council exceeded the recommendations of the ACFM. This pattern dates to the initial comprehensive agreement on fisheries in 1983, in which TACs were fixed on the basis of existing rates of fishing morality and not on a reduction in these rates that would have been necessary to build stocks (Holden 1994, p. 57).[11] Holden states, "It is not surprising that the level of TACs is mainly determined by political decisions because politicians regard it as their responsibility to respond to the pressures of their fishing industries as they consider fit. That is democracy in action." (Holden 1994, p. 70.)

The allocation of TACs is the principal device for distributing potential resource rents in the common fisheries policy (apart from financial subsidies through the structural policy, where the sources of this money are not, of course, fisheries' rents). After long and contentious negotiations, allocation formulas were approved in 1983 and through the principle of "relative stability" have resulted in reasonably constant catch shares among EC members. The three criteria used were (1) historical catch shares, (2) "compensation" for lost fishing opportunities by the extension of 200-mile fishing zones by third countries, and (3) the special needs of countries and regions especially dependent on fishing industry, sometimes known as the Hague Preferences, which include Ireland, Northern Ireland, Scotland, and Northeast England. To adjust different values for different species, quota allocations were converted into "tons of cod equivalent." For example, with a ton of cod at an index of 1, a ton of whiting has a cod equivalent value of 0.86. One ploy used to reach the initial allocation agreement in 1983 was to set TACs well above the levels recommended as necessary to reduce mortality rates. This of course made national quotas more generous and more accept-

11 See Holden's (1994) Tables 4.2 and 4.3 for comparison of recommended and fixed TACs.

able. A second was for the commission to propose TACs that would allow the Hague Preferences to be met, even when these were much higher than recommended levels (Holden 1994, pp. 49–50). In short, scientific advice on maximum sustainable yields was overridden to obtain initial agreement on allocating inflated quotas, and the initial allocation shares have proved to be remarkably stable.

Setting aside the incentive for overfishing from inflated TACs, the EC approach did not promote economic efficiency in fishing effort. The allocation of quotas by country does not favor the least-cost producer. Indeed it reserves a share of catch for the high-cost producers. Eliminating national quotas would have been more efficient. Moreover, quotas by country and species leads to high rates of discards, the difference between what is caught and what is landed. A vessel that catches a species for which its country's quota is filled will have to discard these fish or land them illegally. And because large fish command higher prices per pound, there is an incentive to discard small fish even when the quota has not yet been filled. Finally the CFP's technical regulations, which are partially designed to protect juvenile fish (for example, through mesh size requirements), also had implications for the efficiency of fishing effort. One example was limitations on days at sea – in 1991 to reduce fishing pressure, vessels fishing for cod and haddock in the North Sea were required to tie up at dock for eight consecutive days each calendar month from February through December.

The issue of economic efficiency is not only an EC-level question. The CFP delegates to the member countries responsibility for how they wish to manage their quotas. Thus, even if quotas are not distributed to least-cost fishing countries, an individual country could set up an auction system or tradeable permits system within its country quota, and achieve efficiency at the national, if not at the EC level. Holland has experimented with a domestic transferable permit system but found it necessary to impose days at sea restrictions as well. Other members have been slow to move toward creating permits and property rights within their national quotas.

To summarize, the extension of a 200-mile EEZ in 1977 greatly increased the EC's management area and created a need to allocate valuable property rights. The broad approach was to divide the catch by the national quota rather than national fishing zones. The main allocation criterion was historic shares, modified by lost distant water fishing opportunities and local economic dependence on the fishing sector. Prior to 1983, conservation was undermined by subsidizing and protecting the fishing sector; after 1983, conservation was initially undermined by politically inflated TACs. The efficiency of the fishing effort was eroded by the types of technical regulations used, although EC members were free to seek efficiency by allocating their quotas to their own fishers. It was not until the early 1990s that reducing the overcapacity of the fishing fleet became a serious objective.

4.2 *The Turbot War* (Aquerreta Ferraz 1996; Springer 1997)

In March 1995, the Canadian Navy seized a Spanish fishing vessel, claiming it had violated fishing regulation laws in an area of the high seas close to Canadian jurisdictional waters off Newfoundland. Not only did the incident rouse a political, economic, and diplomatic dispute between Canada and the European Union, but it also revealed the weaknesses in the existing system of fisheries management. From an economic perspective, the "turbot war" illustrates the difficulty in establishing property rights to certain fish stocks, and the consequent dispute over how the benefits from the resource are to be shared.

An understanding of the legal and organizational background to the dispute is useful. Although the 1982 UNCLOS III grants coastal states property rights to fish stocks within their EEZ, these rights are not absolute. Coastal states also have obligations for conservation and optimal utilization of the resources. Moreover, although the convention grants all states the right to fish in the high seas adjacent to the EEZs, these rights are not absolute either. The convention requires states to cooperate in the conservation and management of living resources in the high seas, and further requires states to establish regional fisheries organizations to this end. Finally, and with specific reference to fish stocks that straddle the EEZ and adjacent high seas, the Convention requires states to agree upon conservation measures.

It was within this context and for this purpose that the North Atlantic Fisheries Organization (NAFO) was created and tasked with the management of both fisheries resources beyond the 200-mile EEZ zone and stocks that migrated between the EEZ and the adjacent high seas. Both Canada and the European Union are among its members. The EU's common fisheries policy gives sole authority to the EU Commission to enter into external fisheries negotiations and participate in international fisheries organizations. Thus, although it was a Spanish vessel that precipitated the crisis, the turbot war was essentially between the EU and Canada. Although NAFO has fisheries management responsibilities, it must operate on consensus. Any member can object to proposed measures concerning total allowable catch and national quotas of that catch. A state need only accept decisions to which it has expressly agreed. Despite this restrictive procedure,

NAFO had been successful in 1993 and 1994 in responding to overfishing by establishing fishing moratoria on several species and placing reduced catch limits on others.

An understanding of the fisheries circumstances of Canada and the EU is also helpful. Despite certain conservation measures, Canada's Atlantic fishing industry was in decline. The problems included overcapacity of fishing fleets and very high levels of unemployment in the industry. Traditional groundfish stocks were in decline, and this shifted fishing effort toward turbot. An earlier moratorium on the collapsed cod fishery also contributed to the aggressive Canadian response to the turbot dispute. The EU's circumstances were equally troubled. Although total catch limits had been established, effective limits on fishing effort and reducing the number of vessels active in community waters were difficult to achieve. Market price supports tended to encourage fishing effort. Moreover, it was EU policy to keep community vessels fishing in what had been international waters so that they would not place further stress on already overfished community waters.

The conflict itself has a rather crass flavor. There was no dispute over the total allowed catch, which was set by NAFO at 27,000 tons, down from an actual catch of 60,000 tons in 1994. At a meeting in early 1995, NAFO allocated this quota at 12.6 percent to the EU, 60.4 percent to Canada, and the remaining 26.7 percent to Russia, Japan, and other members. The EU, claiming over half the total, objected, as it had a right to do under NAFO procedures. This objection set aside the NAFO allocation, and the EU promptly and unilaterally set its own quota of 67 percent of the total catch (18,000 tons). Canada responded by amending its fisheries legislation so that it could seize foreign fishing vessels outside its (Canada's) jurisdictional waters and in NAFO regulated waters, if such vessel were contravening prescribed conservation and management measures. Canada followed through with the seizure of the Spanish vessel Estai on March 9, 1995. Although disputed by the EU, Canada claimed to find a hidden hold on the Estai containing 25 tons of flatfish, which was under a NAFO moratorium, and a large proportion (79 percent) of turbot to be immature fish. In this fashion, conservation questions were conflated with distributional issues. The fishing dispute also precipitated a minor trade skirmish, with Canada raising tariffs on EU exports of vodka, perfume, fashion shoes, and glassware.

After some further incidents in which nets were cut, Canada and the EU reached an agreement resolving the dispute. Responding to Canada's conservation concerns, the EU agreed on a number of measures to improve reporting, inspection, and enforcement. On the division of the total annual catch of 27,000 tons to member quotas, Canada received 10,000 (including 7,000 in its jurisdictional waters), and the EU received a quota of 5,013 tons (subsequent to April 16, 1995), not including the estimated 7,000 tons taken by Spanish vessels prior to April 1995. Although this resolution defused international tension, and may improve inspection and enforcement procedures, it did not address central problems such as phasing down the industry and basing fisheries management on efficiency criteria.[12]

4.3 (Mis) Management: U.S. Northeast Fisheries

During the 1960s and early 1970s fisheries off the New England coast experienced greatly increased fishing pressure, with annual catch on the productive Georges Bank rising from about 100,000 metric tons to 427,000 tons. The increase was primarily due to foreign fleets fishing beyond the 12-mile U.S. territorial waters, whose catch rose to 88 percent of the total (WRI 1994). In 1976, the Congress responded by passing the Fisheries Conservation and Management Act (Magnuson Act), establishing U.S. federal government jurisdiction over fish resources up to 200 miles. While conservation motives played a role – the International Commission on Northwest Atlantic Fisheries had warned of overfishing as early as 1964 – the enclosure was mainly motivated by a desire to appropriate to the United States the economic benefits of its coastal fisheries.

The extension of national jurisdiction and the establishment by the Magnuson Act of the New England Management Council under the authority of the National Marine Fisheries Service of the U.S. Department of Commerce provided an opportunity to address the problems of overfishing, overcapitalization, and dissipation of fisheries' rent, but that opportunity was lost or mismanaged for two decades. The evidence of mismanagement is in the catch data, the composition of the catch, and the excessive resources devoted to fishing effort. Figure 15.5 shows U.S. commercial landings for five high-valued groundfish species for the period 1965–1995. The first management plan under the Magnuson Act did attempt to check depleted groundfish stock (cod, haddock, yellowtail, and flounder) through quota, trip, and size limits. But the plan was unpopular among fishermen, who viewed the exclusion of foreign fleets as a bonanza. Quotas were ignored in many instances, fish were mislabelled and landed illegally, and when quotas proved burdensome to fishers, the council accommodated them by inflating the quotas (WRI 1994, p. 188 [citing McHugh 1983]; pp. 87–88; Dorsey 1994). The plan

---

12 The dispute was, however, an impetus to a 1995 United Nations agreement dealing with both migratory and straddling fishstocks.

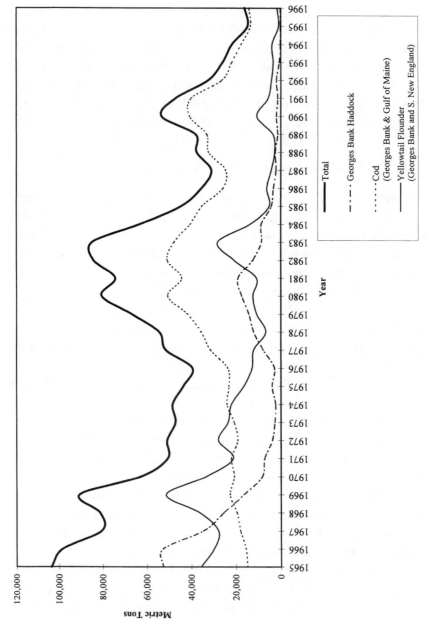

Figure 15.5. *Northeast U.S. commercial fish landings 1965–1996. Source: Derived from NOAA/NMFS Draft Report of the 24th Northeast Regional Stock Assessment Workshop, Stock Assessment Review (SARC), National Fisheries Service, Woods Hole, MA, June 1997*

set no direct limits on fishing mortality and no limits on the number of fishermen. In fact, quotas and trip limits were abandoned in 1982 under an interim groundfish management plan based on the concepts of open access and indirect controls. The latter included minimum fish size and minimum net size, the compliance with which was low, and the closing of some spawning areas. The interim plan was formalized in 1985 with the Multispecies Fisheries Management Plan despite reservations by fishery experts, and indeed in 1988 a technical review concluded that the indirect control plan was working only poorly and that the measures in it were inadequate to rebuild and maintain stocks (Dorsey 1994).

A 1990 report from the Massachusetts Offshore Groundfish Task Force documented the effect of overfishing high-valued species on the composition of stocks (Massachusetts Offshore Groundfish Task Force 1990). In 1963, 55 percent of the fish caught in research trawls were the high-valued cod, haddock, and hakes, and 24 percent were the low-valued dogfish and skates. By 1986, the high-valued species declined to 11 percent and skates and dogfish were 74 percent. The share of flounder also fell dramatically. One implication of this ecological shift is the increased competition for food sources by skates and dogfish that may have impeded the recovery of the desired species. An important proximate cause of depletion of stocks was overcapitalization and the expansion of the fishing fleet and its increasing technological sophistication. The number of otter trawlers, the principal fishing technique, increased from 650 in 1977 to 1,021 in 1984, and the number of days fished increased from about 25,000 in 1977 to almost 50,000 in 1985 before declining to about 43,000 in 1989. New electronic technology increased the technical efficiency with which fish were found and caught. The expansion and upgrading of the fleet was encouraged by federal financial assistance and liberal tax laws (MOGTF 1990, p. iii). Greater fishing efforts did not bring substantially greater revenues. Gross revenue from the New England otter trawler fleet rose from about $215 million in 1980 to a peak of about $260 million in 1982 before falling to less than $200 million by 1988 (all figures in 1990 dollars) (MOGTF 1990, Fig. 4).

The 1990s have seen a series of reforms. These include a numerical definition of overfishing so that the council can be held accountable[13] and temporary closures of parts of the Georges Bank and Southern New England Fisheries and effort and area controls, including restrictions on days at sea and limitations on daily trip catches. The latter appear to be highly

13 In the early 1980s the Interim Plan defined the optimum yield as the amount of fish actually harvested by U.S. fishermen (i.e., any size of the harvest was declared to be optimum in advance) (Dorsey 1994, p. 4).

inefficient as some boats are limited to 88 days per year at sea, and some vessels that are capable of up to a 6,000-lb catch are limited to daily trip limits of 1,000 lbs. Finally, the U.S. Department of Commerce has initiated a $25 million boat buy-back program to reduce the size of the fleet.

The principal factor responsible for this history of mismanagement was the excessive influence of the industry in the New England Fisheries Management Council and the failure of the U.S. Department of Commerce, which approves nominations to the council and has authority over the council's actions, to exercise proper supervision. The short-term interests of the fishing industry in capturing the revenues previously earned by foreign fleets, and in fishing above sustainable yields, dominated conservation and economic efficiency objectives, especially during the 1980s. These unsustainable practices were encouraged by government financial incentives to the industry, and by the adoption by the council of an open-access regime relying on indirect and often unenforced controls (MOGTF 1990, Executive Summary). Political pressures applied by the industry at the local and federal levels were a contributing factor. While the involvement of an industry in its own regulation can in some situations have advantages (Townsend and Pooley 1995), the experience of the New England fisheries provides a strong counterexample. The most basic lesson is that extension of national jurisdiction over international resources does not guarantee efficient management.

4.4 Rights-Based Fishing: New Zealand's ITQ System[14]

Creating marketable rights for fish offers a solution to the problems of open access, overcapitalization, and dissipation of rents from fisheries. In one version of rights-based fishing, government authorities set total allowable catches by species and fishery and allocate rights to that catch to fishers in the form of individual transferable quotas (ITQs). The advantages are that if TACs are set appropriately, catch is limited to sustainable levels. Because the owners of the quotas have a secure and perpetual right to a fraction of the catch, they have less interest in lobbying for inflated TACs. Indeed, the market value of their quotas is directly linked to the health and productivity of the fishery. Because access is restricted to those who own quotas, owning the right to a specific catch encourages efficiency (i.e., efficient levels of boats, gear, and fish-handling techniques). Finally, the marketability of quotas leads to the most efficient fishermen doing the

14 For analysis of New Zealand's ITQ scheme, see Clark, Major, and Mollett (1988) and New Zealand Ministry of Fisheries (1996).

actual fishing (inefficient fishers find it more profitable to sell or lease their quotas.)

New Zealand has the best known ITQ system. It was introduced in 1986 partly in response to evidence of overcapitalization and overfishing in inshore waters and partly to prevent those problems from developing in deep-water fishing within its 200-mile exclusive economic zone. Government authorities set annual TACs by species and management area that are based on sustainable yield estimates. The TACs are then divided into quotas, and fishers have the right to harvest based on their ownership of quotas. The quotas are perpetual and can be bought or sold (with a limit on foreign ownership). The permanent, private right to a share of the total catch moderates fishers' pressure for unsustainably high TACs, as that would force down the current price of their quota assets. The government raises revenues through a levy on quota holdings, not actual catches, reducing the incentive by fishers to misrepresent catch levels. The initial allocation in 1986 was based on investments and catch history of fishers. This allocation was not without problems. Of the 1,800 fishers notified of their catch history, almost 80 percent lodged objections. Also, initially quotas were in tons rather than a percent of TAC, and because total tonnage represented by the quotas exceeded the TAC for some species, the government was forced to buy back quotas.

The system is generally considered successful. Average annual marine catch in tons increased by 152 percent from 1981–83 to 1991–93 (WRI 1996, p. 311). The value of total catch from 1986 to 1995 increased by 80 percent. The overcapitalized fleet has been rationalized and downsized. Handling of fish on board to maximize quality and value has improved. But some problems have emerged. *By-catch* is the incidental catch of one species when targeting a different species for which the fisher has a quota. The management problem is how to avoid wasteful dumping of by-catch overboard without encouraging covert targeting of the by-catch species. The law allows fishers to either buy quotas for their by-catch or surrender the by-catch to the government for a fraction of its value, but this arrangement has not worked well. A related problem is *high-grading*, or keeping only the most valuable (generally the largest) fish to stay within the quota. This, too, is wasteful. There has also been controversy over the conversion factor for translating live catch, for which the quota applies, to processed weight, for at-sea processing plants. Because inspection is in port, the conversion factor can work for or against fishers. Finally, there was a serious legal dispute with the indigenous Maori people who claimed ownership of offshore fishing rights based on a 19th-century treaty. This claim was settled in 1992 but at considerable expense to the government.

Part 4

Sustainable Development

Note to Part 4

Part 4 considers the now fashionable concept of sustainable development. At one level it is a clever term. The word *development* has a positive and attractive ring. And who would favor unsustainable development? But if sustainable development is to serve as a spline to join economic and environmental strategies, it must take a more concrete and objective form. What should be sustained, economic or natural systems? What types of development are unsustainable? What weight should be given to the welfare of today's poor and what weight to future generations? What is the appropriate geographic scope? If sustainability refers to environmental and natural resources, is sustainable development a local, national, or international process? How does the international economic system advance or retard sustainable development? Does sustainability imply limits to economic growth?

Chapter 16 opens with a discussion of natural resource limits in economic development. The notion of limits is old and has proved durable, but the specific resources thought to be limiting have changed over time. The recent view is that the environment may be the binding constraint. Also, sustainable development carries an intergenerational equity connotation. The two notions of limits and equity come together in a "strong" sustainability rule, which would make conservation of the stock of natural capital available for future generations a necessary requirement in a sustainable development program. The necessity for strong sustainability, however, depends in large measure on how easily physical and human capital can substitute for natural capital. If they are good substitutes, a "weak" sustainability rule, which only requires the maintenance of aggregate productive capital, may be sufficient to sustain economic welfare.

The emergence of sustainable development as a benchmark for policy has coincided with attempts to improve the measurement of economic-environment interactions, and these are analyzed in Chapter 17. Much of the measurement effort centers on reforming national income and product accounts. GDP and national income statistics record economic activity by business, government, and households, but there is no explicit sector for nature or natural capital. One reformist view is to more accurately measure sustainable income – the amount of income and output that can be consumed currently while leaving productive capital intact. More controversial reforms would nudge the national accounts toward more accurate measurement of economic welfare, a role they were not designed for, but for which they are often used. A second measurement issue is whether there are any stylized facts connecting environmental quality and economic development. This brings us to the inverted U hypothesis.

Academic discussions of sustainability have a rather dry flavor. It is useful to conclude this section in Chapter 18 with a case study that examines trade, environment, and sustainability in Thailand, a country that has been much lauded for achieving over two decades of rapid economic growth, but which in the process has suffered from acute pollution and natural resource degradation.

16

Perspectives on Sustainable Development

1 Introduction

The term *sustainable development* was popularized in the 1987 report of the World Commission on Environment and Development (Brundtland Commission), *Our Common Future*, although its first general use was in 1980 by the International Union for the Conservation of Nature in *World Strategy: Living Resource Conservation for Sustainable Development*. Since then sustainability has become a principal benchmark against which economic development policies are assessed by national governments, development assistance agencies, and NGOs. Although the adoption of sustainability as a benchmark for development has been hampered because of ambiguities in definition and interpretation, there is a consensus that sustainable development implies an active role for government in efficient and equitable management of natural and environmental resources. This is not a totally new idea. Pigou,[1] writing in 1932, states, "It is the clear duty of Government, which is the trustee for unborn generations as well as for its present citizens, to watch over, and if need be, by legislative enactment, to defend the exhaustible natural resources of this country from rash and reckless spoilation." At one level, this active role fits uneasily with another major trend in the past two decades – deregulation and privatization – in which the driving force for development is an increased role for the private sector and decreased government involvement. At a more basic level, however, both sustainability and the freeing up of private markets seek greater efficiency, although sustainable development stresses intertemporal efficiency and tempers this with a strong dose of equity concerns. Still, tension remains between sustainable development and deregulation with regard to the proper role of markets and governments in stewardship of resources, tension

1 Cited by Krutilla 1967.

that is traced later in this chapter to the Conservation Movement in the United States at the beginning of the 20th century.

The Brundtland Commission defined sustainable development as "development that meets the needs of the present without compromising the ability of future generations to meet their own needs"; and clarified this by calling attention to "the essential needs of the world's poor, to which overriding priority should be given, and to the limits imposed by technology and social organization on the environment's ability to meet present and future needs" (World Commission on Environment and Development 1987). The commission's definition centers on environmental limits, and on intra- and intergenerational equity, although efficiency is stressed elsewhere in the report. The notions of resource limits and equity provide convenient paths to investigating the origins of the concept and are considered in Sections 2 and 3. Section 4 addresses the question of what is to be sustained, Section 5 analyzes policies, and Section 6 examines the international dimension of sustainable development.

2 Changing Views on Resource Limits

The idea of natural resource and environmental limits to economic growth has deep roots, but has often been challenged. Moreover, identifying *which* resources constitute limits has changed from generation to generation. The classical economists writing in the first half of the 19th century were primarily concerned with the availability and cost of primary products. Thomas Malthus stressed the limited availability of agricultural land and David Ricardo elaborated by pointing out that increased output brought land of lower fertility (and lower-grade mineral resources) into production. Together with population increases, the classical models concluded these limits would ultimately bring diminishing returns to labor and capital employed in agriculture. In turn, this would force wages toward a subsistence level (checking population growth) and redistribute income toward rent at the expense of profits, capital accumulation, and economic growth. The classical model was in essence a long-run stagnation model. Somewhat later, John Stuart Mill broadened the notion of natural resource scarcity to include the amenities of nature and the threat to solitude from overcrowding. In this respect, Mill's contribution to the limits debate was to move beyond an impending scarcity of production inputs to a more modern concern with directly consumed environmental amenity services. The eminent economist, Stanley Jevons, writing in the middle of the 19th century, shifted the focus from agriculture to energy and in particular coal, the then dominant nonrenewable natural resource used in production (Jevons 1865). His conclusion was that ultimately the increased scarcity and cost of coal would bring economic stagnation to Britain.

These pessimistic conclusions pointing toward stagnation were refuted during the latter part of the 19th century and the first half of the 20th century by the empirical fact of continued economic growth, whose natural resource base was greatly augmented by new discoveries, technological progress, substitution in energy sources, the application of capital, and the globalization of production and trade in natural resources. Nor was population growth in industrial countries and its pressure on natural resources a burning issue in the first half of the 20th century. Indeed, population decline was of greater concern in Europe. High death rates tended to stabilize population elsewhere. Except for localized crises such as the Dust Bowl in the American plains states in the 1930s, neither natural resources nor environmental degradation were considered to be serious limits to growth, although as described later wasteful resource exploitation was a hot public issue. The limits debate was in suspension.

The early post–World War II era was marked by a greater divergence of views. The Paley Commission, established by President Truman and reporting in 1952, was influenced by World War II and Korean War commodities shortages and found many causes for concern, including evidence of moderate increases in the cost of raw materials (President's Materials Policy Commission 1952). The commission's recommendations included government stockpiling of strategic materials for defense purposes, and greater reliance on imported raw materials. The perspective was national, not global. A decade later, Harold Barnett and Chandler Morse (1963) revisited the natural resource limits question in their influential book, *Scarcity and Economic Growth*. Their conclusions, based on deductive and empirical analysis, were essentially optimistic, a view shared by many economists today. The basic hypothesis was that if natural resources were becoming increasingly scarce, the real cost of extractive output would increase over time. When tested against U.S. data for the period 1870–1957 they found the opposite, that the trend in unit costs of extractive goods as a whole had been downward, not upward. They then tested a weaker hypothesis, that increasing scarcity of natural resources was real but being masked by technological improvements and economies of scale. They found support for this proposition in the forest products sector, but not for other natural-resource-based sectors such as agriculture and minerals. In short, they found little evidence of natural resources as a limit to growth.

The long-term price trend for natural resources also played a critical role in a parallel debate in the early postwar period. The so-called Prebisch thesis, named after a prominent Latin American economist, argued that because of different income elasticities of demand between raw materials and industrial products, and because productivity increases in raw materials tended to be passed forward in lower prices whereas productivity increases in industrial goods were passed back into higher factor incomes, there was a long-term tendency for the terms of trade of commodity-exporting developing countries to deteriorate. The policy implications were import substitution, aggressively pursued in Latin America, and international commodity agreements to limit supply and shore up prices, an idea picked up in the 1970s under the umbrella of a New International Economic Order (see below). The terms-of-trade argument and its policy implications were *not* based on a conservation or sustainability rationale, but did reflect the view that raw material prices were declining over the long term.

Concerns that directly productive natural resources could limit economic growth did not totally disappear. The energy crises of the 1970s, together with world population projections that now appear inflated brought new life to the older Malthusian view. But there were significant modifications. One new view expressed in the 1970s was that the conflation of poverty, population growth, and pressure on the natural resource base, in the context of high energy prices, might not only limit economic growth but combine to cause economic and environmental collapse. The 1970s increase in energy prices coincided with accelerated population growth in developing countries, as mortality rates fell sharply with the introduction of improved sanitation and health services. Erik Eckholm, writing after the first OPEC oil shock, painted a vivid picture of agricultural crisis in which the poor in developing countries are caught in a vicious cycle of deforestation, soil erosion, ever shorter fallow periods for traditional agriculture, and the use of dung for cooking and not as fertilizer for crops, all of which were exacerbated by high prices for commercial fossil fuels and all of which tended to *reduce* productivity of natural resources and compound poverty (Eckholm 1976).

This new perspective is important for three reasons. First, it shifts the focus of the limits debate away from industrial country growth to development in the Third World. In doing so, it contributes to a widespread view, still held by many, that sustainable development is mainly an issue for developing countries.[2] Second, it emphasizes that poverty itself can be a cause of envi-

---

2 The pernicious interaction between poverty and resource degradation is not unknown in U.S. history. Describing conditions in the southern Appalachian mountains at the beginning of the 20th century, Gifford Pinchot, who later became chief forester for the U.S. government, wrote, "These people, poor as the mountain farmer is apt to be, were obliged to use without reserve all the resources of their

ronmental degradation and that sustainable development requires meeting the needs of the *present* generation, an idea picked up in the Brundtland Report. In this sense, a revitalization of intragenerational equity concerns – help for the poor – is not only an ethical issue but a necessary condition for long-term economic growth. Third, there is a recognition that abuse of the natural resource base, occasioned through poverty and population pressure, might not only place a *limit* on economic growth, but cause a pronounced *decline* in economic welfare. In that event, adequate protection of the natural resource base is not a luxury but a prerequisite for sustainable income and development.

At first glance, this vicious circle among population, poverty, and environmental deterioration appeared to be a question of localized collapse – encroachment on marginal lands, exhaustion of specific fisheries, and unsustainable shortening of fallow in regions still relying on slash-and-burn agriculture.[3] But in recent years, there is an increasing recognition that ecological systems are interconnected. For example, biological diversity and genetic resources of international importance can be threatened by local destruction of habitat. Deforestation, directly or indirectly related to poverty, is significant for global warming. Interconnectedness increases the international salience of what had for a time appeared to be localized incidences of unsustainable development.

Some analysts went further, predicting global environmental and economic collapse as successive natural resource and pollution limits were breached. The most dire and influential of these was the report for the Club of Rome entitled *Limits to Growth*, published in 1972. In a technical sense, the authors did not quite predict collapse but rather extrapolated trends to the point of collapse:

> *If the present growth trends* in world population, industrialization, pollution, food production, and resource depletion *continue unchanged*, the limits to growth on this planet will be reached sometime within the next 100 years. The most probable result will be a sudden and uncontrollable decline in the population and industrial capacity. (Meadows et al. 1972, p. 24, italics added)

While *Limits* was severely criticized by economists for failing to incorporate market adjustments for adapting to increasing scarcity and for its idiosyn-

---

scantily productive lands. They were therefore in the habit of cutting all trees that could be used or sold as fuel, fencing, or saw-logs. They turned their cattle into the forest and often burned over their woodlands for the sake of pasturage . . . under such treatment the forest, originally of moderate quality, grew steadily worse . . . the condition of a large part of the forest was deplorable in the extreme." (Trow 1984, p. 59.)

3 For earlier works linking the rise and fall of civilizations to their environmental/resource base, see Edward Hyams (1952) and Vernon Gill Carter and Tom Dale (1955).

cratic treatment of technological change, it did revitalize a dormant debate on physical limits to growth and did add a new limit, pollution, to the earlier concern for population, agriculture, and nonrenewable resources. Its publication at the time of the first oil price shock added greatly to its impact on the public.

Since the 1970s, the limits debate has focused more on ecological and environmental constraints than agriculture and commercialized natural resources. This shift reflects an easing of the energy crisis, considerably more rapid decline in population growth rates than had been anticipated, and an emerging view that securing adequate food supplies is more of an income and distributional issue than an aggregate supply question. It also reflects the growing public awareness of the global environmental threats – greenhouse gases, ozone depletion, loss of biodiversity, nuclear waste disposal – and a new appreciation for basic ecological functions of the environment.

The intellectual underpinning of environmental and ecological limits as opposed to raw material limits can be traced in part to the materials balances approach introduced in the 1970s, which utilizes the first law of thermodynamics – when materials are extracted or harvested from nature, their mass is not significantly altered in production and "consumption" (Boulding 1966; Kneese, Ayres, and d'Arge 1970). It follows that the throughput of an economic system is a flow of wastes, or residuals, disposed of in environmental media, and the capacity of the environment to absorb the wastes is at issue. Moreover, the second law of thermodynamics, which states that any conversion of energy to mechanical work increases entropy, has been invoked (Georgescu-Roegen 1971). *Entropy* is defined as a measure of dissipated or unavailable energy. In this fashion, entropy, and particularly the limit it places on recycling materials, has become another limit to economic growth, although the practical significance is much debated. The existence of a long-run equilibrium between economic and environmental systems, recognizing the first and second laws of thermodynamics and pervasive externalities, has been explored by a number of economists, and we return to it in Section 4.

To summarize, the concept of sustainable development is rooted in a long-standing debate concerning natural and environmental resource limits to economic growth. The terms of the debate have shifted over the years, with greater attention now paid to the residuals of economic activity and the effect these residuals have on the capacity of environmental resources to sustain a variety of life-support and economic functions. The constants in the debate are the degree to which society can rely on prices and markets for substitution as resources become progressively scarcer, and the degree to which technological improvements can push back the limits.

3 The Equity Roots

The intragenerational equity, that is, the distributional component of the Brundtland Commission's definition of sustainable development, has more recent and more political roots. Environmental degradation entered the lexicon of international relations with the 1972 United Nations Conference on the Human Environment. In advance of that conference, it was necessary to persuade developing countries that the environmental *problematique* was more than just industrial pollution, or the "effluence of affluence." The compromise struck in a preparatory meeting in Founex, Switzerland, was to redefine environmental degradation to include not only industrial pollution but the attributes of poverty – unsanitary water supplies, inadequate sewage disposal, urban slums, and overexploitation of renewable resources (Founex Report 1972). This broadening not only allowed developing countries to acknowledge an environmental problem, but, by placing poverty as the overarching problem, outlined the solution as rapid economic growth, preferably with the help of increased financial transfers from rich countries. This idea of additionality in funding found its way 20 years later into the Framework Convention on Climate Change (FCCC) in the form of a commitment to pay full incremental costs, and was a central issue at the 1992 Rio Conference. In retrospect, the Founex compromise, while politically successful in attracting the involvement of poor countries, and while correctly highlighting the important relation between poverty and unsustainable resource use, had two negative consequences. First, by conflating poverty and environmental degradation, it promoted the simplistic idea that economic growth was a necessary and *sufficient* condition for environmental improvement. Second, it raised unrealistic expectations that additional aid from North to South would be forthcoming.

These expectations received a serious jolt with the abortive effort to create a New International Economic Order (NIEO) in the 1970s. Buoyed by the initial success of OPEC in pushing up oil prices in 1972 and by a belief that their position in natural-resources-based exports represented growing international market power, developing countries coalesced behind a broad program to fundamentally alter the balance of international economic relations. The objectives were improved terms of trade through commodity agreements, improved market access for their exports, better terms for technology transfer, regulation of multinational corporations that was more favorable to host countries, and redistribution of income through financial transfers. By and large, the NIEO effort failed as the countries of the South overestimated their market power and underestimated resistance from the industrial countries.

Nevertheless, there were changes underway in the 1970s that reemerged in the 1980s under the rubric of sustainable development. One of these was the popularization of basic human needs as the principal development objective. Basic human needs, as embraced by the World Bank in 1978, has a social equity element. Its achievement was to be accomplished by greatly increasing investment in health, education, nutrition, sanitation, and water supplies (Streeten and Burki 1981). The premise was that investment in human resources is a necessary condition for strong economic growth. Thus provision of basic human needs and economic growth were complementary. This parallels the underlying premise of sustainable development, that protection and conservation of natural and environmental resources is a necessary condition for sustained economic growth, especially in poor countries directly reliant on their natural resource base.

While the concept of basic human needs was sufficiently mainstream to find its way into the World Bank, the 1970s also saw a flowering of other more radical development strategies, elements of which can be found in some versions of sustainable development. These included a stress on national self-sufficiency, the use of "appropriate" (that is, intermediate) technology, ecodevelopment (the use of indigenous materials, for example, bamboo), and grassroots community involvement. The best known appeal for altering development strategy was E. F. Schumacher's *Small Is Beautiful: Economics as if People Mattered* (1973). Some of these ideas have indeed found a home in mainstream development work, especially the value of grassroots community involvement. But the dominant development model for the past 20 years has been the East-Asian example of export-led industrialization, which took a very different path than self-sufficiency, appropriate technology, and ecodevelopment.

It is fair to say that the intragenerational equity component of Brundtland's definition of sustainable development – meeting the essential needs of today's poor, to which overriding priority should be given – was included for the same reasons that the Founex compromise redefined the environmental *problematique* – to bring developing countries on board. And it seems to have met the same fate. Except for the Global Environmental Facility with its limited funds and mandate, the sustainable development debate has lost its intragenerational equity dimension. Indeed, among economists, sustainable development has been analyzed almost exclusively from either an efficiency perspective or an intergenerational equity perspective. Geoffrey Heal (1998), for example, in an excellent exposition of current economic theories of sustainability, exclusively focuses on intertemporal resource allocation and equity, and does not address intragenerational distribution. Of course, this focus does rescue the subject of sustainability from merely an issue for poor countries, but it has a very different emphasis than Brundtland.

The *inter*generational equity element of the commission's definition of sustainable development – that the present generation has a duty and obligation to the welfare of future generations through conservation of environmental resources – can with some stretching be traced to the Conservation Movement of the late 19th and early 20th centuries in the United States. But even here, despite the creation of the great national parks in the United States – Yellowstone in 1872 and Yosemite Valley in 1880 – and reservation of almost 200 million acres in national forests under Theodore Roosevelt, much of the early Conservation Movement was less concerned with intergenerational *equity* and functioned more as a reaction against what was seen as rapacious and wasteful private exploitation. Active government regulation was motivated by efficiency as much as intertemporal equity and stewardship concerns. The blending of efficiency and equity is captured in two quotes. Philip Wells, law officer under Gifford Pinchot at the newly created Forest Service in 1908, defined natural resource policy as the "use of foresight and restraint in the exploitation of the physical sources of wealth as necessary for the perpetuity of civilization, and the welfare of present and future generations." In 1918, the distinguished economist Richard Ely defined conservation as "the preservation of the unimpaired efficiency of the resources of the earth."[4] These definitions, while not inconsistent with a moral obligation to future generations, imply that intertemporal efficiency was an important guiding principle.

The parallels between the Conservation Movement in the United States and current endorsements of sustainable development are many. Both stress the "wise" use of natural resources and the avoidance of waste ("inefficiency" in modern terminology). Many in both movements attribute transcendent value to nature. Both are more than a little vague. President Taft's statement in 1910 resonates in current discussions of sustainable development: "A great many people are in favor of conservation, no matter

---

4 Philip Wells and Richard Ely both cited by Samuel Hays (1959, p. 123). Pinchot, the "father" of scientific forestry in the United States, thought of natural resource scarcity in physical, not economic, terms.

what it means."[5] Nor did the international aspects of conservation go un-
noticed. President Theodore Roosevelt, writing in 1909 to invite the prime
minister of Canada and the president of Mexico to the North American Conservation Conference, noted, "It is evident that natural resources are not
limited by the boundary lines which separate nations." (quoted by Trow
1984, p. 73.)

While the Conservation Movement had both efficiency and equity elements, the connections were not formally analyzed by economists until the
1970s and especially in a seminal study by Talbot Page (1977). One reason
was that neither physical scarcity of materials nor other scarcities – ecological functions, absorption of wastes, and shifting cumulative pollution costs
to future generations – were seen as pressing problems. Intergenerational
equity was deemed unimportant as long as income levels were expected to
rise, which was the prevailing view. Page made two important contributions.
First, he emphasized that natural resources were an inclusive concept, and
that scarcity was not merely the adequacy of material inputs to production
(ores, energy) but was also indexed by pollution and environmental degradation. Second, he presented a formal analysis of two competing criteria for
intertemporal resource allocation, (1) the present value criterion, which is
based on efficiency, and (2) the conservation criterion, which is based on
intergenerational fairness. In this way, he framed the modern question
of intergenerational equity and efficiency, which is considered in the next
section.

4 What Is To Be Sustained?

At the risk of great oversimplification, two broad approaches to sustainability can be identified, ecological and economic. The key ideas in ecological sustainability are that ecosystems, if left unperturbed, organize
themselves into quasi-stable states; that the stability and resiliency of ecosystems (their sustainability) is directly related to the degree of biodiversity,
where biodiversity includes "variety and variability within species, between
species, and of biotic components of ecosystems"[6]; and that because of interdependencies, if one element of an ecosystem is subject to stress and brought
below some threshold level, the ecosystem itself is threatened. It follows that
any economic activity, from resource harvest to residuals disposal, that puts

5 Quoted by John Ise (1920) and again by Barnett and Morse (1963). The Conservation Movement was
  more than technical management of natural resources. It was a political movement and ultimately
  embraced trust busting, immigration limits, and much more.
6 As defined by the United Nations Environment Programme and cited by Mohan Monasinghe and
  Jeffrey McNeely (1995).

stress on elements of an ecosystem has potential sustainability implications. It does not follow, however, that all resource harvesting for economic purposes is unsustainable. Virgin fisheries and forests tend to reach a natural equilibrium stock with zero net growth. A reduction in that stock allows a sustainable yield, the growth increment, to be periodically harvested, provided that collateral ecological effects are minimal. Economics modifies this sustainable physical yield concept by introducing extraction costs and discount rates to estimate sustainable economic yield, or net income.

In contrast to physical or biological sustainability, economists are interested in sustaining income, or welfare, or utility. Typically their interest in the sustainability of ecological systems, or more broadly natural capital, is derivative – does it contribute to sustaining income? Before explaining economic approaches to sustainable development in detail, it should be acknowledged that some economists reject the concept of global sustainability itself as a guiding principle. Wilfred Beckerman (1992; 1994), for example, argues that as a guiding principle global sustainability lacks either a moral basis or an operational value, or both. His argument is that if sustainability implies preserving every component of the environment – in his example, every one of some two million species of beetles – the opportunity costs in terms of continued poverty and disease would be morally indefensible. But any less strict notion of sustaining resources – for example, maintaining a stock of assets that permits a sustained flow of income while allowing for substitution among assets – is not operational, as we do not know today what future preference patterns and future possibilities for technological substitution among assets will be.

4.1 Optimality versus Sustainability

The distinction between optimal and sustainable development paths is a useful place to start. In static (intratemporal) allocation analysis, the optimal allocation of resources ultimately depends on the distribution of assets, or rights to assets, and thus implies a social welfare function with weights attached to different income distributional patterns. The same requirement is present in determining an optimal allocation of resources over time. Optimality requires an explicit or implicit intertemporal social welfare function that assigns weights to the utilities of future generations. Within the framework, an optimal development path is typically formulated to maximize the discounted value of future utilities, and discounting is the procedure through which weights are assigned to the utilities of future generations. A zero discount rate implies equal weights across generations, and a positive discount rate implies that the weight attached to future utility declines. It is important to remember that the weights are determined by the present generation. Future generations cannot participate. It follows that an optimal development path implies a specific distribution of assets, or rights to assets, among generations. Thus, optimality cannot be fully separated from equity, and equity cannot be found through purely economic analysis.

This brings us to the economic concept of sustainability. A plausible attribute of sustainable development might be a requirement of *nondeclining* per capita utility over time. Such a condition squares with at least some notions of intergenerational equity as it protects the well-being of future generations. It also draws attention to the need to sustain the sources of income and utility, which is the stock of productive assets, or capital, and to increase that stock if population is growing. One immediate question is whether an optimal development path is sustainable. The answer depends on how one chooses to model the economy. In general, an optimal development path need not be sustainable, and a sustainable path need not be optimal (Toman, Pezzey, and Krautkraemer 1995). It is relatively easy to construct stylized models in which the optimal consumption path – the path that maximizes discounted utility – leads to steady impoverishment of future generations. For example, in a simple "cake eating" model in which output depends on a nonrenewable resource, the optimal per capita consumption and utility paths decline over time if the rate at which utility is discounted exceeds the (exogenous) rate by which technological progress increases the productivity of the resource input (Pezzey 1992). In more sophisticated models, in which natural resources also provide a directly consumed environmental amenity, or where a reduced stock of the resource adversely affects the production function, the likelihood of an optimal policy leading to impoverishment increases.[7] Nor are these results simply an artifact of nonrenewable resource models. Pezzey presents a simple "corn eating" model in which output depends on a single *renewable* resource. In this system, optimal consumption stays at some minimum subsistence level if the rate at which the renewable resource grows is less than the (exogenous) population growth rate plus the utility discount rate, and under some circumstances can crash to zero even when the resource growth rate exceeds the sum of population growth and discount rates.

The troubling discrepancy between optimality and sustainability models is in large measure a result of discounting, and more specifically intertemporal social welfare functions that are grounded in discounted utilitarian-

---

7 Intertemporal optimization models use mathematical techniques derived from optimal control theory. See Alpha Chiang (1992).

ism. This dilemma has led some economists to seek a "sustainable optimal path" in which some weight is given to present versus future consumption via a discount rate, but some weight is also given to welfare in the very long run. In this fashion, the present generation does not "dictate" the welfare of future generations, but by the same token the welfare of distant generations does not "dictate" the behavior of the present generation (Beltratti, Chichilnisky, and Heal 1995).

The purpose of introducing these models is not to explain reality but to draw attention to the difference between optimality defined as maximizing the sum of discounted utilities and sustaining income levels. Without going into detail, we can list model features that tend to make optimal consumption paths unsustainable – zero or slow technological progress, high population growth rates, high discount rates related to poverty and the preference for present over future consumption, pollution that over time diminishes the productivity of conventional production inputs, and an economic structure that relies heavily on nonrenewable resources or renewable resources exhibiting slow growth rates. Market failures will generally increase the likelihood of unsustainability, but are by no means a necessary condition. If we were convinced that the features just listed either singly or in combination did *not* describe reality, the issue of sustaining income would lose its urgency, and public policy could concentrate on the more traditional concerns of correcting market failures and achieving efficient intertemporal resource use. If, however, there is a real possibility of declining income (utility), the question of intergenerational fairness or equity cannot be avoided.

4.2 Sustainability Rules

A traditional starting point for economic analysis of sustainability is to follow Hicks and define income as the maximum flow of benefits possible from the existing asset base without reducing the flow of future benefits, or the maximum that can be consumed in an accounting period while maintaining capital intact. This approach is helpful in that it is familiar from both personal finances and bears some relation to the concepts underlying national income accounting (see Chapter 17). It also draws attention to the need to maintain the stock of productive assets. Sustainable development is thus a pattern of current consumption that maintains or augments the capital stock on a per capita basis. Beyond this point, however, there is little agreement. The capital stock can be divided into three or possibly four categories – physical or reproducible capital (roads, factories), human capital (skills and knowledge), natural capital (commercialized natural resources, ecological systems that support production, and resources providing directly consumed environmental services), and, perhaps, social capital (the institutions and governance systems within which economic activity takes place).

At this point, the extent of substitutability of one type of capital for another becomes critical. Substitution may be thought of on two levels: the extent to which one type of capital asset can replace another in the production of goods and services; and the extent to which conventional economic goods can substitute for directly consumed environmental services in utility functions. For example, can a country run down its stock of oil and build up its physical and human capital so that real income is maintained or increased? Are there limits to this substitution? To what extent can the products of human capital, say, video games (which we assume require little natural capital) substitute for natural scenic attractions, while maintaining utility? These questions are enormously complicated by uncertainties in new technological substitution opportunities – will natural genetic resources become obsolete with advances in genetic engineering, or become *more* valuable? They are also complicated by our inability to know future tastes and preferences and hence substitution opportunities in consumption. How will future generations value nature? Is utility itself shaped by what is available? The cost of substitution is also at issue. Neoclassical economics assumes substitution of inputs in production processes, but also cautions that the law of diminishing marginal returns implies increasing costs as one input is substituted for another.

A "weak sustainability" rule assumes substitution opportunities among the categories of capital and only requires that the total capital stock (per capita) be kept intact. When nonrenewable resources such as oil or coal are used, the weak sustainability rule implies that the rents from these resources should be invested, if total capital is to be kept intact and consumption levels sustained. This is sometimes known as the Hartwick rule (Hartwick 1977). Doubts about the ability to substitute physical and human capital for natural capital, together with concerns for environmental uncertainties and irreversibilities and, perhaps, a bequest motive, have led some analysts to advocate maintaining a constant stock of natural capital as an essential component of sustainable development (Pearce and Atkinson 1995; Pearce, Barbier, and Markandya 1990). This can be termed a "strong sustainability" rule and has deep roots in the conservation literature. In its more flexible versions, this constraint would accommodate substitutions among categories of natural wealth, for example, substitution of new, renewable energy sources for depletion of nonrenewable fossil fuels, substitution of productive agricultural land for cleared forests, or rehabilitation of fisheries to offset increasing soil salinity, *if* the total stock of natural capital were kept intact. Also, a flexible version of this strong sustainability constraint might allow for some decline in the physical stock of natural capital if systematic progress in technology improved the productivity of natural capital. Finally, some analysts have proposed identifying those components of natural capital that are critical (i.e., of very great value), and limiting the strong sustainability rule to this portion of natural capital, allowing noncritical natural capital to be replaced by other assets. In this connection, it should be remembered that sustaining the stock of natural capital also means sustaining its waste disposal capacity and ability to provide directly consumed environmental services, so that increasing pollution does not interfere with or diminish the productivity of natural or physical capital or impair these directly consumed services. Indeed, in the modern view, an injunction to sustain natural capital has as much to do with rates and forms of waste disposal as it does with harvesting forests or fisheries, depleting nutrients in soils, or conserving nonrenewable resources.

To become operational, strong sustainability must solve two problems. The first is to make different types of natural capital commensurate; that is, changes in, say, soil quality must be made comparable to changes in water quality if the total stock is to be stabilized. Money, or monetary value, is the first choice for the *numeraire* and may work tolerably well if the products of natural capital are commercialized and market prices reflect social costs and values.[8] But many of the important services of natural capital escape markets and market prices, and valuation problems arise. Thus physical as well as monetary indicators of natural capital stock may be needed. The second task is to determine the appropriate geographic or political unit within which the stock of natural capital (or critical natural capital) is to be maintained. Clearly one would not wish to define this unit too narrowly – an urban industrial center can thrive by exchanging the products of physical and human capital for some forms of natural capital. But fixing natural capital at the global level while permitting depletion in some regions and augmentation in another *may* lead to regional impoverishment and compromise the equity aspects of sustainable development. Choosing the appropriate geographic unit for sustaining natural capital is further complicated by differences in the spatial extent of natural capital, for example, between location-specific urban water quality in Jakarta and genetic resources of worldwide value. More generally, if some types of natural capital exist in

8 However, for depletable resources, a rising asset price is associated with stock depletion. Merely maintaining the monetary value of natural capital may conceal increasing physical scarcity.

space x and others in space y, and there is depletion in x but augmentation in y, has natural capital remained unchanged?

There is an understandable tendency to think of sustainability in terms of countries, although there is little ethical or ecological justification for doing so. While we may feel special obligations to our fellow countrymen today, our long-term responsibilities to future generations may well transcend national or political identification – a more generalized obligation to humanity. If so, sustainability at the national level has little meaning. If sustainability rules were followed at the national level, an exporting country drawing down its natural capital would have the responsibility for investing an equivalent amount in other forms of capital (weak sustainability), but would have to acquire secure long-term rights to foreign natural capital if it were to meet the strong sustainability rule. With the possibility of war or expropriation, secure rights are not feasible. Setting up sustainability accounts at the national level to measure changes in natural capital stock would be further complicated by the need to attribute to countries a share in global environmental resources. For example, if genetic diversity is an international resource and it is compromised, national accounts of natural capital stocks should be adjusted downward, but by how much? Also, if the strong sustainability rule is in effect, and if the *numeraire* for natural capital is money, terms-of-trade changes for natural resource importers and exporters would have to be accounted for, although some price changes might be quite unrelated to changes in the resource stock. More specifically, a natural-resource-exporting country that interpreted sustainability as keeping its total capital stock intact would need to invest in physical capital an amount *greater* than its depletion of natural capital if it confronted declining terms of trade (Vincent, Panayotou, and Hartwick 1997; Brekke 1997). Finally, if sustainability rules are to be actually implemented, it will be necessary to identify when and where markets fail to maintain natural capital stock and to develop appropriate correctional policies.

4.3 Sustainability of Income and
Intergenerational Equity

The sustainability rules approach described in Section 4.2 can be thought of as placing a constraint on economic actions – finding the set of policies (prices) that will maximize the net present value of the stream of utilities, subject to the constraint that either the stock of capital or the stock of natural capital does not fall. It has a clear ethical dimension – the present generation has an obligation that future generations possess the capital resources to enjoy welfare at least equal to its own. But the order in which sustainability is addressed may matter. In the sustainability rules approach, a discount rate as determined by the present generation is applied to the welfare of future generations, and then the sustainability constraint of maintaining capital and income that is derived from ethical considerations is imposed. It might be more logical to first agree on the ethical question, that is, the just distribution of rights and assets across generations, and then deduce efficiency prices, including the discount rate. In the latter approach, the discount rate is relieved of its intergenerational equity role, and can be reserved for the important task of achieving intertemporal efficiency (Howarth and Norgaard 1990; 1992).

5 Policies for Sustainable Development

It is easier to agree on policies that would contribute to sustainable development than to define the term itself. Examples of unsustainable or at least inefficient or wasteful practices are numerous. Poor irrigation practices lead to waterlogging and salinization of soils and progressively decrease agricultural productivity. Scarce water in the arid West of the United States is used for water-intensive crops such as alfalfa and cotton due to underpricing. The New England cod, haddock, and flounder fisheries have been greatly depleted. Forest concessionaires in tropical countries high-grade the most valuable species without sustainable management practices. Open-access pasture land is overgrazed in Africa and elsewhere. Pollution in many urban areas, especially developing countries, is increasing. Chemical-intensive agriculture in Europe and elsewhere degrades water resources through runoff and contamination of aquifers.

By and large, the roots of these harmful practices are well known and were reviewed in Chapter 4. The policies and policy reforms needed to curb these abusive practices and nudge development in a sustainable direction are also well known, although admittedly difficult to implement. A first step is to reform government policies that contribute to inefficient use of resources. Of these, subsidies are the most prevalent and the most pernicious. These include subsidies for irrigation, industrial, and household water use; subsidized waste water treatment; pesticide, herbicide, and insecticide subsidies; land subsidies, especially for ill-conceived ranching and agricultural colonization schemes; mining subsidies; energy subsidies, especially fossil fuels; and many others. The removal of these subsidies, some of which support other legitimate social objectives, is not easy and will encounter resistance from vested interests.

At a broader level, whole sectors of the economy may be "subsidized," or artificially promoted by industrial and trade policy. If these sectors are characterized by unregulated externalities or place unwarranted pressure on natural resources, the result is either unsustainable or wasteful use of these resources. One example is the attempt by Indonesia in the 1980s to stimulate downstream processing of tropical timber by restricting export of raw logs. Studies have shown the conversion of logs to processed wood products was inefficient by world technology standards, leading to an unnecessarily high rate of log harvesting. Even more broadly, trade/industrial policies favoring industry over agriculture, including export taxes on agricultural goods and tariffs on imported inputs to agriculture, turn the internal terms of trade against agriculture. While this has the effect of reducing returns to agriculture and may reduce heavy fertilizer and pesticide use, in labor-abundant countries it appears to have had a perverse effect. Capital-intensive urban industrial development fails to absorb surplus rural labor, which, for subsistence reasons, exploits the natural resource base through cultivation of fragile soils, shortened fallow periods, overexploitation of coastal fisheries, and so forth (Panayotou 1993). In short, a sustainable development strategy should not stop at the removal of specific subsidies, but must consider the environmental implications of sector policy.

A further step toward sustainable development is for government to establish, clarify, or enforce private property rights, or to strengthen communal property regimes that effectively regulate access. This is particularly important with regard to land. Without secure property rights, farmers have little incentive for land conservation and improvement through terracing, erosion control, rotation of crops, and other sustainable practices. And without secure tenure, they have greater difficulty in securing loans for conservation. In the forestry sector, long-term concessions are a necessary condition for conservation and replanting (Feder et al. 1988; Mendelsohn 1994). Again, the tools for government to improve property rights and their enforcement are well known – granting secure land tenure, zoning, liability regulations, environmental bonding schemes, establishing tradeable quota rights for fisheries, and so forth.

A third step for governments is to correct for obvious market failures, and in particular externalities and the provision of public goods. There are, of course, serious problems in the valuation of externality damages and public goods and in enforcement, as well as the choice of appropriate instruments, all of which were explored in earlier chapters. Implementing these steps requires a thorough integration of economic and environmental analysis at the project, sector, and macroeconomic levels. The most practical and important legacy of introducing the concept of sustainable development may be stronger efforts at integrating economic-environmental analysis and policy. Having said this, internalizing externalities will not be easy, as industry will point to loss of profits, production, and jobs in the shorts run.

The connections between macroeconomic policies and environmental variables has been under-researched.[9] The debt crisis in the 1980s was addressed with restrictive macroeconomic stabilization and structural adjustment programs supported by the International Monetary Fund (IMF) and the World Bank, and a popular view is that servicing the external debt created increased effort by developing countries to export timber, minerals, and other resource-based products. A study of the Philippines by Wilfredo Cruz and Robert Repetto (1992) suggests this is an oversimplification. They found that in fact production in most natural resource sectors actually contracted during the stabilization/structural adjustment period, in part due to weak export demand but in large part due to the stabilization-induced contraction of the domestic economy. There were two more disturbing conclusions, however. First, Philippine output in both the forestry and fisheries sectors declined not only because of sagging demand, but because both had been badly overexploited in the past and their productive capacity was greatly diminished. In this regard, prior unsustainable practices undercut the resiliency of the Philippine economy during the debt crisis. Second, the severe fall in employment and real incomes led to migration to open-access upland and coastal areas, which resulted in severe, negative effects of deforestation, mangrove conversion, and hillside erosion, as well as even greater pressure on inshore fisheries.

6 The International Dimension

The sustainable development movement has had little apparent effect on changing the levels of international development assistance. In this respect, the intragenerational equity component of Brundtland's stricture has had minimal impact. But attention to sustainable development has reinforced a shift in World Bank funding for environmental protection and has encouraged the IMF to consider the environmental effects of its lending and macroeconomic stabilization advice. Sustainable development has also been popularized in an era characterized by accelerating economic integration

---

9 The International Monetary Fund's official interest in the environment began in 1991, and the Fund held its first seminar on the issue in 1993 (Gandhi 1996). In contrast, the World Bank appointed its first environmental advisor in 1970, with a mandate to review all bank lending for adverse environmental effects.

through trade, foreign investment, and technology flows and by increasing scrutiny of the trade-environment nexus, as well as heightened concern for international environmental degradation. Thus it is useful to reflect on the ways in which the international economy contributes to or retards sustainable development.

The most direct channel is, of course, international trade. The relevant feature of trade is that it separates production and consumption in a spatial sense. Hence consumption activities in one country can affect the environment in the country of production. However, as argued in earlier chapters, this simply means that the exporting country should have adequate environmental protection measures in place. There is nothing inherently unsustainable in the trade relation.[10] Indeed, trade is the vehicle through which a local economy can escape the strict requirement of maintaining its natural capital intact. For example, urban areas can thrive by importing the products of natural capital and combining them with the services of physical and human capital to create goods and services of greater value – the essential nature of the gains from trade. But to realize these gains in a sustainable fashion requires the exporting country to internalize the full social costs of its production in the export price.

The same argument holds for foreign investment. While it is certainly possible for foreign investment to enter a country and despoil the environment, it is not a necessary consequence. Again, the principal responsibility rests with the host government in establishing adequate controls on the foreign investor. Both requirements may be difficult to accomplish in a poor country eager for export earnings and other benefits of foreign investment. Also, political and special-interest pressures opposed to full social cost pricing and strict controls on the environmental performance of multinational corporations (MNCs) may be difficult to resist. There may be scope for international arrangements that assist. These might include simultaneous introduction of minimum environmental protection regulations by principal exporting countries and codes of conduct for MNC environmental performance. But the main point remains. A country is unlikely to achieve sustainable development by selling its products in world markets at less than social costs or by inviting foreign investment to plunder its environment.

There are complications to this simple prescription. One involves transnational externalities. Just as trade separates production and consumption in a spatial sense, transnational externalities separate the activities that generate the externality from those individuals, groups, or countries that bear the

---

10 However, trade requires transportation and transportation is often polluting.

burden. Recall that the externality may occur in either production *or* consumption. Thus it is possible that one country, in internalizing the full social cost to itself of its production or correcting for the external cost to itself of its consumption, may fail to include international interests in its calculus. As pointed out in Chapter 13, this problem is compounded because there is no environmental agency to protect the broader international interest, and international environmental law is not well developed. In this context, international trade may exacerbate unsustainable production and consumption activities by increasing total world output and consumption. It is also possible that trade shifts the location of production toward countries less inclined to internalize international externalities, or countries with open-access natural resource regimes and excessive exploitation levels. For example, U.S. restrictions on domestic logging, mining, and oil exploration and development or Japan's domestic forest conservation practices may shift resource exploitation pressure to developing countries. This would be the raw material analogue of industrial relocation to pollution havens, about which there has been much speculation. In general, however, the environmental costs of such shifts would be borne by the country of production, so the previous point remains relevant – the producing country has principal responsibility for ensuring the appropriate level of environmental protection. When transnational pollution is present, however, one cannot rely on narrow national interest, and some control on relocating polluting activity through trade and foreign investment may be justified. Also, governments are tempted toward policies that shift social costs onto future generations and under these circumstances trade and foreign investment can contribute to unsustainability.

Another trade issue in the context of transnational externalities is the desirability of using trade measures to repair the deficiencies in international environmental governance. It is clear that sustainable development will require measures that go beyond the narrow self-interest of individual countries. As explored in previous chapters, trade restrictions may be needed to secure compliance with MEAs and discourage free riders. Trade and sustainability are linked in yet another way. Trade increases specialization of production within countries and regions of countries. Specialization promotes *monocultures* and the spatial concentration of industry. Monocultures are the antithesis of ecological sustainability – the diversity and resiliency of ecosystems. Concentration and specialization in production is more likely to overwhelm local assimilative capacity. Industrial scale farming of poultry and hogs is a good example. Some concentration of production result from purely domestic trade, but international trade is an increasingly important factor. The long-term implications for environmental stability from globalization of trade and investment remains an open question.

It would be unproductive to conclude this chapter with yet another definition of sustainable development. But there does appear to be sufficient unity to identify three threads that bind the different interpretations. First, the concept of sustainability knits together ecological and environmental systems – natural resources broadly defined – with economic systems. Second, sustainable development reflects a concern for inter- and intragenerational efficiency *and* equity in the use and conservation of natural resources. Third, sustainable development implicitly acknowledges that past and present patterns of economic development have neglected economic-environmental interactions and emphasizes that corrective measures must integrate environmental considerations into conventional economic planning and policy.

17

Measuring Sustainable Development

1 Introduction

This chapter analyzes two issues in the measurement of sustainable development. The first is revising national income accounting to better reflect interactions between economic and environmental systems. The second is the empirical evidence supporting the inverted U hypothesis, which purportedly links environmental indices to per capita income.

Before starting, it is useful to reemphasize that with its multiple and often ambiguous definitions, sustainable development defies measure by a single index.[1] As noted in the previous chapter, even a limited requirement for sustainable development, such as maintaining the stock of natural capital, confronts formidable measurement difficulties: Is the stock to be measured in physical or value units? Over what geographic or political unit is the stock to be maintained? How can depletion or degradation of one form of natural capital, say, biological diversity, be made commensurate with improvements in, say, air quality? Even more fundamentally, if natural capital is valued by the flow of income it generates, how is that flow to be discounted?

Less ambitious attempts to measure aspects of sustainable development can, however, contribute to improved public policy. A preliminary step involves collecting better primary data on the quantity and quality of environmental resource stocks and flows, monetizing these data when feasible,

---

1 If sustainable development is defined narrowly as no decrease in real consumption over time, then an indicator of sustainability is whether gross savings in period t, S_t, exceed depreciation, depletion, and degradation of physical, human, and natural capital during that time period, or

$$S_t \geq \alpha_1 k_P + \alpha_2 k_H + \alpha_3 k_N,$$

where P, H, and N indicate types of capital, and α_1, α_2, and α_3 represent the fraction of the capital lost in that time period. Methods for calculating these variables have not yet been perfected, although some rough estimates are available. See Pearce and Atkinson (1995).

and constructing physical and monetary indices. The results can be used directly for resource management and policy and for testing theoretical propositions linking economic and environmental systems. Also, a "greening" of corporate accounting is taking hold in the business sector. Better data and expanded accounting systems should improve a firm's management of its environmental inputs and outputs. If made public, the accounts should also improve outside surveillance.[2]

Improved data collection should proceed together with the revision of accounting systems or, when necessary, the development of new ones. And accounting systems should be consistent with theory, which guides the choice of what is to be measured. The national income and product accounts are the principal measures of aggregate economic activity. They were developed before the current attention to sustainable development and were not designed to measure economic-environmental interactions. They are, however, widely used not only as a measure of economic activity but as a measure of economic performance and, in a loose sense, economic welfare. The relevant question is whether and how national income and product accounts can be revised to better capture economic-environmental interactions and thus contribute to sustainable development policies.

A full set of national accounts includes asset accounts, which measure stocks and changes in stocks, and flow accounts, which measure output and income in an accounting period. We concentrate on the latter – gross domestic product (GDP), net domestic product (NDP), net national product (NNP), and national income. The reason is that asset accounts are less frequently constructed, and the flow accounts are more widely used as measures of economic performance and economic welfare. If the flow measures are flawed, policy and management mistakes are more likely simply because they are more widely used.

Section 2 explores two aspects of revising the national accounts: the treatment of so-called defensive expenditures and the adjustment of the accounts for depletion or degradation of natural capital. Section 3 follows with a description of three empirical studies that attempt to modify traditional national accounts. The final section shifts gears and examines evidence of

---

2 The ISO 14000 series, described in Chapter 10, is establishing standards for firms for environmental audits, labelling, and life-cycle assessment. Both the Montreal Protocol and the Framework Convention on Climate Change contain reporting requirements that are improving data collection. In the United States, the Environmental Protection Agency collects and disseminates a very large database by industrial plant and by pollutant in its Toxic Release Inventory. But, as noted in Chapter 12, the U.S. Department of Commerce has discontinued its valuable data series on pollution-abatement costs.

the inverted U hypothesis, which suggests that in the longer run economic growth and environmental protection are compatible and reinforcing. An appendix contains the math underlying the user cost and net price methods of calculating depletion of natural capital.

2 Revising National Income Accounts: A Green NNP?

Accounting systems are management systems. If they do not accurately measure what they purport to measure, mistakes in management and policy result. Recent concern for the environment and sustainability has prompted two main objections to traditional national income and product accounts. One criticism is that the statistics include some expenditures that defend against environmental damages occurring during production, but that do not themselves contribute directly to welfare. The specific charge is that some environmental expenditures are defensive and should be treated as expenditures on intermediate, not final, goods and services. By failing to strip out these defensive expenditures, the national accounts overstate true income and welfare.

The second criticism is that the traditional accounts fail to include depletion of natural and environmental resources and residual environmental damages, and therefore present an inaccurate and inflated picture of income, output, and economic growth. Because of greater natural resource dependance, this second criticism, neglect of natural resource depletion, is most often considered in the context of developing countries, but is also relevant for rich countries. The questionable inclusions and exclusions take on added importance because the national accounts are widely used to assess economic performance over time and among countries. These two criticisms delineate the two types of adjustments to national accounts that have been suggested: a more consistent and accurate treatment of environmental defensive expenditures and a more consistent and accurate treatment of depletion of natural capital and residual environmental damages. These criticisms led the United Nations Statistical Office, which has long encouraged the standardization of national accounting systems within its System of National Accounts (SNAs), to publish in 1993 revised SNA guidelines for integrating environmental and economic accounts. The new guidelines are known as SEEA, the System of (integrated) Environmental and Economic Accounts (United Nations 1993). Some national statistical agencies are revising and expanding their accounts to conform to the new guidelines.

2.1 A Confusion of Purposes

Before concluding that traditional SNAs are deficient and need modification, it is useful to sort through their purposes and uses. Historically, the main purpose for the accounts has been for short- and medium-term macroeconomic policy, and, in particular, aggregate demand management. The SNAs are well suited for this purpose. Income and product accounts concentrate on marketed goods and services subject to monetary (market) demand, and ultimately to fiscal and monetary policy. The main exceptions to the market test are government expenditures, the value of whose services is assumed to be equal to their cost, and owner-occupied housing, whose value is imputed. The principal subaccounts – national income and outlay, government receipts and expenditures, savings and investment, personal income and outlay, and foreign transactions – correspond to variables typically found in macroeconomic demand management models, which is not surprising as policy modelling and accounting matured together. The SNAs have proved useful for analyzing trends in aggregate economic activity, business cycles, and the use of macroeconomic tools such as monetary, fiscal, and exchange rate policies. When linked to input-output tables, they can trace the impact of policy on specific sectors. Also, the emphasis on marketed goods and services accords with Pigou's injunction that economists restrict themselves "to that part of social welfare that can be brought directly or indirectly into relation with the measuring rod of money" (Pigou 1932, p. 11). This positive experience with traditional accounts suggests caution in revisions, and the new SEEA makes extensive use of satellite accounts for environmental entries, so that the core accounts can maintain their integrity and traditional functions.

But the national accounts also purport to measure *aggregate income* and have come to serve as measures of *economic performance* and *economic welfare*. At a high level of abstraction and under certain restrictive assumptions, including following an optimal growth path, it can be shown that the theoretical concept of NNP is indeed income in the sense that Hicks employed the term national income – the maximum amount of consumption possible while leaving wealth intact (Weitzman 1976).[3] It should be pointed out that there is a fundamental difference between net national

---

3 As Hartwick and Hageman (1993) point out, if national wealth, $W(t)$, is the present value of the optimal consumption stream through time, then it can be shown that

$$NNP(t) = pW(t)$$

where p is the rate of return to capital. Solving for the optimal consumption path requires techniques derived from optimal control theory. See also Hicks (1946).

product as calculated in this abstract exercise and actual practice. The former requires "shadow" or accounting prices derived from inter- and intratemporal optimization models that accurately reflect economic scarcity. The latter measures market or transactions prices, which is appropriate for economic management. If net national product were calculated on the basis of shadow prices, it would be a better measure of Hicksian income but probably a worse measure for most economic policy management purposes. The two would only converge in a highly idealized economy – perfect competition, no policy-induced distortions (e.g., taxes), perfect knowledge and foresight, and so forth. However, the fact that net product measured at actual transactions prices is not the same as an idealized net product measured at hypothetical shadow prices is no reason not to adjust for the depletion of natural resources if plausible estimates of depletion are available. Such adjustment would subtract the depletion from gross output to derive a new, adjusted net product. That adjusted net product would still diverge from "true" or Hicksian income by the amount that actual transaction prices depart from "shadow" or efficiency prices.

National income and product accounts are also used for international comparisons of economic performance. If they are flawed as measures of income, the comparisons are likely to be flawed. One technical difficulty in comparing per capita income levels is choosing the appropriate exchange rate for converting national currencies. Market or official exchange rates can distort real per capita income differences, especially when there are systematic differences in the price of nontradeable goods, when trade barriers are pervasive, or when capital flows are large. This can be partially corrected by using purchasing power parity exchange rates, although these calculations are complex and are always approximations. International comparisons of income growth rates do not require currency conversions, but do require consistency and accuracy among countries in deflating nominal income to estimate real income.

It is with respect to measuring welfare that national accounts display their greatest weakness. Herein lies a dilemma. On the one hand, national income accounts (and accountants) do not purport to measure welfare. At best, they (imperfectly) measure income. Welfare is a normative concept and in principle income (output) is an objective concept. On the other hand, and for better or worse, national income and output statistics are *de facto* widely used as indices of welfare. The dilemma is whether to insist that national accounts *not* be used as welfare measures, or to accept that they are so used and modify them to bring them closer to measuring welfare. National income (output) and economic welfare are not, of course, totally unrelated.

One could *define* welfare as the present value of society's current and future consumption, in which case, and assuming a theoretically perfect and distortion-free economy, net product is the present value of future consumption and indeed becomes a measure of welfare. But the equivalence of national income and welfare is then an artifact of the *definition* of welfare and the implicit social welfare function. Any other social welfare function that gave additional weight to income to the poor, incorporated the value of leisure and the disutility of work, placed a value on economic security (e.g., the stability of employment), or attempted to value political freedom or physical security would sever the link between national income (product) and welfare.[4]

To summarize, traditional SNAs have been very satisfactory for measuring short-run economic activity and for aggregate demand management. They are less satisfactory for assessing and comparing economic performance because of deficiencies in measuring sustainable income and in particular because of their neglect of depletion of natural capital. They are also widely used as indices of welfare, although they do not purport to measure welfare. The task is to "green" the accounts without unduly departing from their traditional transactions basis or undermining their role in macroeconomic management. This task is complicated because of subtle variations in the purposes of the modifications – to nudge the accounts toward better measurement of sustainable income, make them better measures of welfare, or make them better tools for environmental management. With this background, we turn first to the issue of environmental defensive expenditures and then to depletion of natural capital.

2.2 Defensive Expenditures

As currently compiled, the national accounts are not consistent with respect to defensive expenditures. Specifically, environmental defensive expenditures that mitigate pollution damages and that are made by firms are considered as purchases of intermediate goods and services, whereas similar defensive expenditures by households and government are considered purchases of final goods and services. Consider, for example, three methods for dealing with noise pollution from truck traffic, all assumed to be equally effective – sophisticated muffler systems installed by trucking firms, installation of double-glazed windows by homeowners, and erection of sound barriers by local government. Under current national accounting

---

4 Some expenditures on physical security do get included in the national accounts.

procedures, the expenditures made by trucking firms would be treated as a cost of production (purchase of intermediate goods) and would reduce value added in the trucking sector.[5] Because national income and output are the sum of value added in various industries, it is clear that the pollution-abatement expenditure would not be treated as part of output of final goods and services. This seems appropriate as the expenditure reflects a cost of production.[6]

In contrast, double-glazing by homeowners is treated as an expenditure on final goods and services and would inflate the national income and output accounts. One might argue that the activity of producing and installing the glass does not contribute to national income or welfare in any positive way, it merely moderates harm from a production externality. In this light, the double-glazing is also in the nature of an intermediate good reflecting a cost of production, although undertaken by the homeowner rather than the trucking company. If it were treated as an intermediate good, measured output of final goods and services (GDP, NDP) would be lower than currently reported and would be a more accurate measure of welfare. The asymmetry is also present in national, state, and local government expenditures on pollution abatement (e.g., the government-installed sound barrier), which are also treated as final goods and services. As with the homeowner's defensive expenditure, one could argue that these government expenditures are in the nature of intermediate goods and, if treated as such, they would reduce measured GDP, NDP, and national income. The treatment of indirect costs of production is not a new issue. Simon Kuznets, a pioneer of national income accounting, suggested decades ago that expenditures consequent to an urban pattern of living (e.g., commuter costs) and the major part of government activity are intermediate rather than final expenditures.

Thus there appears to be an asymmetry in the treatment of expenditures mitigating production externalities – if done by firms, they are not counted as part of the output of final goods and services (GDP and NDP), whereas if done by governments or individuals they do show up in GDP and NDP. If these expenditures were deleted, the accounts would better reflect Hicksian income (goods and services available for consumption after leaving wealth intact) and presumably welfare. On reflection, however, there are

---

5 *Value added* is defined as sales minus purchases of intermediate inputs. Of course, value added in the muffler sector may increase, but in a fully employed economy increased output of mufflers merely shifts resources and output away from other sectors.

6 Increased expenditure on pollution abatement *may* reduce investment in new productive capacity and reduce measured GDP in the future. But if the pollution abatement sustains the productivity of environmental capacity whose services enter production functions, GDP is also sustained. In any event, the possible diversion of resources away from conventional investment to environmental protection is a separate issue.

several problems with attempting to strip out defensive expenditures made by consumers and governments. First, it is difficult to draw a line between consumer expenditures that are an indirect cost of producing goods and services and those that make a positive contribution to welfare and probably should be considered expenditures on final goods and services. Double-glazing might simultaneously defend against truck noise and also reduce heating bills. Defending against nature (winter) by home heating is not a cost of production but is properly considered expenditure on final goods. In other words, it would be necessary to distinguish between consumer expenditures designed to negate a cost of production and consumer expenditures that do not. For example, many consumer expenditures to maintain health are in effect protecting against harm, but they are correctly viewed in the national accounts as expenditures on final goods.

Second, the adjustment in a particular accounting period would have to be linked to *incremental* environmental damage during that period. Consider, for example, a steady flow of environmental disamenities from production and an individual who now chooses to protect himself or herself with a defensive expenditure. Surely his or her welfare is increased. To subtract that expenditure from national product would indicate reduced welfare, an incorrect adjustment. The same logic holds for a remedial expenditure by government, for example, cleanup of old waste dumpsites. Such an expenditure represents an investment in a productive asset, the improved land, and is properly part of GDP and NDP. These examples imply that if household and government defensive expenditures were to be stripped out, a baseline stock of environmental assets and flow of disamenities would have to be established and only expenditures made to offset changes in those stocks and flows would be charged against output and income in the current accounting period.[7]

There is a third problem. If the measure of national income were to be stripped of consumer defensive environmental expenditures, it would be logical to also include in income the positive flow of services derived from nature. To some extent this is done when the flow of services enters production functions, although nature is not explicitly credited. Property-type income – rent and profits – include a return to natural capital, which Ricardo called "the original and indestructible powers of the soil," and which more recently has been recognized as the valuable waste disposal service provided by the environment. But environmental services that directly enter utility

7 Furthermore, reclassifying consumer-defensive expenditure would drive a wedge between the product-side value of GDP and the income-side value of GDP, and the current consistency between product expenditures and income would be lost.

functions are not accounted for. The failure to include positive services produced by nature and consumed by households is not unlike the exclusion of services produced and consumed within the household sector. The exclusion is partly for practical reasons of measurement and valuation. In any event, it is not clear that an asymmetrical treatment of adjusting national income downward for defensive expenditures and not adjusting it upward for directly consumed environmental services would nudge national accounts closer to a true measure of either income or welfare.

A final practical and conceptual problem in national accounts is how to treat changes in consumer product characteristics resulting from environmental regulation. Consider, for example, auto emission regulations that have led manufacturers to install catalytic converters. The question is whether to treat the resulting cost and price increase as a price change or a quality change. If the former is chosen, nominal GDP is deflated to obtain real or inflation-adjusted GDP. If the latter is chosen, as it has been in the United States, the cost increase is presumed to reflect improved quality and no adjustment is made to the nominal value of auto sector output or actual consumer expenditures on autos. Thus reported real GDP is higher. However, from a welfare perspective, at least part of the incremental cost in autos is defending against *increased* pollution and does not represent a positive increase in welfare. Measured GDP is greater than a true measure of welfare even if the underlying regulations pass a strict cost-benefit test. But the reduced emissions may also lead to an *improvement* in air quality as compared to the previous accounting period. In that event, real welfare increases and, unless captured elsewhere as an entry for improvement in directly consumed environmental services (which do not currently exist), some portion of the incremental cost and price is properly counted as an element in national income. The same issue arises when considering whether reformulated gasoline should be treated as a price change or quality improvement. Conceptually, one would wish to distinguish between that portion of the expenditure that maintains welfare in the accounting period and that portion that improves welfare. But it is not practical to do so.

To summarize, it is intuitively appealing to try to strip defensive expenditures out of final goods and services and treat them as intermediate expenditures. This is, in fact, done when the expenditures are made by the business sector. To do so for households and government, however, would involve arbitrary and subjective judgements and would nudge the accounts away from their current transactions basis. It is questionable whether the revised accounts would lead to better environmental management.

2.3 Depletion of Natural Capital

The crux of the natural resource capital stock problem can be simply stated. Following Hicks, an economic definition of national income is "the maximum amount that can be consumed in a given period without reducing the amount of possible consumption in a future period" (El Serafy and Lutz 1989, p. 2). This implies that in calculating *sustainable* income, changes in the value of capital that produces income must be adjusted for. Thus there should be entries deducting depreciation, depletion, or degradation of capital (productive assets) from gross output. But there is an asymmetrical treatment of physical, human, and natural capital in SNAs. Depreciation of physical capital is subtracted from GDP to obtain NDP, but by and large there is no similar adjustment for the depletion or degradation of natural capital (or for that matter changes in the stock of human capital).[8] Thus with traditional SNAs the liquidation of renewable and nonrenewable natural resources is recorded as income, distorting the true performance of the economy and contributing to poor resource management decisions.

The need to adjust gross output for depreciation is not a new idea. Adam Smith, writing in 1776, captured the notion of sustainable income and depreciation long before the official compilation of national accounts:

The gross revenue of all the inhabitants of a great country comprehends the whole annual produce of their land and labor; the neat [net] revenue, what remains free to them after the expense of maintaining; first their fixed; and second, their circulating capital; or what, without encroaching upon their capital, they can place in their stock reserved for immediate consumption, or spend upon their subsistence, conveniences, and amusements. Their real wealth too is in proportion, not to their gross, but to their neat revenue (in El Serafy 1989, p. 11).

Pigou also anticipated by 60 years recent calls to revise national income accounts to include depletion of natural capital. In his view, the "national dividend," his term for net national product, will fall short of aggregate output by the amount that agriculture "wastes the productive powers of the soil," and a deduction from aggregate output should be made for the value of minerals used during the accounting period (properly measured by their royalties). Indeed, he anticipates the notion of (weak) sustainability when he asserts that the value of minerals consumed or exported for the importation of consumption goods should be deducted from aggregate output to

---

8 Between 1942 and 1947 the U.S. national accounts did adjust GDP downward for depletion of mineral resources when calculating NDP. But no entries were made for additions to stocks of mineral resources. This asymmetric treatment led to dropping the depletion entry.

determine the national dividend, but minerals embodied in capital goods or that are exported for the importation of capital goods should not be subtracted (Pigou 1932, p. 39). While there is general agreement on the desirability of correcting this defect, there is less agreement on how that should be done.

Which Types of Environmental Capital Should Be Adjusted? One question centers on which types of environmental capital should be adjusted in deriving net national product or national income. The case for including nonrenewable, commercialized mineral resources is strongest on practical grounds, in part because changes in physical stocks can be relatively easily measured – barrels of oil pumped or tons of ore mined – and in part because monetized market data on stocks and flows are more readily available. Adjusting for changes in the stock value of commercialized renewable resources such as fisheries, forests, and agricultural land, which also can be "mined," is more problematic. Market data on the value of stocks are less available – many are not under private ownership. Prices that are available may be substantially distorted by common property ownership. Moreover, biological regeneration functions for fisheries and forests may be uncertain, but necessary, if stock changes are to be measured. Also, depleted renewable resources are more likely to exhibit salvage value – deforested land *may* convert to productive agricultural land – and it would be the *net* loss of asset value, if any, not the gross, that would be needed for adjusting GDP. Nevertheless, depletion of renewable resources is widely considered to be a prime source of *unsustainable* development, and the new SEEA recognizes the desirability of making this adjustment. Finally, adjusting for degradation of noncommercialized environmental capital – waste disposal services, basic ecological functions, and the positive but nonmonetized contribution of the environment to utility and conventional production – poses the most difficult problems. Consider, for example, an accounting period that opened with a certain index level of biological diversity and closed with a lower level. What monetary correction to GDP should be entered to obtain a more accurate measure of national income? More fundamentally, would such revisions of national accounts contribute in any direct way to the institutional and policy changes necessary to protect biological diversity? Rather than burying the loss of biological diversity in aggregate national accounts, would it be better to publicize the loss in some separate accounts?

Natural Capital as Inventory or Fixed Assets There is some debate over whether natural capital should be considered as "inventory" or "fixed assets." In traditional national income accounting, a reduction in the inventory in the current period of, say, autos produced but not sold in the previous accounting period shows up as a reduction in gross and net investment and hence is subtracted from GDP. This allows gross production in the current accounting period to equal gross expenditure on final goods in that period. In contrast, the loss of physical productive capacity or economic value of, say, machinery during the current accounting period is considered "capital consumption" or in common usage, depreciation. The GDP figure is not itself changed because GDP is supposed to measure gross output. But to obtain NDP the capital consumption is subtracted from GDP. In this fashion, NDP is a measure of output available for consumption or new investment.

Natural capital, say, ore in the ground, was not produced in the previous accounting period, but it can be physically depleted by mining in the current period. This suggests that it is closer to fixed assets than inventories. But if depletion of mineral assets were treated the same as depreciation of physical capital, the goal of using national accounts as measures of sustainiblility would be compromised in two respects, according to some analysts. First, the GDP remains untouched and GDP remains the most widely used measure of economic performance. This is a weak argument. GDP is a measure of gross output; NDP is or should be a measure of sustainable production and income. To fiddle with GDP and undermine its integrity simply because it is more widely cited than NDP seems perverse.[9] Second and more legitimately, the simple subtraction from GDP of the net value of natural resources consumed within the accounting period (a capital consumption allowance for natural resources) would produce a NDP that does not necessarily accurately measure sustainable income. For example, in a completely oil-dependent economy, the sale of $1 billion of oil in the accounting period would show up as GDP of $1 billion and NDP of zero (neglecting extraction costs). The implication of zero NDP is that no positive level of current consumption is sustainable. But it is clear that the country could sustain some positive level of income *if* a portion of the receipts were invested in assets with a positive return. This example underscores the issue of whether

---

9 All this depends on what uses GDP and NDP were put to. If the *sole* purpose was to alert policy makers to inefficient resource use, and if the only statistic they looked at was GDP, then one might wish to offer both GDP as currently measured, and GDP adjusted downward by the amount that current resource use departs from optimal use. The discrepancy would then be a measure of nonoptimality in resource use. The downward adjustment would be the net present value of the deviation of future GNPs from their optimal as a result of current resource use practices. For a method of calculation, see Devarajan and Weiner (1995). By this logic, of course, the entire set of national accounts could be cleaned up so that they reflected what an ideal economy with no distortions of any sort might look like.

the national accounts should be concerned with maintaining productive capacity, in which case it is appropriate to list NDP as zero, or with sustainable income, in which case NDP would be positive. This example brings us to the *user cost* versus *net price* question.

Valuing and Adjusting for Depletion of Natural Capital As explained in Appendix 17.1, there is a general agreement that the depletion or degradation of natural capital as a result of production should be adjusted for, and this depletion can be measured by the cost to replace the natural capital used up in production. For nonrenewable resources, this is reasonably clear – oil is pumped, ore is mined, and *ceteris paribus* physical stocks are depleted. The reduction in physical reserves must then be translated into value terms. For monetized renewable resources, the notion is still reasonably clear – the harvest of wood or fish may exceed regeneration, and the physical stock is depleted. In principle, the degradation of nonmonetized natural capital – loss of biodiversity, the role of ecosystems in nutrient recycling, directly consumed environmental services, and assimilation of wastes – should also be monetized, and that portion of degradation attributable to production should be charged against gross output.

Two approaches have been followed in adjusting national accounts for the depletion of natural resources (El Serafy 1989; Hartwick and Hageman 1993; Repetto, Magrath, Wells, Beer, and Rossini 1989). The *user cost* method proposed by El Serafy divides a constant finite stream of net receipts from resource sales, R (i.e., gross receipts less all extraction costs), into two components, that portion which represents true income, X, and that portion, R−X, which, if reinvested at interest rate r, would accumulate to an amount sufficient to generate a constant income of X in perpetuity. In essence, this converts a finite steam of receipts from the depletable resource into an infinite stream of income. In the national accounts, the income portion, X, would be included in GDP, but the user cost, R−X, would be excluded from GDP as it represents a liquidation of assets, not true output and income. (The SNA treatment has been to include all of R in GDP.) While the user cost approach identifies the income component of resource receipts (X) and the user cost or capital consumption element (R−X), there is nothing in the analytical method that obliges the country to set aside a portion of the receipts for investment and the perpetual maintenance of income. The finite stream of receipts might be fully used for current consumption, in which case consumption would exceed *sustainable* income. The user cost method simply calculates the amount needed as a sinking fund to provide a perpetual annuity, but does not require its establishment. With constant net receipts of

R over T years (the lifetime of the oil or mineral resource) the ratio of true income X to total receipts is[10]

$$\frac{X}{R} = 1 - \frac{1}{(1+r)^T}$$

The data requirements of the user cost approach appear minimal – gross receipts and full extraction costs to estimate R, the appropriate discount rate (which in a perfect market is the marginal productivity of capital; see Chapter 4), and the ratio of the current extraction rate to total reserves to calculate the lifetime, T. Note that either a slower extraction rate (larger T) or a higher estimated return on the alternative investment, r, increases the fraction of receipts that should be considered true income. If desired, an adjustment could be made for rising extraction costs which would be reflected in decreasing R over time and thus shorten economic lifetime. New discoveries could be accommodated by extending the lifetime or adjusting upward the extraction rate, either one of which would have the effect of increasing income. However, this method departs from traditions in national income accounting that attempt to use market prices for assets. The user cost method attempts to measure the true income potential of depletable resources, not their market value.

A second approach known as the *net price* method treats the full net receipts or rent from natural resource sales, R, as a cost of production (Repetto et al. 1989). Using this method, depletion of natural capital during an accounting period is calculated by determining the unit price of the resource less all marginal per unit extraction costs, including the cost of the physical capital employed, and multiplying that net return (rent) per unit times the quantity of the resource extracted. As shown in Appendix 17.1, the decrease in the value of the natural resource during the accounting period is equal to the net receipts,

$$\Delta V - = - R.$$

That amount can then be considered a "resource depletion cost" and, together with the depreciation of man-made capital, subtracted from GDP

---

10 A numerical example may be useful. Assume a mine yielding net annual revenue of $1,000 over four years, after which it is fully exhausted, and assume opportunities to invest at 10 percent in perpetuity. Then solving for X,

$$X = 316.99$$

$$R - X = 683.01$$

If $683.01 per year is saved and invested at 10 percent over four years, it cumulates to $3,169.80, which then reinvested at 10 percent yields a perpetual income stream of $316.99.

to obtain a more accurate estimate of NDP.[11] One comment on both methods is the technical difficulty of disentangling the return to physical capital employed in extractive sectors from the rent to the resource itself.[12]

The choice between the two methods, user cost and net price, has theoretical and practical aspects. The user cost method has been shown to be theoretically correct – that is, it produces an accurate measure of the change in the value of the capital asset and hence can be used to determine sustainable income from resource sales – if the flow of net receipts (rents) is constant (Hartwick and Hageman 1993). But rent depends in part on price and in part on marginal extraction costs, which for a depletable resource are expected to change over time. In this sense, the user cost method rests on rather arbitrary assumptions about the time profile of receipts. Also, the underlying assumption is that natural resources can be extracted and converted to some other financial or real asset at a constant rate of return. While this may be true for a small entity – a single mine or a small producing country in the world oil market – and for a limited time, it begs a central question of sustainability: can natural capital be converted to physical or human capital without eroding its return and hence its value?

The net price method has been shown to be theoretically correct if the rent is rising over time at the rate of interest and unit extraction costs are uniform and constant. Under certain restrictive assumptions, Hotelling's rule concludes that the rental earned on the marginal unit of the resource extracted will indeed increase at the rate of interest, but empirical evidence that the rule obtains in the real world is slim. Also, if marginal extraction costs rise over time as less productive grades of ore are mined, the net price method overstates depletion costs. More broadly, unless there are significant new discoveries, the user cost method will produce a higher NDP than the net price method because a portion of the receipts from exploitation are considered income. In the net price method, that portion shows up in revaluation of assets but not in the flow accounts.

It should also be pointed out that both methods, while developed in the context of nonrenewable resources (e.g., mineral deposits), have been applied to renewable resources such as timber and soils.[13] The assumption

---

11 Care must be taken to properly account for salvage values. If a forest is cut and converted to agricultural production, focusing exclusively on the depletion of *forest* resources would neglect the value of newly created agricultural capital.

12 For various methods, see Carson and Landefeld (1994).

13 El Serafy cautions against the user-cost method for renewables on the grounds that resources such as fisheries are subject to open-access problems and overfishing. In that event, he suggests that a conservative approach would be to leave GDP untouched and consider the entire depletion as appropriate to subtract when calculating the NNP. This is the net-price method. (El Serafy 1991, pp. 205–219.)

is that these resources are in practice being depleted or mined. While such calculations are useful in drawing attention to the discrepancies between traditionally measured and sustainable income, they do not themselves point to optimal exploitation policies, as, for example, do the maximum sustainable economic yield models of fisheries. Put somewhat differently, if renewable resources were optimally managed, in many cases there would be neither a user cost nor a depletion charge as the productivity would not be impaired. The net output in the accounting period would be gifts of nature captured by the state through license fees or possibly by private owners. Also, neither method is easily used for degradation of natural capital whose services are not marketed and for which market prices are not available. In that event, the derivation of shadow prices indicating the economic or scarcity value of this type of natural capital would be desirable. The degradation of such capital is costed in the expanded national accounts, SEEA, at their potential restoration or avoidance costs or by contingent valuation methods.

For completeness, we should mention as an alternative to the user cost and net price methods a proposal by Hueting and others that would calculate a hypothetical GDP if appropriate environmental protection and resource conservation measures were undertaken, and which then could be compared to actual measured GDP. The comparison would highlight how far an economy "has drifted away from sustainable economic development" (Hueting 1989, p. 37). The approach is pragmatic rather than theoretical and reflects the view that correct economic (shadow) prices for many environmental functions cannot be determined. To calculate the hypothetical GDP requires estimates of monetary expenditures that would be necessary to meet physical standards for maintaining the availability and quality of environmental functions. The standards would be based on health considerations and sustainable use of renewable resources. The use of nonrenewable resources would be valued at the cost of alternatives and substitutes – i.e., renewable energy as a substitute for fossil fuel use. The main drawback to this scheme from an economic perspective is that the standards would be arbitrary. There is no reason to believe that the benefits of protection and restoration are measured by their costs. It follows that the hypothetical GDP would neither measure economic activity nor necessarily income. Nevertheless, the Hueting approach would be one way of measuring the costs of a "strong" sustainability policy.

There are further complications in accounting for natural capital depletion. As pointed out in Chapter 15, on fisheries, renewable resources under open-access regimes tend to dissipate the resource rent. Market prices for, say, fish are distorted. If the resource stock is declining, the calculation of resource depletion to be subtracted from GDP to arrive at a corrected NDP will be distorted. NDP is then a less accurate measure of sustainable income and welfare. In principle, one could calculate a hypothetical level of national income that would be achieved if resources were being used optimally, but that benchmark would fail to measure true income produced under market distorted conditions. It might be more productive to concentrate research on sector-specific, optimal management problems rather than try to fold this complication into national accounts. Another complication arises from the choice of discount (interest) rates. The user cost method requires an explicit choice of rates; the net price method assumes resource rents increase at the rate of interest. Both implicitly assume the discount or interest rate is exogenous. But as discussed in Chapter 4, the market interest rate may be distorted precisely because the return to physical capital investment does not adjust for unsustainable use of natural resources.

Finally, most of the discussions of revising national income accounts to obtain better measures of income by adjusting for depletion of natural capital take a national perspective. But there are at least two international aspects to consider. First, if revision of SNAs does lead to policy changes that conserve natural capital, this should improve the terms of trade of natural resource exporters. Either slowing the rate of mineral extraction or preserving wilderness and wildlife for international tourism should increase net receipts from natural capital. In principle, anticipated changes in the terms of trade resulting from current economic activities should also be included in measures of national income. Second, a full integration of environment into national accounts would have to incorporate transnational pollution. In a narrow sense, if some of the costs of production can be shunted to other countries, net domestic product and national income for the polluting country will increase, and the national income of receiving countries will decrease. But this parochial perspective is essentially a beggar-thy-neighbor strategy and inconsistent with global environmental values. To be operational, it would require a matrix of monetized transnational environmental spillovers.

3 Some Examples of Green Accounting

There are now some 35 published studies that have attempted to "green" national income accounting in one fashion or another. They are difficult to compare and summarize because their purpose, scope, methodology,

assumptions, and presentation differ widely. As an alternative to an unsatisfactory synthesis, we provide a brief summary of three quite different
studies: (1) an accounting for mineral resources in the United States within
the new Integrated Economic and Environmental Satellite Accounts
(IEESA) prepared by the U.S. Commerce Department's Bureau of
Economic Analysis (BEA) and authored by Carol Carson and Steven
Landefeld; (2) a report analyzing natural resource depreciation in a relatively advanced developing country, Costa Rica, prepared by the Tropical
Science Center in Costa Rica and World Resources Institute, a pioneer in
green national accounting; and (3) a preliminary and tentative exploration
of integrating environmental accounting (the application of SEEA) to
Papua New Guinea, a country that is both natural resource dependent and
at an early stage of development (Carson and Landefeld 1994; Cruz and
Repetto 1991; Bartelmus, Lutz, and Schweinfest 1993).

3.1 U.S. Mineral Resources

The U.S. Department of Commerce study attempts to estimate the asset
value of U.S. mineral resources – additions, depletions, and revaluations –
for oil, gas, coal, and metals for the period 1947 (or in some cases 1958)
to 1991. Four different valuation methods for resource stocks and stock
changes were employed: current rent, net present discounted value (the
range of the discount rate being 3 to 10 percent), a replacement cost technique, and a transactions price method that measures the value of reserves
by what firms pay to acquire new proven reserves. The BEA rejected
the user-cost method because it is more of a welfare-oriented measure
than a market transaction measure, which has been the traditional SNA
approach.

Some of the more interesting results are:

1 The value of additions to mineral stocks has tended to exceed depletion;
   the value of stocks has increased in nominal dollars and shown little
   change in constant dollars. It follows that a national income revision that
   accommodated both depletion and additions to the value of mineral
   stocks would *not* reduce U.S. NDP.
2 As one might expect, during the period when resource rents were rising,
   there were positive changes in resource stocks, and when rents were
   declining, stock changes were negative. Changes in rents presumably
   drove investment in exploration and resource recovery techniques.
3 Separating out the rate of return on the capital employed in the mining

industry from the rent to the resource itself has a dramatic impact on rates of return in the mining sector. The conventional accounts show an average annual rate of return to mining of 23 percent for the 1958–91 period, but stripping out the return to the resource itself leaves rates of return to invested capital between 3.5 and 5.2 percent. This is sufficient to pull down returns to *total* private capital in the United States from 16.1 percent to 14.1–14.9 percent for the 1958–91 period. This result tends to confirm that market rates of interest overestimate the opportunity cost of capital, and, when depletion of natural capital is significant, the social rate of discount should be adjusted downwards accordingly (see Chapter 4).

3.2 Degradation of Renewable Resources: Costa Rica

The joint study by the Tropical Science Center and World Resources Institute attempts to measure the depletion of Costa Rica's natural resources in three areas: deforestation, soil erosion, and overfishing. No attempt was made to make comprehensive estimates of the value of depreciation, for example, the loss of tourist revenue as forests and wildlife are reduced or nonerosion damages to soils. The basic methodologies were to calculate loss of timber in physical and then monetary units using stumpage values, to calculate physical measures of soil erosion and loss of plant nutrients and monetize these by using fertilizer replacement costs, and to estimate maximum sustainable yields for a particular fishery and calculate actual depletion from overfishing.

The precise methodologies are less interesting than attempts to interpret the results. The estimates show that NNP adjusted downward for natural resource depletion was consistently lower in the 1970–1989 period than unadjusted NNP, by roughly 5 to 10 percent. This indicates that real income was indeed lower than measured and reported income. The estimates also show that cumulative depletion of natural resources over the period 1970–1989 totaled some 184 billion colones (U.S. $2.2 billion at 1989 exchange rate), which exceeds the average annual value of GDP during the period. The evidence seems persuasive that the value of natural capital declined during the period. But it is not conclusive. The tourism value of the remaining natural environment has boomed. If this were included, the real value of natural resources may have increased. Also, the impact of resource degradation on economic growth is not clear-cut. If one attributed depletion and degradation to sheer waste (a dissipation of rents) as was apparently the case in the relatively small but mismanaged fisheries sector, then one would conclude that a loss of natural capital each year equivalent to 5 percent of GDP could reduce *potential* growth rate by 1.5–2.0 percent per year, assuming an incremental capital output ratio of 2.5 to 3.0. With a measured annual average growth rate of GDP of 4.6 percent, this implies that the potential growth rate would have been 6.1–6.6 percent, a very large sacrifice of economic well-being. Still, one cannot conclude that the depletion of natural resources *necessarily* reduced real income growth. If the depletion of the natural resources led to increased investment in other productive resources (i.e., physical or human capital), the total capital stock and hence the productive capacity of the economy might have been maintained or increased. The details of the study suggest this was not the case in Costa Rica due to extremely inefficient harvesting of timber and the low agricultural potential of converted land. Still, the possibility exists that depletion of natural resources can be converted to other income-producing assets with little or no loss of income. The important point is that while improved accounting can clarify the consequences of natural resource policy, the actual result depends on how the proceeds from resource sales are split between current consumption and investment.

3.3 Papua New Guinea: Green Accounts in a Primitive Economy

Peter Bartelmus et al. tested the new satellite accounts system of the SEEA in Papua New Guinea (PNG). The results are highly tentative and the report is designed more to understand the application of the system than to derive hard numbers and guide policy. The report produced flow accounts and a balance sheet for subsoil assets. Both the user cost and the net price methods were employed to adjust the accounts for resource depletion. Following the formula proposed by El Serafy, the user costs, or capital consumption element of receipts from mining, were estimated assuming a discount rate of 10 percent and either a direct estimate of the lifespan of individual mines or the ratio of reserves over annual extraction rates. The user cost adjustment was subject to considerable fluctuations over the period (1985–1990) because of additions to reserves (new discoveries) and changes in the importance of various mines with different lifetimes. Both factors cause T, the number of years of the mines' lifetimes used in the formula, to change year by year and hence change the user-cost adjustment. The results show the ratio of user cost to value added in the mining sector to range from 2.6 to 9.5 percent over the period. In the user-cost approach, traditionally measured GDP is adjusted downward by the amount of the user cost. When this is done, the adjusted GDP ranges from 98.6 to 99.7 percent of traditional measured GDP. This can be interpreted as the amount by which traditional accounting overstates the sustainable output of the economy with respect to the extraction of subsoil assets.

The picture is somewhat different if the net price method is used to estimate depletion costs. Here the ratio of depletion to traditionally measured value added in the mining sector ranges from 7 to 48 percent. One implication is that the efficiency of man-made capital in the mining sector, as measured by the capital-to-output ratio, is dramatically reduced when depletion costs are considered. This is consistent with the BEA's analysis of returns in the U.S. mining sector. In the net price method, the depletion costs are subtracted from traditionally measured NDP (which has already subtracted depreciation of physical capital from GDP). When this was done for PNG, the adjusted net product ranged from 91.8 to 99.1 percent of traditionally measured NDP, a much larger downward revision than occurs in the user-cost method. But recall that the net-price method following SEEA guidelines as applied to PNG keeps new discoveries out of the flow accounts and only records them as changes in the asset accounts. The rationale is that new discoveries should not be considered the result of economic production. While this is questionable, it does keep the income and output accounts insulated from erratic fluctuations in discoveries.

The difference in the treatment of new discoveries explains part of the difference between the user-cost method and the net-price method. New discoveries extend the lifetime of mines and reduce the calculated depletion cost in the user-cost method but do not affect depletion costs in the net-price method. The other major difference is that the user cost splits net revenues between "true" income and a user-cost or capital-consumption element.

The PNG report also includes separate estimates for the costs of environmental degradation. The SEEA recommends costing such degradation at its potential restoration or avoidance costs. This represents a practical compromise reflecting the difficulty in placing monetary values on loss of nonmarketed environmental services and in separating out defensive expenditures. Even restoration and avoidance cost data were difficult to acquire in PNG, and an interesting experimental alternative involving compensation payments was used in certain cases. Because of the special social structure and land tenure patterns in PNG, some data on compensation payments to tribal groups for land use losses were available. The report views negotiating for compensation as a "simulated" market to establish monetary values for losses of nonmarketed environmental services. This provided the basis

Table 17.1. *Comparing traditional and green measures of national output:
Papua New Guinea*

	1986	1987	1988	1989	1990
NDP (millions kia)	2,314	2,569	2,863	2,698	2,760
EDPI (in %) NDP	94.5	91.8	96.3	99.1	93.5
EDP2 (in %) NDP	92.2	89.7	94.4	97.1	91.5
Consumption (in %) EDP2	105.4	105.5	94.5	102.1	109.1

Note: NDP is net domestic product traditionally measured. EDP1 is net domestic
product adjusted for mineral resource depletion (net price method). EDP2 is net
domestic product adjusted for mineral resource depletion and estimated degradation in the quality of environmental resources. The authors caution that "given the
many underlying assumptions that had to be made, the values presented here [in
their Table 14] should be interpreted and used with considerable caution."
Source: Calculated from Bartelmus et al. (1993), Table 14, p. 39.

for inferring adjustments to traditionally measured national accounts to
account for environmental degradation. Separate estimates were made for
agriculture, forestry, mining, and energy.

The highly tentative and qualified results show a further reduction in NDP.
Specifically, moving from net domestic product adjusted for natural resource
depletion to net domestic product adjusted for both natural resource depletion and environmental degradation reduces traditionally measured NDP
on average by a further 2.1 percent. Furthermore, the study reports that
national consumption was greater than the twice-adjusted NNP in four of
the five years covered. If correct, the consumption level of the country was
running down the aggregate of its man-made and natural capital, which
would clearly be unsustainable. But recall that these flow measures do not
account for new discoveries and revaluations, which are included on the
balance sheet. Also, no depletion allowance was calculated in the forestry
sector because of a lack of reliable information. For these reasons, it is not
possible to assert unambiguously that Papau New Guinea entered each
subsequent accounting period with a smaller stock of productive assets.
Table 17.1 summarizes the principal findings but, as noted, should be used
with great caution.[14]

14 According to estimates by David Pearce and Giles Atkinson (1995), PNG was not alone in its unsustainable pattern. They found that of 22 countries examined, 8 exhibited depreciation of man-made
   and natural capital in excess of savings, indicating unsustainability. All 8 were developing countries.
   In addition, 3 of the 22 (Mexico, Philippines, United Kingdom) were on the edge, with savings equal
   to depreciation.

4 An Environmental Kuznets Curve?

Over four decades ago, Simon Kuznets found an "inverted U" relationship between income inequality and per capita income (Kuznets 1955). As income increased, inequality first increased and then decreased. More recently, there have been attempts to find a similar relation between environmental quality/pollution variables and income per capita.[15] The hypothesis is that as income increases from a low level, pollution first increases and then, past some turning point in per capita income, starts to decline. If valid, the relation would have major significance for achieving sustainable development. It would imply that, over time and with economic growth, the alleged trade-off between economic growth and environmental quality disappears, although not necessarily automatically. It would also imply that growth-promoting trade liberalization improves environmental quality.

An inverted U relation is plausible and indeed was sketched out in Chapter 2. On the pollution "supply" side, one might identify general stages of development as natural-resource-intensive, industry-intensive, and services- (knowledge-) intensive. If the environmental Kuznets curve measures pollutants typically associated with industrial production (e.g., SO_2), the shifting composition of output and, as modified by trade, consumption should trace out such a curve. Moreover, increasing urbanization, which is associated with higher incomes, could help explain the rising segment of the curve if pollution is primarily measured in urban areas. Additionally, the "demand" for environmental quality and its attainment through pollution abatement may well shift upward at higher income levels. Specifically, the income elasticity of demand for environmental quality may be low at low income levels but substantially higher at high income levels. This demand for environmental quality would tend to be transformed into actual pollution abatement through the political process and government regulations, because pollution levels are not "bought and sold" in the marketplace but to a large extent are supplied through government action. International trade may also contribute to an observed inverted U. If developing countries follow dynamic comparative advantage, moving from a labor-intensive to a capital-intensive production structure before emerging as high-income countries and concentrating on services and technology intensive production, the pollution associated with heavy industry would tend to reach a peak in countries at the midrange of per capita income.[16]

---

15 For a comprehensive review and evidence, see Barbier (1997).
16 In this view, pollution is shunted down the per capita income "ladder." Richard Baldwin (1995) has melded the idea of an "ecological transition" with the demographic transition literature. Abatement lags increasing pollution, producing an inverted U path for pollution. The demographic transition

Econometric studies investigating an environmental Kuznets curve were done by Gene Grossman and Alan Krueger (1993), Grossman (1995), and by Thomas Selden and Daqing Song (1994). The Grossman and Krueger panel study did tend to confirm an inverted U pattern relating per capita income (adjusted on a purchasing-power-parity basis) and a number of the 14 air and water quality indices that were examined, but the results indicate that a time trend, independent of income, was also at work (positively in the case of air quality, negatively in the case of water quality). For some of the environmental variables, ambient concentrations leveled off, but did not decline; also, the per capita income level at which pollution peaked was substantially different among different pollutants. One difficulty in the study is the use of national-level per capita income and generally urban data on pollution levels. In countries such as Thailand with very wide geographic disparities of income, a finding drawn from urban air quality and national per capita income cannot easily be compared with countries in which the urban-rural income disparity is much less. This can affect the calculation of the turning points. Another limitation is that their estimation procedures using reduced-form equations do not shed light on why an inverted U pattern might exist.

Selden and Song use data on the flow of emissions rather than stock measures of ambient quality. Their research is restricted to four air pollutants: particulates, SO_2, oxides of nitrogen, and carbon monoxide. Also, in contrast to Grossman and Krueger's use of urban data, Selden and Song use national-level data on emissions. The difference may be important as pollution can be spatially dispersed, either through technical means (higher smokestacks) or by dispersing industry. Nonetheless, their conclusions are consistent – the air pollution indices exhibit an inverted U relation with per capita GDP.

Before drawing too much comfort for long-term sustainable development from these findings, a number of caveats are in order. First, as a technical matter, the results might simply reflect shunting pollution from relatively high-income to low-income countries, and this relocation could account for the inverted U. As examined earlier, the empirical evidence for shunting is weak, but it remains a possible explanation. With a closed global system, shunting has a finite limit, and the global curve may not resemble the estimated curve drawn from national data. Second, emissions data as used

describes first acceleration and then stabilization of population at high per capita income levels. His somewhat pessimistic conclusion is that the world's poor are in the middle of the demographic transition but in an early stage of the ecological transition, with rapidly rising pollution emission rates.

in the Selden and Song study may not accurately reflect damages for pollutants that accumulate over time. Emission *rates* may fall, but stock *levels* of pollutants may increase. Third, and closely related, neither stock nor flow environmental variables measure damages. It is conceivable that the economic (welfare) damages from pollution continue to rise even as the measured level (stock or flow) declines. For example, urbanization increases the number of people exposed to a constant level of air pollution and hence the damages. Fourth, neither study included certain pollutants of international importance – CO_2 emissions and CFCs. It is plausible that pollution-abatement regulations for *local* pollutants respond to rising per capita income but not for pollutants whose damages are dispersed internationally. This seems reasonable in a political modelling of pollution-abatement policies where local regulation protects against local damages. Fifth, the studies investigate only a subset of elements contributing to environmental degradation. They did not include unsustainable use of natural resources, which is likely to be associated with poverty; they do not include certain environmental quality variables typically of interest to high-income countries such as preservation of wilderness and wildlife; and they do not try to relate more basic ecological variables such as biodiversity to per capita income. For this reason, the empirical relation between income and environmental quality remains partial. Some indices may decrease, some may increase, and some may follow an inverted U pattern. Sixth, and perhaps the most disturbing, the Selden and Song study concludes that because the majority of countries are well below the turning points, global pollution will rise and indeed accelerate over the next three decades. In any event, the existence of an inverted U relation inferred from past data, like the original Kuznets income-inequality relation, does not imply the relation is either desirable or fixed.

Three other empirical studies cast light on the income-environment relation. Cropper and Griffiths (1994) find an inverted U or at least an inverted L relation between income and deforestation for countries in Africa and Latin America. Higher levels of population density shift the curve upwards. The regression variables, however, were not significant in explaining deforestation in Asia.

Nemat Shafik (1994) examined a much wider range of environmental variables and not surprisingly found a wide range of curves. Certain local air pollutants, sulfur dioxide and suspended particulate matter, displayed the inverted U pattern. The deforestation variables were not significant. As one might expect, two variables that are almost hallmarks of poverty, percentage of population lacking safe water and urban sanitation, declined sharply as per capita income increased. One measure of river water quality, dissolved oxygen, worsened steadily as incomes increased. A second river quality measure, the presence of fecal coliform, first increased to a per capita income level of about $1,400, then fell to a very low level at about $11,000 per capita, and then rose again to high levels at income levels above $11,000. Finally, two variables, municipal solid waste per capita and carbon emissions per capita, rose monotonically throughout the income range. Those results suggest that the environmental Kuznets curve is limited to a subset of environmental variables, mainly local air pollutants.

A recent study by Hettige, Mani, and Wheeler concentrates on organic waste discharges from industrial activities (Hettige, Mani, and Wheeler 1999). Two innovative features are the use of actual data on BOD emissions collected by national environmental protection agencies in 13 countries, and an attempt to decompose industrial water pollution into four determinants: total national output, the share of industry in national output, the share of highly polluting sectors in industrial output, and end-of-pipe pollution intensity. The results do not support the inverted U hypothesis, but instead show that industrial water emissions increase with per capita income up to middle income levels (about $7,000 per capita) and then stabilize throughout the high income range. Although the manufacturing share of total output roughly shows an inverted U, the end-of-pipe pollution intensity declines continuously with higher per capita incomes (presumably reflecting increased demand for regulatory strictness), and the BOD intensity of industrial production, reflecting the sectoral composition of industrial output, initially falls but stabilizes in the $4,000–$5,000 region. When combined with increased total output as per capita income rises, the simulations show total organic water pollution remains constant at higher income levels, which gives the inverted L rather than the inverted U pattern.

Appendix 17.1

User-Cost and Net-Price Methods to Value Depletion of Natural Capital[17]

The user-cost and net-price methods of adjusting national income accounts for depletion of natural capital can be shown to be special cases of a more general framework. The general framework is as follows. The present value of an asset under perfect market conditions and optimizing behavior is the sum of the net revenues it will generate discounted to the present. This can be formalized as

---

17 This follows Bartelmus (1997) and Hartwick and Hageman (1993).

$$V_0 = R_0 + \frac{R_1}{1+r} + \frac{R_2}{(1+r)^2} + \cdots \frac{R_T}{(1+r)^T}, \qquad (1)$$

where V_0 is net present value, $R_0 \ldots R_T$ are net returns in time periods $t=0 \ldots t=T$, when the asset fully used up or depleted; r is the appropriate discount rate, assumed constant and equal to the return on the best alternative investment. The Rs should be interpreted as the price per unit minus marginal extraction costs times the quantity extracted in the accounting period. It follows that the value of the asset at the beginning of the following accounting period is

$$V_1 = R_1 + \frac{R_2}{1+r} + \cdots + \frac{R_T}{(1+r)^{T-1}}. \qquad (2)$$

The difference, $V_1 - V_0$, is the change in the economic value of the asset and, with some manipulation,

$$\Delta V = V_1 - V_0 = -R_0 + \frac{V_1}{(1+r)}(r). \qquad (3)$$

The change in the value, ΔV, thus has two components: the loss of value measured by the receipts from current sales, $-R_0$, and the gain in value of the remaining asset as a result of advancing one unit in time,

$$\frac{V_1}{1+r}(r).$$

This gain arises because the stream of returns on the remaining assets, $R_1 \ldots R_T$, is now discounted over one less time period.

We thus have three concepts: R_0, which is the net receipt from sales, sometimes called Hotelling Rent; ΔV, which measures the loss of economic value, or depreciation in the accounting period; and

$$\frac{V_1(r)}{(1+r)},$$

which can be considered the true income in the accounting period. This can be more easily seen if we rearrange

$$R_0 + \Delta V = \frac{V_1}{(1+r)}(r). \qquad (4)$$

Because ΔV is negative, Equation (4) says that after we subtract the loss of value or depreciation from net receipts, the remainder is true income. Put somewhat differently, if the economic depreciation were set aside and invested at r, the value of total assets at t_1, V_1 plus $(\Delta V)(1+r)$, would equal their initial level, V_0.

If good data on the Rs or the Vs were available, putting a monetary value on the depletion of natural capital stock would be straightforward. ΔV could be calculated from discounted net returns using (1) and (2) or by using opening and closing asset values in (3). These data are not readily available, and two alternative approaches have been used. The *user cost* method assumes a finite, constant stream of net returns (the Rs) and converts this to an infinite income stream. Using (1) and (2), and dropping the time subscript on R (as returns are assumed constant),

$$\Delta V = V_1 - V_0 = \frac{-R}{(1+r)^T} \tag{5}$$

and, from (4),

$$R - \frac{R}{(1+r)^T} = X, \tag{6}$$

where X is defined as true income.

This can be rearranged

$$\frac{X}{R} = 1 - \frac{1}{(1+r)^T}, \tag{7}$$

which shows the ratio of true Hicksian income to net receipts.

The net-price approach assumes Hotelling's Rule, that the net price of the marginal unit extracted of a depletable resource increases at the same rate as the discount rate (see Chapter 17). In that event, the value of the resource at any time is

$$V_t = (p_t - c_t)Q = N_t Q, \tag{8}$$

where p is its per unit price, c is the per unit marginal extraction cost, N_t is the net price, and Q is the physical stock of the resource (e.g. tons or barrels).

Then (1) can be written

$$V_0 = (Q_0)(N_0) + Q_1 \frac{(N_0)(1+r)}{1+r} + \cdots + Q_T \frac{(N_0)(1+r)^T}{(1+r)^T}$$
$$= Q(N_0), \tag{9}$$

where the subscript to Q is the amount extracted in various time periods.

In turn, it can be shown that

$$V_1 = (Q - Q_0)N_0(1+r) - Q(N_0) \tag{10}$$

and thus

$$\Delta V = V_1 - V_0 = (Q - Q_0)(N_0)(1+r) - Q(N_0). \tag{11}$$

If the price increase $(N_0)(1+r)$ is thought of as a holding gain, it would be entered as a revaluation in the asset accounts, but would be excluded from the flow accounts as it does not represent production. In that event, the depreciation measured in (11) is deflated by $(1+r)$, and we obtain

$$\Delta V = (Q - Q_0)(N_0) - Q(N_0) = -Q_0(N_0) = -R_0. \tag{12}$$

Comparing (3) and (12)

$$\Delta V = -R_0 + \frac{(V_1)(r)}{(1+r)}$$

$$\Delta V = -R_0.$$

We see that the term $(V_1/1+r)r$ disappears in the net-price method. The reason is that by assuming Hotelling's Rule, the rising net price just offsets the gain in asset value by advancing one time period. Thus in the net-price method the full value of the resource sale R should be considered as depreciation and subtracted from GDP to obtain NNP. The term $(V_1/1+r)r$ vanishes from the calculation of the flow accounts but does turn up in the asset accounts as a positive revaluation. See Chapter 17 for strengths and weaknesses of the user-cost and net-price method.

18

Trade, Environment, and Sustainable Development: Thailand's Mixed Experience

Sitanon Jesdapipat
Faculty of Economics
Chulalongkorn University

1 Introduction

Until recently international trade theory left environmental impacts outside its purview. Now, when they are linked, free trade is often depicted as either a scourge or savior of the world's natural resources. Supporters of free trade rightfully point out that trade brings higher income, modern technology, and better access to environmentally friendly products and techniques. Unfortunately, opponents of unrestrained trade can claim with equal justification that it also has often led to increased pollution and natural resource depletion. In Thailand, rapid economic growth, led mainly by increased international trade, has had dramatic impacts upon the country's physical environment and its natural resource endowment. In addition to current damage to humans and the well-being of the natural ecosystems, these impacts will adversely affect the nation's long-term economic capabilities. Thailand's potential for sustainable development is being challenged. This chapter analyzes the ways in which trade affects Thailand's environment, and in turn, the effects on trade of measures taken to ensure environmental quality. It identifies the key policy measures that are needed for Thailand to reap local benefits while addressing global concerns.

2 Thailand's Trade-Environment Profile

Based on a shift from agriculture to manufacturing and the accompanying movement of people from rural to urban areas, Thailand emerged as one of the world's fastest growing economies. Real GDP growth rates averaged over 10 percent annually in the late 1980s and 7.5 percent for 1991–1996. GNP per capita has also shown remarkable growth, more than doubling between 1989 and 1995 alone.[1] (See Figure 18.1.) Thailand's impressive economic growth is attributable largely to its rapidly expanding participation in international trade. While early policies called for import substitution and an inward-looking economy, subsequent Thai governments have promoted a more open and outwardly focused economic stance based on export promotion policies, hoping to duplicate the experience of the newly industrialized economies of Asia (e.g., Hong Kong, Singapore, South Korea, and Taiwan). In the early phase of development, the country capitalized on its well-endowed natural resource base and its comparative advantage in low-wage and low- or semi-skilled labor. Later on, an export-promotion investment policy captured global demand for somewhat more sophisticated manufactured products, and products processed from natural resources (processed chicken, wood furniture, jewelry). The value of exports nearly doubled between 1990 and 1994, rising from about $24 billion to $46 billion. Imports remained greater than exports, although growing at a slower rate, rising from about $34 billion to $55 billion between 1990 and 1994, and causing serious current account deficits in recent years. A large portion of imports were, however, to supply the booming export sector. Roughly 73 percent of all imports in the first half of the 1990s consisted of raw materials, intermediate materials, or capital goods. Taken together, the total value of imports and exports represented over 67 percent of the nation's GDP in 1994, up from 49 percent in 1980. This demonstrates the growing openness of the Thai economy.

In retrospect, export opportunities induced a dramatic shift in the production structure of the Thai economy. In the early 1960s, primary commodities, including agricultural goods, minerals, and metals, represented 95 percent of exports. Today, manufactured goods fuel the nation's export expansion (see Table 18.1). The pollution-intensive manufacturing sector, which in 1965 represented only 14 percent of GDP (NESDB 1993), more than doubled its share to an estimated 29 percent in 1995 and accounted for over 72 percent of all exports in 1994.[2] Leading exports dominating the top 10 list now are all nonagricultural products, and include computers and electronics, electrical appliances and components, textiles, and processed food products. The trend towards semiskilled manufactured goods is expected to continue.

1 While this chapter was being written, Thailand was going through a tremendous flux that put its economy in a very critical economic crisis. The medium-term perspective is not as rosy as suggested by figures cited herein. The country's currency dropped from an average 25 baht to a dollar to around 50 at the end of 1997 before recovering somewhat. While the causes of the collapse of growth are disputed, there is no indication that inappropriate environmental and natural resource policies were the proximate cause.
2 This figure does not include agro-industry, which represented over 9 percent of exports in 1994. Pollution intensity is defined by the Department of Industry.

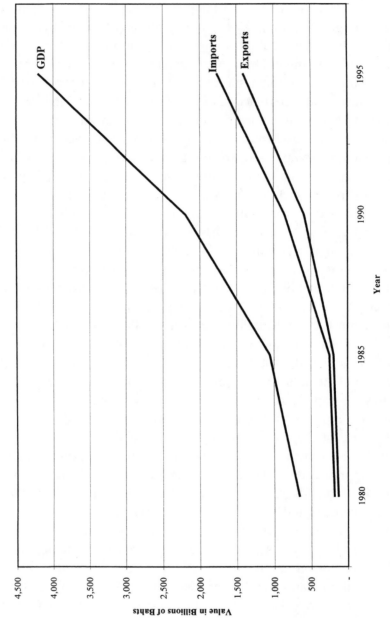

Figure 18.1. *Thailand's exports, imports, and GDP. Sources: Derived from International Monetary Fund, International Financial Statistics, 1998*

Table 18.1. *Percentage Distribution of Thai exports by sector*

	1980	1990	1994
Agriculture (including Fisheries)	48.4	21.3	16.6
Agro-industry	8.2	12.5	9.3
Manufacturing	35.6	63.7	72.1
Mineral	3.8	1.3	1.3
Others	4.0	1.2	0.7
Total	100.0	100.0	100.0

Source: Alpha Research (1995).

Agriculture, once the traditional sector of the Thai economy, has been declining in importance to the nation's trade and its overall economy. While continuing to show overall growth in absolute terms due to higher inputs of capital, the agriculture sector saw its relative contribution to GDP drop from 30 percent in 1965 to below 17 percent in 1994 (NESDB 1993; Alpha Research 1995), and its share of total exports fall from 34 percent in 1986 to 11 percent in 1995. Moreover, growth in the agriculture sector has slowed in recent years due to changes in world market prices and stagnant investment in the sector. Also, expansion of agricultural output has slowed as the land frontier was approached, and growth in land productivity has failed to compensate for the slowdown. Nevertheless, despite its declining importance, agriculture remains responsible for over 60 percent of all employment in Thailand, and therefore any policy that adversely affects the agricultural sector has wide-ranging implications for the whole nation.

In comparison to many developing nations, Thailand has been relatively successful in diversifying its export base, moving away from dependence on commodity exports. However, it is still reliant on a few principal export products: roughly 60 percent of export earnings come from 10 items (see Table 18.2), including electronic goods and parts, textiles, and seafood. In addition, market concentration is high: in 1994 Japan imported more than 76 percent of Thailand's meat (mostly poultry) exports, and Japan and the United States together made up over two-thirds of all Thai exports of seafood (Alpha Research 1995, pp. 74–75), while Singapore alone accounted for over 48 percent of exports of computers and computer parts (BOT 1996, p. 64). Overall, there has been little market diversification in the past two decades,

Table 18.2. *Thailand's top ten exports, 1994*

Product Type	1994 Value (millions of baht)	Share of Total Exports (in %)
1. Textile products (all types)	149,609	13.2
2. Electrical apparatus for breaking circuits (including integrated circuits)	102,438	9.0
3. Computers and parts	92,059	8.1
4. Electrical appliances (all kinds)	88,124	7.7
5. Shrimp (fresh and frozen)	49,155	4.2
6. Precious stones and jewelry	44,684	3.9
7. Rubber	41,820	3.7
8. Footwear	39,258	3.5
9. Rice	39,188	3.4
10. Plastic products[a]	30,351	2.7
Total of Top Ten Exports	676,686	59.5
Total of All Exports	1,137,600	100.0

[a] Preliminary figures for 1995 show the value of exports of plastic products more than doubling to over 61 million baht, giving it a 4.4% share of total exports, and making it Thailand's fifth-leading export for that year.
Source: Calculations based on Bank of Thailand, January 1996.

and exports are concentrated in a few major markets: the United States (21 percent), Japan (17 percent), the EU (15 percent), and Singapore (14 percent) (BOT 1996). This pattern makes Thailand potentially vulnerable to external environmental requirements imposed by importing industrial countries. The vulnerability would be revealed if a dispute concerning shrimp exports and mangrove destruction were to arise between Thailand and the United States. (Jesdapipat and Chatchen 1997).

Thailand's imports are also dependent on these few partners. Japan alone supplied over 30 percent of Thailand's imports in 1994, while the EU accounted for nearly 14 percent and the United States 12 percent. Again, this pattern makes Thailand vulnerable to externally imposed regulation. Higher product and environmental standards by the supplying nations, for instance, could translate into higher costs for imported goods. As much of the imports are for eventual export, this could increase relative prices of Thai exports as well, possibly damaging the country's competitiveness.

The fruits of development have been an impressive reduction in levels of poverty, from about half the population in the 1960s to below 14 percent in the 1990s. (World Bank 1998). Higher levels of income and growing middle and upper classes have led to greater demands for environmental standards, and growing involvement in international trade has also brought about relatively active participation by Thailand in many international multilateral environmental agreements. The industrialization of Thailand, however, has had its costs as well. For instance, Thailand's new-found wealth has not been distributed evenly among the population: the average income of a farmer is roughly one-tenth that of an urban worker in the service or industrial sectors (TCGE 1992, p. 14). This income gap has led to an influx of workers into the urban areas, which account for more than 80 percent of GDP, and whose population is increasing at twice the national average. Urban pollution and environmental problems have become increasingly severe.

For those that do enjoy the fruits of economic growth, higher levels of disposable income have meant higher levels of resource consumption and pollution. A vivid example is the dramatic increase in the number of private automobiles in Bangkok, which has resulted in air pollution at rates up to 5 to 6 times WHO standards. Annual growth of registered passenger cars between 1990 and 1994 was 13 percent and 10 percent for the Kingdom and Bangkok, respectively. Ownership rates in Bangkok increased from 37 percent in 1990 to 53 percent in 1994. Traffic congestion not only adds to levels of air and noise pollution, but it has been estimated that the Thai work force loses 44 working days per year sitting in traffic jams (World Bank 1995b), and total traffic congestion losses may nearly equal one-third of the city's potential GDP. The increased geographic concentration of population and polluting industries in urban areas, especially the Bangkok region, has meant increases in levels of domestic and industrial wastes and pollution and an increase in the number of persons affected by such problems. It is estimated that one in six of all Bangkok residents suffers from allergies or respiratory problems aggravated by air pollution (*Bangkok Post*, February 20, 1996). Development services have been unequal: only 67 percent of Thailand's urban population has access to safe drinking water, this despite an increase in levels of sanitation services, but not sufficient to outpace the rise in polluting sources (WRI 1996).[3]

Trade-led economic growth has had repercussions on the rural and marine environments as well. Deforestation, both for the timber industry and in order to clear land for agriculture, has produced negative consequences such as massive flooding and soil erosion, which is the largest source of soil

---

3 This figure of 67 percent was for 1990, while the figure for a decade earlier was a comparable 65 percent.

nutrient loss (Jesdapipat 1994). Changed land use has also released large amounts of carbon dioxide into the atmosphere.[4] Intensifying agriculture for export has led to a 380 percent increase in the use of fertilizers but has produced just a 25 percent increase in yields between 1980 and 1990 (FAO 1992), degrading both soil and water quality. Intensive use of chemical fertilizer potentially could lead to the long-term nitrification of underground water, which has not been investigated in Thailand. Overfishing in Thailand's coastal waters has depleted local marine resources and forced Thai fishermen to expand into international waters. Large areas of mangrove forests, which are especially productive and important marine-estuary ecosystems, have been cleared for shrimp farming over the last two decades.[5]

It is clear from these examples that Thailand's trade and its environmental quality are inextricably linked and that restrictions on one are likely to have effects upon the other. Until the 1997 crisis, Thailand enjoyed a prospering economy, but this tended to come at the expense of the environment, especially as sufficient earnings have not been invested in environmental protection and conservation. Section 3 examines how measures designed to ensure environmental integrity impact the economy, and Section 4 looks at the effects of environmental regulation upon individual economic sectors.

3 Environmental Measures Affecting Thai Trade

3.1 Domestic Policies

The negative environmental consequences of decades of outward-looking economic policy have taken Thais by surprise. Some of these consequences are physically visible, such as industrial pollution, while others are more subtle, and not yet well understood or convincing (such as the case of nutrient loss due to soil erosion). Only recently has the government attempted to elevate the status of environmental issues in overall policy

---

4 Thailand's total forest area, representing 58 percent of total land area in 1960, was down to less than 26 percent in 1995 and continued to decline despite a logging ban introduced in the late 1980s. Once a major exporter of tropical timber, Thailand has become a net importer of wood. It is estimated that 91 million metric tons of CO_2 were released into the atmosphere in 1991 due to changes in land use (World Resources Institute 1994), and more than half of the nation's total CO_2 emissions are due to deforestation alone (TCGE 1992, p. 67).

5 Arbhabhirama, Phantumvanit, Elkington, and Ingkasuwan (1988) estimate that an area of 38,000 ha or 13 percent of the 287,300 ha of the mangrove resource in 1979 was cleared and converted to coastal aquaculture by 1986. There has been no consensus, however, as to how much of mangrove land has been cleared for aquaculture, especially shrimp farming, over the years. See also Jesdapipat and Chatchen (1997).

directives. Hesitant to impede economic growth, the government is also slowly changing its policy from an emphasis on command-and-control methods to greater reliance on voluntary management practices and market-based instruments.

Authority over environmental issues in Thailand rests with several different governmental agencies. Thailand's first two major pieces of legislation were passed in 1992 in an attempt to coordinate and strengthen domestic environmental policy. The Factory Act implemented by the Ministry of Industry is the first one. It aims to ensure compliance with environmental standards by individual industries, and it devises measures such as business licensing and zoning. The second is the more wide-ranging National Environmental Quality Act (NEQA), which raises environmental issues to the ministerial level from their former position at departmental levels. Its major contributions include the formation of the National Environment Board (NEB), responsible, *inter alia*, for approving environmental legislation, evaluating environmental impact assessments (EIAs), monitoring business compliance with environmental regulations, and the establishing an environmental fund known as Super Fund. The fund is financed in part by fees and penalties collected under the Polluter Pays Principle recently incorporated into Thai law, and by a portion of gasoline taxes. One factor limiting the use of funds has been the lengthy process of approval for use of the monies.

The new legislation provides several other tools for improving environmental performance by businesses. These include mandating the use of EIAs for several types of projects and the promotion of Industrial Estates.[6] The latter, by concentrating businesses, reduces the cost of environmental monitoring and makes available lower cost joint services such as centrally treated wastewater. In addition to the economic incentives provided to companies locating in Industrial Estates, the Polluter Pays Principle is being integrated into policy, with fines being levied against noncompliant firms and subsidies for polluting practices being cut back or phased out. The effectiveness of fines is questionable, however, because enforcement is lax and fines are relatively low, failing to induce a change of production methods. More effective has been the manipulation of subsidies, which, for instance, were successful in promoting the use of unleaded gasoline and reducing lead levels in the air in the Bangkok region by 75 percent between 1990 and 1996.

---

6 It should be noted, however, that due to lack of enforcement and personnel, EIAs are often not acted on and in practice once a project is approved, there is little or no follow-up on measures outlined in the EIA.

Investment policy during the early years sacrificed environmental quality for economic prosperity. Only recently has investment policy taken potential environmental impacts into account through EIA requirements when a project is submitted for promotion by the government. For investment projects not submitted for promotion, the Factory Act is applicable, but not necessarily effective in assuring environmental protection. One question is whether Thailand's proinvestment policy has attracted polluting industries. A survey conducted in 1993 revealed that foreign investors complied with local environmental standards, which they saw as less stringent than their home countries'. (NESDB and IDE 1993). When questioned as to factors influencing location decisions, foreign businesses in Thailand listed wage rates, presence of a developed infrastructure, and access to growing local (domestic and regional) markets as the major criteria. Companies were not worried about having to utilize top-grade technology, since this was often prudent from a purely economic/financial perspective as well. Moreover, according to surveys of American and European companies investing abroad, strong environmental standards may *encourage* investment, as firms mentioned a sufficient supply of clean water and waste treatment/disposal facilities among their concerns when evaluating project sites. The experience of Singapore, with its strict standards, tends to confirm the point.

A principal obstacle to better performance is government officers who still act reactively – in contrast to proactively – in taking an end-of-pipe approach to pollution abatement. This traditional attitude needs to be modified. For instance, the concept behind the Super Fund will have to be enlarged to support adoption of cleaner production and cleaner technology, not just end-of-pipe treatment. The Ministry of Finance itself has to be "educated" about cheaper ways to ally with environment – and even to make more money in a sounder environment in the long run. If Thailand truly believes in the virtues of the market, market-friendly environmental policies need to be devised and implemented.

3.2 *International Environmental Commitments*

Thailand has been a party to several major international agreements that affect the environment and trade. Some of these have entailed significant economic and environmental readjustments. While earlier action in the international sphere has been mostly reactive, Thailand is now taking a more proactive position in dealing with environmental issues of international interest. This section briefly looks at the effects of some of the major agreements to which Thailand is a party.

The Montreal Protocol Thailand is a party to the *Montreal Protocol on Ozone Depleting Substances* (ODSs), which commits parties to control and reduce use of designated chemicals below certain levels and according to a specific time schedule. The protocol also bans Thailand from engaging in trade in these substances with nations not party to the agreement. Because its base year (1986) annual per capita ODS consumption was less than 0.3 kg, Thailand is entitled under Article 5 to a 10-year grace period to meet ODS reduction schedules. It is also eligible for concessional funding from a multilateral fund established to assist developing nations in phasing out the use of ODSs.

Thailand's leading export industries, electronic components and appliances, are also the largest consumers of ODSs, which act as solvents and cleansers in integrated circuits and insulating and blowing agents in refrigeration and air conditioning. Together these industries account for over one-fifth of all Thai exports and are among the nation's fastest growing economic sectors. Thailand's imports of ODSs more than tripled 1986 levels in the first two years after it became a party to the protocol. This was partly a result of companies in more developed nations facing immediate regulation, taking advantage of Thailand's status as an Article 5 nation with a 10-year grace period, and using the nation as an "ODS haven."

ODS use continued to grow until the mid 1990s, especially use of CFC-11 and CFC-12 used for refrigeration and air conditioning. However, Thailand has had success in phasing out several aspects of ODS consumption. In an agreement between Thai, U.S., and Japanese governmental and trade agencies, multinational electronics corporations operating in Thailand were encouraged to phase out ODS use in solvents according to the schedule followed by the companies in their base countries. This alone was a significant step in addressing total ODS consumption, as solvents accounted for over 40 percent of the nation's overall ODS use in the early 1990s, and 97 percent of solvents use was by Japanese and American companies or joint ventures. As a result, Thailand's 1995 consumption of CFC-113, used as a cleansing solvent by the electronics industry, was 90 percent lower than 1992 levels, and only one-third its 1986 levels. Due to the shift in types of ODSs consumed, Thailand's overall ozone depletion potential dropped slightly from 1991–92 levels. Companies have also taken advantage of money made available through the multilateral fund to help in the phaseout transition. As of mid-1995, the multilateral fund had granted over $20 million in phaseout assistance to 32 different companies operating in Thailand.[7] Far from hurting

---

7 Data are from the Department of Industrial Works, the main agency responsible for the implementation.

industry, many of the companies phasing out ODS use increased production efficiency by upgrading facilities and found they were able to recover costs in a reasonable amount of time. This was especially so for companies with large foreign market shares.

The Montreal Protocol has had mixed results for Thailand's economy. It has not had a negative impact on overall trade in electrical and electronic equipment and appliances, which continue to be among Thailand's fastest growing sectors. The phaseout, however, has been seen as prohibitively expensive by many Thai companies, especially small- and medium-sized enterprises (SMEs), and because most of these firms are in the informal sector, it has been difficult for the government to deal effectively with them. While multinational companies have access to technology from their home country and have the financial resources to acquire technology and absorb increased costs until the initial investment is recovered, smaller companies do not have access to the technology, nor do they have easy access to cheap credit. Often it is not cost-effective for a financial institution to extend loans to SMEs. Moreover, some of the technology is only economically feasible at certain levels of scale, meaning that what may be financially attractive for the larger companies may not necessarily be for smaller ones. The Article 5 grace period may have encouraged some companies to wait, hoping for cheaper technology to come along. Fierce competition in the marketplace has also played a role.

While there has been a movement by consumers in many countries away from ODS use, consumers within Thailand and other Article 5 nations still constitute a large market. Producers of ODS-containing goods who are unable or unwilling to phase out can shift markets instead. For instance, only three years before the end of the Article 5 grace period, more than half of the refrigerators sold *within* Thailand still contained ODSs. In contrast, measures that would have restricted trade in products made with, but not containing, ODSs would have had a greater effect on Thai trade than present regulations. Much of the Thai electronic components industry still falls within this category, and much of the market for these products is in non-Article 5 countries. Such measures would probably be found in conflict with WTO trade agreements regarding production process methods, and so their future is unclear.

In summary, Thailand's experience shows that the availability of funding and technology does not guarantee success in a phaseout. After the multilateral fund is allocated to support a phaseout, many more technical details have to be worked out at the implementation level, and only economically viable firms are supported. SMEs, especially those in the informal sector, would need additional policy reform to enable them to benefit from government support. In the case of automobile air-conditioning units, all servicing firms are small ones, and they are not well regulated by government. It is thus difficult to lend any support to help them phase out ODS usage. Furthermore, in addition to funding and technology, competitive pressure is a disincentive to early phaseout.

CITES Thailand is a full party to CITES. In accordance with the convention, the Thai government designated three government agencies to oversee trade in plants, fish, and other animals. Thailand is home to over 4,000 species of plants and animals, including 111 species currently recognized as endangered, and has designated 12.7 percent of its total land as conservation or protected areas (TCGE 1992), thereby preserving natural habitat. Despite these efforts by the Thai government, the CITES committee censured Thailand, claiming that the Kingdom did not have the institutions necessary to effectively deal with illegal trade in several protected species, and more importantly, accusing Thailand of turning a blind eye to such activities. In response to these charges and the economic sanctions that went with them, in 1992, Thailand passed two new laws, and later established the Division of Plant Quarantine to more effectively regulate protected species. These actions were sufficient for the CITES committee to lift sanctions. The protection measures have been only moderately successful, with the Department of Agriculture listing several violations of traffic in endangered species (primarily in wild orchid trade). While the trade was prevented, fines levied in these cases were minimal (between US$ 20–80), and are insufficient to act as a real disincentive to continued smuggling efforts.

Commitment to CITES has, at times, put Thailand at an economic disadvantage. Restrictions against trade in a whole family of wild orchids, because one species among it was listed as endangered, resulted in the loss of export revenue potentially worth millions of U.S. dollars. Eventually orchids were commercially bred in Thailand for export, but by this time breeders in foreign markets had already established themselves and captured markets.

In order to better regulate trade, Thailand has recently amended legislation to require export permits in much flora and fauna trade. Unfortunately trade in endangered species still continues, especially in certain rare plants and in products made from endangered animal species, which are used in many Asian folk medicines and as exotic foods. Because none of Thailand's neighbors – Cambodia, Laos, or Myanmar – are parties to CITES, they do not have wildlife protection laws, much illegal trade is conducted across land borders, which are difficult to effectively patrol. While CITES goes some distance toward conserving rare plants and animals, it is clearly insufficient to guarantee their continued survival. Many in Thailand call for distinguishing between wild and cultivated specimens, in order to reward well-managed plant and animal production. Both from a conservation perspective and an economic perspective, many feel that controlled trade of protected species would be more beneficial than banned trade. This is a hotly debated issue even within Thailand, as there exists the danger that such a move would open rare plants and animals to greater exploitation.

The Basel Convention In an effort to control hazardous waste production and treatment, the Basel Convention on the Control of Transboundary Movements of Hazardous Waste and their Disposal was drafted in 1989. The convention not only deals with restricting international trade in hazardous wastes, especially between developed and developing nations, but also stipulates waste management regulations to be incorporated into the domestic policies of member states. Thailand became a signatory of the convention in 1992, and ratified it late in 1996.

Estimates of the amount of hazardous waste produced in Thailand vary. A comprehensive study done by an American engineering firm in 1989 placed total hazardous waste volume for 1986 at over one million tons. A revised estimate done by the Thai Department of Pollution Control, taking into consideration local coefficients, placed the figure at less then half that (see Table 18.3).

Of the total amount of hazardous wastes produced in Thailand, an estimated 67 percent is produced by metals industries (TEI 1994b, p. 66), with the electrical machinery, chemical, and textiles sectors also ranking as leading sources of waste generation. The problem is becoming more serious, with the growth rate of hazardous waste production far exceeding that of overall economic growth (Table 18.3). National economic policy has encouraged growth in sectors that are highly waste producing,[8] and monitoring the 30,000-plus factories producing hazardous wastes has been lax. Existing facilities for treating hazardous waste are inadequate for appropriately dealing with such massive amounts of waste, with the result that an estimated 75 percent of hazardous wastes are discharged directly into rivers and

---

8 For example, the Board of Investment increased its approval rating for investments in hazardous waste-producing industries from 25 to 55 percent between 1987 and 1989 alone (TEI 1994b, p. 66).

Table 18.3. *Estimates of hazardous waste generation in Thailand*
(tons per year)

Study/Year	1986	1991	1996 (projected)	2001 (projected)
Engineering Science, et al.	1,160,780	1,993,590	3,459,030	5,993,220
Dept. of Pollution Control (MOSTE)	531,154	932,638	1,634,104	2,813,980

Source: TEI (1994b).

landfills, and only about one percent of all hazardous waste is delivered to a legal dump (Moreau 1993).

With regard to trade, no significant exports of hazardous wastes from Thailand are known. Thailand does, however, import wastes, and import levels have risen dramatically since signing the Basel Convention (TEI 1994b, p. 65). This has occurred despite a low recycling rate and a lack of capacity to deal with the wastes. According to the Department of Customs, as of May 1995, 10,000 tons of what was defined as "dangerous materials" had accumulated at the Bangkok Port. The government is currently undertaking measures to better deal with the nation's hazardous waste. It is preparing a licensing scheme for importers and exporters to help improve waste-monitoring capabilities, and has introduced legislation requiring chemicals and other hazardous materials to exit through the country's central port. Efforts are also being made to build more hazardous waste treatment and disposal centers, although large-scale efforts have run into "not-in-my-backyard" opposition from local residents. Encouragement of industrial zones should also help to control hazardous wastes by making the industries easier to monitor, and more importantly, by providing the opportunity for central waste treatment and waste recovery. In practice, however, officials are still struggling with firms' reluctance to ship waste to central facilities for fear that doing so will place them under close supervision.

Efforts to limit waste trade are frustrated by the many illegal shipments via various entry points and with falsified papers, the disguising of wastes by mixing them with legitimate materials/products for import, and the lack of capacity at the port to identify and classify materials as being hazardous. According to the Basel Convention, the responsibility for all of these challenges rests at the national government level with cooperation from countries of origin. Given the scope of the problem, this is an extremely difficult task for present government agencies to handle. Thus far, regional efforts to deal with hazardous waste trade by ASEAN have been very general in nature. If established, a coordinated regional hazardous waste management regime would help in monitoring waste movement and revealing accountability – even within the region itself.

Thailand's biggest challenge with regard to hazardous waste lies not with its import regulation, but with domestic production and disposal, which will continue to grow in importance as industrialization continues and waste levels increase more rapidly than capacity to treat them. Currently less than 2 percent receive adequate treatment. Several creative ideas for new incentives to reduce waste have been suggested, e.g., a "performance bond"-type system in which polluters pay an inflated price for treatment and receive half this sum back upon receipt of the wastes at a central treatment plant. Such plans, however, have yet to be implemented. There is also a need to communicate with the public about a participatory approach to solving the problems and promote capacity building among regulatory officials.

4 Impacts on Specific Sectors

Thailand has faced several trade measures for protection of natural resources and the environment. The United States has been the most active trade partner in imposing unilateral measures on its trading partners, including Thailand. This section examines the impacts on trade and environment in four sectors: timber, marine fisheries and aquaculture, textiles, and electronics.[9]

4.1 The Timber Industry

Thailand's once plentiful forest resources provided much of the country's foreign exchange in its early years of development. The economy of several regions, especially in the northern part of the country, prospered primarily due to the logging industry. In addition, many wood-processing and other related industries developed. With relatively lax restrictions, the deforestation rate in Thailand averaged 3 percent annually over the past three

---

9 A trade sector is a very large and complex focus for analysis, and environmental measures often have different impacts on various subsectors, depending on factors such as company size, destination of exports, specific product type, and specific legislation considered. While an attempt has been made to evaluate major components of a sector as best as possible, there is a possibility of opposite impacts on specific subsectors or individual enterprises.

decades (Royal Forest Dept. 1993, p. 98).[10] The total amount of the country's area covered with forest was estimated at just 26 percent in the mid-1990s, and possibly much lower now, down from 58 percent of the country's land area in 1960 (Royal Forest Dept. 1993, p. 98).[11]

Part of the costs of deforestation has been incurred by the timber industry itself. Due to declining sources of supply, it has experienced a continuous decline in the real value of production since the mid-1970s (TCGE 1992, p. 135). Deforestation also has had negative off-site impacts, for example, on water quality due to increased erosion and on the microclimate, and has contributed to massive flooding. Forest loss has directly impacted other areas of the economy, especially agriculture.[12] After major damage from deforestation in the South, the government initiated a total logging ban in January 1989. This devastated the local logging industry (although there remained limited legal and illegal logging activities), and sent shocks through other wood-processing and wood-related industries. Only those wood-processing industries close to main waterways and railways have remained viable, and they have been forced to adapt their practices to accommodate the new reality.

Many wood-dependent firms have turned to importing wood from neighboring countries, either directly from non-Thai companies or as part of a joint venture. Almost overnight, Thailand went from a major exporter of lumber to the world's fourth-largest importer. There have also been attempts to raise trees for commercial purposes on private land. One very positive result for the wood-based industries in Thailand has been increased production efficiency, including the use of what was formerly considered waste to produce particle board and other products, which can substitute for natural wood in many uses.

The major environmental legislation governing the forestry sector, the 1989 logging ban, has been ineffective in achieving its environmental goal of slowing deforestation rates. But the logging ban does not appear to have been detrimental to the timber sector overall. Since its implementation, exports of wood products actually increased nearly 70 percent, relying on imports of raw materials. Revenues of pulp exports plummeted 91 percent

10 This rate of deforestation was more than double the rate of any of Thailand's Southeast Asian neighbors for the same period. Deforestation in Thailand has come about in three overlapping waves: the first, primarily due to commercial logging of timber for export; the second, due to agricultural expansion, especially growing cash crops for export; and the third, since the late 1980s, due primarily to land speculation, and secondarily, to encroachment by subsistence farmers.

11 The figure of 26 percent is from official Forestry Department statistics. Unofficial informed estimates put the figure much lower, as low as 15 percent.

12 One study found, for instance, that one hectare of forest loss reduced agriculture production by US$ 155, and that this figure increased as deforestation became more severe (TCGE 1992, p. 136).

between 1989 and 1990 immediately after the ban was implemented. Since 1991, however, export levels have increased, and in 1994 they surpassed preban levels by nearly 50 percent. The source of the raw material is mainly eucalyptus plantations (which have themselves raised environmental concerns). Exports of paper products, while remaining stagnant for the first few years after the ban was initiated, were more than four times 1989 levels in 1994 (Alpha Research 1995, pp. 116–120). Such trends are encouraging, and seem to indicate that while this ban, implemented to conserve resources, was damaging to the sector in the short term and to certain subsectors in the long term (e.g., the domestic logging industry and wood-processing centers in remote areas), overall the sector was able to accommodate the measure and continue to grow. Efficiency has been improved, and innovations such as wood substitutes have been introduced.

While the Thai furniture industry has not been severely affected by the logging ban, Thailand has lost business with foreign companies demanding that wood products be certified as coming from sustainably managed sources. Should this trend continue, Thailand's wood industry could suffer significant short-run economic costs, as half of its export of wood products are to the United States and the EU, the markets most likely to make such demands.[13] One survey estimated the costs for certification surveying are between US\$ 0.3 and \$1 per hectare of land in tropical countries, with an additional 1 percent of border prices for the importing nation to identify and trace the chain of custody (Baharuddin 1995, p. 20). Other studies, however, have concluded that better management involved in attaining certification may reduce operating costs, thus lowering the overall costs passed on to buyers (Jonsson and Lingren 1990).

Certification poses difficulties in an international context. In 1994, 87 percent of Thailand's imports of wood and wood products came from the four countries with which it shares a land border (56 percent from Malaysia alone). If Thailand wants a share of the certified market, it would have to ensure that its neighbors change their current forestry practices, a prospect that does not seem to be on the horizon.[14] Should Thailand look for other sources of timber, it would face higher transport costs and increased demand

---

13 The Netherlands, for instance, has already mandated that its timber imports come from sustainable sources, while Austria has declared that a 70 percent tariff will be levied on tropical timber products, with fees going into a fund for reforestation. As for voluntary schemes, their potential to influence markets is debated. Preliminary studies show that so far consumers have not been willing to pay higher prices for certified products (Bourke 1995, p. 17), while others show that in the United Kingdom and the United States, the potential market share for certified products could be as high as 19 percent, with a price increase of up to 13 percent, cited in Baharuddin (1995, p. 20).

14 Two of Thailand's suppliers, Cambodia and Burma, face internal political and social unrest, which makes attempts at monitoring extremely difficult.

on port capacity to receive shipments, which could hurt the industry if costs for such certified wood products were not passed on to the end consumer. Based on studies estimating market potential for certified wood products in the United States and the EU,[15] it is unclear whether incentives will be sufficient to cause the Thai producers to readjust in order to accommodate the certified products market or to continue to ignore such markets. (Note the difference between certifying forest *practices*, over which Thailand has some control, and certifying *products* produced with imported inputs, over which Thailand has little control.)

One idea suggested by some environmentalists is countervailing duties by importing countries on products grown with "environmental subsidies," that is, the costs of unsustainable practices not taken into account in valuing the product (Barbier 1995b, p. 9). Values, however, would be technically difficult to calculate, and such measures would most certainly be brought up as violations of GATT/WTO principles. Such schemes, while potentially threatening to Thai wood industries, are not an immediate worry. More serious would be attempts by nations to impose stricter import requirements, based on their own forestry practices (i.e., the United States subjecting wood imports to the same requirements it places on its logging industry in its Pacific-Northwest region or demanding minimum recycled waste content in paper products). Thailand itself cannot set environmental norms on its foreign suppliers' wood inputs. With few producing countries and many buyers, Thailand would not be able to influence its suppliers to establish a certification scheme – even if it wants to act proactively.

Perhaps the greatest threat to the Thai timber products industry would be an absolute ban on trade in tropical timber, as has been proposed by some nations. While the industry was able to accommodate a domestic ban on logging by relying mostly on imports, a worldwide ban would cut off the overwhelming share of its supplies from its neighbors.[16] Finding nontropical substitutes, when feasible, would likely be prohibitively expensive for most of Thailand's wood export industries. On the other hand, imports of logs have brought an unfair accusation to Thailand that it is exporting its domestic problem to neighboring countries. Thailand is not acting differently in the international marketplace as compared with others. The derived demand is mainly for exports, and only when consumers are ready to pay for the full

---

15 See, for example, ITTO Secretariat (1995).
16 Such a ban may not even achieve the desired results, as it would most likely be implemented by western nations and thus would not stop trade among developing nations themselves and among developing and nonparticipatory western nations. It would, however, damage all industries that used sustainable tropical sources and that depend on western consumers to buy their products.

social cost of sustainable management can Thailand effectively internalize the environmental cost.

4.2 Marine Fisheries and Aquaculture

Unsustainable practices have had serious impacts on renewable natural resources, prompting increasing environmental regulation. Due to lucrative opportunities in the seafood export market, Thailand's marine fisheries industry has expanded exponentially, making Thailand the world's seventh largest marine fishing nation (based on size of catch) and the sixth largest aquaculture producer (World Resources Institute 1994, p. 352). The value of seafood exports doubled between 1990 and 1994 alone (Alpha Research 1995, p. 75) and amounted to roughly 9 percent of Thailand's total export revenue in 1994.[17] Thailand's fishing fleet has grown in size and sophisticated equipment, as companies upgrade and expand their fleets and as more players enter the market.[18]

This increased capacity and greater competition has led to serious overfishing. Maximum sustainable yield for the Gulf of Thailand, the nation's main fishing area, was estimated at 1.7 million tons, while actual catches were in excess of 2 million tons (Kamkredsakul 1996, p. 6). With depleted local stocks, larger fishing vessels have been forced to go farther from Thailand's coasts, often into international, or other nations' waters.[19] Another alternative has been the illegal encroachment of trawlers into protected shallow coastal waters, within the 3,000-meter limit, where trawling activity is especially destructive to both the marine ecology and the livelihood of small-scale fishermen.

In addition to overfishing, the fishing industry also uses illegal and improper fishing methods, such as the use of dynamite and small-mesh nets. These methods tend to kill indiscriminately, including unintended species, as well as immature, nonmarketable fish of commercial species. One estimate put the share of undersized fish caught by the average large trawler at 63 percent (Ridmontri 1996). Damage has been done to the fish population and to the coral, a delicate ecological system and one of the nation's most important tourist attractions. The fisheries industry contributes to and is adversely

17 Including both frozen and canned seafood exports.
18 In addition to larger and faster vessels, there has been a dramatic increase in the use of trawlers, small-mesh driftnets, and other equipment and methods designed to increase yields. Due to both depleted stocks and the increase in the number of participants, however, while total catch figures have risen appreciably, the average amount of catch per trawler has declined significantly (Ridmontri 1996).
19 Thailand, for instance, is the world's largest exporter of canned tuna, none of which is caught in Thai waters.

affected by marine pollution, agricultural runoff, untreated or improperly treated domestic waste, offshore gas and oil operations, land-based water pollution, and the illegal dumping of heavy metals by Thai industries.[20] Ironically, an increasingly significant source of marine pollution is inland and coastal aquaculture practices (New 1990).

Government efforts at national fisheries management have been largely ineffective. Fishing effort ostensibly has been controlled by restrictions on gear (e.g., purse-seine nets), harvest seasons, restricted zones, etc., and these have well-known inefficiencies. More importantly, with over 40,000 legal fishing boats, and only some 50 official vessels, enforcement of regulations has been lacking. Moreover, the government has subsidized diesel fuel for fishing boats at about 20 percent of cost, and given an implicit subsidy to the industry by exempting it from paying minimum wages.

Aquaculture, principally shrimp cultivation, has taken off in the past couple of decades, making Thailand the most important shrimp exporter in the region and giving Thailand a 15 percent share of total world cultured shrimp production in 1991. Most shrimp production is for export; indeed, shrimps and prawns from aquaculture and marine catches accounted for 71 percent of the total value of all of Thailand's 1994 seafood exports (Alpha Research 1995, p. 75). Aquaculture has developed as a booming business in coastal and inland areas and has brought with it its own environmental problems. These include off-site and on-site effects; clearing of ecologically vital mangrove forests; the pollution of water from industry wastes, organic wastes, and chemicals added to stimulate fish growth or prevent disease; and saltwater intrusion into nearby rice farms. Arbhabhirama et al. (1988) estimate that 13 percent of Thailand's total mangrove resources in 1979 were cleared and converted to coastal aquaculture by 1986. The destruction of mangroves, critical in nutrient cycling and filtering, and important as fertile nursery areas for young fish, has negative repercussions on water quality and thus on the fish and wild crustacean populations themselves.

Current government policy for the fisheries and aquaculture industry promotes increased catches, a goal which is at stark cross-purposes with marine life conservation. While there is nominal support for activities such as research and rehabilitation projects, actual practices are not yet evident. Difficulty in checking operational practices (e.g., type of net, use of dynamite, waste treatment) of large numbers of enterprises has made most command-and-control initiatives unenforceable and ineffective. The number, ownership, location, and composition of the fishing fleet are not well

---

20 For more detailed information on marine pollution and its effect on fisheries, see Thoaphom, Atisook, and Vongbudhapitalc (1987); Piyankarnchana (1992); and Kamkredsakul (1996).

known, making it difficult to regulate fishing practices. Government attempts to register prawn farms failed because of the negative connotation associated with industry, and because there were no positive incentives to comply. What change has occurred has been initiated by external sources. Due to the market concentration of Thai seafood exports, measures taken by Japan or the United States are the most likely to affect Thai fishery and aquaculture practices. Strict Japanese food additive regulations have led to controls on antibiotic use. The majority of tuna canneries in Thailand have responded to pressure from U.S. importers to adopt dolphin-safe practices and have ceased purchasing drift-net–caught tuna, and sales of canned tuna have grown since the switchover.

Large mechanized Thai trawlers must now adopt turtle exclusion devices (TEDs) in order to avoid a U.S. ban of shrimp imports from nations whose mechanized fleets are not so equipped. Compliance with U.S. legislation required action by only 13 percent of the total number of fishing vessels, and since most are run by larger companies, they are able to afford the additional costs (Ridmontri 1996). The unilateral U.S. measure was originally opposed by Thai fisheries interests, and the Thai government has appealed to the WTO, claiming it violates rules regarding production and process methods (PPMs). The installation of TEDs has continued, however.

It appears that the fisheries and aquaculture industries will respond to environmental measures provided that compliance is verifiable and that there are sufficient, enforceable penalties for noncompliance. Thus far, measures have come only from outside sources, and although Thai officials have protested many, when implemented the measures have not been significantly detrimental to Thai seafood exports. Measures which involve high compliance costs and mandate severe penalties for noncompliance, however, could have significant negative impacts on Thai exports. If, for instance, avoiding the U.S. shrimp ban entailed equipping *all* vessels with TEDs in order to avoid a ban, the cost of compliance could have been too much for many small-scale fishing vessels, which represent roughly 87 percent of the Thai fleet.

Another development that may affect Thai fisheries' practices is international conflict over marine stocks. As noted, because of dwindling resources Thai vessels have gone farther into non-Thai waters, often bringing them into conflict with vessels of other nations. The increase in number and severity of incidences may provide the incentive to coordinate a regional cooperative fishing management program. As of now, a regional scheme is still lacking, although the sector is engaging in a growing number of joint ventures and bilateral agreements. Such cooperative measures should not only reduce conflict but also reduce overfishing by controlling the number of vessels and catch and improving monitoring of international waters. Aside from joint ventures, other ideas to control overfishing while improving the fishermen's economic situation, include consolidating small fishing companies into larger ones. This would make them easier to monitor and control and would also make it easier for the fishermen to negotiate better terms for loans and credit. Also, there have been calls to better define and publicize fishing zones, which would reduce both overfishing and conflict between competitors within the industry. Regulating other sectors of the economy that contribute to marine pollution would help sustain the fishing industry.

4.3 The Textile Sector

The textile industry has shown continual growth over the past three decades, and textiles have become one of Thailand's leading exports, representing nearly 12 percent of all export revenues in 1994. The textile sector is a large consumer and polluter of water, using water in its washing and dyeing phases and discharging organic and inorganic dyes, bleaches, and other chemicals. In terms of BOD produced, it was found to be the second most polluting industrial sector, and the worst polluter sector in the Bangkok metropolitan region (Qwanruedee 1994; TEI 1994a). The production of textiles also generates air pollutants in the form of chemical-laden vapors and suspended particulate matter.

Several mechanisms exist to reduce water and electricity consumption, increase production efficiency, and reduce pollution in the textile industry. These range from relatively cheap technique modifications, such as adjusting wash cycles, to relatively expensive technologies such as computerized color-matching equipment and wastewater treatment facilities. Studies have found that many of these techniques pay for themselves in reduced inputs and energy consumption and other forms of increased efficiency (TEI 1996). Low capital and start-up costs and a low level of technology has meant that many small- and medium-sized enterprises have entered the textile industry. Indeed, smaller-sized businesses account for roughly half of production capacity. The problem with adopting cleaner practices is that often, even if the new methods or equipment pay for themselves in the long term, initial costs are high and recovery of investment periods are prohibitively long for smaller firms. Because of minimal requirements for entry into the industry, the textile sector is very competitive, especially with countries with low labor and operational costs like China and Indonesia entering the field. Thus Thai companies are very hesitant to take on additional costs.

While some technologies focus on waste minimization and input reduction, which can be profitable, others such as wastewater treatment are purely end-of-pipe measures. This means extra cost burden with no economic return for the producer. A study evaluating costs for basic wastewater treatment in one industrial province in Thailand has shown that costs ranged from an average of 0.5 percent of profits for a basic oxidation ditch process to an average of between 2 and 5 percent for a more sophisticated and effective activated sludge process (Qwanruedee 1994, p. 60). Thus costs for at least basic treatment appear manageable. In the absence of an effective system in which all players are forced to internalize externalities, however, an individual producer has no incentive to change from polluting to cleaner practices, as this will reduce his/her competitiveness and possibly force him/her out of business.

Response to environmental measures has not been uniform in the textile sector. Since large companies are the biggest polluters in terms of overall quantity of wastes produced, have the financial resources to implement better practices, and are the easiest for enforcement agencies to monitor, they have responded better to standards and legislation than have small- and medium-sized enterprises. Small- and medium-size enterprises (SMEs) often tend to ignore these requirements as enforcement is lax and many companies are unregistered and therefore unknown to enforcement agents.

Unlike some sectors that rely on only a few export markets, the Thai textile export market is fairly diverse. Thus textile exporters are not as vulnerable to restrictions imposed unilaterally by a purchasing country as are other sectors. For example, following a German ban of Azo dyestuffs, larger Thai firms exporting to the German market tended to change their practices and sought substitutes. Despite a similar ban against Azo dyes by Thailand itself, smaller companies, unable to afford the change, have simply sought new markets in which the dyes are permitted. This short-term solution will be temporary because they now face more fierce competition from other suppliers with lower labor cost. External voluntary measures such as ecolabelling may have an impact, but only if consumers are willing to pay a higher price for certified goods. Currently all major markets for Thai textiles, with the exception of the Middle East, are implementing or developing ecolabelling schemes for fabrics and garments. Demand for ecolabelled textiles shows strong growth in European markets, with consumers not only wanting to be environmentally responsible but also concerned about fabrics releasing formaldehyde, a known carcinogen (Phantumvanit 1995, p. 15).

To summarize, environmental measures taken in Thailand's export markets will have some effect on improving performance in the Thai textile sector, but for the most part limiting air and water pollution will remain a domestic responsibility. With many clean-technology measures profitable in the long run, the task is to provide favorable credit, especially to SMEs, and to improve monitoring and enforcement. If cleaner technology has a long-term financial return in the form of lower energy, water, and other input requirements, cleaner production could be a win-win solution for the environment *and* trade. Also, it might encourage the Thai industry to shift toward higher value-added products, leaving the lower-end market to new competitors with lower labor costs.

5 Challenges and Opportunities for Sustainable Development

It is time to step back and look at broader issues and lessons. What does Thailand's experience say about the connection between poverty and environment? What can be done to improve the environmental performance of SMEs? How is Thailand affected by international environmental management standards and ecolabelling schemes?

5.1 Poverty and the Environment

The prevailing wisdom is that (1) widespread absolute poverty in rural areas contributes to environmentally abusive practices, (2) rapid economic growth will forestall or alleviate these practices, (3) growth based on an open trade regime and industrialization will create a new set of environmental problems centered on industrial pollution and inadequate urban infrastructure, and (4) at sufficiently high income levels, the demand for environmental quality acting through the political system will surmount the growth of industrial and consumption pollution. The Thai experience provides only very partial support for these propositions.

Thailand has been largely successful at reducing the level of absolute poverty, although those living in poverty remain about 13 percent of the population, and this is again rising due to the current economic crisis. The rapid reduction in poverty did not spare the country from serious degradation of its natural resource base, including forests, soils, fisheries, and natural beauty. And, at the same time, the existence of community forests in economically impoverished areas of northern and northeast Thailand shows that the survival of the poor does not have to be to the detriment of primary resource reserves. Perhaps, more importantly, successes such as community forests demonstrate that policy need not exclusively address issues of poverty before it deals with environmental conservation; rather, it can address both fronts simultaneously by incorporating the local population into resource management. Still, there exists a large portion of the population which, while not living in absolute poverty, are still of very modest means. These people have been a factor in resource depletion and degradation, often being in a position in which they are forced to appropriate virgin lands and deplete natural resources in order to survive. They also are vulnerable to exploitation, having to accept lower standards or to tolerate blatant environmental negligence in order to provide for their basic needs, for example, accepting a hazardous waste-producing company polluting their area because they are desperate for employment. Sometimes they do not know that alternative options exist, and sometimes they lack resources to pursue legal defense of their rights and their local environment.

The poor often suffer the most from environmentally unsound development, being the most directly dependent on primary resources. They also have the least economic weight to oppose measures that adversely affect them. Examples are the conversion of forested land used by the poor for basic building materials, fuel, and food, and the construction of hydroelectric dams, which flood areas cropped by farmers engaging in subsistence agriculture. Experience in Thailand shows that local populations, of varying economic means, can responsibly develop their own areas, especially when given the initial organizational support network by the government or other outside parties. Local populations tend to know best their own needs, and should not be consulted *after* a plan has already been devised, but in the initial planning stage. When a project is considered, the economic hardship incurred by the local population should be taken into account in calculating the cost of such development projects, and in national accounting schemes. Experience also shows that not incorporating the local population into development planning can result in resentment and active opposition by the local stakeholders, which translates into administrative and political problems for the government and the party responsible for the development.

The Thai experience does bear out the third proposition; growth based on trade and industrialization has generated a new set of environmental problems including industrial pollution, urbanization that outstrips basic infrastructure, and urban air pollution (due in large measure to increased private auto use). The evidence on the last proposition, that higher incomes create demand for environmental quality, is inconclusive. Certainly the demand is present, but translating that into effective policies, and actually reaching a turning point in environmental indices, is a work in progress.

5.2 The Question of Size

SMEs face special difficulties in adopting environmentally sound practices and their situation is of particular relevance to Thailand. They account for an overwhelming percentage of total enterprises, and a significant share of production and export capacity and industrial pollution. A survey of Samut Prakarn Province near Bangkok found that 97 percent of all firms were SMEs, with household or cottage industries alone representing 38 percent. These SMEs were responsible for 43 percent of the BOD produced by all industries (Visvanathan and Lien Ha 1994, p. 44).

SMEs are at a disadvantage in accessing and implementing environmentally less damaging production methods for a number of reasons:

1 They have difficulty acquiring information regarding the availability and suitability of environmentally sound technology.
2 They have fewer qualified personnel to operate new technologies.
3 Some technologies are developed by larger firms that offer the technology at prohibitive rates to SMEs.
4 Technologies developed and tailor-made for larger firms may not be applicable to smaller-sized firms.
5 Technologies requiring economies of scale may only be profitable for larger companies.
6 Even when suitable technology is available, SMEs are often unable to finance the lag between installation and the time at which initial investments are recovered.
7 SMEs are often unable to finance projects themselves and are denied the credit granted in the formal sector for high risks.

SMEs have less incentive to implement cleaner production methods as well. Because they exist in highly competitive markets, they cannot pass along extra costs in price if they are not convinced that their competitors will do likewise.[21] Also, many SMEs are not registered, making them difficult to find. While the Department of Industrial Works (DIW) in Thailand is responsible for enforcing environmental regulations in a nondiscriminatory manner, in reality large firms are easier to locate and are potentially larger polluters than individual small firms and therefore account for a large share

---

21 This explains some of the reluctance to phase out CFCs in the refrigeration industry.

of the understaffed DIW's monitoring efforts. Evaluations of SMEs in Thailand suggest that there is great potential for improving their environmental practices, provided the proper support infrastructure and staff are available. While some of the cleaner techniques and technologies are beyond the reach of many SMEs, many practices that are significantly cleaner than present methods are feasible. Perhaps the most important obstacle that needs to be overcome is lack of knowledge of options available. A central information bank and network needs to be established specifically tailored to SMEs' needs. This could be done at a national or a regional level. A means of connecting SMEs with those capable of installing and maintaining new equipment must also be established, as individually many SMEs are unable to employ such people. Financial services, as well, should be viewed as part of a larger approach to promoting cleaner technologies, and they should be tailored to specific SME needs, for example, taking the time estimated to receive a return on initial investments for given technologies into consideration in determining credit terms. Finally, because of the high costs of proper waste treatment for individual businesses, economic incentives need to be provided to encourage SMEs to locate in areas where central treatment systems can be built. Special economic zones for SMEs have been suggested as an attempt to help smaller firms. If such zones were to concentrate same-sector businesses together, as is currently done in the leather-tanning industry, costs could be reduced for central treatment and perhaps for waste recovery as well.

5.3 External Environmental Requirements Including ISO 14000 and Ecolabelling

The evidence reviewed in this chapter displays a mixed trade response to external environmental regulations. The Thai electronics sector has accomplished ODS phaseout better than the refrigeration and air-conditioning sector. Foreign health and safety regulations for seafood exports can be met, but if wood products required certification of originating from sustainably managed forests, Thailand would be disadvantaged. The new challenges will include the ISO 14000 environmental management standards and expanded ecolabelling schemes. Thai firms were slow to seek the earlier ISO 9000 certification for quality management, and are responding more readily to the market challenge of ISO 14000. For example, in 1996 the Thailand Environment Institute launched an ISO 14000 certification workshop, and by mid-1997 two dozen Thai firms had been certified. ISO 14000 has the potential to significantly improve the environmental performance of Thai industry and in many instances will lead to long-term cost savings in water, energy, and materials and improved product quality.

The same potential commercial and environmental advantages and similar trade barrier concerns arise from expanded ecolabelling schemes. (Thailand itself is developing its own scheme, Green Label, which will involve life-cycle assessment.) Assuming mutual recognition and equivalency, the economic benefit of ecolabelling is to gain access to foreign markets. Market potential for ecocertified goods varies depending on sector and designated market. As mentioned earlier, studies show relatively big market potential for ecolabelled goods in the wood-product sector, and demand for verified dolphin-safe tuna has already brought about change in Thailand's marine fisheries practices. At the same time, Thailand, like other developing countries, is concerned that ISO 14000 will become an unnecessary nontariff trade barrier.

6 A Concluding Thought

Thailand is a classic case of a country initially very rich in natural resources that enjoyed sustained high levels of economic growth following liberal trade principles.[22] The improvements in material standards of living, health and nutrition, and economic opportunity for most Thais are very substantial and should not be discounted. But at the same time, much of its natural resource base is severely degraded, and pollution is endemic, especially in urban areas. The appropriate question is not whether this development path was or is sustainable. The central question is whether the accomplishments in terms of GDP growth and related improvement in social welfare could have been accomplished at lower environmental cost. The evidence suggests unnecessarily high costs. Despite short-run financial gains, deforestation, degradation of soils, overfishing, and diminished natural beauty to support ecotourism now leave the economy with a lower stock of productive natural capital. The loss of this natural capital limits real income now and in the future. The earlier failure to disperse industry to appropriately controlled sites in rural regions led to excessive concentration of population and pollution in the Bangkok area, and tended to disrupt stable social relations in rural areas. Investment promotion policy put a high priority on employment and income generation and a low priority on general environmental welfare. Failure to control pollution, especially toxic wastes, puts a substantial

---

22 The 1997–1998 crisis stems from financial excesses and represents a very different form of unsustainable development.

remedial cleanup burden on current and future generations. Had this neglect of the environment been *necessary* for material progress, one might argue that on balance the choice was correct. But the evidence points the other way – virtually the same material progress could have been achieved had strong environmental protection measures been in place. Liberal trade policies were an essential component of this flawed strategy. But ultimately, the defects in domestic development policy, not trade, were responsible for the excessive environmental costs.

19

Looking Back, Looking Forward

It is time to draw together the main themes and conclusions of the book and to look ahead toward the next steps in merging environmental and international economics. Our basic thesis has been that the discipline of economics provides powerful and useful tools for understanding environmental degradation and for devising policies to moderate conflict between economic and environmental systems, and that with some modifications economic analysis can perform these roles in an international context. There is little question that over the past 30 years economics has advanced our understanding of the roots of environmental degradation. The related concepts of externalities, public goods, and open-access common property resources, together with the notion of government failure, provide a coherent and durable explanation of pollution and misuse of natural resources. Economics has also made considerable progress in assisting the formulation of policy. Two notable areas are new, innovative techniques for monetizing environmental damages, permitting environmental policies to be analyzed in a cost-benefit framework, and research showing the efficiency advantages of market-friendly policy instruments such as tradeable permits. Policy analysis has also been assisted by improved data on the links between economic activity and environmental variables and improved accounting techniques, such as the extension of input-output tables linked to environmental vectors and the "greening" of traditional national income accounting.

The limits to economic analysis are also more clearly seen, and this, too, is progress. One limit is grounded in the inherently political nature of environmental policy. All measures to protect and improve the environment involve a rearrangement of property rights, and therefore involve politics and require political analysis. A second limit is ethical, and this limit emerges in a number of ways. Economics *per se* cannot make interpersonal welfare comparisons, and this restricts strong statements concerning welfare

543

improvement resulting from environmental policy when compensation is not paid by gainers to losers. The problem is even more acute with intergenerational welfare transfers because the traditional political protections in a democratic society are absent – future generations do not vote on resource and environmental use today. Sorting out intergenerational efficiency and equity is as much an ethical as an economic challenge. Even more fundamental, economics has to dodge the ethical question of whether nature, including wilderness areas and wildlife, has intrinsic values that cannot be brought within the economist's measuring rod of willingness to pay. The reliance on willingness to pay has a double ethical component. Willingness to pay depends on ability to pay and hence income distribution, an ethical issue. But even if society were satisfied with income distribution, willingness to pay does not protect intrinsic values for nonhuman species. At some point, environmental choices are beyond the reach of economic analysis. A third limit is imperfect knowledge and its close relatives, risk and uncertainty. The traditional economic approach to risk, where probabilities are known, is to calculate and make decisions based on expected values and to acknowledge risk through hedging and insurance. This approach is less satisfactory in those environmental circumstances where uncertainty is great and probabilities not known, where damages are potentially large and irreversible, and when insurance markets are defective or absent. Global warming is the preeminent example, and the role of economic analysis, while valuable, has serious limits.

We have identified two broad areas where environmental and economic systems intersect at the international level – trade and environment, and international externalities – and we have examined the concept of sustainable development as an approach for unifying or reconciling economic and environmental systems. With regard to trade and environment, it is possible to modify the traditional theory and theorems of international trade to accommodate environmental variables, and to conclude that the environment is an additional determinant of comparative advantage. The novelties of the extension are to recognize that (1) environmental endowments and demand for their services differ among countries and thus help determine the pattern of trade, (2) environmental services enter production functions and "shadow prices" for these services are needed if trade is to be efficient, and (3) environmental "markets" are riddled with externality and common property characteristics, which if uncorrected lead to trade distortions. One conclusion is that as countries go about the business of correcting distortions from preexisting environmental externalities, the pattern of comparative advantage, and hence the pattern of international trade will necessarily, and desirably, change. A second theoretical insight is that international trade drives a spatial wedge between those who bear the pollution burden of a production externality and those who consume the product. While this raises the possibility of "environmental exploitation" – one country shifting its resource depletion and pollution burden to another – a better interpretation is that the primary responsibility for environmental protection rests with the producing and exporting country for production externalities, and the responsibility for limiting consumption pollution rests with the importing and consuming country. This division of responsibility is consistent with GATT principles and rules. From a different perspective, the task is to ensure that export and import prices reflect the full social costs of production. If they do not, trade is distorted and the gains from trade may be illusionary.

The models developed in Part 2 in general do not pose a wholly new challenge to, or justify a derogation from, the doctrine of free trade. While it is easy enough to build models (or find real world examples) in which increased exports lead to environmental degradation, perhaps to the extent of negating the putative gains from trade, the underlying cause is inappropriate or absent domestic environmental protection policies, not trade *per se*. The important conclusion here is that trade does alter the level and composition of production and consumption, and appropriate environmental policies must be in place and adjusted accordingly, if trade is to improve welfare. Thus, there is a strong case for jointly formulating trade and environmental policies, especially in trade-dependent countries relying on pollution-intensive industries and natural-resource-intensive sectors. With regard to the theory of policy, that branch of trade theory known as the theory of domestic distortions is directly relevant. A principal conclusion is that trade measures are inefficient (second-best) in correcting domestic environmental externalities.

While inclusion of the environment does not pose a new challenge to free trade, it does provide a twist to many elements of conventional trade and environmental theory. For example, in the case of the optimal tariff to secure a terms-of-trade gain (a valid exception to free trade if welfare is measured at the national level), an optimal environmental tax or standard would be adjusted downward to reflect its terms-of-trade effects. Also, for a popular but narrow strategic trade policy model involving "rent switching," it is possible that manipulation of environmental subsidies and taxes can be used to increase output and welfare in the home country. But it should be emphasized that these examples are both "beggar-thy-neighbor" strategies.

Not all trade-environment policy issues have been resolved, however. A persistent question is whether one or more countries may act as a "pollution haven" in an attempt to improve their competitive position. International trade rules have been developed to address overt "unfair trade" practices, namely dumping and subsidies. These rules are not necessarily grounded in narrow economic analysis, as a case can be made that an importing country, the "dumpee," gains from low-priced, subsidized imports. In practice, antidumping and countervailing duties may be defended on fairness grounds but are often used as covert protection. Nevertheless, it may be necessary to pay some attention to "fair trade" if support for a liberal trade system is to be maintained. In that connection, the unresolved question is what, if any, trade sanctions should be applied to unfair trade based on artificially low or absent environmental protection standards. A related, unresolved question is if, when, and how trade measures should be used when one country damages international resources, or indeed, through transnational pollution, harms the environment of another country. Along the same lines, there is no consensus about when and how to use trade sanctions to promote and enforce multilateral environmental agreements. Trade inducements such as tariff reductions are theoretically superior to trade restrictions, as they liberalize trade and they do not invite (inefficient) coercion, but even here one country may threaten noncooperation to extort a payment. The questions of using trade measures in support of international environmental objectives will be prominent in international negotiations to limit greenhouse gas emissions. It needs repeating that an overarching problem is that there is no effective market in which the environmental preferences of one country can effectively "buy" environmental behavior in a second, and the use of trade measures is viewed as a fallback device.

There are also numerous, divisive trade-environment issues at the level of the WTO and GATT. The contentious issues include whether environmental subsidies identified as nonactionable (i.e., against which countervailing duties cannot be imposed) are too broad or too narrow; GATT's treatment of border adjustments for indirect taxes on inputs to production, which may be antithetical to the goal of internalizing environmental costs; whether GATT has been interpreting its general exception provisions (Article XX) too narrowly and thereby undercutting legitimate national environmental legislation; disputes concerning the "least trade restrictive" tests for product standards in the Technical Barriers to Trade and the Sanitary and Phytosanitary Agreements; the current interpretation of PPMs, which draws a line between the product-related standards that an importing country can legitimately insist on and those it cannot; and the possibility that ecolabelling schemes and ISO environmental standards may be used for covert protection, and, if so, how they might be made subject to GATT disciplines. Some of these issues are variations of long-standing ambiguities in international trade rules. While in aggregate the value of trade in actual environmental disputes is relatively modest, the resolution of these points of contention is important for two reasons. First, so long as they are unresolved, they undermine support for a liberal trade system. As illustrated by President Clinton's failure to gain Fast Track authority in fall 1997, environmental opposition can impede new trade legislation. Second, there is considerable concern in developing countries that trade-environment rules made by industrial countries are manipulated in a fashion that denies the developing countries market access for their exports, thus weakening their commitment to a liberal trade system.

Transnational pollution and the management of international environmental resources has been a fertile area for economic research in the past decade and is likely to remain so. As a result of this research, the basic problem is now better appreciated. The natural environment does not respect political borders. Residents of one country have a direct welfare interest in the condition of certain *international* resources – the climate system, gene pools, biodiversity – and also in the transnational movement of pollutants such as SO_2 and the salinity and sediment load of rivers. Environmentalists and others do not, however, have efficient international markets through which they can express their preferences. Property rights are absent or in dispute. At the same time, the international political system remains centered on the nation state and national sovereignty so that international environmental protection measures must be negotiated, not imposed.

If countries pursue their parochial self-interest, they can and do create externality costs for others. Although there is a principle of international law that states that countries cannot use their territory in a fashion that degrades the environment of another state, the implementation and enforcement of the principle is weak. At the national level, external costs are addressed by national governments either by clarifying property rights and allowing a "market" to develop, by more direct intervention specifying pollution limits (command and control), or by inducing/coercing compliance through subsidies and taxes. At the international level, property rights to environmental resources are ill-defined, and there is no political authority, no supranational EPA, that can compel compliance. Hence it is necessary to reach more or less voluntary agreements among governments. This is the art of negotiating property rights to international resources or, more broadly, providing international collective goods.

Without supranational authority, the problems of controlling transnational pollution and managing international resources combine the task of establishing property rights *and* the Coasian task of delivering an efficient, marketlike solution to externalities and open-access resources. This point is worth emphasizing. Whether the issue is ocean fisheries or global warming or genetic diversity, the resolution requires some agreement first on who has rights to what and, second, how those rights can be "marketized" so that those who wish to "buy" can transact with those who wish to "sell."

One clear difficulty in accomplishing these tasks is differences among countries and cultures in the valuation of environmental services and differences in attitudes toward risk. Both are indirectly related to differences in economic circumstances. Rich countries value environmental amenities services more highly than poor countries. Rich and poor countries also evaluate the risks of environmental disasters and of slow economic growth differently. The differences show up in different discount rates and spill over into different conceptions of intergenerational equity.

Another problem in assigning property rights and negotiating marketlike agreements to protect international environmental resources is strategic behavior. Economic analysis is starting to use game theory and related analytical techniques to analyze states' behavior in managing international environmental resources. The immediate analytical difficulties in this research are twofold. First, once one gets beyond simple, two-country, once-off games, most behavioral models are not robust and general. Second, the underlying premise of most models is that states act in their national interest, and this is highly questionable when environmental protection is involved. To be specific, the current, immediate post-Kyoto debate on global warming in the United States is greatly influenced by special interest group advocacy, and the arguments are almost exclusively focused on U.S. self-interest under a Cournot-like assumption that what the United States does (or does not do) does not effect other countries' behavior. Thus the U.S. position and policy may not accurately reflect U.S. welfare, and its policy may not fully recognize the benefits of a cooperative strategy. If game theory modeling of international environmental management is to be realistic, it must move beyond the assumption that governments negotiate to secure the "national interest." The literature on the political economy of trade policy will be helpful in this regard as will "two-level" game theory.

There is a danger, however, in putting excessive emphasis on the difficulties of controlling international externalities and in managing international resources. Chapters 13 and 15 contain a number of examples where progress has been made. In some instances, for example, ocean fisheries, it has been possible to clarify property rights at the national level and provide the preconditions for effective resource management. Rudimentary international markets have been activated through debt-for-nature swaps, the Global Environmental Facility, and the commercialization of certain biological and genetic resources. Arguably, the threat of trade sanctions played a constructive role in reducing emissions of ozone-depleting substances in the Montreal Protocol. In sum, there are several examples of reasonable success in managing international resources.

The concept of sustainable development has been promoted as a unifying strategy, within which economic growth and environmental protection are to be simultaneously achieved and the interests of future generations protected. There has been some success in this effort. The need to maintain the productivity of renewable resources has achieved higher visibility in development strategies and development-assistance institutions. Incorporating the value of nonmarketed environmental services in cost-benefit analysis is more frequent today than 10 or 20 years ago. The earlier plundering of natural resources for export earning, as was evident in Thailand, or the neglect of the environmental consequences of export-oriented development, as exemplified by Costa Rica in the 1980s, has been moderated if not eliminated. Experiments in revising national income accounts to account for natural resource depletion give a more accurate picture of sustainable development or its absence.

Still, it remains to be seen whether sustainable development is a durable concept, or whether, like its predecessors – the Conservation Movement in the United States in the early part of the 20th century and the flirtations by the international community with basic human needs, ecodevelopment, and "appropriate" technology as guides to development in the 1970s and 1980s – sustainable development will fade into a platitude. The *economics* of sustainable development have taken a singular and perhaps unpromising direction. The admonishment to meet the needs of the present generation and to "address the essential needs of the world's poor, to which overriding priority should be given" (World Commission on Environment and Development, 1987) – the *intra*generational dimension of sustainable development – has been more or less neglected by economists. Instead, economic research has focused on the intergenerational aspect of sustainable development, and in particular devising dynamically optimal consumption paths with and without natural resources, and with and without technological progress. These models are not without their value in clarifying the distinction between optimal and sustainable development paths, in underscoring the importance of technology, and in understanding the extent to which environmental and man-made capital are substitutable in production and in consumption. Most importantly, they redress a long-standing neglect of natural and environmental resources in economic development and growth analysis. But at their high level of abstraction, the models tend to suppress the ethical dimensions of intergenerational use of environmental resources, ignore the international political context in which environmental and natural resources are offered for trade, and skip over the intragenerational component of sustainable development. Looking ahead, these last areas are ripe for further analysis.

References

Abrego, Lisandro, Carlo Perroni, John Whalley, and Randall M. Wigle. 1997. Trade and Environment: Bargaining Outcomes from Linked Negotiations. Working Paper W6216, National Bureau of Economic Research, Cambridge, MA.

Alpha Research Co. Ltd and Manager Information Services (MIS) Co. Ltd. 1995. *Thailand Export Focus 1995*. Pocket edition. Bangkok.

Anderson, Kym. 1992a. Effects on the Environment and Welfare of Liberalizing World Trade: The Cases of Coal and Food. In *The Greening of World Trade Issues*, edited by Kym Anderson and Richard Blackhurst. Ann Arbor: University of Michigan Press.

———. 1992b. The Standard Welfare Economics of Environmental Policies in Open Economies. In *The Greening of World Trade Issues*, edited by Kym Anderson and Richard Blackhurst. Ann Arbor: University of Michigan Press.

Arbhabhirama, A., D. Phantumvanit, J. Elkington, and P. Ingkasuwan. 1988. *Thailand: Natural Resources Profile*. Singapore: Oxford University Press.

Aquerreta-Ferra, Carmen. 1996. The Turbot War: A Study of Fisheries Management. Mimeo. Johns Hopkins University, School of Advanced International Studies.

Baharuddin, Hj. G. 1995. Timber Certification: An Overview. *Unasylva* 46(183). Rome: United Nations Food and Agriculture Organization.

Baldwin, Richard. 1995. Does Sustainability Require Growth? In *The Economics of Sustainable Development*, edited by Ian Goldin and L. Alan Winters. Paris: Organization for Economic Cooperation and Development (OECD).

Bank of Thailand (BOT). 1996. *Monthly Bulletin*, Bangkok.

Bangkok Post, February 20, 1996.

Barbier, Edward B. 1994. Valuing Environmental Functions: Tropical Wetlands. *Land Economics* 70(2):155–73.

———. 1995a. Elephant Ivory and Tropical Timber: The Role of Trade Interventions in Sustainable Management. *Journal of Environment and Development* 4(2).

———. 1995b. Trade in Timber-based Forest Products and the Implications of the Uruguay Round. *Unasylva* 46(183). Rome: United Nations Food and Agriculture Organization.

———. 1997. Introduction to the Environmental Kuznets Curve Special Issue. *Environment and Development Economics* 2(4):369–81.

551

Barbier, Edward, Nancy Bockstael, Joanne Burgess, and Ivar Strand. 1995. The Linkages Between the Timber Trade and Tropical Deforestation – Indonesia. *The World Economy* 18(3):411–22.

Barbier, Edward B., Joanne C. Burgess, Timothy M. Swanson, and David W. Pearce. 1990. *Elephants, Economics and Ivory*. London: Earthscan Publications.

Barnett, Harold J., and Chandler Morse. 1963. *Scarcity and Growth*. Baltimore: Johns Hopkins University Press for Resources for the Future.

Barrett, Scott. 1991. The Problem of Global Environmental Protection. In *Economic Policies Toward the Environment*, edited by Dieter Helm. Oxford: Basil Blackwell.

———. 1993. Strategic Environmental Policy and International Trade. *Journal of Public Economics* 54:325–38.

———. 1994. Self-Enforcing International Agreements. *Oxford Economic Papers* 46:878–94.

———. 1999. The Credibility of Trade Sanctions in International Environmental Agreements. In *Trade, Global Policy, and the Envirnoment*, edited by Per G. Fredricksson. World Bank Discussion Paper no. 402.

Bartelmus, Peter. 1997. The Value of Nature: Valuation and Evaluation in Environmental Accounting. Working paper, United Nations Department of Economic and Social Information and Policy Analysis, New York.

Bartelmus, Peter, Ernst Lutz, and Stefan Schweinfest. 1993. Integrated Environmental and Economic Accounting: A Case Study for Papua New Guinea. Paper presented at symposium, UNSTAT – World Bank, Washington, D.C.

Bateman, Ian J. 1993. Valuation of the Environment, Methods and Techniques: Revealed Preference Methods. In *Sustainable Environmental Economics and Management*, edited by R. Kerry Turner. London: Belhaven Press.

Bateman, Ian J., and R. Kerry Turner. 1993. Valuation of the Environment, Methods and Techniques: the Contingent Valuation Method. In *Sustainable Environmental Economics and Management*, edited by R. Kerry Turner. London: Belhaven Press.

Batra, Raveendra. 1993. *The Myth of Free Trade*. New York: Charles Scribner's Sons.

Baumol, William J., and Wallace E. Oates. 1988. 2d ed. *The Theory of Environmental Policy*. Cambridge: Cambridge University Press.

Beausejour, Louis, Gordon Lenjosek, and Michael Smart. 1995. A CGE Approach to Modelling Carbon Dioxide Emissions Control in Canada and the United States. *World Economy* 18(3):457–88.

Beckerman, Wilfred. 1992. Economic Development and the Environment: Conflict or Complementarity? *Policy Research Working Paper* (August). Office of the Vice President, Development Economics. The World Bank.

———. 1994. Sustainable Development: Is it a Useful Concept? *Environmental Values* 3(3):191–209.

Beghin, John, David Roland-Holst, and Dominique van der Mensbrugghe. 1995. Trade Liberalization and the Environment in the Pacific Basin: Coordinated Approaches to Mexican Trade and Environment Policy. *American Journal of Agricultural Economics* 77(3):778–85.

Beltratti, Andrea. 1996. *Models of Economic Growth with Environmental Assets*. Dordrecht: Kluwer Academic.

Beltratti, Andrea, Graciela Chichilnisky, and Geoffrey M. Heal. 1995. Sustainable Growth and the Green Golden Rule. In *The Economics of Sustainable Development*, edited by Ian Goldin and L. Alan Winters. Cambridge: Cambridge University Press.

Benedick, Richard Elliot. 1991. *Ozone Diplomacy: New Directions in Safeguarding the Planet*. Cambridge, MA: Harvard University Press.

Bergman, Lars. 1995. Environment-economic Interactions in a Computable General Equilibrium Model – A Case Study of Sweden. In *Current Issues in Environmental Economics*, edited by Per-Olar Johansson, Bengt Kriström, and Karl-Göran Mäler. Manchester: Manchester University Press.

Bernstein, Paul, and W. David Montgomery, n.d. How Much Could Kyoto Really Cost? Mimeo. Washington, D.C.: Charles Rivers Associates.

Birdsall, Nancy, and David Wheeler. 1993. Trade Policy and Industrial Pollution in Latin America: Where are the Pollution Havens? *Journal of Environment & Development* 2(1):137–50.

Birnie, Patricia W., and Alan E. Boyle. 1992. *International Law and the Environment*. Oxford: Clarendon Press.

Bishop, Richard C., and Richard T. Woodward. 1995. Valuation of Environmental Quality Under Certainty. In *The Handbook of Environmental Economics*, edited by Daniel W. Bromley. Oxford: Basil Blackwell.

Böhringer, Christoph, and Thomas Rutherford. 1997. Carbon Taxes with Exemptions in an Open Economy: A General Equilibrium Analysis of the German Tax Initiative. *Journal of Environmental Economics and Management* 32(2):189–203.

Boulding, Kenneth E. 1966. The Economics of the Coming Spaceship Earth. In *Environmental Quality in a Growing World*, edited by Henry Jarrett. Baltimore: Johns Hopkins University Press.

Bourke, I. J. 1995. International Trade in Forest Products and the Environment. *Unasylva* 46(183). Rome: United Nations Food and Agriculture Organization.

Bovenborg, A. Lans, and Ruud A. Mooij. 1994. Environmental Levies and Distortionary Taxation. *American Economic Review* 84(4):1085–89.

Boyd, Roy, Kerry Krutilla, and W. Kip Viscusi. 1995. Energy Taxation as a Policy Instrument to Reduce CO_2 Emissions: A Net Benefit Analysis. *Journal of Environmental Economics and Management* 29(1):1–24.

Brack, Duncan. 1996. *International Trade and the Montreal Protocol*. Royal Institute of International Affairs, London: Earthscan.

Brander, James, and Barbara Spencer. 1981. Tariffs and the Extraction of Foreign Monopoly Rents under Potential Entry. *Canadian Journal of Economics* 14(3):371–89.

Brander, James, and M. Scott Taylor. 1998. Open Access Renewable Resources: Trade and Trade Policy in a Two Country Model. *Journal of International Economics* 44(2):181–209.

Brekke, Kjell Arne. 1997. Hicksian Income from Resource Extraction in an Open Economy. *Land Economics* 73(4):516–27.

Bromley, Daniel. 1989. *Economic Interests and Institutions: The Conceptual Foundations of Public Policy*. New York: Basil Blackwell.

Bromley, Daniel, ed. 1995. *The Handbook of Environmental Economics*. Oxford: Basil Blackwell.

Brookshire, David S., Alan Randall, Jr., and John R. Stoll. 1980. Valuing

Increments and Decrements in Natural Resource Service Flows. *American Journal of Agricultural Economics* 62(3):478–88.

Bruce, James P., Hoe-song Yi, and Erik F. Haites, eds. 1996. *Climate Change 1995: Economic and Social Dimensions of Climate Change*. Intergovernmental Panel on Climate Change, Working Group III. Cambridge: Cambridge University Press for the Intergovernmental Panel on Climate Change.

Buchanan, James M. 1967. Cooperation and Conflict in Public-Goods Interaction. *Western Economic Journal* 5:109–21.

———. 1969. External Diseconomies, Corrective Taxes, and Market Structure. *American Economic Review* 59(1):174–77.

Bui, Linda T. M. 1998. Gains from Trade and Strategic Interaction: Equilibrium Acid Rain Abatement in the Eastern United States and Canada. *The American Economic View* 88(4):984–1001.

Bunce, Arthur. 1942. *The Economics of Soil Conservation*. Ames, Iowa: Iowa State College Press.

Bunn, Julie, and David Blaney. 1997. To Trade or Not to Trade: The Basel Convention and the Transboundary Movement and Disposal of Hazardous Wastes. Pew Case Studies in International Affairs, Institute for the Study of Diplomacy.

Burgess, Joanne. 1994. The Environmental Effects of Trade in Endangered Species. In *The Environmental Effects of Trade*. Paris: Organization for Economic Cooperation and Development.

Burniaux, J. M., J. P. Martin, G. Nicoletti, and J. O. Martins. 1992. GREEN, Working Paper 115, Organization for Economic Cooperation and Development, Paris.

Burrows, Paul. 1995. Nonconvexities and the Theory of External Costs. In *The Handbook of Environmental Economics*, edited by Daniel W. Bromley. Oxford: Basil Blackwell.

Burtraw, Dallas. 1996. Cost Saving Without Allowance Trades? *Contemporary Economic Policy* 14(2):79–94.

———. 1998. Cost Savings, Market Performance and Economic Benefits of the U.S. Acid Rain Program. Discussion Paper 98-28, Resources for the Future.

Carraro, Carlo, and Domenico Siniscalco. 1995. Policy Coordination for Sustainability: Commitments, Transfers, and Linked Negotiations. In *The Economics of Sustainable Development*, edited by Ian Goldin and Alan Winters. Cambridge: Cambridge University Press.

Carson, Carol S., and Steven J. Landefeld. 1994. Accounting for Mineral Resources: Issues and BEA's Initial Estimates. U.S. Department of Commerce, *Survey of Current Business* 74(4):50–72.

Carson, Rachel. 1962. *Silent Spring*. Boston: Houghton Mifflin.

Carter, Barry E., and Phillip R. Trimble. 1995. *International Law: Selected Documents*. Boston: Little, Brown.

Carter, Vernon Gill, and Tom Dale. 1955. *Top Soil and Civilization*. Norman: University of Oklahoma Press.

Chander, Parkash, and Henry Tulkens. 1992. Theoretical Foundations of Negotiations and Cost Sharing in Transfrontier Pollution Problems. *European Economic Review* 36(2–3):388–99.

Charnovitz, Steve. 1993a. Encouraging Environmental Cooperation Through the Pelly Amendment. *Journal of Environment and Development* 3(1).

———. 1993b. Environmentalism Confronts GATT Rules: Recent Developments and New Opportunities. *Journal of World Trade* 27(2):37–54.

———. 1994. The World Trade Organization and Environmental Supervisions. *International Environmental Reporter*, Bureau of National Affairs, 26 January.

———. 1997. A Critical Guide to the WTOs Report on Trade and Environment. *Arizona Journal of International and Comparative Law* 14(2):341–79.

Chenery, Hollis, Jere Behrman, and T. N. Srivivasan, eds. 1995. *Handbook of Development Economics*. New York: Elsevier Science Publishing Co.

Chiang, Alpha. 1992. *Elements of Dynamic Optimization*. New York: McGraw-Hill.

Chichilinsky, Graciela. 1994. North-South Trade and the Global Environment. *The American Economic Review* 84(4):851–74.

Chichilinsky, Graciela, and Geoffrey Heal. 1994. Who Should Abate Carbon Emissions? An International Viewpoint. *Economics Letters* 44(4):443–49.

———. 1995. Market for Tradeable CO_2 Emissions Quotas: Principles and Practices. Working paper no. 153, Organization for Economic Cooperation and Development.

Christy, Francis, and Anthony Scott. 1965. *The Commonwealth in Ocean Fisheries*. Baltimore: Johns Hopkins University Press for Resources for the Future.

Churchill, R. R. 1992. EC Fisheries and an EZ-Easy! *Ocean Development and International Law* 23(2–3):145–63.

———. 1993. Fisheries Issues in Maritime Boundary Delimitation. *Marine Policy* 17(1):44–57.

Clark, Colin. 1976. *Mathematical Bioeconomics: The Optimal Management of Renewable Resources*. New York: Wiley.

Clark, Ian N., Philip J. Major, and Nina Mollett. 1988. Development and Implementation of New Zealand's ITQ Management System. *Marine Resources Economics* 5:325–49.

Cline, William R. 1992. *The Economics of Global Warming*. Washington, D.C.: Institute for International Economics.

Coase, Ronald. 1960. The Problem of Social Cost. *Journal of Law and Economics* 3:1–44.

Commoner, Barry. 1972. *The Closing Circle: Nature, Man, and Technology*. New York: Knopf.

Conrad, Klaus. 1993. Taxes and Subsidies for Pollution Intensive Industries as Trade Policy. *Journal of Environmental Economics and Management* 25(2):121–35.

Copeland, Brian. 1994. International Trade and the Environment: Policy Reform in a Polluted Small Open Economy. *Journal of Environmental Economics and Management* 26(1):44–65.

Copeland, Brian, and M. Scott Taylor. 1994. North-South Trade and the Environment. *Quarterly Journal of Economics* 109(3):755–87.

———. 1995a. Trade and the Environment: A Partial Synthesis. *American Journal of Agricultural Economics* 77(3):765–71.

———. 1995b. Trade and Transboundary Pollution. *American Economic Review* 85(4):716–37.

Corden, W. Max. 1997. *Trade Policy and Economic Welfare*. 2d ed. London: Oxford University Press.

Crawford, JoAnn. 1995. Debt-For-Nature Swaps: An Analysis of their Impact on Conservation. Mimeo. Johns Hopkins University, School of Advanced International Studies (January).

Cropper, Maureen, and Charles Griffiths. 1994. The Interactions of Population Growth and Environmental Quality. *American Economic Review* 84:250–54.

Cruz, Wilfredo and Robert Repetto. 1992. *The Environmental Effects of Stabilization and Structural Adjustment Programs: The Philippines Case.* Washington, D.C.: World Resources Institute.

———. 1991. *Accounts Overdue: National Resource Depletion in Costa Rica.* Washington, D.C.: World Resources Institute.

Cutter Information Corp. 1997. Public Sector Tests the Use of Environmental Management Systems. *Business and Environment: ISO Update.* Arlington, MA.

Dasgupta, Partha S., and Geoffrey M. Heal. 1979. *Economic Theory and Exhaustible Resources.* Cambridge: Cambridge University Press.

Dasgupta, Partha, Karl-Göran Mäler, and Alessandro Vercelli, eds. 1997. *The Economics of Transnational Commons.* Oxford: Clarendon Press.

Dasgupta, Susmita, Benoit Laplante, and Nlandu Mamingi. 1999. Pollution and Capital Markets in Developing Countries. In *Trade, Global Policy, and the Environment*, edited by Per G. Fredriksson. World Bank Discussion Paper no. 402.

Dean, A. 1995. Costs of Cutting CO_2 Emissions: Evidence from Top Down Models. In *Climate Change, Economic Instruments, and Income Distribution.* Paris: Organization for Economic Cooperation and Development.

Dean, Judith M. 1992. Trade and the Environment: A Survey of the Literature. In *International Trade and the Environment*, edited by Patrick Low. Discussion paper 159, World Bank.

———. 1995. Export Bans, Environment, and Developing Country Welfare. *Review of International Economics* 3(3):319–29.

———. 1999. Testing the Impact of Trade Liberalization on the Environment: Theory and Evidence. In *Trade, Global Policy, and the Environment*, edited by Per G. Fredricksson. World Bank Discussion Paper no. 402.

Dean, Judith M. and Shubhashis Gangopadhyay. 1997. Export Bans, Environmental Protection, and Unemployment. *Review of Development Economics* 1(3):324–36.

Demsetz, Harold. 1967. Toward a Theory of Property Rights. *American Economic Association Papers and Proceedings* 57(2).

Devarajan, Shantayanan, and Robert Weiner. 1995. Natural Resource Depletion and National Income Accounting: Is GNP in Kuwait and Norway Really so High? Working paper no. 95-13, George Washington University School of Business and Management (June).

Dixon, Martin, and Robert McCorquodale. 1991. *Cases and Materials in International Law.* London: Blackstone Press.

Dorfman, Robert. 1997. Protecting the Transnational Commons. In *The Economics of Transnational Commons*, edited by Partha Dasgupta, Karl-Göran Mäler, and Alessandro Verecelli. Oxford: Clarendon Press.

Dorfman, Robert, and Nancy S. Dorfman, eds. 1993. *Economics of Environment: Selected Readings*, 3d ed. New York: Norton.

Dorsey, Eleanor M. 1994. The 602 Guidelines on Overfishing: A Perspective From New England. In *Conserving America's Fisheries*, edited by R. H. Stroud. Proceedings of a National Symposium on the Magnuson Act, New Orleans, Louisiana, 8–10 March 1993. Savannah, GA: National Coalition for Marine Conservation.

Dua, André, and Daniel C. Esty. 1997. *Sustaining the Asia Pacific Miracle: Environmental Protection and Economic Integration.* Washington, D.C.: Institute for International Economics.

Ecchia, Giulio, and Marco Mariotti. 1997. The Stability of International Environmental Coalitions with Farsighted Countries: Some Theoretical Observations. In *Environmental Agreements and Negotiations: Strategic Policy Issues*, edited by Carlo Carraro. London: Edgar Elgar.

Eckholm, Erik. 1976. *Losing Ground: Environmental Stress and World Food Prospects*. 1d ed. New York: Norton.

El Serafy, Salah. 1989. The Proper Calculation of Income from Depletable Natural Resources. In *Environmental Accounting for Sustainable Development: Selected Papers from Joint UNEP/World Bank Workshops*, edited by Yusuf Ahmed, Salah El Serafy, and Ernst Lutz. Washington, D.C.: World Bank.

El Serafy, Salah. 1991. Natural Resource Accounting: An Overview. In *Development Research: The Environmental Challenge*, edited by James Winpenny. London: Overseas Development Institute.

El Serafy, Salah, and Ernst Lutz. 1989. Environmental and Resource Accounting: An Overview. In *Environmental Accounting for Sustainable Development: Selected Papers from Joint UNEP/World Bank Workshops*, edited by Yusuf Ahmed, Salah El Serafy, and Ernst Lutz. Washington, D.C.: World Bank.

Eliste, Paavo, and Per G. Fredriksson. 1999. The Political Economy of Environmental Regulations, Government Assistance, and Foreign Trade. In *Trade, Global Policy, and the Environment*, edited by Per G. Fredriksson. World Bank Discussion Paper no. 402. Washington, D.C.: The World Bank.

Eskeland, Gunnar S., and Ann E. Harrison. 1997. Moving to Greener Pastures? Multinationals and the Pollution-haven Hypothesis. Policy research working paper 1744 (March). Washington, D.C.: The World Bank.

Esty, Daniel C. 1994. *Greening the GATT: Trade, Environment, and the Future*. Washington, D.C.: Institute for International Economics.

European Commission. 1995. *Agenda 2000*. Vol. 1, Commission Communication: For a Stronger and Wider Union.

Falk, Ita, and Robert Mendelsohn. 1993. The Economics of Controlling Stock Pollutants: An Efficient Strategy for Greenhouse Gases. *Journal of Environmental Economics and Management* 25(1):76–88.

Farvar, M. Taghi, and John P. Milton, eds. 1972. *The Careless Technology: Ecology and International Development*. Conference on the Ecological Aspects of International Development. Garden City, NY: Natural History Press.

Farzin, Yehaneh Hossein. 1992. The Time Path of Scarcity Rent in the Theory of Exhaustible Resources. *Economic Journal* 102(413):813–30.

Feder, Gershon, Tongroj Onchan, Yongyuth Chalamwong, and Chira Hongladarom. 1988. *Land Policies and Farm Productivity in Thailand*. Baltimore: Johns Hopkins University Press for the World Bank.

Felder, Stefan, and Thomas F. Rutherford. 1993. Unilateral CO_2 Reductions and Carbon Leakage: The Consequences of International Trade in Oil and Basic Materials. *Journal of Environmental Economics and Management* 25(2):162–76.

Ferrantino, Michael J., and Linda A. Linkins. The Effects of Global Trade Liberalization on Toxic Emissions in Industry. *Weltwirtshaftliches Archiv*. Forthcoming.

Fiedor, Boguslaw. 1994. Interlinkages Between Environment and Trade: A Case Study of Poland. Wroclaw Academy of Economics, Report to UNCTAD.

Food and Agriculture Organization of the United Nations (FAO). 1992. Selected

Indicators of Food and Agricultural Development 1981–1991. Bangkok: Regional Office for Asia and the Pacific.

———. 1997. *The State of World Fisheries and Aquaculture 1996*. Rome: FAO.

Founex Report. 1972. Development and Environment, Report and Working Papers of a Panel of Experts Convened by the Secretary General of the United Nations Conference on the Human Environment. Paris: Mouton.

Frankhauser, Samuel. 1995. *Valuing Climate Change. The Economics of the Greenhouse*. London: Earthscan.

Freeman III, A. Myrick. 1993. *The Measurement of Environmental and Resource Values: Theory and Methods*. Washington, D.C.: Resources for the Future.

Gandhi, Ved Parkash, ed. 1996. *Macroeconomics and the Environment: Proceedings of a Seminar May 1995*. Washington, D.C.: International Monetary Fund.

Gaviria, Diana, Rafael Gómez, Lili Ho, and Adriana Soto. 1994. Reconciliation of Trade and Environment Policies: The Case Study of Colombia. Report prepared by National Planning Department and Ministry of Foreign Trade for UNCTAD (May).

Georgescu-Roegen, Nicholas. 1971. *The Entropy Law and the Economic Process*. Cambridge, MA: Harvard University Press.

Global Environmental Facility (GEF). 1996. Incremental Costs. GEF Council Meeting, 29 February, Washington, D.C.

Golich, Viki L., and Terry Forrest-Young. 1993. Resolution of the United States-Canadian Conflict Over Acid Rain Controls. *Journal of Environment and Development* 2(1):63–110.

Golombek, Rolf, Catherine Hagem, and Michael Hoel. 1994. The Design of a Carbon Tax in an Incomplete International Climate Agreement. In *Trade, Innovation, Environment*, edited by Carlo Carravo. Dordrecht: Kluwer Academic Publishers.

Goodstein, Eban S. 1995a. *Economics and the Environment*. Englewood Cliffs, NJ: Simon and Schuster.

———. 1995b. The Economic Roots of Environmental Decline: Property Rights or Path Dependence? *Journal of Economic Issues* 29(4):1029–43.

Gordon, H. Scott. 1954. The Economic Theory of A Common-Property Resource: The Fishery. *Journal of Political Economy* 62:124–42.

Goulder, Lawrence H. 1995. Effects of Carbon Taxes in an Economy with Prior Tax Distortions: An Intertemporal General Equilibrium Analysis. *Journal of Environmental Economics and Management* 29(3):271–97.

Goulder, Lawrence, Ian Parry, and Dallas Burtraw. 1997. Revenue-Raising vs. Other Approaches to Environmental Protection: The Critical Significance of Pre-Existing Tax Distortions. *RAND Journal of Economics* 28:708–31.

Graham-Tomasi, Theodore. 1995. Quasi-option Value. In *The Handbook of Environmental Economics*, edited by Daniel W. Bromley. Oxford: Basil Blackwell.

Grossman, Gene M. 1995. Pollution and Growth: What Do We Know? In *The Economics of Sustainable Development*, edited by Ian Goldin and L. Alan Winters. Cambridge: Cambridge University Press.

Grossman, Gene M., and Alan B. Krueger. 1993. Environmental Impacts of a North American Free Trade Agreement. In *The Mexico-U.S. Free Trade Agreement*, edited by Peter Garber. Cambridge, MA: MIT Press.

Grubb, Michael, Matthias Koch, Koy Thompson, Abby Munson, and Francis Sullivan. 1993. *The Earth Summit Agreements: A Guide and Assessment*. London: The Royal Institute of International Affairs, Earthscan.

Grubb, Michael, and James Sebenius. 1992. Participation, Allocation and Adaptability in International Tradeable Emission Permit Systems for Greenhouse Gas Control. *Climate Change: Designing a Tradeable Permit System*. Paris: Organization for Economic Cooperation and Development.

Grubel, Herbert G. 1976. Some Effects of Environmental Controls on International Trade: The Heckscher-Ohlin Model. In *Studies in International Environmental Economics*, edited by Ingo Walter. New York: John Wiley & Sons.

Grübler, Arnulf, S. Messner, L. Schrattenholzer, and A. Schäfer. 1993. Emission Reduction at the Global Level. Cited in *Economic and Social Dimensions of Climate Change* edited by Bruce et al. Intergovernmental Panel on Climate Change, Working Group III. Cambridge: Cambridge University Press.

Grübler, Arnulf, and Nebojsa Nakićenović. 1992. International Burden Sharing in Greenhouse Gas Reduction. Environment working paper no. 55, World Bank.

Gullison, Raymond E., and Elizabeth Losos. 1993. The Role of Foreign Debt in Deforestation in Latin America. *Conservation Biology* 7(1).

Hardin, Garrett. 1968. The Tragedy of the Commons. *Science* 162:1243–48. Reprinted in *Economics of the Environment: Selected Readings*, edited by Robert Dorfman and Nancy Dorfman. 1993. 3d ed. New York: Norton.

Hartwick, John M. 1977. Intergenerational Equity and Investing Rents from Exhaustible Resources. *American Economic Review* 67(5):972–74.

Hartwick, John M., and Anja Hageman. 1993. Economic Depreciation of Mineral Stocks and the Contribution of El Serafy. In *Toward Improved Accounting for the Environment*, edited by Ernst Lutz. UNSTAT – World Bank Symposium, Washington, D.C.:211–35.

Hays, Samuel P. 1959. *Conservation and the Gospel of Efficiency*. Cambridge, MA: Harvard University Press.

Heal, Geoffrey. 1998. *Valuing the Future: Economic Theory and Sustainability*. New York: Columbia University Press.

Hettige, Hemanala, Muthulcumara Mani, and David Wheeler. 1999. Industrial Pollution in Economic Development: Kuznets Revisited. In *Trade, Global Policy, and the Environment*, edited by Per G. Fredricksson. World Bank Discussion Paper no. 402.

Hicks, John. 1939. *Value and Capital*. Oxford: The Clarendon Press.

Holden, Michael. 1994. *The Common Fisheries Policy: Origin, Evaluation and Future*. Oxford: Fishing News Books.

Hotelling, Harold. 1931. The Economics of Exhaustible Resources. *Journal of Political Economy* 39:137–75.

Houghton, John Theodore, et al., 1996. *Climate Change 1995: The Science of Climate Change*. Intergovernmental Panel on Climate Change, Working Group I. Cambridge: Cambridge University Press.

Housman, Robert. 1994. Mr. Housman speaking for the Center for International Environmental Law on Behalf of the Sierra Club and Defenders of Wildlife to the U.S. Senate Committee on Commerce, Science and Transportation, Subcommittee on Foreign Commerce and Tourism, 3 February.

Howarth, Richard B., and Richard Norgaard B. 1992. Environmental Valuation Under Sustainable Development. *American Economic Review* 82(2):473–77.

———. 1990. International Resource Rights, Efficiency, and Social Optimality. *Land Economics* 66(1):1–11.

Hueting, Roefie. 1989. Correcting National Income Accounts for Environmental Losses: Toward a Practical Solution. In *Environmental Accounting for*

Sustainable Development: Selected Papers from Joint UNEP/World Bank Workshops, edited by Yusuf Ahmed, Salah El Serafy, and Ernst Lutz. Washington, D.C.: World Bank.

Hufschmidt, Maynard, D. E. James, A. D. Meister, B. T. Bower, and J. A. Dixon. 1983. *Environment, Natural Systems, and Development: An Economic Valuation Guide*. Baltimore: Johns Hopkins University Press.

Huppes, G., E. van der Voet, W. van der Naald, P. Maxson, and G. Vonkeman. 1992. *New Market Oriented Instruments for Environmental Policies*. London: Graham and Trotman for the Commission of the European Communities.

Hyams, Edward. 1952. *Soil and Civilization*. London: Thames and Hudson.

Intal, Ponciano, Erlinda Medalla, Marian de los Angeles, Danilo Israel, Virginia Piñeda, Paul Quintos, and Elizabeth Tan. 1994. Trade and Environment Linkages: The Case of the Philippines. PDFI for UNCTAD.

Interlaboratory Working Group on Energy Efficient and Low Carbon Technologies. 1997. Scenarios of U.S. Carbon Reductions. Prepared for the U.S. Department of Energy.

International Environmental Reporter. 1997. Environmental Commissioner Ritt Bjerregaard quoted, 20(19).

International Legal Affairs. 1992. 31(4).

International Monetary Fund. 1998. *International Financial Statistics Yearbook*. Washington, D.C.: IMF.

Ise, John. 1920. *The U.S. Forest Policy*. New Haven: Yale University Press.

International Tropical Timber Organization (ITTO) Secretariat. 1995. The Uncertain Benefits of Certification. *Tropical Forest Update* 5(4).

Jaffee, Adam B., Steven R. Peterson, Paul R. Portney, and Robert Stavins. 1995. Environmental Regulations and the Competitiveness of U.S. Manufacturing: What Does the Evidence Tell Us? *Journal of Economic Literature* 33(1):132–63.

Jenkins, Glenn. 1997. Project Analysis and the World Bank. *American Economic Review* 87(2):38–42.

Jesdapipat, Sitanon. 1994. Agricultural Trade and the Environment. Research report submitted to Thailand Development Research Institute.

Jesdapipat, Sitanon, and Piyawadee Chatchen. 1997. Eco-tax, Shrimp farming and Mangrove. Paper presented at the Sixth National Workshop on Mangrove Protection and Conservation, 28 August, in Haad Yai, Thailand.

Jevons, William Stanley. 1865. *The Coal Question: An Inquiry Concerning the Progress of the Nation, and the Probable Exhaustion of our Coal Mines*. London: Macmillan.

Johnson, Harry G. 1966. Optimal Trade Intervention in the Presence of Domestic Distortions. In *Trade, Growth, and the Balance of Payments*, edited by Robert E. Baldwin, et al. Amsterdam: North Holland.

Johnston, Douglas M. 1965. *The International Law of Fisheries: A Framework for Policy-oriented Inquiries*. New Haven: Yale University Press.

Jonsson, T., and P. Lingren. 1990. Logging Technologies for Tropical Forests – For or Against? Cited in Hj. G. Baharuddin (1995). Kista, Sweden: Forest Operations Institute.

Jorgenson, Dale W., and Peter J. Wilcoxen. 1993a. Reducing U.S. Carbon Emissions: An Econometric General Equilibrium Assessment. *Resource and Energy Economics* 15(1):7–25.

Jorgenson, Dale W., and Peter J. Wilcoxen. 1993b. Energy, the Environment, and Economic Growth. In *Handbook of Natural Resources and Energy*

Economics, edited by Allen V. Kneese and James L. Sweeney. Amsterdam: North Holland.

Joskow, Paul L., Richard Schmalensee, and Elizabeth M. Bailey. 1998. The Market for Sulfur Dioxide Emissions. *The American Economic Review* 88(4):669–85.

Kamkredsakul, Jay. 1996. Fishing for the Answers. *The Bangkok Post*, 25 March, Sunday Magazine.

Kanbur, Ravi, Michael Keen, and Sweder van Wijnbergen. 1995. Industrial Competitiveness, Environmental Regulation and Direct Foreign Investment. In *The Economics of Sustainable Development*, edited by Ian Goldin and L. Alan Winters. Cambridge: Cambridge University Press.

Khalid, Abdul Rahim, and J. B. Braden. 1993. Welfare Effects of Environmental Regulation in an Open Economy: The Case of Malaysian Palm Oil. *Journal of Agricultural Economics* 44(1):25–37.

Kneese, Allen V., and Blair T. Bower. 1968. *Managing Water Quality: Economics, Technology, Institutions*. Baltimore: Johns Hopkins University Press for Resources for the Future.

Kneese, Allen V., Robert U. Ayres, and Ralph C. d'Arge. 1970. *Economics and the Environment: A Materials Balance Approach*. Baltimore: Johns Hopkins University Press for Resources for the Future.

Krautkraemer, Jeffery A. 1998. Nonrenewable Resource Scarcity. *Journal of Economic Literature* 36(4):2065–107.

Krutilla, Kerry. 1991. Environmental Regulation in an Open Economy. *Journal of Environmental Economics and Management* 20:127–42.

Krutilla, John V. 1967. Conservation Reconsidered. *American Economic Review* 57(4):777–86.

Krutilla, John V., and Anthony C. Fisher. 1985. *The Economics of Natural Environments: Studies in the Valuation of Commodity and Amenity Resources*. 2d ed. Washington, D.C.: Resources for the Future.

Kummer, Kalharina. 1994. *Transboundary Movements of Hazardous Wastes at the Interface of Environment and Trade*. Geneva: United Nations Environment Programme.

Kuznets, Simon. 1955. Economic Growth and Income Inequality. *American Economic Review* 45(1):1–28.

Landefield, J. Steven, and Eugene P. Seskin. 1993. The Economic Value of Life: Linking Theory to Practice" reprinted in Robert Dorfman and Nancy Dorfman, eds. *Economics of the Environment*. 3d ed. New York: Norton.

Legault, L. J. H. 1971. The Freedom of the Seas: A Licence to Pollute? *University of Toronto Law Journal* 21(2):211–21.

Lesser, Jonathan A., Daniel E. Dodds, and Richard O. Zerbe, Jr. 1997. *Environmental Economics and Policy*. Reading, MA: Addison-Wesley.

Lester, A. P. 1963. River Pollution in International Law. *American Journal of International Law* 57:828–53.

Lind, Robert C. 1982. *Discounting for Time and Risk in Energy Policy*. Baltimore, MD: Johns Hopkins Press for Resources for the Future.

———. 1990. Reassessing the Government's Discount Rate Policy in Light of New Theory and Data in a World Economy with a High Degree of Capital Mobility. *Journal of Environmental Economics and Management* 18(2), Part 2:S8–28.

Lindahl-Kiessling, Kerstin, and Hans Landsberg. 1994. *Population, Economic Development, and the Environment*. Oxford: Oxford University Press.

Lloyd, Peter J. 1992. The Problem of Optimal Environmental Policy Choice. In *The Greening of World Trade Issues*, edited by Kym Anderson and Richard Blackhurst. Ann Arbor: The University of Michigan Press.

Low, Patrick. 1992. Trade Measures and Environmental Quality: The Implications for Mexico's Exports. In *International Trade and the Environment*, edited by Patrick Low. World Bank Discussion Paper 159. Washington, D.C.: IBRD/The World Bank.

Low, Patrick, and Alexander Yeats. 1992. Do "Dirty" Industries Migrate? In *International Trade and the Environment*, edited by Patrick Low. World Bank Discussion Paper 159. Washington, D.C.: IBRD/The World Bank.

Lucas, Robert E. B., David Wheeler, and Hemamala Hettige. 1992. Economic Development, Environmental Regulation and the International Migration of Toxic Industrial Pollution: 1960–1988. In *International Trade and the Environment*, edited by Patrick Low. World Bank Discussion Paper 159. Washington, D.C.: IBRD/The World Bank.

MacIlwain, Colin. *Nature.* 1998. When Rhetoric Hits Reality in Debate on Bioprospecting. 392:535–40.

MacNeill, Jim, Pieter Winsemius, and Taizo Yakushiji. 1991. *Beyond Interdependence: The Meshing of the World's Economy and the Earth's Ecology.* New York: Oxford University Press. Trilateral Commission.

Mäler, Karl-Göran. 1991. International Environmental Problems. In *Economic Policy Toward the Environment*, edited by Dieter Helm. Oxford: Blackwell.

Mani, Muthukumara, and David Wheeler. 1997. In Search of Pollution Havens? Dirty Industry in the World Economy 1960–1995. World Bank Environment, Growth, Poverty Working Paper 16 (April).

Marglin, Stephen A. 1963. The Social Rate of Discount and the Optimal Rate of Investment. *Quarterly Journal of Economics* 77:95–111.

Margolis, Howard. 1991. Free Riding Versus Cooperation. In *Strategy and Choice*, edited by Richard J. Zeckhauser. Cambridge, MA: MIT Press.

Markandya, Anil. 1992. The Value of the Environment: A State of the Art Survey. In *Environmental Economics: A Reader*, edited by Anil Markandya and Julie Richardson. New York: St. Martin's Press.

Markandya, Anil, L. Emerton, and S. Mwale. 1998. Preferential Trading Arrangements Between Kenya and the EU: A Case Study of the Environmental Effects of the Horticulture Industry. World Bank Conference on Trade, Global Policy, and the Environment, Washinston, D.C., 21–22 April.

Markandya, Anil, and Julie Richardson. 1992. *Environmental Economics: A Reader.* New York: St. Martin's Press.

Marks, Matthew, and Harold Malmgren. 1975. Negotiating Nontariff Distortions to Trade. *Law and Policy in International Business* 7.

Massachusetts Offshore Groundfish Task Force (MOGTF). 1990. New England Groundfish in Crisis – Again. Publication No. 16, 551-42-200-1-91-CR. (December).

McGuire, Martin C. 1982. Regulation, Factor Rewards, and International Trade. *Journal of Public Economics* 17(3):335–54.

McHugh, John Laurence. 1983. Jeffersonian Democracy and the Fisheries Revisited. In *Global Fisheries: Perspectives for the '80s*, edited by Brian Rothchild. New York: Springer-Verlag 1983:87–8.

McKibben, Warwick, Robert Shackleton, and Peter Wilcoxen. 1998. The Potential Effects of International Carbon Emission Trading Under the Kyoto Protocol.

Working paper no. 98/9, Australian National University, Research School of Pacific and Asian Studies.

Meadows, Donella H., Dennis L. Meadows, Jorgen Randers, and William W. Behrens. 1972. *The Limits to Growth: A Report for the Club of Rome's Project on the Predicament of Mankind*. New York: Universe Books.

Mendelsohn, Robert. 1994. Property Rights and Tropical Deforestation. *Oxford Economic Papers* 46:750–56.

Mendelsohn, Robert. 1999. *The Greening of Global Warming*. Washington, D.C.: American Enterprise Institute.

Merrifield, John D. 1988. The Impact of Selected Abatement Strategies on Transnational Pollution, the Terms of Trade, and Factor Rewards: A General Equilibrium Approach. *Journal of Environmental Economics and Management* 15(3):259–84.

Meyer, Stephen. 1992. Environmentalism and Economic Prosperity: Testing the Environmental Impact Hypothesis. Mimeo. MIT Project on Environmental Politics and Policy (October).

Mintzer, Irving M., and J. Amber Leonard, eds. 1994. *Negotiating Climate Change: The Inside Story of the Rio Convention*. Cambridge: Cambridge University Press.

Mishan, Edward J. 1988. *Cost Benefit Analysis: An Informal Introduction*. 4d ed. London: Unwin Hyman.

Mitchell, Ronald. 1994. *International Oil Pollution at Sea*. Cambridge, MA: MIT Press.

———. 1993. International Oil Pollution of the Oceans. In *Institutions for the Earth: Sources of Effective International Environmental Protection*, edited by Peter M. Haas, Robert O. Keohane, and Marc A. Levy. Cambridge, MA: MIT Press.

Mitchell, Robert C., and Richard T. Carson. 1989. *Using Surveys to Value Public Goods: The Contingent Valuation Method*. Washington, D.C.: Resouces for the Future.

Molina, M.J., and F.S. Rowland. 1974. Stratospheric Sink for Chlorofluoromethanes – Chlorine Atom – Catalyzed Destruction of Ozone. *Nature* 249:810.

Mollerus, Roland. 1995. Environmental Standards: Impact on SELA's Competitiveness and Market Access. In *Trade and Environment: International Debate*. UNCTAD/SELA.

Munasinghe, Mohan, and Jeffrey McNeely. 1995. Key Concepts and Terminology of Sustainable Development. In *Defining and Measuring Sustainable Development*, edited by Mohan Munasinghe and Walter Shearer. Washington, D.C.: IBRD/The World Bank.

Moreau, R. 1993. The Next Miracle: Turning Green into Gold. *Newsweek*, 25 October.

Munro, Gordon R., and Anthony D. Scott. 1985. The Economics of Fisheries Management. In *Handbook of Natural Resource and Energy Economies*, edited by Allen V. Kneese and James L. Sweeney. Amsterdam: North Holland.

Musgrave, Richard Abel. 1959. *The Theory of Public Finance: A Study in Public Economy*. New York: McGraw-Hill.

National Economic and Social Development Board (NESDB). 1993. *Thailand 2000: A Guide to Sustainable Growth and Competitiveness*. Bangkok: Office of the Prime Minister, Royal Thai Government.

National Economic and Social Development Board (NESDB) and Institute of Developing Economies. 1993. *Report on Development and Environment: The Case of Thailand*. Bangkok, A Joint Study Project (March).

Neher, Philip A. 1990. *National Resource Economics: Conservation and Exploitation*. Cambridge: Cambridge University Press.

New, M. 1990. Shrimp Farming Experiences Environmental Problems. EC, *Fisheries Cooperation Bulletin* 3(3).

New Zealand Ministry of Fisheries. 1996. Fisheries Management in a Property Rights Regime: The New Zealand Experience. July.

National Oceanic and Atmospheric Administration/National Marine Fisheries Service. 1997. Report of the 24th Northeast Regional Stock Assessment Workshop (Draft 23 June). Stock Assessments Review Committee (SARC), Consensus Summary of Assessments.

Nordhaus, William D. 1993. Reflections on the Economics of Climate Change. *Journal of Economic Perspectives* (7)4:11–25.

Nordhaus, William D., and Zili Yang. 1996. A Regional Dynamic General-Equilibrium Model of Alternative Climate-Change Strategies. *American Economic Review* 86(4) (September):741–65.

Norgaard, Richard B., and Richard B. Howarth. 1992. Economics, Ethics, and the Environment. In *Energy Environment Connection*, edited by Jack M. Hollander. Washington, D.C.: Island Press. Also in Robert Costanza. 1991. *Ecological Economics: The Science and Management of Sustainability*. New York: Columbia University Press.

Norton, Bryan G., and Michael A. Toman. 1995. Sustainability: Ecological and Economic Perspectives. *Resources for the Future*. Discussion Paper 95-34 (July).

Oates, Wallace E. 1995. Green Taxes: Can We Protect the Environment and Improve the Tax System at the Same Time? *Southern Economic Journal* 61(4) (April):915–22.

Ogg, Clayton W., and John D. Sutton. 1988. Discussion: Linkages Between Soil Conservation Policy and Trade Policy. In *Agricultural Trade and Natural Resources: Discovering the Critical Linkages*, edited by John D. Sutton. Boulder: Lynne Rienner Publishers.

Olson, Mancur, and Richard Zeckhauser. 1966. An Economic Theory of Alliances. *Review of Economics and Statistics* 48(3):266–79.

Organization for Economic Cooperation and Development (OECD). 1972. Recommendations of the Council on Guiding Principles Concerning International Economic Aspects of Environmental Policy. Organization for Economic Cooperation and Development Doc. C (72) 128, 26 May. Reprinted in *The Polluter Pays Principle: Definition, Analysis, Implementation*. 1975. Paris: Organization for Economic Cooperation and Development.

———. 1974. Recommendation of the Council on the Implementation of the Polluter-Pays Principle. Organization for Economic Cooperation and Development Doc. C (74) 223, 14 November.

———. 1975. *The Polluter Pays Principle: Definition, Analysis, Implementation*. Paris: OECD.

———. 1989. *Economic Instruments for Environmental Protection*. Paris: Organization for Economic Cooperation and Development.

———. 1991. *Recommendation of the Council on the Use of Economic Instruments in Environmental Policy*. OECD, 31 January.

———. 1992. Financial Assistance Systems for Pollution Prevention and Control in OECD Countries. OECD Environment Monograph No. 33.

———. 1993. Trade and Environment. OECD/GD (93)99. June. Paris: OECD.

———. 1994a. *The Environmental Effects of Trade*. Paris: OECD.

———. 1994b. *Life-cycle Management and Trade*. Paris: OECD.

Orrego Vicuña, Francisco. 1993. Toward an Effective Management of High Seas Fisheries and the Settlement of Pending Issues of the Law of the Sea. *Ocean Development and International Law* 24(1):81–92.

Ostrom, Elinor. 1990. *Governing the Commons: The Evolution of Institutions for Collective Action*. Cambridge: Cambridge University Press.

Page, Talbot. 1977. *Conservation and Economic Efficiency: An Approach to Materials Policy*. Baltimore: Johns Hopkins University Press for Resources for the Future.

Palmer, Karen, Wallace E. Oates, and Paul R. Portney. 1995. Tightening Environmental Standards: The Benefit-Cost or the No-Cost Paradigm? *Journal of Economic Perspectives* 9(4) (Fall):119–32.

Panayotou, Theodore. 1993. *Green Markets: The Economics of Sustainable Development*. San Francisco: ICS Press.

———. 1995. Conservation of Biodiversity and Economic Development: The Concept of Transferable Development Rights. In *Biodiversity Conservation: Problems and Policies*, edited by Charles A. Perrings, K.-G. Mäler, C. Floke, C. S. Holling, and B.-O. Jansson. Dordrecht: Klewer Academic Publishers.

Parikh, Jyoti. 1994. Trade and Environment Linkages: A Case Study of India. Mimeo. Bombay: Indira Gandhi Institute of Development Research for UNDP/UNCTAD.

Park, Chris. 1987. *Acid Rain: Rhetoric and Reality*. London: Methuen.

Parry, Ian W. H. 1995. Pollution Taxes and Revenue Recycling. *Journal of Environmental Economics and Management* 29(3):S64–77.

———. 1999. Carbon Abatement: Lessons From Second-Best Economics. In *Trade, Global Policy, and The Environment*, edited by Per g. Fredricksson. World Bank Discussion Paper No. 402.

Pearce, David W., and Giles Atkinson. 1995. Measuring Sustainable Development. In *The Handbook of Environmental Economics*, edited by Daniel W. Bromley. Oxford: Basil Blackwell.

Pearce, David W., Edward Barbier, and Anil Markandya. 1990. *Sustainable Development: Economics and Environment in the Third World*. Aldershot, Hants, England: Edward Elgar.

Pearce, David W., and Avil Markandya. 1989. *Environmental Policy Benefits: Monetary Valuation*. Paris: Organization for Economic Cooperation and Development.

Pearce, David W., and R. Kerry Turner. 1990. *Economics of Natural Resources and the Environment*. Baltimore: Johns Hopkins University Press.

Pearson, Charles. 1975. *International Marine Environment Policy*. Baltimore: Johns Hopkins University Press.

———. 1976. International Externalities: The Ocean Environment. In *Studies in International Environmental Economics*, edited by Ingo Walter. New York: Wiley.

———. 1982. Environmental Policies and Their Trade Implications for Developing Countries, with Special Reference to Fish and Shellfish, Fruit and Vegetables. United Nations Conference on Trade and Development (UNCTAD). UNCTAD/ST/MD/26 (October).

Pearson, Charles, ed. 1987. *Multinational Corporations, Environment and the Third World: Business Matters*. Durham: Duke University Press.

———. 1994a. Testing the System: GATT+PPP=? *Cornell International Law Journal* 27(3):553–75.

———. 1994b. Trade and Environment: The U.S. Experience. In *Trade and the Environment: International Debate*. Permanent Secretariat of the Latin American Economic System (SELA) and United Nations Conference on Trade and Development (UNCTAD), SP/DRE/Di No. 4 October. Caracas: SELA/UNCTAD.

———. 1996. Enhancing Trade and Environment Linkages in Selected Environmentally Vulnerable Export-Oriented Sectors of the ESCAP Region. In ESCAP/UNCTAD *Studies in Trade and Investment* number 21. New York: United Nations.

Pearson, Charles, and Anthony Pryor. 1978. *Environment: North and South: An Economic Interpretation*. New York: John Wiley & Sons.

Pearson, Charles, and Wendy Takacs. 1971. International Economic Implications of Environmental Control and Pollution Abatement Programs. In *United States International Economic Policy in an Interdependent World*. Papers submitted to the Commission on International Trade and Investment Policy, Vol. 1. Washington, D.C.: U.S. Government Printing Office.

Perman, Roger, Yue Ma, and James McGilvray. 1996. *Natural Resource and Environmental Economics*. London: Longman.

Perrings, Charles. 1987. *Economy and Environment: A Theoretical Essay on the Interdependence of Economic and Environmental Systems*. Cambridge: Cambridge University Press.

———. 1991. Reserved Rationality and the Precautionary Principle: Technological Change, Time and Uncertainty in Environmental Decision Making. In *Ecological Economics: The Science and Management of Sustainability*, edited by Robert Costanza. New York: Columbia University Press.

Pethig, Rüdiger. 1976. Pollution, Welfare, and Environmental Policy in the Theory of Comparative Advantage. *Journal of Environmental Economics and Management* 2(3):160–69.

Pezzey, John. 1992. *Sustainable Development Concepts*. World Bank Environment Paper No. 2. Washington, D.C.: The World Bank.

Phantumvanit, Dhira. 1995. Linking Trade and the Environment. *Quarterly Environment Journal* 3(1). Bangkok: Thailand Environmental Institute.

Piggot, John, John Whalley, and Randall Wigle. 1992. International Linkages and Carbon Reduction Initiatives. In *The Greening of World Trade Issues*, edited by Kym Anderson and Richard Blackhurst. Ann Arbor: University of Michigan Press.

Pigou, Arthur Cecil. 1932. *The Economics of Welfare*. 4d ed. London: Macmillan.

Piyankarnchana, T. 1992. Implementation of the Montreal Protocol on Land-Based Pollution in Southeast Asia. In Southeast Asian Programme on Ocean Law, Policy and Management, *SEAPOL International Conference on the Implementation of the Law of the Sea Convention in the 1990s: Marine Environmental Protection and Other Issues*, Denpasar (Bali), Indonesia, 28–30 May. Proceedings, Published by the Center for Archipelago, Law and Development Studies, Bandung, May 1992.

Pizer, William. 1997. Prices vs. Quantities Revisited: The Case of Climate Change. Discussion Paper 98-02, Resources for the Future.

Porter, Michael E., and Claas van der Linde. 1995. Toward a New Conception of the Environment-Competitiveness Relationship. *Journal of Economic Perspectives* 9(4):97–118.

President's Materials Policy Commission. 1952. *Resources for Freedom.* Washington, D.C.: Government Printing Office.

Quirk, James, and Katsuaki Terasawa. 1991. Choosing a Government Discount Rate: An Alternative Approach. *Journal of Environmental Economics and Management* 20(1):16–28.

Qwanruedee, Limvorapitak. 1994. Application of Polluter-Pays-Principle for Industrial Wastewater Management in Samut Prakan Province. *Quarterly Environment Journal* 2(1). Bangkok: Thailand Environmental Institute.

Randall, Alan. 1983. The Problem of Market Failure. *Natural Resources Journal* 23(1):131–48.

Raucher, Michael. 1994. On Ecological Dumping. *Oxford Economic Papers* 46(5):822–40.

———. 1997. *International Trade, Factor Movements, and the Environment.* New York: Oxford University Press.

Raustiala, Kal. 1995. The Political Implications of the Enforcement Provisions of the NAFTA Environmental Side Agreement: The CEC as a Model for Future Accords. *Environmental Law* 25(1).

Ready, Richard C. 1995. Environmental Valuation Under Uncertainty. In *The Handbook of Environmental Economics*, edited by Daniel W. Bromley. Oxford: Basil Blackwell.

Repetto, Robert C. 1993. Complimentarities Between Trade and Environmental Policies. In Durwood Zaelke, Paul Orbuch, and Robert Houseman, eds. *Trade and the Environment: Law, Economics and Policy.* Washington, D.C.: Island Press for the Center for Resource Economics.

———. 1995. Jobs, Competitiveness, and Environmental Regulation: What Are the Real Issues? Washington, D.C.: World Resources Institute.

Repetto, Robert, and Duncan Austin. 1997. *The Costs of Climate Protection: A Guide for the Perplexed.* Washington D.C.: World Resources Institute.

Repetto, Robert, Roger C. Dower, Robin Jenkins, and Jacqueline Geoghegan. 1992. Green Fees – How a Tax Shift Can Work for the Environment and the Economy. Washington, D.C.: World Resources Institute.

Repetto, Robert, William Magrath, Michael Wells, Christine Beer, and Fabrizio Rossini. 1989. *Wasting Assets: Natural Assets in the National Income Accounts.* Washington, D.C.: World Resources Institute.

Resources for the Future. 1996. Rights Based Fishing: Transition to a New Industry. *Resources* 124.

Richardson, J. David, and John H. Mutti. 1976. Industrial Displacement Through Environmental Controls: The International Competitive Aspects. In *Studies in International Environmental Economics*, edited by Ingo Walter. New York: John Wiley & Sons.

Ridmontri, Chakrit. 1996. Shrimp Import Ban Could be Good for Resources. *Bangkok Post*, 17 March.

Riedel, Walter V., et al. 1993. *Biodiversity Prospecting: Using Genetic Resources for Sustainable Development.* Washington, D.C.: World Resources Institute.

Roberts, Marc J., and Michael Spence. 1976. Effluent Charges and Licenses Under Uncertainty. *Journal of Public Economics* 5(3–4) (April/May):193–208.

Ruishu, Lu. 1993. Study on Environmental Protection and Foreign Trade Development in China. Report to UNCTAD, September.

Runge, C. Ford. 1994a. The Environmental Effects of Trade in the Agriculture Sector. In *The Environmental Effects of Trade*. Paris: OECD.

———. 1994b. *Freer Trade, Protected Environment: Balancing Trade Liberalization and Environmental Interests*. New York: Council on Foreign Relations Press.

Runge, C. Ford, James P. Houck, and Daniel Halbach. 1988. Implications of Environmental Regulations for Competitiveness in Agricultural Trade. In *Agricultural Trade and Natural Resources: Discovering the Critical Linkages*, edited by John Sutton. Boulder: Lynne Rienner Publishers.

Safadi, Raed. 1994. Trade and Environment: OECD Procedural Guidelines. In *Trade and the Environment: International Debate*. Permanent Secretariat of the Latin American Economic System (SELA) and United Nations Conference on Trade and Development (UNCTAD), SP/DRE/Di No. 4. October. Caracas: SELA/UNCTAD.

Salzman, James. 1997. Informing the Green Consumer: The Debate Over the Use and Abuse of Environmental Labels. *Journal of Industrial Ecology* 1(2):11–21.

Sandler, Todd. 1993. Tropical Deforestation: Markets and Market Failure. *Land Economics* 63(3):225–33.

———. 1997. *Global Challenges: An Approach to Environmental, Political, and Economic Problems*. Cambridge: Cambridge University Press.

Schelling, Thomas. 1995. Intergenerational Discounting. *Energy Policy* 23(4/5):395–401.

Schumacher, Ernst Friedrich. 1973. *Small is Beautiful: Economics as if People Mattered*. New York: Harper and Row.

Scott, Anthony. 1986. The Canadian-American Problem of Acid Rain. *Natural Resources Journal* 26(2):337–58.

Scott, Maurice. 1995. What Sustains Economic Development? In *The Economics of Sustainable Development*, edited by Ian Goldin and Alan L. Winters. Cambridge: Cambridge University Press.

Sedjo, Roger A. 1992. Property Rights, Genetic Resources, and Biotechnological Change. *Journal of Law and Economics* 35(1) (April):199–213.

Selden, Thomas M., and Daqing Song. 1994. "Environmental Quality and Development: Is There a Kuznets Curve for Air Pollution Emissions." *Journal of Environmental Economics and Management* 27(2):147–62.

Sen, A.K. 1967. Isolation, Assurance and the Social Rate of Discount. *Quarterly Journal of Economics* 81:112–24.

Shah, Anwar, and Bjorn Larsen. 1992. Carbon Taxes, The Greenhouse Effect, and Developing Countries. Working paper WPS 957, World Bank.

Shaifik, Nemat. 1994. Economic Development and Environmental Quality: an Econometric Analysis. *Oxford Economic Papers* 46(2):757–73.

Shrybman, Steven. 1991. Selling the Environment Short: An Environmental Assessment of the First Two Years of Free Trade Between Canada and the United States. May. Toronto: Canadian Environmental Law Association.

———. 1991–92. Trading Away the Environment. *World Policy Journal* 9(1):93–110.

Siebert, Horst. 1977. Environmental Quality and the Gains from Trade. *Kyklos* 30(4):657–73.

———. 1987. *Economics of the Environment*. New York: Springer Books.

———. 1990. The Harmonization Issue in Europe: Prior Agreement or a

Competititve Process? In *The Completion of the Internal Market*, edited by Horst Siebert. Tubingen: J.C.B. Mohr.

Simpson, David R., Roger A. Sedjo, and John W. Reid. 1996. Valuing Biodiversity for Use in Pharmaceutical Research. *Journal of Political Economy* 104(1):163–85.

Sinden, John A., and Albert C. Worrell. 1979. *Unpriced Values: Decisions Without Market Prices*. New York: Wiley.

Sjöstedt, Gunnar, ed. 1993. *International Environmental Negotiations*. Newbury Park: Sage.

Snape, Richard H. 1992. The Environment, International Trade and Competitiveness. In *The Greening of World Trade Issues*, edited by Kym Anderson and Richard Blackhurst. Ann Arbor: The University of Michigan Press.

Sohngen, Brent, and Robert Mendelsohn. 1998. Valuing the Impact of Large-Scale Ecological Change in a Market: The Effects of Climate Change on U.S. Timber. *The American Economic Review* 88(4):686–710.

Solow, Robert. 1974. Intergeneration Equity and Exhaustible Resources. *Review of Economic Studies*, Symposium on the Economics of Exhaustible Resources, 29–45.

Song, Yann-Huei. 1995. The EC's Common Fisheries Policy in the 1990s. *Ocean Development and International Law* 26(1):31–56.

Sorsa, Piritta. 1993. Competitiveness and Environmental Standards. Paper presented to Nordic Trade and Environment Seminar, Helsinki, Finland, 24–25 May.

Springer, Allen L. 1997. The Canadian Turbot War with Spain: Unilateral Action in Defense of Environmental Interests. *Journal of Environment and Development* 6(1):26–60.

Squire, Lyn, and Herman van der Tak. 1975. *Economic Analysis of Projects*. Baltimore: Johns Hopkins University Press for the World Bank.

Starrett, D. A., and R. Zeckhauser. 1992. Treating External Diseconomies – Markets or Taxes? In *Environmental Economics: A Reader*, edited by Anil Markandya and Julie Richardson. New York: St. Martin's Press.

Stevens, Candice. 1994. Interpreting the Polluter Pays Principle in the Trade and Environment Context. *Cornell International Law Journal* 27(3):577–90.

Streeten, Paul, and Shahid Javed Burki. 1981. *First Things First: Meeting Basic Human Needs in the Developing Countries*. New York: Oxford University Press for the World Bank.

Strutt, Anna, and Kym Anderson. 1998. Will Trade Liberalization Harm the Environment? The Case of Indonesia to 2020. World Bank Conference on Trade, Global Policy, and the Environment, Washington, D.C., 21–22 April.

Sugden, Robert. 1984. Reciprocity: The Supply of Public Goods Through Voluntary Contributions. *The Economic Journal* 94(376):772–87.

Sutton, John D., ed. 1988. *Agricultural Trade and Natural Resources: Discovering the Critical Linkages*. Boulder: Lynne Rienner Publishers.

Swanson, Timothy. 1991. The Regulation of Oceanic Resources: An Examination of the International Community's Record in the Regulation of One Global Resource. In *Economic Policy Towards the Environment*, edited by Dieter Helm. Oxford: Basil Blackwell.

Sykes, Alan O. 1995. *Product Standards for Internationally Integrated Goods Markets*. Washington, D.C.: Brookings Institution.

Szell, Patrick. 1993. Negotiations on the Ozone Layer. In *International Environmental Negotiations*, edited by Gunnar Sjöstedt. Newbury Park: Sage.

Technical Committee on the Global Environment (TCGE). 1992. *Thailand National Report to UNCED 1992*. Bangkok.

Thailand Environment Institute (TEI). 1994a. Applying Polluter-Pays-Principle – Time for Action. Research paper presented at Thailand Environment Institute Annual Conference, 29 July.

———. 1994b. The Internal Linkages Between Trade and Environment: Thailand. Report submitted to UNCTAD/UNDP, June.

———. 1996. *Thailand's Trade and Environment*. Report submitted to the ASEAN Secretariat. Bangkok.

Thoaphom, G., K. Atisook, Y. Lertreungdej, and A. Vongbudhapitalc. 1987. Insecticide and PCB Residues in Mollusks and Sea Water. Proceedings of the Fourth Seminar on the Water Quality and the Quality of Living Resources in Thai Waters, 7–9 July, Surat Thani, National Research Council of Thailand.

Tietenberg, Thomas H. 1996. *Environmental and Natural Resource Economics*. 4d ed. New York: HarperCollins.

Tobey, James A. 1990. The Effects of Domestic Environmental Policies on Patterns of World Trade: An Empirical Test. *Kyklos* 43(2):191–209.

Tol, R.S.J. 1995. The Damage Costs of Climate Change. *Environmental and Resource Economics* 5:353–74.

Toman, Michael A. 1986. "Depletion Effects" and Nonrenewable Resource Supply: A Diagrammatic Supply. *Land Economics* 62(4):341–52.

Toman, Michael, John Pezzey, and Jeffrey Krautkraemer. 1995. Neoclassical Economic Growth Theory and "Sustainability." In *The Handbook of Environmental Economics*, edited by Daniel W. Bromley. Oxford: Basil Blackwell.

Townsend, Ralph, and Samuel Pooley. 1995. Distributed Governance in Fisheries. In *Property Rights and the Environment: Social and Ecological Issues*, edited by Susan Hanna and Mohan Munasinghe. Washington, D.C.: Beijer International Institute of Ecological Economics and the World Bank.

Trow, George. 1984. Annals of Discourse: The Harvard Black Rock Forest. *The New Yorker*, 11 June.

Ulph, Alistair. 1994. Environmental Policy, Plant Location and Government Protection. In *Trade, Innovation, Environment*, edited by Carlo Carraro. Dordrecht: Kluwer Academic Publishers.

United Nations. 1993. *Handbook of National Accounting: Integrated Environmental and Economic Accounting*. Department for Economic and Social Information and Policy Analysis. Statistical Division. New York: United Nations.

———. 1998. Department of Economic and Social Affairs, Population Division. *World Population Projections to 2150*. New York: United Nations.

United Nations Development Programme, United Nations Environment Programme, and World Bank. 1994. *Global Environmental Facility: Independent Evaluation of the Pilot Phase* (May). Washington, D.C.: World Bank.

United States Commission on International Trade and Investment Policy. 1971. *United States International Economic Policy in an Interdependent World*, Vol. 1. Washington, D.C.: U.S. Government Printing Office.

United States Department of Energy, Energy Information Administration. 1998.

Impacts of the Kyoto Protocol on U.S. Energy Markets and Economic Activity. Washington, D.C. SR/OIAF/98-03(s).

United States Environmental Protection Agency (EPA). 1995. Human Health Benefits from Sulfate Reductions Under Title IV of the 1990 Clean Air Act Amendments. Office of Air and Radiation (November).

United States General Accounting Office (GAO). 1990. Food Safety and Quality: Five Countries' Efforts to Meet U.S. Requirements in Imported Produce. GAO/RCED-90-55. March. Washington, D.C.: GAO.

———. 1991. International Food Safety: Comparison of U.S. and Codex Pesticide Standards. GAO/PEMD-91-22. August. Washington, D.C.: GAO.

United States International Trade Commission (USITC). 1991. *International Agreements to Protect the Environmental Wildlife*. Report to the Committee on Finance, U.S. Senate. USITC Publication. 2351. January. Washington, D.C.: USITC.

Uzawa, Hirofumi. 1991. Global Warming Initiatives: the Pacific Rim. In *Global Warming: Economic Policy Responses*, edited by Rudiger Dornbusch and James M. Poterba. Cambridge, MA: MIT Press.

Van Grasstek, Craig. 1992. The Political Economy of Trade and the Environment in the United States. In *International Trade and the Environment*, edited by Patrick Low. World Bank Discussion Paper 159. Washington, D.C.: IBRD/The World Bank.

Vatn, Arild, and Daniel W. Bromley. 1995. Choices With Prices Without Apologies. In *The Handbook of Environmental Economics*, edited by Daniel W. Bromley. Oxford: Basil Blackwell.

Vincent, Jeffrey R., Theodore Panayotou, and John M. Hartwick. 1997. Resource Depletion and Sustainability in Small Open Economies. *Journal of Environmental Economies and Management* 33(3):274–86.

Visvanathan, C., and N. T. Lien Ha. 1994. Waste Minimization: An Effective Pollution Abatement Tool for Small and Medium Scale Industries. *Quarterly Environment Journal* 2(1). Bangkok: Thailand Environmental Institute.

Vogel, David. 1995. *Trading Up: Consumer and Environmental Regulation in a Global Economy*. Cambridge: Harvard University Press.

Von Moltke, Konrad. 1994. The World Trade Organization: Its Implications for Sustainable Development. *Journal of Environment and Development* 3(1).

Walter, Ingo. 1974. International Trade and Resource Diversion: The Case of Environmental Management. *Weltwirtschaftliches Archiv* 110:482–93.

———. 1975. *International Economics of Pollution*. New York: Wiley.

Ward, Barbara, and Rene Dubos. 1972. *Only One Earth: The Care and Maintenance of a Small Planet*. New York: Norton.

Ward, Justin. 1993. Environmental Strategies for Agricultural Trade. In *Trade and the Environment: Law, Economics and Policy*, edited by Durwood Zaelke, Paul Orbuch, and Robert F. Housman. Washington, D.C.: Island Press for the Center for Resource Economics.

Watson, Robert, Marufu Zinyowera, Richard Moss, and David Dokken, eds., 1996. *Climate Change 1995: Impacts, Adaptations and Mitigation* Intergovernmental Panel on Climate Change, Working Group II. Cambridge: Cambridge University Press for the International Panel on Climate Change.

Weitzman, Martin L. 1974. Prices vs. Quantities. *Review of Economic Studies* 41(4):477–91.

———. 1976. On the Welfare Significance of National Product in a Dynamic Economy. *Quarterly Journal of Economics* 90(1):156–62.

Weitzman, Martin L. 1994. On the 'Environmental' Discount Rate. *Journal of Environmental Economics and Management* 26(2):200–9.

Whalley, John, and Randall Wigle. 1991. The International Incidence of Carbon Taxes. In *Global Warming: Economic Policy Responses*, edited by Rudiger Dornbusch and James M. Poterba. Cambridge, MA: MIT Press.

Wheeler, David, and Paul Martin. 1992. Prices, Policy and the International Diffusion of Clean Technology: The Case of Wood Pulp Production. In *International Trade and the Environment*, edited by Patrick Low. World Bank Discussion Paper 159. Washington, D.C.: IBRD/The World Bank.

Willig, Robert. 1976. Consumer Surplus Without Apology. *American Economic Review* 66(4):509–97.

World Bank. 1998. *World Development Report 1998/99*. New York: Oxford University Press.

World Bank. 1995a. Monitoring Environmental Progress: A Report on Work in Progress. Environmentally Sustainable Development Series. Washington, D.C.: ESD, World Bank.

World Bank. 1995b. *World Development Report*. New York: Oxford University Press.

World Commission on Environment and Development. 1987. *Our Common Future*. Oxford: Oxford University Press.

World Resources Institute, United Nations Environment Programme, United Nations Development Programme. 1994. *World Resources 1994–95*. New York: Oxford University Press.

World Resources Institute (WRI), United Nations Environment Programme, United Nations Development Programme, The World Bank. 1996. *World Resources 1996–97*. New York: Oxford University Press.

World Resources Institute. 1998. Building a Safe Climate, Sound Business Future. Washington, D.C.: World Resources Institute's Climate Protection Initiative.

World Trade Organization (WTO). 1996. *Report (1996) of the Committee on Trade and Environment*. WTO Doc. WT/CTE/W/40 (November 7).

Yellen, Janet. 1998. Chair CEA, Testimony before the Senate Foreign Affairs Committee, 4 March.

Yergin, Daniel. 1991. *The Prize*. New York: Simon and Schuster.

Index

accounting rate of interest (ARI), 84
additionality, 261, 368
Agreement on Technical Barriers to Trade
  (Standards Code), 288
agreements, international: cost burdensharing in
  negotiations, 347–8; sanctions in negotiating,
  347; side payments in negotiating, 346–8
agreements, international environmental:
  compensation systems, 367–71; emergence of
  free-rider behavior, 353; models, 345–53,
  378–84; relation to WTO, 297–8; Thai
  participation in, 522–8; trade effects of, 327,
  331–3
air pollution: Clean Air Act, 164, 166, 260; Trail
  Smelter case, 7, 374–5; U.S. air quality
  standards, 164. *See also* global warming;
  greenhouse gases
Anderson, Kym, 337
annuity formula, 79n1
aquaculture, Thailand, 533–4
Aquerreta-Ferra, Carmen, 451–3
Arrhenius, Svante, 385
Article XX. *See* General Agreement on Tariffs
  and Trade (GATT)
Asean Free Trade Agreement (AFTA), proposed,
  267
Asia Pacific Economic Cooperation (APEC),
  262, 267
assimilative capacity, 174, 177, 184, 483
Association of Southeast Asian Nations
  (ASEAN), 262
assurance problem, 91
Atkinson, Giles, 485, 506
Austin, Duncan, 415n25
Ayres, Robert, 468

backup (backstop) technology, 101n15
balance of payments: with pollution abatement,
  176–7
Baldwin, Richard, 507n16
Barbier, Edward, 276, 337n12, 376, 476, 507n15
Barnett, Harold, 465
Barrett, Scott, 197, 353–4, 357

Bartelmus, Peter, 504, 510n17
Basel Convention: Thailand's participation in,
  526–8; trade provisions, 277
Bateman, Ian J., 129–33
Baumol, William J., 176–7
BEA (Bureau of Economic Analysis), U.S.
  Department of Commerce, 502, 505
Beausejour, Louis, 119
Beckerman, Wilfred, 473
beggar-thy-neighbor tariff, 246
Beghin, John, 322–3
Beltratti, Andrea, 7n5, 475
Benedick, Richard, 362–3
benefit principle, 350n6, 351
benefits: benefit function in pollution abatement,
  117–19; cost benefit analysis, 127, 399–403;
  intertemporal weighting of, 78
bequest motive, 122
Bergman, Lars, 119
Bering Sea Fur Seal Arbitration, 7–8
Berlin Climate Summit, 426–7
best available technology (BAT), 164
best practical technology (BPT), 164
bias: under common law, 147; in contingent
  valuation, 135
biodiversity: commercial market in, 373–4;
  Convention on Biological Diversity, 368,
  373–4
Birdsall, Nancy, 334
Böhringer, Christoph, 425
border adjustment, 265–6; GATT rules, 289–90
Boulding, Kenneth, 468
Boyd, Roy, 415
Brack, Duncan, 362
Braden, J. D., 323
Bruce, James P., 404, 407, 413, 415
Brundtland Commission, 9, 259; definition of
  sustainable development, 464;
  intergenerational equity notion of, 471
Bui, Linda T. M., 378
Burgess, Joanne, 276, 376
Bush, George, 378
Butraw, Dallas, 166, 414

573

CAFE standards. *See* Corporate Average Fuel Economy (CAFE standards)

capital: marginal productivity of, 79–80, 92

capital, natural: depletion of, 494–501, 504–5, 510–13; environment as, 24; as inventory or fixed asset, 495–7; valuing and adjusting for depletion of, 497–501

capital, natural (environmental): adjustment of, 495

capital stock: consumption with sustainable development, 475–8; substitutability of one type for another, 476; in sustainability concept, 111–13

carbon: fossil fuels content, 389–90; problem of leakage, 422–3; tools for reducing emissions, 415

carbon dioxide: (CO_2) concentrations, 388–9; emissions by country and region, 391; emissions by industrial source, 391–2; emissions per capita, 392, 394; emissions per unit GNP, 392–3, 395; Kaya identity to predict emissions, 393, 396; world emissions by source, 388–9

carbon tax: analyses of economic impact, 412–15; compared to permit system, 420–1; cost by region, 407–9; double dividend arising from, 413–14; equalizing by fuel, 416; harmonizing across countries, 416–17; as tool to reduce carbon emissions, 415–25

Caribbean Basin Economic Recovery Act: proposed modification of, 278

Carraro, Carlo, 354–5

Carson, Carol, 502

Carson, Richard, 123

Carter administration, 377

Charnovitz, Steve, 279, 289n6, 375–6

Chichilnisky, Graciela, 188–9, 417, 475

chlorofluorocarbons (CFCs): in global warming, 388–9; phaseout under Montreal Protocol, 332–3, 362–3; regulation under Montreal Protocol, 276; Thailand's consumption, 523–4

Christy, Francis, 430–1

Churchill, R. R., 447–51

Classical model, 5, 464

Clean Air Act: amendments, 166; passage, 164, 260

Clean Development Mechanism (CDM), 428

climate change: economic analysis of, 386–7; Framework Convention on Climate Change (FCCC), 368, 425–6; implications of, 8. *See also* Kyoto Protocol

Cline, William, 385, 402, 407n15

Clinton Administration: standard related to government paper purchases, 274

Club of Rome report. *See Limits to Growth*

Coase, R. H., 6

Coase Theorem, 6, 42; review of, 67–70; transaction costs in, 67–9, 145–6

Coasian markets, 42, 145–8, 346

Codex Alimentarius standards, 326

command-and-control standards: for pollution abatement, 148–53

common property resources (CPRs): open-access, 59–63; open access fisheries, 439–40; privatization of, 60; restricted access, 59–60; as source of market failure, 53

comparative advantage: environment as, 172, 176–7, 180, 183, 188; in H-O trade model, 217; of Thailand, 515

compensating surplus (CS), 75

compensating variation (CV), 49, 70–5; divergence between EV and, 140–1

compensation: Hicks-Kaldor hypothetical compensation test, 51; potential intergenerational, 109–10

competitive disadvantage, 307–8

competitive effect, 240

competitiveness: controls on global warming related to, 424; empirical studies, 310–15; as trade-environment policy issue, 264–7, 307–23

competitiveness effect: circumstances for loss of, 250; on developing countries of environmental protection costs, 320–3; on industrialized countries of pollution abatement and control costs, 316–19

computable general equilibrium (CGE) modelling, 119

Conference on Environment and Development (Rio Conference), 264, 368

Conference on the Human Environment (Stockholm Conference), 259, 260, 368, 375

congestion, 63–4

Conservation Movement, United States, 471–2

consumer pays principle, 284

consumers: consumer surplus as welfare measure, 43–50; consumption of public good, 349–50; green consumerism, 271

consumption: externalities, 236, 241; first-best policy response to externalities, 236; isolation paradox of individual, 91; nonrivalry and nonexcludability in, 53–6; predicted levels of energy consumption, 396–7; shadow pricing, 84; social value of, 240; time preference for present over future, 79–81

contingent valuation, 133–5; WTP and WTA discrepancies, 140

Convention Establishing the Latin American Economic System (SELA), 304

Convention on Biological Diversity, 368, 373–4

Convention on Climate Change. *See* Framework Convention on Climate Change

Convention on Fishing and Conservation of the Living Resources of the High Seas, 443

Convention on International Trade in Endangered Species (CITES): African elephant under, 376–7; Thailand's participation in, 525–6; trade restrictions, 276–7, 376

Convention on the Continental Shelf: Law of the Sea Conference (UNCLOS I), 444

Convention on the High Seas, 443

Copeland, Brian, 183–7, 190–1, 195, 336

Corden, W. Max, 241

Corporate Average Fuel Economy (CAFE standards), 269

cost benefit analysis, 116–19; global warming in context of, 399–403

cost effectiveness, or least-cost analysis: to value environmental problems, 137–8

costs: burdensharing, 347–8; of carbon tax by region, 407–9; of environmental degradation, 125–7; of global warming, 409; internalizing environmental, 249–50; intertemporal weighting of, 78; of uncorrected externalities, 248–57. *See also* environmental protection costs; opportunity costs; transaction costs; user costs

Council on Environmental Quality, United States, 260, 261

Cournot assumption, 197–8, 380–2

COW (crude oil washing) equipment, 366

CPRs. *See* common property resources

Crawford, JoAnn, 370–1

Cropper, Maureen, 509

Cruz, Wilfredo, 481, 502

CV. *See* compensating variation

Daly, Herman, 7n5

d'Arge, Ralph, 468

Dasgupta, Partha, 5, 7n4

data sources: environmental protection costs, 308–9; EPA Toxic Release Inventory Data, 311; FDA import detentions, 323–6; OECD harmonized system for classification of goods, 326–7; OECD pollution-abatement cost, 308; Repetto's analysis, 314; Toxic Release Inventory, 335

Dean, Judith, 191–3, 310, 336–7

debt and environment, 196

debt for nature swaps, 370–1

defensive expenditures: global warming, 400; national income accounts, 490–3

deforestation: implications of, 8; Thailand, 519–20, 528–32

degradation, environmental: in Costa Rica, 503–4; costs of, 125–7; economic analysis of, 19–20; examples of, 115; explanations for, 24–5, 53; market and government failure related to, 53–70; NDP adjusted for, 506; pollution as example of, 115; slowing or arresting, 26

Demsetz, Harold, 60, 373, 432

depletion of natural capital: user cost and net price methods to value, 497–501, 504–5, 510–13

depreciation: gross output adjusted for, 494

developed countries: costs from global warming, 409; damages from global warming, 406

developing countries: competitiveness, 320–3; costs from global warming, 409; costs of remedial pollution cleanup, 321; damages from global warming, 406; effect on competitiveness of environmental protection costs, 320–3; emissions reduction under Kyoto Protocol, 427; models of environmental protection in, 322–3; New International Economic Order of, 469–70; pollution abatement technology, 321; small- and medium-sized enterprises in, 321

development assistance, international: sustainable development movement effect on, 481–4

discounting: defined, 78; determinants of, 79–82; explanation in financial terms, 78–9; resource allocation of fixed supply, 96–105; resource allocation of renewable resources, 105–8

discount rate: choice with user cost and net price methods, 501; environmental, 86–94; in environmental decisions, 84; in equilibrium, 81; in fisheries model, 441–3; high and low, 86–94; as rationing device, 83; relation to intergenerational equity, 111–13; in renewable resource management, 105–8; social rate of, 81; social rate of time discount, 88; under sustainability rules approach, 479; with taxes, 81–3. *See also* social rate of time preference (SRTP)

distortion, domestic: by-product, 241; domestic measure to deal with, 237–41; trade measure to deal with, 241–8

distributional effects, international: of Pareto tax or tradeable permit system, 255–7; of policy to internalize externalities, 254–5; of uncorrected externalities, 249–54

Dorsey, Eleanor, 453, 455

double dividend hypothesis, 158, 162–3, 413–14

Dua, André, 361

Ecchia, Giulio, 355

Echeverria, Luis, 377

Eckholm, Erik, 466

ecoduties, 265

ecoimperialism, 280

ecolabelling: criticism of, 273; distinct from single-issue and warning labels, 272; function and intent of, 271–3; under GATT, 295–7; harmonized systems of, 273; Thailand, 540–1; as trade barrier, 273

economic activity: allocation model linking environment and, 27–34; effect on environmental resources, 4–7, 24–5; interaction with environmental resources, 21–7; national income and product accounts measure, 486

economic growth: relation of environment to, 5–6

economic growth, Thailand: effect on rural and marine environments, 519–20; effects of, 514–19

economic integration: related to the environment, 262

ecosystems: with ecological sustainability, 472–3

ecotourism, 359

efficiency: in allocation of pollution abatement, 149–52, 156; dynamically defined, 96; intergenerational, 108–13; intertemporal, 97–9; in resource allocation, 50–2; of tax on emissions, 152–3

Eliste, Paavo, 319

El Serafy, Salah, 494, 497, 499n13, 504

Ely, Richard, 471

Emerton, L., 337

emissions trading: under Clean Air Act, 166; for global warming, 419, 427–8

enclosure movement, 432
Enterprise for the Americas Initiative, 370
enterprises, small- and medium-sized: in developing countries, 321
entropy, 468
environment: comparative advantage related to, 176–83; contribution to output, 174–6; defined, 24; dual role for, 21; impact of trade and trade liberalization on, 333–7; linked to trade and comparative advantage, 176–7; as natural capital, 24; as nontradeable consumption good, 201; in Ricardian and H-O trade models, 173–4, 177–9, 182; six cases illustrating effect of trade on, 200–202; trade measures related to, 275–80; waste disposal function of, 174–6. *See also* resources, environmental
environmental goods: unpriced, 141
environmental impact assessments (EIAs): European Union (EU), 300; Thailand, 521–2
environmental issues: intergenerational equity considerations for current, 110; North-South, 183–9, 298; related to congestible public goods, 56
environmental management systems (EMS): British Standards Institute, 275; under ISO, 274–5
environmental movement: criticism of GATT rules, 289; objectives related to NAFTA, 303; trade-environment concerns, 262–4
environmental policy: blended with strategic trade policy, 197–9; effect on trade, 189–93; effects of, 145, 174; gains and losses, 248–57; interaction between countries with, 179–80; internalizing costs to correct, 249; partial equilibrium analysis applied to, 236
environmental protection: debt for nature swaps, 370–2; as economic activity, 5; modeling of developing country, 322–4; optimal, 115–19
Environmental Protection Agency (EPA), United States, 164, 260
environmental protection costs: averting damage, 136–7; data on, 308–9; for developing countries, 320–3; effect on competitiveness, 320–3; for industrialized countries, 316–19
environmental quality: ambient standards, 266–7; determinants of, 170; in Thailand linked to trade, 520; welfare measures of changes in, 75–6
environmental services: absence of international markets for, 341–2; as consumer and producer goods, 27–34; defined, 24; in H-O trade model, 173; inputs to production, 23–4; monetary valuation of, 123–6; in static and intertemporal allocation models, 27–37; valuation concepts, 120–3; valuation other than monetary, 136–8
equilibrium analysis, partial: applied to trade and environmental policy, 236
equity: intergenerational, 108–13, 471, 478–9; intragenerational, 469–70; in resource allocation, 50–2
equivalence of import and export taxes, 252
equivalent surplus, 75

equivalent variation (EV), 49, 70–5; divergence between CV and, 140–1
Eskeland, Gunnar S., 319–20
Esty, Daniel, 258–9, 303, 361
European Community: Common Fisheries Policy, 447–51; EC Commission advisory committee on fisheries management, 449. *See also* European Union (EU)
European Court of Justice, 299, 301
European Union (EU): Common Agricultural Policy, 281; emissions reduction under Kyoto Protocol, 427; Environmental Management Auditing Scheme, 275; role in turbot war, 451–3; trade and environment, 299–302
EV. *See* equivalent variation (EV)
exclusive economic zones (EEZs): EC fisheries management area under, 450; national control of ocean fisheries under, 431; under UNCLOS III provisions (1982), 445–6
existence or nonuse value. *See* intrinsic value
exploitation rate: of fixed resource, 96–105
exports: by-product distortion with tax on, 241–2; effect of pollution tax on, 179; optimal second-best tax on, 243; tax equal or not equal to tax on imports, 252–3; Thailand, 515, 517–18
externalities: Coasian bargaining internalizes, 145–6; conditions for nonconvexities produced by, 154; cost of consumption, 249; in cost of production, 249; defined, 56; distinction between international and domestic management of, 342; distributional effects of uncorrected, 249–54; domestic and international, 57; external economies and diseconomies, 56; immediate and delayed, 58; import-competing production, 237–40; international environmental spillovers as, 341; intertemporal, 146–7; origin and impact, 57; Pigou's tax remedy to correct, 6; of production in export industry, 238–40; as source of market failure, 53; tangible and intangible damages, 58; transnational, 482–3; unidirectional and reciprocal, 57; unregulated, 46f, 58–9
externalities, international: application of Coase Theorem to, 70, 147; using Coasian bargaining with, 146
externalities, international environmental: Coasian markets under, 70, 147; compensation systems to manage, 367–71; interests and behavior of countries, 344, 351–3; international law to manage, 374–5; managing by international conventions, 362–7; measurement of damages, 344–5, 348–50; property rights and commercial market development, 358–9; self-interest as moderator, 358; side payments as incentive to cooperate, 359; trade measures to manage, 375–7; unidirectional and reciprocal, 343–53
externality theory: of Coase, 6; Pigou's formulation, 6
extinction, 439, 442–3
extraction costs, 103

factor price equalization theorem, 181
Factory Act, Thailand, 521–2
Falk, Ita, 400
Ferrantino, Michael, 335–6
first-best theory, 236, 241, 245. *See also*
    second-best theory
fisheries: economics of, 432; open access, 439–41;
    property rights related to, 446; Thailand, 532–5.
    See also ocean fisheries; total allowable catch
    (TAC)
fisheries agreements: early international, 443;
    North-East Atlantic Fisheries Convention, 444
fisheries management: EC common fisheries
    policy, 447–51; efficiency in, 441; extension of
    national jurisdiction, 444–6; global framework
    for, 443; rights-based fishing, 456–7; turbot war,
    451–3; U.S. Northeast fisheries, 453–6
Fisherman' Protective Act, United States: Pelly
    Amendment trade-related provision, 278, 375
fish stock: discount rate with zero harvest cost,
    441–2; maximizing economic profit, 433–9
Food and Agriculture Organization (FAO):
    fishery yield and revenue estimates: 430
forced-rider problem, 280
Founex Symposium, 260, 264, 469–70
Framework Convention on Climate Change
    (FCCC), 370; as response to global warming,
    425–6; trade provisions, 277–8
Frankhauser, Samuel, 404, 406–7
Fredricksson, Per G., 319
Freeman, A. Myrick III, 124–7, 129n10, 134
free-rider behavior: in allocating cost of public
    good, 351; circumstances for, 54; post-
    agreement emergence, 353; in restricting access
    to common property resources, 353; trade and
    economic sanctions to curtail, 359–60

game theory, 352n7, 355, 548
Gangopadhyay, Shubhashish, 191–3
Gaviria, Diana, 330–2
GEF. *See* Global Environment Facility (GEF)
General Agreement on Tariffs and Trade
    (GATT): Agreement on Agriculture, 290;
    compatibility of U.S. environmental laws with,
    279; ecolabelling under, 295–7;
    environmentally-related product standards,
    292–7; general exceptions provisions (Article
    XX), 292–3, 297; major trade-related principles,
    288; MFN principle, 288; North-South debates,
    298; rules distinguishing between products and
    product standards, 268; rules for economic
    relations, 10; Subsidies Code, 291–2; subsidy
    and border adjustment rules, 289–92; U.S.-
    Canadian fisheries disputes, 293; U.S.-EC
    Superfund dispute, 286, 292; U.S.-Mexico
    tuna/dolphin dispute, 263, 294, 303; U.S.-
    Thailand tobacco dispute, 293–4; Working
    Group on Trade and Environment, 264.
    See also World Trade Organization (WTO)
General Agreement on Tariffs and Trade
    (GATT), Uruguay Round: Agreement on
    Sanitary and Phytosanitary Measures (SPS),

295–7, 304; Agreement on Technical Barriers to
    Trade (TBT), 294–7, 326; agreements emerging
    from, 326; subsidy and border adjustment rules,
    289–92; Uruguay Round Agreement, 259, 289
Generalized System of Preferences (GSP), 278
Georgescu-Roegen, Nicholas, 7n5, 468
Global Environmental Organization, proposed,
    11
Global Environment Facility (GEF), 367–70
global warming: cost benefit framework, 399–403;
    costs and damages from, 406, 409; differences
    among countries in damages, 406; FCCC as
    response to, 425–6; IPCC estimates of grain
    production with, 406; trade consequences of
    limiting, 424–5; as transboundary
    environmental issue, 387; uncertainty of science
    about, 386. *See also* climate change
Global Warming Potential, 388n5
Goodstein, Eban, 144n2, 154n15
Gordon, H. Scott, 6
Goulder, Lawrence H., 162, 414
government: discriminatory procurement by, 274;
    as economic agent, 56–7; as supplier of public
    goods, 71
government failure, 65–6
government policy: choice of command-and-
    control or market-based, 148–53; command-
    and-control measures, 144–5; criteria for policy
    analysis, 145; economic instruments for
    pollution abatement, 165–6; to establish and
    enforce property rights, 480; incentive or
    market-based approach, 144–5; to internalze
    environmental externalities, 254; related to
    environmental degradation, 65–6. *See also*
    command-and-control standards; public policy;
    tax system; tradeable permits (quotas); trade
    policy
government role: in Coasian solutions, 146–7; in
    correction of market failure, 480; in making
    policy for sustainable development, 479–81; in
    provision of information, 144
greenhouse gases: changes in concentrations over
    time, 388–9; concerns related to, 8; as public
    bad, 387. *See also* carbon dioxide (CO_2/d);
    chlorofluorocarbons (CFCs); methane (CH_4);
    perfluorocarbon (CF_4)
Griffiths, Charles, 509
gross domestic product (GDP). *See* national
    income and product accounts; net domestic
    product
Grossman, Gene, 311, 335, 508
Grotius, Hugo, 59
Grubel, Herbert, 178
Grübler, Arnulf, 407

Hague Preferences: allocation of total allowable
    catch under, 449–50
Hardin, Garrett, 59
harmonizing: carbon tax, 416–17; ecolabelling,
    273; harmonized system (HS) for classification
    of goods, 326–7; product standards, 270–1
Harrison, Ann E., 319–20

Harrod-Domar model, 5
Hartwick rule (of weak sustainability), 476
Heal, Geoffrey, 7n4, 417, 471, 475
health: valuation of, 138–40
Heckscher-Ohlin (HO) trade model. *See* trade models with environment
hedonic pricing, 127–9
Hettige, Hemamala, 311–12, 334, 510
Hicks, John R., 475, 488, 494
Hicks-Kaldor hypothetical compensation test, 51n4
Holden, Michael, 447–51
Hotelling, H., 6, 100
Hotelling's rule, 100, 104, 499, 512
Howarth, Richard, 111, 479
Hueting, Roefie, 500
hydrochlorofluorocarbons (HCFCs), 363, 388–9

income: Hicks's definition of national, 494; sustainability of, 478–9. *See also* national income accounting; national income and product accounts
income distribution: Pareto criterion, 51–2; redistribution to equalize marginal abatement costs, 417; relation between income per capita and (Kuznets), 507
individual transferable quotas (ITQs), 456–7
input-output table, 19, 308, 310
Intal, Ponciano, 322
Intergovernmental Maritime Consultative Organization (IMO), 365
Intergovernmental Panel on Climate Change (IPCC): emissions scenarios, 396, 398; estimates of grain production with global warming, 406; human influence on global climate, 385
International Dolphin Conservation Act, 279
International Monetary Fund (IMF), 481
International Organization for Standardization (ISO), 268, 274; ISO 14000 environmental management systems (EMS), 274–5; ISO 9000 Standard Series on Quality Management and Assurance, 274
International Tropical Timber Agreement, 304
intrinsic value, 120, 122
investment: environmental screening of new, 304; related to sustainable development, 482; shadow pricing of, 84–6, 89
isolation paradox, 91

Jaffee, Adam, 311
Jesdapipat, Sitanon, 514
Jevons, W. Stanley, 464–5
joint implementation, 416, 426–8
Jorgenson, Dale W., 315, 414

Kaldor-Hicks hypothetical compensation test, 109n25
Kaya identity, 393, 396
Khalid, Abdul Rahmin, 323
Kneese, Alan, 7n4, 468
Krueger, Alan, 311, 335, 508
Krutilla, John, 246, 415

Kuznet curve, environmental, 507–10
Kuznets, Simon, 491, 507
Kyoto Protocol, 300; binding emission-reduction targets under, 422, 427; flexibility mechanisms, 427–9; joint implementation concept, 416

Lacey Act Amendments (1981), 278
Landefeld, Steven, 502
Larsen, Bjorn, 418–19
law, international environmental: to manage externalities, 374–5
Law of the Sea: Exclusive Economic Zone, 359
Law of the Sea Conference (UNCLOS I), 443–4
life: valuation of, 138–40
life-cycle assessment (LCA), 273
Limits to Growth, 259, 467
Lindahl Prices: in provision of public goods, 350–1; public-good cost allocation analysis using, 406
Linkins, Linda, 335–6
LOT (load on top) system, 367
Low, Patrick, 312–13
Lucas, Robert E., 311–12, 334

McGuire, Martin, 181, 195
MacIlwain, Colin, 374
McKibben, Warwick, 424
Magnuson Act (Fisheries Conservation and Management Act), United States, 453
Mäler, Karl-Göran, 355–6
Malthus, Thomas, 464
Mani, Muthukumara, 313–14, 510
Marine Mammal Protection Act (1972), 263, 278, 294
Mariotti, Marco, 355
Markandya, Anil, 337
market failure: conditions for, 91; environmental degradation related to, 53–70; examples of, 60–5; government role to correct, 480; identification of, 19–20; international, 2–3; related to CPRs, 59–60; sources of, 53
markets: Coasian, 42, 67–70, 145–8; surrogate approaches, 127–33; in tradeable permits, 155–6, 166
MARPOL 73/78, 366–7
Marshallian demand, 70
Martin, Paul, 334
materials balance-accounting approach, 24–6, 468
MEAs. *See* multinational environmental protection agreements
Mendelson, Robert, 400
Merrifield, John, 182–3
methane: (CH_4) emissions from anthropogenic sources, 391–3; as greenhouse gas, 388–9; sources of emissions, 388, 390
Meyer, Stephen, 313
Mill, John Suart, 464
Mintzer, Irving, 399n8
Mishan, Edward J., 110
modelling, top-down and bottom-up, 413
Mollerus, Roland, 312–13, 327
monocultures, 483

Montreal Protocol: costs to Colombian government of, 332; London Revisions, 363, 364, 368; Multilateral Fund, 332, 364, 368; ozone-depleting substances (ODS), 332, 359, 362–3, 523–5; prohibited export and import of controlled substances, 364; Thailand's participation in, 523–5; trade provisions, 276
Morse, Chandler, 465
most-favored-nation (MFN) trading status, 288
Mulroney, Brian, 378
multinational environmental protection agreements (MEAs), 262, 275, 323–33; negotiation of, 378–84; relation to WTO rules, 297–8; with trade provisions, 276–8
Mutti, John, 310
mutual recognition doctrine: under Single European Act, 299, 301
Mwale, S,, 337

Nash equilibrium, 352n7, 378, 380–1
National Environmental Policy Act, United States, 260
National Environmental Quality Act, Thailand, 521
national income accounting: measuring depletion of Costa Rica's renewable resources, 503–4; in Papua New Guinea, 504–6; valuation of U.S. mineral resources, 502–3
national income accounts: inclusion of depletion of natural capital, 494; revising, 487–501
national income and product accounts: as measures of economic activity, 485–6; objections to, 487; used to compare economic performance, 489
Neher, Philip, 433
net domestic product (NDP): adjusted for mineral resource depletion and environmental resource degradation, 506; measured output of goods and services, 491; as measure of sustainable income, production, or welfare, 496, 501
net domestic product (NDP), Papua New Guinea: adjusted for mineral resource depletion, 506; measures of national output, 505–6
net national product (NNP), 486, 488–9, 494; Costa Rica, 503; Papua, New Guinea: 506
net present value (NPV) formula, 79
net price method: to adjust for depletion of natural resources, 498–501, 510–13; adjustment in Papua New Guinea, 505
New International Economic Order (NIEO), 469–70
New Zealand, ITQ system, 456–7
Nixon, Richard M., 377
nonconvexity issue, 153–4, 235
nongovernmental organizations (NGOs): role in debt for nature swaps, 370–2
nontariff trade barrier (NTB): discriminatory government procurement as, 274; ecolabels as, 273
Nordhaus, William, 387, 402, 409

no-regrets measures, 412–13
Norgaard, Richard, 111, 479
North American Free Trade Agreement (NAFTA): Commission on Environmental Cooperation, 306; creation, 263; environmental agreements emerging from, 326; environmental implications and issues, 282, 302–3; environmental screening of new investment, 304; process and production methods (PPM), 304–5; product standards, 304; side agreement to create Commission on Environmental Cooperation, 306; trade and investment under, 262; trade obligations of MEAs, 305; trade policy debate, 259; trade sanction provisions, 305
North Atlantic Fisheries Organization (NAFO), 451–2
North-East Atlantic Fisheries Convention, 444
North Sea Overfishing Convention, 7, 443
North-South issues: debates under GATT/WTO system, 298; environmental, 183–9
NTB. *See* nontariff trade barrier (NTB)

Oates, Wallace, 162, 176–7
Ocean Dumping Convention (1972), 365–6
ocean fisheries: problem of open-access, 439–41; solving problem of open-access, 443
OECD. *See* Organisation for Economic Cooperation and Development
open access: common property resources, 59–65; to fisheries, 432, 439–41
open-access theory: dissipation of resource rent under, 500–501
opportunity costs: in cost-benefit analysis, 127; defined, 44; to environmental protection, 26; to preserve unmarketed environmental services, 136
optimal control theory, 400
optimal development *vs.* sustainable development, 473–5
optimal exploitation concept, 432
optimal harvest rate model, 105–8
option value, 121–2
Organisation for Economic Cooperation and Development (OECD): environmental standards, 287; injunction against use of border adjustment, 285, 287; Polluter Pays Principle (PPP), 52, 165, 249, 254, 261, 265, 283–8, 299–300, 521; recommendations related to environmental policies, 261, 287; User Pays Principle (UPP), 285–6
ozone-depleting substances (ODS), 332, 359, 362–3, 523–5; international conventions related to, 362–5; Thailand's consumption, 523–5
ozone depletion, 8

Page, Talbot, 7n4, 472
Paley Commission (President's Materials Policy Commission), 465
Panayotou, Theodore, 358, 480
Pareto criterion, or Pareto optimality: described, 50–1; requirements of, 109

Parry, Ian, 162, 414n23
Pearce, David, 6n3, 441n8, 476, 485, 506n14
Pearson, Charles, 106n22, 116, 283n1, 320, 323–5
perfluorocarbon (CF₄), 388–9
permits. *See* quotas, tradeable
Perrings, Charles, 7n5
Pethig, Rüdiger, 179–80
Pezzey, John, 474
Piggott, John, 315
Pigou, A. C., 6, 463, 488, 494–5
Pinchot, Gifford, 471
Pizer, William, 421
Polluter Pays Principle (PPP): of financing environmental protection, 52, 165, 249; financing of abatement spending under, 265; OECD recommendation, 261; significance of, 283–8; under Single European Act, 299–300; success of, 286–7; in Thai policy, 521; trade dispute related to, 286; violation of, 254
pollution: developing countries' costs of remedial cleanup, 321; as example of environmental degradation, 115; inverted U path of levels of, 34; marine pollution in Thailand, 532–3; strategic game of reciprocal, 352–3; in Thailand, 519; trade as vehicle to shift, 179–80; transfrontier, 341; valuation of damage done by, 127. *See also* water pollution
pollution abatement: access to technology in developing countries, 321; allocation under tradeable permits scheme, 156; command-and-control standards for, 148–53; convexity issue, 154–5; costs under PPP, 284; economic instruments for, 164–5; effect of incomplete coverage by scheme for, 422; effect on balance of payments with, 176–7; efficiency in allocation of, 149–50; in internationally shared resource, 345–9; measures in Europe, 164; model with scenarios of policies for, 409–11; of ocean pollution, 365–7; selection of benefit function, 117–19; selection of optimal level of, 116–17, 153; subsidies to alleviate costs, 161–2; uniform tax on emissions, 149–52; U.S. costs as effect on competitiveness, 316–19
pollution haven, 1, 298, 303, 314
population growth, 16
Porter hypothesis, 314, 322
PPM. *See* process and production methods
Prebisch thesis, 466
precautionary principle, 412
preferences: of future generations, 122; homothetic, 35; willingness to pay as evidence of: 122–3. *See also* social rate of time preference (SRTP); time preference
preventative action: under Single European Act, 299
Prevention of Pollution from Ships Convention. *See* MARPOL
prices: in distribution of welfare across generations, 111; of factors of production, 181; hedonic, 127–9; Pareto-efficient, 111; shadow pricing, 84–6, 89; time path of prices, 96–105; unpriced environmental goods, 141; welfare

effects of change in, 71–5. *See also* compensating variation (CV); equivalent variation (EV); Lindahl Prices; net price method
process and production methods (PPM), 271, 275
producer surplus: as welfare measure, 43–50
production: environmental regulation of, 264–7; externality affecting production functions, 228–35
production externalities: effect of uncorrected, 236; first-best policy response, 236; in import-competing and export, 237–40
productivity approach, 124–7; to valuation of life and health, 138–9
product life-cycle (PLC) management, 272
product standards: of Codex Alimentarius, 326; ISO goals related to, 274; justification for environmentally related, 268–70; under NAFTA, 304; national standards as trade barriers, 270; UNCTAD information about, 330–3
product standards, internationally harmonized: justification for, 270; objection to, 270–1; views of environmental community, 271
prospect theory, 143
protectionism: covert, 270; under EU common Agricultural Policy, 281; of OECD countries, 281
public bads, international, 387
public goods: allocating cost of supplying, 350; biological resources as, 373; congestible, 56–8, 60; examples of pure, 54–5; link to externalities, 58–9; naturally occurring, 54–5; nonrivalrous and nonexcludable pure, 53–4, 58, 373; optimal provision of, 55; as source of market failure, 53–4; supplied by government, 71
public goods, international, 56; climate as, 417; Lindahl Prices in allocation of cost of, 350–1; pollution abatement in shared resource, 347–9
public policy: related to environmental degradation, 20; for sustainable development, 479–81. *See also* environmental policy; government policy; trade policy

quotas, tradeable: carbon tax superior to system of, 420–1; establishing regime for, 421–2; international allocation of, 419; as tool to reduce carbon emissions, 415–25

radiative forcing, 388n4
Raucher, Michael, 196
Reagan, Ronald, 377–8
regulation: design and performance, 268–9. *See also* standards
regulation, environmental: criteria for policy analysis, 145; of production, 264–7; of products, 267–75, 323–33; of sulfur dioxide emissions, 166; U.S. command-and-control measures, 163–4
regulation, technical: mandatory nature of, 268; as trade barriers, 270

Reid, John W., 373–4
rent switching, 197
Repetto, Robert, 192, 281, 314–15, 415n25, 481, 498, 502
replacement project approach, 137
res communis, 59
res nullius, 59
resource allocation: in Coase Theorem, 67–70, 146; efficient, 50–1; intra- or intertemporal optimal, 473
resource allocation, intertemporal: discounting of renewable resources, 105–8; discounting of resources in fixed supply, 96–105
resource allocation model, 27–37; formalized, 38–41
resource depletion cost, 498
resource recovery, 25–6
resources: consumption in Thailand, 519; degradation of renewable resources in Costa Rica, 503–4; *res communis* and *res nullius*, 59; social cost of exploiting, 60; valuation of damage to productive, 124–7
resources, environmental: assimilative capacity, 25; as common property, 34; contribution to economic goods, 23–4; debate about international, 1–4; economic activity linked to, 22–7; effect of economic activity on, 24–5; effect of SRTP on, 112–13; hedonic pricing, 127–9; as producer goods, 23
resources, mineral: adjustment for depletion and degradation, 506; asset value of U.S., 502–3
resources, natural: conservation of, 8; economic activity linked to, 22–7; Hotelling's theory, 6; renewable and nonrenewable, 23
resources, natural and environmental, 77
resources, renewable, 23; discount rate in management of, 96–108; optimal fallow period model for soil resources, 105–8
Ricardian trade model. *See* trade models with environment
Ricardo, David, 173, 464, 492
Richardson, J. D., 310
Rio Conference. *See* United Nations Conference on Environment and Development (UNCED)
risk premium: related to environmental uncertainty, 87
Roosevelt, Theodore, 471, 472
Runge, Ford, 281, 361
Russia: emissions reduction under Kyoto Protocol, 427
Rutherford, Thomas, 425

Salinity Control Act, United States, 377
Sanchez, Rafael, 327–30
Santiago Declaration, 444
SBTs (segregated ballast tanks), 366
Schelling, Thomas, 405, 411
Schumacher, E. F., 470
Second Best Theory, 15, 49–50, 162–3, 241–8
Sedjo, Roger A., 373–4
SEEAs. *See* System of Environmental and Economic Accounts (SEEAs), United Nations

Selden, Thomas, 508–9
shadow pricing: of investment and consumption, 84–6, 89
Shafik, Nemat, 509–10
Shah, Anwar, 418–19
Siebert, Horst, 178–9
Simpson, David R., 373–4
Single European Act (1987), 299, 304
Siniscalco, Domenico, 354–5
Smith, Adam, 494
Snape, Richard, 252
SNAs. *See* System of National Accounts, United Nations
social rate of time preference (SRTP): conditions for downward adjustment, 90; defined, 84; effect on intergenerational equity or distribution, 405; literature of, 92; in management of environmental resources, 112–13; relation to time preference of individuals, 85–6
social utility function, intertemporal, 80–1
Solow, Robert, 7n7
Solow-Swan model, 5
Song, Daqing, 508–9
Song, Yann-Huei, 447–51
Sorsa, Piritta, 312
specialization, 473
spillovers. *See* externalities
Springer, Allen, 451
SPS. *See* General Agreement on Tariffs and Trade (GATT), Uruguay Round
SRTP. *See* social rate of time preference (SRTP)
Stackleberg type negotiations, 382–3
standards: Agreement on Technical Barriers to Trade, 288; ambient *vs.* emission, 266–7; command-and-control, 148–53; compatibility, 268–9; design and performance, 268; environmentally related standards directed toward products, 267–75; environmental standards in Thailand, 519; quality, 268–9. *See also* International Organization for Standardization (ISO); product standards
Stevens, Candice, 281, 286
Stockholm Conference. *See* Conference on the Human Environment (Stockholm Conference)
Stopler-Samuelson Theorem, 181
subsidiarity principle: under Single European Act, 299–300, 361
subsidies: elimination for sustainable development, 479–80; GATT rules, 289–91; to natural resources, 320; uncorrected externalities as (implicit) social, 239–40, 249–50
substitutability: of natural and other capital, 111–12, 476
sulfur dioxide (SO_2): U.S.-Canada acid rain dispute, 377; U.S. permit trading program, 166
sustainability: ecological, 472–3; economic, 472–5; of income, 478–9; intergenerational, 108–13, 478–9; relation to property rights, 65; rules, 475–9

sustainable development: concept of, 468–9; of
    Conservation Movement, 471; effect on
    international development assistance, 481–4;
    intertemporal resource allocation and equity
    notion, 471; intragenerational equity concept,
    469–71; measurement of, 485; policies for,
    479–81; as policy benchmark, 461–3; Thailand,
    537–42. *See also* optimal development
sustainable yield, fisheries, 433–9
Swanson, Timothy, 353, 356
System of Environmental and Economic
    Accounts (SEEAs), United Nations, 487–8,
    495, 500, 504–5
System of National Accounts (SNAs), United
    Nations, 487–90, 494, 501
Szell, Patrick, 362

Taft, William Henry, 471–2
Takacs, Wendy, 281
tariffs: beggar-thy-neighbor, 246; optimal, 246,
    248; reduction, 190–1
tax: to correct externalities (Pigou), 6; discount
    rate with, 81–3; on exports and imports, 241–3,
    252–3
tax, effluent and emission: advantages and
    disadvantages, 156–61; under double dividend
    hypothesis, 162–3; efficiency of, 152–3; rates for
    mixed pollutants, 164–5. *See also* carbon tax
tax, Pareto: international distributional effects,
    255–7
tax, Pigovian: with convexities, 154–5; to correct
    production externalities, 209–10, 243–5;
    defined, 47; environmental taxes related to,
    152–3; on externalities, 236–7; for Pareto
    optimum outcome, 153–54; on production,
    209–10; second-best, 163, 246–8; welfare
    produced by, 153–4, 247–8
taxes occultes, 291
tax system: conditions for distortions in, 163; for
    pollution abatement, 149–53
Taylor, M. Scott, 183–7, 336
TBT. *See* General Agreement on Tariffs and
    Trade (GATT), Uruguay Round
textile industry, Thailand, 535–7
Tietenberg, Thomas, 9n12
time preference: for present over future
    consumption, 79–82; relation of SRTP to
    individual, 85–6; of savers, 85–6; social rate of,
    78; with taxes, 83. *See also* social rate of time
    preference (SRTP)
Tobey, James, 310–11
Tol, R. S. J., 403, 406–7
Toman, Michael, 103
total allowable catch (TAC): allocation under EC
    fisheries management, 449–50; under North-
    East Atlantic Fisheries Convention, 444
trade: barriers to, 270; benefits to sustainable
    development, 482; cases illustrating effects on
    environment, 200–202; effect of environmental
    policy on, 178–9; effect of product standards
    with environmental orientation on, 267–75;
    effect on the environment, 333–7; effects of

environmentally related product standards on,
    323; effects of environmental policy on, 174; in
    forest products in Thailand, 528–32; increases
    specialization, 483; influence on Thailand's
    economic growth, 515; terms-of-trade effect,
    193–7, 246–8; in Thailand linked to
    environmental quality, 520; transnational
    externalities in context of, 482–3; welfare gains
    from trade, 178–9. *See also* exports;
    protectionism
tradeable permits (quotas): advantages and
    disadvantages, 156–61; under Clean Air Act,
    166; compared to effluent and emission taxes,
    155–61; in controlling global warming, 419–23;
    under double dividend hypothesis, 162–3; as
    incentive for pollution abatement, 152–53;
    international distributional effect, 155–7;
    markets for, 155–6, 166; property rights in, 155;
    supply and demand for, 156–7; U.S. proposal
    for international, 166
trade measures: to deal with carbon leakage, 423;
    environmental objectives, 275–80; NAFTA
    environment-related, 305; restrictions proposed
    to control carbon leakage, 423
trade models with environment, 217–28; H-O,
    177–8; mixed, 228–35; Ricardian, 203–16
trade policy: effect of liberalization, 333–7; effect
    on environmental resources, 189–93; North-
    South, 183–9; partial equilibrium analysis
    applied to, 236; related to ecolabelling, 272;
    related to Marine Mammal Protection Act,
    278; rent switching, 197; strategic, 197–9
trade theory: optimal export tariff under, 246;
    strategic, 197–9
Trail Smelter case, 7, 374–5
transaction costs: in Coase Theorem, 67–9, 145
transfer coefficients, 153
travel cost method. *See* valuation, monetary
triple dividend, 415
Tropical Science Center, 503
Trudeau, Pierre, 377
Truman, Harry S., 444, 465
Turner, Kerry R., 6n3, 134n11, 441n8

UNCED. *See* United Nations Conference on
    Environment and Development (UNCED)
United Nations: Convention on Biological
    Diversity, 368; Convention on Climate Change
    (Rio Conference), 368; Environment
    Programme (UNEP), 260; Framework
    Convention on Climate Change, 370, 425–6;
    Law of the Sea Conference (UNCLOS I),
    443–4; Law of the Sea Conference (UNCLOS
    III), 445; Resolution on the Charter of
    Economic Rights and Duties of States, 375
United Nations Conference on Environment and
    Development (UNCED) (Rio Conference),
    264, 387; payment for environmental costs, 284
United Nations Conference on the Human
    Environment, 7
United Nations Conference on Trade and
    Development (UNCTAD), 261, 330–3

United Nations Development Programme (UNDP), 368

United Nations Environment Programme (UNEP), 368

United Nations Statistical Office: System of Environmental and Economic Accounts, 487; System of National Accounts, 487

United States: emissions reduction under Kyoto Protocol, 427; Environmental Protection Agency (EPA), 164, 260; fisheries conservation, 275, 278, 453; water pollution control, 164, 261, 377

U.S.-Canada International Joint Commission: Arbitration Tribunal, 374–5

U.S.-Canadian Boundary Waters Treaty, 7

U.S.-Canadian Free Trade Agreement, 263

U.S. General Accounting Office (GAO), 326

UPP. *See* User Pays Principle

user cost method: to adjust for depletion of natural resources, 497–500, 510–13; adjustment in Papua New Guinea, 504–5

user costs: in discounting fixed resource, 97–105

User Pays Principle (UPP), 285–6

use value, 121

Uzawa, Hirofumi, 416

valuation: net price method, 497–501, 505, 510–13; of U.S. mineral resources, 502–3; user cost method, 497–500, 504–5, 510–13

valuation, monetary: alternatives to, 136–8; classification by environmental damages, 123–7; contingent valuation techniques, 133–5; hedonic pricing techniques for, 124, 127–9; travel cost techniques for, 124, 129–33

valuation of life and health: productivity approach to, 138–9; willingness to pay techniques, 139

value, environmental, 120–3; use value, 120

Vercelli, Alessandro, 5

Victim Pays Principle, 345–6

Vienna Convention, 362

Viscusi, W. Kip, 415

von Moltke, Konrad, 259

Walter, Ingo, 177–8

water: European water treaties, 7; regional management of, 7

water pollution: controls in Europe, 164; controls in United States for, 164

Water Pollution Control Act, United States, 261

Weitzman, Martin, 93, 158

welfare: consumer and producer surpluses as measure of, 43–50, 70–6; distribution across generations, 111; effect in Coase Theorem, 68; effect of changes in environmental quality, 75–6; effect of correcting production eternalities, 46f, 68–9; effect of environmental policy on, 178–9; effect of price change, 71–5; with externalities in import and export production, 237–40; intergenerational transfers of, 109–10; monetary measure of, 43–50; produced by Pigovian tax, 153–5, 247–8; using national accounts to measure, 489–90. *See also* compensating variation (CV); equivalent variation (EV); willingness to accept (WTA); willingness to pay (WTP)

Wells, Philip, 471

Western Hemisphere Free Trade Agreement, 267

Whalley, John, 315, 418

Wheeler, David, 311–14, 334, 510

Wigle, Randall, 315, 418

Wilcoxen, Peter J., 315, 414, 424

Willig, Robert, 74

willingness to accept (WTA), 71–5; discrepancies between WTP and, 142–3; estimates of, 141–2

willingness to pay (WTP), 15, 71–5; discrepancies between WTA and, 142–3; as evidence of preferences, 122–3; techniques to value life and health, 139–40

World Bank, 14; basic human needs, 470; environmental unit, 260; funding for environmental protection, 481; in implementation of GEF, 368; implementation of Montreal Multilateral Fund, 368

World Commission on Environment and Development (Bruntland Commission), 259

World Energy Council, 396

World Environmental Organization (WEO), 361

World Resources Institute: energy consumption projections, 396–7; measuring Costa Rica's natural resource depletion, 503; possible climate stabilization paths, 398–9

World Trade Organization (WTO): Committee on Trade and Environment, 287–9, 297; Government Procurement Code, 274; major trade-related principles, 288; North-South debates, 298; relation to multinational environmental protection agreements (MEAs), 297–8; subsidy and border adjustment rules, 289–92; as successor to GATT, 10–11; Trade and Environment Committee, 263; trade dispute settlement process, 259

WTA. *See* willingness to accept

WTP. *See* willingness to pay

Yang, Zili, 402, 409

Yeats, Alexander, 312

Yellen, Janet, 428